MW00358476

NEW NORDIC
COLOUR

NEW NORDIC COLOUR

DECORATING WITH A VIBRANT MODERN PALETTE

ANTONIA AF PETERSENS

Photography by
BETH EVANS

RYLAND PETERS & SMALL
LONDON • NEW YORK

Senior designer Toni Kay
Senior commissioning editor
 Annabel Morgan
Location research Jess Walton
Head of Production
 Patricia Harrington
Art director Leslie Harrington
Editorial director Julia Charles
Publisher Cindy Richards

Styling Sania Pell

First published in 2017 by
Ryland Peters & Small
20–21 Jockey's Fields,
London WC1R 4BW
and
341 East 116th Street
New York, NY 10029

www.rylandpeters.com

Text copyright ©
Antonia af Petersens 2017
Design and photographs copyright
© Ryland Peters & Small 2017

10 9 8 7 6 5 4 3 2 1

ISBN 978-1-84975-875-8

A CIP record for this book is available
from the British Library.

Library of Congress CIP data has been
applied for.

Printed and bound in China

CONTENTS

INTRODUCTION **6**

WHAT IS THE NEW NORDIC COLOUR? **10**

THE NORDIC WAY WITH COLOUR **18**

DARK ECLECTIC **28**

BOLD ACCENTS **70**

MAJESTIC PASTELS **104**

SOURCES **152**

PICTURE CREDITS **156**

INDEX **158**

ACKNOWLEDGMENTS **160**

INTRODUCTION

To many of us, the term 'Nordic colour' may seem like something of a contradiction in terms. The quintessential Nordic home is not known for its vibrant use of colour. Instead, the classic Scandi look, as seen in interiors magazines and Nordic Noir TV series, boasts white walls, white floors, black-framed windows, tasteful black and white prints on the walls and a smattering of leafy houseplants.

The geographical position of the Nordic region results in striking seasonal variations – long days that stretch into light evenings in the summer, and almost never-ending darkness and extreme cold during the autumn and winter months. Unsurprisingly, the meteorological conditions dictate how people work, play and live in the region, and the scant daylight during the winter is the main reason that Scandinavians constantly seek light, brightness and warmth.

However, in recent years something has changed. The Nordic colour palette is slowly moving away from cool whites and pale greys, and stronger, bolder hues are making an appearance in Nordic homes. The common denominator is that white walls have been replaced with bold colourful shades, but it is possible to determine three different strands within this new approach.

The first style I have dubbed Dark Eclectic. Perhaps as a reaction to spacious, pared-down, white, bright interiors, Dark Eclectic is typified by a use of deep, intense hues: dusk blue, storm grey and forest green, inspired by the dramatic tones of the Nordic landscape. Leafy plants and natural materials – wood, leather, straw – combined with eclectic details all come together to create a well-balanced interior that is shown to best advantage against a dark background.

The next style, Bold Accents, provides variety and choice. Pale walls may remain in some homes, yet they are enlivened by vivid, striking accents in the shape of decorative detailing, colourful kitchen cabinets and bold furniture. This style embraces brave details that stand out and add character to an interior.

Lastly, we will focus on a lighter interpretation of Nordic colour in the form of Majestic Pastels. This look is not so much about delicate sugared-almond hues but instead focuses on strong, sophisticated pastel shades with a fresh, bold feel.

Why did Scandinavians suddenly start to welcome colour, and how is it being used? In this book we will dive deep into the phenomenon of New Nordic Colour and learn how to embrace modern colour the Scandinavian way.

WHAT IS THE NEW NORDIC COLOUR?

THE STORY OF NORDIC COLOUR

There is a popular belief that Nordic interiors have always been light, bright and white. But the pale, walls and minimalist interiors that have dominated Scandinavian homes in recent years have their roots in a style that emerged in the last century.

In reality, many design movements have influenced the region's interiors over the centuries and the new Nordic use of colour is not really new at all, at least not if we take a closer look at how colour has been used in this region in the past.

The white, minimalist interiors so typical of Scandinavian homes in the past few decades date back to the Stockholm Exhibition of 1930, which established functionalism as the dominant style in the Nordic region. The exhibition showcased

a modernist lifestyle, with model housing boasting pared-down furnishings, large windows and clean white walls – a seductive vision of contemporary living.

After the Second World War, the term 'Scandinavian Modern' was coined by the Anglo-American design world in the 1950s. The style emerged via several exhibitions featuring design from Nordic countries and the establishment of Scandinavian design as a commodity put names such as Alvar Aalto, Hans J Wegner, Bruno Mathsson and Finn Juhl on the map and paved the way for manufacturers to produce 'products for good living'. Scandinavian Modern interiors were cultured and restrained, with pale walls, natural wood and beautiful, functional furniture. It was around this time that Scandinavian interiors became synonymous with good taste, and the stereotype has persisted ever since.

But modernism is only one side of the story. The Baroque period featured gold accents and rich hues while in 18th-century Sweden the Gustavian style espoused elegantly muted pastels. The Arts and Crafts movement that developed in England during the late 19th century spread to the Nordic region, bringing with it a colour palette of natural pigments: earthy brown, forest green, poppy red and deep plum.

During the 1920s, the Swedish Grace movement was famous for its playful Neoclassical style and subdued Art Deco hues. And we only need to rewind a few decades to find colourful walls in Nordic homes. In the 1970s, Scandinavians painted and papered with strong colours and bold patterns. The 1980s saw a revival of the Gustavian style and a sophisticated palette of pale pink, sky blue and apricot. The 1990s turned to earthy natural tones such as terracotta, cobalt blue and pistachio green, before colours once again lightened, and turned slowly to white, grey and beige.

So the concept of Nordic colour is not exactly a new one. But, as this book will reveal, after a long period of neutral colour and minimal decor, we are currently witnessing a new and exciting infusion of bold, beautiful and refreshing colour.

EMBRACING NEW NORDIC COLOUR

A look in the rear-view mirror proves that history always repeats itself. Trends are cyclical and, believe it or not, what's on trend today will look decidedly passé five or ten years down the line.

When it comes to new trends, the fashion industry is the first to react, but the interior decoration and design industry is never far behind. New technology and social media have made the tempo faster, which, in turn, makes trend cycles shorter. Trends often represent a reaction to what has gone before, but they are also affected by politics, societal movements and changing demographics.

When it comes to colour, the theory is that trends repeat in cycles of 10–15 years. When our surroundings are white and neutral, we grow bored after a while and start to move towards the other end of the spectrum, and that pattern is evident in interior design over the centuries. In the last 15 years, neutral colours such as white and grey have dominated Scandinavian homes. But, in tune with the trend cycle, the palette is changing. At Nordic design expositions and fairs, interior design is gravitating towards clearer, stronger colours — orange, pink, red and even brown. And this shift is likely to be a reaction to the recent dominance of minimalist white.

We will see this new trend for colour taking hold internationally, but Nordic homes are early adopters. Given their geographical, social and cultural environment, Swedes, Danes, Norwegians and Finns are able to carry out extensive home redecoration, since they not only have the desire but also the means to do so. As colour trends start to develop, Scandinavians have been swift to embrace them.

NEUTRALS

The two non-chromatic elementary colours are white and black, with the popular greyscale in between them. Even though it may not seem like it, white is a colour and comes in a variety of shades. Yellow undertones create a warmer, creamier white, while those with blue undertones are crisper and colder. Among Swedes, the search for the perfect white paint has resulted in the term 'Stockholm White' — a white colour with subtle yellow and grey undertones that has become synonymous with standard white.

White and pale greys go nicely with both hot and cold hues, and make an ideal backdrop if you want to let your possessions play a starring role. Mid-greys create a soft, moody feel and are versatile. The Nordic landscape harmonizes with grey most of the year, so it is possible to find inspiration outdoors — think of freshly fallen snow, cloud cover or frozen lakes.

BLUE AND GREEN

As the trend cycle slowly moves from white to grey to colour, blue and green shades are often the first step on the way. Recently, darker and greener greys have increased in popularity and a dark petrol blue shade reminiscent of inland lakes has also appeared.

Green and blue are colours that remind us of the landscape — sky, sea, grassy fields, woods — and they are also excellent accents. The blue palette is incredibly comprehensive, ranging from violet, with red undertones, to green shades via turquoise. In Scandinavia, there is a new interest in deep, subdued tones such as airforce blue and navy.

Green is produced by mixing blue and yellow, and its character changes depending on how much of each is used in the mixing process. It evokes a sense of calm and serenity, and is therefore a popular choice for bedrooms. In Scandinavia, green hues are mainly represented by grey-green tones with lots of white or black in them. Think of sage, moss green or khaki, forest green and seaweed.

RED AND YELLOW

As we move around the colour wheel, we eventually come to hot colours such as red and yellow. Scandinavians tend to be attracted to blackened or muted versions of these shades and, as with blue and green, dirtier shades have proved popular in the transition from white to colour. Powdery pink, for example, is seen a lot, often with putty undertones that prevent it from being too sugary sweet. Bold, deep red tones are also popular but they are not vibrant, instead flirting with natural reds such as lingonberry, rust and terracotta.

In the middle of the red-yellow tonality we find orange hues. These warm colours bring mustard, clay and earth to mind — hues that are not traditionally associated with Scandinavia, but which in recent years have become more popular.

Bright red is dramatic and intense and therefore suitable for social spaces such as living rooms or dining rooms. Yellow, on the other hand, is a refreshing colour that provides warmth and is cheerful and optimistic. Both colours are perfect used as accents as well as colour blocks.

DARK NEUTRALS

Research within colour psychology predicts that chromatic or strongly pigmented colours grow darker and moodier as the trend cycle moves towards dark neutrals such as charcoal and mahogany. In the same way as white, black makes a perfect understated backdrop. Mixing black with small amounts of red creates a warmer black that is easy to live with.

After the recent craze for all shades of grey, there is a new interest in warm, dark brown hues. Experiment with shades of chocolate, rust, coffee or bark, and use your favourite hue to paint an entire room or just one wall. Dark walls create depth and make accents and luxurious materials stand out.

THE NORDIC
WAY WITH
COLOUR

DARK ECLECTIC

Perhaps the most popular new Nordic palette is one that I have dubbed Dark Eclectic. It represents a reaction against the bright, white-painted spaces that we associate with Scandinavian style; pale hues have been replaced by darker colours such as storm grey, forest green and indigo.

Nature is a huge source of interior inspiration in Scandinavia, perhaps now more than ever. Increasingly crowded cities and a rapid rate of urbanization have led to a yearning for the natural environment and these desires are reflected in interior trends that embrace natural colours, textures and materials.

The 'eclectic' part of this style is something of a backlash against the minimalism popular in recent years. Instead of a clean, pared-down look, Scandinavians now like to mix it up and the new darker palette is accompanied by global influences from all over the world teamed with personal mementoes, antique furniture, plants and artworks.

GET THE LOOK

Daylight — or the lack of it — is something to bear in mind when choosing darker colours. Before you fall in love with a specific shade, buy a few sample pots and try colours on the wall or on a piece of lining paper. You will be surprised how much the appearance of a colour changes during the day as the daylight moves around a room.

White reflects light, while black absorbs it. The same applies to gloss levels in paint — a high-gloss finish reflects light, while a matte finish does not. When sombre colours are in vogue, it is important to know how to create a sense of light and space in a room even when the walls are dark. One trick is to paint the ceiling a lighter shade than the walls. It does not have to be white, but as the ceiling reflects a lot of the natural daylight, it will work well if the colour is slightly paler.

It is easy to produce a sleek, seamless effect with paint and there is a current trend to paint floors, walls and even the ceiling in the same hue. Rooms that are painted tone-on-tone can fool the eye and create the impression that a room is larger than it really is. Paint architectural features and woodwork the same colour as the walls and ceiling and allow furniture to bring contrast to the room.

BOLD ACCENTS

Another way to interpret Nordic colour is by focusing on bold accent colours. If Dark Eclectic draws inspiration from the colours of the natural landscape, this palette embraces the details that stand out and add character. Think of deep red lingonberries, blooming poppy fields or the vivid yellow leaves of the northern birch forests in early autumn. Very bright colours can be overpowering, but they feel less challenging when used as accents.

A colour accent is one used to bring emphasis and contrast to a scheme. Depending on how you combine colours, you can either accentuate or soften them. Some designers suggest that you pair up colours that sit close to each other on the colour wheel — so-called analogous colours, such as green and yellow or red and purple. Another way of creating contrast is to combine complementary colours, i.e. ones that sit directly opposite each other on the spectrum, such as green and red.

Colours of the same hue, or basic colour, can have a different chroma, saturation (intensity) and value (lightness/darkness of the colour). By taking into account these characteristics, you will be able to match contrasting colours that share the same nuances.

Scandinavian homes have traditionally been associated with a minimalist style – far from what we think of when we refer to colourful and bold. But flexible, creative and adventurous are also adjectives that can be used to describe the Scandis. Compared to other Europeans, young Swedes and Danes are the first to leave home, and tend to move several times in search of education, employment and travel. These circumstances have resulted in a sense of adventure and a playful, lighthearted approach to home decor.

GET THE LOOK

Choose one colour to use as a common thread through your space, then combine it with a complementary colour. Many paint companies have done the job for you and developed colour palettes where each hue is easy to match with another. Focus on one or two large areas or elements and match them with smaller details in the form of textiles or smaller objects.

Bold details can be balanced by neutral walls or teamed with an accent wall. Choose your colour with care, as it plays an important role in how the room will appear. To create a sense of space and light, use a lighter neutral on the walls and pick out the woodwork and architectural details in a darker hue. A long, narrow room will feel wider and squarer if the two shorter walls are painted in a darker shade.

Bold Accents is a look that's easy to achieve and will suit anyone who likes variety and change. Base your interior decisions on the room's size, light and layout, and experiment with colour on the floor, walls, furniture, fixtures and fittings. Even if your tastes tend to change, it's worth investing in classic designs in good materials and experimenting with wall colour when you feel the need for something new.

MAJESTIC PASTELS

For those who love colour but prefer lighter hues, pastels are a great alternative. Again, it's essential to take natural light and the aspect of a space into account when choosing colours. Light from the north or north-west will make colours look cooler and harder, and you may want to compensate by choosing a warm hue. Conversely, rooms with light from the south and east feel warm and bright. In Nordic homes, a pastel palette can intensify cold northern light in a beautiful way.

It is possible to draw parallels between the pastel colours that are appearing now and the hues that were popular in Scandinavia during the Gustavian era of the 1780s. The pastel shades so popular then are back — pearly grey, duck egg blue and salmon pink. Then, as now, clean lines were characteristic, but today it is a contemporary austerity that is desirable, rather than classic shapes. You can mix pastel-painted walls with natural materials such as stone and wood. Also consider teaming them with mirrors or shiny metals. Reflective surfaces create the illusion of a luminous interior by reflecting light and offering contrast to a muted background.

GET THE LOOK

Shades of pink and pale blue go well together. Pink is a warm colour and balances blue-grey hues effectively. It brings a sense of energy and peace, while blues are calming and refreshing. As modern pastels have black undertones, shades of grey will harmonize with them perfectly. If you are tempted by grey, bear in mind that it can be perceived as cold with a hint of mauve in north-facing rooms. To avoid a chilly effect, opt for a warm grey with yellow or red undertones.

In addition to colour, finish also plays an important role. When using modern pastels, opt for matte colours with low gloss levels to create a velvety, textured effect.

DARK
ECLECTIC

DARK AND HANDSOME

Five floors above Copenhagen's busy streets perches a penthouse apartment with
wide-ranging views. Here, interior designer and store owner Michala Jessen has created
her own universe, with personal treasures showcased against a dark, monochromatic
backdrop. Michala has embraced the apartment's modernist architecture and its sleek
lines offer an interesting counterpoint to a collection of handcrafted pieces, artworks
and tactile textiles. Michala has followed her own style compass to create a home
that combines urban glamour with eclectic charm.

ABOVE LEFT AND RIGHT Michala Jessen's apartment is filled with
personal objects and pieces from her shop, Rue Verte. The spherical table
lamp is by the Italian glass studio Gallotti & Radice. Michala's boyfriend,
Danish artist Morten Angelo, created several of the artworks in her
apartment; the painting in the kitchen is one of them.

OPPOSITE The dark colours in every room melt together in a
harmonious way, while the finishes and materials add contrast. In the
living room, the walls are painted a deep, dark green that verges on
black. The ceiling is painted the same colour, but instead of a matte
finish, Michala has used a high gloss to bounce light around the interior.

In the very heart of Copenhagen in elegant Frederiksstaden, just a stone's throw from the city's most historic sights, Michala and her son live in this considered, elegant apartment on the top floor of a 1950s block. The penthouse boasts a 120 sq.m./1291 sq.ft. wraparound terrace and sunlight floods in from the large windows. The apartment has the famous 18th-century Frederiks Kirke as a neighbour, and its stately Rococo architecture and patinated copper dome is reflected in the decor of the apartment, where dark, dull green-painted walls provide a backdrop for glittering steel, gleaming brass and plush textiles.

Michala opened her high-end interior design store Rue Verte in 1994. Located in a 250-year-old listed building nearby, it is decorated just like a private home. Many of the pieces in Michala's apartment can also be found in the store and it has a similar colour scheme. However, Rue Verte has a very different energy to the apartment, because of its original architectural mouldings and the building's quirky nooks and crannies.

Thanks to the success of her store, Michala has had a great deal of experience in helping people decorate their homes. Her philosophy is to first consider a home's location before deciding on the style of decor, and to embrace a property's original architecture instead of trying to work against or around it. Her own home is proof that Michala practises what she preaches. As this is a city-centre apartment surrounded by sweeping views of the urban skyline, she decided to give the space a cosmopolitan vibe with a sophisticated, sombre colour palette. The petrol green and dark grey hues give the modern architecture a sense of authority, and painting the ceilings the same colour as the walls gives the space a seamless feel. Finding the right shades was not easy — Michala tested 13 colours before she found exactly the right ones.

The building's modernist architecture is reflected in the open-plan kitchen, where the brushed stainless-steel surfaces are reminiscent of mid-20th-century tableware from Sweden and Denmark as well as aircraft galley kitchens. When Michala renovated the apartment a few years ago, she knocked out the wall between the kitchen and the living area to create an airier feel and a social connection between the two spaces.

A sense of timelessness is evident here. Michala explains that she has made decorative decisions based on her own taste rather than passing trends. To stay true to her individual sense of style, she tends to avoid reading interiors magazines and

OPPOSITE AND ABOVE
Behind the doors of a vintage wooden cabinet lies a treasure trove of tableware from all around the world. The handmade ceramics and lustrous metalware bring visual interest and a sense of history to the interior.

THIS PAGE In the open-plan living area, daylight bounces off the shiny metal and translucent glass surfaces. The glorious emerald-coloured velvet modular couch from Italian company Meridiani stands out against the subdued tones of deepest green and aubergine. To furnish the apartment, Michala chose to combine modern Danish craftsmanship with brands from southern Europe. The wire bar stool in the foreground is from Overgaard & Dyrman, while many of the light fittings were designed by Michala and her colleagues.

OPPOSITE Unlike the contemporary styling of the rest of the apartment, stepping into the bedroom feels like visiting a Venetian palace. The walls are painted in a mossy blue-green and a varied mix of fabrics with different textures creates contrast. Washed linen sheets, a knitted throw and lustrous velvet curtains meet delicate lace on the artwork above the bed, which is by photographer and visual artist Trine Søndergaard.

draws inspiration from her travels and from hotels and restaurants all over the world. She describes how, when she was choosing the materials for the kitchen, brass and copper were in vogue, but she opted for stainless steel instead – a material she loves, regardless of what is currently in fashion. This is the perfect illustration of her belief that if you create an interior that is rooted in your own personal taste, you won't tire of it.

The reflective surfaces, unusual lamps and gloss-painted ceilings in the living room all amplify the daylight, which brightens up the penthouse. Michala says she put a lot of time and effort into choosing lighting, partly because the decorative

light fittings create a dramatic effect against the monochrome walls, but also because good artificial lighting is a necessity in Denmark during the dark winter months.

Michala's apartment breathes sophisticated glamour. The atmosphere is part luxury hotel, part art gallery. Here and there, beloved objects demand our attention. Art, modern furniture and ethnic pieces from around the globe have been carefully chosen and curated by Michala. The colour palette may make a bold statement, but it is the eclectic mix of personal treasures that really makes her home stand out from the crowd.

ABOVE To the left of the window are narrow shelves that house decorative pieces, books and scented candles. Putting a traditional glass display cloche over scented candles not only looks attractive but also preserves the aromas and protects the candle from dust.

LEFT In the bedroom, as in the living room, Michala has chosen pieces of furniture that stand out against the dark backdrop. The rich yellow velvet armchair positioned in one corner of the room echoes golden accents elsewhere and glows in the sunlight that shines into the apartment all day long.

CALM AND COLLECTED

The home of Norway's brightest design exports and boutique owners,
Jannicke Kråkvik and Alessandro D'Orazio, could not be described as a typically
Scandinavian interior. The overall impression is of a dark, eclectic, almost Parisian
elegance, yet there is still something about the space that is identifiably
Scandinavian – it is calm, ordered and functional. What stands out the most
are the shadowy grey-blue walls, which bring a poetic serenity to the interior and
echo the waters of the Indre Oslofjord just outside their Oslo apartment.

OPPOSITE The kitchen units were handmade by Frama, a Danish
design studio and frequent collaborator with the Kråkvik & D'Orazio
creative studio. It was built as a mobile studio kitchen, but fits perfectly
in this imposing room with its high ceilings and original stucco
cornicing/crown moldings.

ABOVE LEFT AND RIGHT The couple collect Japanese pottery
and these are a few of their favourite pieces. The kitchen cabinets
were constructed from Douglas fir, stone and steel, and have a black
countertop, sink and tap/faucet. Irregular wooden chopping boards
add some character to the austere lines.

The couple have lived and worked together since 2003, and their creative studio, Kråkvik & D'Orazio, is celebrated for its projects both with Norwegian brands in Scandinavia and worldwide. The company undertakes interior design projects as well as commercial styling commissions. The couple have an experimental approach to colour and, thanks to a close collaboration with the Norwegian paint label Jotun and the company's creative director Lisbeth Larsen, Jannicke and Alessandro have learned a great deal about how colours interact and complement each other.

Their apartment is situated in a period property dating back to 1899. The main part of the interior consists of three beautifully proportioned rooms arranged *en enfilade* and all the original architectural features and ornamental mouldings are still intact.

LEFT The main living rooms overlook the street and are all painted a smoky grey-blue colour from Norwegian paint brand Jotun. The bedroom is at one end of the enfilade and the kitchen at the other, with the living room in between. Jannicke says they always have the doors open to keep the energy flowing through the space.

PAGE 42 The wooden floors of the apartment were treated with linseed oil to achieve a pale, creamy bone shade. On the wall behind the double door is the steel Eiffel lamp from Danish brand Frama.

PAGE 43 A textured brass folding screen seems to positively glow against the shadowy backdrop. The chair is by Harry Bertoia for Knoll and the lamp is an Akari Light Sculpture by lighting maestro Isamu Noguchi. The open doorway provides a glimpse into the hallway, where the walls have been left bare as a reminder of the apartment's history.

THIS PAGE Around the table stands a mix of vintage Thonet bentwood chairs and Chair One B by Konstantin Grcic for Magis. Coincidentally, the kitchen table is almost exactly the same colour as the walls. It came from their boutique, Kollekted By, but now fits in perfectly here. Jannicke says you cannot plan your home too closely – it's important to leave some space for happy accidents.

ABOVE LEFT Jannicke and Alessandro like to collect ceramics while on their travels. They are both passionate about Norwegian and Japanese crafts.

ABOVE RIGHT The couple use a lot of greenery in their styling work and when a project is finished they tend to bring any unwanted plants home with them. Their indoor garden started with one plant; now they have a small jungle. The wall art is by the photographer Sigve Asplund, a friend of the couple, and the plant artwork on the floor is by Danish sculptor Martin Erik Andersen.

OPPOSITE The sleek, minimal Modern Line sofa is from Danish brand Gubi, while the cork and black marble Sintra side table is by Frama and available from the couple's boutique, Kollekted By.

To demarcate between this area and the newly renovated study/office space and bathroom in the other part of the apartment, Jannicke and Alessandro painted the sections in very different colours. In the new bathroom and home office area, raw concrete floors are teamed with very light pink walls. In the enfilade rooms, which feature tall windows overlooking the street, the wooden floorboards were bleached to a pale buff hue and the doors, walls and architraves were painted a rich, stately grey-blue. Jannicke says that the smoky blue tone creates a calm, coherent atmosphere that ties everything together and works as a backdrop for their carefully chosen furnishings. With white walls, she says, the contrasts are sometimes too conspicuous.

Jannicke's advice is to bravely embrace colour. As the walls play a dominant role in any space, a coat of paint can have a transformative effect. Ringing the changes with paint is not expensive, and to keep costs down you can even do it yourself. Jannicke and Alessandro have a design philosophy that they adhere to both when it comes to professional projects and home — they always keep one wall bare in every room and prefer to pare down the contents rather than add to them. The result is that special treasures can enjoy the spotlight.

In the course of their job, Jannicke and Alessandro have access to a huge range of different furnishing and decorative products, and this has made them very discriminating when it comes to choosing items for their own home — objects are carefully considered

LEFT The chair is the Gaudi, designed by Vico Magistretti in 1970 for Italian brand Artemide. Its glossy grass green curves pop against the subdued grey wall. In every room, at least one wall remains bare — Jannicke says it's a good way to achieve a sense of balance and give space to the things you really love.

OPPOSITE The other part of the apartment has a very different feeling and a more modern vibe. Before the renovation, this office was a small kitchen, but Jannicke and Alessandro decided to move it to one of the larger rooms. The unusual wooden storage chest is the Sutoa from Frama.

before they cross the threshold. So what has made the grade? Some pieces were brought back from foreign flea markets, others were designed by Norwegian craftspeople and many items were handpicked from their own boutique, Kollekted By, which they opened in 2013 in Oslo's trendy Grünerløkka district. For obvious reasons, their store and home have many similarities.

The apartment appears carefully composed, with its dark walls, leafy plants, feature lighting, treasured pieces and contrasting textures creating a sense of calm completeness. But in reality, it seems that the interior came together without too much thought or forward planning. For a couple of the international design world's most celebrated stylists, Jannicke

and Alessandro have an unusually relaxed approach to their own home. They say there was not any specific concept, plan or source of inspiration behind the decor — their living space has just evolved naturally, one step at a time.

The couple purchased the apartment in the early 2000s and for many years lived with it just as it was. Two years ago, they felt the time was finally right for a complete renovation. But even once the wheels had been put in motion, the couple were in no hurry and the refurbishment proved to be a slow and steady process, taking about a year to accomplish. This was partly due to the lead time for the kitchen, which was made by Danish studio Frama. The minimalist, contemporary look of the kitchen cabinets, constructed from Douglas fir, stone and steel, provides an unexpected contrast to the apartment's stately architecture and ornate stucco ceiling mouldings.

Calmness and contrast are qualities that characterize Jannicke and Alessandro's relationship as much as their home. They met at a birthday party 15 years ago, moved in together and have never looked back. Alessandro's Italian roots and Jannicke's Norwegian heritage have come together to create a unique sense of style that is both Italian and Scandinavian, sophisticated and functional, masculine and feminine, eclectic and minimalistic. And perhaps it's because they haven't tried too hard that their apartment comes so close to perfection.

OPPOSITE The bed is dressed in minimalist fashion as the couple favour plain linen sheets in white and pale grey. The striking woven blanket placed on top was made by young Dutch textile designer Mae Engelgeer. It brings a note of colour and comfort to the space.

ABOVE RIGHT In the bedroom, Alessandro designed a whole wall of storage and left one small opening in the middle, which is now home to a stack of books and a vase designed by Norwegian ceramic artist Lillian Tørlen. The couple discovered her work at

an exhibition where her ceramics had been attached to different surfaces in a room — the ceiling, corners and so on.

BELOW RIGHT The 90° Shelf Wall Light is by Frama and acts as both bedside light and handy shelf. Its simple, industrial styling is elevated by the rich glow of the brass, which looks particularly effective against the grey wall.

JEWELLED HUES

Behind the brick facade of a 1930s townhouse in Copenhagen lies a hidden gem.
Goldsmith and jewellery designer Rebekka Notkin and her family live in this Art
Deco-inspired home against a backdrop of Danish vintage finds, a fine glass
collection and rich, jewel-coloured walls. The skills and aesthetics of Rebekka's
profession of jewellery designer is reflected in the home's perfectly balanced
spaces and the soul of the house whispers that everything here has a story.
Rebekka's magical home is certainly one of a kind.

ABOVE LEFT The hand-painted cranes on the living room wall are
one of the reasons Rebekka could never imagine moving from here. By
De Gournay, they are painted in a special colourway on blue-grey dyed
silk. The rattan armchair came from a store in Tisvilde in North Zealand.
Together with the broad-leaf fig, this area feels like an exotic garden.

ABOVE RIGHT The turquoise pot with a surface pattern was, like
everything in this home, chosen for its good looks. The little bowl on the
lower level of the side table was designed by Bjørn Wiinblad, a Danish
designer who had great success worldwide during the mid-20th century
and has enjoyed a revival in recent years.

THIS PAGE The arresting artwork is by Rebekka's friend Asger Mortensen, while the white glass pieces on top of the 1930s trolley are part of Rebekka's collection of vintage opaline glass.

THIS PAGE AND OPPOSITE The kitchen successfully combines classical glamour and Scandinavian modernity. The pairing of yellow gold and red gemstones is a timeless motif in jewellery design. Here, the colour combination is recreated in the form of kitchen cabinets painted a deep, ruby red and subtle brass detailing. The windows are unencumbered by curtains or blinds, which allows light to flow in and highlight the simple aesthetic of the lamps, the brass details and the clean modern lines.

LEFT Rebekka and her husband have tried to preserve as many of the house's architectural details as possible. The original staircase and doors are still intact, while the old pine floor has been oiled in a dark hue to create a solid foundation for the rooms and complement the jewel- coloured walls.

PAGES 50 AND 51 The narrow hallway leads to an entrance room decorated with prints and art by Danish artists Tal R and Evren Tekinoktay from the Schäfer Grafisk Værksted. The dull blue walls provide the perfect backdrop for the distinctive artworks, glass sculptures and brass decorations.

Sometimes it's not until you step into a colourful interior that you realize how much you miss joyful, vibrant colours in a world of white, minimalist spaces. Colour and pattern add character, spark positive energy and kick-start creativity. That's exactly what happens when you enter Danish jewellery designer Rebekka Notkin's home. Every vase, painting and candleholder in here tells a special story and the house has the atmosphere of a fantasy universe from a childhood dream.

Rebekka's brick townhouse dates from the 1930s and is located in Frederiksberg, a fashionable, leafy neighbourhood in the Danish capital. The house is part of a historic terrace designed by Thorkild Henningsen, a famous Danish architect active during the transition from Neoclassicism to functionalism in the early 1900s. The dignified brick facade conceals a well-preserved home with many original features and a unique atmosphere.

The house was originally built for an artist, something revealed by the huge studio window upstairs. And, in a case of history repeating itself, almost 100 years later goldsmith and jewellery designer Rebekka Notkin and her family live here. Rebekka believes there is a special atmosphere in the house and she and her husband have tried to

LEFT AND RIGHT
The dusky blue walls of
the living room provide
a subdued backdrop
for furniture, art and
decorative details. Above
the sofa hangs a poetic
artwork by Astrid Kruse
Jensen, named 'Within
the Landscape'. The
Spanish Chairs are a
Danish design classic,
originally designed by
Børge Mogensen in 1958,
and the circular table
decorated with birds
by Bjørn Wiinblad dates
back to the 1960s and is
a treasured possession.
Rebekka found it while on
vacation in Hamburg and
took a detour to buy the
table on her way home.

preserve it by making sensitive renovations and retaining as many architectural features
as possible. The stairways and doors are all original, while the old pine floors have been oiled
to a dark brown hue to create a solid base for the rooms and highlight the coloured walls.

The house is an endless source of inspiration for Rebekka. An ornamental detail on the
brick facade or an architectural feature might provide the idea for a new piece of jewellery,
and at the same time some of the colour combinations here are drawn from her designs.
In the kitchen, for example, a gold-painted wall is combined with glinting brass fixtures
and glossy, deep ruby red cabinets.

Rebekka opened her first boutique and atelier in Copenhagen in 1997 after finishing her
goldsmith training. Her passionate approach to craftsmanship, and especially metalworking,
was inherited from her father, who was a goldsmith by profession, and her grandfather, who
was a dental technician. Rebekka inherited their tools and still uses them today. Nowadays,
she has two entrancing boutiques, one on fashionable Bredgade in Copenhagen and the other
in Hamburg, where she sells her sought-after pieces – all individually designed and inspired
by history, myth and fantasy.

It is possible to draw parallels between Rebekka's designs and the decoration of her home.
Both are strongly inspired by the Art Deco era, with its eclectic feminine mix of patterns,

LEFT AND ABOVE In the bedroom, Rebekka chose a dramatic crimson for the walls. The generous size of the room and the daylight that floods in from a skylight balance out the bold shade. The mood is calm and cosy thanks to the simple furnishings, and the bed is the focal point. Delicate floral patterns, a feminine still life with perfumes and the fresh, flamingo pink walls give the room a romantic yet avant-garde vibe.

materials, textures and colours. The clear hues of petrol blue, rich red and dusty green are a perfect backdrop for her elegant still lifes. Most of the objects are chosen for their beauty rather than their functionality. Rebekka explains that she is drawn to the Art Deco movement because of its decadence and spirit of optimism. It was also the first time that many female artists gained recognition and were able to shape their own style of expression.

Rebekka's own creative streak has been evident for as long as she can remember. She was the kind of child who spent a lot of time alone in her bedroom, decorating the walls of her dolls' house with wallpaper or creating elaborate narratives about other worlds. In her adult life, she tries to maintain that spirit of imagination, along with a sense of restrained elegance.

Her house is a short cycle ride from work and school, but the great location is not the only reason that Rebekka cannot imagine moving. In the living room, one wall is decorated with an exquisite hand-painted silk wallpaper depicting a group of cranes. 'It would be awful to abandon them,' she says.

As you walk around Rebekka's house, it wouldn't be a surprise to stumble across a Narnia-like alternative universe at the back of a wardrobe, or a tiny walnut-shell cradle on a windowsill. The house is full of quirky treasures found at auctions and flea markets. Rebekka says that when her children's friends come over to play they say that the house is special. The truth is you don't have to be a child to find it alluring — this elegant wonderland makes everyone believe in fairy tales again.

THIS PAGE Rebekka is drawn to naturalistic patterns, shapes and colours. There are plants and flowers throughout her home, not least in the bedroom where the sheets and coverlet feature soft florals, green leaves and waving palm trees.

A MODERN CLASSIC

Behind a sober, classical facade in Copenhagen's redeveloped Islands Brygge district lies interior designer Anders Krakau's handsome apartment. This sophisticated space boasts graceful proportions and original period features teamed with sleek modern furnishings. When it came to choosing a colour scheme, Anders drew his inspiration from the Nordic autumn, opting for a subtle palette of warm, dark hues. Despite the sombre tones of the decor, his apartment is still remarkably light and open in feel.

As with many cities, Copenhagen has an old industrial district that within just a few decades has been transformed from an undesirable and dilapidated spot to a fashionable, sought-after neighbourhood. Islands Brygge is a harbourfront area that was established through a programme of land reclamation that began in the 1880s. Its name translates roughly to Iceland Wharf, and it was from here that ships sailed to and from Iceland, which was at that time a Danish colony. During the first half of the 20th century, Islands Brygge was heavily industrialized, but during the second half of the century the industries based here entered a long decline and the district became derelict.

OPPOSITE When Anders moved into the apartment, the kitchen was a rather antiseptic white space. To give it more character and bring it into line with the rest of the apartment, Anders painted the cabinets in a dark greenish black and replaced the handles with burnished brass knobs that he designed himself.

ABOVE LEFT To achieve a coordinated and harmonious look throughout the apartment,

Anders opted for a palette of dark, moody shades that share the same tonal values.

ABOVE CENTRE On a brass table top is a cluster of ceramic bowls and a vintage wooden bowl from Indonesia.

ABOVE RIGHT In the living room, the grey-brown linen-covered sofa is from French brand La Fibule and perfectly matches the warm grey walls.

However, in the past 20 years the area has undergone a massive programme of redevelopment and it is now one of the city's trendiest and most popular neighbourhoods. Islands Brygge is characterized by a mixture of old buildings and new developments, and many of the original structures have now been converted into sought-after residential units. A couple of years ago, designer Anders Krakau moved into this apartment, which is located in a Nordic Classicist building dating back to 1920.

Anders knew that he wanted to give his new home a dark and moody look and, in search of an array of dark tones that would work well together, he looked at colour schemes based on those seen in nature. Scandinavians have a deep love of and sense of connection with the natural world around them, as

ABOVE In the kitchen, the bowls, plates and cups on the countertop come from Anders' own brand, Arrondissement Copenhagen. The ceramics are made of natural brown clay moulded by hand and their dark lustre is due to smoke firing at a certain temperature.

OPPOSITE Circular dining tables usually result in convivial conversations. This one was designed by Anders himself and is made from concrete and iron. The pendant light is the burnished brass and blown glass Bolle by Gallotti & Radice. Anders' elegant dining chairs are upholstered in a beautiful velvet fabric and, like many of the other furnishings in the apartment, come from Rue Verte, the boutique that he co-owns.

summed up by the Norwegian word *friluftsliv*, which describes an ancient Nordic appreciation of and closeness to nature. With its fallen leaves, shorter days and misty mornings, autumn is Anders' favourite season and so he decided to take it as his inspiration for the decor of the apartment. He chose a limited palette of rich, mellow grey-browns and darkest forest green in a chalky, flat finish from British paint brand Zoffany.

To prevent the interior from becoming too dark and sombre, Anders was careful to make sure there was enough contrast to enliven the spaces. The woodwork, architraves and ceilings are painted a bright, crisp white throughout and bring definition to the well-proportioned rooms. Anders has incorporated reflective surfaces such as glass and dull metal to bounce natural light around the rooms, while antique furnishings in dark polished wood contribute a rich, subtle glow of their own. The white details frame the rooms to perfection and stand out against the dark walls, while the light oak floors were treated with a brown wax oil to create a dark, matte finish that looks as if it has developed over the years.

Anders co-owns renowned Copenhagen concept store Rue Verte with Michala Jessen (see her home on pages 30—37) and they make several trips each year to the major design fairs in Paris, Milan and London to source new stock. As can be seen in the store, unlike the traditional Scandinavian style, with its natural materials, austere lines and organic shapes,

OPPOSITE The photograph hanging above the sofa is by Anders' friend Josephine Alberthe and was taken in the Kongens Have (King's Garden) park in central Copenhagen. The Eclipse chandelier from British brand Ochre is made from dark horn and is one of Anders' favourite pieces.

BELOW LEFT The elegant dark wood and rattan rocking chair is an heirloom handed down from Anders' girlfriend's grandparents. A pile of coffee-table books doubles as a side table in this tranquil reading corner.

BELOW RIGHT A generously stocked drinks trolley or bar harks back to a more elegant time and makes pre-dinner drinks something of an occasion. Anders' home bar is also a beautiful addition to the decor, with its crystal decanters, cut glass and vintage cocktail shaker.

Anders is drawn to a more luxurious look, with tactile velvet curtains and upholstery and polished dark wood furniture – a style that is more common in France and Italy. However, the harbourfront location of the apartment is also referenced in the décor – industrial-luxe materials including raw linen, leather and unpolished iron all put in an appearance and contrast beautifully with the calm, classical vibe.

Many of the handsome pieces in the apartment were sourced by Anders on his travels, but quite often he has a vision of a particular item or object that proves impossible to find. His solution? To design it himself, of course. In 2015, together with Therese Torgersen, Anders established Arrondissement Copenhagen, a Danish company that creates timeless, high-quality, custom-made furniture, and their designs can be found throughout the apartment.

Good craftsmanship is at the heart of the Arrondissement concept and the materials are chosen with great care and attention to detail. Ceramic bowls and plates are handmade from natural brown clay, fired in a wood-burning kiln and smoked at a high temperature to create a dense lustre. Tables are crafted from tarnished iron and hand-finished leather, while the knobs on Anders' kitchen cabinets were specially made of burnished brass that will slowly develop a rich patina. All the designs have longevity in mind and Arrondissement pieces will only grow more beautiful with the passage of time.

OPPOSITE The apartment is situated in a building built in the Nordic Classicism style of the 1920s. The large windows allow natural daylight to flood into the interior and to accentuate the graceful architectural features. Anders painted all the ceilings and the woodwork a clean, crisp white to provide definition and frame the moody hues that cover the walls. When the daylight fades away, the Eclipse chandelier casts a rich, mellow light and provides the room with a glamorous focal point.

ABOVE AND BELOW RIGHT Every room in the apartment is painted in a carefully chosen hue from English brand Zoffany, renowned for the great depth of colour of their paints. The furnishings are minimal, but every piece tells a story. Next to an old Chinese table stands a leather chair that Anders inherited from his grandfather (above right), while beside this small velvet-covered ottoman is a Circle side table from Anders' company Arrondissment Copenhagen (below right).

LEFT In the bedroom, a wooden dressing table enjoys pride of place. It was inherited from Anders' girfriend's grandparents and is adorned with a brass lamp, jewellery display and a scented candle that add a glamorous touch. In this room, Anders retained the original dado rail/chair rail and painted the wall beneath it white to provide contrast with the dark floor.

OPPOSITE Anders designed a bespoke storage unit to hold clothes and accessories in the bedroom. The doors have bevelled panels that give the cabinets the same traditional character as the architectural features in the rest of the apartment. The bed is dressed in soft linens in restful hues of dark brown and midnight blue. The wall lamp in brass from Restart Milano provides light to read by.

In Anders' bedroom, he designed a practical custom-built fitted wardrobe/closet that surrounds the bed and offers ample storage space. It was especially designed to match the apartment's architectural features and the bevelled panels on the doors give the unit a traditional character that ties in with the room's original dado rail/chair rail and window frames. The cabinetry has been painted the same soft, sludgy khaki hue as the rest of the room so that it appears to just blend into the walls.

During the last hundred years, Islands Brygge has changed from a gritty working-class waterfront area with many small factories and workers' housing into a fashionable residential quarter. The imaginative redevelopment has brought new life and new inhabitants into the area, and the recently established shops, restaurants, harbour park, open-air swimming pool and the varied architecture positioned right by the water's edge make this neighbourhood an attractive place to live.

BOLD
ACCENTS

BRINGING COLOUR TO LIFE

With a passion for colour, a working life that has honed his sense for shades and hues and a willingness to experiment, it comes as no surprise that white is out of the picture in designer Daniel Heckscher's apartment. The 1980s building's apricot facade, along with his daughter's love of pink, influenced his choice of wall colour, while the complementary blue on the floor is a reference to the family's former house in the Stockholm archipelago. This is a home that pushes the boundaries and celebrates the sheer sensual pleasure of vibrant colour.

ABOVE LEFT The herringbone hall floor is the only white detail in the apartment. The pattern is formed by narrow rectangular tiles and meets a pink standard tile that is set on the diagonal on the walls. The coloured grouting between the tiles is a detail that creates contrast and provides an intriguing visual effect.

ABOVE RIGHT The same type of standard square tile appears in the kitchen, but in a light green hue. Daniel knocked through part of the wall between the kitchen and living room when he bought the apartment. The opening creates an airy space and the marble-topped bar is the family's favourite place to eat breakfast in the mornings.

THIS PAGE The salmon pink walls are in tune with the pastel pink facade of the block, which can be seen from the apartment's balcony. The moulding that covers the bottom part of the wall is painted the same blue as the floors, and to create a seamless effect, the ceiling is a light grey-blue hue.

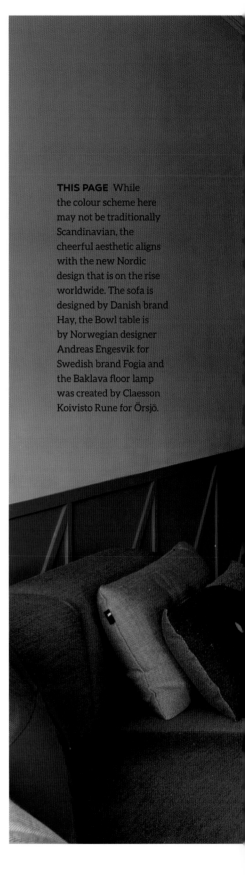

THIS PAGE While the colour scheme here may not be traditionally Scandinavian, the cheerful aesthetic aligns with the new Nordic design that is on the rise worldwide. The sofa is designed by Danish brand Hay, the Bowl table is by Norwegian designer Andreas Engesvik for Swedish brand Fogia and the Baklava floor lamp was created by Claesson Koivisto Rune for Örsjö.

ABOVE LEFT The modernist mouldings with diagonal stripes give character to the walls in the living room. The diagonal motif is repeated in the herringbone tile on the hallway floor. When Daniel bought the apartment, it was essentially a white box – the ideal opportunity for a designer to try out new, playful ideas.

ABOVE RIGHT The home is filled with items that have special meaning for Daniel. The small green marble table by Nick Ross was found at the Örnsbergsauktionen, an artist-run auction of studio-produced design and craft objects by Swedish and international designers held once a year, just outside of Stockholm.

A 30-minute drive from central Stockholm, in one of the archipelago's many bays, stands an apartment block dating back to 1988. The building itself, boasting a pastel apricot facade that stands out among the pines of the neighbourhood, is fairly typical of 1980s architecture, but a spectacular surprise awaits inside.

This is the home of interior architect Daniel Heckscher and his two children, Otis and India. The rich, saturated colours that dominate the space might seem daring at first sight, but the bold shades here make perfect sense when you learn that Daniel is part of Swedish design studio Note, which has gained a reputation worldwide for projects with adventurous palettes.

Daniel describes himself as drawn to design that affects people and evokes some sort of emotional response or leaves a lasting impression. It might be hard to pinpoint exactly what that impression is, or difficult to feel it right away, but you will take something with you when you leave. For him, this compact apartment offered somewhere to experiment in a playful way.

The warm orange-pink hue in the living area makes reference to the exterior of the apartment building (which is visible from the living room and kitchen area), and it was also chosen by Daniel's daughter India. He asked both children which colours they would like to have in their new home and India opted for pink, while son Otis wanted gold and black. To avoid too much

of a mismatch, Daniel plumped for a soothing pink palette and gave his son a new bicycle helmet in his favourite colours instead.

The children were at the forefront of Daniel's mind when it came to decorating the apartment. The kitchen tiles and the saturated blue of the flooring and wall mouldings are reminiscent of their previous home, where the family lived before Daniel's divorce. He explains that it felt right to use a colour scheme that the children were already familiar with. The colours in the living area set the tone for the rest of the apartment; deep blue-green and powdery pink mingle with bright yellow accents and a playful mix of patterns and textures. The ceramic herringbone tiles in the hallway are the only touch of white in the interior.

Daniel was partly educated abroad. Despite a background in economics, he was attracted to a more creative profession and was close to 30 when he began studying interior and spatial design, first in Milan and then at the prestigious Konstfack (University of Arts, Crafts and Design) in Stockholm. Although his career change came relatively late in life, strong colour and form have always fascinated him, and his love of colour was only enhanced by time spent abroad.

Daniel's theory is that many people opt for white or neutral interiors because they are nervous about choosing the 'right' colour and are frightened of making a mistake. However, life is not colourless. Even on the greyest winter day in Sweden, a thousand different shades can be seen just outside the window. He points out that few people would choose white or grey as their favourite colour and therefore it's strange that so many of us choose to decorate our homes in this way.

To anyone used to images of pared-back or monochrome Scandinavian interiors and stark white walls, the dramatic colour choices in this home might not seem to be traditionally Nordic.

OPPOSITE Daniel emphasizes that many of the materials used in his home were far from expensive, but they were chosen with care. The coloured tiles and grouting make all the difference in the kitchen, while the lamp from Established & Sons and the stools from Cappellini offer colourful contrasting accents.

ABOVE The oil painting is by Daniel's grandfather, who worked in a bank for his whole life but was also a talented artist. On the wall behind hangs a print by Mari Helen Wahlberg, a classmate of Daniel's from Konstfack. The sleek chair is from Muuto and the candlesticks are from Normann Copenhagen and Iittala.

On the other hand, when it comes to design and decoration, this apartment is identifiably Scandinavian in the sense that it manages to be uncluttered and functional yet still warm and welcoming. The tiled hall floor can be mopped quickly and easily after muddy mountain bikes and slushy shoes have made their mark. Daniel has also paid a great deal of attention to the lighting, which has to work well because the family spend most of the time in their apartment when it is dark outside. Nordic homes need effective lighting to cater for the long winters, while summer days tend to be spent out of doors.

Even though the family love their home and are very happy here, Daniel admits that part of him longs to get his teeth into an exciting new project. But as he wants to remain in the same area, it's a bit of a Catch-22. Moreover, it would be difficult to introduce any new colours into the apartment, as everything is so harmoniously matched. One thing is for sure, the current colour palette is perfect — and leaves no one untouched.

ABOVE AND OPPOSITE Instead of a traditional headboard, Daniel attached a framework of diagonal strips to the wall behind the bed to create a decorative panelled effect. The tranquil blue-green tone is a restful shade for a bedroom and recurs in the adjacent kids' room and in the hall. As those spaces have less natural daylight, Daniel used a slightly lighter shade of paint there, but clever lighting makes the difference in colour almost imperceptible. The rule of thumb is that the closer to a light source you are, the darker you can afford to go.

SECOND TIME AROUND

A spacious and serene villa in the peaceful Copenhagen suburb of Gentofte is
home to Danish art collector and gallerist Sara Lysgaard. Once decorated in a
fashionably pale and pared-down Scandinavian palette, her recently redecorated
home boldly embraces colour and pattern. A break-up a few years ago proved
a turning point both personally and stylistically, and gave Sara the opportunity
to develop her own vision. The result is a glamorous yet playful interior full of
art and colour that gives her energy and inspiration.

ABOVE LEFT Sara Lysgaard grew up surrounded by art – a legacy that
has continued into her adult life. In a corner of her living room hangs a
piece by British artist David Shrigley alongside a small Bubbly lamp by
Rosie Li, a puddle sculpture on the floor by art group AKassen and a
playful neon piece by Gun Gordillo.

ABOVE RIGHT Sara turned to Jannik Martensen-Larsen, owner
of Copenhagen's renowned Tapet-Café, for help in finding the right
colour palette, rugs and texiles for her home. It took the two of them
just 30 minutes to make their decisions. Sara chose Farrow & Ball paint
throughout and the petrol blue-grey in the living room is Inchyra Blue.

PAGE 81 The flooring throughout the house was treated with white hard wax to achieve a light, semi-matte finish. It's a perfect match for the grey Wishbone or Y-chairs from Hans J Wegner that surround a marble-topped dining table by another iconic Danish designer, Poul Kjærholm. The geometric Lina pendant light in brass hanging above the table is by the Chinese-born American designer Rosie Li and was inspired by 1960s Italian lighting. The red box made from salvaged materials just seen on the floor behind the table is by Brooklyn-based artist Graham Collins.

Once a popular summer retreat for Copenhagen's wealthy bourgeoisie, Gentofte is now a leafy, pleasant suburb located just ten minutes away from the city centre. The house where Sara lives was originally a large family home complete with gardens and stables, but it has been converted into separate units that now house six families. Her portion of the house is split over two floors and has its own lovely garden.

Sara moved in seven years ago, along with her boyfriend. Their newly renovated house was a clean white shell with white walls, white curtains and bleached wooden floors. Simple and stylish, the pared-down, typically Scandinavian interior suited the couple perfectly at the time. But times change, and when Sara's relationship came to an end, she decided that she wanted to remain in the house but to make a fresh start and create a new home to suit her new life.

Sara began the process by putting all of her furniture, art and other possessions into storage, leaving her with a blank canvas. Realizing that she had a new appetite for bold colour, she turned to Jannik Martensen-Larsen — a friend who also happens to be the owner of celebrated Danish design company Tapet-Café, which was founded in 1974 and is located in an old house close by in Gentofte. Sara asked Jannik to realize her vision

ABOVE AND OPPOSITE Sara chooses art by instinct and she has the same philosophy when it comes to selecting furniture. In the living room, the yellow velvet chaise longue from Danish company Eilersen is accompanied by the Diamond table from FOS and green and blue Lens tables with resin tops by British designers McCollin Bryan. The Moroccan rug is vintage, from Copenhagen store The Apartment. Daylight is reflected in the mirror piece by Henry Krokatsis and Adonis artwork by Elmgreen & Dragset.

PAGE 84 The living room has all the ingredients that are important for a warm and welcoming home: plants, textiles, light and colour. The elegant lines of the Gubi sofa are softened by cushions from Tapet-Café and the artwork is by Tom Humphreys.

PAGE 85 The French doors are screened by simple white curtains. The artwork is by David Shrigley and the floral rug is Fleurelle by Helene Blanche, a famous Danish textile designer and Jannik's wife.

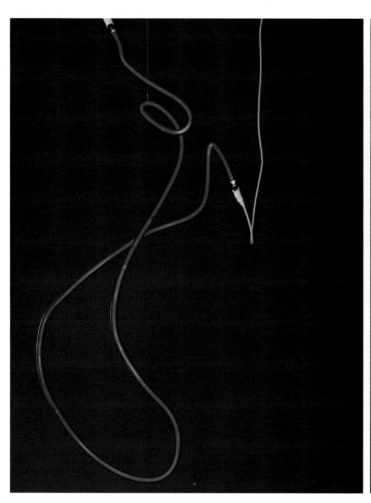

ABOVE LEFT The sculptural blue neon squiggle is by the Swedish-Danish artist Gun Gordillo. She has been working with light for more than 25 years, making the pieces herself in her studio. Well known in the Scandinavian art world, she is now popular on the international stage as well.

ABOVE RIGHT Paint-splattered coffee mugs from the LA-based ceramic artist Peter Shire reflect the changes in Sara's home over the past few years — from plain white to a vibrant spectrum of colour.

OPPOSITE A wooden staircase leads upstairs. The walls are Light Blue from Farrow & Ball and in the stairwell hangs an installation with soccer balls by Colombian artist Dario Escobar. The two paintings hung adjacent to each other in the corner are by New York-based artist Landon Metz. The timeless kitchen boasts glossy, white cabinets and had just been installed by the previous owner when Sara moved in, almost seven years ago.

of a home filled with timeless yet bold colours and richly patterned textiles in matching hues. With Jannik's encouragement and collaboration, Sara was able to commit to her vision of a colourful home.

The results are breathtaking. A palette of petrol blue, peppermint, powder pink, grass green and citrus yellow is combined with attention-grabbing artworks, patterned rugs and eclectic furnishings. Sara does not miss her all-white interior, saying that, while it suited her at the time, in retrospect it was bland and didn't make enough of a statement. Her attitude towards colour has undergone a complete change during the past few years, and Sara describes herself as something of a colour addict now, automatically opting for rich, vibrant shades when it comes to clothing, furniture and art. She explains that the transformation of her home has allowed her to be true to herself and her own personal tastes.

Sara grew up in a home that was filled with art. At the tender age of 18, she asked her father to withdraw all the funds from her childhood savings account so that she could buy her first piece. Today, as well as an art collector, Sara is

EXISTENCE
WHAT DOES
IT MATTER
I EXIST
ON THE BEST
TERMS
I CAN
THE PAST IS NOW PART OF MY
FUTURE
TH PRESENT
IS WELL OUT OF

OPPOSITE AND BELOW Sara's bedroom is painted in Setting Plaster by Farrow & Ball – a soft, restful pink. The large artwork is by Michael Bevilacqua and the cerise lamp is vintage, as is the vibrant Moroccan rug on the floor. The pink artwork hanging above a low stool is by Danish artist Troels Sandegaard (below), while the two works on the floor are by Morten Ernlund Jørgensen.

RIGHT Sara describes her bedroom as a beautiful, soft bubble. Previously the walls were white, but thanks to the high ceiling and the large windows, Sara says the room was almost too dazzlingly bright. The eyes artwork to the left of the bed is by Sven Dalsgaard.

owner of a holding company that makes various investments, and, until recently, was a partner in a gallery in Mallorca. As part of her job, Sara travels to art fairs around the world and cities such as Venice, New York and Paris, among others, and says she feels privileged to be able to visit some of the world's most beautiful cities on a regular basis. However, despite the globe trotting to glamorous destinations, Sara says that landing at Copenhagen airport is her favourite feeling. During her travels she leads a busy and sociable existence, so for her home is a place to retreat, rest and recharge the batteries.

Sara's art collection is eclectic and diverse, encompassing paintings, photographs, drawings, sculptures and more. Each and every piece has a story behind it and was chosen with thought, love and care. When it comes to buying, Sara looks for works that she has an immediate connection with and which speak to her in some way. It used to be believed that white walls provided the best backdrop for contemporary art, but in recent years they have started to look slightly outdated and most galleries have embraced softer hues. The strong, saturated wall colours in Sara's home perfectly showcase her collection, although Sara declares

LEFT Upstairs is a home office-cum-guest room. The slanted ceiling was painted in Farrow & Ball's Stone Blue and the walls in contrasting Calke Green for a fresh, playful effect. The elegantly minimal table lamp on the desk is the Get Set by Michael Anastassiades and the wall is hung with colourful pieces by several different artists.

OPPOSITE The white sofa from Meridiani doubles up as a bed for overnight guests. The green walls set off the vibrant orange artwork by French artist Philippe Parreno that hangs behind the sofa and the large-scale abstract painting by Clare Woods with its warm orange and brown tones. The rug is by Richard Colman for Danish brand Hay.

that neither the colour palette nor the furnishings were deliberately chosen to match the art. Friends and acquaintances have sometimes sought her advice on buying artworks to match a decorative scheme, but Sara maintains that art should be chosen because it sparks an emotional connection, not purely to match an interior decorator's mood board.

When she talks about her home, Sarah compares it to life in general: always changing, constantly evolving. The original decor — white, cool and pared-down — has developed into something colourful, confident and bold, and for the first time in a long while, Sara feels that her surroundings are completely in tune with her personality.

THIS PAGE Isabelle's apartment is located in Stockholm's bohemian SoFo district. The family's previous home was in the same neighbourhood and they only moved a few blocks to their new home. The apartment is a maisonette/duplex and the kids have their own space downstairs, while the living areas occupy the top floor.

DREAMING IN COLOUR

In the heart of Stockholm, interior designer, blogger and TV personality Isabelle McAllister has created a family home that's full of fun, distinctive designs and brave colour choices. It's a warm, convivial space furnished with flea-market bargains, quirky antiques and upcycled pieces, and the relaxed vibe signals that the inhabitants don't take themselves too seriously. Environmental awareness, untrammelled creativity and a passion for colour and pattern have all made their mark on Isabelle's cosy loft apartment.

ABOVE LEFT Concrete tiles by Scandinavian design trio Claesson Koivisto Rune for Marrakech Design cover the wall behind the hob/stovetop. The emerald green works well against the plaster pink walls and granite countertop, and the graphic detailing and asymmetrical arrangement make a bold design statement.

ABOVE RIGHT Isabelle chose an eco-friendly kitchen from Finnish company Puustelli Miinus. The materials and manufacturing process are non-toxic and all the parts can be reused or recycled. As a result, its carbon footprint is about 50 per cent less than a standard kitchen. The kitchen counter is extra deep to provide additional work space.

THIS PAGE Isabelle adores colour but says that finding the right combinations can sometimes be a challenge. The wall behind the wall tiles was originally mint green and the kitchen cabinets were a mid-blue. She thinks the current scheme of dusty pink walls and dark green cabinets suits the space much better. The bench in the foreground is a vintage Indian piece, the leaf wall lamp was found in Belgium and the wall-mounted pineapple sconce came from a market in Berlin.

OPPOSITE The powdery pink colour of the walls matches Isabelle's wedding dress, partly concealed by an oil painting to the right of the chimneybreast. In Isabelle's opinion, saturated pastels are a better base for a room than white – they add warmth and subtlety and don't get dirty and dingy. Just blending white paint with a few drops of pigment will result in more interesting walls.

BELOW LEFT AND RIGHT The apartment is filled with unique pieces and quirky details. The vintage Öglan cafe chairs from Ikea and the bubblegum pink table (seen opposite) were used in a job Isabelle did where children were allowed to paint an apartment that was for sale. A closer look at the chairs reveals that they are beautifully sprinkled with drops of cerise and orange paint.

As soon as you enter Isabelle McAllister's apartment, it is obvious that she is not afraid of colour. A plaster pink sitting room, forest green bedroom and a bathroom tiled in peppermint green are not unusual by Isabelle's standards. She is known as a colour advocate and uses television appearances, magazine articles and her blog to encourage her fellow Swedes to embrace colour and creativity. Paint and colour make Isabelle happy and she believes that it is difficult to design a cosy, beautiful home only using white — in her opinion, monochromatic interiors may be photogenic, but they are very hard to live in. Isabelle's theory is that the minimalist white homes we see all over social media are like pop songs – we listen to them on the radio and eventually we start to sing along, but is it because we actually like the music, or because we've heard it so many times that the tune has taken root in our brains? As for the old decorating rule that white is the only colour to use if you want to make a room appear lighter, she points out that we no longer live in the 17th century — effective lighting is available at the flick of a switch.

Isabelle's aesthetic is one of cheerful imperfection. Her bold tastes and resourceful attitude were instilled in her during her childhood, as both her parents worked with colour and design. Her mother is originally from Belgium and when Isabelle was a teenager the family moved there. She learned Flemish and began a course at art school, only to drop out and start designing lamps and styling homes instead. Her father, a scrap dealer and salvage merchant, still helps out with many of her projects and has a solution for every problem.

Isabelle's apartment is divided over two floors and the communal areas occupy the attic space. The open-plan living room-cum-kitchen has slanting ceilings, wooden beams and a huge fireplace taking up most of one wall, which posed something of a challenge when they first moved in. To begin with, Isabelle painted the kitchen cabinets sea blue and the walls of the kitchen area mint green, but after a while she reconsidered and repainted the walls a muted pink and the cabinets dark grey-brown. She says she often defaults to dusty pastels — they are neutral, soft and timeless, and combine happily with many other colours.

Isabelle didn't start with a grand plan or vision for the apartment. Instead, she likes to make a start decorating and see where she ends up. Her home is somewhere that allows her to experiment and try new things – when inspiration strikes, she unearths an old tin of paint from her cache and her husband comes home that night to discover that the furniture or walls have changed colour. For example, Isabelle recently repainted the bedroom a soft, luxurious dark green shade. She hasn't changed anything else in the room, but both she and her husband have noticed that now they use the room much more, going in there to read or relax.

Most of the items in Isabelle's apartment were discovered in flea markets and antiques shops, both

OPPOSITE Against the gallery wall stands a workbench that was previously used for carpentry work in the family's country house in Sweden's Dalarna province. The pink armchair was bought in Paris by Isabelle's mother many years ago and was reupholstered by Isabelle's father. Her parents are creatives who have worked with colour and design all their lives.

ABOVE A string of lights playfully delineates the slope of the roof. The old storage cabinet, which is on wheels, looks as if it might have had a previous life in a hospital or dental practice. Isabelle found it in a flea market.

OPPOSITE AND PAGE 102
The bedroom was recently repainted after a family holiday to Milan, where Isabelle was inspired by the decor of the hotel they stayed in. Isabelle is a dab hand at crafting and upcycling – she made the ochre cushions herself from old bath towels.

ABOVE LEFT In the bedroom, ornate vintage lamps featuring lustrous gold-coloured leaves stand out beautifully against the deep, dark green walls. Since the room was repainted, Isabelle finds it a much more welcoming and relaxing space.

ABOVE RIGHT The apartment has numerous charming yet awkward nooks and crannies. Isabelle had some fun with paint tester pots in this little niche in a corner of the bedroom. The ceiling is the same pink as the living room, while a small area of floor is painted a vibrant mustard yellow.

PAGE 103 The mint green and grey bathroom was newly renovated when the family moved in and Isabelle thought it would be very wasteful to tear everything out and start again. Instead, she is thinking about a few small changes to make the space truly her own.

at home and abroad. Upcycling is her speciality subject and she says a lick of paint or a length of fabric gives most items a new lease of life. Hunting for treasure at flea markets is one of her favourite activities. The most important thing for Isabelle is falling in love with an object. She is not interested in status symbols or iconic designer pieces and values character, comfort and personality in a home over impersonal perfection.

This is a friendly, easy-going space where everyone feels at home. Isabelle has allowed her kids free rein in their own rooms — her son has covered his walls with posters of footballers/soccer players and Isabelle was a little surprised when her pre-teen daughter wanted to paint her bedroom walls white. But then her daughter also recently suggested that they could transform a pair of her trousers into cool, bespangled shorts to wear to a party — so the creativity, recycling gene and desire to go one's own way seems to have been transmitted to the next generation too.

MAJESTIC
PASTELS

EMBRACING HISTORY

In this majestic residence in the affluent Östermalm district of central Stockholm, three perfectly preserved traditional ceramic-tiled stoves dating back to the 19th century provided the inspiration for a colour scheme that encompasses every aspect of the decor. Note Design Studio was tasked with adapting the period interior to make it suitable for modern family life. Their solution was to use a palette of warm pastel hues and to introduce a variety of interesting textures and patterns to provide further visual interest.

On the fourth floor of an unremarkable building in a quiet corner of Östermalm is an entirely remarkable modern family home. The rooms are lofty and imposing, and their stately period features are decorated in an unexpected palette of creamy pastel tones. The colour scheme manages to be distinctive without being overly dramatic or attention seeking — the main living rooms are bathed in a gentle, welcoming wash of colour that gives the impression that the sun is shining in through the tall windows all year round. As you wander from room to room, the subtlety of the scheme becomes apparent. Delicate hues of buttery yellow, mossy green, apricot and pale grey wash over the walls and

ABOVE LEFT AND RIGHT In the kitchen of this astonishing apartment the buttercup yellow walls give everything a warm, sun-kissed glow. Light wood furniture harmonizes perfectly with wall cupboards painted a saturated golden shade.

ABOVE CENTRE The kitchen island is made from polished terrazzo. This lively material is flecked with yellow, black and

grey, and picks up the colours that run through the apartment. The clean modern lines of the island contrast with the original architecture features in the room.

OPPOSITE The window treatments were kept very simple so as not to compete with the architectural details. The curtains match the walls and ceilings, and the fabric has a loose weave that allows daylight to shine through.

ceilings and, despite the splendour of the 19th-century architecture, the overall effect is surprisingly modern.

It's hard to believe that just a year or so ago, this tranquil, elegant interior was an impersonal, tired-looking office space with white walls and ugly modern spotlights disfiguring the tall ceilings. The apartment had been used as the headquarters of a Danish fashion brand for a couple of decades and did not have a kitchen, bathroom or any proper storage facilities. But many of the building's original features were still intact, including the wooden parquet flooring and decorative plaster ceiling mouldings, and the space still had something of

its former grandeur. It was at this point that its new owner approached Swedish design studio Note and asked for their help in transforming the apartment into a beautiful, practical family home that retained the interior's period detailing.

The Note team was headed by interior architect Susanna Wåhlin. Instead of trying to recreate a 19th-century interior, she and her colleagues decided to take it in a contemporary direction while retaining the architectural integrity of the space. One of the things that first caught Susanna's eye were the *kakelugnar* or original Swedish ceramic-tiled stoves that occupied three of the rooms in the apartment. Despite the interior's previous

OPPOSITE AND ABOVE The homeowner particularly enjoys cooking and wanted a spacious and functional kitchen. Note Design Studio were inspired by traditional Italian country kitchens, where the layout is based around various unfitted elements. The refrigerator and freezer are concealed in the freestanding khaki cupboard at one end of the room.

incarnation as an office space, the stoves had been well maintained and their distinctive glazed majolica tiles in shades of green, pink and buttery cream provided Susanna and the Note team with inspiration for a colour scheme for the rest of the home.

As work started on the apartment, other colours came to light and were added to the palette one by one, until it encompassed eight harmonious pastel tones. When a wall was demolished to provide access to plumbing pipes, it revealed an old door frame painted in a rich mustard yellow hue that has been used to adorn new storage cabinets. When the floors were sanded, beautifully patterned parquet became apparent. Each room had its own individual design and Susanna found the graphic Viennese Cross pattern of the parquet in the bedroom especially appealing. The team from Note decided to utilize its symmetrical cross pattern as a recurrent motif that would unite all the new elements in the apartment.

Wall-mounted storage cabinets were designed to hold all the necessities of everyday life and these were either made to be freestanding or attached to the walls a couple of feet up from the floor. This was to prevent any damage to the original skirting/base boards and meet the client's request that the refurbishment must respect the 19th-century splendour of the interior. The new floating cabinets are pleasingly functional and give a sense of lightness and space. All the new cabinetry features diagonal markings that mimic the pattern of the parquet flooring, as do two new walls that were constructed.

ABOVE LEFT AND RIGHT Note were responsible for choosing everything in the apartment, from paint colours to furniture to even the smallest decorative details. When it came to selecting the tableware and household utensils, they opted for contemporary shapes and textures that complemented the sophisticated colour scheme of the interior rather than the original style of the apartment.

ABOVE CENTRE The glassware collection Tela from Danish Hay has a subtle smoked colour and interesting texture that stand out against the soft yellow walls. The design was originally formed by experimenting with blowing molten glass into stitched textile bags.

OPPOSITE The splendid architectural features in this interior are its crowning glory. Built in the neo-Renaissance or Renaissance Revival style, the apartment boasts grandiose decorations such as the pediments above the doorways and the ornate plaster mouldings that adorn the cornices/crown moldings.

PAGE 114 Black details bring a little drama and definition to the tranquil decor. In the sitting room, the airy Vertigo pendant lamp by Constance Guisset for French brand Petite Friture almost seems to spread its wings and hover above the furniture. When the light is switched on, it casts elegant, attenuated shadows over the ceiling and walls.

PAGE 115 The main rooms in the apartment are arranged *en enfilade* and from the bedroom it is possible to look straight ahead through the kitchen and into the sitting room at the other end of the space. The Beetle upholstered chair and footstool from Gubi provide a vibrant pop of colour against the calm, pastel backdrop, as does the leafy plant in the foreground.

OPPOSITE In the sitting room, the furniture is arranged around the glorious *kakelugn* stove, with its rococo detailing. The quilted lounge chairs in a punchy coral shade were created by Note Design Studio for Danish brand Won. The cushioned inside of the chair was inspired by a mango fruit that has been sliced into squares before being pushed inside out. The terrazzo-topped coffee table is the Tabula, also by Note.

ABOVE The matte paint on the walls tends to absorb more light than a normal emulsion and so several contemporary lamps have been used to offer increased illumination and mood lighting. The black table lamp is the Mayfair from Spanish lighting brand Vibia.

RIGHT In Swedish bourgeois residences of the late 19th century, lavish decorative ceramic stoves were generally installed in the living room. The intricate decorative details and delicate hues of this example inspired Susanna Wåhlin of Note Design Studio to decorate the rest of the apartment in the same palette.

OPPOSITE The perfectly preserved corner stove in the bedroom is covered with majolica glazed tiles in tones of rich olive green. This type of masonry stove is very typical of the era when the house was built and is characterized by its dark tiles and their bold relief patterns. They were once to be found in almost every Swedish home, but during the early 20th century the vogue for tiled stoves slowly died out, thanks to the development of central heating and electricity.

BELOW The walls and ceilings are all painted with Pashmina paint from Swedish brand Alcro, which gives a luxurious, extremely matte effect. The wall colour in the bedroom was chosen to match the tiled stove and the green-grey tone gives the room a serene, restful mood.

RIGHT The specially designed bed is reminiscent of a Japanese futon and its angular form provides an interesting contrast to the classical ceiling rose. Like the cabinetry, the bed was built by a carpentry company that Note often collaborate with and the frame was spray-painted to achieve an immaculate finish.

For a contemporary look, in each room the walls, ceilings and mouldings were all painted the same colour, creating a calm, spacious effect. The paint used was from Swedish brand Alcro and the finish is flat with an almost velvety texture. To offer a subtle contrast, the imposing door surrounds, with their beautiful pediments and dentil mouldings, were painted a soft greenish-grey shade, as were the tall skirting/base boards, window niches and radiators.

When it came to furnishing the apartment, Note Design Studio chose modern Scandinavian designs with clean lines and simple forms, including several of their own products. The materials vary from natural unvarnished wood to powder-coated metal to sleek terrazzo.

ABOVE All the parquet floors in the apartment were sanded, then treated with a white wax oil. The upholstered pink Beetle lounge chair and footstool are from Danish brand Gubi and provide a vivid pop of colour in the otherwise tranquil green bedroom.

ABOVE RIGHT AND OPPOSITE The walls in the study are painted a muted shade of apricot. The sofa is the upholstered Beetle from Gubi, while the floor lamp is the Silo by Note. The strong olive green of the bookshelf (seen opposite) echoes the colour of the tiled stove in the bedroom. The black desk and slender desk lamp add a little definition to the pastel scheme.

The kitchen is at the very heart of the apartment and the walls are painted a buttery light yellow. The kitchen cabinets echo the dark green hue of the tiled stove in the bedroom and feature a simple grid design on their doors. Instead of opting for classic marble, the rectangular kitchen island was crafted from functional polished terrazzo flecked with yellow, black, grey and white. Above the practical limestone splashback, Row white wall lamps from Atelier Areti were fitted to cast task light onto the worksurface, while the powder-coated Silo Trio lamp in yellow by Note hangs over the long wooden dining table.

The master bedroom is painted in a light olive green that takes its cue from the tiled stove that occupies one corner. The rest of the room has been kept deliberately simple so as not to detract from this striking feature and the ornate plaster ceiling rose. The wall behind the bed has been panelled and features the same symmetrical cross device that appears elsewhere in the apartment. In the bathroom, the gentle colour scheme and matte finishes reoccur in the form of powdery, unglazed Pico wall tiles from Italian brand Mutina. Even in here the concept is clear — calm shades, modern design and interesting textures perfectly complement the lavish period splendour of this unique apartment.

THIS PAGE The hallway is full of warmth, light and colour. The Alexandrie wallpaper from Pierre Frey features exotic vegetation and swaying palm trees, and sets the colour palette for the rest of the apartment. The wall panelling was fitted when Rikke and her fiancé renovated the apartment.

A HINT OF THE TROPICS

When interior stylist Rikke Bye Andersen moved into this period apartment in central Oslo, it was in need of some tender loving care. Over the decades, the soul of the 19th-century apartment had been eradicated by a series of refurbishments and renovations, so Rikke and her fiancé decided to restore the space to its former glory. The new parquet flooring and reinstated architectural features are faithful to the building's past, while the decor and furnishings are an eclectic mix of colours and styles. The result? A touch of the tropics in the middle of the city.

ABOVE LEFT Rikke has always loved blue and green shades and for the hall walls she chose Teresa's Green from Farrow & Ball — a warm, rich aqua blue. The finish is matte and the colour picks up those in the wallpaper. The white stoneware Dot vase comes from House Doctor DK and has an interesting irregular surface and ivory-white glaze.

ABOVE RIGHT Yellow is a recurring accent colour in Rikke's home. In the entrance hall is a low bench with a cushion covered in a vivid mustard fabric (see picture opposite), and on the kitchen countertop stands an anglepoise lamp in a lemon yellow shade. The primary colour pops against the soft pastel walls.

BELOW At one end of the kitchen stands a pretty antique wooden side table decorated with fresh flowers, books and ornamental items including a coral under a glass display bell. On the wall above hangs a portrait of Mao by Andy Warhol dating back to the early 1970s. In Rikke's home, pieces of art, textiles and small treasures contribute splashes of colour.

RIGHT In the kitchen, all the cabinets and appliances were covered with new fronts in a peppermint shade dubbed Aerugo Green from Swedish brand Superfront. This particular design is called Illusion, as its subtle pattern seems to change as light shifts during the course of the day. Some people see squares, others a zigzag pattern or box. The glossy marble worktop adds a classic element.

Located in the Majorstuen neighbourhood in western Oslo, Rikke's apartment is part of an old townhouse dating back to 1904. During the past hundred or so years, the apartment had undergone multiple renovations and most of the original architectural features had been torn out. When she first moved in, Rikke herself experimented with various different colour palettes and decorative styles, but recently she and her fiancé decided to go back to the drawing board and take on the challenge of a full restoration and refurbishment.

Visiting their neighbours gave the couple an invaluable insight into the apartment's original architecture and how it once looked. To recreate the same feel in her home, Rikke installed a *kakelugn* – a traditional tiled stove – in the living room, covered the walls of the hallway with dado-height panelling, and reinstated the cornices/crown moldings on the ceilings. On the floors, parquet was laid in a classic Dutch pattern.

The newly refurbished apartment was decorated in a carefully chosen palette of calm pastels and furnished with a mixture of modern and retro pieces. Rikke is drawn to soft shades

THIS PAGE The kitchen and living room are open plan. Rikke opted for cool pastels here, saying that she prefers them to vibrant hues, as they create a timeless look that can be quickly updated by adding new textiles and decorative items. The pared-back decor makes the room feel lighter and draws the attention to the red dining table from Muuto and the classic CH24 Wishbone or Y-chairs by Hans J Wegner.

LEFT The living room is filled with Scandinavian design classics both old and new. The art on the wall includes works by Scandinavian artists Marit Geraldine Bostad, Johs. Bøe and Souvanni Asmussen, and harmonizes with the gentle pastel colour scheme. The large green painting is by Marit Geraldine Bostad and is entitled 'Shy but Not', which seems to sum up this soft yet colourful home perfectly.

on the walls – she feels they create a timeless backdrop that can be updated by changing decorative details, textiles and other pieces in step with different seasons and passing trends.

The apartment is full of colourful details and observant visitors will recognize several patterns by well-known 1930s designers. Rikke is greatly inspired by the classic Swedish brand Svenskt Tenn and the work of its great designers Josef Frank and Estrid Ericson. Together, Ericson and Frank transformed rigid Scandinavian functionalism into something much more inviting, joyful and vibrant. Their version of Scandinavian style was bold and sophisticated, and included pattern and colour while maintaining a sense of simplicity. The same characteristics can be seen in Rikke's home.

The public areas, such as the hallway, living room and kitchen, feature bold patterns and quirky

OPPOSITE AND LEFT Rikke and her fiancé laid new parquet floors throughout the apartment. The wood has an antique finish and a slightly matte surface treatment, which means that the colour changes in different lights. In the small home office-cum-guest room, the warm beige walls match the flooring perfectly.

LEFT For this room, Rikke chose an earthy beige hue with pinkish undertones called Soft Skin from Norwegian paint brand Jotun. Its matte finish gives a densely pigmented effect. This space doubles up as a guest room and has a calm, relaxing mood. The photos on the wall are by Esther Haase and Mikal Strøm, and their candy-coloured pastels echo the colours that Rikke has used elsewhere in the apartment.

BELOW To create a luxe hotel vibe, Rikke and her fiancé installed a small sink and mirror in the guest room — a very practical addition in a small apartment and one that allows visitors to freshen up in the privacy of their own room.

decorative pieces and are furnished with a selection of mid-century Scandinavian design classics. But this home is not all about retro styling — there is more than a smattering of contemporary art and modern furniture in organic shapes. The bedrooms are more tranquil, and are decorated and furnished with a calm simplicity.

When Rikke and her fiancé renovated the apartment, they reconfigured the kitchen and living room to create an open-plan layout that not only makes the space feel much bigger and brighter but also means it is perfect for entertaining. Lighting is important here. The sitting room boasts a Louis Poulsen Panthella floor lamp by Danish designer Verner Panton and a George Nelson Bubble Saucer pendant light that was originally inspired by a set of silk-covered Swedish hanging lamps. Over the kitchen table hangs the Semi brass pendant light from Danish brand Gubi, and the white wall lamps in the kitchen are the PH 2/1 — the smallest members of the famous PH3 family

ABOVE A notebook covered with Celotocaulis, a Josef Frank design dating back to 1930, takes pride of place on Rikke's small marble bedside table..

LEFT Both the guest room and the bedroom have built-in shelves painted the same colour as the walls. This creates a unified look and provides a soft, subtle backdrop for the cheerful items arranged on the shelves.

designed by Poul Henningsen in the 1950s. Rikke was determined she wanted to fit these lamps above the kitchen worksurface, and therefore the couple opted for roomy base cabinets rather than wall cupboards. To add colour and visual interest, they replaced the existing Ikea kitchen doors with peppermint green ones from Swedish brand Superfront, which produces new fronts especially designed to fit Ikea kitchen cabinets. This particular design is called Illusion, thanks to its subtle pattern that appears differently as light shifts during the course of the day.

Rikke runs her own company offering styling and interior design for magazines, advertising campaigns, private homes and offices. In order to stay true to her own unique sense of style, she has tried to create a home that reflects her own tastes and personality yet is neutral and timeless. It's no surprise to hear that Rikke's professional skills came in useful during the refurb – she put together detailed mood boards before the renovation got underway and she has changed the fabric on various pieces of furniture and repainted the apartment herself several times.

The result is a home that's unmistakably Scandinavian yet boasts a very up-to-date colour scheme. After more than a hundred years, this apartment has finally been restored to its former glory, but it is the colourful details that bring it to life.

THIS PAGE The bedroom is painted in Peignoir from Farrow & Ball – a soft, greyish pink shade that provides a sophisticated backdrop for the raspberry and aqua accents that spice up the room. The handmade cushions on the bed are by Danish designer Christina Lundsteen and Rikke reupholstered the Ikea headboard herself. Both thick curtains and sheer voile panels hang at the windows, allowing Rikke and her fiancé to adjust the light levels as necessary.

A SOPHISTICATED SPACE

This airy apartment with views over Stockholm has been transformed from a white, minimalist and rather impersonal space into a warm and welcoming home. When businessman Stefan Lundborg and his family decided to leave the suburbs and move back into the centre of town, they wanted a home that both lent itself to entertaining and offered a tranquil, functional base for everyday life. With the help of a calm palette, elegant furnishings and a smattering of Nordic design classics, this apartment meets their requirements perfectly.

For most parents there comes a time when little kids grow into big kids and nobody wants to kick a ball around the garden anymore. After many happy years living in Stockholm's pleasant suburbs, this happened to Stefan Lundborg, his partner and their teenage sons. The whole family yearned for the faster pace of urban life and decided to leave their comfortable suburban existence for a new start in the city centre.

In a tall 1930s house in central Stockholm, the family found an apartment that caught their attention. The huge balcony offering astonishing views over the city was a great attraction, but the modern black and white interior did not appeal. The white walls,

ABOVE LEFT AND CENTRE Sand, clay and cashmere were materials that inspired the colour palette in this apartment. The walls and ceilings are painted shades of apricot pink and sandy beige, which creates a soft, hazy atmosphere. The space works wonderfully for family life and is also great for entertaining. Stefan and his partner have demanding jobs and travel extensively, so their priority was a relaxing home that was a joy to return to.

ABOVE RIGHT The silver jug on the fireplace was inherited, while the candleholder was a gift from good friends. The latter is very appropriately called 'The Knot of Friendship' and was designed by Josef Frank for Svenskt Tenn in 1938, a year before the outbreak of the Second World War, as a symbol of peace and friendship.

THIS PAGE At first, Stefan and his wife were unsure about the pinky beige colour that covers the walls. What had looked like a soft neutral on the colour card proved to be a much more definite colour on the walls and ceilings. After a little while, and once the furniture was in place, the couple fell in love with the calming hue.

large glass partitions and black elements felt hard and inhospitable. The family decided that if they were going to make a major lifestyle change, they wanted their new home to be different and special with a spin on modern Scandinavian design.

Both Stefan and his partner work in the world of finance and travel a great deal for work. They wanted a home that was easy to live in and relaxing to come back to, but also suitable for entertaining business associates and friends from all over the world. To make their dreams a reality, Stefan contacted Stockholm-based design studio Note. The brief was to create a warm, cosy space with a homey, welcoming atmosphere and a timeless, sophisticated vibe. Note put together a mood board that attempted to capture those feelings, drawing inspiration from images of an Italian piazza, a pirouetting ballerina, a cashmere coat and a pair of sand-coloured sneakers.

ABOVE The painting hanging on the wall by the stairs is by Swedish artist and songwriter Ulf Lundell. Stefan bought it many years ago as he is a great fan of Lundell's music.

LEFT When the family moved in, there was a heavy oak staircase with glass panels leading up to the loft area. To create a neater look, it was replaced with a specially designed staircase by Note Design Studio. The new version has taller risers and is painted the same colour as the wall to blend in. The handrail is covered in a tactile leather strap.

OPPOSITE The open-plan layout contains many different social spaces, which allows the whole family to be together even while engaged with varying activities in different areas. The staircase leads up to a mezzanine level, while the spacious seating area has two long, low sofas upholstered in putty pink and sky blue arranged around the glossy Zorro table by Note.

LEFT AND ABOVE Before the apartment was renovated, there was little or no effective storage. The tall dormer windows and roof angles made it impossible to fit wall cabinets, so Note Design Studio suggested constructing low-level units holding deep drawers. These create a long horizontal line that grounds the space nicely. The warm steel blue colour reappears in the master bedroom and on shelves and doors throughout. The pale wood dining table and the gently padded Beetle chairs from Danish brand Gubi echo the soft pastel shade of the sloping ceiling.

The high ceilings, sharp roof angles and narrow dormer windows of the apartment made it difficult to use curtains to soften the space. Instead, the walls and ceilings were painted in a palette of gentle pastel hues to create a calm and composed atmosphere. The colour scheme consists of three soft shades – apricot pink, warm sandy beige and a smoky grey-blue – and painting the ceilings the same subtle colour as the walls produces a sleek, seamless effect. However, it took the family some time to get used to the results – Stefan says that the first time he and his partner saw the painted walls they were in a state of shock. Shades that had looked subtle and knocked back on the colour chart made much more of a statement when they covered all the walls and ceilings.

OPPOSITE The apartment is located in an unusually tall house in the southern part of Stockholm's centre. This means that it has magnificent views of the city and light flows in all day long. It is lovely most of the time, but can be quite confusing during midsummer, when the nights are almost non-existent, admits Stefan. The blue-grey storage units run throughout the interior and provide a strong base for the decor and the high ceilings.

LEFT The stepped staircase form is a motif that's repeated in several places – here on the side of the chimney breast. The glass vase is called Äng, which means meadow in Swedish, and is from modern Swedish design brand Klong.

BELOW Open fireplaces are a typical feature of Swedish homes and this example has a rugged, functional charm. The oak parquet flooring was sanded and treated with a little white lacquer to create a dull lustre that complements the walls.

To foster a sense of comfort and ease, the apartment is furnished with soft upholstered pieces in elegant, simple shapes. The interior plays with typical Nordic materials, a timeless colour palette and a sleek international vibe.

One of Stefan's more practical requirements was plenty of storage. The tall ceilings and awkward slanting roofs of the top-floor apartment made it difficult to construct full-height storage, so Note suggested fitting low-level, deep drawer units throughout the apartment. Painted a soft grey-blue, these units contribute a strong horizontal element that counteracts the high ceilings and adds a unifying feature to the interior.

The blue colour reappears in the master bedroom. This space was relatively small, so it was decided to enhance the feeling of intimacy and enclosure by painting the room dark blue. Stefan says the dark walls create a soothing cave-like atmosphere and, even though they live in the middle of a noisy city, the couple sleep undisturbed.

The beautiful, sculptural staircase that leads up to the mezzanine level is another feature that

THIS PAGE From this small dining area, the family enjoys views across the Stockholm rooftops. The soft beige of the walls feels even warmer when the sun shines in. The chairs are part of the Spine collection by Space Copenhagen for Fredericia Furniture. The design is influenced by Børge Mogensen but with a modern touch.

ABOVE LEFT The traditional Windsor chair has been synonymous with Swedish design since Carl Malmsten created his Lilla Åland chair in 1942 and can be found in many Swedish and Norwegian summer cottages. This version is the J110 from Hay. Its tall back and armrests create a regal, refined look, and its austere form looks striking silhouetted against the soft wall colour.

ABOVE RIGHT The blue-grey hue is picked up again on the desk, while the tan leather of the desk chair pops up throughout the apartment on details such as the the staircase handrail. The articulated black floor lamp stands ready to take over once night falls and the daylight fades away.

PAGES 140 AND 141 To create an intimate feel in the small master bedroom, the space was painted a rich, saturated steel blue. The textiles were chosen to match: the cotton bedspread is Quilt Sideways by All The Way To Paris for Hay. Plenty of effective lighting was planned to compensate for the dark walls, and the wall-mounted Bestlite lamps provide focused light to read by. The wall behind the bed is covered with a wooden panel with an incised grid design that brings the monochromatic scheme texture and visual interest.

transformed the apartment. Note replaced a large staircase with glass sections with a neat, economical flight of stairs sprayed the same colour as the walls and accompanied by slender metal banisters and a handrail covered in wound leather.

The sunlight that shines uninterrupted through the high windows also makes its mark on the interior. In the kitchen, where the family likes to meet for breakfast with coffee and the morning papers, natural light plays over the beige walls. Nowadays the family love the soft colour palette and the homey atmosphere delights guests. The open-plan layout of the interior allows them to spend time together without necessarily doing the same thing or even being in the same space – one teenage son can watch TV on the sofa while the other studies at the dining table and Stefan prepares supper in the kitchen, chatting to both of them at the same time. This is a home that perfectly balances the sophisticated and the social.

THIS PAGE Mikkel and Mette designed the house themselves, drawing inspiration from classic Danish barn architecture. The tiled chimney in the centre of the space is both beautiful and functional, as it serves to support the roof construction.

AT HOME WITH NATURE

At the northernmost edge of Zealand, Danish craftsmanship and exotic treasures from all over the world coexist happily beneath the soaring roof of a newly built home. The photographer Mikkel Adsbøl, his wife Mette and their two sons moved here a few years ago, after the couple had designed the house of their dreams. Mikkel and Mette's home exudes a very Scandinavian type of luxury. There is no gilt or bling here. Instead, functional solutions, robust materials, a cosy atmosphere and close proximity to nature are valued above all else.

Weary of urban life, Mikkel and Mette dreamed of a new start in the countryside north of Copenhagen. Mette had a vision of life at the water's edge, while Mikkel wanted their children to grow up surrounded by fields and woodland. The couple found the perfect plot overlooking a lake and at the edge of one of the country's largest forests, and here they built a long, low, whitewashed house inspired by traditional Danish barn architecture. The location is idyllic and the views from the house are constantly changing, depending on the season, time of day and weather.

Mikkel and Mette share a typically Nordic love of nature and this is evident both indoors and out. When they designed the

ABOVE LEFT Many of the unique decorative pieces were bought abroad and shipped back home. This old urn close to the doorway planted up with a *Monstera deliciosa* was found on a trip to France.

ABOVE CENTRE The walls of the main living area are painted Bagdad Grey — a calming blue-grey shade from Danish paint brand Flügger that was inspired by colours used in

historic Danish buildings. The piece of carved wood hanging on the hall wall was originally from a house in India.

ABOVE RIGHT For a family with children, storage is of paramount importance. The Adsbøl family planned ample storage space when they designed the house, including this long run of built-in cupboards/closets in the hallway.

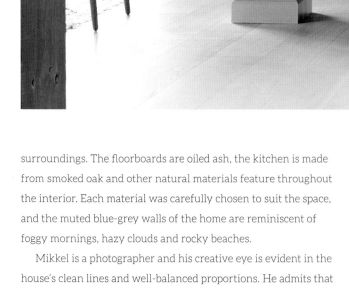

ABOVE The window separating the entrance hall from the living room is more than 100 years old and was salvaged from the B&W shipyard in Copenhagen. The elegant OW150 daybed is a Danish classic designed by Ole Wanscher in 1950 and the angled brass wall lights are from Tine K.

RIGHT The kitchen was handcrafted in smoked oak by Københavns Møbelsnedkeri. Mikkel and Mette bought it before they had made a start on the house and have used the rich tones of the smoked oak as a recurrent motif. The brass pendant light was custom made.

house, the couple created mood boards and collated colour samples and materials to make it easier to visualize the final result. Their previous home was decorated in lighter tones, but in this location they decided to create a scheme based around the clear, restful blue-grey hues so often found in the Nordic landscape. Building a home from scratch allowed Mette and Mikkel to choose materials and textures in tune with the

surroundings. The floorboards are oiled ash, the kitchen is made from smoked oak and other natural materials feature throughout the interior. Each material was carefully chosen to suit the space, and the muted blue-grey walls of the home are reminiscent of foggy mornings, hazy clouds and rocky beaches.

Mikkel is a photographer and his creative eye is evident in the house's clean lines and well-balanced proportions. He admits that

he employed photographic techniques such as negative space when designing the house and that he naturally inclines towards a limited colour palette. Sticking to one main colour but using different tones on textiles, walls and woodwork has brought the space a soft, soothing atmosphere.

The calm blue shades used throughout go well with the brass details and soaring wooden ceilings in the living area and kitchen. In fact, the smoked oak kitchen sets the style for the whole house. Mikkel found it in a showroom four years before they built the house and fell in love with its rich hues, strong lines and incredible craftsmanship. The couple bought, dismantled and stored the units and then, several years later, installed them in their newly built house. Mikkel says the kitchen is one of his favourite places and he loves to cook there.

The huge exposed beams that support the roof were sourced abroad because it was impossible to find local timbers that were large enough. They have been stained a rich, dark brown to match the kitchen units and the planked roof. Mikkel adds that guests often like to knock on the timbers and to handle other objects in their home. It's as if we are fascinated with quality materials, as they are so rare nowadays.

Everything in this house was done with love and care. The walls were hand-painted and the furniture made by skilled craftsmen, while many decorative pieces were either designed by Mikkel and Mette or bought on trips around the world. The rugs came from the souk in Marrakech and the couple shipped container-loads of antiques back from India, Bali and Thailand.

When they planned the layout of the house, Mikkel and Mette divided it into two parts — an airy, sociable space that's home to the kitchen, dining area and living room, and a more intimate and relaxed zone at the other end of the barn. That feeling of cosiness and comfort is something the family want visitors to experience as well and so they planned spare bedrooms for overnight guests.

Friends warned the couple that they would miss Copenhagen and feel isolated, but they have been proved wrong. The family are happier than ever. The children play outside and love to drive an old Ferguson tractor around the plot, while Mikkel's 30-minute commute to work in Copenhagen allows him valuable thinking time every day. This home offers the best of all worlds.

OPPOSITE The floors are made of wide oiled ash planks. The eating area is home to a dining table from Koch Køkken and the chairs around the table are Hans J Wegner's CH33 and the CH26 armchair. A feeling of cosiness and comfort is highly important to the Adsbøls. They have achieved it by mixing new pieces, design classics, antiquities and finds from their travels in an eclectic mix.

LEFT Lighting often poses a challenge in a space with high ceilings. The solution here was to combine recessed spotlights with decorative fixtures at different levels. The wall lamps here are the Brass Swing Arm light by Danish brand Tine K.

ABOVE The Beni Ourain rug just glimpsed in the corner of this picture was sourced, like all the rugs in the home, in Morocco, where Mikkel and Mette bought them in the Marrakech souk. The lounge chair is the classic CH22 designed by Hans J Wegner in the 1950s.

THIS PAGE Mikkel and Mette created mood boards to ensure a balanced, coherent interior style. In front of the windows hang blue curtains that match the velvet-covered armchair from Frits Henningsen. The sofa is from Italian company Meridiani.

ABOVE LEFT The bathroom exudes unassuming luxury. The antique mirrors, taps/faucets and Bestlite wall lamps in brass stand out against the indigo blue walls. The granite sinks were shipped back to Denmark from Bali and are placed on washstands from Københavns Møbelsnedkeri. The flooring is Jura limestone containing many fossils.

LEFT The bathroom is painted in a water-resistant paint suitable for wet rooms. Mikkel and Mette initially chose a delicate powder pink colour for the bathroom, but it was recently repainted in this rich, saturated blue — a hue that emphasizes the brass details and dark wood details. The elegant hand sculpture was bought in Thailand.

ABOVE Like much of the lighting in the house, the fixtures in the bedroom were designed by Mikkel and custom made for the house. The vases were bought in Morocco and the Gustavian chair once belonged to Mette's ancestors but has been recovered in a new fabric.

OPPOSITE The calm, serene blue colour scheme links every room in the barn together. In the bedroom, the comfy feeling is amplified by all the blue textiles. The dark blue velvet curtains from Dedar block out the daylight and the soft washed linen sheets echo the hue on the wall.

SOURCES

FURNITURE

Arrondissement Copenhagen
www.arrondissment-cph.com
Danish furniture brand co-owned by Anders Krakau of Rue Verte.

Carl Hansen & Son
www.carlhansen.com
Founded in 1905, this famous firm produces designs by Scandinavian design giants such as Hans J Wegner and Poul Kjaerholm, among others.

La Fibule
www.lafibule.fr
Luxurious contemporary furniture, sofas and lighting from a French furniture brand.

Fredericia
www.fredericia.com
Danish design house dating back to 1911 and producing many Scandinavian design classics.

Fogia
Swedish brand that collaborates with selected Scandi designers.

Gubi
Møntergade 19
1140 København K
Denmark
+45 53 61 63 68
www.gubi.com
Danish designer furniture and lighting brand.

Hay DK
Østergade 61
1100 København K
Denmark
+45 42 82 08 20
www.hay.dk
Danish brand offering affordable designs with a modern aesthetic.

Kollekted By
Rathkes gate 4
0558 Oslo
Norway
+47 400 42 743
www.kollektedby.no
Jannicke Krakvik and Alessandro D'Orazio's store in Oslo.

Meridiani
www.meridiani.it
Elegant contemporary Italian furniture from a Milan-based firm.

Muuto
www.muuto.com
Modern Scandinavian furniture, lighting and accessories, including tableware and textiles. Visit their website for your nearest stockist.

Normann Copenhagen
Østerbrogade 70
2100 København Ø
Denmark
+45 35 27 05 40
www.normann-copenhagen.com
As the name suggests, a Danish design company producing furniture, lighting, kitchenware, textiles and decorative accessories.

Ochre
www.ochre.net
Beautifully crafted, elegant, contemporary lighting and furniture from a New York/London-based British brand.

Overgaard & Dyrman
www.oandd.dk
Contemporary Danish furniture maker merging traditional craftsmanship with modern technology and sold through Rue Verte (see above), among others.

Rue Verte
Ny Østergade 11
1101 København K
Denmark
+45 33 12 55 55
www.rueverte.dk
High-end interiors store co-owned by Anders Krakau (pp. 60–69) and Michala Jessen (pp. 28–37).

Won
www.wondesign.dk
Innovative young Danish design brand producing fresh and appealing furniture designs.

LIGHTING

Artemide
www.artemide.com
Renowned Italian lighting and furniture brand.

Atelier Areti
www.atelierareti.com
European design studio producing stunning lighting designs.

Gallotti & Radice
www.gallottiradice.com
Sophisticated and luxurious Italian lighting, glassware and furnishings.

Louis Poulsen Lighting
www.louispoulsen.com
Renowned Danish lighting manufacturer producing lighting designs by iconic Scandinavian designers including Poul Henningsen and Verner Panton.

Tine K Home
Overgade 14
5000 Odense C
Denmark
+45 27 82 85 21
www.tinekhome.com
Danish lifestyle brand offering simple, understated tableware, textiles, lighting and some very elegant furniture.

Orsjö Belysnig
www.orsjo.com
Swedish lighting brand producing exciting collaborations with Scandinavia's leading designers, including Claesson Koivisto Rune and Note Design Studio.

Restart Milano
www.restartmilano.com
Elegant minimalist furniture and lighting.

Vibia
www.vibia.com
Beautiful, dramatic and architectural lighting designs from this Spanish brand.

PAINT, WALLPAPER, FABRICS AND FLOORS

Alcro
www.alcro.se
Swedish paint brand.

Dinesen
Søtorvet 5
1371 København K
Denmark
+45 33 11 21 40
www.dinesen.com
Danish wooden flooring company producing good-quality solid oak and fir floors in a wide range of sizes and finishes.

Jotun
www.jotun.com
Norwegian paint company.

Marrakech Design
www.marrakechdesign.se
Swedish company specializing in encaustic cement tiles for walls and floors, with exclusive designs from Scandinavian designers Claesson Koivisto Rune and Mats Theselius.

Mutina
www.mutina.it
Remarkable Italian ceramic tiles designed in collaboration with leading designers.

Svenskt Tenn
Strandvägen 5
114 51 Stockholm
Sweden
+46 8 670 16 00
www.svenskttenn.se
Historic Swedish interior design company famous for Josef Frank's bold and colourful fabric designs as well as homewares, furniture, decorative pieces and jewellery.

Tapet-Café
Brogårdsvej 23
2820 Gentofte
Denmark
+45 39 65 66 30
www.tapet-café.dk

Printed textiles, wallpaper, rugs, Farrow & Ball paints, upholstery and custom-made soft furnishings. Interior design service available.

Zoffany
www.zoffany.com
British paint company.

KITCHENS

Frama
www.framacph.com
Danish design studio specializing in elegant, refined furniture, lighting and a unique, freestanding low-tech kitchen system made from Douglas fir, marble, melamine and steel and designed to move house with you.

KBH Københavns Møbelsnedkeri
Sturlasgade 14
2300 København S
Denmark
+45 33 31 30 30
www.kbhsnedkeri.dk
Custom-built handmade furniture and kitchens plus a 'new classics' collection of handcrafted chairs, tables, cabinetry and lighting.

Koch Køkken
Birkerød Kongevej 137 C
3460 Birkerød
Denmark
+45 40 41 07 08
www.kochkoekken.dk
High-end Danish kitchen company producing quietly elegant handcrafted kitchens.

Puustelli Miinus
www.puustellimiinus.com
Eco-friendly Finnish kitchen company. The Miinus Kitchen is produced using ecologically friendly, non-toxic methods and has a low carbon footprint. It has great longevity and is entirely reusable and recyclable. Visit their website for details of stockists.

Superfront
www.superfront.com
Ingenious Swedish brand offering high-quality cabinet fronts, legs, knobs and handles that work with popular Ikea kitchen designs as well as the Swedish superstore's wardrobes and other storage.

DECORATIVE ITEMS AND ACCESSORIES

Bjørn Wiinblad
www.bjornwiinblad-denmark.com
Decorative items, ceramics and glassware designed by the Danish designer and illustrator.

House Doctor DK
www.housedoctor.dk
Fun, trend-led wall décor, home office supplies, storage, cushions and lighting.

Iittala
www.iittala.com
Beautiful, simple glassware from a historic Finnish company.

Rebekka Notkin
Bredgade 25A
1260 København K
Denmark
+45 33 32 02 60
www.rebekkanotkin.com
Exquisite pieces from jeweller Rebekka Notkin (see her home on pp. 50–59).

Lillian Tørlen
www.lilliantorlen.no
Norwegian ceramic artist.

PICTURE CREDITS

Front endpapers: *above centre left* The home of interior stylist Rikke Bye-Anderson in Oslo; *Above centre right* Note Design Studio; *Above right* The home of art collector Sara Lysgaard; *Below right* The home of Stefan Lundborg, designed by Note Design Studio; *Below centre right* Note Design Studio; *Below centre left* The home of Daniel Heckscher, Interior Architect at Note Design Studio, Stockholm; *Below left* House and interior designed by Mette and Mikkel Beck Adsbøl.

Back endpapers: *above left* The home of art collector Sara Lysgaard; *Above centre left* The home of interior stylist Rikke Bye-Anderson in Oslo; *Above centre right* Note Design Studio; *Below right* House and interior designed by Mette and Mikkel Beck Adsbøl; *Below centre right* Note Design Studio; *Below centre left* The home of Daniel Heckscher, Interior Architect at Note Design Studio, Stockholm; *Below left* The home of Stefan Lundborg, designed by Note Design Studio.

1 The home of interior stylist Rikke Bye-Anderson in Oslo; **2** The home of Creative Director and TV host Isabelle McAllister in Stockholm www.isabelle.se; **3** Note Design Studio; **4** House and interiors is designed by Mette and Mikkel Beck Adsbøl; **5** The home of Daniel Heckscher, Interior Architect at Note Design Studio, Stockholm; **6** The home of interior stylist Rikke Bye-Anderson in Oslo; **7** *left and right* The home of Daniel Heckscher, Interior Architect at Note Design Studio, Stockholm; **7** *centre and* **9** The home of interior designer Michala Jessen in Copenhagen www.rueverte.dk; **10–11** House and interior designed by Mette and Mikkel Beck Adsbøl; **12–13** The home of art collector Sara Lysgaard; **14** Note Design Studio; **16** Kråkvik & D'Orazio; **17** The home of interior designer Michala Jessen in Copenhagen www.rueverte.dk; **18–19** The home of jewellery designer Rebekka Notkin in Copenhagen; **20** *left* The home of Stefan

Lundborg, designed by Note Design Studio; **20** *centre* The home of interior designer Michala Jessen in Copenhagen www.rueverte.dk; **20** *right and* **21** The home of Anders Krakau interior designer at Rue Verte, Copenhagen; **22** The home of art collector Sara Lysgaard; **23** The home of Daniel Heckscher, Interior Architect at Note Design Studio, Stockholm; **24** The home of Stefan Lundborg, designed by Note Design Studio; **25** *above* The home of interior stylist Rikke Bye-Anderson in Oslo; **25** *below* House and interior designed by Mette and Mikkel Beck Adsbøl; **26–27** The home of interior designer Michala Jessen in Copenhagen www.rueverte.dk; **28–29** The home of jewellery designer Rebekka Notkin in Copenhagen; **30–37** The home of interior designer Michala Jessen in Copenhagen www.rueverte.dk; **38–49** Kråkvik and D'Orazio; **50–59** The home of jewellery designer Rebekka Notkin in Copenhagen; **60–69** The home of Anders Krakau interior designer at Rue Verte, Copenhagen; **70–71** The home of art collector Sara Lysgaard; **72–79** The home of Daniel Heckscher, Interior Architect at Note Design Studio, Stockholm; **80–91** The home of art collector Sara Lysgaard; **92–103** The home of Creative Director and TV host Isabelle McAllister in Stockholm www.isabelle.se; **104–105** The home of interior stylist Rikke Bye-Anderson in Oslo; **106–119** Note Design Studio; **120–129** The home of interior stylist Rikke Bye-Anderson in Oslo; **130–141** The home of Stefan Lundborg, designed by Note Design Studio; **142–151** House and interior designed Mette and Mikkel Beck Adsbøl; **152** Kråkvik and D'Orazio; **153** The home of jewellery designer Rebekka Notkin in Copenhagen; **154–155** The home of Creative Director and TV host Isabelle McAllister in Stockholm www.isabelle.se; **157** *above left and below right* Note Design Studio; **157** *above right* The home of Creative Director and TV host Isabelle McAllister in Stockholm www.isabelle.se; **157** *below left and* **160** The home of Daniel Heckscher, Interior Architect at Note Design Studio, Stockholm.

BUSINESS CREDITS

Mikkel Adsbøl
Interiors and food
photographer
Struenseegade 15A 1 sal tv.
2200 Copenhagen
Denmark
T: +45 51 92 57 00
E: mikkel@mikkeladsbol.dk
www.mikkeladsbol.dk
and also
www.kbhsnedkeri.dk
www.koekkenskaberne.dk
www.kmldesign.wordpress.com
www.comfortbeds.dk
Front endpapers below left, 4, 10–11, 25 below, 142–151, Back endpapers below left.

Rikke Bye-Anderson
Interior Stylist
www.rikkesroom.blogg.no

Front endpapers above centre left, 1, 6, 25 above, 104–105, 120–129, Back endpapers centre left.

Kråkvik & D'Orazio
St Halvards gate 1C
0192 Oslo
Norway
T: +47 452 38 185
T: +47 900 72 718
E: post@krakvikdorazio.no
www.krakvikdorazio.no
Pages 16, 38–49, 152.

Miss McAllister
Creative Agency
www.isabelle.se
www.dosfamily.com
Pages 2, 92–103, 154–155, 157 above right.

Note Design Studio
Nytorgsgatan 23
116 40 Stockholm
Sweden
T: +46 (0)8 656 88 04
E: info@notedesignstudio.se
www.notedesignstudio.se
Front endpapers above centre right, below right, below centre right and below centre left, pages 3, 5, 7 left, 7 right, 14, 20 left, 23, 24, 72–79, 106–111, 130–141, 157 above left, 157 below right, 157 below left, 160, Back endpapers above centre right, below centre right, below centre left, below left.

Rebekka Notkin Jewellery
Bredgade 25
1260 Copenhagen K
Denmark
T: +45 33 32 02 60
E: RN@rebekkanotkin.com
Pages 18–19, 28–29, 50–59, 153.

Rue Verte
Ny Østergade 11
1101 Copenhagen
Denmark
T: +45 33 12 55 55
E: contact@rueverte.dk
www.rueverte.dk
Product Design:
www.arrondissement-cph.com
Pages 7 centre, 9, 17, 20 centre, 20 right, 21, 26, 27, 30–37, 60–69.

INDEX

Italic pagination refers to captions.

A
Aalto, Alvar 12
accent colours/Bold Accents 22, 71
   blues and greens 15
   bringing colour to life 72–79
   detailing 8, *121*
   dreaming in colour 92–103
   second time around 80–91
Adsbøl, Mikkel and Mette 142–51
Akari Light Sculpture 40
AKassen sculpture *80*
Alberthe, Josephine 64
Alcro paint 117, *117*
All The Way To Paris, quilt *139*
Anastassiades, Michael *90*
Andersen, Martin Erik 44
Äng vase *137*
Angelo, Morten *30*
The Apartment 82
Arondissement Copenhagen 62, 67, *67*
art collector 80–91
Art Deco 50, 57, 58
Artemide, Gaudi chair 46
Arts and Craft movement 12
Asmussen, Souvanni *125*
Asplund, Sigve 44
Atelier Areti lamps 118

B
Baklava lamp 74
bathroom 101, 118, *150*
bedroom
   Bold Accents 78, 89, 99, *101*
   Dark Eclectic 37, 38, 40, 49, 58, 59, 68, *68*
   Majestic Pastels 117, 118, *128*, *129*, *139*, *150*
Bertola, Harry *40*
Bevilacqua, Michael *89*
black, use of 16
Blanche, Helene *82*
blue 15, 25
Bøe, Johs. *125*
Bostad, Marit Geraldine *125*
brown, use of 16
Bye-Andersen, Rikke 120–29

C
Cappellini, stools *77*
ceiling
   contrast colour 64, 67
   light impact 20, 30, 37
   mouldings 110, 117, 122
ceramics *see* pottery/ceramics
chairs *see* seating
Claesson Koivisto Rune 74
Collins, Graham *82*
Colman, Richard *90*
colour, introduction 7–8, 15
complementary colours 22, 72
concrete
   floors 44, 46
   tiles *93*
contrast
   accent colours 22
   dark colours 64, 67, 68

D
Dalsgaard, Sven *89*
Danish barn architecture 143
dark colours/Dark Eclectic 8, 20, 28
   calm and collected 38–49
   dark and handsome 30–37
   jewelled hues 50–59
   modern classic 60–69
   neutrals 16
De Gournay 50
decorative items, display 44, 46
dining areas
   Bold Accent 82, 95, 96
   Dark Eclectic 62
   Majestic Pastels 123, *135*, *138*, *147*

D'Orazio, Alessandro 39–49
drinks trolley 64

E
earth colours 12, 16
Eilersen, chaise longue *82*
Elmgreen & Dragset *82*
Engelgeer, Mae *49*
Engesvik, Andreas 74
environmental awareness 93
Ericson, Estrid *125*
Ernlund Jørgensen, Morten *89*
Escobar, Dario 86
Established & Sons *77*

F
Farrow & Ball paint 80, 86, 89, 90, *121*, *129*
fireplace *137*
Fleurelle rug *82*
floors
   concrete 44, 46
   herringbone tiles 72
   Jura limestone *150*
   painting 20, *101*
   parquet 110, 118, 121, 122, *127*, *137*
   rugs 82, 89, 90, *147*
   wooden 40, 44, 57, 64, *82*, 144, *147*
Flügger paint 143
Fogia, Bowl table 74
FOS, Diamond table *82*
Frama
   kitchen units 39, 49
   lighting 40, 49
   side table 44
   storage chest 46
Frank, Josef *125*, *128*, 130
Fredericia Furniture 138
Frey, Pierre 120
furniture, as contrast 20, *82*

G
Gallotti & Radice 30, 62
Gaudi chair 46
Gordillo, Gun 80, 86
Grcic, Konstantin 41
green, use of 15, 20
grey, use of 15, 16, 20, 25
Gubi

seating 44, 82, 113, 118, *135*
   Semi pendant light *127*
guest room 90, *127*, *128*
Guisset, Constance *113*
Gustavian style 12, *150*

H
Haase, Esther *127*
hallways 55, 72, 78, 86, 120–21, 122, 143
Hay
   J110 Windsor chair *139*
   Quilt Sideways *139*
   rug 90
   sofa 74
   Tela glassware 110
Heckscher, Daniel 72–79
Henningsen, Frits *149*
Henningsen, Poul *128*
Henningsen, Thorkild 55
House Doctor DK, Dot vase *121*
hue
   accent colours 22
   pastels 25
Humphreys, Tom *82*

I J
Iittala *77*
indigo 20
Jessen, Michala 30–37, 64
Jotun paint 40, *127*
Juhl, Finn 12

K
kitchen
   Bold Accents 72, 77, *77*, 86, 93, 95, 99
   Dark Eclectic 30, 33, 39, 41, 54, 61, 62
   Majestic Pastels 106, 109, 110, 118, 122, 123, *127*, *128*, 144, *145*
Kjærholm, Poul *82*
Klong, Äng vase *137*
Knoll 40
Københavns Møbelsnedkeri 144, *150*
Koch Køkken, table *147* *93*
Kollekted By 41, 44, 46
Krakau, Anders 61–69

Kråkvik, Jannicke 39–49
Krokatsis, Henry 82
Kruse Jensen, Astrid 57

L
La Fibule sofa 61
Lens table 82
Li, Rosie 80, 82
light 7, 20, 25, 78, 99, 137
lighting
    Bold Accents 74, 77, 78, 80, 82, 89, 90, 95, 96, 99, 101
    Dark Eclectic 30, 37, 40, 49, 62, 64, 68
    Majestic Pastels 113, 118, 118, 127, 139, 144, 147, 150
living area
    Bold Accents 73, 74, 74, 77, 80, 82, 92, 99, 99
    Dark Eclectic 34, 40, 50, 57, 61, 64, 66
    Majestic Pastels 113, 122, 125, 127–28, 131, 132, 139, 144, 147, 149
Louis Poulsen Panthella lamp 127
Lundborg, Stefan 130–41
Lundell, Ulf 132
Lundsteen, Christina 129
Lysgaard, Sara 12, 80–91

M
Magis 41
Magistretti, Vico 46
Malmsten, Carl 139
Mango chair, Won 113
Marrakech Design 93
Martensen-Larsen, Jannik 80, 82, 86
Mathsson, Bruno 12
Mayfair lamp 113
McAllister, Isabelle 92–103
McCollin Bryan, Lens table 82
Meridiani, sofa 34, 90, 149
metal 33, 34, 37, 64
Metz, Landon 86
minimalist interiors 7, 12
modernist decor 12, 74
Mogensen, Børge 57, 138
Mortensen, Asger 51

mouldings
    modernist 74, 78
    plaster ceiling 110, 117, 122
Mutina, Pico tiles 118
Muuto, dining table 123

N
Nelson, George, pendant light 127
neutral colours
    dark 16
    use of 15
Noguchi, Isamu 40
Nordic Classicism style 62, 66
Normann Copenhagen 77
Note Design Studio 74, 106–19, 132–41
Notkin, Rebekka 50–59

O
Ochre, chandelier 64
office/study
    Bold Accent 90
    Dark Eclectic 46
    Majestic Pastels 118, 127, 128, 139
Öglan chairs 96
orange, use of 16
Örnsbergsauktionen 74
Örsjö, Baklava lamp 74
Overgaard & Dyrman 34

P
paint
    Alcro 117, 117
    Farrow & Ball 80, 86, 89, 90, 121, 129
    finish impact 20, 25, 30
    Flügger 143
    Jotun 40, 127
    Zoffany 64, 67
Panton, Verner 127
Parreno, Philippe 90
pastels/Majestic Pastels 8, 25, 105
    at home with nature 142–51
    embracing history 106–19
    hint of the tropics 120–29
    sophisticated space 130–41

Petite Friture, Vertigo lamp 113
pink 16, 25
plants 44, 50, 59, 120, 143
pottery/ceramics
    Arondissement Copenhagen 62, 67
    Bjørn Wiinblad 50
    Dot vase 121
    Indonesian 61
    Japanese 39, 44
    Lillian Tørlen 49
    Peter Shire 86
    tiled stove 109–10, 113, 117, 122
Puustelli Miinus 93

R
recycling 99, 101, 144
red, use of 16
Restart Milano 68
Ross, Nick 74
Rue Verte 33, 62, 64
rugs 82, 89, 90, 147

S
Sandegaard, Troels 89
Scandinavian Modern style 12
Schäfer Grafisk Værksted 55
sculpture 40, 55, 80, 86
seating
    Bold Accents 74, 77, 82, 90, 96
    Dark Eclectic 34, 40, 41, 44, 46, 61
    Majestic Pastels 113, 123, 138–39, 144, 147, 149, 150
shades, similar 20, 78
shelving, painted 128, 130
Shire, Peter 86
Shrigley, David 80, 82
Silo lamp 118
Søndergaard, Trine 37
Space Copenhagen 138
Spine chairs 138
stairs 86, 132, 137, 139
Stockholm Exhibition (1930) 12
stove
    tiled 109–10, 113, 117, 122

tiled chimney 142
Strøm, Mikal 127
study see office/study
Superfront, door fronts 122, 128
Svenskt Tenn 125, 130
Swedish Grace movement 12

T
tableware 33, 62, 110
Tabula table 113
Tal R 55
Tapet-Café 80, 82, 82
Tekinoktay, Evren 55
Tela glassware 110
Thonet, chairs 41
Tibia, Mayfair lamp 113
tiles
    ceramic 72, 77, 77, 78, 118
    chimney 142
    concrete 93
    stoves 109–10, 113, 117, 122
Tine K, Brass Swing Arm light 147
Torgersen, Therese 67
Tørlen, Lillian 49

U V
upcycling 99, 101
Vertigo lamp 113

W
Wahlberg, Mari Helen 77
Wåhlin, Susanna 109
wallpaper
    Alexandrie 120
    hand-painted 50, 58
Wanscher, Ole 144
Warhol, Andy 122
Wegner, Hans J. 12, 82, 123, 147
white, use of 15
Wiinblad, Bjørn 50, 57
Won Mango chair 113
Woods, Clare 90

Y Z
yellow, use of 16
Zoffany paint 64, 67
Zorro table 132

ACKNOWLEDGMENTS

Thank you to everyone at Ryland Peters & Small for making this book so beautiful and inspirational. I am particularly grateful to Annabel, for kindly guiding me through the process, and also to Sara, for sowing the seed for this project. Beth and Sania, thank you for travelling Scandinavia and taking photographs that capture the extraordinary uniqueness of each location.

There were a few friends and family members who offered proofreading eyes along the way — my beloved Axel, Ann, Fabian, Saga and Erik, your help was invaluable.

Last but not least, I would like to thank all the homeowners for sharing their personal thoughts about colour and Scandinavian style. You have made me, and I hope many others, abandon white walls in favour of dynamic, vibrant colour.

ESSENTIALS
of
DISCRETE
MATHEMATICS

—Fourth Edition—

DAVID J. HUNTER, PhD
Westmont College

JONES & BARTLETT
LEARNING

World Headquarters
Jones & Bartlett Learning
5 Wall Street
Burlington, MA 01803
978-443-5000
info@jblearning.com
www.jblearning.com

Jones & Bartlett Learning books and products are available through most bookstores and online booksellers. To contact Jones & Bartlett Learning directly, call 800-832-0034, fax 978-443-8000, or visit our website, www.jblearning.com.

Production Credits

VP, Product Development: Christine Emerton
Director of Product Management: Laura Pagluica
Product Manager: Edward Hinman
Content Strategist: Melissa Duffy
Content Coordinator: Paula-Yuan Gregory
Project Manager: Kristen Rogers
Digital Project Specialist: Rachel DiMaggio
Director of Marketing: Andrea DeFronzo
Production Services Manager: Colleen Lamy
VP, Manufacturing and Inventory Control: Therese Connell
Product Fulfillment Manager: Wendy Kilborn

Composition: Exela Technologies
Project Management: Exela Technologies
Cover Design: Briana Yates
Media Development Editor: Faith Brosnan
Rights & Permissions Manager: John Rusk
Rights Specialist: James Fortney
Cover Image: © VRVIRUS/Shutterstock
    Image ID: 1749505577
Printing and Binding: McNaughton & Gunn

Library of Congress Cataloging-in-Publication Data
Names: Hunter, David James, 1968- author.
Title: Essentials of discrete mathematics / David Hunter.
Description: Fourth edition. | Burlington, MA : Jones & Bartlett Learning, [2022] | Includes bibliographical references and index. |
    Summary: "Essentials of Discrete Mathematics is designed for the one-semester undergraduate discrete math course. This course geared towards math and computer science majors. The textbook is organized around five types of mathematical thinking, with each chapter addressing a different type of thinking: logical, relational, recursive, quantitative, and analytical. The final chapter, "Thinking Through Applications" looks at different ways that discrete math thinking can be applied. Applications are included throughout the textbook and are sourced from a variety of disciplines, including biology, economics, music, and more"– Provided by publisher.
Identifiers: LCCN 2020044756 | ISBN 9781284184761 (paperback)
Subjects: LCSH: Computer science–Mathematics.
Classification: LCC QA76.9.M35 H867 2022 | DDC 004.01/5113–dc23
LC record available at https://lccn.loc.gov/2020044756

6048
Printed in the United States of America
25 24 23 22 21   10 9 8 7 6 5 4 3 2 1

Table of Contents

Preface   ix
    Introduction   ix
    What's New in the *Fourth Edition*   x
    How to Use this Book   x
    About the Cover   xi
    Supplements   xi
    Acknowledgments   xi

Chapter 1   **Logical Thinking**   1
    1.1 Formal Logic   1
        1.1.1 Preview Questions   2
        1.1.2 Connectives and Propositions   2
        1.1.3 Truth Tables   3
        1.1.4 Activities   5
        1.1.5 Logical Equivalences   5
        Exercises 1.1   7
    1.2 Propositional Logic   11
        1.2.1 Tautologies and Contradictions   11
        1.2.2 Derivation Rules   13
        1.2.3 Proof Sequences   15
        1.2.4 Forward–Backward   15
        Exercises 1.2   17
    1.3 Predicate Logic   20
        1.3.1 Predicates   21
        1.3.2 Quantifiers   21
        1.3.3 Translation   22
        1.3.4 Negation   23
        1.3.5 Two Common Constructions   25
        Exercises 1.3   26
    1.4 Logic in Mathematics   31
        1.4.1 The Role of Definitions in Mathematics   31
        1.4.2 Other Types of Mathematical Statements   32
        1.4.3 Counterexamples   33
        1.4.4 Axiomatic Systems   33
        Exercises 1.4   36
    1.5 Methods of Proof   39
        1.5.1 Direct Proofs   39
        1.5.2 Proof by Contraposition   41

	1.5.3 Proof by Contradiction	43
	Exercises 1.5	44
Chapter 2	**Relational Thinking**	47
	2.1 Graphs	48
	2.1.1 Edges and Vertices	48
	2.1.2 Terminology	49
	2.1.3 Modeling Relationships with Graphs	50
	Exercises 2.1	54
	2.2 Sets	57
	2.2.1 Membership and Containment	58
	2.2.2 New Sets from Old	59
	2.2.3 Identities	62
	Exercises 2.2	63
	2.3 Functions	66
	2.3.1 Definition and Examples	66
	2.3.2 One-to-One and Onto Functions	69
	2.3.3 New Functions from Old	72
	Exercises 2.3	74
	2.4 Relations and Equivalences	76
	2.4.1 Definition and Examples	77
	2.4.2 Graphs of Relations	77
	2.4.3 Relations vs. Functions	78
	2.4.4 Equivalence Relations	79
	2.4.5 Modular Arithmetic	82
	Exercises 2.4	84
	2.5 Partial Orderings	86
	2.5.1 Definition and Examples	87
	2.5.2 Hasse Diagrams	88
	2.5.3 Topological Sorting	89
	2.5.4 Isomorphisms	91
	2.5.5 Boolean Algebras	93
	Exercises 2.5	94
	2.6 Graph Theory	97
	2.6.1 Graphs: Formal Definitions	97
	2.6.2 Isomorphisms of Graphs	98
	2.6.3 Degree Counting	99
	2.6.4 Euler Paths and Circuits	100
	2.6.5 Hamilton Paths and Circuits	101
	2.6.6 Trees	102
	Exercises 2.6	104
Chapter 3	**Recursive Thinking**	107
	3.1 Recurrence Relations	108
	3.1.1 Definition and Examples	108
	3.1.2 The Fibonacci Sequence	109
	3.1.3 Modeling with Recurrence Relations	111
	Exercises 3.1	113
	3.2 Closed-Form Solutions and Induction	116
	3.2.1 Guessing a Closed-Form Solution	117
	3.2.2 Polynomial Sequences: Using Differences	118
	3.2.3 Inductively Verifying a Solution	119
	Exercises 3.2	123
	3.3 Recursive Definitions	125
	3.3.1 Definition and Examples	126
	3.3.2 Writing Recursive Definitions	128
	3.3.3 Recursive Geometry	130

3.3.4 Recursive Jokes   132
Exercises 3.3   132
3.4 Proof by Induction   136
3.4.1 The Principle of Induction   136
3.4.2 Examples   137
3.4.3 Strong Induction   140
3.4.4 Structural Induction   142
Exercises 3.4   144
3.5 Recursive Data Structures   146
3.5.1 Lists   146
3.5.2 Efficiency   149
3.5.3 Binary Search Trees Revisited   150
Exercises 3.5   152

Chapter 4   Quantitative Thinking   155
4.1 Basic Counting Techniques   156
4.1.1 Addition   156
4.1.2 Multiplication   157
4.1.3 Mixing Addition and Multiplication   159
Exercises 4.1   161
4.2 Selections and Arrangements   163
4.2.1 Permutations: The Arrangement Principle   164
4.2.2 Combinations: The Selection Principle   165
4.2.3 The Binomial Theorem   167
Exercises 4.2   169
4.3 Counting with Functions   172
4.3.1 One-to-One Correspondences   173
4.3.2 The Pigeonhole Principle   176
4.3.3 The Generalized Pigeonhole Principle   176
4.3.4 Ramsey Theory   177
Exercises 4.3   177
4.4 Discrete Probability   181
4.4.1 Definitions and Examples   182
4.4.2 Applications   183
4.4.3 Expected Value   186
4.4.4 Conditional Probability   187
Exercises 4.4   189
4.5 Counting Operations in Algorithms   191
4.5.1 Algorithms   192
4.5.2 Pseudocode   192
4.5.3 Sequences of Operations   193
4.5.4 Loops   194
4.5.5 Arrays   196
4.5.6 Sorting   197
Exercises 4.5   199
4.6 Estimation   202
4.6.1 Growth of Functions   203
4.6.2 Estimation Targets   207
4.6.3 Properties of Big-Θ 208
Exercises 4.6   209

Chapter 5   Analytical Thinking   213
5.1 Algorithms   213
5.1.1 More Pseudocode   214
5.1.2 Preconditions and Postconditions   215
5.1.3 Iterative Algorithms   216
5.1.4 Functions and Recursive Algorithms   218
Exercises 5.1   221

5.2	Three Common Types of Algorithms	224
	5.2.1 Traversal Algorithms	225
	5.2.2 Greedy Algorithms	228
	5.2.3 Divide-and-Conquer Algorithms	231
	Exercises 5.2	234
5.3	Algorithm Complexity	237
	5.3.1 The Good, the Bad, and the Average	238
	5.3.2 Approximate Complexity Calculations	241
	Exercises 5.3	243
5.4	Bounds on Complexity	247
	5.4.1 Algorithms as Decisions	248
	5.4.2 A Lower Bound	250
	5.4.3 Searching an Array	251
	5.4.4 Sorting	252
	5.4.5 *P* vs. *NP*	252
	Exercises 5.4	253
5.5	Program Verification	256
	5.5.1 Verification vs. Testing	256
	5.5.2 Verifying Recursive Algorithms	257
	5.5.3 Searching and Sorting	258
	5.5.4 Towers of Hanoi	260
	Exercises 5.5	262
5.6	Loop Invariants	264
	5.6.1 Verifying Iterative Algorithms	265
	5.6.2 Searching and Sorting	268
	5.6.3 Using Invariants to Design Algorithms	270
	Exercises 5.6	272
Chapter 6	**Thinking Through Applications**	277
6.1	Patterns in DNA	278
	6.1.1 Mutations and Phylogenetic Distance	278
	6.1.2 Phylogenetic Trees	279
	6.1.3 UPGMA	280
	Exercises 6.1	282
6.2	Social Networks	283
	6.2.1 Definitions and Terminology	284
	6.2.2 Notions of Equivalence	285
	6.2.3 Hierarchical Clustering	287
	6.2.4 Signed Graphs and Balance	290
	Exercises 6.2	291
6.3	Structure of Languages	292
	6.3.1 Terminology	293
	6.3.2 Finite-State Machines	294
	6.3.3 Recursion	296
	6.3.4 Further Issues in Linguistics	298
	Exercises 6.3	299
6.4	Discrete-Time Population Models	300
	6.4.1 Recursive Models for Population Growth	301
	6.4.2 Fixed Points, Equilibrium, and Chaos	302
	6.4.3 Predator–Prey Systems	304
	6.4.4 The SIR Model	304
	Exercises 6.4	307
6.5	Twelve-Tone Music	308
	6.5.1 Twelve-Tone Composition	309
	6.5.2 Listing All Permutations	309
	6.5.3 Transformations of Tone Rows	310

6.5.4 Equivalence Classes and Symmetry   311
Exercises 6.5   312

Hints, Answers, and Solutions to Selected Exercises   315
1.1 Formal Logic   315
1.2 Propositional Logic   317
1.3 Predicate Logic   318
1.4 Logic in Mathematics   319
1.5 Methods of Proof   319
2.1 Graphs   321
2.2 Sets   322
2.3 Functions   323
2.4 Relations and Equivalences   324
2.5 Partial Orderings   325
2.6 Graph Theory   327
3.1 Recurrence Relations   327
3.2 Closed-Form Solutions and Induction   328
3.3 Recursive Definitions   330
3.4 Proof by Induction   331
3.5 Recursive Data Structures   332
4.1 Basic Counting Techniques   333
4.2 Selections and Arrangements   334
4.3 Counting with Functions   335
4.4 Discrete Probability   335
4.5 Counting Operations in Algorithms   336
4.6 Estimation   337
5.1 Algorithms   338
5.2 Three Common Types of Algorithms   339
5.3 Algorithm Complexity   340
5.4 Bounds on Complexity   341
5.5 Program Verification   341
5.6 Loop Invariants   342

Selected References   345
Index   347
Index of Symbols   353

Preface

Introduction

The fourth edition of *Essentials of Discrete Mathematics* is the product of nearly two decades of dialog with colleagues and students. This comprehensive revision retains the one-semester focus of the text while facilitating the use of active and inquiry-based pedagogy. The text is designed for first- or second-year computer science and mathematics majors in discrete mathematics courses, and can also serve students in other disciplines.

The original motivation for writing this book stemmed from a 2004 workshop on discrete mathematics, led by Bill Marion at Valparaiso University and funded by the National Science Foundation (NSF). It was there that I rediscovered my affinity for the rich collection of mathematical topics found in the traditional syllabus of a discrete mathematics course. While these topics have always been among my favorites, I struggled to find a textbook that organized them in a coherent and compelling way. It seemed to me that while most presentations of discrete mathematics provided an excellent set of tools, they lacked a central theme that would highlight both the utility and the beauty of the subject.

Further study in computer science or mathematics requires familiarity with a variety of discrete structures, such as sets, functions, strings, graphs, trees, and many others. Each of these structures can be considered from several different mathematical viewpoints: logical, relational, recursive, quantitative, and analytical. Therefore, the first five chapters of this book are organized around these five types of mathematical thinking.

Chapter 1: **Logical Thinking.** Since every statement in mathematics has a logical foundation, it is essential to learn how to think logically. We will explore logic formally (that is, symbolically), and then consider how logic is used in mathematical statements and arguments.

Chapter 2: **Relational Thinking.** Most mathematical problems contain different objects that are related to each other in certain ways. The mathematical structures of sets, relations, functions, and graphs describe these relationships. Finding relationships among objects is often the first step in solving a mathematical problem.

Chapter 3: **Recursive Thinking.** Many objects in nature have recursive structures: a branch of a tree looks like a smaller tree, an ocean swell has the same shape as the ripples formed by its splashes, an onion holds a smaller onion under its outer layer. Finding similar traits in mathematical objects unleashes a powerful tool. We will study recurrence relations for a concrete introduction to this concept, after which we will consider more general recursive structures. Mathematical induction will be the natural way to prove facts about recursively-defined objects.

Chapter 4: **Quantitative Thinking.** Some of the most powerful theorems in mathematics are theorems that count something. After exploring different enumeration techniques, we will consider applications, including a first look at how to count operations in an algorithm. We will also practice the art of estimation—a valuable skill when precise enumeration is difficult.

Chapter 5: **Analytical Thinking.** Algorithms are generally regarded as the domain of computer scientists, but mathematicians use algorithms all the time. And since many applications of discrete mathematics come in the form of an algorithm, it is important to be able to understand and analyze them. This chapter brings together themes from earlier in the book: we apply quantitative and relational thinking to the study of algorithm complexity, and then apply logical and recursive thinking to the study of program correctness. Although this material will be challenging, it is intended for a broad audience, including students who have had little or no experience in programming.

Applications appear throughout the text, and the final chapter, **Thinking Through Applications**, explores several uses of discrete mathematical thinking in a variety of disciplines. These case studies—taken from biology, sociology, linguistics, physics, chemistry, and economics—are appropriate for independent study, and they could even inspire undergraduate research projects. Furthermore, they illustrate the diverse ways that discrete techniques arise in modern scholarship.

This book will give the beginning computer science student a strong background in the types of mathematical thinking used in upper-division courses. But I am writing with a larger group of students in mind. Students in any technical discipline will benefit from learning how to think mathematically. My hope is that a course using this text will make a fundamental contribution to a general liberal arts education. Since mathematical ideas undergird so many different areas of study, it makes sense to take this course early, even in the first semester of the first year.

Finally, I intend this book as a serious invitation to the discipline of mathematics. Although a course or two in calculus is the generally accepted place to begin the study of college-level mathematics, I believe that the material in this book is a better introduction to what mathematics is all about. Mathematicians prove theorems. So, throughout the book, there are exercises designed to develop the skills of reading and writing proofs. Any student wishing to go on to more theoretical upper-division mathematics courses will find this preparation valuable.

What's New in the *Fourth Edition*

The extensive revisions in this fourth edition have been brewing at least since 2012, when my appreciation for inquiry-based learning was rekindled at another NSF-funded workshop, organized by Doug Moore and Bill Jacob at the University of California, Santa Barbara. Since then I have converted all my courses, including discrete mathematics, to employ inquiry-based pedagogy. This edition features 60 new activities, which are the product of several years of collaborations and classroom testing. These activities can be done by groups of students cooperatively in class, or they can function as individual investigations, whether in-person, remotely, or in some hybrid arrangement.

While students can now explore most of the course content through these activities, all of the material from the first three editions remains, with some of the exposition streamlined to accommodate the new format. In particular, the exercises and the detailed back-of-book solutions will be familiar to instructors who have used previous editions.

How to Use This Book

This book is designed to present a coherent one-semester course in the essentials of discrete mathematics for several different audiences. The following diagram describes the dependencies among the sections of this book. Regardless of audience, a course should cover the sections labeled "Core" in the diagram: 1.1–1.5, 2.1–2.4, 3.1–3.4, 4.1–4.3, 4.5, and 5.1.

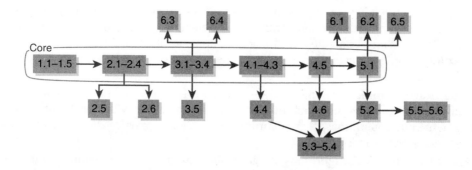

Beyond the 18 core sections, instructors have many options for additional sections to include, depending on the audience. A one-semester course should be able to cover approximately 5–8 additional sections. The following table shows three possible course outlines, each with a different focus.

Computer Science Emphasis	Mathematics Emphasis	Interdisciplinary
1.1–1.5	1.1–1.5	1.1–1.5
2.1–2.4	2.1–2.6	2.1–2.4
3.1–3.5	3.1–3.4	3.1–3.4
4.1–4.6	4.1–4.5	4.1–4.3, 4.5
5.1–5.2	5.1	5.1
5.3–5.4 and/or 5.5-5.6	6.3, 6.4, 6.5	6.1–6.5

Some subsections in the core (3.2.2, 4.2.3, and 4.3.4) have been marked with a double-dagger symbol (‡) to indicate that these subsections may safely be omitted without disrupting the continuity of the material. Answers and hints to selected problems can be found at the end of the book. Exercises requiring extra effort or insight have been marked with an asterisk (∗).

About the Cover

The Fibonacci sequence $1, 1, 2, 3, 5, 8, 13, 21, 34, 55, 89, \ldots$ is a famous example of recursion; each number in this sequence is the sum of the two numbers that precede it. The flower pictured on the front cover of this book exhibits 34:55 Fibonacci phyllotaxis: the central disk has 34 spirals in one direction and 55 in the other. This specimen continues the theme of the cover illustrations for the first three editions of this text: an 8:13 pine cone, a 13:21 *Santolina* flower, and a 21:34 *Asteraceae* flower, respectively. You can read more about Fibonacci numbers in Section 3.1.2.

Supplements

- *Instructor's Solutions Manual*

- *Lecture slides in PowerPoint format*

- *WebAssign*™, developed by instructors for instructors, is a premier independent online teaching and learning environment, guiding several million students through their academic careers since 1997.

- *eBook format.* As an added convenience, this complete textbook is now available in eBook format for purchase by the student through WebAssign.

- *Activity Workbook*

- *Instructor Activity Guide*

Acknowledgments

My understanding of inquiry-based learning has been influenced by colleagues over the years, including Ted Mahavier, Stan Yoshinobu, Brian Katz, Volker Ecke, Christine von Renesse, Elizabeth Thoren, Ray Rosentrater, Michael Everest, and many others. Much of the inspiration for the new material in the *Fourth Edition* comes from these creative and devoted teachers. In addition, the following colleagues have provided valuable input and suggestions:

Vladimir Akis; California State University, Los Angeles
Wasim A. Al-Hamdani; Kentucky State University
Sven Anderson; Bard College
Daniel Birmajer; Nazareth College of Rochester
Miklos Bona; University of Florida
Kyle Calderhead; Malone University
Douglas Childers; Georgia Military College
Quinn Culver; Fordham University
Dana Dahlstrom; University of California, San Diego
Susanne Doree; Augsburg College
Howard Francis; University of Pikeville

Richard Freda; Farmingdale State College
Arturo Gonzalez Gutierrez; Universidad Autónoma de Querétaro, Mexico
Peter B. Henderson; Butler University
Brian Hopkins; St. Peter's College
Uwe Kaiser; Boise State University
Lazaros D. Kikas; University of Detroit Mercy
Zachary Kudlak; Mount Saint Mary College
Bill Marion; Valparaiso University
Bonita M. McVey; St. Norbert College
Darren A. Narayan; Rochester Institute of Technology
Hemant Pendharkar; Worcester State University
Frank Ritter; The Pennsylvania State University
C. Ray Rosentrater; Westmont College
Caroline Shapcott; Indiana University at South Bend
Fereja Mohammed Tahir; Illinois Central College
David Tannor; Cornerstone University
Richard L. Stankewitz; Ball State University
Relja Vulanovic; Kentucky State University

Also, I would like to express my appreciation to the team at Jones & Bartlett Learning. In particular I would like to thank Product Manager, Edward Hinman and Melissa Duffy, Content Strategist.

Finally, I am deeply thankful to my wife Patti, whose support, patience, and encouragement sustained me throughout this project.

Chapter 1

Logical Thinking

Mathematicians are in the business of stating things precisely. When you read a mathematical statement, you should take every word seriously; good mathematical language conveys a clear, unambiguous message. In order to read and write mathematics, you must practice the art of logical thinking. The goal of this chapter is to help you communicate mathematically by understanding the basics of logic.

A word of warning: mathematical logic can be difficult—especially the first time you see it. This chapter begins with the study of formal, or symbolic, logic, and then applies this study to the language of mathematics. Expect things to be a bit foggy at first, but eventually (we hope) the fog will clear. When it does, mathematical statements will start making more sense to you.

1.1 Formal Logic

Notation is an important part of mathematical language. Mathematicians' blackboards are often filled with an assortment of strange characters and symbols; such a display can be intimidating to the novice, but there's a good reason for communicating this way. Often, the act of reducing a problem to symbolic language helps us see what

Figure 1.1 Symbols are an important part of the language of mathematics.

1

is really going on. Instead of operating in the fuzzy world of prose, we translate a problem to notation and then perform well-defined symbolic manipulations on that notation. This is the essence of the powerful tool called *formalism*. In this section, we explore how a formal approach to logic can help us avoid errors in reasoning.

A note on terminology: we'll use the word *formal* to describe a process that relies on manipulating notation. Often, people use this word to mean "rigorous," but that's not our intention. A formal argument can be rigorous, but so can an argument that does not rely on symbols.

One nice feature of formalism is that it allows you to work without having to think about what all the symbols mean. In this sense, formal logic is really "logical *not*-thinking." Why is this an advantage? Formal calculations are less prone to error. You are already familiar with this phenomenon: much of the arithmetic you learned in school was formal. You have a well-defined symbolic algorithm for multiplying numbers using pencil and paper, and you can quite effectively multiply three-digit numbers without thinking much about what you are really doing. Of course, formalism is pointless if you don't know what you are doing; at the end of any formal calculation, it is important to be able to interpret the results.

1.1.1   Preview Questions

Every section of this book begins with some open-ended *preview questions* that are designed to help you begin thinking about the ideas that follow. Often, these questions will introduce unfamiliar concepts, and they do not call for complete solutions. To get the most out of these problems, spend a little time thinking about them on your own, write down some preliminary responses, and make a note of any questions that you have.

Preview 1.1

1. Westley, standing with his hands behind his back, claims that he is holding a quarter in his left hand and a $20 bill in his right hand. You believe he is lying. What would you have to show to demonstrate that he is lying? Invent a diagram, chart, or symbols to illustrate all the possible scenarios.

2. Buttercup knows whether or not Westley is lying. She promises that if Westley is lying, she will give you a cookie. Buttercup always keeps her promises. Suppose she does not give you a cookie; what can you conclude? Suppose she gives you a cookie; what can you conclude? Illustrate your thinking in some organized way.

3. Camp Halcyon and Camp Placid are two summer camps with the following daily policies on pool use and cleanup duties.

    Camp Halcyon's Policy: If you used the pool in the afternoon and you didn't clean up after lunch, then you must clean up after dinner.

    Camp Placid's Policy: You must do at least one of the following: (a) Stay out of the pool in the afternoon, (b) clean up after lunch, or (c) clean up after dinner.

    How do these policies differ?

1.1.2   Connectives and Propositions

In order to formalize logic, we need a system for translating statements into symbols. We'll start with a precise definition of *statement*.

Definition 1.1 A *statement* (also known as a *proposition*) is a declarative sentence that is either true or false, but not both.

The following are examples of statements:

- 7 is odd.

- $1 + 1 = 4$

- If it is raining, then the ground is wet.

- Our professor is from Mars.

Note that we don't need to be able to decide whether a statement is true or false in order for it to be a statement. Either our professor is from Mars or our professor is not from Mars, though we may not be sure which is the case.

How can a declarative sentence fail to be a statement? There are two main ways. A declarative sentence may contain an unspecified term:

> x is even.

In this case, x is called a *free variable*. The truth of the sentence depends on the value of x, so if that value is not specified, we can't regard this sentence as a statement. A second type of declarative non-statement can happen when a sentence is *self-referential*:

> This sentence is false.

We can't decide whether or not the above sentence is true. If we say it is true, then it claims to be false; if we say it is false, then it appears to be true.

Often, a complicated statement consists of several simple statements joined together by words such as "and," "or," "if . . . then," etc. These connecting words are represented by the five *logical connectives* shown in the following table. Logical connectives are useful for decomposing compound statements into simpler ones, because they highlight important logical properties of a statement.

Name	Symbol
and	$\wedge$
or	$\vee$
not	$\neg$
implies (if . . . then)	$\rightarrow$
if and only if	$\leftrightarrow$

In order to use a formal system for logic, we must be able to *translate* between a statement in English and its formal counterpart. We do this by assigning letters for simple statements and then building expressions with connectives.

Example 1.1 If p is the statement "you are wearing shoes" and q is the statement "you can't cut your toenails," then $p \rightarrow q$ represents the statement, "If you are wearing shoes, then you can't cut your toenails." We may choose to express this statement differently in English: "You can't cut your toenails if you are wearing shoes," or "Wearing shoes makes it impossible to cut your toenails." The statement $\neg q$ translates literally as "It is not the case that you can't cut your toenails." Of course, in English, we would prefer to say simply, "You can cut your toenails," but this involves using logic, as we will see in the next section.

1.1.3 Truth Tables

We haven't finished setting up our formal system for logic because we haven't been specific about the meaning of the logical connectives. Of course, the names of each connective suggest how they should be used, but in order to make statements with mathematical precision, we need to know exactly what each connective means.

Defining the meaning of a mathematical symbol is harder than it might seem. Even the $+$ symbol from ordinary arithmetic is problematic. Although we all have an intuitive understanding of addition—it describes how to combine two quantities—it is hard to express this concept in words without appealing to our intuition. What does "combine" mean, exactly? What are "quantities," really?

One simple, but obviously impractical, way to define the $+$ sign would be to list all possible addition problems, as in the following table. Of course, such a table could never end, but it would, in theory, give us a precise definition of the $+$ sign.

x	y	$x+y$
0	0	0
0	1	1
1	0	1
1	1	2
2	1	3
$\vdots$	$\vdots$	$\vdots$

The situation in logic is easier to handle. Any statement has two possible values: true (T) or false (F). So when we use variables such as p or q for statements in logic, we can think of them as unknowns that can take one of only two values: T or F. This makes it possible to define the meaning of each connective using tables; instead of infinitely many values for numbers x and y, we have only two choices for each variable p and q.

We will now stipulate the meaning of each logical connective by listing the T/F values for every possible case. The simplest example is the "not" connective, $\neg$. If p is true, then $\neg p$ should be false, and *vice versa*.

p	$\neg p$
T	F
F	T

This table of values is called a *truth table*; it defines the T/F values for the connective.

The "and" and "or" connectives are defined by the following truth tables. Since we have two variables, and each can be either T or F, we need four cases.

p	q	$p \wedge q$
T	T	T
T	F	F
F	T	F
F	F	F

p	q	$p \vee q$
T	T	T
T	F	T
F	T	T
F	F	F

The definition of the "and" connective $\wedge$ is what you would expect: in order for $p \wedge q$ to be true, p must be true *and* q must be true. The "or" connective $\vee$ is a little less obvious. Notice that our definition stipulates that $p \vee q$ is true whenever p is true, or q is true, or both are true. This can be different from the way "or" is used in everyday speech. When you are offered "soup or salad" in a restaurant, your server isn't expecting you to say "both."

The "if and only if" connective says that two statements have exactly the same truth values. Thus, its truth table is as follows.

p	q	$p \leftrightarrow q$
T	T	T
T	F	F
F	T	F
F	F	T

Sometimes authors will write "iff" as an abbreviation for "if and only if."

The "if . . . then" connective has the least intuitive definition.

p	q	$p \rightarrow q$
T	T	T
T	F	F
F	T	T
F	F	T

To understand the motivation for this definition, let $p \rightarrow q$ be the statement of Example 1.1:

"If you are wearing shoes, then you can't cut your toenails."

In order to demonstrate that this statement is false, you would have to be able to cut your toenails while wearing shoes. In any other situation, you would have to concede that the statement is not false (and if a statement is not false, it must be true). If you are not wearing shoes, then maybe you can cut your toenails or maybe you can't, for some other reason. This doesn't contradict the statement $p \rightarrow q$.

Put another way, if you live in a world without shoes, then the statement is *vacuously* true; since you can never actually wear shoes, it isn't false to say that "*If* you are wearing shoes," then anything is possible. This explains the last two lines of the truth table; if p is false, then $p \rightarrow q$ is true, no matter what q is.

Often, mathematicians use the word "implies" as a synonym for the $\rightarrow$ connective. "If p then q" means the same thing as "p implies q," namely that q is a necessary consequence of p. Like many words in the English language, "imply" has multiple meanings. Sometimes it means "to indicate or suggest," as in, "She didn't say she wanted to leave, but she implied it." The mathematical usage is stronger, expressing a forced relationship: "$x > 3$ implies $x^2 > 3$." It is important to recognize when common words have special meanings in mathematical writing; Exercise 32 at the end of this section explores another example, the word "only."

1.1.4 Activities

The *activity* below will help you practice using truth tables while previewing some of the results that we will discuss later. In the same way, the activities that you will encounter throughout this text will encourage you to process new ideas and explore their consequences. Ideally, you will work cooperatively with others on these activities, so you can share ideas and compare answers.

Activity 1.1.1: Truth Tables

1. Complete the missing columns in the following truth table.

p	q	$p \vee q$	$p \wedge q$	$p \rightarrow q$	$\neg p$	$\neg p \vee q$	$\neg q$	$\neg q \rightarrow \neg p$	$\neg(p \wedge q)$	$\neg(p \vee q)$	$\neg p \wedge \neg q$	$\neg p \vee \neg q$
T	T	T	T	T	F							
T	F	T	F	F	F							
F	T	T	F	T	T							
F	F	F	F	T	T							

2. In the truth table above, find three different statements that have the same T/F values for all cases.
3. Compare the truth tables for $\neg(p \wedge q)$, $\neg(p \vee q)$, $\neg p \wedge \neg q$, and $\neg p \vee \neg q$. Is there a rule for logical connectives that resembles the distributive property from algebra?

1.1.5 Logical Equivalences

Definition 1.2 Two statements are *logically equivalent* if they have the same T/F values for all cases, that is, if they have the same truth tables.

There are some logical equivalences that come up often in mathematics, and also in life in general.

Example 1.2 Consider the following theorem from high school geometry. (Recall that two angles are *supplementary* if their angle measures sum to 180°.)

If a quadrilateral has a pair of parallel sides, then it has a pair of supplementary angles.

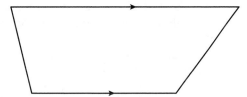

This theorem is of the form $p \rightarrow q$, where p is the statement that the quadrilateral has a pair of parallel sides, and q is the statement that the quadrilateral has a pair of supplementary angles.

We can state a different theorem, represented by $\neg q \rightarrow \neg p$.

If a quadrilateral does not have a pair of supplementary angles, then it does not have a pair of parallel sides.

We know that this second theorem is logically equivalent to the first because the formal statement $p \rightarrow q$ is logically equivalent to the formal statement $\neg q \rightarrow \neg p$, as the following truth table shows.

p	q	$p \rightarrow q$	$\neg q$	$\neg p$	$\neg q \rightarrow \neg p$
T	T	T	F	F	T
T	F	F	T	F	F
F	T	T	F	T	T
F	F	T	T	T	T

Notice that the column for $p \to q$ matches the column for $\neg q \to \neg p$. Since the first theorem is a true theorem from geometry, so is the second.

Now consider a different variation on this theorem.

> If a quadrilateral has a pair of supplementary angles, then it has a pair of parallel sides.

It turns out that this statement is not true, in general, in geometry. (Can you draw an example of a quadrilateral for which it fails to be true?) In propositional logic, this statement is of the form $q \to p$. The following truth table shows that $q \to p$ is *not* logically equivalent to $p \to q$, because the T/F values are different in the second and third rows.

p	q	$p \to q$	$q \to p$
T	T	T	T
T	F	F	T
F	T	T	F
F	F	T	T

The statement $\neg q \to \neg p$ is called the *contrapositive* of $p \to q$, and the statement $q \to p$ is called the *converse*. The truth tables above prove that, for any statement s, the contrapositive of s is logically equivalent to s, while the converse of s may not be.

There are lots of situations where assuming the converse can cause trouble. For example, suppose that the following statement is true.

> If a company is not participating in illegal accounting practices, then an audit will turn up no evidence of wrongdoing.

It is certainly reasonable to assume this, since there couldn't be evidence of wrongdoing if no such wrongdoing exists. However, the converse is probably not true:

> If an audit turns up no evidence of wrongdoing, then the company is not participating in illegal accounting practices.

After all, it is possible that the auditors missed something.

At this point, you might object that formal logic seems like a lot of trouble to go through just to verify deductions like this last example. This sort of thing is just common sense, right? Well, maybe. But something that appears obvious to you may not be obvious to someone else. Furthermore, our system of formal logic can deal with more complicated situations, where our common sense might fail us. The solution to the next example uses formal logic. Before you look at this solution, try to solve the problem using "common sense." Although the formal approach takes a little time, it resolves any doubt you might have about your own reasoning process.

Example 1.3 If Aaron is late, then Bill is late, and, if both Aaron and Bill are late, then class is boring. Suppose that class is not boring. What can you conclude about Aaron?

Solution: Let's begin by translating the first sentence into the symbols of logic, using the following statements.

$$p = \text{``Aaron is late.''}$$
$$q = \text{``Bill is late.''}$$
$$r = \text{``Class is boring.''}$$

Let S be the statement "If Aaron is late, then Bill is late, and, if both Aaron and Bill are late, then class is boring." In symbols, S translates to the following.

$$S = (p \to q) \wedge [(p \wedge q) \to r]$$

Now let's construct a truth table for S. We do this by constructing truth tables for the different parts of S, starting inside the parentheses and working our way out.

Row #	p	q	r	$p \to q$	$p \wedge q$	$(p \wedge q) \to r$	S
1.	T	T	T	T	T	T	T
2.	T	T	F	T	T	F	F
3.	T	F	T	F	F	T	F
4.	T	F	F	F	F	T	F
5.	F	T	T	T	F	T	T
6.	F	T	F	T	F	T	T
7.	F	F	T	T	F	T	T
8.	F	F	F	T	F	T	T

You should check that the last column is the result of "and-ing" the column for $p \to q$ with the column for $(p \wedge q) \to r$.

We are interested in the possible values of p. It is given that S is true, so we can eliminate rows 2, 3, and 4, the rows where S is false. If we further assume that class is not boring, we can also eliminate the rows where r is true, namely the odd-numbered rows. The rows that remain are the only possible T/F values for p, q, and r: rows 6 and 8. In both of these rows, p is false. In other words, Aaron is not late.   ◇

Activity 1.1.2: Truth Tables and Deduction

Let the following statements be given.

$$p = \text{"You used the pool in the afternoon."}$$
$$q = \text{"You cleaned up after lunch."}$$
$$r = \text{"You must clean up after dinner."}$$

1. Use connectives to translate the following statement into formal logic.

    If you used the pool in the afternoon and you didn't clean up after lunch, then you must clean up after dinner.

2. Construct a truth table for the formal logic statement that you found in part (1). The eight rows of your table should correspond to the eight different possibilities for p, q, and r.

3. Suppose that the statement given in part (1) is false. What must be true about your pool usage and cleanup duties? Explain how to justify your answer using the truth table.

Exercises 1.1

---

1. Let the following statements be given.

    $$p = \text{"There is water in the cylinders."}$$
    $$q = \text{"The head gasket is blown."}$$
    $$r = \text{"The car will start."}$$

    (a) Translate the following statement into symbols of formal logic.

    If the head gasket is blown and there's water in the cylinders, then the car won't start.

    (b) Translate the formal statement $r \to \neg(q \vee p)$ into everyday English.

2. Let the following statements be given.

$$p = \text{"You are in Seoul."}$$
$$q = \text{"You are in Kwangju."}$$
$$r = \text{"You are in South Korea."}$$

(a) Translate the following statement into symbols of formal logic.

If you are not in South Korea, then you are not in Seoul or Kwangju.

(b) Translate the formal statement $q \rightarrow (r \wedge \neg p)$ into everyday English.

3. Let the following statements be given.

$$p = \text{"You can vote."}$$
$$q = \text{"You are under 18 years old."}$$
$$r = \text{"You are from Mars."}$$

(a) Translate the following statement into symbols of formal logic.

You can't vote if you are under 18 years old or you are from Mars.

(b) Give the contrapositive of this statement in the symbols of formal logic.

(c) Give the contrapositive in English.

4. Let s be the following statement.

If you are studying hard, then you are staying up late at night.

(a) Give the converse of s.

(b) Give the contrapositive of s.

5. Let s be the following statement.

If it is raining, then the ground is wet.

(a) Give the converse of s.

(b) Give the contrapositive of s.

6. Give an example of a quadrilateral that shows that the *converse* of the following statement is false.

If a quadrilateral has a pair of parallel sides, then it has a pair of supplementary angles.

7. We say that two ordered pairs (a, b) and (c, d) are *equal* when $a = c$ and $b = d$. Let s be the following statement.

If $(a, b) = (c, d)$, then $a = c$.

(a) Is this statement true?

(b) Write down the converse of s.

(c) Is the converse of s true? Explain.

8. Give an example of a true if–then statement whose converse is also true.

9. Show that $p \leftrightarrow q$ is logically equivalent to $(p \rightarrow q) \wedge (q \rightarrow p)$ using truth tables.

10. Use truth tables to establish the following equivalences.

(a) Show that $\neg(p \vee q)$ is logically equivalent to $\neg p \wedge \neg q$.

(b) Show that $\neg(p \wedge q)$ is logically equivalent to $\neg p \vee \neg q$.

These equivalences are known as *De Morgan's laws*, after the 19th-century logician Augustus De Morgan.

11. Are the statements $\neg(p \rightarrow q)$ and $\neg p \rightarrow \neg q$ logically equivalent? Justify your answer using truth tables.

12. Use truth tables to show that $(a \vee b) \wedge (\neg(a \wedge b))$ is logically equivalent to $a \leftrightarrow \neg b$. (This arrangement of T/F values is sometimes called the *exclusive or* of a and b.)

13. Use a truth table to prove that the statement $[(p \lor q) \land (\neg p)] \to q$ is always true, no matter what p and q are.

14. Let the following statements be given.

$$p = \text{"Andy is hungry."}$$
$$q = \text{"The refrigerator is empty."}$$
$$r = \text{"Andy is mad."}$$

(a) Use connectives to translate the following statement into formal logic.

If Andy is hungry and the refrigerator is empty, then Andy is mad.

(b) Construct a truth table for the statement in part (a).

(c) Suppose that the statement given in part (a) is true, and suppose also that Andy is not mad and the refrigerator is empty. Is Andy hungry? Explain how to justify your answer using the truth table.

15. Let A be the statement $p \to (q \land \neg r)$. Let B be the statement $q \leftrightarrow r$.

(a) Construct truth tables for A and B.

(b) Suppose statements A and B are both true. What can you conclude about statement p? Explain your answer using the truth table.

16. Use truth tables to prove the following *distributive properties* for propositional logic.

(a) $p \land (q \lor r)$ is logically equivalent to $(p \land q) \lor (p \land r)$.

(b) $p \lor (q \land r)$ is logically equivalent to $(p \lor q) \land (p \lor r)$.

17. Use truth tables to prove the *associative properties* for propositional logic.

(a) $p \lor (q \lor r)$ is logically equivalent to $(p \lor q) \lor r$.

(b) $p \land (q \land r)$ is logically equivalent to $(p \land q) \land r$.

18. Mathematicians say that "statement P is *stronger* than statement Q" if Q is true whenever P is true, but not conversely. (In other words, "P is stronger than Q" means that $P \to Q$ is always true, but $Q \to P$ is not true, in general.) Use truth tables to show the following.

(a) $a \land b$ is stronger than a.

(b) a is stronger than $a \lor b$.

(c) $a \land b$ is stronger than $a \lor b$.

(d) b is stronger than $a \to b$.

19. Suppose Q is a quadrilateral. Which statement is stronger? Explain.

- Q is a square.

- Q is a rectangle.

20. Which statement is stronger? Explain.

- Manchester United is the best football team in England.

- Manchester United is the best football team in Europe.

21. Which statement is stronger? Explain.

- n is divisible by 3.

- n is divisible by 12.

22. Mathematicians say that "Statement P is a *sufficient condition* for statement Q" if $P \to Q$ is true. In other words, in order to know that Q is true, it is sufficient to know that P is true. Let x be an integer. Give a sufficient condition on x for $x/2$ to be an even integer.

23. Mathematicians say that "Statement P is a *necessary condition* for statement Q" if $Q \to P$ is true. In other words, in order for Q to be true, P must be true. Let $n \geq 1$ be a natural number. Give a necessary but not sufficient condition on n for $n + 2$ to be prime.

24. Let Q be a quadrilateral. Give a sufficient but not necessary condition for Q to be a parallelogram.

25. Write the statement "P is necessary and sufficient for Q" in the symbols of formal logic, using as few connectives as possible.

26. Often a complicated expression in formal logic can be simplified. For example, consider the statement $S = (p \wedge q) \vee (p \wedge \neg q)$.

    (a) Construct a truth table for S.

    (b) Find a simpler expression that is logically equivalent to S.

27. Consider the statement $S = [\neg(p \rightarrow q)] \vee [\neg(p \vee q)]$.

    (a) Construct a truth table for S.

    (b) Find a simpler expression that is logically equivalent to S.

28. The NAND connective $\uparrow$ is defined by the following truth table. Use truth tables to show that $p \uparrow q$ is logically equivalent to $\neg(p \wedge q)$. (This explains the name NAND: Not AND.)

p	q	$p \uparrow q$
T	T	F
T	F	T
F	T	T
F	F	T

29. The NAND connective is important because it only takes two transistors to build an electronic circuit that computes the NAND of two signals:

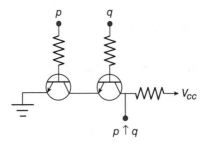

Such a circuit is called a *logic gate*. Moreover, it is possible to build logic gates for the other logical connectives entirely out of NAND gates. Prove this fact by proving the following equivalences, using truth tables.

    (a) $(p \uparrow q) \uparrow (p \uparrow q)$ is logically equivalent to $p \wedge q$.

    (b) $(p \uparrow p) \uparrow (q \uparrow q)$ is logically equivalent to $p \vee q$.

    (c) $p \uparrow (q \uparrow q)$ is logically equivalent to $p \rightarrow q$.

30. Write $\neg p$ in terms of p and $\uparrow$.

31. A technician suspects that one or more of the processors in a distributed system is not working properly. The processors, A, B, and C, are all capable of reporting information about the status (working or not working) of the processors in the system. The technician is unsure whether a processor is really not working, or whether the problem is in the status reporting routines in one or more of the processors. After polling each processor, the technician receives the following status reports.

    • Processor A reports that processor B is not working and processor C is working.

    • Processor B reports that A is working if and only if B is working.

    • Processor C reports that at least one of the other two processors is not working.

    Help the technician by answering the following questions.

    (a) Let $a =$ "A is working," $b =$ "B is working," and $c =$ "C is working." Write the three status reports in terms of a, b, and c, using the symbols of formal logic.

    (b) Complete the following truth table.

a	b	c	A's report	B's report	C's report
T	T	T			
T	T	F			
T	F	T			
T	F	F			
F	T	T			
F	T	F			
F	F	T			
F	F	F			

(c) Assuming that all of the status reports are true, which processor(s) is/are working?

(d) Assuming that all of the processors are working, which status report(s) is/are false?

(e) Assuming that a processor's status report is true if and only if the processor is working, what is the status of each processor?

32. Use the symbols of propositional logic to explain the difference between the following two statements.

> My team will win if I yell at the TV.
> My team will win only if I yell at the TV.

Look up the word "only" in a dictionary. This word has several different meanings. Which meaning applies when we use the phrase "if and only if" in logic?

1.2 Propositional Logic

After working through the exercises of the previous section, you may have noticed a serious limitation of the truth table approach. Each time you add a new statement to a truth table, you must double the number of rows. This makes truth table analysis unwieldy for all but the simplest examples.

In this section, we will develop a system of rules for manipulating formulas in symbolic logic. This system, called the *propositional calculus*, will allow us to make logical deductions formally. There are at least three reasons for doing this.

1. These formal methods are useful for analyzing complex logical problems, especially where truth tables are impractical.

2. The derivation rules we will study are commonly used in mathematical discourse.

3. The system of derivation rules and proof sequences is a simple example of mathematical proof.

Of these three, the last is the most important. The mechanical process of writing proof sequences in propositional calculus will prepare us for writing more complicated proofs in other areas of mathematics.

1.2.1 Tautologies and Contradictions

Preview 1.2

1. Explain how the answers to the following two questions are related.

> If you pass all the exams, will you pass the course?
>
> Is it possible to pass all the exams and fail the course?

2. Consider the following statement.

> If you have a ticket, then, as long as you are wearing a shirt, you may enter the theater, unless you aren't wearing shoes.

Write a simpler statement that expresses the same policy. Explain how you know that your statement is equivalent.

3. Suppose that a natural number n is *gaunt* if it satisfies the following condition.

If n is even, then 10 divides n, and, if n is odd, then 5 divides n.

List the first 6 gaunt numbers. Is there a simpler way to define the condition of "gauntness"?

There are some statements in formal logic that are always true, no matter what the T/F values of the component statements are. For example, the truth table for $(p \wedge q) \to p$ is as follows.

p	q	$p \wedge q$	$(p \wedge q) \to p$
T	T	T	T
T	F	F	T
F	T	F	T
F	F	F	T

Such a statement is called a *tautology*, and we write $(p \wedge q) \Rightarrow p$ to indicate this fact. The notation $A \Rightarrow B$ means that the statement $A \to B$ is true in all cases; in other words, the truth table for $A \to B$ is all Ts. Similarly, $A \Leftrightarrow B$ denotes that $A \leftrightarrow B$ is a tautology.

Example 1.4 In Activity 1.1.1 you proved the tautologies $\neg(p \vee q) \Leftrightarrow \neg p \wedge \neg q$ and $\neg(p \wedge q) \Leftrightarrow \neg p \vee \neg q$.

When a tautology is of the form $(C \wedge D) \Rightarrow E$, we often prefer to write

$$\left. \begin{array}{c} C \\ D \end{array} \right\} \Rightarrow E$$

instead. This notation highlights the fact that if you know both C and D, then you can conclude E. The use of the $\wedge$ connective is implicit.

Example 1.5 Use a truth table to prove the following.

$$\left. \begin{array}{c} p \\ p \to q \end{array} \right\} \Rightarrow q$$

Solution: Let S be the statement $[p \wedge (p \to q)] \to q$. We construct our truth table by building up the parts of S, working from inside the parentheses outward.

p	q	$p \to q$	$p \wedge (p \to q)$	S
T	T	T	T	T
T	F	F	F	T
F	T	T	F	T
F	F	T	F	T

Since the column for S is all Ts, this proves that S is a tautology.   ◇

The tautology in Example 1.5 is known as *modus ponens*, which is Latin for "affirmative mode." This concept goes back at least as far as the Stoic philosophers of ancient Greece, who stated it as follows.

If the first, then the second;
but the first;
therefore the second.

In the exercises, you will have the opportunity to prove a related result called *modus tollens* ("denial mode"). In the symbols of logic, this tautology is as follows.

$$\left. \begin{array}{c} \neg q \\ p \to q \end{array} \right\} \Rightarrow \neg p$$

There are also statements in formal logic that are never true. A statement whose truth table contains all Fs is called a *contradiction*.

Example 1.6 Use a truth table to show that $p \wedge \neg p$ is a contradiction.

Solution:

p	$\neg p$	$p \wedge \neg p$
T	F	F
F	T	F

In other words, a statement and its negation can never both be true.   ◇

A statement in propositional logic that is neither a tautology nor a contradiction is called a *contingency*. A contingency has both Ts and Fs in its truth table, so its truth is "contingent" on the T/F values of its component statements. For example, $p \wedge q$, $p \vee q$, and $p \rightarrow q$ are all contingencies.

1.2.2 Derivation Rules

Tautologies are important because they show how one statement may be logically deduced from another. For example, suppose we know that the following statements are true.

> Our professor does not own a spaceship.
> If our professor is from Mars, then our professor owns a spaceship.

We can apply the *modus tollens* tautology to deduce that "Our professor is not from Mars." This is a valid argument, or *derivation*, that allows us to conclude this last statement given the first two.

Every tautology can be used as a rule to justify deriving a new statement from an old one. There are two types of derivation rules: equivalence rules and inference rules. Equivalence rules describe logical equivalences, while inference rules describe when a weaker statement can be deduced from a stronger statement. The equivalence rules given in Table 1.1 could all be checked using truth tables. If A and B are statements (possibly composed of many other statements joined by connectives), then the tautology $A \Leftrightarrow B$ is another way of saying that A and B are logically equivalent.[1]

Equivalence	Name
$p \Leftrightarrow \neg\neg p$	double negation
$p \rightarrow q \Leftrightarrow \neg p \vee q$	implication
$\neg(p \wedge q) \Leftrightarrow \neg p \vee \neg q$	De Morgan's laws
$\neg(p \vee q) \Leftrightarrow \neg p \wedge \neg q$	
$p \vee q \Leftrightarrow q \vee p$	commutativity
$p \wedge q \Leftrightarrow q \wedge p$	
$p \wedge (q \wedge r) \Leftrightarrow (p \wedge q) \wedge r$	associativity
$p \vee (q \vee r) \Leftrightarrow (p \vee q) \vee r$	

Table 1.1 Equivalence Rules

An equivalence rule of the form $A \Leftrightarrow B$ can do three things:

1. Given A, deduce B.

2. Given B, deduce A.

3. Given a statement containing statement A, deduce the same statement, but with statement A replaced by statement B.

---

1. A word on notation: We typically use $p, q, r, \ldots$ to stand for simple statements, and we use $A, B, C, \ldots$ to denote statements that are (possibly) made up of simple statements and logical connectives. This convention, however, is purely expository and doesn't signify any difference in meaning.

The third option is a form of *substitution*. For example, given the following statement,

If Micah is not sick and Micah is not tired, then Micah can play.

we can deduce the following using De Morgan's laws.

If it is not the case that Micah is sick or tired, then Micah can play.

Activity 1.2.1: Using Equivalence Rules

In Activity 1.1.2, you translated the statement "If you used the pool in the afternoon and you didn't clean up after lunch, then you must clean up after dinner" into formal logic, using the following variables.

$$p = \text{"You used the pool in the afternoon."}$$

$$q = \text{"You cleaned up after lunch."}$$

$$r = \text{"You must clean up after dinner."}$$

1. Use the *implication* rule to rewrite your formal logic statement so that it doesn't contain the $\rightarrow$ connective.
2. Use *De Morgan's laws* to rewrite the resulting statement from part (1) so that it doesn't contain the $\wedge$ connective.
3. Use equivalence rules to simplify the *negation* of your statement from part (2) so that it doesn't use parentheses.
4. Without using truth tables, can you give an alternative explanation for your conclusion in part (3) of Activity 1.1.2?

In addition to equivalence rules, there are also inference rules for propositional logic. Unlike equivalence rules, inference rules work in only one direction. An inference rule of the form $A \Rightarrow B$ allows you to do only one thing:

1. Given A, deduce B.

In other words, you can conclude a weaker statement, B, if you have already established a stronger statement, A. For example, *modus tollens* is an inference rule: the weaker statement B:

Our professor is not from Mars.

follows from the stronger statement A:

Our professor does not own a spaceship, and if our professor is from Mars, then our professor owns a spaceship.

If A is true, then B must be true, but not *vice versa*. (Our professor might own a spaceship and be from Jupiter, for instance.) Table 1.2 lists some useful inference rules, all of which can be verified using truth tables.

Inference	Name
$\left.\begin{array}{l} p \\ q \end{array}\right\} \Rightarrow p \wedge q$	conjunction
$\left.\begin{array}{l} p \\ p \rightarrow q \end{array}\right\} \Rightarrow q$	*modus ponens*
$\left.\begin{array}{l} \neg q \\ p \rightarrow q \end{array}\right\} \Rightarrow \neg p$	*modus tollens*
$p \wedge q \Rightarrow p$	simplification
$p \Rightarrow p \vee q$	addition

Table 1.2 Inference Rules

1.2.3   Proof Sequences

We now have enough tools to derive some new tautologies from old ones. A *proof sequence* is a sequence of statements and reasons to justify an assertion of the form $A \Rightarrow C$. The first statement, A, is given. (Often, there are several given statements.) The proof sequence can then list statements $B_1, B_2, B_3, \ldots$, etc., as long as each new statement can be derived from a previous statement (or statements) using some derivation rule. Of course, this sequence of statements must culminate in C, the statement we are trying to prove, given A.

Example 1.7 Write a proof sequence for the assertion

$$\left. \begin{array}{c} p \\ p \to q \\ q \to r \end{array} \right\} \Rightarrow r.$$

Solution:

Statements	Reasons
1. p	given
2. $p \to q$	given
3. $q \to r$	given
4. q	*modus ponens*, 1, 2
5. r	*modus ponens*, 4, 3

$\diamond$

Every time we prove something, we get a new inference rule. The rules in Table 1.2 are enough to get us started, but we should feel free to use proven assertions in future proofs. For example, the assertion proved in Example 1.7 illustrates the *transitive* property of the $\to$ connective.

Another thing to notice about Example 1.7 is that it was pretty easy—we just had to apply *modus ponens* twice. Compare this with the truth table approach: the truth table for

$$[p \wedge (p \to q) \wedge (q \to r)] \to r$$

would consist of eight rows and several columns. Truth tables are easier to do, but they can be much more tedious.

Proof sequences should remind you of the types of proofs you did in high school geometry. The rules are simple: start with the given, see what you can deduce, and end with what you are trying to prove. Here's a harder example.

Example 1.8 Prove:

$$\left. \begin{array}{c} p \vee q \\ \neg p \end{array} \right\} \Rightarrow q$$

Solution:

Statements	Reasons
1. $p \vee q$	given
2. $\neg p$	given
3. $\neg(\neg p) \vee q$	double negation, 1
4. $\neg p \to q$	implication, 3
5. q	*modus ponens*, 4, 2

$\diamond$

Notice that in step 3 of this proof, we used one of the equivalence rules (double negation) to make a substitution in the formula. This is allowed: since $\neg(\neg p)$ is logically equivalent to p, it can take the place of p in any formula.

1.2.4   Forward–Backward

If you are having trouble coming up with a proof sequence, try the "forward–backward" approach: consider statements that are one step forward from the given, and also statements that are one step backward from the statement you are trying to prove. Repeat this process, forging a path of deductions forward from the given and backward from the final statement. If all goes well, you will discover a way to make these paths meet in the middle. The next example illustrates this technique.

Example 1.9 In Section 1.1, we used truth tables to show that a statement is logically equivalent to its contrapositive. In this example we will construct a proof sequence for one direction of this logical equivalence:

$$p \to q \;\Rightarrow\; \neg q \to \neg p$$

Solution: We apply the forward–backward approach. The only given statement is $p \to q$, so we search our derivation rules for something that follows from this statement. The only candidate is $\neg p \vee q$, by the implication rule, so we tentatively use this as the second step of the proof sequence. Now we consider the statement we are trying to prove, $\neg q \to \neg p$, and we look backward for a statement from which this statement follows. Since implication is an equivalence rule, we can also use it to move backward to the statement $\neg(\neg q) \vee \neg p$, which we propose as the second-to-last statement of our proof. By moving forward one step from the given and backward one step from the goal, we have reduced the task of proving

$$p \to q \;\Rightarrow\; \neg q \to \neg p$$

to the (hopefully) simpler task of proving

$$\neg p \vee q \;\Rightarrow\; \neg(\neg q) \vee \neg p.$$

Now it is fairly easy to see how to finish the proof: we can switch the $\vee$ statement around using commutativity and simplify using double negation. We can now write down the proof sequence.

Statements	Reasons
1. $p \to q$	given
2. $\neg p \vee q$	implication
3. $q \vee \neg p$	commutativity
4. $\neg(\neg q) \vee \neg p$	double negation
5. $\neg q \to \neg p$	implication

We used the forward–backward approach to move forward from step 1 to step 2, and again to move backward from step 5 to step 4. Then we connected step 2 to step 4 with a simple proof sequence.   ◇

You may have noticed that in Section 1.1, we proved the stronger statement

$$p \to q \;\Leftrightarrow\; \neg q \to \neg p$$

using truth tables; the above example proves only the "$\Rightarrow$" direction of this equivalence. To prove the other direction, we need another proof sequence. However, in this case, this other proof sequence is easy to write down, because all of the derivation rules we used were reversible. Implication, commutativity, and double negation are all equivalence rules, so we could write down a new proof sequence with the order of the steps reversed, and we would have a valid proof of the "$\Leftarrow$" direction.

Activity 1.2.2: Proof Sequences

1. Fill in the reasons in the following proof sequence. Make sure you indicate which step(s) each derivation rule refers to.

Statements	Reasons
1. $\neg[(p \wedge \neg q) \to r]$	given
2. $\neg[\neg(p \wedge \neg q) \vee r]$	
3. $\neg[(\neg p \vee \neg\neg q) \vee r]$	
4. $\neg[(\neg p \vee q) \vee r]$	
5. $\neg(\neg p \vee q) \wedge \neg r$	
6. $(\neg\neg p \wedge \neg q) \wedge \neg r$	
7. $(p \wedge \neg q) \wedge \neg r$	
8. $p \wedge (\neg q \wedge \neg r)$	
9. p	

2. Notice that the "given" in step 1 of the above proof sequence is the *negation* of formal logic translation of the pool policy from Activity 1.1.2. In other words, we start by assuming that the pool policy has been violated. Interpret what the conclusion of this sequence tells you in context by completing the sentence: "If you violated the pool policy, then _____."

Exercises 1.2

1. Use truth tables to establish the *modus tollens* tautology:

$$\left.\begin{array}{r} \neg q \\ p \to q \end{array}\right\} \Rightarrow \neg p$$

2. Fill in the reasons in the following proof sequence. Make sure you indicate which step(s) each derivation rule refers to.

Statements	Reasons
1. $q \wedge r$	given
2. $\neg(\neg p \wedge q)$	given
3. $\neg\neg p \vee \neg q$	
4. $p \vee \neg q$	
5. $\neg q \vee p$	
6. $q \to p$	
7. q	
8. p	

3. Fill in the reasons in the following proof sequence. Make sure you indicate which step(s) each derivation rule refers to.

Statements	Reasons
1. $(p \wedge q) \to r$	given
2. $\neg(p \wedge q) \vee r$	
3. $(\neg p \vee \neg q) \vee r$	
4. $\neg p \vee (\neg q \vee r)$	
5. $p \to (\neg q \vee r)$	

4. Is the proof in Exercise 2 reversible? Why or why not?

5. Is the proof in Exercise 3 reversible? Why or why not?

6. Fill in the reasons in the following proof sequence. Make sure you indicate which step(s) each derivation rule refers to.

Statements	Reasons
1. $p \wedge (q \vee r)$	given
2. $\neg(p \wedge q)$	given
3. $\neg p \vee \neg q$	
4. $\neg q \vee \neg p$	
5. $q \to \neg p$	
6. p	
7. $\neg(\neg p)$	
8. $\neg q$	
9. $(q \vee r) \wedge p$	
10. $q \vee r$	
11. $r \vee q$	
12. $\neg(\neg r) \vee q$	
13. $\neg r \to q$	
14. $\neg(\neg r)$	
15. r	
16. $p \wedge r$	

7. Justify each conclusion with a derivation rule.

    (a) If Joe is artistic, he must also be creative. Joe is not creative. Therefore, Joe is not artistic.

    (b) Lingli is both athletic and intelligent. Therefore, Lingli is athletic.

    (c) If Monique is 18 years old, then she may vote. Monique is 18 years old. Therefore, Monique may vote.

    (d) Marianne has never been north of Saskatoon or south of Santo Domingo. In other words, she has never been north of Saskatoon and she has never been south of Santo Domingo.

8. Which derivation rule justifies the following argument?

    If n is a multiple of 4, then n is even. However, n is not even. Therefore, n is not a multiple of 4.

9. Let x and y be integers. Given the statement

    $x > y$ or x is odd.

    what statement follows by the implication rule?

10. Let Q be a quadrilateral. Given the statements

    If Q is a rhombus, then Q is a parallelogram.
    Q is not a parallelogram.

    what statement follows by *modus tollens*?

11. Let x and y be numbers. Simplify the following statement using De Morgan's laws and double negation.

    It is not the case that x is not greater than 3 and y is not found.

12. Write a statement that follows from the statement

    It is sunny and warm today.

    by the simplification rule.

13. Write a statement that follows from the statement

    This soup tastes funny.

    by the addition rule.

14. Recall Exercise 31 of Section 1.1. Suppose that all of the following status reports are correct:

    • Processor B is not working and processor C is working.

    • Processor A is working if and only if processor B is working.

    • At least one of the two processors A and B is not working.

    Let $a =$ "A is working," $b =$ "B is working," and $c =$ "C is working."

    (a) If you haven't already done so, write each status report in terms of a, b, and c, using the symbols of formal logic.

    (b) How would you justify the conclusion that B is not working? (In other words, given the statements in part (a), which derivation rule allows you to conclude $\neg b$?)

    (c) How would you justify the conclusion that C is working?

    (d) Write a proof sequence to conclude that A is not working. (In other words, given the statements in part (a), write a proof sequence to conclude $\neg a$.)

15. Write a proof sequence for the following assertion. Justify each step.

$$\left. \begin{array}{c} p \to \neg q \\ r \to (p \wedge q) \end{array} \right\} \Rightarrow \neg r$$

16. Write a proof sequence for the following assertion. Justify each step.

$$\left.\begin{array}{l} p \\ p \to r \\ q \to \neg r \end{array}\right\} \Rightarrow \neg q$$

17. Write a proof sequence for the following assertion. Justify each step.

$$\left.\begin{array}{l} p \to q \\ p \wedge r \end{array}\right\} \Rightarrow q \wedge r$$

18. Write a proof sequence for the following assertion. Justify one of the steps in your proof using the result of Example 1.8.

$$\left.\begin{array}{l} \neg(a \wedge \neg b) \\ \neg b \end{array}\right\} \Rightarrow \neg a$$

19. Write a proof sequence to establish that $p \Leftrightarrow p \wedge p$ is a tautology.

20. Write a proof sequence to establish that $p \Leftrightarrow p \vee p$ is a tautology. (Hint: Use De Morgan's laws and Exercise 19.)

21. Write a proof sequence for the following assertion. Justify each step.

$$\neg(\neg p \to q) \vee (\neg p \wedge \neg q) \Rightarrow \neg p \wedge \neg q$$

22. Write a proof sequence for the following assertion. Justify each step.

$$(p \vee q) \vee (p \vee r) \Rightarrow \neg r \to (p \vee q)$$

23. Consider the following assertion.

$$\neg(\neg p \vee q) \Rightarrow p \vee q$$

   (a) Find a statement that is one step forward from the given.
   (b) Find a statement that is one step backward from the goal. (Use the addition rule—in reverse—to find a statement from which the goal will follow.)
   (c) Give a proof sequence for the assertion.
   (d) Is your proof reversible? Why or why not?

24. Use a truth table to show that

$$\left.\begin{array}{l} p \to q \\ \neg p \end{array}\right\} \overset{?}{\Rightarrow} \neg q$$

is not a tautology. (This example shows that substitution isn't valid for inference rules, in general. Substituting the weaker statement, q, for the stronger statement, p, in the expression "$\neg p$" doesn't work.)

25. (a) Fill in the reasons in the following proof sequence. Make sure you indicate which step(s) each derivation rule refers to.

Statements	Reasons
1. $p \to (q \to r)$	given
2. $\neg p \vee (q \to r)$	
3. $\neg p \vee (\neg q \vee r)$	
4. $(\neg p \vee \neg q) \vee r$	
5. $\neg(p \wedge q) \vee r$	
6. $(p \wedge q) \to r$	

   (b) Explain why the proof in part (a) is reversible.
   (c) The proof in part (a) (along with its reverse) establishes the following tautology:

$$p \to (q \to r) \Leftrightarrow (p \wedge q) \to r$$

Therefore, to prove an assertion of the form $A \Rightarrow B \rightarrow C$, it is sufficient to prove

$$\left.\begin{matrix} A \\ B \end{matrix}\right\} \Rightarrow C$$

instead. Use this fact to rewrite the tautology

$$p \wedge (q \rightarrow r) \Rightarrow q \rightarrow (p \wedge r)$$

as a tautology of the form

$$\left.\begin{matrix} A \\ B \end{matrix}\right\} \Rightarrow C,$$

where C does not contain the $\rightarrow$ connective. (The process of rewriting a tautology this way is called the *deduction method*.)

(d) Give a proof sequence for the rewritten tautology in part (c).

26. This exercise will lead you through a proof of the *distributive property* of $\wedge$ over $\vee$. We will prove:

$$p \wedge (q \vee r) \Rightarrow (p \wedge q) \vee (p \wedge r).$$

(a) The above assertion is the same as the following:

$$p \wedge (q \vee r) \Rightarrow \neg(p \wedge q) \rightarrow (p \wedge r).$$

Why?

(b) Use the deduction method from Exercise 25(c) to rewrite the tautology from part (a).

(c) Prove your rewritten tautology.

27. Use a truth table to show that $(a \rightarrow b) \wedge (a \wedge \neg b)$ is a contradiction.

28. Is $a \rightarrow \neg a$ a contradiction? Why or why not?

1.3 Predicate Logic

When we defined statements, we said that a sentence of the form "x is even" is not a statement, because its T/F value depends on x. Mathematical writing, however, almost always deals with sentences of this type; we often express mathematical ideas in terms of some unknown variable. This section explains how to extend our formal system of logic to deal with this situation.

Preview 1.3

1. The diagram below shows a standard brick pattern (a "running bond" pattern) composed of two different colors of bricks. The bricklayer had certain rules in mind governing the arrangement of the colors. Devise some possible rules, written as logical statements. Your statements should be as specific as possible but should also hold true for every brick in the pattern.

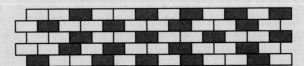

2. Nikola bets you $5 that every player on his basketball team will score a point or earn an assist in tonight's game. What must happen for you to win the bet? Express this condition in the simplest, most natural way possible, and explain your reasoning.

3. For each of the following statements, give a list of natural numbers that satisfies the statement. Can you find a single list that satisfies both statements?

   Statement p: There is a number in the list that is greater than every other number in the list.

   Statement q: Every number in the list is less than some other number in the list.

1.3.1 Predicates

Definition 1.3 A *predicate* is a declarative sentence whose T/F value depends on one or more variables. In other words, a predicate is a declarative sentence with variables, and after those variables have been given specific values the sentence becomes a statement.

We use function notation to denote predicates. For example,

$$P(x) = \text{"}x \text{ is even,"} \text{ and}$$

$$Q(x,y) = \text{"}x \text{ is heavier than } y\text{"}$$

are predicates. The statement $P(8)$ is true, while the statement $Q(\text{feather}, \text{brick})$ is false.

Implicit in a predicate is the *domain* (or *universe*) of values that the variable(s) can take. For $P(x)$, the domain could be the integers; for $Q(x,y)$, the domain could be some collection of physical objects. We will usually state the domain along with the predicate, unless it is clear from the context.

Equations are predicates. For example, if $E(x)$ stands for the equation $x^2 - x - 6 = 0$, then $E(3)$ is true and $E(4)$ is false. We regard equations as declarative sentences, where the $=$ sign plays the role of a verb.

1.3.2 Quantifiers

By themselves, predicates aren't statements because they contain free variables. We can make them into statements by plugging in specific values of the domain, but often we would like to describe a range of values for the variables in a predicate. A *quantifier* modifies a predicate by describing whether some or all elements of the domain satisfy the predicate.

We will need only two quantifiers: universal and existential. The *universal quantifier* "for all" is denoted by $\forall$. So the statement

$$(\forall x)P(x)$$

says that $P(x)$ is true *for all* x in the domain. The *existential quantifier* "there exists" is denoted by $\exists$. The statement

$$(\exists x)P(x)$$

says that *there exists* an element x of the domain such that $P(x)$ is true; in other words, $P(x)$ is true *for some* x in the domain.

For example, if $E(x)$ is the real number equation $x^2 - x - 6 = 0$, then the expression $(\exists x)E(x)$ says, "There is some real number x such that $x^2 - x - 6 = 0$," or more simply, "The equation $x^2 - x - 6 = 0$ has a solution." The variable x is no longer a free variable, since the $\exists$ quantifier changes the role it plays in the sentence.

If $Z(x)$ represents the real number equation $x \cdot 0 = 0$, the expression $(\forall x)Z(x)$ means "For all real numbers x, $x \cdot 0 = 0$." Again, this is a sentence without free variables, since the range of possible values for x is clearly specified.

When we put a quantifier in front of a predicate, we form a *quantified statement*. Since the quantifier restricts the range of values for the variables in the predicate, the quantified statement is either true or false (but not both). In the above examples, $(\exists x)E(x)$ and $(\forall x)Z(x)$ are both true, while the statement $(\forall x)E(x)$ is false, since there are some real numbers that do not satisfy the equation $x^2 - x - 6 = 0$.

The real power of predicate logic comes from combining quantifiers, predicates, and the symbols of propositional logic. For example, if we would like to claim that there is a negative number that satisfies the equation $x^2 - x - 6 = 0$, we could define a new predicate

$$N(x) = \text{"}x \text{ is negative."}$$

Then the statement

$$(\exists x)(N(x) \wedge E(x))$$

translates as "There exists some real number x such that x is negative and $x^2 - x - 6 = 0$."

The *scope* of a quantifier is the part of the formula to which the quantifier refers. In a complicated formula in predicate logic, it is important to use parentheses to indicate the scope of each quantifier. In general, the scope is what lies inside the set of parentheses right after the quantifier:

$$(\forall x)(\dots \text{scope of } \forall \dots), \quad (\exists x)(\dots \text{scope of } \exists \dots).$$

In the statement $(\exists x)(N(x) \wedge E(x))$, the scope of the $\exists$ quantifier is the expression $N(x) \wedge E(x)$.

1.3.3 Translation

There are lots of different ways to write quantified statements in English. Translating back and forth between English statements and predicate logic is a skill that takes practice.

Example 1.10 Using all cars as a domain, if

$$P(x) = \text{``}x \text{ gets good mileage.''}$$
$$Q(x) = \text{``}x \text{ is large.''}$$

then the statement $(\forall x)(Q(x) \rightarrow \neg P(x))$ could be translated very literally as

"For all cars x, if x is large, then x does not get good mileage."

However, a more natural translation of the same statement is

"All large cars get bad mileage."

or

"There aren't any large cars that get good mileage."

If we wanted to say the opposite—that is, that there are some large cars that get good mileage—we could write the following.

$$(\exists x)(P(x) \wedge Q(x))$$

We'll give a formal proof that this negation is correct in Example 1.13.

The next example shows how a seemingly simple mathematical statement yields a rather complicated formula in predicate logic. The careful use of predicates can help reveal the logical structure of a mathematical claim.

Example 1.11 In the domain of all integers, let $P(x) = \text{``}x \text{ is even.''}$ We can express the fact that the sum of an even number with an odd number is odd as follows.

$$(\forall x)(\forall y)[(P(x) \wedge \neg P(y)) \rightarrow (\neg P(x + y))]$$

Of course, the literal translation of this quantified statement is "For all integers x and for all integers y, if x is even and y is not even, then $x + y$ is not even," but we normally say something informal like "An even plus an odd is odd."

This last example used two universal quantifiers to express a fact about an arbitrary pair x, y of integers. The next example shows what can happen when you combine universal and existential quantifiers in the same statement.

Example 1.12 In the domain of all real numbers, let $G(x, y)$ be the predicate "$x > y$." The statement

$$(\forall y)(\exists x) G(x, y)$$

says literally that "For all numbers y, there exists some number x such that $x > y$," or more simply, "Given any number y, there is some number that is greater than y." This statement is clearly true: the number $y + 1$ is always greater than y, for example. However, the statement

$$(\exists x)(\forall y)G(x,y)$$

translates literally as "There exists a number x such that, for all numbers y, $x > y$." In simpler language, this statement says, "There is some number that is greater than any other number." This statement is clearly false, because there is no largest number.

The order of the quantifiers matters. In both of these statements, a claim is made that x is greater than y. In the first statement, you are first given an arbitrary number y, then the claim is that it is possible to find some x that is greater than it. However, the second statement claims there is some number x, such that, given any other y, x will be the greater number. In the second statement, you must decide on what x is before you pick y. In the first statement, you pick y first, then you can decide on x.

Activity 1.3.1: Translating Quantified Statements

1. In the domain of natural numbers, let $P(x)$ be the statement "x is even" and let $Q(x)$ be the statement "x is a multiple of 10." Translate the following statements into natural English statements, and decide which of them are true.

    (a) $(\forall x)(P(x) \to Q(x))$

    (b) $(\forall x)(Q(x) \to P(x))$

    (c) $(\exists x)(Q(x) \land P(x))$

2. Let $P(x,y)$ be the statement "$x^2 + y = 7$" in the domain of all real numbers.

    (a) When using more than one quantifier in a formula, we read them from left to right, and we don't always write all the parentheses. For example, the expression $(\forall y)(\exists x)P(x,y)$ means $(\forall y)[(\exists x)P(x,y)]$, translated as, "For all y, there is some x such that $x^2 + y = 7$." Decide whether each of the following expressions is true or false. Give a brief justification for each answer.

        i $(\forall y)(\exists x)P(x,y)$

        ii $(\forall x)(\exists y)P(x,y)$

        iii $(\exists y)(\forall x)P(x,y)$

        iv $(\exists x)(\exists y)P(x,y)$

        v $(\exists y)(\exists x)P(x,y)$

        vi $(\forall x)(\forall y)P(x,y)$

        vii $(\forall y)(\forall x)P(x,y)$

    (b) Based on these examples, when do you think it is permissible to switch the order of quantifiers?

1.3.4 Negation

In mathematical arguments, it is often important to be able to accurately express the logical opposite, or *negation* of a quantified statement. The next activity encourages you to discover some formal rules for doing so.

Activity 1.3.2: Negating Quantified Statements

1. Let $H(x)$ be the statement "x is happy," where the domain is the set of dogs.

    (a) How would you write the statement "all dogs are happy" in the symbols of predicate logic?

    (b) The **negation** of a statement is its logical opposite; it is true when the statement is false, and false when the statement is true. For each of the following statements, decide whether the statement correctly expresses the negation of the statement "all dogs are happy."

i All dogs are not happy.

ii Not all dogs are happy.

iii Some dogs are not happy.

(c) For each statement in (b) that correctly expresses the negation of the statement "all dogs are happy," write the statement in the symbols of predicate logic.

2. Let X be the set of real numbers in the interval $0 < x \leq 1$. Consider the following statement.

For every number x in X, there is a number y in X such that $y < x$.

(a) Decide whether this statement is true or false.

(b) Write the negation of this statement in English.

(c) Write the above statement, and its negation, in the symbols of predicate logic.

3. Based on your work above, state some symbolic rules you can use to negate a quantified statement.

The preceding activity suggests the following *negation rules* for predicate logic.

Equivalence	Name
$\neg[(\forall x)P(x)] \Leftrightarrow (\exists x)(\neg P(x))$	universal negation
$\neg[(\exists x)P(x)] \Leftrightarrow (\forall x)(\neg P(x))$	existential negation

It is easy to see the pattern of these two rules: to negate a quantified statement, bring the negation inside the quantifier, and switch the quantifier.

Let's interpret the negation rules in the context of an example. In the domain of all people, let $L(x)$ stand for "x is a liar." The universal negation rule says that the negation of "All people are liars" is "There exists a person who is not a liar." In symbols,

$$\neg[(\forall x)L(x)] \Leftrightarrow (\exists x)(\neg L(x)).$$

Similarly, the existential negation rule says that the negation of "There exists a liar" is "There are no liars."

Example 1.13 In Example 1.10, we discussed what the negation of the statement

"All large cars get bad mileage."

should be. We can answer this question by negating the formal statement

$$(\forall x)(Q(x) \rightarrow \neg P(x)) \tag{1.3.1}$$

using a proof sequence. We'll suppose as given the negation of statement 1.3.1, and deduce an equivalent statement.

Statements	Reasons
1. $\neg[(\forall x)(Q(x) \rightarrow \neg P(x))]$	given
2. $(\exists x)\neg(Q(x) \rightarrow \neg P(x))$	universal negation
3. $(\exists x)\neg(\neg Q(x) \vee \neg P(x))$	implication
4. $(\exists x)(\neg(\neg Q(x)) \wedge \neg(\neg P(x)))$	De Morgan's law
5. $(\exists x)(Q(x) \wedge P(x))$	double negation
6. $(\exists x)(P(x) \wedge Q(x))$	commutativity

Notice that the result of our formal argument agrees with the intuitive negation we did in Example 1.10: There exists some car that is both large and gets good mileage.

Example 1.14 Let the domain be all faces of the following truncated icosahedron (also known as a soccer ball).

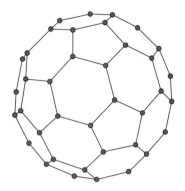

Consider the following predicates:

$$P(x) = \text{``}x \text{ is a pentagon.''}$$
$$H(x) = \text{``}x \text{ is a hexagon.''}$$
$$B(x,y) = \text{``}x \text{ borders } y.\text{''}$$

Here we say that two polygons border each other if they share an edge. We also stipulate that a polygon cannot border itself. Confirm that the following observations are true for any truncated icosahedron.

1. No two pentagons border each other.

2. Every pentagon borders some hexagon.

3. Every hexagon borders another hexagon.

Write these statements in predicate logic and negate them. Simplify the negated statements so that no quantifier or connective lies within the scope of a negation. Translate your negated statement back into English.

Solution: The formalizations of these statements are as follows.

1. $(\forall x)(\forall y)((P(x) \wedge P(y)) \rightarrow \neg B(x,y))$

2. $(\forall x)(P(x) \rightarrow (\exists y)(H(y) \wedge B(x,y)))$

3. $(\forall x)(H(x) \rightarrow (\exists y)(H(y) \wedge B(x,y)))$

We'll negate (2), and leave the others as exercises. See if you can figure out the reasons for each equivalence.

$$\neg[(\forall x)(P(x) \rightarrow (\exists y)(H(y) \wedge B(x,y)))] \Leftrightarrow (\exists x)[\neg(P(x) \rightarrow (\exists y)(H(y) \wedge B(x,y)))]$$
$$\Leftrightarrow (\exists x)[\neg(\neg P(x) \vee (\exists y)(H(y) \wedge B(x,y)))]$$
$$\Leftrightarrow (\exists x)[\neg\neg P(x) \wedge \neg(\exists y)(H(y) \wedge B(x,y))]$$
$$\Leftrightarrow (\exists x)[\neg\neg P(x) \wedge (\forall y)\neg(H(y) \wedge B(x,y))]$$
$$\Leftrightarrow (\exists x)(P(x) \wedge (\forall y)\neg(H(y) \wedge B(x,y)))$$
$$\Leftrightarrow (\exists x)(P(x) \wedge (\forall y)(\neg H(y) \vee \neg B(x,y)))$$
$$\Leftrightarrow (\exists x)(P(x) \wedge (\forall y)(H(y) \rightarrow \neg B(x,y)))$$

This last statement says that there exists an x such that x is a pentagon and, for any y, if y is a hexagon, then x does not border y. In other words, there is some pentagon that borders no hexagon. If you found a solid with this property, it couldn't be a truncated icosahedron.   ◇

1.3.5 Two Common Constructions

There are two expressions that come up often, and knowing the predicate logic for these expressions makes translation much easier. The first is the statement

All ⟨blanks⟩ are ⟨something⟩.

For example, "All baseball players are rich," or "All oysters taste funny." In general, if $P(x)$ and $Q(x)$ are the predicates "x is ⟨blank⟩" and "x is ⟨something⟩," respectively, then the predicate logic expression

$$(\forall x)(P(x) \rightarrow Q(x))$$

translates as "For all x, if x is ⟨blank⟩, then x is ⟨something⟩." Put more simply, "All x's with property ⟨blank⟩ must have property ⟨something⟩," or even simpler, "All ⟨blanks⟩ are ⟨something⟩." In the domain of all people, if $R(x)$ stands for "x is rich" and $B(x)$ stands for "x is a baseball player," then $(\forall x)(B(x) \rightarrow R(x))$ is the statement "All baseball players are rich."

The second construction is of the form

There is a ⟨blank⟩ that is ⟨something⟩.

For example, "There is a rich baseball player," or "There is a funny-tasting oyster." This expression has the following form in predicate logic.

$$(\exists x)(P(x) \wedge Q(x))$$

Note that this translates literally as "There is some x such that x is ⟨blank⟩ and x is ⟨something⟩," which is what we want. In the domain of shellfish, if $O(x)$ is the predicate "x is an oyster" and $F(x)$ is the predicate "x tastes funny," then $(\exists x)(F(x) \wedge O(x))$ would translate as "There is a funny-tasting oyster." Note that you could also say "There is an oyster that tastes funny," "Some oysters taste funny," or, more awkwardly, "There is a funny-tasting shellfish that is an oyster." These statements all mean the same thing.

Exercises 1.3

1. In the domain of integers, let $P(x, y)$ be the predicate "$x \cdot y = 12$." Tell whether each of the following statements is true or false.

   (a) $P(3, 4)$

   (b) $P(3, 5)$

   (c) $P(2, 6) \vee P(3, 7)$

   (d) $(\forall x)(\forall y)(P(x, y) \rightarrow P(y, x))$

   (e) $(\forall x)(\exists y)P(x, y)$

2. In the domain of all penguins, let $D(x)$ be the predicate "x is dangerous." Translate the following quantified statements into simple, everyday English.

   (a) $(\forall x)D(x)$

   (b) $(\exists x)D(x)$

   (c) $\neg(\exists x)D(x)$

   (d) $(\exists x)\neg D(x)$

3. In the domain of all movies, let $V(x)$ be the predicate "x is violent." Write the following statements in the symbols of predicate logic.

   (a) Some movies are violent.

   (b) Some movies are not violent.

   (c) No movies are violent.

   (d) All movies are violent.

4. Let the following predicates be given. The domain is all mammals.

$$L(x) = \text{"}x \text{ is a lion."}$$

$$F(x) = \text{"}x \text{ is fuzzy."}$$

Translate the following statements into predicate logic.

(a) All lions are fuzzy.

(b) Some lions are fuzzy.

5. In the domain of all books, consider the following predicates.

$$H(x) = \text{"}x \text{ is heavy."}$$

$$C(x) = \text{"}x \text{ is confusing."}$$

Translate the following statements in predicate logic into ordinary English.

(a) $(\forall x)(H(x) \rightarrow C(x))$

(b) $(\exists x)(C(x) \wedge H(x))$

(c) $(\forall x)(C(x) \vee H(x))$

(d) $(\exists x)(H(x) \wedge \neg C(x))$

6. The domain of the following predicates is the set of all plants.

$$P(x) = \text{"}x \text{ is poisonous."}$$

$$Q(x) = \text{"Jeff has eaten } x \text{."}$$

Translate the following statements into predicate logic.

(a) Some plants are poisonous.

(b) Jeff has never eaten a poisonous plant.

(c) There are some nonpoisonous plants that Jeff has never eaten.

7. In the domain of nonzero integers, let $I(x,y)$ be the predicate "x/y is an integer." Determine whether the following statements are true or false, and explain why.

(a) $(\forall y)(\exists x)I(x,y)$

(b) $(\exists x)(\forall y)I(x,y)$

8. In the domain of integers, consider the following predicates: Let $N(x)$ be the statement "$x \neq 0$." Let $P(x,y)$ be the statement "$xy = 1$."

(a) Translate the following statement into the symbols of predicate logic.

   For all integers x, there is some integer y such that if $x \neq 0$, then $xy = 1$.

(b) Write the negation of your answer to part (a) in the symbols of predicate logic. Simplify your answer so that it uses the $\wedge$ connective.

(c) Translate your answer from part (b) into an English sentence.

(d) Which statement, (a) or (b), is true in the domain of integers? Explain.

9. Let $P(x,y,z)$ be the predicate "$x + y = z$."

(a) Simplify the statement $\neg(\forall x)(\forall y)(\exists z)P(x,y,z)$ so that no quantifier lies within the scope of a negation.

(b) Is the statement $(\forall x)(\forall y)(\exists z)P(x,y,z)$ true in the domain of all integers? Explain why or why not.

(c) Is the statement $(\forall x)(\forall y)(\exists z)P(x,y,z)$ true in the domain of all integers between 1 and 100? Explain why or why not.

10. The domain of the following predicates is the set of all traders who work at the Tokyo Stock Exchange.

$$P(x,y) = \text{"}x \text{ makes more money than } y \text{."}$$

$$Q(x,y) = \text{"}x \neq y\text{"}$$

Translate the following predicate logic statements into *ordinary, everyday* English. (Don't simply give a word-for-word translation; try to write sentences that make sense.)

(a) $(\forall x)(\exists y)P(x,y)$

(b) $(\exists y)(\forall x)(Q(x,y) \rightarrow P(x,y))$

(c) Which statement is impossible in this context? Why?

11. Translate the following statements into predicate logic using the two common constructions in Section 1.3.5. State what your predicates are, along with the domain of each.

(a) All natural numbers are integers.

(b) Some integers are natural numbers.

(c) All the streets in Cozumel, Mexico, are one-way.

(d) Some streets in London don't have modern curb cuts.

12. Write the following statements in predicate logic. Define your predicates. Use the domain of all quadrilaterals.

(a) All rhombuses are parallelograms.

(b) Some parallelograms are not rhombuses.

13. Let the following predicates be given. The domain is all people.

$$R(x) = \text{``}x \text{ is rude.''}$$
$$\neg R(x) = \text{``}x \text{ is pleasant.''}$$
$$C(x) = \text{``}x \text{ is a child.''}$$

(a) Write the following statement in predicate logic.

There is at least one rude child.

(b) Formally negate your statement from part (a).

(c) Write the English translation of your negated statement.

14. In the domain of all people, consider the following predicate.

$$P(x,y) = \text{``}x \text{ needs to love } y.''$$

(a) Write the statement "Everybody needs somebody to love" in predicate logic.

(b) Formally negate your statement from part (a).

(c) Write the English translation of your negated statement.

15. The domain for this problem is some unspecified collection of numbers. Consider the predicate

$$P(x,y) = \text{``}x \text{ is greater than } y.''$$

(a) Translate the following statement into predicate logic.

Every number has a number that is greater than it.

(b) Negate your expression from part (a), and simplify it so that no quantifier or connective lies within the scope of a negation.

(c) Translate your expression from part (b) into understandable English. Don't use variables in your English translation.

16. Any equation or inequality with variables in it is a predicate in the domain of real numbers. For each of the following statements, tell whether the statement is true or false.

(a) $(\forall x)(x^2 > x)$

(b) $(\exists x)(x^2 - 2 = 1)$

(c) $(\exists x)(x^2 + 2 = 1)$

(d) $(\forall x)(\exists y)(x^2 + y = 4)$

(e) $(\exists y)(\forall x)(x^2 + y = 4)$

17. The domain of the following predicates is all integers greater than 1.

$$P(x) = \text{``}x \text{ is prime.''}$$

$$Q(x,y) = \text{``}x \text{ divides } y.\text{''}$$

Consider the following statement.

> For every x that is not prime, there is some prime y that divides it.

(a) Write the statement in predicate logic.

(b) Formally negate the statement.

(c) Write the English translation of your negated statement.

18. Write the following statement in predicate logic, and negate it. Say what your predicates are, along with the domains.

> Let x and y be real numbers. If x is rational and y is irrational, then $x + y$ is irrational.

19. Refer to Example 1.14.

(a) Give the reasons for each $\Leftrightarrow$ step in the simplification of the formal negation of statement (2).

(b) Give the formal negation of statement (1). Simplify your answer so that no quantifier or connective lies within the scope of a negation. Translate your negated statement back into English.

(c) Give the formal negation of statement (3). Simplify your answer. Translate your negated statement back into English.

20. Let the following predicates be given in the domain of all triangles.

$$R(x) = \text{``}x \text{ is a right triangle.''}$$

$$B(x) = \text{``}x \text{ has an obtuse angle.''}$$

Consider the following statements.

$$S_1 = \neg(\exists x)(R(x) \wedge B(x))$$

$$S_2 = (\forall x)(R(x) \rightarrow \neg B(x))$$

(a) Write a proof sequence to show that $S_1 \Leftrightarrow S_2$.

(b) Write S_1 in ordinary English.

(c) Write S_2 in ordinary English.

21. Let the following predicates be given. The domain is all computer science classes.

$$I(x) = \text{``}x \text{ is interesting.''}$$

$$U(x) = \text{``}x \text{ is useful.''}$$

$$H(x,y) = \text{``}x \text{ is harder than } y.\text{''}$$

$$M(x,y) = \text{``}x \text{ has more students than } y.\text{''}$$

(a) Write the following statements in predicate logic.

    i All interesting CS classes are useful.

ii There are some useful CS classes that are not interesting.

iii Every interesting CS class has more students than any non-interesting CS class.

(b) Write the following predicate logic statement in everyday English. Don't just give a word-for-word translation; your sentence should make sense.

$$(\exists x)[I(x) \wedge (\forall y)(H(x,y) \to M(y,x))]$$

(c) Formally negate the statement from part (b). Simplify your negation so that no quantifier lies within the scope of a negation. State which derivation rules you are using.

(d) Give a translation of your negated statement in everyday English.

22. Let the following predicates be given. The domain is all cars.

$$F(x) = \text{``}x \text{ is fast.''}$$

$$S(x) = \text{``}x \text{ is a sports car.''}$$

$$E(x) = \text{``}x \text{ is expensive.''}$$

$$A(x,y) = \text{``}x \text{ is safer than } y.\text{''}$$

(a) Write the following statements in predicate logic.

i All sports cars are fast.

ii There are fast cars that aren't sports cars.

iii Every fast sports car is expensive.

(b) Write the following predicate logic statement in everyday English. Don't just give a word-for-word translation; your sentence should make sense.

$$(\forall x)[S(x) \to (\exists y)(E(y) \wedge A(y,x))]$$

(c) Formally negate the statement from part (b). Simplify your negation so that no quantifier or connective lies within the scope of a negation. State which derivation rules you are using.

(d) Give a translation of your negated statement in everyday English.

23. Let $P(x)$ be a predicate in the domain consisting of just the numbers 0 and 1. Let p be the statement $P(0)$ and let q be the statement $P(1)$.

(a) Write $(\forall x)P(x)$ as a propositional logic formula using p and q.

(b) Write $(\exists x)P(x)$ as a propositional logic formula using p and q.

(c) In this situation, which derivation rule from propositional logic corresponds to the universal and existential negation rules of predicate logic?

24. (a) Give an example of a pair of predicates $P(x)$ and $Q(x)$ in some domain to show that the $\exists$ quantifier does not distribute over the $\wedge$ connective. That is, give an example to show that the statements

$$(\exists x)(P(x) \wedge Q(x)) \quad \text{and} \quad (\exists x)P(x) \wedge (\exists x)Q(x)$$

are not logically equivalent.

(b) It is true, however, that $\exists$ distributes over $\vee$. That is,

$$(\exists x)(P(x) \vee Q(x)) \;\Leftrightarrow\; (\exists x)P(x) \vee (\exists x)Q(x)$$

is an equivalence rule for predicate logic. Verify that your example from part (a) satisfies this equivalence.

25. (a) Give an example to show that ∀ does not distribute over ∨.

    (b) It is a fact that ∀ distributes over ∧. Check that your example from part (a) satisfies this equivalence rule.

1.4 Logic in Mathematics

There is much more that we could say about symbolic logic; we have only scratched the surface. But we have developed enough tools to help us think carefully about the types of language mathematicians use. This section provides an overview of the basic mathematical "parts of speech."

Most mathematics textbooks (including this one) label important statements with a heading, such as "Theorem," "Definition," or "Proof." The name of each statement describes the role it plays in the logical development of the subject. Therefore, it is important to understand the meanings of these different statement labels.

Preview 1.4

---

1. Explain why an integer cannot be both even and odd.

2. Draw a diagram consisting of straight line segments in which every line segment intersects exactly four other line segments.

3. Recall that a *prime number* is a natural number n such that $n > 1$ and n has no divisors other than n and 1. Prove or disprove the following: Every prime number greater than 3 is the sum of two prime numbers.

1.4.1 The Role of Definitions in Mathematics

When we call a statement a "definition" in mathematics, we mean something different from the usual everyday notion. Everyday definitions are *descriptive.* The thing being defined already exists, and the purpose of the definition is to describe the thing. When a dictionary defines some term, it is characterizing the way the term is commonly used. For example, if we looked up the definition of "mortadella" in the *Oxford English Dictionary* (OED), we would read the following.

> Any of several types of Italian (esp. Bolognese) sausage; (now) spec. a thick smooth-textured pork sausage containing pieces of fat and typically served in slices.

The authors of the OED have done their best to describe what is meant by the term "mortadella." A good dictionary definition is one that does a good job describing something.

In mathematics, by contrast, a *definition* is a statement that stipulates the meaning of a new term, symbol, or object. For example, a plane geometry textbook may define parallel lines as follows.

Definition 1.4 Two lines are *parallel* if they have no points in common.

The job of this definition is not to describe parallel lines, but rather to specify exactly what we mean when we use the word "parallel." Once parallel lines have been defined in this way, the statement "l and m are parallel" means "l and m have no points in common." We may have some intuitive idea of what l and m might look like (e.g., they must run in the same direction), but for the purposes of any future arguments, the only thing we really *know* about l and m is that they don't intersect each other.

The meaning of a mathematical statement depends on the definitions of the terms involved. If you don't understand a mathematical statement, start looking at the definitions of all the terms. These definitions stipulate the meanings of the terms. The statement won't make sense without them.

For example, consider preview question 1.4.1 at the beginning of this section. We already know what even and odd numbers are; we all come to this problem with a previously learned *concept image* of "even" and "odd." Our concept image is what we think of when we hear the term: an even number ends in an even digit, an odd number can't be divided in half evenly, "2, 4, 6, 8; who do we appreciate," etc. When writing mathematically, however, it is important not to rely too heavily on these concept images. Any mathematical statement about even and odd numbers derives its meaning from definitions. We choose to specify these as follows.

Definition 1.5 An integer n is *even* if $n = 2k$ for some integer k.

Definition 1.6 An integer n is *odd* if $n = 2k + 1$ for some integer k.

Given these definitions, we can justify the statement "17 is odd" by noting that $17 = 2 \cdot 8 + 1$. In fact, this equation is precisely the meaning of the statement that "17 is odd"; there is some integer k (in this case, $k = 8$) such that $17 = 2k + 1$. You already "knew" that 17 is odd, but in order to mathematically *prove* that 17 is odd, you need to use the definition.

Mathematical definitions must be extremely precise, and this can make them somewhat limited. Often, our concept image contains much more information than the definition supplies. For example, we probably all agree that it is impossible for a number to be both even and odd, but this fact doesn't follow immediately from Definitions 1.5 and 1.6. To say that some given number n is even means that $n = 2k_1$ for some integer k_1, and to say that it is odd is to say that $n = 2k_2 + 1$ for some integer k_2. (Note that k_1 and k_2 may be different.) Now, is this possible? It would imply that $2k_1 = 2k_2 + 1$, which says that $1 = 2(k_1 - k_2)$, showing that 1 is even, by Definition 1.5. At this point we might object that 1 is odd, so it can't be even, but this reasoning is circular: we were trying to show that a number cannot be both even and odd. We haven't yet shown this fact, so we can't use this fact in our argument. It turns out that Definitions 1.5 and 1.6 alone are not enough to show that a number can't be both even and odd; to do so requires more facts about integers, as we will see in Section 1.5.

One reasonable objection to the above discussion is that our definition of odd integers was too limiting; why not define an odd integer to be an integer that isn't even? This is certainly permissible, but then it would be hard[2] to show that an odd integer n can be written as $2k + 1$ for some integer k. And we can't have two definitions for the same term. Stipulating a definition usually involves a choice on the part of the author, but once this choice is made, we are stuck with it. We have chosen to define odd integers as in Definition 1.6, so this is what we mean when we say "odd."

Since definitions are stipulative, they are logically "if and only if" statements. However, it is common to write definitions in the form

[Object] x is [defined term] if [defining property about x].

The foregoing examples all take this form. In predicate logic, if

$$D(x) = x \text{ is [defined term]}$$

$$P(x) = \text{[defining property about } x\text{]}$$

then the above definition really means $(\forall x)(P(x) \leftrightarrow D(x))$. However, this is not what the definition says at face value. Definitions look like "if ... then" statements, but we interpret them as "if and only if" statements because they are definitions. For example, Definition 1.4 is stipulating the property that defines all parallel lines, not just a property some parallel lines might have. Strictly speaking, we really should use "if and only if" instead of "if" in our definitions. But the use of "if" is so widespread that most mathematicians would find a definition like

Two lines are *parallel* if and only if they have no points in common.

awkward to read. Since this statement is a definition, it is redundant to say "if and only if."

1.4.2 Other Types of Mathematical Statements

Definitions are a crucial part of mathematics, but there are other kinds of statements that occur frequently in mathematical writing. Any mathematical system needs to start with some assumptions. Without any statements to build on, we would never be able to prove any new statements. Statements that are assumed without proof are called *postulates* or *axioms*. For example, the following is a standard axiom about the natural numbers.

If n is a natural number, so is $n + 1$.

Axioms are typically very basic, fundamental statements about the objects they describe. Any theorem in mathematics is based on the assumption of some set of underlying axioms. So to say theorems are "true" is not to say they are true in any absolute sense, only that they are true, given that some specified set of axioms is true.

---

2. Actually, it would be impossible, without further information.

A *theorem* is a statement that follows logically from statements we have already established or taken as given. Before a statement can be called a theorem, we must be able to prove it. A *proof* is a valid argument, based on axioms, definitions, and proven theorems, that demonstrates the truth of a statement. The derivation sequences that we did in Section 1.2 were very basic mathematical proofs. We will see more interesting examples of proofs in the next section.

We also use the terms *lemma, proposition,* and *corollary* to refer to specific kinds of theorems. Usually authors will label a result a lemma if they are using it to prove another result. Some authors make no distinction between a theorem and a proposition, but the latter often refers to a result that is perhaps not as significant as a full-fledged theorem. A corollary is a theorem that follows immediately from another result via a short argument.

One last word on terminology: A statement that we intend to prove is called a *claim*. A statement that we can't yet prove but that we suspect is true is called a *conjecture*.

1.4.3 Counterexamples

Often, mathematical statements are of the form

$$(\forall x)P(x). \tag{1.4.1}$$

We saw in the previous section that the negation of statement 1.4.1 is

$$(\exists x)\neg P(x). \tag{1.4.2}$$

So either statement 1.4.1 is true or statement 1.4.2 is true, but not both. If we can find a single value for x that makes $\neg P(x)$ true, then we know that statement 1.4.2 is true, and therefore we also know that statement 1.4.1 is false.

For example, we might be tempted to make the following statement.

$$\text{Every prime number is odd.} \tag{1.4.3}$$

But 2 is an example of a prime number that is not odd, so statement 1.4.3 is false. A particular value that shows a statement to be false is called a *counterexample* to the statement.

Another common logical form in mathematics is the universal if–then statement, $(\forall x)(P(x) \rightarrow Q(x))$. To find a counterexample to a statement of this form, we need to find some x that satisfies its negation, $(\exists x)\neg(P(x) \rightarrow Q(x))$. This last statement is equivalent (using implication and De Morgan's law) to $(\exists x)(P(x) \wedge \neg Q(x))$. So a counterexample is something that satisfies P and violates Q.

Example 1.15 Find a counterexample to the following statement.

For all sequences of numbers $a_1, a_2, a_3, \ldots$, if $a_1 < a_2 < a_3 < \cdots$, then some a_i must be positive.

Solution: By the above discussion, we need an example of a sequence that satisfies the "if" part of the statement and violates the "then" part. In other words, we need to find an increasing sequence that is always negative. Something with a horizontal asymptote will work: $a_n = -1/n$ is one example. Note that $-1 < -1/2 < -1/3 < \cdots$, but all the terms are less than zero. ◇

1.4.4 Axiomatic Systems

Activity 1.4.1: Undefined Terms and Axioms

An axiomatic system is a collection of words, called *undefined terms*, and rules, called *axioms*. The properties of the undefined terms are stipulated by the axioms. Here's an example.

Undefined terms: container, object, contain

Axioms:

1. Every container contains exactly two objects.

2. Every pair of objects is contained in exactly one container.

3. There are exactly four objects.

1. Draw a picture of objects and containers such that all three axioms are satisfied. You will have to decide what an object and a container look like, and what it looks like for a container to contain an object.

2. How many containers did you have in your picture in part (1)? Could you have predicted this from the axioms?

3. Write the negation of Axiom 1 in English in the form "Some container _____."

4. Draw a picture of objects and containers such that Axioms 2 and 3 are satisfied, but Axiom 1 is not.

5. If you only have to satisfy Axioms 2 and 3, is there any limit on the number of containers you could have?

In rigorous, modern treatments of mathematics, any system (e.g., plane geometry, the real numbers) must be clearly and unambiguously defined from the start. The definitions should leave nothing to intuition; they mean what they say and nothing more. It is important to be clear about the assumptions, or axioms, for the system. Every theorem in the system must be proved with a valid argument, using only the definitions, axioms, and previously proved theorems of the system.

This sounds good, but it is actually impossible. It is impossible because we can't define everything; before we write the first definition we have to have some words in our vocabulary. These starting words are called *undefined terms*. An undefined term has no meaning—it is an abstraction. Its meaning comes from the role it plays in the axioms of the system. A collection of undefined terms and axioms is called an *axiomatic system*.

Axiomatic systems for familiar mathematics such as plane geometry and the real number system are actually quite complicated and beyond the scope of an introductory course. Here we will look at some very simple axiomatic systems to get a feel for how they work. This will also give us some experience with logic in mathematics.

The first example defines a "finite geometry," that is, a system for geometry with a finite number of points. Although this system speaks of "points" and "lines," these terms don't mean the same thing they meant in high school geometry. In fact, these terms don't mean anything at all, to begin with at least. The only thing we know about points and lines is that they satisfy the given axioms.

Example 1.16 Axiomatic system for a four-point geometry.

> *Undefined terms:* point, line, is on
>
> *Axioms:*
>
> 1. For every pair of distinct points x and y, there is a unique line l such that x is on l and y is on l.
>
> 2. Given a line l and a point x that is not on l, there is a unique line m such that x is on m and no point on l is also on m.
>
> 3. There are exactly four points.
>
> 4. It is impossible for three points to be on the same line.

Notice that these axioms use terms from logic in addition to the undefined terms. We are also using numbers ("four" and "three"), even though we haven't defined an axiomatic system for the natural numbers. In this case, our use of numbers is more a convenient shorthand than anything; we aren't relying on any properties of the natural numbers such as addition, ordering, divisibility, etc.

It is common to use an existing system to define a new axiomatic system. For example, some modern treatments of plane geometry use axioms that rely on the real number system. The axioms in Example 1.16 use constructions from predicate logic. In any event, these prerequisite systems can also be defined axiomatically, so systems that use them are still fundamentally axiomatic.

Definitions can help make an axiomatic system more user-friendly. In the four-point geometry of Example 1.16, we could make the following definitions. In these (and other) definitions, the word being defined is in *italics*.

Definition 1.7 A line l *passes through* a point x if x is on l.

Definition 1.7 gives us a convenient alternative to using the undefined term "is on." For example, in the first axiom, it is a bit awkward to say "x is on l and y is on l," but Definition 1.7 allows us to rephrase this as "l passes through x and y." The definition doesn't add any new features to the system; it just helps us describe things more easily. This is basically what any definition in mathematics does. The following definition is a slight restatement of Definition 1.4, modified to fit the terminology of this system.

Definition 1.8 Two lines, l and m, are *parallel* if there is no point x, such that x is on l and x is on m.

Now we could rephrase the second axiom of Example 1.16 as follows.

2. Given a line l and a point x that is not on l, there is a unique line m passing through x such that m is parallel to l.

A simple theorem and proof would appear as follows.

Theorem 1.1 *In the axiomatic system of Example 1.16, there are at least two distinct lines.*

Proof   By Axiom 3, there are distinct points x, y, and z. By Axiom 1, there is a line l_1 through x and y, and a line l_2 through y and z. By Axiom 4, x, y, and z are not on the same line, so l_1 and l_2 must be distinct lines.   □

A *model* of an axiomatic system is an interpretation in some context in which all the undefined terms have meanings and all the axioms hold. Models are important because they show that it is possible for all the axioms to be true, at least in some context. And any theorem that follows from the axioms must also be true for any valid model.

Let's make a model for the system in Example 1.16. Let a "point" be a dot, and let a "line" be a simple closed loop. A point "is on" a line if the dot is inside the loop:

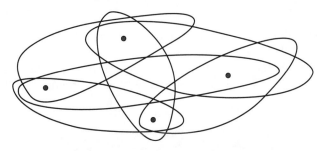

It is easy to check that all the axioms hold, though this model doesn't really match our concept image of points and lines in ordinary geometry. We may think we know what points and lines should look like, but mathematically speaking we only know whatever we can prove about them using the axioms. (In the exercises you will construct a more intuitive model for this system.)

The mathematician David Hilbert (1862–1943) was largely responsible for developing the modern approach to axiomatics. Hilbert, reflecting on the abstract nature of axiomatic systems, remarked, "Instead of points, lines, and planes, one must be able to say at all times tables, chairs, and beer mugs" [24]. If we used a word processor to replace every occurrence of "point" with "table" and every occurrence of "line" with "chair" in the above axioms, definitions, theorem, and proof, the theorem would still hold, and the proof would still be valid.

The following activity will give you some practice thinking abstractly about axiomatic systems. The choice of the words used for undefined terms emphasizes that these terms, by themselves, carry no meaning.

Activity 1.4.2: Models for Axiomatic Systems

Consider the zork-gork-snork axiomatic system.

Undefined terms: zork, gork, snork

Axioms:
1. For every pair of zorks z_1 and z_2, there is exactly one gork g such that z_1 snorks g and z_2 snorks g.
2. For every pair of gorks g_1 and g_2, there is a zork z that snorks both g_1 and g_2.
3. There are at least four distinct zorks, no three of which snork the same gork.

1. Let g_1 and g_2 be a pair of gorks. Fill in the blanks in the following proof that, given a pair of gorks, there is a *exactly one* zork that snorks both of them.

   Let g_1 and g_2 be a given pair of gorks. By Axiom ____, some zork z snorks both of them. Suppose another zork z' also snorks both g_1 and g_2. Then ____ and ____ are each snorked by both ____ and ____, contradicting Axiom ____. So there can't be such a zork z', and therefore there is only one zork that snorks both gorks.

2. Draw a model for this system in which a zork is a point, a gork is a line, and "snorks" means "lies on." Use as few zorks as possible.

3. In your model, are there three gorks that are snorked by the same zork? Must this always be the case?

The next example is referred to in the exercises.

Example 1.17 Badda-Bing axiomatic system.

> *Undefined terms:* badda, bing, hit
> *Axioms:*
>
>   1. Every badda hits exactly four bings.
>   2. Every bing is hit by exactly two baddas.
>   3. If x and y are distinct baddas, each hitting bing q, then there are no other bings hit by both x and y.
>   4. There is at least one bing.

One possible model for the Badda-Bing system is shown in Figure 1.2. The picture shows an infinite collection of squares; the central square connects to four other squares whose sides are half as long. Each of these squares connects to three other smaller squares, and each of those connects to three others, and so on. This is an example of a *fractal*—a shape with some sort of infinitely repetitive geometric structure. (We'll say more about fractals in Chapter 3.)

Figure 1.2 A fractal model for the Badda-Bing geometry.

In this model, a "badda" is a square, and a "bing" is a corner, or *vertex,* of a square. A square "hits" a vertex if the vertex belongs to the square. Since every square has four vertices, Axiom 1 is satisfied. Axiom 2 holds because every vertex in the model belongs to exactly two squares. Axiom 3 is a little harder to see: if squares x and y share a vertex q, there is no way they can share another vertex. And Axiom 4 is obviously true—there are lots of bings.

Exercises 1.4

1. Look up the word "root" in a dictionary. It should have several different definitions. Find a definition that is (a) descriptive and another definition that is (b) stipulative.

2. Find another word in the English language that has both descriptive and stipulative definitions.

3. Use Definition 1.5 to explain why 104 is an even integer.

4. Let n be an integer. Use Definition 1.6 to explain why $2n + 7$ is an odd integer.

5. Let n_1 and n_2 be even integers.

    (a) Use Definition 1.5 to write n_1 and n_2 in terms of integers k_1 and k_2, respectively.

    (b) Write the product $n_1 n_2$ in terms of k_1 and k_2. Simplify your answer.

    (c) Write the sum $n_1 + n_2$ in terms of k_1 and k_2. Simplify your answer.

6. Consider the following definition of the "$\triangleleft$" symbol.

    Definition. Let x and y be integers. Write $x \triangleleft y$ if $3x + 5y = 7k$ for some integer k.

    (a) Show that $1 \triangleleft 5$, $3 \triangleleft 1$, and $0 \triangleleft 7$.

    (b) Find a counterexample to the following statement:

    If $a \triangleleft b$ and $c \triangleleft d$, then $a \cdot c \triangleleft b \cdot d$.

7. Give three adjectives that describe your concept image of a circle.

8. There are several different models for geometries in which the points are ordered pairs (x, y) of real numbers; we plot these points in the usual way in the xy-plane. In such a geometry, there can be a formula for the *distance* between two points (x_1, y_1) and (x_2, y_2). For example, in Euclidean geometry, distance is given by the usual Euclidean distance formula:

$$\text{Distance} = \sqrt{(x_2 - x_1)^2 + (y_2 - y_1)^2}$$

In any geometry with a distance formula, we can define a *circle* as follows.

Definition 1.9 A *circle* centered at (a, b) with radius r is the collection of all points (x, y) whose distance from (a, b) is r.

    (a) Use Definition 1.9 to give an equation for the circle with radius 5 centered at $(0, 0)$ in the Euclidean plane.

    (b) Plot the circle from part (a) in the xy-plane.

    (c) In the *Taxicab geometry*, the distance between two points (x_1, y_1) and (x_2, y_2) is given by the following formula.

$$\text{Distance} = |x_2 - x_1| + |y_2 - y_1|$$

    (This is called "taxicab" distance because it models the distance you would have to travel if you were restricted to driving on a rectangular city grid.) In this model, use Definition 1.9 to plot the "circle" with radius 5 centered at $(0, 0)$.

    (d) Which type of circle (Euclidean or taxicab) agrees with your concept image of circle?

9. Consider the lines $y = 2x + 1$ and $y = x + 2$ in the usual xy-plane. Use Definition 1.4 to explain why these lines are not parallel. Be specific.

10. Consider the domain of all quadrilaterals. Let

$$A(x) = \text{"x has four right angles."}$$
$$R(x) = \text{"x is a rectangle."}$$

Write the meaning of each mathematical statement in predicate logic, keeping in mind the logical distinction between definitions and theorems.

    (a) **Definition.** A quadrilateral is a *rectangle* if it has four right angles.

    (b) **Theorem.** A quadrilateral is a rectangle if it has four right angles.

11. Write Definition 1.5 in predicate logic. Use the predicate $E(x) = \text{"$x$ is even"}$ in the domain of integers.

12. Let the following statements be given.

    Definition. A triangle is *scalene* if all of its sides have different lengths.

    Theorem. A triangle is scalene if it is a right triangle that is not isosceles.

Suppose $\triangle ABC$ is a scalene triangle. Which of the following conclusions are valid? Why or why not?

    (a) All of the sides of $\triangle ABC$ have different lengths.

    (b) $\triangle ABC$ is a right triangle that is not isosceles.

13. What is the difference between an axiom and a theorem?

14. Let $P(n, x, y, z)$ be the predicate "$x^n + y^n = z^n$."

   (a) Write the following statement in predicate logic, using positive integers as the domain.

   > For every positive integer n, there exist positive integers $x, y,$ and z such that $x^n + y^n = z^n$.

   (b) Formally negate your predicate logic statement from part (a). Simplify so that no quantifier lies within the scope of a negation.

   (c) In order to produce a counterexample to the statement in part (a), what, specifically, would you have to find?

15. Find a counterexample for each statement.

   (a) If n is prime, then $2^n - 1$ is prime.

   (b) Every triangle has at least one obtuse angle.[3]

   (c) For all real numbers x, $x^2 \geq x$.

   (d) For every positive nonprime integer n, if some prime p divides n, then some other prime q (with $q \neq p$) also divides n.

16. Find a counterexample for each statement.

   (a) If all the sides of a quadrilateral have equal lengths, then the diagonals of the quadrilateral have equal lengths.

   (b) For every real number $N > 0$, there is some real number x such that $Nx > x$.

   (c) Let $l, m,$ and n be lines in the plane. If $l \perp m$ and n intersects l, then n intersects m.

   (d) If p is prime, then $p^2 + 4$ is prime.

17. Which of the statements in the previous problem can be proved as theorems?

18. Consider the following theorem.

   > **Theorem.** Let x be a wamel. If x has been schlumpfed, then x is a borfin.

   Answer the following questions.

   (a) Give the converse of this theorem.

   (b) Give the contrapositive of this theorem.

   (c) Which statement, (a) or (b), is logically equivalent to the Theorem?

19. Draw a model for the axiomatic system of four-point geometry (Example 1.16), where a "line" is a line segment, a "point" is an endpoint of a line segment, and a point "is on" a line if it is one of its endpoints.

20. In four-point geometry, use the axioms to explain why every point is on three different lines.

21. In four-point geometry, is it possible for two different lines to both pass through two given distinct points? Explain why or why not using the axioms.

22. In four-point geometry, do triangles exist? In other words, is it possible to have three distinct points, not on the same line, such that a line passes through each pair of points? Why or why not?

23. In four-point geometry, state a good definition to stipulate what it means for two lines to *intersect*.

24. Consider the following model for four-point geometry.

   Points: 1, 2, 3, 4

   Lines: $\boxed{1\ 2}$, $\boxed{1\ 3}$, $\boxed{1\ 4}$, $\boxed{2\ 3}$, $\boxed{2\ 4}$, $\boxed{3\ 4}$

   A point "is on" a line if the line's box contains the point.

   (a) Give a pair of parallel lines in this model. (Refer to Definition 1.8.)

   (b) Give a pair of intersecting lines in this model. (Use your definition from Exercise 23.)

25. Explain why, in the axiomatic system of Example 1.17, there must be at least seven distinct bings.

---

3. An angle is *obtuse* if it has measure greater than $90°$.

26. Consider the following definition in the system of Example 1.17.

    > **Definition.** Let x and y be distinct baddas. We say that a bing q is a *boom* of x and y, if x hits q and y hits q.

    Rewrite Axiom 3 using this definition.

27. In the context of Example 1.17, consider the following predicates.

    $$N(x,y) = \text{“}x \neq y.\text{”}$$
    $$D(x) = \text{“}x \text{ is a badda.”}$$
    $$G(x) = \text{“}x \text{ is a bing.”}$$
    $$H(x,y) = \text{“}x \text{ hits } y.\text{”}$$

    Use these predicates to write Axiom 3 in predicate logic.

28. Refer to Example 1.17 and Figure 1.2. Describe a different model, using squares and vertices, where all the squares are the same size.

29. In the axiomatic system of Example 1.17, let a "badda" be a line segment, let a "bing" be a point, and say that a line segment "hits" a point if it passes through it. In the diagram below, there are 4 baddas and 12 bings. Is this a model for the system? Which of the axioms does this model satisfy? Explain.

30. Describe a model for Example 1.17 with 10 bings, where a "badda" is a line segment and a "bing" is a point.

1.5 Methods of Proof

The types of proofs we did in Section 1.2 were fairly mechanical. We started with the given and constructed a sequence of conclusions, each justified by a deduction rule. We were able to write proofs this way because our mathematical system, propositional logic, was fairly small. Most mathematical contexts are much more complicated; there are more definitions, more axioms, and more complex statements to analyze. These more complicated situations do not easily lend themselves to the kind of structured proof sequences of Section 1.2. In this section we will look at some of the ways proofs are done in mathematics.

Preview 1.5

1. Suppose that a and b are odd integers. What can be said about their sum $a + b$? Explain your reasoning.
2. What can be said about the sum of two even integers? Explain.

1.5.1 Direct Proofs

The structure of a proof sequence in propositional logic is straightforward: in order to prove $A \Rightarrow C$, we prove a sequence of results.

$$A \Rightarrow B_1 \Rightarrow B_2 \Rightarrow \cdots \Rightarrow B_n \Rightarrow C$$

A *direct proof* in mathematics has the same logic, but we don't usually write such proofs as lists of statement and reasons. Instead, this linear chain of implications is couched in mathematical prose and written in paragraph form.

Example 1.18 The proof of Theorem 1.1 on page 35 is a direct proof. Although this proof takes the form of a paragraph, the logical sequence of implications is easy to see.

There are distinct points x, y, and z.

$\Rightarrow$ There is a line l_1 through x and y, and a line l_2 through y and z.

$\Rightarrow x, y$, and z are not on the same line, so $l_1 \neq l_2$.

These three statements are justified by Axioms 3, 1, and 4, respectively.

Example 1.19 Prove the following statement.

For all real numbers x, if $x > 1$, then $x^2 > 1$.

Proof Let x be a real number, and suppose $x > 1$. Multiplying both sides of this inequality by a positive number preserves the inequality, so we can multiply both sides by x to obtain $x^2 > x$. Since $x > 1$, we have $x^2 > x > 1$, or $x^2 > 1$, as required. $\square$

It is worth looking back at this proof. The chain of implications is as follows.

$$x > 1 \;\Rightarrow\; x^2 > x \;\Rightarrow\; x^2 > 1 \tag{1.5.1}$$

Each conclusion is justified by an elementary fact from high school algebra, and the results are packaged in paragraph form. More precisely, the statement we were proving was actually a quantified statement of the form $(\forall x)(P(x) \to Q(x))$, where $P(x)$ means "$x > 1$" and $Q(x)$ means "$x^2 > 1$." We see that the sequence of implications in Equation (1.5.1) is true no matter what value we initially choose for x. This is the meaning of the introductory phrase "Let x be a real number." We assume nothing about x other than that it is a real number; it is arbitrary in every other respect. We then treat $P(x)$ as given and try to conclude $Q(x)$. Since x could have been any real number to start with, we have proved the implication for *all* x.

We state this type of proof as our first "Rule of Thumb" for proving theorems.

Rule of Thumb 1.1 To prove a statement of the form $(\forall x)(P(x) \to Q(x))$, begin your proof with a sentence of the form

Let x be [an element of the domain], and suppose $P(x)$.

A direct proof is then a sequence of justified conclusions culminating in $Q(x)$.

Activity 1.5.1: Direct Proofs

Recall that we define an integer n to be *even* if $n = 2k$ for some integer k. For the problems below, use the predicate $E(x)$ for "x is even."

1. Consider the statement: "For all integers n, if n is even, then n^2 is even."

   (a) Write this statement in predicate logic.

   (b) Fill in the blanks in the following proof of this statement.

   Let n be an integer, and suppose that _____. By the definition of *even*, $n =$ ____ for some integer k. Therefore, $n^2 =$ ____ $= 2 \cdot$ ____, so by the definition of *even*, n^2 is even.

2. Consider the statement: "For all integers a and b, if a is even and b is even, then $a + b$ is even."

   (a) Write this statement in predicate logic.

   (b) Fill in the blanks in the following proof of this statement.

   Let a and b be integers, and suppose that _____. By the definition of *even*, $a =$ ____ for some integer k_1 and $b =$ ____ for some integer k_2. Therefore, ... (Finish the proof.)

Before we look at another example of direct proof, we will need some tools for dealing with integers. We'll start with a definition for what it means for an integer x to *divide* another integer y.

Definition 1.10 An integer x *divides* an integer y if there is some integer k such that $y = kx$.

We write $x \mid y$ to denote that x divides y. An identical definition holds for natural numbers (i.e., positive integers). Just replace the three occurrences of "integer" in Definition 1.10 with "natural number."

We are not going to develop a rigorous axiomatic approach to the integers; such a treatment is beyond the scope of this course. When you deal with integer equations, feel free to use elementary facts from high school algebra. You can add something to both sides of an equation, use the distributive property, combine terms, and so on. However, there are certain facts about the integers that we will state as axioms, because they justify important steps in the proofs that follow.

Axiom 1.1 If a and b are integers, so are $a + b$ and $a \cdot b$.

Axiom 1.1 describes the *closure* property of the integers under addition and multiplication. Most number systems are closed under these two operations; you can't get a new kind of number by adding or multiplying. On the other hand, the integers are not closed under division: $2/3$ is not an integer, even though 2 and 3 are.

Example 1.20 Prove the following.

For all integers a, b, and c, if $a \mid b$ and $a \mid c$, then $a \mid (b + c)$.

Proof Let integers a, b, and c be given, and suppose $a \mid b$ and $a \mid c$. Then, by Definition 1.10, there is some integer k_1 such that $b = k_1 a$ and there is some integer k_2 such that $c = k_2 a$. Therefore,

$$b + c = k_1 a + k_2 a = (k_1 + k_2)a.$$

By Axiom 1.1, $k_1 + k_2$ is an integer, so $a \mid (b + c)$, again by Definition 1.10. $\square$

Notice that this proof illustrates how definitions are used in mathematics. We used the definition of "divides" in order to translate the given statement into an equation, we did some simple algebra on this equation to obtain a new equation, and we used the definition again to translate the new equation into the statement we were trying to prove. The following "flow chart" illustrates this proof technique.

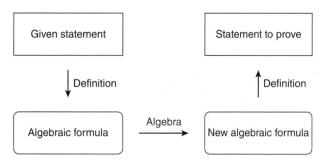

1.5.2   Proof by Contraposition

Sometimes it is hard to see how to get a direct proof started. If you get stuck (and you will), try proving the contrapositive. This is certainly permitted, since the contrapositive of a statement is its logical equivalent. We can state this as another rule of thumb.

Rule of Thumb 1.2 To prove a statement of the form $(\forall x)(P(x) \rightarrow Q(x))$, begin your proof with a sentence of the form

Let x be [an element of the domain], and suppose $\neg Q(x)$.

A proof by contraposition is then a sequence of justified conclusions culminating in $\neg P(x)$.

Example 1.21 Suppose x and y are positive real numbers such that the geometric mean $\sqrt{xy}$ is different from the arithmetic mean $\frac{x+y}{2}$. Then $x \neq y$.

Proof (By contraposition.) Let x and y be positive real numbers, and suppose $x = y$. then

$$
\begin{aligned}
\sqrt{xy} &= \sqrt{x^2} && \text{since } x = y \\
&= x && \text{since } x \text{ is positive} \\
&= \frac{x+x}{2} && \text{using arithmetic} \\
&= \frac{x+y}{2} && \text{since } x = y
\end{aligned}
$$

$\square$

Contraposition isn't a radically new proof technique; a proof of a statement by contraposition is just a direct proof of the statement's contrapositive. In Example 1.21, the form of the statement to prove gave a clue that a proof by contraposition would work. If A is the statement "$\sqrt{xy} = \frac{x+y}{2}$" and B is the statement "$x = y$," then the statement to prove has the form $\neg A \to \neg B$. The contrapositive of this statement is $B \to A$, so our proof started with the assumption that $x = y$ and concluded that $\sqrt{xy} = \frac{x+y}{2}$.

For the next example we need some facts from the system of plane geometry that you studied in high school. Henceforth, we'll refer to this type of geometry as *Euclidean* geometry. The following theorem, which we will not prove, is true in Euclidean geometry.

Theorem 1.2 *The sum of the measures of the angles of any triangle equals* $180°$.

The definition of *parallel* that we used in four-point geometry also works in Euclidean geometry. Although the wording of the following definition is a little different, the content is fundamentally the same.

Definition 1.11 Two lines are parallel if they do not intersect.

We'll use these two statements in the next example.

Example 1.22 Prove:

> If two lines are cut by a transversal such that a pair of interior angles are supplementary, then the lines are parallel.

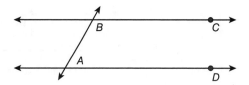

Proof (By contraposition.) Suppose we are given two lines cut by a transversal as shown above, and suppose the lines are not parallel. Then, by the definition of parallel lines, the lines intersect. Without loss of generality, suppose they intersect on the right at point X. (If they intersect on the left, the same argument will work.)

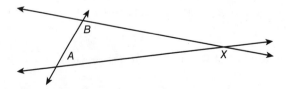

By Theorem 1.2, the sum of the angles of $\triangle XAB$ is $180°$. Since $\angle X$ has measure greater than 0, the sum of the measures of $\angle A$ and $\angle B$ must be less than $180°$, so $\angle A$ and $\angle B$ can't be supplementary. $\square$

1.5.3 Proof by Contradiction

Sometimes even a simple-looking statement can be hard to prove directly, with or without contraposition. In this case, it sometimes helps to try a *proof by contradiction*. The idea is a little counterintuitive. To prove statement A, suppose its negation $\neg A$ is true. Then argue, as in a direct proof, until you reach a statement that you know to be false. You will have established the sequence

$$\neg A \Rightarrow B_1 \Rightarrow B_2 \Rightarrow \cdots \Rightarrow B_n \Rightarrow \mathbf{F}$$

where $\mathbf{F}$ represents a statement that is always false, that is, a contradiction. Taking contrapositives of this chain gives us a sequence

$$A \Leftarrow \neg B_1 \Leftarrow \neg B_2 \Leftarrow \cdots \Leftarrow \neg B_n \Leftarrow \mathbf{T}$$

and since $\mathbf{T}$ is always true (i.e., a tautology) it follows that A is true also. To sum up:

Rule of Thumb 1.3 To prove a statement A by contradiction, begin your proof with the following sentence:

Suppose, to the contrary, that $\neg A$.

Then argue, as in a direct proof, until you reach a contradiction.

This next example is similar to Example 1.22. In fact, it is a weaker statement, so the proof given in Example 1.22 could also be used to prove it. But it makes a nice example of the contradiction method.

Example 1.23 In Euclidean geometry, prove:

If two lines share a common perpendicular, then the lines are parallel.

Before stating the proof, notice that this theorem is of the following form.

$$(\forall x)(\forall y)(C(x,y) \rightarrow P(x,y))$$

Here $C(x,y)$ means "x and y share a common perpendicular," and $P(x,y)$ means "$x \parallel y$." You can check that the formal negation of this statement is the following.

$$(\exists x)(\exists y)(C(x,y) \wedge \neg P(x,y))$$

The translation of this last statement is "There exist lines that share a common perpendicular but are not parallel." So we use this statement to start our proof by contradiction.

Proof (By contradiction.) Suppose, to the contrary, that line AB is a common perpendicular to lines AC and BD, and also that AC and BD are not parallel. Then, by Definition 1.11, AC and BD intersect in some point X. But then $\triangle ABX$ has two right angles (and a third angle of nonzero measure), contradicting Theorem 1.2.   □

The next results rely on properties of even and odd numbers, so we need to use these definitions in our arguments. Recall:

Definition 1.5. An integer n is even if $n = 2k$ for some integer k.

Definition 1.6. An integer n is odd if $n = 2k + 1$ for some integer k.

As we discussed in Section 1.4.1, these definitions alone don't imply that every integer is either even or odd. We'll state this fact as an axiom.[4]

Axiom 1.2 For all integers n, $\neg(n$ is even$) \Leftrightarrow (n$ is odd$)$.

---

4. In a more rigorous treatment of number theory, this fact could be proved using the division algorithm, which would follow from the well-ordering principle.

In other words, any integer is either even or odd, but never both. This axiom is the key to proving the following lemma.

Lemma 1.1 Let n be an integer. If n^2 is even, then n is even.

The following activity will lead you through two different proofs of this lemma.

Activity 1.5.2: Proofs by Contraposition and Contradiction

Consider statement P: "For all integers n, if n^2 is even, then n is even."

1. Write statement P in predicate logic. Use $E(x)$ for "x is even."
2. Write the contrapositive of statement P in predicate logic. Use $O(x)$ for "x is odd."
3. Give a direct proof of the contrapositive of statement P.
4. Write the negation of P in predicate logic. Use rules of logic to write this statement using the $\exists$ quantifier and the $\wedge$ connective, and translate this negation back into English.
5. Assume that the negation of P is true. Prove that this assumption leads to a contradiction.

Our final example is a classic proof by contradiction. Recall that a *rational* number is a number that can be written as a/b, where a and b are integers with $b \neq 0$.

Example 1.24 Prove that $\sqrt{2}$ is irrational.

Proof (By contradiction.) Suppose, to the contrary, that $\sqrt{2}$ is rational, so there are integers a and b such that $a/b = \sqrt{2}$, and a and b can be chosen so that the fraction a/b is in lowest terms. Then $a^2/b^2 = 2$, so $a^2 = 2b^2$, that is, a^2 is even. By Lemma 1.1, a is even. Therefore, $a = 2k$ for some integer k, so $a^2 = 4k^2$. But now we have $b^2 = a^2/2 = 2k^2$, so b^2 is even, and therefore, by the lemma again, b is even as well. We have shown that a and b are both even, which contradicts the assumption that a/b is in lowest terms. $\qquad\square$

Exercises 1.5

1. Consider the following statement.

   > For all integers x, if $4 \mid x$, then x is even.

   (a) Write this statement in predicate logic in the domain of integers. Say what your predicates are.
   (b) Apply Rule of Thumb 1.1 to write down the first sentence of a direct proof of this statement.
   (c) Use Definition 1.10 to translate your supposition in part (b) into algebra.
   (d) Finish the proof of the statement.

2. Give a direct proof:

   > Let a, b, and c be integers. If $a \mid b$ and $a \mid c$, then $a \mid (b \cdot c)$.

   Remember that you must use the definition of $\mid$ in your proof.

3. Prove: Let a, b, and c be integers. If $(a \cdot b) \mid c$, then $a \mid c$.

4. Give a direct proof.

   > Let a, b, and c be integers. If $a \mid b$ and $b \mid c$, then $a \mid c$.

5. Give a direct proof of the following statement in Euclidean geometry. Cite any theorems you use.

   > The sum of the measures of the angles of a parallelogram is $360°$.

6. Prove:

   For all integers n, if n^2 is odd, then n is odd.

   Use a proof by contraposition, as in Lemma 1.1.

7. Prove the following statement by contraposition.

   Let x be an integer. If $x^2 + x + 1$ is even, then x is odd.

   Make sure that your proof makes appropriate use of Definitions 1.5 and 1.6.

8. Prove that the sum of two even integers is even.

9. Prove that the sum of an even integer and an odd integer is odd.

10. Prove that the sum of two odd integers is even.

11. Write a proof by contradiction of the following.

    Let x and y be integers. If x and y satisfy the equation

    $$3x + 5y = 153$$

    then at least one of x and y is odd.

12. Prove the following statement in Euclidean geometry. Use a proof by contradiction.

    A triangle cannot have more than one obtuse angle.

13. Let "$x \nmid y$" denote "x does not divide y." Prove by any method.

    Let a and b be integers. If $5 \nmid ab$, then $5 \nmid a$ and $5 \nmid b$.

14. Consider the following definition.

    Definition. An integer n is *sane* if $3 \mid (n^2 + 2n)$.

    (a) Give a counterexample to the following: All odd integers are sane.
    (b) Give a direct proof of the following: If $3 \mid n$, then n is sane.
    (c) Prove by contradiction: If $n = 3j + 2$ for some integer j, then n is not sane.

15. Recall Exercise 6 of Section 1.4. Consider the following definition of the "$\lhd$" symbol.

    Definition. Let x and y be integers. Write $x \lhd y$ if $3x + 5y = 7k$ for some integer k.

    Give a direct proof of the following statement.

    If $a \lhd b$ and $c \lhd d$, then $a + c \lhd b + d$.

16. Consider the following definitions.

    Definition. An integer n is *alphic* if $n = 4k + 1$ for some integer k.
    Definition. An integer n is *gammic* if $n = 4k + 3$ for some integer k.

    (a) Show that 19 is gammic.
    (b) Suppose that x is alphic and y is gammic. Prove that $x + y$ is even.
    (c) Prove by contraposition: If x is not odd, then x is not alphic.

17. Prove that the rational numbers are closed under multiplication. That is, prove that, if a and b are rational numbers, then $a \cdot b$ is a rational number.

18. Prove that the rational numbers are closed under addition.

19. Prove: Let x and y be real numbers with $x \neq 0$. If x is rational and y is irrational, then $x \cdot y$ is irrational.

20. Prove: Let x and y be real numbers. If x is rational and y is irrational, then $x + y$ is irrational.

21. Consider the following definition.

> **Definition.** An integer n is *frumpable* if $n^2 + 2n$ is odd.

Prove: All frumpable numbers are odd.

22. Recall the Badda-Bing axiomatic system of Example 1.17. Prove:

> If q and r are distinct bings, both of which are hit by baddas x and y, then $x = y$.

23. Two common axioms for geometry are as follows. The undefined terms are "point," "line," and "is on."

1. For every pair of points x and y, there is a unique line such that x is on l and y is on l.
2. Given a line l and a point x that is not on l, there is a unique line m such that x is on m and no point on l is also on m.

Recall that two lines l and m are *parallel* if there is no point on both l and m. In this case we write $l \parallel m$. Use this definition along with the above two axioms to prove the following.

> Let l, m, and n be distinct lines. If $l \parallel m$ and $m \parallel n$, then $l \parallel n$.

24. Recall Example 1.16. In the axiomatic system for four-point geometry, prove the following assertion using a proof by contradiction:

> Suppose that a and b are distinct points on line u. Let v be a line such that $u \neq v$. Then a is not on v or b is not on v.

25. The following axioms characterize *projective geometry*. The undefined terms are "point," "line," and "is on."

1. For every pair of distinct points x and y, there is a unique line l such that x is on l and y is on l.
2. For every pair of lines l and m, there is a point x on both l and m.
3. There are (at least) four distinct points, no three of which are on the same line.

Prove the following statements in projective geometry.

(a) There are no parallel lines.
(b) For every pair of lines l and m, there is exactly one point x on both l and m.
(c) There are (at least) four distinct lines such that no point is on three of them.

Chapter 2

Relational Thinking

Most quantitative problems involve several different interrelated objects: market forces determine the price of a commodity, steps in a manufacturing process depend on other steps, virus-infected computers can slow network traffic, etc. In order to analyze these relationships, it helps to think mathematically about them.

In this chapter, we will explore different ways that the elements of a set can be related to each other or to the elements of another set. These relationships can be described by mathematical objects such as functions, relations, and graphs. Our goal is to develop the ability to see mathematical relationships between objects, which in turn will enable us to apply tools from discrete mathematics.

Figure 2.1 A circuit board contains an intricate system of mathematical relationships. Concepts such as connectivity, interdependence, and modularity can be expressed in the language of mathematics.

Preview 2.1

Two natural numbers are called *relatively prime* if they have no common divisors, other than 1.

1. Arrange the natural numbers 3, 4, 5, 6, 7, 8 in the shape of a hexagon and draw line segments between all pairs of these numbers that are relatively prime.

2. If three numbers in this diagram are connected by line segments that form a triangle, what must be true about these three numbers?

3. If a is relatively prime to b, and b is relatively prime to c, must a be relatively prime to c? How can the diagram help answer this question?

4. Can you find four of these numbers that are all relatively prime to each other? What pattern would four such numbers have to make in this diagram?

2.1 Graphs

When faced with a difficult problem in mathematics, it often helps to draw a picture. If the problem involves a discrete collection of interrelated objects, it is natural to sketch the objects and draw lines between them to indicate the relationships. A *graph* is the mathematical version of such a sketch. In this section, we will study a few basic definitions about graphs and then explore some ways to use graphs to model mathematical relationships. Our approach here will be informal; later in the chapter, we will look at graphs from a more rigorous point of view.

2.1.1 Edges and Vertices

In Section 2.6, we will give a mathematical definition of a graph, and we will prove several theorems about graphs. For now, however, just think of a graph informally as a diagram of dots, called *vertices*, connected by lines or curves, called *edges*. The edges of a graph may have arrows on them; in this case, the graph is called a *directed* graph. A graph without arrows on the edges is called an *undirected* graph.

When we draw a graph, it doesn't really matter where we put the vertices or whether we draw the edges as curved or straight; the thing that matters is whether or not two given vertices are connected by an edge (or edges).

Example 2.1 The Pregel River divided the Prussian city of Königsberg (now Kaliningrad, Russia) into four sections. These sections were connected by seven bridges, as shown below.

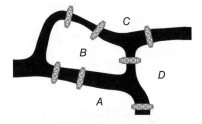

If we draw a vertex for each land mass and an edge for each bridge, we can represent the city as the following graph.

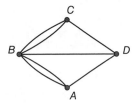

Notice that there are some double edges; these reflect the presence of two bridges connecting the same pair of land masses.

The bridges of Königsberg inspired the great 18th-century mathematician Leonhard Euler to think about the kinds of relationships that graphs express. In March of 1736, Euler wrote the following to a colleague:

> A problem was posed to me about an island in the city of Königsberg, surrounded by a river spanned by seven bridges, and I was asked whether someone could traverse the separate bridges in a connected walk in such a way that each bridge is crossed only once. I was informed that hitherto no one had demonstrated the possibility of doing this, or shown that it is impossible. This question is so banal, but seemed to me worthy of attention in that geometry, nor algebra, nor even the art of counting was sufficient to solve it. [10]

Although Euler did not use modern notation and terminology, his paper on the Königsberg bridges is widely regarded as the start of modern graph theory. [16]

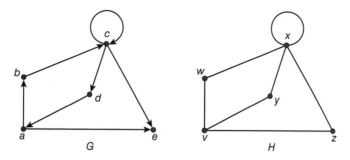

Figure 2.2 Graph H is the underlying undirected graph of the directed graph G.

2.1.2   Terminology

In order to work with graphs, it helps to define some terms. The *degree* of a vertex is the number of times an edge touches it. This is different than the number of edges touching it, because an edge may form a *loop*, as in Figure 2.2. In graph H, vertex x has degree 5. In a directed graph, we can speak of the *indegree* (the number of edges coming in to the vertex) and the *outdegree* (the number of edges going out). In Figure 2.2, vertex a of graph G has indegree 1 and outdegree 2.

A *path* in a graph is a sequence

$$v_0, e_1, v_1, e_2, v_2, \ldots, v_{n-1}, e_n, v_n$$

of vertices v_i and edges e_j such that edge e_i connects vertices v_{i-1} and v_i. Here $n \geq 1$. A *circuit* is a path that ends where it begins, so $v_0 = v_n$. An undirected graph is *connected* if there is a path connecting any two vertices. A directed graph is connected if the underlying undirected graph is.

In Figure 2.2, graph H is connected, and, therefore, so is graph G. There is a circuit in graph H going around the large quadrilateral: start at vertex v, follow the edges clockwise through vertices w, x, and z, and return to vertex v. However, the corresponding sequence is not a circuit in graph G because the edge from a to e goes in the wrong direction.

Why do we need all of these terms? One reason is that terminology makes it easier to make *precise* descriptions of the relationships that graphs define. Let's take another look at the bridges of Königsberg. In his 1736 paper, Euler made the following observations (quoted in Ref. [16]).

1. The number of bridges written next to the letters A, B, C, etc., together add up to twice the total number of bridges. The reason for this is that, in the calculation where every bridge leading to a given area is counted, each bridge is counted twice, once for each of the two areas that it joins.

2. If there are more than two areas to which an odd number of bridges lead, then such a journey is impossible.

3. If, however, the number of bridges is odd for exactly two areas, then the journey is possible if it starts in either of these two areas.

4. If, finally, there are no areas to which an odd number of bridges lead, then the required journey can be accomplished starting from any area.

We can use modern terminology to restate these observations. Let's define an *Euler path* (resp. *circuit*) as a path (resp. circuit) that uses every edge of the graph exactly once.

1. In any graph, the sum of the degrees of the vertices equals twice the number of edges, because each edge contributes 2 to the sum of the degrees.

2. If a graph has more than two vertices of odd degree, it does not have an Euler path.

3. If a connected graph has exactly two vertices, v and w, of odd degree, then there is an Euler path from v to w.

4. If all the vertices of a connected graph have even degree, then the graph has an Euler circuit.

The vertices A, B, C, and D of the graph of Example 2.1 have degrees 3, 5, 3, and 3, respectively. Therefore, (if we trust Euler), this graph does not have an Euler path. In the language of bridges, there is no way a connected walk can cross each bridge exactly once.

2.1.3   Modeling Relationships with Graphs

In addition to the "banal" problem of walking over bridges, there are many other applications of graphs for problems involving relationships.

Activity 2.1.1: Graph Models

Each vertex in the diagram below represents a web page on the topic of twelve-tone music. The arrows represent links: an arrow from vertex *x* to vertex *y* indicates that web page *x* has a link to web page *y*.

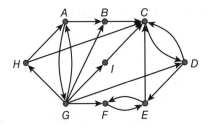

1. Compute the indegree and outdegree of each vertex.

2. Based solely on the indegrees and outdegrees, which web page do you think is the most authoritative? In other words, which web page is most likely to contain correct information?

3. Based solely on the indegrees and outdegrees, which web page do you think is the most informative? In other words, if you wanted to learn about twelve-tone music, which would be the best page to start at?

4. Add up all the indegrees, and add up all the outdegrees. What do you notice? Can you explain why every directed graph must have this property?

Example 2.2 A college registrar would like to schedule the following courses in as few time slots as possible: Physics, Computer Science, Chemistry, Calculus, Discrete Math, Biology, and Psychology. However, from previous experience, the following pairs of classes always have students in common, so they can't be scheduled in the same time slot:

Physics and Computer Science
Physics and Chemistry
Calculus and Chemistry
Calculus and Physics
Calculus and Computer Science
Calculus and Discrete Math
Calculus and Biology
Discrete Math and Computer Science
Discrete Math and Biology
Psychology and Biology
Psychology and Chemistry

What is the fewest number of time slots needed to schedule all of these classes without conflicts?

Solution: The natural way to model this problem with a graph is to make each course into a vertex and connect any two vertices that represent courses that cannot be scheduled in the same time slot. Figure 2.3 shows this graph.

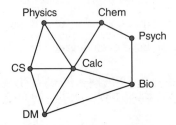

Figure 2.3 Graph for Example 2.2.

Let's start with Calculus: call its time slot A. None of the courses that share an edge with Calculus can be in time slot A, so pick one, say, Computer Science, and call its time slot B. Now Physics shares edges with both Calculus and Computer Science, so this forces us to use a third time slot, C, for Physics.

We should note at this point that all of our choices have been forced so far—we are going to need at least three time slots. The question remains whether we need more than three slots. Notice that we can assign Chemistry to slot B (since it doesn't share an edge with Computer Science) and we can assign Discrete Math to slot C (since it doesn't conflict with Physics). This allows us to use B for Biology and either A or C for Psychology, showing that three time slots are sufficient.   ◇

This scheduling problem is an example of graph coloring. A *coloring* for a graph is an assignment of different values (colors) to each vertex such that no two vertices of the same color share an edge. In Example 2.2, the "colors" were the time slots A, B, and C.

We call a graph *planar* if it can be written down (on a "planar" sheet of paper) without any edges crossing each other. The graph in Figure 2.3 is an example of a planar graph. The famous Four Color Theorem states that any planar graph can be colored with at most four colors.[1] A consequence of the Four Color Theorem is that cartographers need only four colors of ink: it is always possible to color the regions of a planar map (e.g., the states in a map of the United States) with at most four colors, so that no two adjacent regions have the same color.

Activity 2.1.2: Avoiding Conflicts

Each vertex in the graph below represents an animal that needs to be transported to the zoo. Two vertices are connected by an edge whenever the corresponding animals cannot be placed in the same cage (i.e., the edges represent pairs of animals that would harm each other if caged together). What is the fewest number of cages needed to transport these animals? Use graph coloring to find a conflict-free way to assign them to cages.

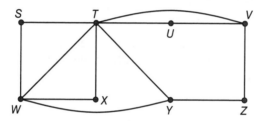

Example 2.3 Several departments around campus have wireless access points (WAPs), but problems arise if two WAPs within 200 feet of each other are operating on the same frequency. Suppose the departments with WAPs are situated as follows.

Department:	Is within 200 feet of departments:
Math	Physics, Psychology, Chemistry, Sociology
Sociology	History, English, Economics, Math, Chemistry, Psychology
Physics	Math, Chemistry
Psychology	Math, Chemistry, Sociology, Economics
History	Sociology, English
English	Economics, Sociology, History
Economics	English, Sociology, Psychology
Chemistry	Math, Psychology, Sociology, Physics

What is the fewest number of frequencies needed? How could these frequencies be assigned to departments?

Solution: Figure 2.4 shows a graph model for this situation, along with a possible coloring. We leave it as an exercise to check that four colors (frequencies) are needed.   ◇

In Example 2.3, we modeled the positions of the departments by drawing an edge between any two departments that were "close"—i.e., within 200 feet of each other. If we had more specific data, we could make our model

---

1. Although this result is very simple to state, the only known proofs to date are extremely complicated.

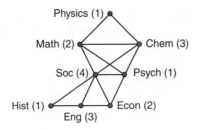

Figure 2.4 Graph for Example 2.3. Colors/frequencies: 1, 2, 3, 4.

say *how* close each department is to the others by putting numbers on each edge indicating the distance between two departments. A graph with numerical values, or *weights*, on its edges is called a *network*. Networks can be directed or undirected, depending on what they are intended to model.

Example 2.4 The following table lists some pairwise driving distances (in miles) on selected routes between some California cities.

	B	E	F	L	N	S
Barstow						
Eureka						
Fresno	245	450				
Los Angeles	115	645	220			
Needles	145		385	260		
San Diego	175			125	320	

Figure 2.5 shows the graph for this network. Writing the distance data in this format makes it easier to answer certain questions. How far is it from San Diego to Fresno (using these routes)? If we travel from Needles to Fresno via Barstow, how much longer will it take?

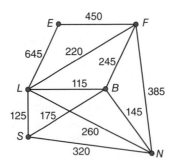

Figure 2.5 A network showing mileage between cities.

The above examples show how versatile graph models are; often, it helps to add extra structure to a graph (for example, colors or weights) to suit a particular application. The next example illustrates another way to add information to a graph model by specifying how the graph is drawn.

Example 2.5 The custom dictionary in a spell-checker keeps track of words that you don't want flagged as misspellings but aren't in the standard dictionary. These words get added one at a time, in no particular order, but it is necessary to keep them organized so that searching the list is easy. Suppose your custom dictionary contains the following words:

macchiato, poset, phat, complexify, jazzed, sheafify, clueless

What is an efficient way to organize this data?

One possible organizational structure is a graph model called a *binary search tree*. The rules for constructing a binary search tree are simple. Start with an item (chosen arbitrarily) at the top of the tree. This is the *root* node of the tree. The root has (at most) two edges touching it, one going down to the right, and one going down to the left. These are the *children* of the root node. In fact, every node in a binary search tree can have up to two children, one on the right, and one on the left. The only condition is that the right child (along with its "descendants") must come after its parent in alphabetical (or numerical) order, and the left child and its descendants must come before its parent. For example, in the following tree, x has right child r and left child l, so this data must have the order l, x, r.

Let's place the data from Example 2.5 into a binary search tree. Start with "macchiato" at the root of the tree. The next word, "poset," comes after "macchiato" in alphabetical order, so "poset" becomes the right child of "macchiato." We would then place the next word, "phat," to the right of "macchiato," but since that spot is taken, and since "phat" precedes "poset" in alphabetical order, we make "phat" the left child of "poset." We continue in this manner, finding the new position for each new word by moving down the tree. At each branch we move right or left, depending on where the new word falls in the alphabet. Figure 2.6 shows the first few steps of this process, along with the final result.

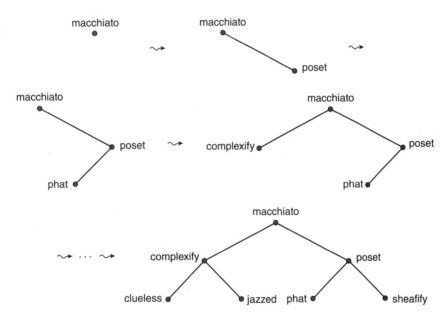

Figure 2.6 Constructing the binary search tree for Example 2.5.

The reason this graph is called a "search" tree is that it makes finding an element in the tree easy. If you are looking for a word in a binary search tree, you go through the same procedure as if you were adding the word to the tree; if you don't come across the word, it isn't there.

For large data sets, this process goes very quickly, since you don't need to look at every element. For example, to find "poset" in the tree in Figure 2.6, we have to look at only two words. To establish that "iPod" is not in the tree, we need to check only three. Each comparison moves the search one level down the tree, and each level contains twice the number of elements as the level before. So, for example, a balanced binary search tree with

$$255 = 1 + 2 + 4 + 8 + 16 + 32 + 64 + 128$$

elements requires at most eight comparisons to search it completely. See Figure 2.7.

Note that a binary search tree contains more information than its graph structure conveys. The branches of the tree always go downward, and it matters whether they go to the left or to the right. Technically, a binary search tree is a directed graph, with all of the edges pointing downward, away from the root. But most books (including this one) omit the arrows.

Figure 2.7   A balanced binary search tree with 255 nodes requires at most eight comparisons to search it completely.

1. Consider the following undirected graph.

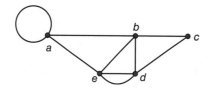

   (a) How many edges are there in this graph?

   (b) Give the degree of each vertex.

   (c) Do these numbers agree with Euler's first observation?

2. Consider the following directed graph.

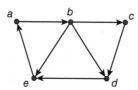

   (a) Give the indegree of each vertex.

   (b) Give the outdegree of each vertex.

   (c) Compute the sum of the indegrees and the sum of the outdegrees. What do you notice?

3. A circuit is *simple* if it has no repeated edges. Draw a connected, undirected graph with seven vertices and no simple circuits. How many edges does it have?

4. Draw an undirected graph with six vertices, each of degree 3, such that the graph is:

   (a) Connected.

   (b) Not connected.

5. A graph is called *simple* if it has no multiple edges or loops. (The graphs in Figures 2.3, 2.4, and 2.5 are simple, but the graphs in Example 2.1 and Figure 2.2 are not simple.) Draw five different connected, simple, undirected graphs with four vertices.

6. An undirected graph is called *complete* if every vertex shares an edge with every other vertex. Draw a complete graph on five vertices. How many edges does it have?

7. Recall Example 2.1. The diagram below shows modern-day Kaliningrad, in which two of the bridges from Euler's day no longer exist. Represent these five bridges and four land masses as an undirected graph. Is it possible to travel an Euler path on this graph? Why or why not?

8. Does the following graph have an Euler path? Why or why not?

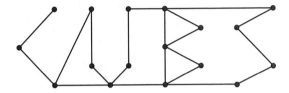

9. Consider the following graph.

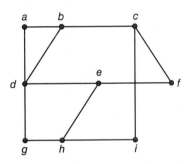

   (a) Without adding new vertices, add a single edge to the graph so that the new graph will have an Euler path. Which vertices does your new edge connect?

   (b) In addition to the edge from part (a), add a second edge (using the existing vertices) so that the resulting graph will have an Euler circuit. Which vertices does your second new edge connect?

10. Think of the Internet as one big graph, where each web page is a vertex and each link is an edge.

   (a) Is this a directed graph? Why or why not?

   (b) Is this graph connected? Why or why not?

   (c) Is this graph complete? Why or why not?

   (d) Is this graph simple? Why or why not?

   (e) For a given web page p, what does the outdegree of p represent?

   (f) For a given web page p, what does the indegree of p represent?

11. Consider the graph in Example 2.3. The graph in Figure 2.4 shows a possible coloring using four colors. Explain why this graph cannot be colored using fewer than four colors.

12. Find a map of the United States. Draw a graph whose vertices represent the states of Illinois, Missouri, Tennessee, Virginia, West Virginia, Ohio, Indiana, and Kentucky. Draw an edge between any two vertices whose states share a common border. Explain why it takes four colors to color this graph (and hence also to distinguish these states on a map).

13. As in Exercise 12, draw a graph representing the border relationships for the states of Washington, Oregon, Idaho, California, Nevada, and Utah. What is the fewest number of colors needed to color this graph? Justify your answer.

14. Represent the 13 regions in South America (12 countries plus the territory of French Guiana) as a graph. What is the fewest number of colors needed to color this graph?

15. Using as few groups as possible, put the words `fish`, `sit`, `stay`, `play`, `diet`, `tree`, `duck`, `dog`, and `hen` into groups such that none of the words in a group have any letters in common. Use a graph model and graph coloring. Justify your answer: explain why your grouping uses the fewest groups possible.

16. Give an example of a graph that requires five colors to make a valid coloring. (Note that, by the Four Color Theorem, your example cannot be planar.)

17. Compute the minimal number of colors needed to color the following graph. Show that your answer is big enough (by describing a coloring), and explain why the graph cannot be colored in fewer colors.

18. Color the vertices of the following graph so that no vertices of the same color share an edge. Use as few colors as possible. Explain why the graph cannot be colored using fewer colors. Be specific.

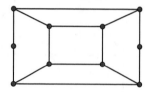

19. Color the vertices of the following graph with as few colors as possible so that no two vertices of the same color are connected by an edge. Explain why fewer colors cannot be used.

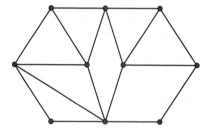

20. A round-robin tournament among four teams—Canadiens, Canucks, Flames, and Oilers—have the following results: Canucks defeat Canadiens; Canucks defeat Flames; Canucks defeat Oilers; Canadiens defeat Oilers; Flames defeat Canadiens; Oilers defeat Flames.

    (a) Model these results with a directed graph, where each vertex represents a team and each edge represents a game, pointing from the winner to the loser.

    (b) Find a circuit in this graph.

    (c) Explain why the existence of a circuit in such a graph makes it hard to rank the teams from best to worst.

21. Consider the network in Example 2.4. Plan a round trip starting and ending at San Diego that visits all the other cities in as few miles as possible. In other words, find a circuit that contains every vertex and has minimal weight.

22. Construct a directed network whose vertices represent the numbers 11, 12, 13, 15, 17 and whose weights tell how much you must add to get from one vertex to another. Include only edges of positive weight.

23. A car rental company has three locations in Mexico City: the International Airport, Oficina Vallejo, and Downtown. Customers can drop off their vehicles at any of these locations. Based on prior experience, the company expects that, at the end of each day, 40% of the cars that begin the day at the Airport will end up Downtown, 50% will return to the Airport, and 10% will be at Oficina Vallejo. Similarly, 60% of the Oficina Vallejo cars will end up Downtown, with 30% returning to Oficina Vallejo and 10% to the Airport. Finally, 30% of the Downtown cars will end up at each of the other locations, with 40% staying at the Downtown location.

    Model this situation with a directed network. If the company starts with all of its cars at the Airport, how will the cars be distributed after two days of rentals?

24. Consider the list of numbers 123, 684, 121, 511, 602, 50, 43.

    (a) Place the numbers, in the order given, into a binary search tree.

    (b) The *height* of a binary search tree is the maximum number of edges you have to go through to reach the bottom of the tree, starting at the root. What is the height of the tree in part (a)?

    (c) Reorder the numbers so that when they are put into a binary search tree, the height of the resulting tree is less than the height of the tree in part (a). Give both your new list and the search tree it produces.

25. Place each list of numbers into a binary search tree. Add the numbers to each tree in the order they are listed.

    (a) 2, 1, 4, 3, 5

    (b) 5, 4, 3, 2, 1

26. Put the words Cheddar, Swiss, Brie, Panela, Stilton, Mozzarella, and Gouda into a binary search tree with the smallest height possible.

27. Put the words i, will, not, eat, them, with, a, and fox into a binary search tree. Add them to the tree in the order given.

28. Place the words lust, gluttony, greed, sloth, wrath, envy, and pride in a binary search tree. Add the words to the tree in the order given.

29. Sociologists use graphs to model social relationships. A *social network* (not to be confused with a network) is a graph where the nodes represent "actors" (e.g., people, companies) and the edges represent relationships, or "ties," between actors (e.g., friendships, business partnerships). Consider the following social network.

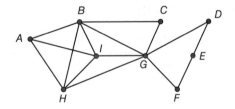

    (a) A *clique* in a social network is a group of actors who all have ties to each other. What is the largest clique in this social network?

    (b) If you had to choose the most important actor in this social network, who would you pick? Why?

    (c) Suppose the actors represent people and the ties represent acquaintances. If the people in this social network continue to interact, which two (currently unacquainted) actors would you most expect to become acquainted? Which two actors are the least likely to become acquainted? Why?

2.2   Sets

The applications from the previous section should convince you that graphs are a powerful mathematical tool. However, our viewpoint wasn't very rigorous; in order to prove useful theorems about graphs, we need to consider some more mathematical structures that describe relationships.

Preview 2.2

1. A certain discrete mathematics class consists of 21 students. Of these, 10 plan to major in mathematics and 13 plan to major in computer science. Five students are not planning to major in either subject. How many students plan to major in both subjects? Draw a diagram to explain your reasoning.

2. Consider the following collections of natural numbers.

    Collection T: All multiples of 2.
    Collection R: All multiples of 3.
    Collection S: All multiples of 5.

    (a) Where do T, R, and S overlap? In other words, which numbers do all three collections have in common?

    (b) Describe an infinite list of natural numbers, none of which are in T, R, or S.

3. Can you describe an infinite collection of infinite lists of natural numbers, such that none of the lists have any numbers in common?

Preview questions 2.2.1–3 have a common theme: very often, mathematical statements deal with groups of objects that share some property. This section introduces the standard notation and terminology that mathematicians use to express these types of statements.

The simplest way to describe a collection of related objects is as a *set*. Think of the set S as a container where an object x is something that S contains.

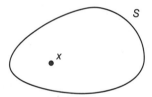

We write $x \in S$ to denote that x is contained in S. We also say that "x is a member of S," "x is an element of S," or more simply, "x is in S." If we want to express that x is *not* an element of S, we can write $x \notin S$.

2.2.1   Membership and Containment

We can describe examples of sets by listing the elements in the set or by describing the properties that an element in the set has. To say that set S consists of the elements $x_1, x_2, \ldots, x_n$, we write

$$S = \{x_1, x_2, \ldots, x_n\}.$$

Suppose there is some property p that some of the elements of a set S have. We can describe the set of all elements of S that have property p as

$$\{x \in S \mid x \text{ has property } p\}.$$

This is sometimes called "set builder" notation, because it explains how to build a list of all the elements of a set.

Example 2.6 Let $A = \{1, 2, 3, 4, 5, 6, 7, 8\}$. Then $2 \in A$ and $9 \notin A$. If $B = \{x \in A \mid x \text{ is odd}\}$, then the elements of B are $1, 3, 5, 7$.

Example 2.7 There are some common sets that have specific names. The set of integers is denoted by $\mathbf{Z}$, and the set of positive integers, or *natural numbers* is written as $\mathbf{N}$. Note that $0 \in \mathbf{Z}$, but $0 \notin \mathbf{N}$. We use $\mathbf{R}$ for the set of real numbers, and $\mathbf{Q}$ for the set of rational numbers.[2]

---

2. Recall that a rational number is a number that can be written as a fraction a/b, where a and b are integers.

Example 2.8 Let P be the set of all polygons. So P contains all triangles, squares, pentagons, etc. If c is a circle, then $c \notin P$. We could describe the set H of all hexagons in set builder notation as $H = \{x \in P \mid x \text{ has six sides}\}$.

The language of sets is convenient for describing groups of objects that are related by some common property. Often, some property implies another; for example, all integers are real numbers. In terms of sets, this means that the set $\mathbf{Z}$ is contained in the set $\mathbf{R}$. In general, the predicate logic statement that

$$(\forall x)(x \in A \rightarrow x \in B) \tag{2.2.2}$$

is written as $A \subseteq B$, and we say "A is contained in B," or "A is a subset of B," or "B contains A." We can express this relationship pictorially using the following *Venn diagram*.

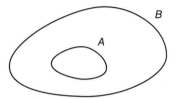

Example 2.9 In Example 2.6, $B \subseteq A$. We have noted that $\mathbf{Z} \subseteq \mathbf{R}$ in Example 2.7, and we could also say that $\mathbf{N} \subseteq \mathbf{Z}$, $\mathbf{Z} \subseteq \mathbf{Q}$, and $\mathbf{Q} \subseteq \mathbf{R}$. This chain of relationships could also be written as $\mathbf{N} \subseteq \mathbf{Z} \subseteq \mathbf{Q} \subseteq \mathbf{R}$.

Example 2.10 In Example 2.8, $H \subseteq P$, but $P \nsubseteq H$, because not every polygon is a hexagon.

Example 2.11 The *empty set* $\emptyset$ is the set that contains no elements. Therefore, the empty set is a subset of any set, that is, $\emptyset \subseteq X$ for all X. This is because the statement $x \in \emptyset$ is false for any x, so the implication $(\forall x)(x \in \emptyset \rightarrow x \in X)$ must be true. (See the truth table for the "$\rightarrow$" connective on page 4.)

2.2.2   New Sets from Old

Sets describe relationships, but the language of sets can also describe the logic of how things are related. We have seen one example of this already: statement 2.2.2 shows how to interpret the $\subseteq$ symbol in terms of a predicate logic statement containing the $\rightarrow$ connective; the relationship of containment has the logic of an implication. The connectives $\vee$, $\wedge$, $\neg$, and $\leftrightarrow$ also have set-theoretic counterparts.

The *union* $A \cup B$ of two sets A and B is the set containing all the elements of both A and B put together. An element is in the union of two sets A and B if the element is in A, or B, or both. In set builder notation,

$$A \cup B = \{x \mid (x \in A) \vee (x \in B)\}.$$

This translates to the following equivalence rule in predicate logic.

$$(\forall x)[x \in A \cup B \Leftrightarrow (x \in A) \vee (x \in B)]$$

The statement $x \in A \cup B$ is logically equivalent to the statement $(x \in A) \vee (x \in B)$. This fact is important when writing proofs; one of these statements can always be replaced by the other.

Think of "union" as the set-theoretic counterpart of the logical "or." In the following Venn diagram, $A \cup B$ is the shaded area:

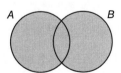

The *intersection* $A \cap B$ is the set containing all the elements that A and B have in common. In order for an element to be in the intersection of A and B, the element must be in both sets. Therefore, we write the intersection as

$$A \cap B = \{x \mid (x \in A) \wedge (x \in B)\}$$

in set builder notation. This implies the following logical equivalence for all x.

$$x \in A \cap B \iff (x \in A) \wedge (x \in B)$$

In the following Venn diagram, the shaded area represents $A \cap B$:

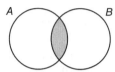

Implicit in the above predicate logic statements is a domain, or *universal set U*, of which every set is a subset. If we know what the domain U is, we can speak of the *complement A′* of A, which is the set

$$A' = \{x \in U \mid x \notin A\}.$$

We usually draw U as a big rectangle, so the shaded area below represents A'.

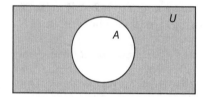

Note that we could also write $A' = \{x \in U \mid \neg(x \in A)\}$ to make the use of the $\neg$ connective explicit.

We say that two sets are equal if they have the same elements. So the statement "$A = B$" translates to the following statement in predicate logic:

$$(\forall x)(x \in A \leftrightarrow x \in B).$$

This translation is important when it comes to proving that two sets are equal. A proof that $A = B$ usually consists of two direct proofs: given $x \in A$, prove that $x \in B$, and conversely, given $x \in B$, prove that $x \in A$. In other words, showing $A = B$ amounts to showing that $A \subseteq B$ and $B \subseteq A$.

Example 2.12 Let the following sets be given.

$$X = \{n \in \mathbf{Z} \mid n = 2k \text{ for some odd integer } k\}$$
$$F = \{n \in \mathbf{Z} \mid n = 4k \text{ for some integer } k\}$$
$$E = \{n \in \mathbf{Z} \mid n \text{ is even}\}$$

1. Prove that $F \subseteq E$.
2. Prove that $X = E \cap F'$.

Proof of 1 Let $x \in F$. By the definition of F, $x = 4k$ for some integer k. We can write this equation as $x = 2(2k)$, so x is even by Definition 1.5. Therefore, $x \in E$. □

Proof of 2 (We first show that $X \subseteq E \cap F'$.) Let $x \in X$. Then $x = 2k$ for some odd integer k, so x is even. Therefore, $x \in E$. Suppose, to the contrary, that $x \in F$. Then $x = 4j$ for some integer j. This implies that $2k = 4j$, or $k = 2j$, which contradicts that k is odd. Therefore, $x \in F'$. Since $x \in E$ and $x \in F'$, we have shown that $x \in E \cap F'$.

(We now show that $E \cap F' \subseteq X$.) Suppose $x \in E \cap F'$, so $x \in E$ and $x \in F'$. Since $x \in E$, $x = 2k$ for some integer k. Suppose, to the contrary, that k is even. Then $k = 2l$ for some integer l, so $x = 2(2l) = 4l$. But this contradicts that $x \in F'$. Therefore, k must be odd. This establishes that $x \in X$. □

These proofs illustrate how to translate back and forth between the language of sets and the language of logic. For example, the statement "$x \in E \cap F'$" was translated as "$x \in E$ and $x \in F'$." In general, any statement involving sets and the symbols $\cap$, $\cup$, $\subseteq$, $=$, and $'$ translates into a logical statement using the connectives $\wedge$, $\vee$, $\rightarrow$, $\leftrightarrow$, and $\neg$, respectively. So all the work we did in propositional and predicate logic (Sections 1.2 and 1.3) will now pay off when dealing with sets.

Think of the symbols $\cap$, $\cup$, $\subseteq$, $=$, and $'$ as tools for making new sets from old ones. For example, given two sets, A and B, we can build a new set, $A \cap B$, consisting of all the elements the two sets have have in common. We can also take two sets A and B and form their *Cartesian product* $A \times B$. The Cartesian product is just the set of all ordered pairs where the first item comes from the first set and the second item comes from the second set. Formally,

$$A \times B = \{(a, b) \mid a \in A \text{ and } b \in B\}.$$

We can also have ordered triples, quadruples, and so on. The set

$$A_1 \times A_2 \times \cdots \times A_n = \{(a_1, a_2, \ldots, a_n) \mid a_i \in A_i\}$$

is the set of ordered n-tuples where the ith item comes from set A_i.

Two ordered pairs are equal if and only if their corresponding parts are equal. In other words,

$$(a, b) = (c, d) \iff a = c \text{ and } b = d.$$

You are already quite familiar with the Cartesian product $\mathbf{R} \times \mathbf{R}$, the set of all ordered pairs of real numbers. This set is the usual Cartesian plane from high school algebra.

One last construction that is sometimes useful is the *power set* $\mathcal{P}(S)$ of the set S. The power set of S is the set of all subsets of S: $\mathcal{P}(S) = \{X \mid X \subseteq S\}$. Note that the empty set $\emptyset$ is a member of $\mathcal{P}(S)$, no matter what S is, because the empty set is a subset of any set.

Example 2.13 Suppose you want to form a study group with some of the other students in your class. If S is the set of all students in your class, then $\mathcal{P}(S)$ is the set of all possible study groups you could form. (The empty set would represent the decision not to form a study group at all!)

Example 2.14 Let $A = \{1, 2, 3, 4, 5\}$, $B = \{4, 5, 6, 7, 8\}$, and suppose the universal set is $U = \{1, 2, \ldots 10\}$. Then

$$A \cup B = \{1, 2, \ldots, 8\}$$
$$A \cap B = \{4, 5\}$$
$$B' = \{1, 2, 3, 9, 10\}$$
$$(A \cap B) \times A = \{(4, 1), (4, 2), (4, 3), (4, 4), (4, 5), (5, 1), (5, 2), (5, 3), (5, 4), (5, 5)\}$$
$$\mathcal{P}(A \cap B) = \{\emptyset, \{4\}, \{5\}, \{4, 5\}\}$$

Notice that, while A and B are sets of numbers, the sets you construct from A and B may have different kinds of elements. For example, $(A \cap B) \times A$ is a set of ordered pairs, and $\mathcal{P}(A \cap B)$ is a set of sets.

Activity 2.2.1: Set Notation

For the following questions, let V be the set of vertices in the graph below, and let E be the set of edges.

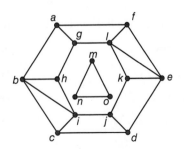

1. Write V in roster form.

2. Compute $|E|$.

3. Let $R = \{x \in V \mid \text{there is a path from } a \text{ to } x\}$. Write R' in roster form.

4. Let $D_3 = \{x \in V \mid x \text{ has degree 3}\}$ and let $T = \{x \in V \mid x \text{ is part of a triangular subgraph}\}$. Does $D_3 = T$? Prove or disprove.

5. Let $D_4 = \{x \in V \mid x \text{ has degree 4}\}$. Write $D_4 \cup (D_3 \cap T)$ in roster form.

6. Write R in terms of D_3 and D_4.

7. Let $N = \{a, h, i, c\}$. Using the fact that each of these vertices shares an edge with b, write N in set-builder form.

8. Write $\{a, h, c\}$ in terms of N and D_3.

9. Let $N \times R' = \{(x, y) \mid x \in N \text{ and } y \in R'\}$. Write $N \times R'$ in roster form.

2.2.3 Identities

Since there is such a direct relationship between logic and set theory, we can write down many facts about sets that follow immediately from things we know from our study of logic. For example, the addition inference rule $p \Rightarrow p \vee q$ allows us to prove the identity $A \subseteq A \cup B$ in set theory.

Proof that $A \subseteq A \cup B$. Let $x \in A$. By the addition rule, $(x \in A) \vee (x \in B)$. By the definition of set union, $x \in A \cup B$, as required. ◻

De Morgan's laws for sets follow from the equivalence rule of the same name.

Theorem 2.1 *Let A and B be sets. Then*

1. $(A \cup B)' = A' \cap B'$

2. $(A \cap B)' = A' \cup B'$

The proof of this theorem illustrates how to prove set equalities.

Proof We will prove part 1. (Part 2 is similar.) Let $x \in (A \cup B)'$. In other words, if $P(x)$ is the statement "$x \in A$" and $Q(x)$ is the statement "$x \in B$," we are starting with the assumption $\neg(P(x) \vee Q(x))$. By De Morgan's laws for propositional logic, this is equivalent to $\neg P(x) \wedge \neg Q(x)$, which, in the language of set theory, is the same as $x \in A' \cap B'$. We have shown that

$$x \in (A \cup B)' \quad \Leftrightarrow \quad x \in A' \cap B',$$

hence the sets $(A \cup B)'$ and $A' \cap B'$ are equal. ◻

Take a look back at this proof, and notice two things. First, the proof establishes an "if and only if" claim, since all of its deductions are based on logical equivalences. Second, the proof illustrates that the way to show an equality $U = V$ of sets is to show that $x \in U \Leftrightarrow x \in V$.

The proof of Theorem 2.1 consists of a simple chain of equivalences. When the structure of a proof is this basic, we might opt to write it in the following format.

Proof of Theorem 2.1, "$\Leftrightarrow$" version. We will prove part 1. (Part 2 is similar.)

$$
\begin{aligned}
x \in (A \cup B)' &\Leftrightarrow \neg(x \in A \cup B) && \text{Definition of } ' \\
&\Leftrightarrow \neg[(x \in A) \vee (x \in B)] && \text{Definition of } \cup \\
&\Leftrightarrow \neg(x \in A) \wedge \neg(x \in B) && \text{De Morgan's law (logic)} \\
&\Leftrightarrow (x \in A') \wedge (x \in B') && \text{Definition of } ' \\
&\Leftrightarrow x \in A' \cap B' && \text{Definition of } \cap
\end{aligned}
$$

Therefore, the sets $(A \cup B)'$ and $A' \cap B'$ are equal. ◻

Proofs of identities can often be written in this format. Notice that each "$\Leftrightarrow$" is justified by a reason in the rightmost column.

Activity 2.2.2: Proving Set Containment

Let $E = \{x \in \mathbf{Z} \mid x = 2k \text{ for some } k \in \mathbf{Z}\}$, and let $S = \{x \in \mathbf{Z} \mid x = 6k + 4 \text{ for some } k \in \mathbf{Z}\}$.

1. Complete the following proof that $S \subseteq E$.

   Let $x \in S$. Since $x \in S$, _____. Factoring out a 2 gives $x =$ _____.
   Therefore, _____, as required.

2. Is $E \subseteq S$? Explain.

3. Does $E = S$? Explain.

Sets that contain a finite number of elements are called *finite sets*. It is convenient to denote the number of elements in a finite set S by $|S|$. For example, if S is the set containing all the members of the Unites States House of Representatives, then $|S| = 435$.

One handy rule dealing with set sizes is the *inclusion–exclusion principle*.

$$|A \cup B| = |A| + |B| - |A \cap B| \tag{2.2.3}$$

It is easy to see why this rule must hold by looking at the Venn diagrams for $A \cup B$ and $A \cap B$ at the beginning of Section 2.2.2. Counting the elements of $A \cup B$ by counting the elements in A and B and adding would double-count the elements that lie in $A \cap B$. This is the reason for the "$- |A \cap B|$" on the right-hand side of Equation 2.2.3. This equation can help organize counting problems involving sets that overlap.

Example 2.15 The Masters of the Universe Society at a certain college accepts members who have 1600 SAT scores or 4.0 GPAs in high school. Of the 11 members of the society, 8 had 1600 SAT scores, and 5 had 4.0 GPAs. How many members had both 1600 SAT scores and 4.0 GPAs?

Solution: Let A be the set of members with 1600 SAT scores, and let B be the set of members with 4.0 GPAs. Then $A \cap B$ is the set of members with both. By the inclusion–exclusion principle (Equation 2.2.3), $11 = 8 + 5 - |A \cap B|$, so there are two members with both 1600 SAT scores and 4.0 GPAs. $\diamond$

We will apply the inclusion–exclusion principle to harder counting problems in Chapter 4.

Exercises 2.2

1. Draw Venn diagrams to illustrate De Morgan's laws for sets (Theorem 2.1).

2. Draw a Venn diagram to show the region $A \cap B'$. This region is also denoted $A \setminus B$, and is called the *set difference*.

3. Let $A = \{2, 3, 4\}$, $B = \{3, 4, 5, 6\}$, and suppose the universal set is $U = \{1, 2, \ldots, 9\}$. List all the elements in the following sets.

   (a) $(A \cup B)'$

   (b) $(A \cap B) \times A$

   (c) $\mathcal{P}(B \setminus A)$

4. Let the following sets be given.

$$G = \text{the set of all good citizens.}$$
$$C = \text{the set of all charitable people.}$$
$$P = \text{the set of all polite people.}$$

Write the statement, "Everyone who is charitable and polite is a good citizen," in the language of set theory.

5. Consider the following sets. The universal set for this problem is **N**.

$$A = \text{The set of all even numbers.}$$
$$B = \text{The set of all prime numbers.}$$
$$C = \text{The set of all perfect squares.}$$
$$D = \text{The set of all multiples of 10.}$$

Using **only** the symbols 3, $A, B, C, D, \mathbf{N}, \in, \subseteq, =, \neq, \cap, \cup, \times, \,', \emptyset, ($ and $)$, write the following statements in set notation.

(a) None of the perfect squares are prime numbers.

(b) All multiples of 10 are even numbers.

(c) The number 3 is a prime number that is not even.

(d) If you take all the prime numbers, all the even numbers, all the perfect squares, and all the multiples of 10, you still won't have all the natural numbers.

6. Consider the following sets. The universal set U for this problem is the set of all residents of India.

$$A = \text{the set of all English speakers.}$$
$$B = \text{the set of all Hindi speakers.}$$
$$C = \text{the set of all Urdu speakers.}$$

Express the following sets in the symbols of set theory.

(a) Residents of India who speak English, Hindi, and Urdu.

(b) Residents of India who do not speak English, Hindi, or Urdu.

(c) Residents of India who speak English, but not Hindi or Urdu.

7. Consider the following sets. The universal set for this problem is the set of all quadrilaterals.

$$A = \text{The set of all parallelograms.}$$
$$B = \text{The set of all rhombuses.}$$
$$C = \text{The set of all rectangles.}$$
$$D = \text{The set of all trapezoids.}$$

Using **only** the symbols x, $A, B, C, D, \in, \subseteq, =, \neq, \cap, \cup, \times, \,', \emptyset, ($ and $)$, write the following statements in set notation.

(a) The polygon x is a parallelogram, but it isn't a rhombus.

(b) There are other quadrilaterals besides parallelograms and trapezoids.

(c) Both rectangles and rhombuses are types of parallelograms.

8. Let the following sets be given. The universal set for this problem is the set of all students at some university.

$$F = \text{the set of all freshmen.}$$
$$S = \text{the set of all seniors.}$$
$$M = \text{the set of all math majors.}$$
$$C = \text{the set of all CS majors.}$$

(a) Using only the symbols $F, S, M, C, |\;|, \cap, \cup, \,',$ and $>$, translate the following statement into the language of set theory.

There are more freshmen who aren't math majors than there are senior CS majors.

(b) Translate the following statement in set theory into everyday English.

$$(F \cap M) \subseteq C$$

9. Let E be the set of even numbers, and let P be the set of prime numbers. Use set notation to express the following statement: "2 is the only even prime number."

10. Two sets are called *disjoint* if they have no elements in common, i.e., if their intersection is the empty set. Prove that finite sets A and B are disjoint if and only if $|A| + |B| = |A \cup B|$. Use the definition of $\emptyset$ and the inclusion–exclusion principle (Equation 2.2.3) in your proof.

11. In a class of 40 students, everyone has either a pierced nose or a pierced ear. The professor asks everyone with a pierced nose to raise their hands. Nine hands go up. Then the professor asked everyone with a pierced ear to do likewise. This time there are 34 hands raised. How many students have piercings both on their ears and their noses?

12. How many integers in the set $\{n \in \mathbf{Z} \mid 1 \leq n \leq 700\}$ are divisible by 2 or 7?

13. Let A, B, and C be sets, and let $X = A \cup B$.

    (a) Write $|X \cap C|$ in terms of $|A \cap C|$, $|B \cap C|$, and $|A \cap B \cap C|$. Hint: In the following Venn diagram, $X \cap C$ is the shaded area.

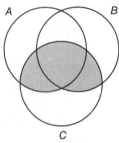

    (b) Write $|A \cup B \cup C|$ in terms of A, B, C, $|A \cap B|$, $|A \cap C|$, $|B \cap C|$, and $|A \cap B \cap C|$. (The result is the inclusion–exclusion principle for three sets.)

14. How many integers in the set $\{n \in \mathbf{Z} \mid 1 \leq n \leq 700\}$ are divisible by 2, 5, or 7?

15. Write down all elements of $(\{1, 2, 3\} \cap \{2, 3, 4, 5\}) \cup \{6, 7\}$.

16. Write down all elements of $\{A, B, C\} \times \{H, K\}$.

17. Let $S = \{a, b, c\}$. Write down all the elements in the following sets.

    (a) $S \times S$

    (b) $\mathcal{P}(S)$

18. An integer solution to the equation $3x + 4 = 7y$ is an ordered pair of integers (x, y) that satisfies the equation. For example, $(1, 1)$ is one such solution. Write the set of all integer solutions to the equation $3x + 4 = 7y$ in set builder notation.

19. Use Definition 1.6 to write the set of odd integers in set builder notation.

20. List all the elements of $\mathcal{P}(\mathcal{P}(\{1\}))$.

21. List all of the elements $S \in \mathcal{P}(\{1, 2, 3, 4\})$ such that $|S| = 3$.

22. Let $X = \{1, 2\}$ and let $Y = \{1, 2, 3\}$. List all of the elements in the set $(X \times Y) \cap (Y \times X)$.

23. Prove part 2 of Theorem 2.1.

24. Give a direct proof that for any set S, $(S')' = S$. (Hint: Follow the format of the proof of Theorem 2.1. You need to show that

$$x \in (S')' \Leftrightarrow x \in S$$

for all x in S. Translate this statement into a statement in predicate logic, and use an equivalence rule from Section 1.2.)

25. Let E be the set of all even integers, and let O be the set of all odd integers.

    (a) Explain why $E \cup O \subseteq \mathbf{Z}$.

    (b) Explain why $\mathbf{Z} \subseteq E \cup O$.

26. Let $X = \{n \in \mathbf{Z} \mid n = x + y \text{ for some } x, y \in O\}$, where O is the set of all odd integers. Let E be the set of even integers.

    (a) Prove that $X \subseteq E$.

    (b) Prove that $E \subseteq X$.

27. Let X, Y, and Z be sets. Use the distributive property from propositional logic (Exercise 16 in Section 1.1) to prove that

$$X \cap (Y \cup Z) = (X \cap Y) \cup (X \cap Z).$$

28. Let A and B be sets. Prove that $A \cap B \subseteq A \cup B$.

29. Let X be a finite set with $|X| > 1$. What is the difference between $P_1 = X \times X$ and $P_2 = \{S \in \mathcal{P}(X) \mid |S| = 2\}$? Which set, P_1 or P_2, has more elements?

30. Draw an undirected graph G with the following properties. The vertices of G correspond to the elements of $\mathcal{P}(\{0, 1\})$. Two vertices (corresponding to $A, B \in \mathcal{P}(\{0, 1\})$) are connected by an edge if and only if $A \cap B = \emptyset$.

31. Repeat Exercise 30 using $\mathcal{P}(\{0, 1, 2\})$ instead of $\mathcal{P}(\{0, 1\})$.

32. Let X be any finite set. Consider the graph G described in Exercise 30, replacing $\mathcal{P}(\{0, 1\})$ with $\mathcal{P}(X)$. Explain why G must be a connected graph.

2.3   Functions

You have probably seen functions before. For example, in high school algebra, you learned how to graph functions like

$$f(x) = x^2 - 3x + 2 \tag{2.3.1}$$

and do various calculations. But this is a very specific kind of function; in this section we will look at functions from a more general perspective, using the language of sets.

Like sets, functions describe mathematical relationships. In this type of relationship, the value of one object is completely determined by the value of another. In Equation 2.3.1, the value of $f(x)$ is forced if we know x's value.

Definition 2.1 An *f-graph* is a directed graph where each vertex has outdegree 1.

Preview 2.3

1. Give an example of an f-graph with at least five vertices. Invent a shorthand notation that encodes all the information needed to reconstruct the graph.

2. An f-graph is called *epi* if each vertex has indegree 1. Give an example of an epi f-graph and an example of a non-epi f-graph. What do you observe about the properties of epi f-graphs?

3. Let E be the set of even integers and let O be the set of odd integers. Suppose that a computer is programmed to input a sequence of elements of E and output a sequence of elements of O according to some rule. You run a test of this program using $12, 6, 8, 10, 2$ as input, and the computer outputs $81, 9, 25, 49, 1$. What rule does the computer appear to be using?

2.3.1   Definition and Examples

Definition 2.2 A *function* from a set X to a set Y is a well-defined rule that assigns a single element of Y to each element of X. If f is such a function, we write

$$f : X \longrightarrow Y$$

and we denote the element of Y assigned to $x \in X$ by $f(x)$. The set X is called the *domain* of the function, and the set Y is called the *codomain*.

Example 2.16 Let $X = \{1, 2, 3\}$ and $Y = \{1, 2, 3, 4\}$. The formula $f(x) = x + 1$ defines a function $f : X \longrightarrow Y$. For this function, $f(1) = 2$, $f(2) = 3$, and $f(3) = 4$. The following diagram shows one way to represent this function graphically.

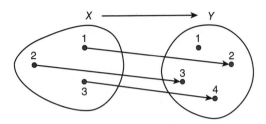

Example 2.17 The formula $f(x) = x^2 - 3x + 2$ defines a function $f : \mathbf{R} \longrightarrow \mathbf{R}$.

Example 2.18 Let W be the set of all words in this book, and let L be the set of all letters in the alphabet. Define a function $f : W \longrightarrow L$ by setting $f(w)$ equal to the first letter in the word w. Notice that the choice of word w completely determines $f(w)$, the first letter in the word.

Example 2.19 A propositional statement in two variables defines a function

$$w : \{T, F\} \times \{T, F\} \longrightarrow \{T, F\}$$

where $w(A, B)$ is the truth value of the statement when the variables have truth values A and B. For example, the statement $A \vee B$ defines a function whose values are given by the following table of values.

A	B	$w(A, B)$
T	T	T
T	F	T
F	T	T
F	F	F

Example 2.20 Let F be the set of all nonempty finite sets of integers, so $F \subseteq \mathcal{P}(\mathbf{Z})$. Define a function $s : F \longrightarrow \mathbf{Z}$ by setting $s(X)$ to be the sum of all the elements of X. For example, $s(\{1, 2, 3\}) = 6$.

Another word for function is *map*. This reflects the thinking that a function is a way of describing a route from one set to another. In Example 2.20, we are describing a way to get from a finite set of integers to a particular integer; i.e., we are describing a map from the set of all finite sets of integers to the set of integers. This function maps the set $\{1, 2, 3\}$ to the integer 6.

We can represent a function by a graph. The vertices of the graph represent the elements of the domain and codomain of the function. For each element in the domain, there is a directed edge to some element in the codomain.

Example 2.21 Let $N = \{-2, -1, 0, 1, 2\}$. Define a function $s : N \longrightarrow N$ by $s(n) = n^2 - 2$. Represent this function with a directed graph.

Solution: Since the domain and codomain are the same set, we can represent the function with an f-graph, as in preview questions 2.3.1–2:

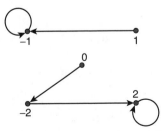

Alternatively, we can represent the domain separately from the codomain. Following the $s : N \longrightarrow N$ notation, we put the vertices for the domain on the left and the vertices for the codomain on the right.

Notice that the definition of a function restricts the features of the graph. Every vertex representing an element of the domain must have outdegree 1. As an exercise, think about what the f-graph representing the following function would look like.

Example 2.22 Let X be a set. Then the *identity* function $1_X : X \longrightarrow X$ is defined by $1_X(x) = x$.

The $f(x)$ notation suggests the most important aspect of the definition of function: the value of the function is completely determined by the object you "plug in" to the function. More precisely, the condition that a function must be *well defined* means that $f(x)$ has a value for every x in the domain, and

$$a = b \implies f(a) = f(b)$$

for any a and b in the domain.

A proposed function $f: X \longrightarrow Y$ can fail to be well defined in two ways: (1) some x in the domain X can fail to have a y in the codomain to which to map, or (2) some x in the domain can be mapped (ambiguously) to two different y's in the codomain.

Example 2.23 Let P be the set of all people (alive or dead). Let $m: P \longrightarrow P$ be such that $m(x)$ is the birth mother of x. We have to make some reasonable biological assumptions to regard this as a well-defined function: everybody has a birth mother (e.g., no clones) and no person can have two different birth mothers.

Think of functions as tools for describing relationships between the elements of a set, or the elements of two different sets. In our list of functions above, Example 2.23 describes the maternal relationships of all people (alive or dead), while Example 2.20 shows how to describe sets of integers with integers. Example 2.22 is rather trivial and describes a trivial relationship that the elements of any set have.

It might seem obvious that functions given by formulas are always well defined, but difficulties can arise if there is more than one way to write the same element of the domain, as in the following example.

Example 2.24 Let $\mathbf{Q} = \{x/y \mid x, y \in \mathbf{Z}, y \neq 0\}$ be the set of rational numbers. Let $f(x/y) = x + y$ for any $x/y \in \mathbf{Q}$. Does this yield a well-defined function $f: \mathbf{Q} \longrightarrow \mathbf{Z}$?

Solution: No. As a counterexample, note that $2/3 = 4/6$, but

$$f(2/3) = 2 + 3 = 5 \neq f(4/6) = 4 + 6 = 10,$$

so f is not well defined.

When defining a function on a domain like this, it is wise to check that your function is well defined.

Example 2.25 Show that the function $f: \mathbf{Q} \longrightarrow \mathbf{Q}$ defined by

$$f(x/y) = \frac{x+y}{y}$$

is well defined.

Proof Let $a/b = c/d \in \mathbf{Q}$. Then

$$f(a/b) = \frac{a+b}{b}$$

$$= \frac{a}{b} + \frac{b}{b}$$

$$= \frac{c}{d} + \frac{d}{d}$$

$$= \frac{c+d}{d}$$

$$= f(c/d)$$

so f is well defined. $\qquad\square$

Activity 2.3.1: Functions, Domain, Codomain

For the following directed graph, let $E = \{I, J, K, L, M\}$ and let $V = \{a, b, c, d\}$.

For each definition of f below, determine if f is a function. If it is a function, state its domain and codomain in the form "$f : X \longrightarrow Y$" and give a table of values that lists each element x of the domain along with the corresponding element $f(x)$ of the codomain. If the given f is not a function, explain why not.

1. If x is an edge, then $f(x)$ is the vertex that the edge points to.
2. If x is a vertex, then $f(x)$ is the edge that points to it.
3. If x is a vertex, then $f(x)$ is the indegree of x.
4. If x is a natural number, then $f(x)$ is the vertex whose outdegree is x.
5. If x is a subset of V of size 2, then $f(x)$ is the edge connecting the two vertices in x.
6. If x is an edge, then $f(x) = (v_1, v_2)$ such that x goes from v_1 to v_2.
7. If x is a subset of V, then $f(x)$ is the sum of the indegrees of the vertices in x.
8. If x is a vertex, then $f(x)$ is the set of all vertices that can be reached by following a directed path starting at x.

2.3.2 One-to-One and Onto Functions

Just as it is useful to describe different properties that relationships have, it is useful to name certain properties of functions.

Definition 2.3 A function $f : X \longrightarrow Y$ is *injective* (or *one-to-one*) if, for all a and b in X, $f(a) = f(b)$ implies that $a = b$. In this case we say that f is a *one-to-one mapping* from X to Y.

Definition 2.4 A function $f : X \longrightarrow Y$ is *surjective* (or *onto*) if, for all $y \in Y$, there exists an $x \in X$ such that $f(x) = y$. In this case we say that f *maps X onto Y*.

From this point on, we will use the less formal terms *one-to-one* and *onto* to describe injective and surjective functions.[3] The graphs in Figures 2.8 and 2.9 illustrate why these terms are appropriate. A one-to-one function will always map different elements of the domain to different elements of the codomain. In other words, at most *one*

---

3. Note that we are now using the word "onto" as an adjective, as well as a preposition.

element of the domain maps to any *one* element of the codomain. In terms of graph theory, the indegree of every vertex in the codomain is at most 1.

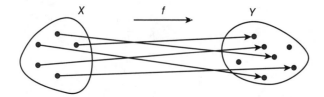

Figure 2.8 A one-to-one function maps each element of X to a different element of Y.

We use the term *image* to describe the set of all values a function can take. An onto function has every element of the codomain in its image. Figure 2.9 illustrates an onto function. Notice that the domain gets mapped *onto* the entire codomain. In the graph of an onto function, the indegree of every vertex in the codomain is at least 1.

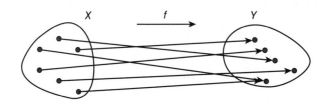

Figure 2.9 An onto function maps something onto each element of Y.

Remember (Section 1.4.1) how definitions are used in mathematics: in order to prove a function is one-to-one or onto, we almost always have to use the definition.

Example 2.26 Prove that the function $f \colon \mathbf{Z} \longrightarrow \mathbf{Z}$ defined by $f(x) = 2x + 1$ is one-to-one.

Proof Let $a, b \in \mathbf{Z}$ and suppose $f(a) = f(b)$. Then

$$2a + 1 = 2b + 1$$
$$2a = 2b$$
$$a = b$$

We have shown that $f(a) = f(b)$ implies that $a = b$, i.e., that f is one-to-one.   □

Let $\lfloor x \rfloor$ denote the greatest integer less than or equal to x. So, for example, $\lfloor 4.3 \rfloor = 4$, $\lfloor -2.1 \rfloor = -3$, and $\lfloor 17 \rfloor = 17$. The function that maps x to $\lfloor x \rfloor$ is called the *floor* function.

Example 2.27 Let $f \colon \mathbf{R} \longrightarrow \mathbf{Z}$ be defined by $f(x) = \lfloor x \rfloor$. Prove that f maps $\mathbf{R}$ onto $\mathbf{Z}$.

Proof Let $n \in \mathbf{Z}$. Then, since $\mathbf{Z} \subseteq \mathbf{R}$, $n \in \mathbf{R}$ as well. But since n is an integer, $\lfloor n \rfloor = n$. Therefore, $f(n) = n$.   □

The proofs in the last two examples are standard. To prove a function f is one-to-one, suppose $f(a) = f(b)$ and show $a = b$. To show that a function f is onto, let y be some element of the codomain, and find some x in the domain such that $f(x) = y$.

To prove that a function is *not* one-to-one or onto, look for a counterexample. The function in Example 2.26 is not onto because, for example, $38 \in \mathbf{Z}$, but there is no integer x such that $2x + 1 = 38$. Likewise, the function in Example 2.27 is not one-to-one because $\lfloor 9.3 \rfloor = \lfloor 9.8 \rfloor$, but $9.3 \neq 9.8$. Note that these two examples show that one-to-one is not the same as onto.

Activity 2.3.2: Proving that is a Function is One-to-one or Onto

1. Let $f : \mathbf{N} \longrightarrow \mathbf{N}$ be defined by $f(x) = 10x + 5$. Complete the following proof that f is one-to-one.

   Let $a, b \in \mathbf{N}$ and suppose that _____. Using the formula for the function f gives the equation _____, which simplifies to _____. This proves that f is one-to-one.

2. Let O be the set of odd integers. Define a function $g : O \longrightarrow \mathbf{Z}$ by $g(x) = \dfrac{x+1}{2}$. Prove that g is onto.

   Let $n \in \mathbf{Z}$ be given. Consider the integer $j =$ _____. First, notice that $j \in O$, since $j = 2\cdot$ _____$+1$. Second, using the formula for g gives $g(j) =$ _____ $= n$, which proves that g is onto.

3. Let X be the set of all nonempty subsets of natural numbers. Define a function $m : X \longrightarrow \mathbf{N}$ by taking $m(S)$ to be the smallest number in the set S. Give a counterexample to show that m is not one-to-one.

4. Let T be the set of all triangles, and define $A : T \longrightarrow \mathbf{R}$ by taking $A(t)$ to be the degree measure of the largest angle of the triangle t. Explain why A is not onto.

Of course, it is possible for a function to be both one-to-one and onto; the identity function of Example 2.22 is one example. Such a function is called a *one-to-one correspondence*, or more formally, a *bijection*. Compare the following example to Example 2.26.

Example 2.28 Prove that the function $f : \mathbf{R} \longrightarrow \mathbf{R}$ defined by $f(x) = 2x + 1$ is a one-to-one correspondence.

Proof We need to show that f is both one-to-one and onto. The proof that it is one-to-one is exactly the same as in Example 2.26. To prove that f is onto, let $y \in \mathbf{R}$ be any real number. Set $x = (y - 1)/2$. Then $x \in \mathbf{R}$ and

$$
\begin{aligned}
f(x) &= f((y-1)/2) \\
&= 2[(y-1)/2] + 1 \\
&= y - 1 + 1 \\
&= y
\end{aligned}
$$

Thus f is onto as well.   □

Example 2.29 Let $E = \{n \in \mathbf{Z} \mid n \text{ is even}\}$ and let $O = \{n \in \mathbf{Z} \mid n \text{ is odd}\}$. Define a function $f : E \times O \longrightarrow \mathbf{Z}$ by $f(x,y) = x + y$. Is f one-to-one and/or onto? Prove or disprove.

Solution: We first show that f is not onto. Suppose, to the contrary, that f is onto. Since $2 \in \mathbf{Z}$ is an element of the codomain, there is some ordered pair $(x,y) \in E \times O$ such that $f(x,y) = x + y = 2$. But since x is even and y is odd, $x + y$ is odd, by Exercise 9 of Section 1.5. This contradicts that 2 is even.

We next show that f is not one-to-one. Notice that $f(4, -3) = 1 = f(6, -5)$, but $(4, -3) \neq (6, -5)$. This counterexample shows that f is not one-to-one.   ◇

Example 2.30 Let P be a set of n points lying on a circle. Draw lines connecting every point to every other point. Suppose that the points are arranged so that no three of these lines intersect in a single point inside the circle. The following diagram shows a possible such configuration when $n = 8$.

Let X be the set of all points of intersection of the lines in the interior of the circle (note that the points in P are not included in X). Let Y be the set of all sets of four of the points on the circle, that is,

$$Y = \{\{A, B, C, D\} \subseteq P \mid A, B, C, D \text{ are all distinct}\}.$$

Describe a one-to-one correspondence $f : X \longrightarrow Y$. Show that your function is both one-to-one and onto.

Solution: Let $H \in X$ be a point of intersection. Then H lies on exactly two lines, so we can define $f(H)$ to be the set containing the four distinct endpoints of these two lines.

We prove that f is one-to-one by contraposition. Suppose H and K are two distinct points of intersection, so $H \neq K$. If l_1 and l_2 are the two lines intersecting at H, then at least one of the lines intersecting at K must be different from l_1 and l_2, since two lines can intersect in at most one point. Call this third line l_3. Then $f(K)$ contains the endpoints of l_3, but $f(H)$ does not. Hence, $f(K) \neq f(H)$.

To show that f is onto, let $\{A, B, C, D\} \subseteq P$. Without loss of generality, we can relabel these points (if necessary) so that A, B, C, D are in order as you travel clockwise around the circle. Let l_1 be the line through A and C, and let l_2 be the line through B and D. Since B is on the arc going clockwise from A to C, and D is on the arc going counterclockwise from A to C, line l_1 separates B and D, so lines l_1 and l_2 intersect. Call this point of intersection H. Then $f(H) = \{A, B, C, D\}$, as required. $\diamond$

Think of a one-to-one correspondence $f : X \longrightarrow Y$ as a way to assign every element of X to a unique element of Y, and *vice versa*. We sometimes write

$$X \longleftrightarrow Y$$

to emphasize the symmetry of the relationship that a one-to-one correspondence defines. Every element of one set has a unique partner in the other set.

Activity 2.3.3: Constructing One-to-one Correspondences

For each given X and Y, describe a function $f : X \longrightarrow Y$ such that f is a one-to-one correspondence. (You don't need to prove that it is.)

1. $X = \{x \in \mathbf{Z} \mid x = 2k \text{ for some } k \in \mathbf{Z}\}$, $Y = \{x \in \mathbf{Z} \mid x = 6k + 4 \text{ for some } k \in \mathbf{Z}\}$.

2. X is the set of edges in the complete graph K_n on n vertices, V is the vertex set of K_n, and Y is the set of subsets of V of size 2.

3. $S = \{s_1, s_2, \ldots, s_n\}$ is a set of size n, $X = \mathcal{P}(S)$ is the power set of S, and Y is the set of all functions from S to the set $\{0, 1\}$. That is, $Y = \{f \mid f : S \longrightarrow \{0, 1\}\}$.

2.3.3 New Functions from Old

There are some common ways to make new functions out of old ones. One such construction is the *composition* of two functions. If $f : X \longrightarrow Y$ and $g : Y \longrightarrow Z$, then $g \circ f$ is a function from X to Z defined by $(g \circ f)(x) = g(f(x))$.

Example 2.31 Let $f : \mathbf{R} \longrightarrow \mathbf{R}$ be defined by $f(x) = \lfloor x \rfloor$, and let $g : \mathbf{R} \longrightarrow \mathbf{R}$ be defined by $g(x) = 3x$. Then

$$\begin{aligned}
(g \circ f)(2.4) &= g(f(2.4)) \\
&= g(2) \\
&= 6
\end{aligned}$$

and

$$\begin{aligned}
(f \circ g)(2.4) &= f(g(2.4)) \\
&= f(7.2) \\
&= 7
\end{aligned}$$

This example shows that $f \circ g$ can be different from $g \circ f$. And note one potentially confusing thing about the notation: In the composition $g \circ f$, we do f first, and then apply g to the result. Order matters, in general.

Sometimes we would like to be able to "undo" a function, so that it maps back to where it came from. If $f: X \longrightarrow Y$ is a function, then the *inverse* of f is the function

$$f^{-1} : Y \longrightarrow X$$

that has the property that $f^{-1} \circ f = 1_X$ and $f \circ f^{-1} = 1_Y$.

Not all functions have inverses. If $f: X \longrightarrow Y$ has an inverse, then, for any $y \in Y, f(f^{-1}(y)) = y$, so f must map X onto Y. In addition, if $f(a) = f(b)$, then we can apply f^{-1} to both sides of this equation to get $a = b$, so f must be one-to-one also. So we see that if a function has an inverse, it must be a one-to-one correspondence.

Conversely, we can construct the inverse of any one-to-one correspondence $f: X \longrightarrow Y$ by taking $f^{-1}(y)$ to be the unique element of X that maps onto y. We know such an element exists, because f is onto, and we know this element is unique, since f is one-to-one. This is the only choice we have for f^{-1}; see Exercise 28.

Example 2.32 If $f: \mathbf{R} \longrightarrow \{y \in \mathbf{R} \mid y > 0\}$ is the function $f(x) = 2^x$, then the inverse of f is given by $f^{-1}(x) = \log_2 x$.

In this last example, we could have defined $f(x) = 2^x$ as a function from $\mathbf{R}$ to $\mathbf{R}$, but then it wouldn't be invertible because it wouldn't be onto.

One final way to construct functions is by *restriction*. If $f: X \longrightarrow Y$ is some function, and $H \subseteq X$, then the restriction of f to H is the function

$$f|_H : H \longrightarrow Y$$

defined by taking $f|_H(x) = f(x)$. In other words, we just restrict the domain to a smaller set, and use the same rule that assigns an element of the codomain to each element of this smaller domain. Why bother? Sometimes the new, restricted function is simpler to describe, or has other desirable properties.

Example 2.33 Let D be the unit disk in $\mathbf{R}^2$, that is,

$$D = \{(x,y) \in \mathbf{R}^2 \mid x^2 + y^2 \leq 1\}$$

and let $D^* = D \setminus \{(0,0)\}$. Let $S^1 = \{(x,y) \in \mathbf{R}^2 \mid x^2 + y^2 = 1\}$ be the unit circle. Define a function $p: D^* \longrightarrow S^1$ by projecting straight out along a radius until you reach the boundary of the disk. See the following picture.

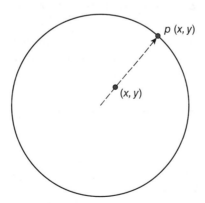

Getting a formula for p might be a little messy, but things can be cleaner if we consider a restriction. Let H be the circle of radius $\frac{1}{2}$:

$$H = \left\{(x,y) \in \mathbf{R}^2 \mid x^2 + y^2 = \frac{1}{4}\right\}$$

We'll leave it as an exercise to show that $p|_H(x,y) = (2x, 2y)$.

Exercises 2.3

1. Let X be a set with four elements. Represent the identity function 1_X of Example 2.22 with a directed graph in two different ways:

   (a) as an f-graph with four vertices.

   (b) with eight vertices, four for the domain and four for the codomain.

2. See Definitions 2.3 and 2.4. Write the definitions of one-to-one and onto in terms of predicate logic.

3. Show that the function of Example 2.20 is not one-to-one.

4. Show that the function of Example 2.20 is onto.

5. Several languages are spoken in India; let L be the set of all such languages, and let U be the set of all residents of India. Explain why the proposed function $f \colon U \longrightarrow L$ defined by

   $$f(u) = \text{the language that } u \text{ speaks}$$

   is not well defined.

6. Let P be a set of people, and let Q be a set of occupations. Define a function $f \colon P \longrightarrow Q$ by setting $f(p)$ equal to p's occupation. What must be true about the people in P for f to be a well-defined function?

7. Is the function of Example 2.23 onto? Why or why not? Is it one-to-one? Why or why not?

8. Consider Example 2.23. Let y be some person. What is the relationship of $(m \circ m)(y)$ to y?

9. Is the function depicted in Figure 2.8 onto? Why or why not?

10. Is the function depicted in Figure 2.9 one-to-one? Why or why not?

11. Explain why the proof in Example 2.28 could not be used to prove that the function in Example 2.26 is onto.

12. Consider the situation of Example 2.30. Describe a different one-to-one correspondence $g \colon Y \longrightarrow X$. Show that your function is both one-to-one and onto.

13. Consider the negation function $n \colon \{T, F\} \longrightarrow \{T, F\}$ given by $n(x) = \neg x$. Is n a one-to-one correspondence? What is n^{-1}?

14. Define a function $f \colon \mathbf{R} \longrightarrow \mathbf{R}$ by the formula $f(x) = 3x - 5$.

    (a) Prove that f is one-to-one.

    (b) Prove that f is onto.

15. Let $\mathbf{Z}$ denote the set of integers, let $\mathbf{Z}^*$ denote the set of nonzero integers, and let $\mathbf{Q}$ be the set of all rational numbers. Define a function $g \colon \mathbf{Z} \times \mathbf{Z}^* \longrightarrow \mathbf{Q}$ by $g(a, b) = a/b$. Explain why g is not one-to-one. Be specific.

16. Let E be the set of edges in the directed graph below, and let V be the set of vertices. Define a function $h \colon E \longrightarrow V$ as follows: For any edge $e \in E$, let $h(e)$ be the vertex that edge e points at. Explain why this function is not onto. Be specific.

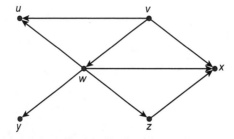

17. Define a function $f \colon \mathbf{Z} \longrightarrow \mathbf{Z} \times \mathbf{Z}$ by $f(x) = (2x + 3, x - 4)$.

    (a) Is f one-to-one? Prove or disprove.

    (b) Does f map $\mathbf{Z}$ onto $\mathbf{Z} \times \mathbf{Z}$? Prove or disprove.

18. Define a map $t \colon \mathbf{R} \times \mathbf{R} \longrightarrow \mathbf{R} \times \mathbf{R}$ by $t(a, b) = (a + b, a - b)$. Prove that t is a one-to-one correspondence.

19. Let X be a set. Define a map $d: X \longrightarrow X \times X$ by $d(x) = (x, x)$.

(a) Is d one-to-one? Prove or disprove.

(b) Is d onto? Prove or disprove.

20. Let G be the following directed graph.

Let V be the set of vertices in G and let E be the set of edges in G. This graph describes a function

$$i : E \longrightarrow V \times V$$

where $i(e) = (a, b)$ if edge e goes from vertex a to vertex b.

(a) List the values of $i(e_1), i(e_2), \ldots, i(e_8)$.

(b) Is the function i one-to-one? Why or why not?

(c) Is the function i onto? Why or why not?

21. Let G be a simple, connected, undirected graph. Let V be the set of vertices in G, and let

$$P = \{\{v_1, v_2\} \mid v_1, v_2 \in V, v_1 \neq v_2\}$$

be the set of all unordered pairs of vertices. Let E be the set of all edges in G. Define a function $f: E \longrightarrow P$ as follows: If $e \in E$ is an edge in G, then $f(e) = \{a, b\}$, where a and b are the vertices that e touches.

(a) Explain why $f(e)$ is always a set of size 2. (This better be true, or f is not well defined.)

(b) Is f one-to-one? Prove or disprove.

(c) Does f map E onto P? Prove or disprove.

22. Let $S = \{0, 1, 2, 3, 4, 5\}$, and let $\mathcal{P}(S)^*$ be the set of all nonempty subsets of S. Define a function $m: \mathcal{P}(S)^* \longrightarrow S$ by

$$m(H) = \text{ the largest element in } H$$

for any nonempty subset $H \subseteq S$.

(a) Is m one-to-one? Why or why not?

(b) Does m map $\mathcal{P}(S)^*$ onto S? Why or why not?

23. Let $X = \{n \in \mathbf{N} \mid n \text{ divides } 30030\}$, and define a function $f: X \longrightarrow X$ by

$$f(n) = \frac{30030}{n}.$$

(a) Prove that f is one-to-one.

(b) Prove that f is onto.

24. Let $f: \mathbf{Z} \longrightarrow \mathbf{Z}$ be defined as

$$f(x) = \begin{cases} x + 3 & \text{if } x \text{ is odd} \\ x - 5 & \text{if } x \text{ is even} \end{cases}.$$

(a) Show that f is a one-to-one correspondence.

(b) Find a formula for f^{-1}.

25. Define a function $f: \mathbf{N} \longrightarrow \mathbf{Z}$ by

$$f(n) = \begin{cases} n/2 & \text{if } n \text{ is even} \\ (1-n)/2 & \text{if } n \text{ is odd} \end{cases}.$$

   (a) Show that f is one-to-one correspondence.

   (b) Find a formula for f^{-1}.

26. Define a function $g: \mathbf{Z} \longrightarrow \mathbf{N}$, by $g(z) = z^2 + 1$.

   (a) Prove that g is not one-to-one.

   (b) Prove that g is not onto.

27. Compute the inverse of $f(x) = x^3 + 1$. Check your answer by showing that $f(f^{-1}(x)) = x$ and $f^{-1}(f(x)) = x$.

28. Suppose that $f: X \longrightarrow Y$ has two inverses, g and h. Prove that $g = h$; that is, prove that for all $y \in Y$, $g(y) = h(y)$.

29. Define functions $f, g: \mathbf{N} \longrightarrow \mathbf{N}$ by

$$f(x) = 2x$$
$$g(x) = \lfloor x/2 \rfloor$$

   Is $f \circ g$ the same as $g \circ f$? Explain.

30. Let $f: X \longrightarrow Y$ and $g: Y \longrightarrow Z$ be one-to-one correspondences. Prove that $(g \circ f)^{-1} = f^{-1} \circ g^{-1}$.

31. Complete Example 2.33. That is, show that $p|_H(x, y) = (2x, 2y)$.

32. Let $q: \mathbf{R}^2 \longrightarrow \mathbf{R}^2$ be given by $q(x, y) = (x, 0)$. Geometrically, q is called the *projection* onto the x-axis, because it maps any point straight down (or up) to the x-axis. Let $q|_{D^*}$ be the restriction of q to the unit disk, and let p be the function defined in Example 2.33. Draw a **well-labeled** picture to show that

$$p \circ q|_{D^*} \neq q|_{D^*} \circ p.$$

33. Suppose $f: X \longrightarrow Y$ and $g: Y \longrightarrow Z$ are both onto. Prove that $g \circ f$ is onto.

*34. Suppose $f: X \longrightarrow Y$ and $g: Y \longrightarrow Z$ are both one-to-one. Prove that $g \circ f$ is one-to-one.

*35. Let $f: X \longrightarrow Y$ and $g: Y \longrightarrow Z$ be functions such that $h = g \circ f$ is a one-to-one correspondence.

   (a) Prove that f is one-to-one.

   (b) Prove that g is onto.

*36. Let $f: X \longrightarrow Y$ be a function. For any subset $U \subseteq X$, define the set $f(U)$:

$$f(U) = \{y \in Y \mid y = f(x) \text{ for some } x \in U\}.$$

   In particular, $f(X)$ is the image of f.

   (a) Let $A \subseteq X$ and $B \subseteq X$. Does $f(A \cap B) = f(A) \cap f(B)$ in general? Prove it, or give a counterexample.

   (b) Let $A \subseteq X$ and $B \subseteq X$. Does $f(A \cup B) = f(A) \cup f(B)$ in general? Prove it, or give a counterexample.

   Hint: Refer to Exercise 24 of Section 1.3.

2.4   Relations and Equivalences

Although functions are used in almost every area of mathematics, many relationships are not functional. For example, we could never define a function $b(x)$ that gives the brother of x, because x might have more than one brother (or no brothers at all). A *relation* is a more general mathematical object that describes these kinds of relationships.

Definition 2.5 An *r-graph* is a directed graph with no multiple edges. That is, for all vertices u, v, there can be at most one edge from u to v.

Preview 2.4

1. Recall Definition 2.1. Is every f-graph also an r-graph? Explain.

2. Give an example of an r-graph with at least five vertices that is not an f-graph. Invent a shorthand notation that encodes all the information needed to reconstruct the graph.

3. Construct a directed graph whose vertices represent the integers $1, 2, 3, 4, 5$, where there is an edge from vertex n to vertex m iff $m - n$ is even. What properties do you notice about this graph? Would these properties remain if the graph were constructed using a longer list of integers?

2.4.1 Definition and Examples

Definition 2.6 A *relation* on a set S is a subset of $S \times S$. If R is a relation on S, we denote the set along with its relation as (S, R). We say that "a is related to b" if $(a, b) \in R$, which we sometimes write as $a R b$. If $(a, b) \notin R$, then a is not related to b; in symbols, $a \not\mathrel{R} b$.

Some books call this a "binary relation." It is easy to see how you could generalize this definition: you could have a relation between a pair of sets, or a relation among a list of sets, but these other kinds of relations are less commonly seen.

Example 2.34 The symbols $=, <, >, \leq, \geq$ all define relations on $\mathbf{Z}$ (or on any set of numbers). For example, if $S = \{1, 2, 3\}$, then the relation on S defined by $<$ is the set $\{(1, 2), (1, 3), (2, 3)\}$.

Example 2.35 Let P be the set of all people, living or dead. For any $a, b \in P$, let $a R b$ if a and b are (or were) brothers. Then R is a relation on P, and the ordered pair $(\text{Cain}, \text{Abel}) \in R$.

Example 2.36 Let W be the set of all web pages. Then

$$L = \{(a, b) \in W \times W \mid a \text{ has a link to } b\}$$

is a relation on W. In other words, $a L b$ if page a links to page b.

Example 2.37 Let $a, b \in \mathbf{Z}$. If, for some $n \in \mathbf{Z}$, $n \mid (a - b)$, we say that "a is equivalent to b modulo n." The notation for this relation is

$$a \equiv b \quad \mathrm{mod}\ n.$$

For example, $1, 4, 7, 10, 13, \dots$ are all equivalent to 1 modulo 3.
  Notice that

$$
\begin{aligned}
a \equiv b \quad \mathrm{mod}\ n &\Leftrightarrow n \mid (a - b) \\
&\Leftrightarrow a - b = kn \text{ for some } k \in \mathbf{Z} \\
&\Leftrightarrow a = b + kn \text{ for some } k \in \mathbf{Z},
\end{aligned}
$$

so adding any multiple of n to a number b gives a number that is equivalent to b modulo n.

2.4.2 Graphs of Relations

Preview questions 2.4.1–3 illustrate that relations and graphs are similar concepts. Given a relation, there is a graph that models it.

Definition 2.7 Let R be a relation on a set X. The *directed graph* associated with (X, R) is the graph whose vertices correspond to the elements of X, with a directed edge from vertex x to vertex y whenever $x R y$.

Example 2.38 The "|" relation on the set $X = \{2, 3, 4, 6\}$ has the following graph.

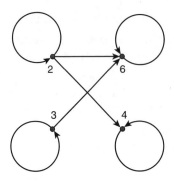

Often, a relation R will have the property that $x \, R \, y$ if and only if $y \, R \, x$. Such a relation is called *symmetric*. For a symmetric relation, the arrows would come in pairs—one in each direction. In this case, we replace the two arrows by a single edge and omit the arrowheads.

Definition 2.8 Let R be a relation on a set X, and suppose $x \, R \, y \Leftrightarrow y \, R \, x$ for all $x, y \in X$. The *undirected graph* associated with (X, R) is the graph whose vertices correspond to the elements of X, with an (undirected) edge joining any two vertices x and y for which $x \, R \, y$.

Example 2.39 Define a relation on the set $X = \{2, 3, 4, 6\}$ by setting $a \, R \, b$ whenever $ab < 13$. Since $ab < 13 \Leftrightarrow ba < 13$, this is a symmetric relation, and so can be represented by the following undirected graph.

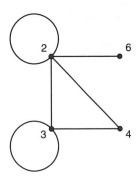

Every relation yields a graph, but there are graphs that don't have relations associated to them. One example is the graph of the Königsberg bridges in Example 2.1. The double edges in this graph cannot be represented by a relation, because any ordered pair (x, y) can occur at most once in the Cartesian product $X \times X$.

2.4.3   Relations vs. Functions

What's the difference between a relation and a function? Strictly speaking, a relation on X is a function $X \longrightarrow X$ if each $x \in X$ occurs exactly once as the first element of an ordered pair. But this description is fairly mechanical; what does it really mean? Think of a function as a way of describing how the elements in one set *depend* on the elements in another set. When we graph a function $y = f(x)$, we usually say that y is the *dependent* variable and x is the *independent* variable. This means we get to pick x, and y depends on what we choose for x.

We can't view relations this way, because any given x may be related to several other elements or none at all. Instead, think of relations as describing comparisons within a set or links between elements of a set.

Example 2.40 Let $X = \{2, 3, 4, 5, 6, 7, 8\}$, and say that two elements $a, b \in X$ are related if $a \mid b$ and $a \neq b$. We can represent this relation with a directed graph: the elements of X are the vertices, and there is a directed edge from distinct vertices a and b whenever $a \mid b$.

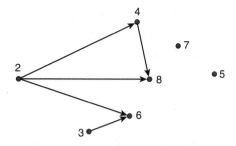

This example shows that the relationships described by a relation aren't constrained the way relationships described by a function are: the element 2 is related to three other elements, while 5 and 7 aren't related to anything. Thus this relation does not describe a function on X.

Activity 2.4.1: Reflexive, Symmetric, and Transitive Relations

A relation R on a set S is *reflexive* if every element is related to itself. That is, for any $a \in S$, $a R a$.
A relation R on a set S is *symmetric* if it can be flipped. That is, for any $a, b \in S$, $a R b \Leftrightarrow b R a$.
A relation R on a set S is *transitive* if, for any $a, b, c \in S$, if $a R b$ and $b R c$, then $a R c$.

1. The three connected, directed graphs below represent relations on the set of vertices: $u R v$ if there is a directed edge from u to v. For each graph, determine which of the three properties (reflexive, symmetric, transitive) the relation satisfies.

2. Draw a directed graph with four vertices that represents a relation that is reflexive, symmetric, and transitive. Is there more than one such graph? Draw two such graphs, if possible.

3. Define a relation $\lhd$ on $\{1, 2, 3, 4, 5\}$ by $a \lhd b$ if $a - b$ is even. Use the graph from preview question 2.4.3 to determine whether $\lhd$ is reflexive, symmetric, and/or transitive.

4. Define a relation $\models$ on $\{1, 2, 3, 4, 5\}$ by $a \models b$ if $a - b$ is odd. Is $\models$ reflexive? symmetric? transitive?

2.4.4 Equivalence Relations

Definition 2.9 A relation R on a set S is an *equivalence relation* if it satisfies all three of the following properties.

1. *Reflexivity.* For any $a \in S$, $a R a$.

2. *Symmetry.* For any $a, b \in S$, $a R b \Leftrightarrow b R a$.

3. *Transitivity.* For any $a, b, c \in S$, if $a R b$ and $b R c$, then $a R c$.

In other words, an equivalence relation is a relation that is reflexive, symmetric, and transitive.

Example 2.41 The relation on $\mathbf{Z}$ defined by $=$ is an equivalence relation, because equality is reflexive, symmetric, and transitive.

The idea of an equivalence relation might seem abstract at first, but you are already quite familiar with an important example: fractions. In elementary school, you learned that equivalent fractions represent the same number; for instance, $\frac{3}{6}$ is the same as $\frac{1}{2}$. The next example shows how to prove that this notion is an equivalence relation on the set S of all symbols of the form $\frac{x}{y}$, where x and y are integers. Be careful: the set S is a set of symbols, not a set of numbers. Two different symbols in S can represent the same number; this is the point of the equivalence relation.

Example 2.42 Let S be the set of all symbols of the form $\frac{x}{y}$, where x and y are integers with $y \neq 0$. In other words, $S = \left\{ \frac{x}{y} \mid x, y \in \mathbf{Z}, y \neq 0 \right\}$. Define a relation R on S as follows. For any elements $\frac{x}{y}$ and $\frac{z}{w}$ in S, $\frac{x}{y} R \frac{z}{w}$ if $xw = yz$. The proof that R is an equivalence relation has three parts:

Proof

1. *Reflexivity.* Suppose that $\frac{x}{y} \in S$. Since $xy = yx$, we have $\frac{x}{y} R \frac{x}{y}$.

2. *Symmetry.* Suppose that $\frac{x}{y}, \frac{z}{w} \in S$ and suppose that $\frac{x}{y} R \frac{z}{w}$. By the definition of R, this means that $xw = yz$, which is the same thing as saying $zy = wx$. Thus $\frac{z}{w} R \frac{x}{y}$, as required.

3. *Transitivity.* Let $\frac{x}{y}, \frac{z}{w}, \frac{p}{q} \in S$ with $\frac{x}{y} R \frac{z}{w}$ and $\frac{z}{w} R \frac{p}{q}$. Then $xw = yz$ and $zq = wp$. Using substitution, $xq = yzq/w = ywp/w = yp$. This shows that $\frac{x}{y} R \frac{p}{q}$, as required. □

The next example is a little less familiar, but notice that the proof follows the same template.

Example 2.43 Given any function $f: X \to Y$, define a relation on X as follows. For any $a, b \in X$, $a R b$ if $f(a) = f(b)$. The proof that R is an equivalence relation has three parts:

Proof

1. *Reflexivity.* Suppose that $a \in X$. Since f is a well-defined function, $f(a) = f(a)$, so $a R a$.

2. *Symmetry.* Suppose that $a, b \in X$ and that $a R b$. By the definition of R, this means that $f(a) = f(b)$, which is the same thing as saying $f(b) = f(a)$. Thus $b R a$, as required.

3. *Transitivity.* Let $a, b, c \in X$ with $a R b$ and $b R c$. Then $f(a) = f(b)$ and $f(b) = f(c)$, so by substitution, $f(a) = f(c)$. This shows that $a R c$. □

Activity 2.4.2: Proving a Relation is an Equivalence Relation

A relation is an *equivalence relation* if it is reflexive, symmetric, and transitive. To prove that a relation is an equivalence relation, you need to write three direct proofs, one for each property.

Define a relation R on $\mathbf{Z}$ by $a R b$ if $a = b + 5k$ for some integer k.

1. Complete the following proof that R is reflexive.

   Let $a \in$ ____. Since $a = a + 5 \cdot$ ____, $a R a$, as required.

2. Complete the following proof that R is symmetric.

   Let $a, b \in \mathbf{Z}$ and suppose that $a R b$. By the definition of R, $a =$ _____ for some integer k. Using algebra, $b =$ _____, which shows that _____, as required.

3. Complete the following proof that R is transitive.

   Let $a, b, c \in \mathbf{Z}$ and suppose that _____ and _____. By the definition of R, $a =$ _____ for some integer k_1 and $b =$ _____ for some integer k_2. Substituting the second equation into the first gives $a =$ _____ $= c + 5($ _____$)$, which shows that _____, as required.

Example 2.44 Say that two computers on a network are related if it is possible to establish a network connection between the two (e.g., it is possible to ping one from another). In order for this to be an equivalence relation, any computer must be able to ping itself (reflexive), any computer must be able to return a ping (symmetric), and any computer must be able to pass along a ping to any other computer that it can ping (transitive).

Example 2.45 A *partition* of a set S is a set P of nonempty subsets of S with the following properties.

1. For any $a \in S$, there is some set $X \in P$ such that $a \in X$. The elements of P are called the *blocks* of the partition.

2. If $X, Y \in P$ are distinct blocks, then $X \cap Y = \emptyset$.

Informally, a partition is a way of dividing a set into nonoverlapping pieces; in a Venn diagram, a partition looks like an arrangement of walls, where the blocks of the partition are the rooms:

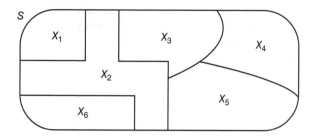

Suppose P is a partition of S. Define a relation on S by setting $a \, R \, b$ if a and b belong to the same block. We can prove that R is an equivalence relation.

Proof

1. *Reflexivity.* Suppose that $a \in S$. Then a must be in some block X, and a is evidently in the same block as itself. So $a \, R \, a$.

2. *Symmetry.* Suppose that $a, b \in S$ and suppose that $a \, R \, b$. Thus a and b are in the same block, which is the same as saying that b and a are in the same block. Therefore, $b \, R \, a$.

3. *Transitivity.* Let $a, b, c \in S$ with $a \, R \, b$ and $b \, R \, c$. Then a and b are in the same block, and b and c are in the same block, so a and c are in the same block. Therefore, $a \, R \, c$, as required. □

Example 2.45 shows that every partition determines an equivalence relation. It is also true that every equivalence relation determines a partition. Partitions and equivalence relations are essentially the same thing.

Theorem 2.2 *Let R be an equivalence relation on a set S. For any element $x \in S$, define $R_x = \{a \in X \mid x \, R \, a\}$, the set of all elements related to x. Let P be the collection of distinct subsets of S formed in this way, that is, $P = \{R_x \mid x \in S\}$. Then P is a partition of S.*

A formal proof of this theorem takes a little bit of work, and we'll omit the proof for the sake of brevity. Informally, such a proof must show that the two properties of a partition are satisfied. The first property is easy: for any $a \in S$, there is a block containing a, namely R_a. The second property is the hard part. Roughly speaking, the transitive and symmetric properties guarantee that if two blocks overlap at all, then they must overlap completely.

The sets R_x are called the *equivalence classes* formed by the equivalence relation. A set S partitioned into equivalence classes looks like this:

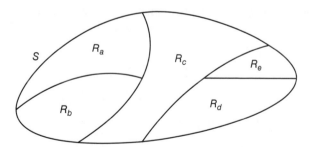

In this picture, the elements $a, b, c, d, e \in S$ are called equivalence class *representatives*. As the name suggests, there is usually a choice of representatives for a given equivalence class. By Theorem 2.2, different equivalence classes must have nonequivalent representatives.

Example 2.46 Let W be the set of all words in the sentence, "There are more things in heaven and earth, Horatio, than are dreamt of in your philosophy." Define a relation R on W as follows: for any words $w_1, w_2 \in W$, $w_1 \, R \, w_2$ if the first letter of w_1 is the same as the first letter of w_2, without regard to upper or lower cases. (Exercise: show this is an equivalence relation.) The equivalence classes are the sets of all words beginning with the same letter. For example, $R_{\text{things}} = \{\text{There, things, than}\}$.

Activity 2.4.3: Equivalence Relations and Equivalence Classes

If a relation R on a set S is reflexive, symmetric, and transitive, it is called an *equivalence relation*. For any $a \in S$, the set $\{x \in S \mid x R a\}$ is called the *equivalence class* represented by a, denoted $[a]$.

1. In the graph below, define $a R b$ if there is a path from vertex a to vertex b. For this equivalence relation, write the equivalence classes $[t]$, $[x]$, $[s]$, and $[p]$ in roster form.

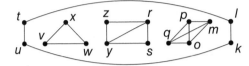

2. Let $S = \{0, 1, 2, 3 \ldots 19\}$, and define $a R b$ iff $a - b$ is a multiple of 5. How many different equivalence classes are there? Write each equivalence class in roster form, and label each set as $[k]$ for some choice of representative k.

3. More generally, we define *equivalence modulo n* on $\mathbf{Z}$ as $a R b$ if $a - b$ is a multiple of n. In this case we write "$a \equiv b \mod n$." Consider the equivalence relation modulo 7 on $\mathbf{Z}$. The equivalence classes modulo 7 are $[0], [1], [2], [3], [4], [5], [6]$.

   (a) Write down three different members of $[2]$.

   (b) Write down three different members of $[3]$.

   (c) If $x \in [2]$ and $y \in [3]$, what equivalence class is $x + y$ in? (Try some examples from parts (a) and (b).)

   (d) If $x \in [2]$ and $y \in [3]$, what equivalence class is xy in?

4. Without using a calculator, can you (quickly) find the equivalence class of $24(12 \cdot 47 + 60 \cdot 35)$ modulo 11?

2.4.5   Modular Arithmetic

Consider the "$\equiv \mod n$" relation of Example 2.37. To check that this is an equivalence relation, we need to prove that it is reflexive, symmetric, and transitive. We'll show transitivity, and leave the proofs of the other two properties as exercises.

Lemma 2.1 The "$\equiv \mod n$" relation on $\mathbf{Z}$ is transitive.

Proof Let $a, b, c \in \mathbf{Z}$, and suppose that $a \equiv b \mod n$ and $b \equiv c \mod n$. This means that $a = b + kn$ and $b = c + ln$ for some integers k and l. Substituting the second equation into the first, we find that $a = (c + ln) + kn = c + (l + k)n$, so $a \equiv c \mod n$, as required for transitivity. □

The set of equivalence classes formed by this equivalence relation is called the *integers modulo n*, and is denoted $\mathbf{Z}/n$. We use $[k]$ to denote the equivalence class of k. For example, the elements of $\mathbf{Z}/3$ are

$$[0] = \{\ldots, -9, -6, -3, 0, 3, 6, 9, \ldots\}$$
$$[1] = \{\ldots, -8, -5, -2, 1, 4, 7, 10, \ldots\}$$
$$[2] = \{\ldots, -7, -4, -1, 2, 5, 8, 11, \ldots\}.$$

The next result is the basis for modular arithmetic.

Proposition 2.1 Let $[a]$ and $[b]$ be equivalence classes in $\mathbf{Z}/n$. Suppose that $x \in [a]$ and $y \in [b]$. Then $x + y \in [a + b]$ and $xy \in [ab]$.

Proof Let $[a], [b] \in \mathbf{Z}/n$, and let $x \in [a]$ and $y \in [b]$. By the definition of $\equiv \mod n$, $x = a + kn$ and $y = b + ln$ for some integers k and l. Therefore,

$$x + y = (a + kn) + (b + ln) = (a + b) + (k + l)n$$

and

$$xy = (a + kn)(b + ln) = ab + aln + bkn + kln^2 = ab + (al + bk + kln)n,$$

so $x + y \equiv a + b \mod n$ and $xy \equiv ab \mod n$, as required. □

What is so important about this proposition? It shows that if we add or multiply equivalence class *representatives* (no matter which ones we choose), we get a representative of the "right" equivalence class. For example, in $\mathbf{Z}/3$, $-6 \in [0]$ and $11 \in [2]$. Their sum, $-6 + 11 = 5$, is in $[2]$, the natural value for the "sum" of $[0]$ and $[2]$.

In other words, the operations of addition and multiplication on *equivalence classes* are well defined:

$$[a] + [b] = [a + b]$$
$$[a] \cdot [b] = [ab].$$

This means we can add and multiply elements in $\mathbf{Z}/n$ by adding and multiplying the numbers we use to represent the equivalence class. These are the operations of *modular arithmetic*. For example, in the modular arithmetic of $\mathbf{Z}/12$, $[6] + [8] = [2]$ because $14 \equiv 2 \mod 12$.

We usually represent an equivalence class in $\mathbf{Z}/n$ by its least non-negative representative, so the operations of modular arithmetic really are just the ordinary arithmetic operations followed by taking the remainder upon division by n.

Although the elements of $\mathbf{Z}/n$ are technically sets of numbers (equivalence classes), we can think of them as a new type of number with new rules for multiplication and addition. Sometimes, we'll even omit the [ ]s around these numbers if the meaning is clear from the context.

Example 2.47 The following tables show how to add and multiply in $\mathbf{Z}/6$.

+	0	1	2	3	4	5
0	0	1	2	3	4	5
1	1	2	3	4	5	0
2	2	3	4	5	0	1
3	3	4	5	0	1	2
4	4	5	0	1	2	3
5	5	0	1	2	3	4

·	0	1	2	3	4	5
0	0	0	0	0	0	0
1	0	1	2	3	4	5
2	0	2	4	0	2	4
3	0	3	0	3	0	3
4	0	4	2	0	4	2
5	0	5	4	3	2	1

Notice the patterns in these tables. The "numbers" 0 and 1 in $\mathbf{Z}/6$ add and multiply as they do in standard integer arithmetic, but the other numbers behave differently. For example, $5 \in \mathbf{Z}/6$ acts like -1, both for addition and for multiplication. This reflects the fact that $[5] = [-1]$ as equivalence classes in $\mathbf{Z}/6$.

Modular arithmetic can come in quite handy. For example, if we want a counter to keep track of an n-stage process that needs to be repeated several times, we would start at $[0]$ and add $[1]$ in $\mathbf{Z}/n$ at each stage, and the counter would cycle through n values and repeat. Another application—ISBN check digits—appears in the following activity, and also in the exercises.

Activity 2.4.4: Modular Arithmetic

1. Compute $3 \cdot 4 + 2 \mod 5$.
2. Compute $1923 \cdot 845834 + 123482 \mod 5$. (Remember that you can mod first, then multiply and add.)
3. Compute $2^2 \mod 5$, $2^3 \mod 5$, and $2^4 \mod 5$.
4. Compute $2^{10000007} \mod 5$.
5. Ten-digit ISBN numbers used a check digit scheme to determine the 10th digit of a book's ISBN number. If the first nine digits of an ISBN number are $a_1a_2a_3a_4a_5a_6a_7a_8a_9$, the tenth digit is given by the formula $a_{10} = (1a_1 + 2a_2 + 3a_3 + 4a_4 + 5a_5 + 6a_6 + 7a_7 + 8a_8 + 9a_9) \mod 11$, where $a_{10} = $ X if this value is 10.

   (a) Calculate the tenth digit of the ISBN whose first nine digits are 229332131.

   (b) Calculate the tenth digit of the ISBN whose first nine digits are 292332131.

   (c) Notice that in parts (a) and (b), switching adjacent digits changed the ISBN check digit. Can you explain why switching adjacent digits will always change the check digit?

Exercises 2.4

1. Let $X = \{0, 1, 2, 3, 4\}$. Draw the graph associated with the $<$ relation on X. Should this graph be directed or undirected?

2. Let $X = \{0, 1, 2, 3, 4\}$. Define a relation R on X such that $x \, R \, y$ if $x + y = 4$. Draw the graph associated with this relation. Should this graph be directed or undirected?

For Exercises 3–6, define a relation $\rightleftharpoons$ on the set S of all strings of letters: two strings are related if you can get one from the other by reversing one pair of adjacent letters. For example, cow $\rightleftharpoons$ ocw but cow $\not\rightleftharpoons$ woc.

3. Consider all the strings you can form with the letters c, a, and t (there are six). Draw the graph whose nodes are these six strings and whose edges represent the $\rightleftharpoons$ relation. Should this be a directed or an undirected graph?

4. Find an Euler path in the graph you made in Exercise 3.

5. Consider the graph formed by the $\rightleftharpoons$ relation on the set of all the strings you can form from the letters l, y, n, and x. Does this graph have an Euler path? Why or why not?

6. Does the graph of the $\rightleftharpoons$ relation on the set of all strings formed from the letters l, e, o, p, a, r, and d have an Euler path? Why or why not?

7. Suppose you wanted to model an equivalence relation with a graph. Would you use a directed or an undirected graph? What would the equivalence classes look like? Explain.

8. The "$\equiv$ mod 3" relation is an equivalence relation on the set $\{1, 2, 3, 4, 5, 6, 7\}$. List the equivalence classes.

9. Define a relation on $\mathbf{Z}$ by $a \, R \, b$ if $a^2 = b^2$.
   (a) Prove that R is an equivalence relation.
   (b) Describe the equivalence classes.

10. Define a relation on $\mathbf{Z}$ by setting $x \, R \, y$ if xy is even.
    (a) Give a counterexample to show that R is not reflexive.
    (b) Give a counterexample to show that R is not transitive.

11. Explain why the web linking relation in Example 2.36 is not an equivalence relation. (You only need to give one reason why it fails to be an equivalence relation.)

12. Prove that the relation defined in Example 2.46 is an equivalence relation.

13. The following set R defines an equivalence relation on the set $\{1, 2, 3\}$, where $a \, R \, b$ means that $(a, b) \in R$.

$$R = \{(1, 1), (2, 2), (3, 3), (2, 3), (3, 2)\}$$

   What are the equivalence classes?

14. Give a specific reason why the following set R does not define an equivalence relation on the set $\{1, 2, 3, 4\}$.

$$R = \{(1, 1), (2, 2), (3, 3), (4, 4), (2, 3), (3, 2), (2, 4), (4, 2)\}$$

15. Explain why the relation R on $\{0, 1, 2\}$ given by

$$R = \{(0, 0), (1, 1), (2, 2), (0, 1), (1, 0), (1, 2), (2, 1)\}$$

   is not an equivalence relation. Be specific.

16. Let $A = \{1, 2\}$. Write out the subset of $A \times A$ defined by the $\leq$ relation on A.

17. Let $X = \{0, 1\}$.
    (a) List (as subsets of $X \times X$) all possible relations on X.
    (b) Which of the relations in part (a) are equivalence relations?

18. Let X be a nonempty set. Define a relation R on the power set $\mathcal{P}(X)$ by

$$A \, R \, B \iff A \cap B = \emptyset$$

   for $A, B \in \mathcal{P}(X)$. Determine whether this relation is reflexive, symmetric, and/or transitive.

19. Let S be the set of all provinces in Canada. For $a, b \in S$, let $a \, R \, b$ if a and b border each other. Which properties of an equivalence relation (reflexive, symmetric, transitive) does the relation R satisfy?

20. Let T be the set of all movie actors and actresses. For $x, y \in T$, define $x \, R \, y$ if there is some movie that both x and y appear in. Which properties of equivalence relations does R satisfy?

21. Let W be the set of words in the English language. Define a relation R on W by

$$w_1 \, R \, w_2 \iff w_1 \text{ and } w_2 \text{ have a letter in common.}$$

   Which properties of equivalence relations does R satisfy? Explain.

22. Let W be the set of words in the English language. Define a relation S on W by

$$w_1 \, S \, w_2 \iff w_1 \text{ has at least as many letters as } w_2.$$

   Which properties of equivalence relations does S satisfy? Explain.

23. Let X be a finite set. For subsets $A, B \in \mathcal{P}(X)$, let $A \, R \, B$ if $|A| = |B|$. This is an equivalence relation on $\mathcal{P}(X)$. If $X = \{1, 2, 3\}$, list the equivalence classes.

24. A playground consists of several structures, some of which are connected by bridges. The ground is covered with bark chips. Define a relation on the set of structures on the playground as follows: two structures are related if it is possible for a child to get from one to the other without walking on the bark chips (otherwise known as "hot lava").

   (a) Can you imagine a playground for which this would not be an equivalence relation? Explain.

   (b) Suppose this relation is an equivalence. In the language of playground equipment, describe the equivalence classes.

25. Let G be a connected, undirected graph, and let V be the set of all vertices in G. Define a relation R on V as follows: for any vertices $a, b \in V$, $a \, R \, b$ if there is a path from a to b with an even number of edges. (A path may use the same edge more than once.) Prove that R is an equivalence relation.

26. Suppose the equivalence relation of Exercise 25 is defined on the vertices of the following graph. What are the equivalence classes?

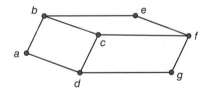

27. Recall the definition of even numbers.
   Definition. An integer n is even if $n = 2k$ for some integer k.
   Define a relation R on $\mathbf{Z}$ by $x \, R \, y$ if $x + y$ is even.

   (a) Show that R is an equivalence relation.

   (b) Describe the equivalence classes formed by this relation.

28. Lemma 2.1 states that the "$\equiv$ mod n" relation on $\mathbf{Z}$ is transitive. Show that it is also symmetric and reflexive.

29. Compute the following arithmetic problems in $\mathbf{Z}/8$. Represent your answer with the least positive representative of the appropriate equivalence class.

   (a) $[3] + [7]$

   (b) $[2] \cdot ([4] + [5])$

   (c) $([3] + [4]) \cdot ([5] + [6])$

30. For any $[x] \in \mathbf{Z}/n$ and any $k \in \mathbf{Z}$, we can define $k[x]$ by

$$k[x] = \underbrace{[x] + [x] + \cdots + [x]}_{k \text{ times}}$$

where the result is an element of $\mathbf{Z}/n$. We say $k[x]$ is a *multiple* of $[x]$.

(a) List all the multiples of $[3]$ in $\mathbf{Z}/9$.

(b) List all the multiples of $[3]$ in $\mathbf{Z}/8$.

31. Consider the function $p: \mathbf{Z} \longrightarrow \mathbf{Z}/n$ defined by $p(k) = [k]$. Prove that this function is onto but not one-to-one.

32. Construct the addition and multiplication tables for $\mathbf{Z}/4$.

33. Construct the multiplication table for $\mathbf{Z}/11$.

Exercises 34–40 deal with the method of using *check digits* in ISBN numbers. Prior to 2007, every commercially available book was given a 10-digit International Standard Book Number, usually printed on the back cover next to the barcode. The final character of this 10-digit string is a special digit used to check for errors in typing the ISBN number. If the first nine digits of an ISBN number are $a_1 a_2 a_3 a_4 a_5 a_6 a_7 a_8 a_9$, the tenth digit is given by the formula

$$a_{10} = (1a_1 + 2a_2 + 3a_3 + 4a_4 + 5a_5 + 6a_6 + 7a_7 + 8a_8 + 9a_9) \mod 11,$$

where $a_{10} = \mathrm{X}$ if this value is 10.

34. Calculate the tenth digit of the ISBN whose first nine digits are 039481500.

35. Suppose $a_1 a_2 a_3 a_4 a_5 a_6 a_7 a_8 a_9 a_{10}$ is a valid ISBN number. Show that

$$(1a_1 + 2a_2 + 3a_3 + 4a_4 + 5a_5 + 6a_6 + 7a_7 + 8a_8 + 9a_9 + 10a_{10}) \equiv 0 \mod 11.$$

36. Is 0060324814 a valid ISBN number?

*37. Show that the check digit will always detect the error of switching two adjacent digits. That is, show that $a_1 \cdots a_k a_{k+1} \cdots a_9$ and $a_1 \cdots a_{k+1} a_k \cdots a_9$ have different check digits.

*38. Show that the check digit will always detect the error of changing a single digit. Hint: The proof has something to do with the multiplication table for $\mathbf{Z}/11$ (Exercise 33).

*39. Unfortunately, there were too many books and not enough ISBN numbers; since January 2007, ISBN numbers have been 13 digits long. The check digit scheme for 13-digit ISBN numbers is different. Explain why the obvious modification to the old system won't work. That is, find a 12-digit string $a_1 a_2 \cdots a_{12}$ where the quantity

$$(1a_1 + 2a_2 + \cdots + 12a_{12}) \mod 14$$

doesn't change after changing a single digit.

*40. Will the "obvious modification" in Exercise 39 detect the error of switching two adjacent digits?

2.5 Partial Orderings

Most of the relationships modeled in the previous section express sameness; an equivalence relation is a mathematical way of describing how two objects are similar. However, there are many situations in which we would like to quantify how objects of a set are different from each other. The relations in this section will give us a mathematical way to analyze comparisons and rankings.

Preview 2.5

1. Construct a directed graph whose vertices represent the integers $1, 2, \ldots, 5$, where there is an edge from vertex n to vertex m iff $m - n$ is a positive even number. Compare the properties of this graph with the graph in preview question 2.4.3.

2. A *round robin* is a type of tournament in which each participant plays every other participant exactly once. In a sport without ties (e.g., tennis), will a round robin always produce a clear tournament champion? Justify your answer with an example.

3. Under what conditions will a round-robin tournament give a well-defined ranking of all tournament participants? Give two examples with at least four participants: one example where you can decide first, second, third, and fourth place, and another example where you cannot decide such a ranking.

2.5.1 Definition and Examples

In addition to equivalence relations, there is another type of relation that is worth studying as a special case. Compare the following with Definition 2.9.

Definition 2.10 A relation R on a set S is a *partial ordering* if it satisfies all three of the following properties.

1. *Reflexivity.* For any $a \in S$, $a R a$.

2. *Transitivity.* For any $a, b, c \in S$, if $a R b$ and $b R c$, then $a R c$.

3. *Antisymmetry.* For any $a, b \in S$, if $a R b$ and $b R a$, then $a = b$.

The reflexivity and transitivity properties are the same as in the definition of an equivalence relation, but the third property is new: it is called "antisymmetry" because it says that $a R b$ *never* happens when $b R a$, unless $a = b$.

Example 2.48 If S is a set of numbers, then $\leq$ defines a partial ordering on S.

Since Example 2.48 is a natural example of a relation that is reflexive, antisymmetric, and transitive, we will often use the symbol $\preceq$ to represent a generic partial ordering relation (instead of R). This notation has the advantage of allowing us to write $a \prec b$ when $a \preceq b$ and $a \neq b$.

Example 2.49 Let S be any set, and let $\mathcal{P}(S)$ be the power set of S. Then $\subseteq$ defines a partial ordering on $\mathcal{P}(S)$.

Proof Let $A \in \mathcal{P}(S)$. Then $A \subseteq A$, since $x \in A$ obviously implies that $x \in A$. So $\subseteq$ is reflexive.

Let $A, B, C \in \mathcal{P}(S)$, and suppose $A \subseteq B$ and $B \subseteq C$. Then for all $x \in S$, $x \in A \Rightarrow x \in B$ and $x \in B \Rightarrow x \in C$, so $x \in A \Rightarrow x \in C$. Thus $A \subseteq C$, so $\subseteq$ is transitive.

Finally, let $A, B \in \mathcal{P}(S)$, and suppose that $A \subseteq B$ and $B \subseteq A$. Then $x \in A \Leftrightarrow x \in B$, so $A = B$. Therefore, $\subseteq$ is antisymmetric. $\qquad\square$

Example 2.50 The "divides" relation $\mid$ defines a partial ordering on $\mathbf{N}$. The proof of this is an exercise.

If a set X has a partial ordering $\preceq$ on it, we say that $(X, \preceq)$ is a partially ordered set, or *poset*, for short. In a poset, it is possible to have elements a and b such that neither $a \preceq b$ nor $b \preceq a$. Such elements are called *incomparable*. In Example 2.50, 12 and 25 are incomparable because $12 \nmid 25$ and $25 \nmid 12$.

If a poset $(X, \preceq)$ has no incomparable elements, it is called a *total ordering*. For example, the real numbers $\mathbf{R}$ are totally ordered by the $\leq$ relation.

Activity 2.5.1: Partial Orders and Hasse Diagrams

If a relation R on a set S is called *antisymmetric* if $a R b$ and $b R a$ implies $a = b$, for all $a, b \in S$.
If a relation is reflexive, transitive, and antisymmetric, it is called a *partial order*.
Define a relation $\mid$ on $\mathbf{N}$ by $a \mid b$ if $b = ka$ for some $k \in \mathbf{N}$. (We read "$a \mid b$" as "a divides b.")

1. Complete the following proof that the divides relation $\mid$ is antisymmetric on $\mathbf{N}$.

   Let $a, b \in \mathbf{N}$ and suppose that _____ and _____. By the definition of "$\mid$", _____ for some $k_1 \in \mathbf{N}$ and _____ for some $k_2 \in \mathbf{N}$. Substituting the second equation into the first gives the equation _____, which simplifies to $k_1 k_2 = 1$. Since k_1 and k_2 are both natural numbers, they must both equal 1. Therefore, _____, as required.

2. For any set X, the $\subseteq$ relation is a partial order on the power set $\mathcal{P}(X)$. Partial orders can be illustrated by a *Hasse diagram*. For example, if $X = \{0, 1\}$, the Hasse diagram for the $\subseteq$ relation on $\mathcal{P}(X)$ is the following:

Fill in the missing entries in the Hasse diagram below for the $\subseteq$ relation on $\mathcal{P}(\{2,3,5\})$.

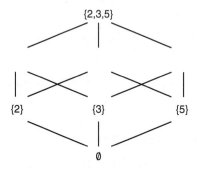

3. Draw the Hasse diagram for the divides relation | on the set $S = \{1, 2, 3, 5, 6, 10, 15, 30\}$. Show that it has the same shape as the Hasse diagram you drew in Question 2. Describe a natural one-to-one correspondence between $\mathcal{P}(\{2, 3, 5\})$ and S.

2.5.2   Hasse Diagrams

In the last section, we saw that the key fact about equivalence relations was that they break a set up into partitions. Partial orderings are important because they define a hierarchy among the elements of a set. We use *Hasse diagrams* to describe this hierarchy graphically.

Suppose $\preceq$ is a partial ordering on a set X. A Hasse diagram for $(X, \preceq)$ consists of a label, or *node*, for each element in the set, along with lines connecting related nodes. More specifically, if x, y are distinct elements of X with $x \preceq y$, and there are no elements z such that $x \prec z \prec y$, then there should be an upward sloping line from node x to node y in the Hasse diagram.

Example 2.51 Let $T = \{1, 2, 3\}$ and consider the poset $(\mathcal{P}(T), \subseteq)$. Since there are eight subsets of T, the Hasse diagram has eight nodes. See Figure 2.10. Note that by following the edges up the diagram, you move from one set to another set that contains it. And since $\subseteq$ is transitive, every set you encounter as you move up the diagram will contain the set where you started.

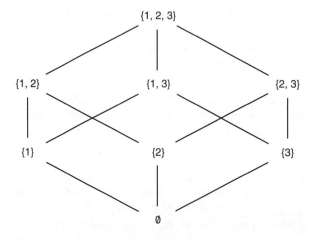

Figure 2.10 The Hasse diagram for $(\mathcal{P}(\{1, 2, 3\}), \subseteq)$.

Like binary search trees, Hasse diagrams are graphs with extra information encoded in the way the graph is drawn. Traditionally, Hasse diagrams don't have arrows, but the edges are, in fact, directed: in an edge between nodes x and y, x is drawn above y when $y \preceq x$.

Example 2.52 Let $X = \{2, 3, 4, 6, 8\}$, and say two elements $a, b \in X$ are related if $a \mid b$. Figure 2.11 shows the Hasse diagram for this poset. Compare this to the graph in Example 2.40, and notice that there are no edges in the Hasse diagram between related nodes that are connected by a sequence of edges. Here we don't need an edge between 2 and 8, since you can get there via node 4.

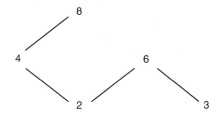

Figure 2.11 The Hasse diagram for $(X, |)$.

A partial order on a set gives you a way of comparing elements and ranking them. In this ranking system, there are often least elements and greatest elements. If $(X, \preceq)$ is a poset, we say that an element $m \in X$ is *minimal* if there is no $x \in X$ $(x \neq m)$ such that $x \preceq m$. Similarly, we say that an element $M \in X$ is *maximal* if there is no $x \in X$ $(x \neq M)$ such that $M \preceq x$. For example, in Figure 2.11, the minimal elements are 2 and 3 and the maximal elements are 6 and 8. In Figure 2.10, $\emptyset$ is minimal and $\{1, 2, 3\}$ is maximal.

2.5.3   Topological Sorting

Partial orderings are useful for describing the relationships among the parts of a complex process, such as manufacturing assembly or scheduling. Suppose that some process consists of a finite set, T, of tasks. Some tasks are dependent on others being done first. (For example, when you get dressed, you must put on your socks before putting on your shoes.) If $x, y \in T$ are two tasks, let $x \preceq y$ if x must be done before y. This is a partial ordering.

In most real-world applications, $(T, \preceq)$ won't be a totally ordered set. This is because some steps of the process do not depend on other steps being done first. (You can put your watch on at any time in the process of getting dressed.) However, if we want to create a schedule in which all of the tasks in T are done in some sequential order, we need to create a total ordering on T. (At some point, we just need to decide on an order to put our clothes on.) Furthermore, this total ordering must be compatible with the partial ordering. In other words, we need a total order relation $\preceq_t$ such that

$$x \preceq y \Rightarrow x \preceq_t y$$

for all $x, y \in T$. The technique of finding such a total ordering is known as *topological sorting*.

Performing a topological sort involves making an ordered list of all the tasks. Represent the partial ordering on T with a Hasse diagram. Then repeat the following steps until there are no more tasks.

- Choose a minimal element in your Hasse diagram. (Note that you can always find a minimal element, but there might be more than one.) Add this element to the end of the list you are making.

- Remove the element from your Hasse diagram.

Example 2.53 Julia is interested in completing a Computer Science minor and has several courses left to take. Some of the courses have prerequisite courses that must be taken first.

Courses Needed	Prerequisites
Calculus I	
Calculus II	Calculus I
Calculus III	Calculus II
Linear Algebra	Calculus II
Programming II	Calculus I
Software Development	Programming II
3D Computer Graphics	Calculus III, Linear Algebra, Programming II

In what order must Julia take these courses to ensure that she will satisfy the prerequisites for each course? Is this ordering unique? What is the minimum number of semesters it will take Julia to finish?

Solution: We start with a Hasse diagram for this poset.

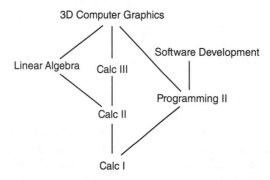

To perform a topological sort, we start by choosing a minimal element in the Hasse diagram. The only minimal element is Calculus I, so that must be Julia's first class. We then remove Calculus I from the diagram.

After Calculus I has been removed, there are two minimal elements: Calculus II and Programming II. Julia could take either of these next, so the ordering of courses is not unique. Let's choose Calculus II as the second course, and remove it from the diagram. This leaves Linear Algebra, Calculus III, and Programming II as minimal elements. Julia needs to take all three before she takes 3D Computer Graphics, and she needs to take Programming II before she takes software development. Again, the ordering is not unique. One allowable order for the remaining classes is Calculus III, Programming II, Software Development, Linear Algebra, and, finally, 3D Computer Graphics.

If we are trying to minimize the number of semesters, we repeat the process, except at each stage we choose *all* the minimal elements, so Julia takes as many courses as she is allowed to take each semester. This would yield the following schedule.

Semester	Courses
1	Calculus I
2	Calculus II, Programming II
3	Calculus III, Linear Algebra, Software Development
4	3D Computer Graphics

◇

Topological sorting is a pretty simple technique, once you have written the dependencies in the form of a Hasse diagram. This simplicity illustrates the power of a graphical approach to a discrete problem.

Activity 2.5.2: Topological Sorting

When making pizza, certain steps have to be done before others. The following chart lists several steps in the pizza-making process, along with prerequisite steps that must be done first.

Step	Prerequisite step(s)
Make the sauce	Mince the garlic
Make the crust	Proof the yeast
Bake pizza	Assemble pizza
Assemble pizza	Make the sauce, make the crust, prepare the toppings
Prepare the toppings	Brown the sausage, sauté the vegetables, grate the cheese
Sauté the vegetables	Cut the vegetables, mince the garlic

1. Draw a Hasse diagram representing this information. The nodes of the diagram should be steps in the pizza-making process. For each node, there should be an upward-sloping line to any step that is listed as a prerequisite in the chart.

2. List the pizza-making steps in the order they must be performed. Is there more than one way to order these steps?

3. The process of obtaining an ordered sequence from a partial order is called *topological sorting*. Write two or three careful sentences describing how to perform a topological sort, given a Hasse diagram for a partial order.

2.5.4   Isomorphisms

Sometimes two problems are so closely related that solving one gives a solution to the other. When two mathematical objects are fundamentally the same in every aspect of structure and function, we can define a map called an *isomorphism* to describe the similarity.

Example 2.54 Let $F \subseteq \mathbf{N}$ be the set of all factors of 30, and consider the poset $(F, |)$ given by the "divides" relation. As in Example 2.52, we can construct the Hasse diagram for this partially ordered set. See Figure 2.12.

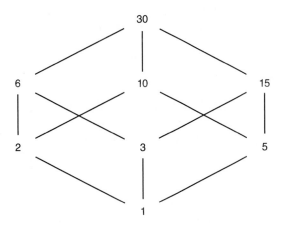

Figure 2.12 The Hasse diagram for $(F, |)$.

Notice how this Hasse diagram has the same structure as the Hasse diagram for $(\mathcal{P}(\{1, 2, 3\}), \subseteq)$ in Example 2.51. These two posets are the same in a very specific way.

Definition 2.11 Let $(X_1, \preceq_1)$ and $(X_2, \preceq_2)$ be partially ordered sets. Then $(X_1, \preceq_1)$ is *isomorphic* to $(X_2, \preceq_2)$ if there is a one-to-one correspondence $f : X_1 \longrightarrow X_2$ such that

$$a \preceq_1 b \iff f(a) \preceq_2 f(b)$$

for all $a, b \in X_1$. In this case, we say that f is an *isomorphism* and we write $(X_1, \preceq_1) \cong (X_2, \preceq_2)$ to denote that these posets are isomorphic.

The following table defines a one-to-one correspondence $f\colon \mathcal{P}(\{1,2,3\}) \longrightarrow F$ that describes the isomorphism between $(F, |)$ and $(\mathcal{P}(\{1,2,3\}), \subseteq)$.

X	$\emptyset$	$\{1\}$	$\{2\}$	$\{3\}$	$\{1,2\}$	$\{1,3\}$	$\{2,3\}$	$\{1,2,3\}$
$f(X)$	1	2	3	5	6	10	15	30

Since every element of F appears exactly once in this table, f is a one-to-one correspondence. To see that $X \subseteq Y$ if and only if $f(X) \mid f(Y)$ for all $X, Y \subseteq \{1,2,3\}$, it is sufficient to observe that the edges in the Hasse diagram for $(F, |)$ correspond exactly to the edges in the Hasse diagram for $(\mathcal{P}(\{1,2,3\}), \subseteq)$, and that this correspondence is given by f. This shows that $(F, |) \cong (\mathcal{P}(\{1,2,3\}), \subseteq)$.

At this point it is natural to wonder whether this isomorphism is a happy coincidence, or perhaps there is something deeper going on. Are the partial orders given by $\subseteq$ and $|$ related in some fundamental way? In the exercises, you will have the opportunity to check that the Hasse diagrams for these relations agree when applied to the factors of $210 = 2 \cdot 3 \cdot 5 \cdot 7$ and the set $\{1,2,3,4\}$. But will this always happen?

Let's take a closer look at the relationship between the posets $(F, |)$ and $(\mathcal{P}(\{1,2,3\}), \subseteq)$. Since $30 = 2 \cdot 3 \cdot 5$, every factor of 30 can be written (uniquely) as a product of the form

$$\begin{pmatrix} 2 \\ \text{or} \\ 1 \end{pmatrix} \begin{pmatrix} 3 \\ \text{or} \\ 1 \end{pmatrix} \begin{pmatrix} 5 \\ \text{or} \\ 1 \end{pmatrix}.$$

Choosing a factor $k \in F$ amounts to choosing whether or not to include each prime 2, 3, or 5 in this product. Similarly, choosing a subset X of the set $\{1,2,3\}$ amounts to choosing which of the three members $1,2,3$ to include in X. This explains why the above function f is a one-to-one correspondence. The number $3 \cdot 5$ corresponds to the subset $\{2,3\}$, for example.

Furthermore, under this one-to-one correspondence, the $|$ relation plays exactly the same role as the $\subseteq$ relation. Checking, for example, that $3 \cdot 5 \mid 2 \cdot 3 \cdot 5$ is the same as checking that all of the factors on the left are included on the right, while checking that $\{2,3\} \subseteq \{1,2,3\}$ involves checking that all of the elements on the left are included on the right. This explains why f is order-preserving.

The proof of the following theorem generalizes this observation.

Theorem 2.3 *Let $q = p_1 p_2 \cdots p_n$ be the product of the first n primes, and let $F \subseteq \mathbf{N}$ be the set of all factors of q. Then $(F, |) \cong (\mathcal{P}(\{1, 2, \cdots, n\}), \subseteq)$.*

Proof   Define a function $f\colon \mathcal{P}(\{1, 2, \ldots, n\}) \longrightarrow F$ by setting $f(X)$ to be the product of all the p_i's with $i \in X$. For example,

$$f(\{1,3\}) = p_1 p_3 = 2 \cdot 5 = 10.$$

Also, define $f(\emptyset) = 1$. In product notation,

$$f(X) = \prod_{i \in X} p_i$$

expresses the fact that $f(X)$ is the product of all the p_i's having $i \in X$. We claim that f is a one-to-one correspondence. □

Proof that f is a one-to-one correspondence   Let $k \in F$ be a factor of q. Since q is a product of distinct primes, any factor of q must be a product of these primes. Therefore, $k = \prod_{i \in X} p_i$ for some $X \in \mathcal{P}(\{1, 2, \ldots, n\})$. So f is onto.

To show that f is one-to-one, suppose that X and Y are subsets of $\{1, 2, \ldots, n\}$ with $f(X) = f(Y)$; that is,

$$\prod_{i \in X} p_i = \prod_{i \in Y} p_i.$$

Since the prime factorization of a number is unique, X and Y must have the same elements, so $X = Y$.   □

To show that f is an isomorphism, we also need to show that $X \subseteq Y$ if and only if $f(X) \mid f(Y)$. This property of isomorphisms is called "preserving" the partial ordering.

Proof that f is order-preserving Suppose that $X \subseteq Y$ for some $X, Y \subseteq \{1, 2, \ldots, n\}$. Then Y consists of two parts: those elements in X and those not in X. In symbols, $Y = X \cup (Y \setminus X)$ is a union of disjoint sets. Therefore,

$$\prod_{i \in Y} p_i = \left(\prod_{i \in X} p_i \right) \left(\prod_{i \in Y \setminus X} p_i \right)$$

$$= \left(\prod_{i \in X} p_i \right) \cdot k$$

where $k \in \mathbf{N}$. In other words, $f(Y) = k \cdot f(X)$, so $f(X) \mid f(Y)$.

Conversely, suppose $f(X) \mid f(Y)$ for some $X, Y \subseteq \{1, 2, \ldots, n\}$. Then

$$\prod_{i \in Y} p_i = k \left(\prod_{i \in X} p_i \right)$$

for some $k \in \mathbf{N}$. Since prime factorizations are unique, every p_i factor on the right side of this equation must also be on the left side. Therefore, $X \subseteq Y$. $\qquad\square$

The above theorem tells us that these posets will always be isomorphic, and the proof tells us *why* they are isomorphic. In short, choosing a factor of q amounts to choosing a list of prime numbers, and this choice corresponds to a choice of a subset of $\{1, 2, \ldots, n\}$. The whole proof is based on this observation.

2.5.5   Boolean Algebras ‡

The isomorphic posets described by the Hasse diagrams in Figures 2.11 and 2.12 are examples of a special kind of partially ordered set called a *Boolean algebra*. These mathematical structures highlight a beautiful connection between partial orders and propositional logic.

Let $(X, \preceq)$ be a poset. For any elements $a, b \in X$, define the *meet* of a and b (denoted $a \wedge b$) to be the greatest lower bound of a and b, if such a lower bound exists. Formally, $a \wedge b$ is an element of X with the following properties.

1. $a \wedge b \preceq a$ and $a \wedge b \preceq b$.

2. If some $x \in X$ satisfies $x \preceq a$ and $x \preceq b$, then $x \preceq a \wedge b$.

It follows from property 2 that if the meet of two elements exists, then it is unique. Similarly, we can define the *join* of $a, b \in X$ to be the element $a \vee b \in X$ satisfying

1. $a \preceq a \vee b$ and $b \preceq a \vee b$.

2. If some $x \in X$ satisfies $a \preceq x$ and $b \preceq x$, then $a \vee b \preceq x$.

if such an element exists.

Example 2.55 In Example 2.52, $4 \wedge 6 = 2$, $2 \vee 3 = 6$, but $4 \vee 6$ does not exist. In Example 2.51, $\{1\} \vee \{2, 3\} = \{1, 2, 3\}$ and $\{1\} \wedge \{2, 3\} = \emptyset$.

If every pair of elements $a, b \in X$ has both a meet and a join, then $(X, \preceq)$ is called a *lattice*. The notation for meet and join is the same as the notation for "and" and "or" in propositional logic, and this is no accident. In a lattice, meet and join satisfy the following properties, for all $a, b, c \in X$.

1. (Commutativity) $a \wedge b = b \wedge a$ and $a \vee b = b \vee a$.

2. (Associativity) $a \vee (b \vee c) = (a \vee b) \vee c$ and $a \wedge (b \wedge c) = (a \wedge b) \wedge c$.

3. (Absorption) $a \vee (a \wedge b) = a$ and $a \wedge (a \vee b) = a$.

If, in addition, a lattice has the following three properties, it is called a *Boolean algebra*.

4. (Distributivity) $a \vee (b \wedge c) = (a \vee b) \wedge (a \vee c)$ and $a \wedge (b \vee c) = (a \wedge b) \vee (a \wedge c)$.

5. (Boundedness) There exist elements $\mathbf{0}, \mathbf{1} \in X$ such that $x \preceq \mathbf{1}$ and $\mathbf{0} \preceq x$ for all $x \in X$.

6. (Complements) For any $x \in X$ there exists an element $\neg x \in X$ such that $x \wedge \neg x = \mathbf{0}$ and $x \vee \neg x = \mathbf{1}$.

From our study of set theory, we know that the poset $(\mathcal{P}(\{1, 2, \ldots, n\}), \subseteq)$ satisfies all the properties of a Boolean algebra. The correspondence is suggested by the set notation: meet is $\cap$, join is $\cup$, $\mathbf{0}$ is $\emptyset$, $\mathbf{1}$ is $\{1, 2, \ldots, n\}$, and $\neg$ is the set complement. The next theorem states that this is the only finite Boolean algebra, up to isomorphism.

Theorem 2.4 *Let X be a finite set. Suppose that the poset $(X, \preceq)$ is a Boolean algebra. Then $|X| = 2^n$ for some $n \in \mathbf{N}$, and*

$$(X, \preceq) \cong (\mathcal{P}(\{1, 2, \ldots, n\}), \subseteq).$$

The proof of this theorem is beyond the scope of this book, as are the theories of lattices and Boolean algebras. But the above definitions are still worth knowing, because they illustrate the rich connections between set theory, propositional logic, and partial orders.

Exercises 2.5

1. Refer to Definition 1.10. Show that the divisibility relation | makes the set **N** of natural numbers a partially ordered set.

2. Explain why the divisibility relation | does not define a partial ordering on the set **Z** of integers.

3. Consider the poset $(\mathbf{N}, |)$. Are there any minimal elements? Are there any maximal elements? Explain.

4. Let $A = \{a, b, c, \ldots, z\}$. In the poset $(\mathcal{P}(A), \subseteq)$, find a pair of incomparable elements.

5. Let W be the set of all web pages. For $x, y \in W$, let $x \, R \, y$ if you can navigate from x to y by following links. (Let's say it is always possible to "navigate" from a page to itself; just do nothing.) Explain why R is not a partial ordering.

6. Let a relation R be defined on the set of real numbers as follows:

$$x \, R \, y \quad \Leftrightarrow \quad 2x + y = 3$$

   Prove that this relation is antisymmetric.

7. Explain why the relation R on $\{0, 1, 2, 3\}$ given by

$$R = \{(0, 0), (1, 1), (2, 2), (3, 3), (0, 1), (1, 2), (2, 3), (0, 2), (1, 3)\}$$

   is **not** a partial ordering on $\{0, 1, 2, 3\}$. Be specific.

8. Explain why the relation R on $\{0, 1, 2, 3\}$ given by

$$R = \{(0, 0), (1, 1), (2, 2), (3, 3), (0, 1), (1, 2), (0, 2), (2, 1)\}$$

   is **not** a partial ordering on $\{0, 1, 2, 3\}$. Be specific.

9. The Hasse diagram below defines a partial ordering on the set $\{0, 1, 2, 3\}$. Give the set of ordered pairs corresponding to this relation.

10. The Hasse diagram below defines a partial ordering on the set $\{0, 1, 2, 3\}$. Give the set of ordered pairs corresponding to this relation.

11. The divides relation "|" defines a partial ordering on the set $\{1, 2, 3, 6, 8, 10\}$. Draw the Hasse diagram for this poset. What are the maximal elements?

12. Let $S = \{1, 2, 3, 5, 10, 15, 20\}$. It is a fact that $(S, |)$ is a poset. Draw its Hasse diagram.

13. Let X be a set of different nonzero monetary values (in U.S. or Canadian cents). In other words, $X \subseteq \mathbf{N}$. Define a relation $\models$ on X as follows. For $a, b \in X$, $a \models b$ if b can be obtained from a by adding a (possibly empty) collection of dimes (10 cents) and quarters (25 cents). So, for example, $25 \models 35$, but $25 \not\models 30$. Prove that $\models$ is a partial ordering on X.

14. Let $X = \{5, 10, 15, 20, 25, 30, 35, 40\}$, and let $\models$ be as in Problem 13.

    (a) Draw the Hasse diagram for the poset $(X, \models)$.

    (b) List all minimal elements of $(X, \models)$.

    (c) Give a pair of incomparable elements in $(X, \models)$.

15. Let X be the following set (of sets of letters).

$$X = \{\{b\}, \{b, e\}, \{b, r\}, \{b, e, r\}, \{a, r\}, \{b, a, r\}, \{b, e, a, r, s\}\}$$

Then X is a partially ordered set under the $\subseteq$ relation.

    (a) Draw the Hasse diagram for this partial ordering.

    (b) Name all minimal elements, if any exist.

    (c) Name a pair of incomparable elements, if any exist.

16. Let $A = \{a, b, c\}$. Use Hasse diagrams to describe all partial orderings on A for which a is a minimal element. (There are 10.)

17. Suppose you want to write a program that will collect information on a customer's tastes and customize web content accordingly. By monitoring online shopping habits, you are able to collect a set of pairwise preferences on a set X of products. If $x, y \in X$ are two different products, we say that $x \preceq y$ if the customer prefers y over x. (In order to satisfy the reflexive property, we stipulate that $x \preceq x$ for all $x \in X$.) Suppose you know the following things about your customer.

Customer prefers:	Over:
lettuce	broccoli
cabbage	broccoli
tomatoes	cabbage
carrots	cabbage
carrots	lettuce
asparagus	lettuce
mushrooms	tomatoes
corn	tomatoes
corn	carrots
eggplant	carrots
eggplant	asparagus
onions	mushrooms
onions	corn

In order for $(X, \preceq)$ to be a poset, we must also assume that the customer's preferences are transitive.

    (a) Draw the Hasse diagram for $(X, \preceq)$.

    (b) What is/are the customer's favorite vegetable(s)? (I.e., what are the maximal element(s)?) What is/are the least favorite?

    (c) Use topological sorting to rank order these vegetables according to the customer's preferences. Is the ranking unique?

18. A *partition* of a positive integer n is a list of positive integers $a_1, a_2, \ldots, a_k$ such that $a_1 + a_2 + \cdots + a_k = n$. For example, the following are distinct partitions of 5.

$$5 \quad 1,1,1,2 \quad 1,2,2 \quad 1,1,1,1,1$$

The order of the list doesn't matter; $1, 2, 2$ is the same partition as $2, 1, 2$. There is a natural partial ordering on the set of partitions of n: if P_1 and P_2 are partitions, define $P_1 \preceq P_2$ if P_1 can be obtained by combining parts of P_2. For example, $1, 2, 2 \preceq 1, 1, 1, 1, 1$ because $1, 2, 2 = 1, 1 + 1, 1 + 1$. On the other hand, $2, 3$ and $1, 4$ are incomparable elements in this poset.

(a) Write the partitions of 6 in a Hasse diagram. (There are 11 partitions of 6.)

(b) Is this a total ordering? Why or why not?

19. Let $X = \{1, 2, 3, 4\}$. Draw the Hasse diagram for the poset $(\mathcal{P}(X), \subseteq)$.

20. Let $F \subseteq \mathbf{N}$ be the set of all factors of 210. Draw the Hasse diagrams for $(F, |)$ and $(\mathcal{P}(\{1, 2, 3, 4\}), \subseteq)$ in a way that shows these two posets are isomorphic.

21. Let $A \subseteq \mathbf{N}$ be the set of all factors of 12, and let $B \subseteq \mathbf{N}$ be the set of all factors of n. Find a natural number $n \neq 12$ so that $(A, |) \cong (B, |)$. Give a table of values for the one-to-one correspondence that describes the isomorphism.

22. Let B be the set of all four-digit binary strings; that is,

$$B = \{0000, 0001, 0010, 0011, \ldots, 1110, 1111\}.$$

Define a relation $\lhd$ on B as follows: Let $x, y \in B$, where $x = x_1 x_2 x_3 x_4$ and $y = y_1 y_2 y_3 y_4$. We say that $x \lhd y$ if $x_i \leq y_i$ for $i = 1, 2, 3, 4$. In other words, $x \lhd y$ if y has a 1 in every position where x does. So, for example, $0101 \lhd 0111$ and $0000 \lhd 0011$, but $1010 \ntriangleleft 0111$. The relation $\lhd$ is called the *bitwise* $\leq$. Show that $(B, \lhd)$ is a poset.

23. Prove that $(B, \lhd) \cong (\mathcal{P}(\{1, 2, 3, 4\}), \subseteq)$.

24. In $(B, \lhd)$, give a counterexample to show that

$$0000, 0001, 0010, 0011, 0100, 0101, 0110, 0111, 1001, 1000, 1010, 0011, 1100, 1101, 1110, 1111$$

is not a valid topological sort of the elements of B.

25. Perform a topological sort on the elements of B.

26. Let $F \subseteq \mathbf{N}$ be the set of all factors of 210. In the poset $(F, |)$, find the following.

(a) $30 \wedge 21$, the meet of 30 and 21.

(b) $35 \vee 15$, join of 35 and 15.

(c) $2 \wedge 7$.

(d) $2 \vee 7$.

(e) $\neg 30$, the complement of 30.

27. Let $W = \{a, b, c, d, e, f, g, h, i, j, k, l\}$. Define a partial order on W by the following Hasse diagram.

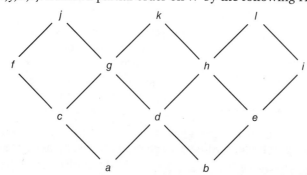

(a) Find two elements of W whose meet exists but whose join does not exist.

(b) Find two elements of W whose join exists but whose meet does not exist.

(c) Find two elements of W whose meet and join both do not exist.

28. Let $m, n \in \mathbf{Z}$ and suppose $m \leq n$. In the poset $(\mathbf{Z}, \leq)$, what are $m \wedge n$ and $m \vee n$?

29. Let T be the set of all two-digit ternary strings; that is,

$$T = \{00, 01, 02, 10, 11, 12, 20, 21, 22\}.$$

   Consider the poset $(T, \lhd)$, where $\lhd$ is the bitwise $\leq$. Let $F \subseteq \mathbf{N}$ be the set of all factors of 36. Draw Hasse diagrams to show that $(T, \lhd) \cong (F, |)$.

30. Consider the poset $(T, \lhd)$ of the previous problem. This poset is, in fact, a lattice.

    (a) Theorem 2.4 can be used to show that $(T, \lhd)$ is not a Boolean algebra. How?

    (b) Find an element of $(T, \lhd)$ that has no complement. Explain why.

31. Let P be a set of posets. Prove that $\cong$ is an equivalence relation on P.

2.6   Graph Theory

We began this chapter with an informal introduction to graphs, and we have seen several ways to model mathematical relationships with them. We have also studied how sets, functions, and relations express these ideas in formal mathematical language. Now that we have developed this new machinery, we can revisit graphs from a more rigorous perspective. In this section we explore how to prove theorems about graphs. Some of the topics in this section—in particular, some of the proofs—will be quite challenging, because the viewpoint here will be more theoretical than in preceding sections. Fasten your seat belts.

Preview 2.6

---

1. Preview questions 2.3.1–2 asked you to invent shorthand notation that encoded all the information necessary to recreate certain types of graphs. Repeat this task for a general undirected graph. That is, invent a way of describing an undirected graph using symbols and instructions so that someone could recreate a picture of the graph using your symbols and instructions. Be as concise as possible.

2. Is it possible to create an undirected graph with three vertices such that each vertex has odd degree? Give an example, or explain why it isn't possible.

3. Give three examples of connected graphs having 8 vertices and 7 edges. What do your graphs have in common? Formulate a conjecture.

4. Verify that each of the following graphs can be colored using two colors. What other properties do these graphs share? Make a conjecture about two-colorable graphs.

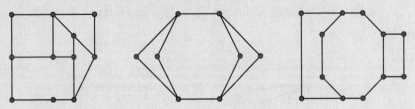

2.6.1   Graphs: Formal Definitions

In Section 2.1, we gave an informal description of a graph in terms of dots and lines. In preview question 2.6.1, you thought about ways to represent graphs formally, using symbols. Now that we have discussed sets and functions, we can give a mathematical definition. Warning: Giving a definition of a graph is tricky; choices need to be made, and other books might make different choices.

Definition 2.12 A *directed graph* G is a finite set of vertices V_G and a finite set of edges E_G, along with a function $i: E_G \longrightarrow V_G \times V_G$. For any edge $e \in E_G$, if $i(e) = (a, b)$, we say that edge e *joins* vertex a to vertex b.

Note that this definition allows for loops (when $a = b$) and multiple edges (when $i(e_1) = i(e_2)$ for $e_1 \neq e_2$).[4] The definition of an undirected graph differs only in the way the word "join" is defined.

Definition 2.13 An *undirected graph* G is a finite set of vertices V_G and a finite set of edges E_G, along with a function $i\colon E_G \longrightarrow V_G \times V_G$. For any edge $e \in E_G$, if $i(e) = (a, b)$, we say that vertices a and b are *joined* by edge e, or equivalently, *e joins a to b* and *e joins b to a*. (Here it is possible that $a = b$; if $i(e) = (a, a)$, then e is a loop *joining* a to itself.)

These definitions have the advantage of treating both directed and undirected graphs with the same notation. However, a disadvantage to this choice of definitions is that any undirected edge can be represented formally in two different ways. If the undirected edge e joins vertex a to vertex b, then we could define $i(e) = (a, b)$, or we could define $i(e) = (b, a)$.

While these definitions are mathematically rigorous, they can be hard to conceptualize. It is still important to think of a graph as a picture: each vertex corresponds to a dot, and each edge corresponds to an arrow (for directed graphs) or a line (for undirected graphs).

2.6.2   Isomorphisms of Graphs

What really matters about a graph is the relationship it describes among its vertices. You can draw a given graph any way you choose, as long as you connect the vertices correctly. Two graphs that share the same fundamental structure are called *isomorphic*. The precise definition is similar to the definition of isomorphic posets. Note that, since Definitions 2.12 and 2.13 both stipulate the meaning of the word "join," the following definition can apply to directed and undirected graphs simultaneously.

Definition 2.14 Let G be a graph with vertex set V_G and edge set E_G, and let H be a graph with vertex set V_H and edge set E_H. Then G is *isomorphic* to H if there are one-to-one correspondences

$$\alpha : V_G \longrightarrow V_H \quad \text{and} \quad \beta : E_G \longrightarrow E_H$$

such that, for any edge $e \in E_G$,

$$e \text{ joins vertex } v \text{ to vertex } w \quad \Leftrightarrow \quad \beta(e) \text{ joins vertex } \alpha(v) \text{ to vertex } \alpha(w).$$

In this case, we write $G \cong H$.

For example, the graphs in Figure 2.13 are isomorphic. The one-to-one correspondence of vertices is given by $\alpha(x_i) = y_i$, and the correspondence of edges is given by $\beta(a_i) = b_i$. By inspecting the graphs, it is evident that the criterion

$$a_i \text{ joins vertex } x_j \text{ to vertex } x_k \quad \Leftrightarrow \quad b_i \text{ joins vertex } y_j \text{ to vertex } y_k$$

holds for all i, j, and k.

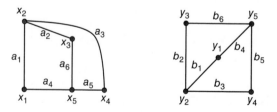

Figure 2.13 Two isomorphic graphs.

Definition 2.14 is quite complicated, but it applies to any graph. For graphs without multiple edges, the following theorem gives a simpler condition to check.

---

4. Some authors call this a "multigraph."

Theorem 2.5 *Let G and H be graphs without multiple edges, with vertex sets V_G and V_H, respectively. For vertices x and y, write $x R y$ if an edge joins x to y. If there is a one-to-one correspondence $f: V_G \longrightarrow V_H$ with the property that*

$$x R y \Leftrightarrow f(x) R f(y)$$

for all $x, y \in V_G$, then $G \cong H$.

Proof   We need to check that all the conditions of Definition 2.14 are satisfied. Let α be the given one-to-one correspondence $f: V_G \longrightarrow V_H$. We define $\beta: E_G \longrightarrow E_H$ as follows. Given an edge $e \in E_G$, let x and y be the vertices that e joins, so $x R y$. Define $\beta(e) \in E_H$ to be the edge between $f(x)$ and $f(y)$. We know there is an edge joining $f(x)$ to $f(y)$ because $x R y \Rightarrow f(x) R f(y)$. Since H has no multiple edges, there is only one such edge. So β is well defined.

To show that β is onto, let $a \in E_H$ be an edge of H, and let v and w be the vertices that a joins. Then there exist $p, q \in V_G$ such that $f(p) = v$ and $f(q) = w$, since f is onto. Furthermore, there is an edge joining p to q, since $f(p) R f(q)$. So this edge in E_G maps to a via β.

To show that β is one-to-one, suppose $e_1, e_2 \in E_G$ with $\beta(e_1) = \beta(e_2)$. Let x_1, y_1 and x_2, y_2 be the vertices joined by e_1 and e_2, respectively. Then $\beta(e_1)$ joins $f(x_1)$ to $f(y_1)$, and it also joins $f(x_2)$ to $f(y_2)$. Therefore, $f(x_1) = f(x_2)$ and $f(y_1) = f(y_2)$, so $x_1 = x_2$ and $y_1 = y_2$, since f is one-to-one. Since G has no multiple edges, $e_1 = e_2$.

We have shown that β is a one-to-one correspondence. By the way we defined β,

$$e \text{ joins vertex } v \text{ to vertex } w \quad \Leftrightarrow \quad \beta(e) \text{ joins vertex } \alpha(v) \text{ to vertex } \alpha(w).$$

so $G \cong H$.   □

It is usually tricky to prove that two graphs are isomorphic, but it is less tricky to use Theorem 2.5 than Definition 2.14. To check that the two graphs in Figure 2.13 are isomorphic using the theorem, we need only to define a function f on vertices by $f(x_i) = y_i$. Since each pair of vertices defines at most one edge, there is no need for a separate function on edges. Of course, we must also check that f is a one-to-one correspondence, and that an edge joins x_i to x_j whenever an edge joins y_i to y_j.

It follows immediately from the definition that isomorphic graphs must have the same number of vertices and the same number of edges. It is also true, but harder to show, that corresponding vertices of isomorphic graphs must have the same degree. This is left as Exercise 1.

In fact, an isomorphism between two graphs guarantees that the graphs share any property having to do with the structure of the graph. For example, if $G \cong H$, and G has an Euler circuit, then so does H. If G is planar, so is H. The only differences between isomorphic graphs lie in the way they are labeled and drawn.

2.6.3   Degree Counting

In Section 2.1, we stated several observations of Euler, which we now make precise with modern statements and proofs. The first theorem describes a useful condition on the degrees of the vertices in any graph. First we must be precise about the meaning of "degree."

Definition 2.15 Let G be an undirected graph, and let $x \in V_G$ be a vertex. Let D_1 be the set of all edges $e \in E_G$ such that $i(e) = (x, b)$ for some b, and let D_2 be the set of all edges $e \in E_G$ such that $i(e) = (a, x)$ for some a. Then the *degree* of x is $|D_1| + |D_2|$.

In other words, in an undirected graph, the degree of a vertex is the number of edges that join to it, where loops are counted twice. It is left as an exercise to write down similar definitions for the *indegree* and *outdegree* of a vertex in a directed graph.

Theorem 2.6 *(Euler) Let G be an undirected graph. The sum of the degrees of the vertices of G equals twice the number of edges in G.*

Proof   Since each edge joins two vertices (or possibly a single vertex to itself), each edge contributes 2 to the sum of the degrees of the vertices.   □

This simple theorem is surprisingly useful. In the discussion of the Königsberg bridges, it tells us that it is impossible to have exactly one island with an odd number of bridges to it: if one vertex had odd degree and the rest even, the sum of the degrees would be odd, contradicting the theorem. By the same reasoning, the number of odd-degree vertices must be even.

Example 2.56 There are 11 teams in a broomball league. The league organizer decides that each team will play five games against different opponents. Explain why this idea won't work.

Solution: The situation can be modeled by a graph. The 11 teams are the vertices, and the edges join pairs of teams that will play each other. Since the organizer wants each team to play five games, the degree of each vertex is 5. This means that the sum of the degrees of the vertices is 55, contradicting Theorem 2.6.   ◇

One thing to notice about this problem is that we were able to model and solve this problem using graphs, but we never had to actually try to draw the graph. Theorems (like 2.6) that tell you when you *can't* do something can save you a lot of work.

2.6.4   Euler Paths and Circuits

Recall the definitions of paths and circuits.

Definition 2.16 Let G be a graph. A *path* in G is a sequence

$$v_0, e_1, v_1, e_2, v_2, \ldots, v_{n-1}, e_n, v_n$$

of vertices v_i and edges e_i such that edge e_i joins vertex v_{i-1} to vertex v_i, where $n \geq 1$. A *circuit* is a path with $v_0 = v_n$. A path or a circuit is called *simple* if $e_1, e_2, \ldots, e_n$ are all distinct. Recall that a graph is *connected* if there is a path connecting any two vertices.

An Euler path (resp. Euler circuit) in an undirected graph G is a simple path (resp. simple circuit) using all the edges of G. Euler's theorems on these constructions are interesting because they describe local conditions (the degrees of vertices) that completely determine the existence of a global object (an Euler path or circuit). Such theorems should surprise us; they are amazing in the same way that taking the temperature of the area under our tongue can tell us that our immune system is fighting off a virus. Euler managed to discover the perfect "symptom" to test.

Theorem 2.7 *If all the vertices of a connected, undirected graph G have even degree, then G has an Euler circuit.*

Proof   Choose any vertex v of G. Follow a sequence of contiguous edges and vertices, starting with v, without repeating any edges. Since every vertex has even degree, this sequence will never get stuck at any vertex $w \neq v$, because any edge we follow in to w will have another edge to follow out from w. Since there are a finite number of edges, this sequence must end, so it must produce a circuit ending at v. Call this circuit C_1.

If C_1 contains all the edges of G, we are done. If not, remove the edges of C_1 from G. The resulting graph G' will still have all vertices of even degree, because every edge in C_1 going in to a vertex had a matching edge going out. Now repeat the construction of the previous paragraph, choosing a vertex v' of positive degree in G', to get another circuit C_2. Continue repeating this construction, producing circuits $C_3, C_4, \ldots, C_k$, until all the edges have been used.

By construction, every edge of G appears exactly once in the list of circuits $C_1, C_2, \ldots, C_k$. Since G is connected, every circuit C_i must share a vertex with some other circuit C_j. We can therefore combine any such pair C_i, C_j of circuits into a new circuit by starting at this common vertex, following circuit C_i, and then following C_j. This combining process reduces the number of circuits on our list by one. Continue until one circuit remains. By construction, this remaining circuit is an Euler circuit.   □

The preceding is an example of a *constructive* proof; it describes how to construct the hypothesized object. As such, this proof has added value because it gives us a way to tell a computer how to produce an Euler circuit. The kind of exact language required to write a proof is similar to the kind of instructions you need to give to a computer to get it to do what you want.

The converse of Theorem 2.7 is also true, and easier to prove.

Theorem 2.8 *If a graph G has an Euler circuit, then all the vertices of G have even degree.*

Proof   Let v be a vertex in G. If the degree of v is zero, there is nothing to prove. If the degree of v is nonzero, then some edges on the Euler circuit touch it, and since the Euler circuit contains all of G's edges, the number of touches by these edges equals the degree of v. If we traverse the circuit, starting and ending at v, we must leave v the same number of times as we return to v. Therefore, the number of touches by an edge in the Euler circuit is even.   □

Euler's observations about paths have related proofs. These are left as exercises.

Activity 2.6.1: Two-colorable Graphs

An undirected graph is *two-colorable* if there is an assignment of two colors to the vertices of the graph so that no two vertices of the same color share an edge. In this activity we will prove that a graph is two-colorable if and only if every circuit in the graph has even length.

1. Suppose that G is a two-colorable graph, and that $v_0, e_1, v_1, e_2, v_2, \ldots, v_{n-1}, e_n, v_n$ is a circuit of length n in G, where $v_n = v_0$. Explain why n must be even.

2. Conversely, suppose that every circuit in a graph G has even length. Prove that G is two-colorable, using the following argument.

   (a) Without loss of generality, suppose G is connected. Pick any vertex $v_0 \in V_G$. Define a function $d : V_G \longrightarrow \mathbf{Z}$ by setting $d(v)$ to be the length of the shortest path from v_0 to v, where $d(v_0) = 0$. Illustrate this construction using one of the graphs from preview question 2.6.4.

   (b) Assign the color red to the vertices in the set $R = \{v \in V_G \mid d(v)$ is even$\}$, and assign the color blue to the vertices in the set $B = \{v \in V_G \mid d(v)$ is odd$\}$. Prove that this assignment is a valid two-coloring of G. (Hint: Show that if two vertices of the same color were to share an edge, then there would be a circuit of odd length.)

2.6.5 Hamilton Paths and Circuits

Euler's theorems tell us just about all there is to know about the existence of paths and circuits that visit every edge of a graph exactly once. So it is natural to ask the same questions about paths and circuits that visit every *vertex* of a graph exactly once. These constructions are named in honor of the 19th-century Irish mathematician William Rowan Hamilton.

Definition 2.17 A *Hamilton path* in a graph G is a path

$$v_0, e_1, v_1, e_2, \ldots, e_n, v_n$$

such that $v_0, v_1, \ldots, v_n$ is a duplicate-free list of all the vertices in G. A *Hamilton circuit* is a circuit of the form $v_0, e_1, v_1, e_2, \ldots, e_n, v_n, e_{n+1}, v_0$, where $v_0, e_1, v_1, e_2, \ldots, e_n, v_n$ is a Hamilton path.

Although it is easy to tell whether a given graph has an Euler circuit, it is actually quite difficult, in general, to determine whether a graph has a Hamilton circuit. For graphs without too many vertices, it usually isn't hard to find a Hamilton circuit when it is possible to do so. However, for graphs that don't have Hamilton circuits, it is often very tricky to prove that this is the case. The next two examples illustrate this phenomenon.

Example 2.57 Find a Hamilton circuit in the following graph.

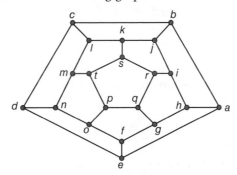

Solution: One possible Hamilton circuit can be found as follows. (Try this with a piece of tracing paper.) Starting at vertex a, travel counterclockwise around the outer ring. Notice that you can't go back to a until you have visited all the vertices, so you will need to change direction when you get to e. Go from e to f, and then go around clockwise from there, but you must change direction again at i in order to leave room to get back to a. Then it is easy to see how to finish. The sequence of vertices

$$a, b, c, d, e, f, o, n, m, l, k, j, i, r, s, t, p, q, g, h, a$$

forms a Hamilton circuit. $\diamond$

Example 2.58 Prove that the following graph has no Hamilton circuit.

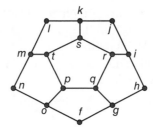

Proof Notice that this graph has five vertices of degree 2: f, h, j, l, n. Any Hamilton circuit must pass through these vertices, so it must include the edges that touch these vertices. But this makes it impossible to leave the outer ring: we can't add edges to those forced by the vertices f, h, j, l, n because that would involve including three edges at some vertex, which can't happen in a Hamilton circuit: if a single vertex touches three edges in a path, the vertex must occur twice in that path.   □

The previous two arguments are *ad hoc*; they don't generalize well to other examples the way Euler's theorems do. There are existence theorems about Hamilton circuits, but they are quite difficult to prove, and they don't give a complete characterization of graphs containing Hamilton circuits. In fact, the problem of finding a Hamilton circuit in a graph belongs to a famous class of problems called *NP-complete*. Roughly speaking, these are problems that are difficult to solve, but whose solutions are easy to check.[5] It may not be clear whether a given graph has a Hamilton circuit, but it is really easy to check the answer of a student who claims to have found one.

Euler and Hamilton circuits raise interesting mathematical questions, but they also have several important applications. For example, consider a graph model of a network of roads (edges) connecting various points of interest (vertices). A street cleaner would be interested in an Euler circuit, because it would provide a way to go down every street without having to retrace any steps. On the other hand, a salesperson wanting an efficient route through each point of interest might find a Hamilton circuit more useful.

2.6.6   Trees

In Section 2.1, we saw how to organize data using a binary search tree. In future chapters, we will see several other uses for trees of various types. We wrap up our look at the mathematical theory of graphs with some theorems about trees in general.

Definition 2.18 A *tree* is a graph T with a specified vertex r, called the *root*, with the property that, for any vertex v in T ($v \neq r$), there is a unique simple path from r to v.

This definition works for directed or undirected graphs. Usually we draw trees as undirected graphs, but we often draw the tree with the root at the top and an implicit downward direction on all the edges. The next theorem gives an alternate characterization of a tree.

Theorem 2.9 *Let G be an undirected graph, and let $r \in G$. Then G is a tree with root r if and only if G is connected and has no simple circuits.*

Proof ($\Rightarrow$) Suppose that G is an undirected tree with root r. Let a, b be two vertices in G. By Definition 2.18, there are paths from r to a and r to b. Therefore, there is a path from a to b via r, so G is connected.

Suppose, to the contrary, that

$$v_0, e_1, v_1, e_2, \ldots, v_{k-1}, e_k, v_0$$

---

5. We will say more about NP-completeness in Chapter 5.

is a simple circuit in G. We can relabel this circuit, if necessary, so that $v_0 \neq r$. If $r = v_i$ for some i, then

$$v_0, e_1, \ldots, r \quad \text{and} \quad r, e_{i+1}, \ldots, e_k, v_0$$

are two different simple paths from v_0 to r, contradicting the definition of a tree. If $r \neq v_i$ for any i, then there is a simple path from r to v_0, and combining this path with the sequence

$$e_1, v_1, e_2, \ldots, v_{k-1}, e_k, v_0$$

yields another simple path from r to v_0, a contradiction.

($\Leftarrow$) Now suppose that G is a connected undirected graph with no simple circuits. Let $v \neq r$ be a vertex in G. Since G is connected, there is a path from r to v. If this path does not repeat any vertices, then it does not repeat any edges, so it is simple. If this path has the form

$$r, e_1, \ldots, e_i, a, e_{i+1}, \ldots, e_k, a, e_{k+1}, \ldots, e_n, v$$

for some vertex a, then we can replace it with a shorter path

$$r, e_1, \ldots, e_i, a, e_{k+1}, \ldots, e_n, v$$

that still goes from r to v. Furthermore, we can repeat this shortening procedure until there are no repeated vertices. So there is a simple path from r to v. To show that G is a tree with root r, we need to show that this path is unique. But if there were two distinct simple paths

$$r, e_1, v_1, \ldots, v_{n-1}, e_n, v \quad \text{and} \quad r, d_1, w_1, \ldots, w_{m-1}, d_m, v$$

from r to v, we could combine them to form a circuit

$$r, e_1, v_1, \ldots, v_{n-1}, e_n, v, d_m, w_{m-1}, \ldots, w_1, d_1, r$$

in G. While this circuit may not be simple, it must contain a simple circuit, since there is at least one d_i that differs from all the e_j's. (This detail is left as Exercise 26.) This contradicts that G has no simple circuits. $\square$

An important consequence of Theorem 2.9 is that you can choose any vertex to be the root of an undirected tree. Figure 2.14 shows the same undirected tree drawn three different ways: first (a) without a root, then (b) with root r_1, and finally (c) with root r_2. Imagine that the graph is made of beads and string. In graph (a), pick up the bead that you want to be the root (r_1 or r_2), and let the rest of the beads hang down to get graphs (b) or (c). This process is intuitively obvious, but the previous proof gives us a solid mathematical justification: if a graph G is connected and has no simple circuits, it is a tree with root r, for any vertex r in G. And any undirected tree is a connected graph with no simple circuits, so any vertex can be the root. A corollary follows from this observation.

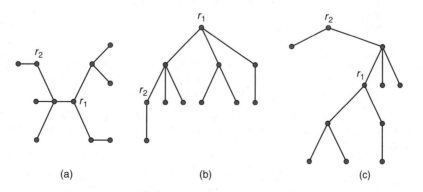

Figure 2.14 You can choose the root in an undirected tree.

Corollary 2.1 In an undirected tree, there is a unique simple path between any two vertices in the tree.

Proof Let a, b be two vertices in an undirected tree T. Then T can be viewed as a tree with root a, so by Definition 2.18 there is a unique simple path from a to b.   □

The characterization of trees in Definition 2.18 implies quite a lot about the structure of these graphs. Let v be a nonroot vertex of a tree T. Since there is a unique simple path from the root r of T to v, there is a well-defined natural number $d(v)$ that equals the number of edges in this path. Call the number $d(v)$ the *depth* of the vertex v. By convention, $d(r) = 0$. The *height* of the tree T is the maximum value of $d(v)$ over all the vertices v in T. For example, the tree in Figure 2.14(c) has height 4, and $d(r_1) = 2$ in this tree. Of course, the depth function and the height of a tree depend on the choice of root; the tree in Figure 2.14(b) has height 3.

Another implication of the definition is that we can make an undirected tree into a directed tree in a well-defined way, by choosing a direction on each edge away from the root. More precisely, start at the root, and direct each edge outward. These edges will end in vertices of depth 1, and all the vertices of depth 1 will now have directed edges to them. Repeat this process, forming directed edges to all the vertices of depth 2, then 3, etc., until all the vertices (and hence all the edges) have been covered. Thus, every edge will point from a vertex of depth i to a vertex of depth $i + 1$. This construction explains why it isn't really necessary to draw the directions on the edges of a tree, as long as we designate a root. It also helps us prove the following fact.

Theorem 2.10 *Let T be a tree with n vertices. Then T has $n - 1$ edges.*

Proof Suppose T is a tree with n vertices, and let r be the root of T. By the above construction, we can make T into a directed tree, if necessary, without changing the number of edges and vertices. Every edge must point to a nonroot vertex. Furthermore, every nonroot vertex has a single edge pointing to it, since there is a unique path to each vertex from the root. So the number of edges equals the number of nonroot vertices: $n - 1$.   □

Exercises 2.6

1. See Definitions 2.14 and 2.15. Let G and H be isomorphic, undirected graphs with vertex bijection α and edge bijection β. Let $x \in V_G$ be a vertex in G. Prove that the degree of x equals the degree of $\alpha(x)$.

2. Draw two nonisomorphic, undirected graphs, each having four vertices and four edges. Explain how you know they are not isomorphic.

3. Find a pair, G and H, of isomorphic graphs among the four graphs below, and give the one-to-one correspondence $\alpha : V_G \longrightarrow V_H$ of vertices. (For each vertex of G, tell to which vertex of H it corresponds.)

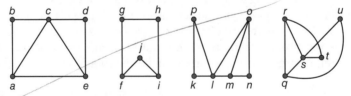

4. Give a rigorous definition for the *indegree* and *outdegree* of a vertex in a directed graph. (Model your definition on Definition 2.15.)

5. Let X be a finite set, and let $\mathcal{P}(X)$ be the power set of X. Let G be the graph whose vertices represent the elements of $\mathcal{P}(X)$, where A and B are joined by an edge if $A \cap B = \emptyset$. Similarly, let H be the graph with a vertex for each element of $\mathcal{P}(X)$, but where A and B share an edge if $A \cup B = X$. Prove that G is isomorphic to H.

6. Let (X_1, R_1) and (X_2, R_2) be isomorphic partial orders. Let G_1 and G_2 be their respective associated graphs, as defined in Definition 2.7. Prove that G_1 and G_2 are isomorphic graphs.

7. Let R_1 and R_2 be relations on a set X. Give a reasonable definition for an isomorphism of relations.

8. Speaking to a congregation of 97 people, a pastor instructs everyone to stand and shake hands with *exactly* three other people. (The pastor is not included in the hand-shaking activity.) Use a graph model to explain why this cannot be done. What do the vertices and edges represent? Why is this activity impossible?

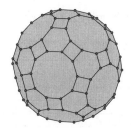

Figure 2.15 A truncated icosidodecahedron. See Exercises 16 and 19.

9. Between 1970 and 1975, the National Football League was divided into two conferences, with 13 teams in each conference. Each team played 14 games in a season. Would it have been possible for each team to play 11 games against teams from its own conference and 3 games against teams from the other conference? Use a graph model to answer this question (without drawing the graph).

10. A league of 10 teams is playing a "round-robin" style tournament, where each team plays every other team exactly once. How many games total need to be played? Justify your answer using a graph model—say what the vertices and edges of your graph represent, and what (if any) theorems you use.

11. The *complete* graph on n vertices (denoted K_n) is the undirected graph with exactly one edge between every pair of distinct vertices. Use Theorem 2.6 to derive a formula for the number of edges in K_n.

12. Recall the definition of K_n in Exercise 11. What is the fewest number of colors needed to color the vertices of K_n such that no two vertices of the same color are joined by an edge?

13. The *complete bipartite graph* $K_{m,n}$ is the simple undirected graph with $m + n$ vertices split into two sets V_1 and V_2 ($|V_1| = m$, $|V_2| = n$) such that vertices x, y share an edge if and only if $x \in V_1$ and $y \in V_2$. For example, $K_{3,4}$ is the following graph, where V_1 is the top row of vertices and V_2 is the bottom row.

Use Theorem 2.6 to derive a formula for the number of edges in $K_{m,n}$.

14. Recall the definition of $K_{m,n}$ in Exercise 13. What is the fewest number of colors needed to color the vertices of $K_{m,n}$ such that no two vertices of the same color are joined by an edge?

15. Prove that every circuit in $K_{m,n}$ has an even number of edges.

16. A truncated icosidodecahedron (also known as a "great rhombicosidodecahedron" or "omnitruncated icosidodecahedron") is a polyhedron with 120 vertices. Each vertex looks the same: a square, a hexagon, and a decagon come together at each vertex. How many edges does a truncated icosidodecahedron have? Explain how you arrive at your answer. (Note: The picture in Figure 2.15 doesn't show the vertices or edges on the back of the polyhedron.)

17. Prove the following theorem of Euler.

    Theorem 2.11 *If a connected, undirected graph has exactly two vertices v and w of odd degree, then there is an Euler path from v to w.*

18. Prove the following theorem of Euler.

    Theorem 2.12 *If an undirected graph has more than two vertices of odd degree, it does not have an Euler path.*

    Hint: Try a proof by contradiction, and model your argument on the proof of Theorem 2.8.

19. Is there an Euler path on the graph formed by the vertices and edges of a truncated icosidodecahedron? Why or why not?

20. The following graph has 45 vertices.

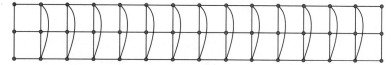

    (a) Does this graph have an Euler circuit? Why or why not?

    (b) Does this graph have an Euler path? Why or why not?

(c) The graph below is a copy of the above graph, but with some additional edges added so that all of the vertices in the resulting graph have degree four.

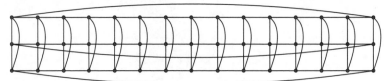

How many edges does this new graph have? Explain how you can use a theorem from this section to make counting the edges easier.

21. Prove that K_n, the complete graph on n vertices, has a Hamilton circuit for all $n \geq 3$.

22. For what values of n does K_n have an Euler circuit? Explain.

23. See Exercise 13. Find conditions on m and n that ensure that $K_{m,n}$ has an Euler circuit.

24. Find a Hamilton circuit in the following graph.

25. Explain why the following graph does not have a Hamilton circuit.

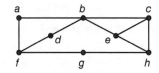

26. Finish the proof of Theorem 2.9 by proving that, if a graph G has a circuit with some edge e that differs from all the other edges in the circuit, then G has a simple circuit. (Hint: Focus on the sequence of vertices in the given circuit.)

27. Copy the three graphs from Figure 2.14 and label the vertices to show that the graphs are isomorphic.

28. Let G be a graph with vertex set V_G and edge set E_G. A *subgraph* of G is a graph with vertex set $V_H \subseteq V_G$ and edge set $E_H \subseteq E_G$. Write down all the subgraphs of the following graph.

29. Let G be a graph with vertex set V_G and edge set E_G. Let $V \subseteq V_G$ and $E \subseteq E_G$. Is there always a subgraph of G with vertex set V and edge set E? Explain.

30. Let G be a connected, undirected graph. Prove that there is a subgraph T of G such that T contains all the vertices of G, and T is a tree. (Such a subgraph is called a *spanning tree*.) Give a constructive proof that explains how to construct a spanning tree of a graph.

Chapter 3
Recursive Thinking

The branches of a blue spruce tree (Figure 3.1) follow an interesting pattern. The trunk of the tree is a large central stem, with branches coming off each side. These branches also have thinner stems coming off them, and so on, until you reach the level of the needles. A branch looks like a smaller copy of the whole tree, and even a small twig looks like a miniature branch. This is a picture of recursion.

The natural phenomenon of recursion pervades many areas of mathematics. In this chapter, you will learn how to work with recursive structures. You will develop the ability to see recursive patterns in mathematical objects. And you will study mathematical induction, a powerful tool for proving theorems about recursive structures.

Figure 3.1 A recursive blue spruce.

3.1   Recurrence Relations

Preview 3.1

1. The figure below shows the first three squares in a sequence $q_0, q_1, q_2, \ldots$ of squares divided into square regions. The next square in the sequence is formed by drawing a "+" inside each region of the previous square. How many nonoverlapping square regions are there in each of the first five squares q_1, q_2, q_3, q_4, q_5?

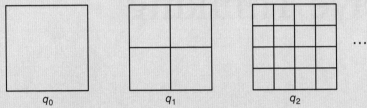

$$q_0 \qquad\qquad q_1 \qquad\qquad q_2$$

2. Laura is given a starting salary of \$2,000 and is promised a 10% raise every month. What will her monthly salaries be for the next three months?

3. The *odd numbers* are the numbers in the sequence $1, 3, 5, 7, 9, \ldots$. Define the sequence of *S-numbers* as follows:

> The first S-number is 1.
> The second S-number is the sum of the first S-number and the second odd number.
> The third S-number is the sum of the second S-number and the third odd number.
> The fourth S-number is the sum of the third S-number and the fourth odd number, etc., ...

Compute the first seven S-numbers. Make a conjecture.

3.1.1   Definition and Examples

The simplest and most concrete type of recursive object in mathematics is a *recurrence relation*. Suppose we wish to define a function $P\colon \mathbf{N} \longrightarrow \mathbf{Z}$ that inputs a natural number and returns an integer. The easiest way to do this is to give an explicit formula:

$$P(n) = \frac{n(n + 1)}{2}. \tag{3.1.2}$$

To evaluate $P(n)$ for some given n, you just plug n into the formula.

It is always nice to have an explicit formula for a function, but sometimes these are hard to come by. Often, a function comes up in mathematics that is natural to define recursively. Here is a second way of defining our function $P(n)$:

$$P(n) = \begin{cases} 1 & \text{if } n = 1 \\ n + P(n - 1) & \text{if } n > 1. \end{cases} \tag{3.1.3}$$

This is a *recursive definition* because P is defined in terms of itself: P occurs in the formula that defines P. This may seem a little sneaky, but it is perfectly legal. For any $n \in \mathbf{N}$, we can use the definition in Equation 3.1.3 to compute $P(n)$.

Example 3.1 Use Equation 3.1.3 to compute $P(5)$.

Solution: We'll compute $P(5)$ two different ways. The first approach is called "bottom-up" because we start at the bottom with $P(1)$ and work our way up to $P(5)$. By the first part of the definition, $P(1) = 1$. By the second part of the definition, with $n = 2$, we get $P(2) = 2 + P(1) = 2 + 1 = 3$. Again, by the second part with $n = 3$, $P(3) = 3 + P(2) = 3 + 3 = 6$. Repeating this process, $P(4) = 4 + 6 = 10$, and finally, $P(5) = 5 + 10 = 15$.

Alternatively, we can do a "top-down" computation. Whenever $n > 1$, we can apply the second part of the function definition to replace "$P(n)$" with "$n + P(n-1)$." This replacement justifies the first four uses of the $=$ sign.

$$P(5) = 5 + P(4)$$
$$= 5 + 4 + P(3)$$
$$= 5 + 4 + 3 + P(2)$$
$$= 5 + 4 + 3 + 2 + P(1)$$
$$= 5 + 4 + 3 + 2 + 1$$
$$= 15.$$

The second-to-last $=$ sign is the result of applying the first part of the definition to replace "$P(1)$" with "1."   ◇

Note that the equation

$$P(n) = n + P(n-1)$$

by itself would not define a recurrence relation, because the bottom-up calculation could never get started, and the top-down calculation would never stop. A well-defined recurrence relation needs a nonrecursive *base case* that gives at least one value of the function explicitly.

Activity 3.1.1: Recurrence Relations

1. Define $S(n)$ by the following recurrence relation.

$$S(n) = \begin{cases} 1 & \text{if } n = 1 \\ 2n - 1 + S(n-1) & \text{if } n > 1. \end{cases}$$

   (a) Compute $S(4)$ using a "bottom-up" evaluation: Compute $S(1)$, $S(2)$, $S(3)$, and then $S(4)$.

   (b) Fill in the blanks in the "top-down" evaluation of $S(5)$.

$$S(5) = \underline{\qquad} + S(4)$$
$$= \underline{\qquad} + \underline{\qquad} + S(3)$$
$$= \underline{\qquad} + \underline{\qquad} + \underline{\qquad} + S(2)$$
$$= \underline{\qquad} + \underline{\qquad} + \underline{\qquad} + \underline{\qquad} + S(1)$$
$$= \underline{\qquad} + \underline{\qquad} + \underline{\qquad} + \underline{\qquad} + \underline{\qquad}$$

2. The *Fibonacci numbers* $F(n)$ satisfy the following recurrence relation.

$$F(n) = \begin{cases} 1 & \text{if } n = 1 \text{ or } n = 2 \\ F(n-1) + F(n-2) & \text{if } n > 2. \end{cases}$$

   The sequence $F(1), F(2), F(3), \ldots$ is called the *Fibonacci sequence*. Write the first seven terms of the Fibonacci sequence.

3.1.2 The Fibonacci Sequence

One of the earliest examples of recursive thinking is the famous Fibonacci sequence. In the early 13th century, the Italian mathematician Leonardo Pisano[1] Fibonacci proposed the following problem. [10]

---

1. "Pisano" means "of Pisa." In fact, if you visit Pisa, Italy, you will find a statue of Fibonacci in the Camposanto, near the famous leaning tower.

Figure 3.2 Fibonacci numbers appear in many different kinds of plant growth, including this pine cone. Image courtesy of Pau Atela and Christophe Golé. [3]

Courtesy of Pau Atela and Christophe Golé. [3] – Phyllotaxis. Retrieved September 6, 2007 from the Smith College Website: http://maven
.smith.edu/phyllo/index.html

> A certain man put a pair of rabbits in a place surrounded on all sides by a wall. How many pairs of rabbits can be produced from that pair in a year if it is supposed that every month each pair begets a new pair which from the second month on becomes productive?

Let $F(n)$ represent the number of pairs of rabbits present on month n. Assuming that it takes two months for the first pair of rabbits to become productive, we have

$$F(1) = F(2) = 1$$

as a base case, and the first pair of offspring show up on the third month, so $F(3) = 2$. Every month, the number of new pairs of rabbits equals the number of rabbits present two months before. So we can define a recurrence relation as follows.

Definition 3.1 The *Fibonacci numbers* $F(n)$ satisfy the following recurrence relation:

$$F(n) = \begin{cases} 1 & \text{if } n = 1 \text{ or } n = 2 \\ F(n-1) + F(n-2) & \text{if } n > 2. \end{cases}$$

The sequence $F(1), F(2), F(3), \ldots$ is called the *Fibonacci sequence*.

The second part of this definition, $F(n) = F(n-1) + F(n-2)$, is the recursive part. The $F(n-1)$ term represents the number of rabbit pairs present the previous month. The $F(n-2)$ term represents the number of new rabbit pairs—equal to the number of rabbit pairs present two months ago. Therefore, the sum of these two terms is the total number of rabbit pairs present for month n, the current month. The first few terms of the famous Fibonacci sequence are then

$$1, 1, 2, 3, 5, 8, 13, 21, 34, \ldots.$$

Despite its somewhat whimsical origins, the Fibonacci sequence has a remarkable number of applications. This sequence of numbers is found in a variety of contexts, including plant growth, stock prices, architecture, music, and drainage patterns.

Example 3.2 The pine cone in Figure 3.2 contains Fibonacci numbers. Notice the spiral patterns emanating out from the center, both in clockwise and counterclockwise directions. There are $F(6) = 8$ counterclockwise spirals and $F(7) = 13$ clockwise spirals. Many flowers exhibit a similar pattern. For example, the *Santolina chamaecyparissus* typically has $F(7) = 13$ counterclockwise spirals and $F(8) = 21$ clockwise spirals, and many members of the *Asteraceae* family have $F(8) = 21$ spirals in one direction and $F(9) = 34$ spirals in the other. The flower pictured on the front cover of this book goes one level further, with $F(9) = 34$ and $F(10) = 55$ spirals in its seed cone.

These patterns are not simply coincidental. Fibonacci patterns are often found in nature where growth occurs in stages, with each successive stage dependent on previous stages. The recursive nature of plant growth is reflected in the presence of recursively defined sequences. The study of leaf patterns in plants is called *phyllotaxis*, and the more general study of how shapes form in living things is called *morphogenesis*. These studies apply recursive ideas.

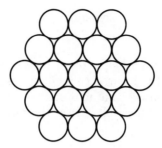

Figure 3.3 Circles packed to form a hexagon.

3.1.3   Modeling with Recurrence Relations

Fibonacci's rabbit example shows how to think recursively about a problem by describing it with a recurrence relation. Remember that any recurrence relation has two parts: a base case that describes some initial conditions, and a recursive case that describes a future value in terms of previous values. Armed with this way of thinking, we can model other problems using recurrence relations.

Example 3.3 Ursula the Usurer lends money at outrageous rates of interest. She demands to be paid 10% interest *per week* on a loan, compounded weekly. Suppose you borrow \$500 from Ursula. If you wait four weeks to pay her back, how much will you owe?

Solution: Let $M(n)$ be how much money you owe Ursula on the nth week. Initially, you owe \$500, so $M(0) = 500$. Each subsequent week, the amount you owe increases by 10%. Therefore, we have the following recurrence relation:

$$M(n) = \begin{cases} 500 & \text{if } n = 0 \\ 1.10 \cdot M(n-1) & \text{if } n > 0. \end{cases}$$

Then the amount you owe after four weeks is

$$
\begin{aligned}
M(4) &= 1.10 \cdot M(3) \\
&= 1.10 \cdot 1.10 \cdot M(2) \\
&= 1.10 \cdot 1.10 \cdot 1.10 \cdot M(1) \\
&= 1.10 \cdot 1.10 \cdot 1.10 \cdot 1.10 \cdot M(0) \\
&= 1.10 \cdot 1.10 \cdot 1.10 \cdot 1.10 \cdot 500 \\
&= \$732.05.
\end{aligned}
$$

$\diamond$

Example 3.4 If you have ever tried making patterns with a collection of coins, you have probably noticed that you can make hexagons in a natural way by packing circles as tightly as possible. Figure 3.3 shows how 19 circles fit into a hexagonal shape with 3 circles on each edge. Let $H(n)$ be the number of circles you need to form a hexagon with n circles on each edge. From Figure 3.3, it is clear that $H(2) = 7$ and $H(3) = 19$. Find a recurrence relation for $H(n)$.

Solution: The base case of the recurrence relation could be $H(2) = 7$, or we could agree that $H(1) = 1$, representing a "trivial" hexagon with just one circle. For the recursive case, we need to describe how to make a hexagonal pattern of edge size n from a hexagonal pattern of edge size $n - 1$. We would need to add six edges, each made up of n circles, but each circle on a vertex of the new hexagon will be included in two edges. Thus, the number of circles added will be $6n - 6$; subtracting 6 accounts for double-counting the circles on the vertices. This gives the following recurrence relation:

$$H(n) = \begin{cases} 1 & \text{if } n = 1 \\ H(n-1) + 6n - 6 & \text{if } n > 1. \end{cases}$$

If you don't quite believe in this formula, try some calculations: $H(2) = H(1) + 6 \cdot 2 - 6 = 7, H(3) = H(2) + 6 \cdot 3 - 6 = 19$, etc. ◇

To construct a recurrence relation, it often helps to see how successive cases of the problem are built on previous ones, like the layers of an onion. The recurrence relation describes how to count the next layer in terms of the previous one(s). If $P(n)$ is the function we want to describe recursively, think of $P(n)$ as the general case of the problem, while $P(n-1)$ represents the next simplest case. The recursive part of the recurrence relation is then an equation of the form

$$P(n) = \text{ some function of } P(n-1) \text{ and } n$$

that describes how to add a layer to your onion. The next few examples illustrate this paradigm.

Example 3.5 Let X be a finite set with n elements. Find a recurrence relation $C(n)$ for the number of elements in the power set $\mathcal{P}(X)$.

Solution: The base case is when $n = 0$ and X is the empty set, in which case $\mathcal{P}(X) = \{\emptyset\}$, so $C(0) = 1$. Now suppose $|X| = n$ for some $n > 0$. Choose some element $x \in X$ and let $X' = X \setminus \{x\}$. Then X' has $n - 1$ elements, so $|\mathcal{P}(X')| = C(n-1)$. Furthermore, every subset of X is either a subset of X' or a subset of the form $U \cup \{x\}$, where $U \subseteq X'$, and these two cases are mutually exclusive. Therefore, $\mathcal{P}(X)$ has twice as many elements as $\mathcal{P}(X')$. So

$$C(n) = \begin{cases} 1 & \text{if } n = 0 \\ 2 \cdot C(n-1) & \text{if } n > 0 \end{cases}$$

is a recurrence relation for $|\mathcal{P}(X)|$. ◇

Recall that the *depth* $d(v)$ of a vertex v in a binary tree is the number of edges in the path from the root to v. The *height* of a binary tree is the maximum value of $d(v)$ over all the vertices in the tree. A *leaf* is a node with no children.

Example 3.6 Call a binary tree *perfect* if every leaf has depth n and every nonleaf node has two children. For example,

is a perfect binary tree of height 3. Let T be a perfect binary tree of height n. Find a recurrence relation $V(n)$ for the number of nodes in T.

Solution: Notice that a perfect tree of height n has two perfect trees of height $n - 1$ inside of it.

In addition to the nodes in T_1 and T_2, there is one more node: the root. Therefore, a perfect binary tree of height n has

$$V(n) = \begin{cases} 1 & \text{if } n = 0 \\ 2 \cdot V(n-1) + 1 & \text{if } n > 0 \end{cases}$$

nodes. ◇

Example 3.7 Recall that the complete graph K_n on n vertices is the undirected graph that has exactly one edge between every pair of vertices. Find a recurrence relation $E(n)$ for the number of edges in K_n.

Solution: Given a complete graph on $n - 1$ vertices, we can add a vertex and edges to make a complete graph on n vertices. We need to add $n - 1$ new edges, because the new vertex needs to be connected to all of the vertices of the original given graph. For example, the following figure shows how to make K_5 from K_4.

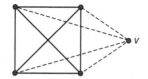

The new vertex is labeled v, and the four new edges are dashed. A complete graph on one vertex has no edges, so we obtain the following recurrence relation:

$$E(n) = \begin{cases} 0 & \text{if } n = 1 \\ E(n-1) + n - 1 & \text{if } n > 1. \end{cases}$$

Activity 3.1.2: Modeling with Recurrence Relations

1. Let $T(n)$ be the number of circles needed to form a triangle with n circles on each side, such as in the following sequence.

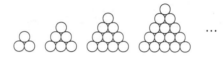

   (a) Write down a formula for a recurrence relation for $T(n)$.

   (b) Check your answer by computing $T(2)$, $T(3)$, $T(4)$, and $T(5)$, and comparing to the picture above.

2. The *half-life* of a radioactive element is the amount of time it takes for half of the mass of a sample to decay; a sample loses half of its mass over its half-life. Nobelium-259 has a half-life of approximately one hour. Suppose a 2048-atom sample of Nobelium-259 is allowed to decay.

   (a) Give a recurrence relation for $A(n)$, the number of atoms remaining after n hours.

   (b) How long will it take for there to be only a single atom remaining?

Look back at the examples in this section and see if you can recognize the recursive way of thinking. A power set contains all the elements of a smaller power set, and more. A perfect binary tree has two smaller perfect binary trees inside it. And a complete graph on $n - 1$ vertices can be augmented to form a complete graph on n vertices. The hard part of these problems was identifying the recursive structure in these objects; this structure made writing down the recurrence relation a fairly straightforward task.

Exercises 3.1

1. Refer to the recurrence relation for the Fibonacci sequence in Definition 3.1.

   (a) Answer Fibonacci's question by calculating $F(12)$.

   (b) Write $F(1000)$ in terms of $F(999)$ and $F(998)$.

   (c) Write $F(1000)$ in terms of $F(998)$ and $F(997)$.

2. In Fibonacci's model, rabbits live forever. The following modification of Definition 3.1 accounts for dying rabbits:

$$G(n) = \begin{cases} 0 & \text{if } n \leq 0 \\ 1 & \text{if } n = 1 \text{ or } n = 2 \\ G(n-1) + G(n-2) - G(n-8) & \text{if } n > 2. \end{cases}$$

(a) Compute $G(n)$ for $n = 1, 2, \ldots, 12$.

(b) In this modified model, how long do rabbits live?

3. Consider the following recurrence relation:

$$H(n) = \begin{cases} 0 & \text{if } n \leq 0 \\ 1 & \text{if } n = 1 \text{ or } n = 2 \\ H(n-1) + H(n-2) - H(n-3) & \text{if } n > 2. \end{cases}$$

(a) Compute $H(n)$ for $n = 1, 2, \ldots, 10$.

(b) Using the pattern from part (a), guess what $H(100)$ is.

4. The *Lucas numbers* $L(n)$ have almost the same definition as the Fibonacci numbers:

$$L(n) = \begin{cases} 1 & \text{if } n = 1 \\ 3 & \text{if } n = 2 \\ L(n-1) + L(n-2) & \text{if } n > 2. \end{cases}$$

(a) How is the definition of $L(n)$ different from the definition of $F(n)$ in Definition 3.1?

(b) Compute the first 12 Lucas numbers.

5. Compute the first seven terms of the following recurrence relations:

(a) $C(n)$ of Example 3.5.

(b) $V(n)$ of Example 3.6.

(c) $E(n)$ of Example 3.7.

6. Consider the following recurrence relation.

$$P(n) = \begin{cases} 0 & \text{if } n = 0 \\ [P(n-1)]^2 - n & \text{if } n > 0 \end{cases}$$

Use this recurrence relation to compute $P(1)$, $P(2)$, $P(3)$, and $P(4)$.

7. Given the following definition, compute $P(4)$.

$$P(n) = \begin{cases} 1 & \text{if } n = 0 \\ n \cdot [P(n-1)] & \text{if } n > 0 \end{cases}$$

8. Given the following definition, compute $Q(5)$.

$$Q(n) = \begin{cases} 0 & \text{if } n = 0 \\ 1 & \text{if } n = 1 \\ 2 & \text{if } n = 2 \\ Q(n-1) + Q(n-2) + Q(n-3) & \text{if } n > 2 \end{cases}$$

9. Consider the recurrence relation defined in Example 3.3. Suppose that, as in the example, you borrow $500, but you pay her back $100 each week. Each week, Ursula charges you 10% interest on the amount you still owe, after your $100 payment is taken into account.

(a) Write down a recurrence relation for $M(n)$, the amount owed after n weeks.

(b) How much will you owe after four weeks?

10. Every year, Alice gets a raise of $3,000 plus 5% of her previous year's salary. Her starting salary is $50,000. Give a recurrence relation for $S(n)$, Alice's salary after n years, for $n \geq 0$.

11. Suppose that today (year 0) your car is worth $10,000. Each year your car loses 10% of its value, but at the end of each year you add customizations to your car that increase its value by $50. Write a recurrence relation to model this situation.

12. Refer to Example 3.4. Calculate $H(7)$.

13. Circles can be packed into the shape of an equilateral triangle. Let $T(n)$ be the number of circles needed to form a triangle with n circles on each edge. From Figure 3.3 (or by experimenting with coins), it is easy to see that $T(2) = 3$ and $T(3) = 6$. Write down a recurrence relation for $T(n)$.

14. Let $H(n)$ be as in Example 3.4, and let $T(n)$ be as in Exercise 13. Write $H(n)$ in terms of $T(n-1)$. Explain your reasoning. The following diagram may be helpful.

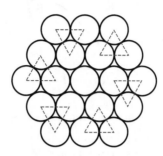

15. At the beginning of each day, Andrew adds one gallon of water to his bird bath. Each day, one-third of the water in the bird bath evaporates. At the end of day 0, the bird bath contains 8 gallons of water. Give a recurrence relation for $W(n)$, the amount of water in the bird bath at the end of day n.

16. Recall that the factorial function is defined as $n! = 1 \cdot 2 \cdot 3 \cdots \cdot (n-1) \cdot n$ and, by convention, $0! = 1$. Give a recurrence relation for $n!$.

17. Let $S(n) = 1^2 + 2^2 + \cdots + n^2$ be the sum of the first n perfect squares. Find a recurrence relation for $S(n)$.

18. The ancient Indian game of *Chaturanga*—from which the modern game of chess was apparently derived—was played on a board with 64 squares. A certain folktale tells the story of a Raja who promised a reward of one grain of rice on the first square of the board, two grains on the second square, four on the third, and so on, doubling the number of grains on each successive square.

    (a) Write a recurrence relation for $R(n)$, the number of grains of rice on the nth square.

    (b) Compute $R(64)$. Assuming a grain of rice weighs 25 milligrams, how many kilograms of rice must be placed on the 64th square?

19. Find recurrence relations that yield the following sequences:

    (a) $5, 10, 15, 20, 25, 30, \ldots$

    (b) $5, 11, 18, 26, 35, 45, \ldots$

20. Give a recurrence relation that describes the sequence $3, 6, 12, 24, 48, 96, 192, \ldots$.

21. Give a recurrence relation that describes the sequence $1, 1, 3, 3, 5, 5, 7, 7, 9, 9, \ldots$.

22. Let $f: \mathbf{N} \longrightarrow \mathbf{R}$ be any function on the natural numbers. The sum of the first n values of $f(n)$ is written as

$$\sum_{k=1}^{n} f(k) = f(1) + f(2) + \cdots + f(n)$$

    in *sigma notation*.

    (a) Write $1^2 + 2^2 + \cdots + n^2$ in sigma notation.

    (b) Give a recurrence relation for $\displaystyle\sum_{k=1}^{n} f(k)$.

23. Let $f: \mathbf{N} \longrightarrow \mathbf{R}$ be any function on the natural numbers. The product of the first n values of $f(n)$ is written as

$$\prod_{k=1}^{n} f(k) = f(1) \cdot f(2) \cdots \cdot f(n)$$

    in *product notation*.

(a) Write $n!$ in product notation, for $n > 0$.

(b) Give a recurrence relation for $\prod\limits_{k=1}^{n} f(k)$.

24. *Calculus required.* Use the reduction formula

$$\int x^n e^x \, dx = x^n e^x - n \int x^{n-1} e^x \, dx$$

to give a simple (noncalculus) recurrence relation for

$$I(n) = \int_0^1 x^n e^x \, dx$$

where $n \geq 0$. Make sure that your recurrence relation has a base case.

25. Suppose we model the spread of a virus in a certain population as follows. On day 1, one person is infected. On each subsequent day, each infected person gives the cold to two others.

(a) Write down a recurrence relation for this model.

(b) What are some of the limitations of this model? How does it fail to be realistic?

26. Let X be a set with n elements. Let $E \subseteq P(X)$ be the set of all subsets of X with an even number of elements, and let $O \subseteq P(X)$ be the subsets of X with an odd number of elements. Let $E(n) = |E|$ and $O(n) = |O|$.

(a) Find a recurrence relation for $E(n)$ in terms of $O(n-1)$ and $E(n-1)$.

(b) Find a recurrence relation for $O(n)$ in terms of $O(n-1)$ and $E(n-1)$.

(c) Find the first five values of $E(n)$ and $O(n)$.

27. The *complete bipartite graph* $K_{m,n}$ is the simple undirected graph with $m + n$ vertices split into two sets V_1 and V_2 ($|V_1| = m$, $|V_2| = n$) such that vertices x, y share an edge if and only if $x \in V_1$ and $y \in V_2$. For example, $K_{3,4}$ is the following graph.

(a) Find a recurrence relation for the number of edges in $K_{3,n}$.

(b) Find a recurrence relation for the number of edges in $K_{n,n}$.

3.2   Closed-Form Solutions and Induction

Although recurrence relations have a certain elegant quality, it can be tedious to compute with them. For example, armed only with Definition 3.1, it would take 998 steps to compute the Fibonacci number $F(1000)$. In this section we will explore ways to find a nonrecursive closed-form solution to a recurrence relation. Much more than appears here could be said about solving recurrence relations. The essential concept in this section is the idea of mathematical induction, the method by which we verify the correctness of a closed-form solution.

Preview 3.2

1. Consider the following variation of the Fibonacci numbers.

$$E(n) = \begin{cases} 4 & \text{if } n = 1 \\ 2 & \text{if } n = 2 \\ E(n-1) + E(n-2) & \text{if } n > 2. \end{cases}$$

Explain why $E(n)$ will always be even, for all $n \geq 0$.

2. Give an example of a sequence of numbers in which each number (after the first) is the sum of all the numbers that come before it. What must be true about such a sequence? How do you know?

3. Consider the following sequence.

$$3, 7, 11, 15, 19, 23, 27 \ldots$$

Describe this sequence (a) using a recurrence relation and (b) some other way.

3.2.1 Guessing a Closed-Form Solution

Suppose that $P(n)$ is a function defined by a recurrence relation. We would like to have an expression

$$P(n) = \text{a nonrecursive function of } n$$

because then we could just calculate $P(n)$ by plugging n into the formula, rather than by using the recurrence relation over and over. A formula like this is called a *closed-form solution* to the recurrence relation. Recall Example 3.1: we found that the first five values of the recurrence relation

$$P(n) = \begin{cases} 1 & \text{if } n = 1 \\ n + P(n-1) & \text{if } n > 1 \end{cases}$$

were $1, 3, 6, 10$, and 15. A closed-form solution to this recurrence relation is

$$P(n) = \frac{n(n+1)}{2}.$$

We can check that the values of $P(n)$ given by this nonrecursive formula match the values given by the recurrence relation:

n	1	2	3	4	5
$\frac{n(n+1)}{2}$	1	3	6	10	15

This table of values is pretty convincing evidence that we have found the right closed-form solution, but it is not a proof. Later in this section we will see how to verify that such a solution is correct, but first we will consider the problem of finding closed-form solutions.

Given a recurrence relation, the most general way of finding a closed-form solution is by guessing. Unfortunately, this is also the hardest technique to master.

Example 3.8 Find a closed-form solution for the recurrence relation from Example 3.3:

$$M(n) = \begin{cases} 500 & \text{if } n = 0 \\ 1.10 \cdot M(n-1) & \text{if } n > 0. \end{cases} \tag{3.2.1}$$

Solution: It almost always helps to write out the first few values of $M(n)$. In this case, it also helps to leave things unsimplified: the pattern is easier to see if you don't multiply out the terms.

$$
\begin{aligned}
M(0) &= 500 \\
M(1) &= 500 \cdot 1.10 & &= 500(1.10)^1 \\
M(2) &= 500 \cdot 1.10 \cdot 1.10 & &= 500(1.10)^2 \\
M(3) &= 500 \cdot 1.10 \cdot 1.10 \cdot 1.10 & &= 500(1.10)^3 \\
M(4) &= 500 \cdot 1.10 \cdot 1.10 \cdot 1.10 \cdot 1.10 &&= 500(1.10)^4.
\end{aligned}
$$

The evident pattern in these calculations suggests that

$$M(n) = 500(1.10)^n \tag{3.2.2}$$

is a closed-form solution to the recurrence relation. $\diamond$

Please note: *This is only a guess.* We haven't *proved* that Equation 3.2.2 represents the same function as Equation 3.2.1. There is still more work to do. Stay tuned.

Activity 3.2.1: Closed-form Solutions to Recurrence Relations

Define a function $t : \mathbf{N} \longrightarrow \mathbf{N}$ by the closed-form formula $t(n) = \dfrac{n^2 + n}{2}$.

1. Write $t(n - 1)$ in terms of n, and simplify your answer.
2. Write the expression $t(n - 1) + n$ in terms of n, and simplify your answer as much as possible.
3. Compare your result in question 2 to the given formula for $t(n)$.
4. Describe the sequence $t(1), t(2), t(3), t(4), t(5), \ldots$ using a recurrence relation.

3.2.2 Polynomial Sequences: Using Differences ‡

Finding a closed-form solution for $P(n)$ can be thought of as guessing a formula for the sequence $P(0), P(1), P(2), \ldots$. If we knew that

$$P(n) = \text{a polynomial function of } n$$

then it would be easier to guess at a formula. One way to detect such a sequence is to look at the differences between terms. Given any sequence

$$a_0, a_1, a_2, a_3, \ldots, a_{n-1}, a_n$$

the differences

$$a_1 - a_0, a_2 - a_1, a_3 - a_2, \ldots, a_n - a_{n-1}$$

form another sequence, called the *sequence of differences*. A linear sequence will have a constant sequence of differences (because a line has constant slope). Using algebra, it is possible to show that a quadratic sequence will have a linear sequence of differences, a cubic sequence will have a quadratic sequence of differences, etc. Given a sequence, we can calculate its sequence of differences, then calculate the sequence of differences of that, and so on. If we eventually end up with a constant sequence, then we have reason to believe that the original sequence is given by a polynomial function. The degree of the conjectured polynomial is the number of times we had to calculate the sequence of differences. The next example illustrates this technique.

Example 3.9 Find a closed-form solution for the recurrence relation from Example 3.4:

$$H(n) = \begin{cases} 1 & \text{if } n = 1 \\ H(n - 1) + 6n - 6 & \text{if } n > 1. \end{cases} \tag{3.2.3}$$

Solution: Calculate the first few terms, and then look at sequences of differences:

$$
\begin{array}{ccccccccccc}
1 & & 7 & & 19 & & 37 & & 61 & & 91 \\
& 6 & & 12 & & 18 & & 24 & & 30 & \\
& & 6 & & 6 & & 6 & & 6 & &
\end{array}
$$

The second sequence of differences is constant. This suggests that the sequence may have a formula of the form

$$H(n) = An^2 + Bn + C,$$

so all we need to do is find A, B, and C. Using $H(1) = 1$, $H(2) = 7$, and $H(3) = 19$, we get a system of three equations in three variables:

$$1 = A + B + C$$
$$7 = 4A + 2B + C$$
$$19 = 9A + 3B + C.$$

Solving this system is a simple—but somewhat lengthy—exercise in algebra. (Add/subtract equations to eliminate variables, etc. We'll omit the details.) The solution is $A = 3$, $B = -3$, and $C = 1$, so

$$H(n) = 3n^2 - 3n + 1 \tag{3.2.4}$$

is a good candidate for a closed-form solution. $\diamond$

The technique of using sequences of differences is more of a "brute force" approach than pure guessing; there are certain mechanical procedures you go through in order to arrive at a formula. But the result of these procedures is still only a guess. To be sure that our guess is right, we need to *prove* that the formula matches the recurrence relation for all n.

3.2.3 Inductively Verifying a Solution

If we use Equation 3.2.4 to calculate the first six values of $H(n)$, we get 1, 7, 19, 37, 61, and 91. These numbers match the values given by the recurrence relation in Equation 3.2.3 perfectly. This is pretty good evidence that Equation 3.2.4 is the correct closed-form solution for the recurrence relation. But this is not a proof. For all we know, the 7th value won't match, or the 8th, or the 739th. Without a proof, we can't be sure.

The general template for verifying a solution to a recurrence relation follows. We have

$$R(n) = \text{some recurrence relation}$$
$$f(n) = \text{hypothesized closed-form formula},$$

and we would like to show that $R(n) = f(n)$ for all values of n. For the purposes of this discussion, let's say that the first value of n for which $R(n)$ is defined is $n = 1$. As we have seen, recurrence relations usually start at $n = 1$ or $n = 0$, but any starting value of n is possible.

To prove that $R(n) = f(n)$ for all $n \geq 1$, we need to use the technique of *mathematical induction*. The idea of this kind of proof is analogous to climbing a staircase. Going up a staircase is a fairly repetitive task; if you know how to ascend one stairstep, you know how to ascend a staircase of any height. Of course, you need to start at the bottom of the staircase. In the proof, this is the base case.

Base Case: Verify that $R(1) = f(1)$.

Checking the base case is usually fairly easy. After all, you probably wouldn't have chosen $f(n)$ as a candidate solution if it didn't at least match for the case $n = 1$.

Next, you must be able to take one step up the staircase. Note that it doesn't matter where on the staircase you are; taking one step up requires the same amount of skill, whether you are at the bottom, top, or somewhere in the middle. So let's suppose, for the sake of the argument, you are standing on the $(k-1)$th stair. This is the inductive hypothesis.

Inductive Hypothesis: Let $k > 1$ be some integer. Suppose as *inductive hypothesis* that $R(k-1) = f(k-1)$.

The inductive hypothesis will be a crucial part of our proof. Any valid proof by induction must use the inductive hypothesis somewhere in its argument.

Finally, you need to be able to go up to the next stairstep. See Figure 3.4.

Inductive Step: Prove that $R(k) = f(k)$.

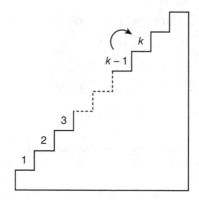

Figure 3.4 The inductive step shows that you can climb up one stairstep.

To do this, use the recurrence relation to compute the kth value. When you need to plug in the $(k-1)$th value, use the inductive hypothesis. Then use algebra to show that the answer matches the closed-form solution.

Why does this work? An induction argument proves the following assertion:

Let $k > 1$. If the recurrence relation matches the closed-form solution for $n = k - 1$, then the recurrence relation matches the closed-form solution for $n = k$.

In other words,

$$R(k-1) = f(k-1) \;\Rightarrow\; R(k) = f(k).$$

Since our proof supposed an arbitrary value of k, we are allowed to apply this assertion for *any* particular value of $k > 1$. Using $k = 2$, we get the assertion

If the recurrence relation matches the closed-form solution for $n = 1$, then the recurrence relation matches the closed-form solution for $n = 2$.

But we know that the recurrence relation matches the closed-form solution for $n = 1$; this was the base case. Therefore, the above assertion (and *modus ponens*) tells us that they match for $n = 2$. Now apply the assertion again, with $k = 3$:

If the recurrence relation matches the closed-form solution for $n = 2$, then the recurrence relation matches the closed-form solution for $n = 3$.

So we know they match for $n = 3$. By repeating this argument, we can verify the cases $n = 4, 5, 6, \ldots$, up to whatever number we wish. In other words, the recurrence relation matches the closed-form solution for *any* value of n. This is exactly what we needed to show. In the symbols of logic, an induction argument establishes the following chain of implications:

$$R(1) = f(1) \Rightarrow R(2) = f(2)$$
$$\Rightarrow R(3) = f(3)$$
$$\Rightarrow R(4) = f(4)$$
$$\Rightarrow \cdots.$$

The base case gets this chain of implications started, and since the inductive step works for any value of k, we are allowed to continue the chain of implications indefinitely to conclude that $R(n) = f(n)$ for any $n \geq 1$. The following example shows what a typical proof by induction should look like.

Example 3.10 Let $H(n)$ be defined by the following recurrence relation:

$$H(n) = \begin{cases} 1 & \text{if } n = 1 \\ H(n-1) + 6n - 6 & \text{if } n > 1. \end{cases}$$

Let $f(n) = 3n^2 - 3n + 1$. Prove that $H(n) = f(n)$ for all $n \geq 1$.

Proof We use induction on n.

> **Base Case:** If $n = 1$, the recurrence relation says that $H(1) = 1$, and the formula says that $f(1) = 3 \cdot 1^2 - 3 \cdot 1 + 1$, which is 1, so they match.
>
> **Inductive Hypothesis:** Suppose as inductive hypothesis that
>
> $$H(k - 1) = 3(k - 1)^2 - 3(k - 1) + 1$$
>
> for some $k > 1$.
>
> **Inductive Step:** Using the recurrence relation,
>
> $$H(k) = H(k - 1) + 6k - 6, \text{ by the second part of the recurrence relation}$$
>
> $$= 3(k - 1)^2 - 3(k - 1) + 1 + 6k - 6, \text{ by inductive hypothesis}$$
>
> $$= 3k^2 - 6k + 3 - 3k + 3 + 1 + 6k - 6$$
>
> $$= 3k^2 - 3k + 1.$$

So, by induction, $H(n) = f(n)$ for all $n \geq 1$.   □

The solution of Example 3.10 makes a good proof template for verifying a closed-form solution to a simple recurrence relation; such a proof almost always should look like this. The next example establishes a closed-form solution to the recurrence relation of Example 3.5 for the number of elements in a power set. The proof is very similar to Example 3.10, but the induction starts at $n = 0$ instead of $n = 1$.

Example 3.11 Let $C(n)$ be defined by the following recurrence relation:

$$C(n) = \begin{cases} 1 & \text{if } n = 0 \\ 2 \cdot C(n - 1) & \text{if } n > 0. \end{cases}$$

Prove that $C(n) = 2^n$ for all $n \geq 0$.

Proof We use induction on n. Let $f(n) = 2^n$.

> **Base Case:** If $n = 0$, the recurrence relation says that $C(0) = 1$, and the formula says that $f(0) = 2^0 = 1$, so $C(0) = f(0)$.
>
> **Inductive Hypothesis:** Let $k > 0$. Suppose as inductive hypothesis that $C(k - 1) = 2^{k-1}$.
>
> **Inductive Step:** Using the recurrence relation,
>
> $$C(k) = 2 \cdot C(k - 1), \text{ by the second part of the recurrence relation}$$
>
> $$= 2 \cdot 2^{k-1}, \text{ by inductive hypothesis}$$
>
> $$= 2^k.$$

So, by induction, $C(n) = 2^n$ for all $n \geq 0$.   □

Take a moment to compare the proofs in Examples 3.10 and 3.11. In the exercises at the end of this section, you should mimic these examples when you are asked to prove that a given recurrence relation has a given closed-form solution. It is important to master this standard type of proof.

Activity 3.2.2: Proofs by Induction

---

1. Let $S(n)$ be defined by the following recurrence relation.

$$S(n) = \begin{cases} 1 & \text{if } n = 1 \\ S(n - 1) + 2n - 1 & \text{if } n > 1 \end{cases}$$

Let $s(n) = n^2$. Fill in the blanks in the following proof that $S(n) = s(n)$ for all $n \geq 1$.

We use induction on n.

Base Case: If $n = 1$, the recurrence relation says that $S(1) =$_____, and the closed-form formula says that $s(1) =$_____, so $S(1) = s(1)$.

Inductive Hypothesis: Let $k > 1$. Suppose as inductive hypothesis that $S(k - 1) =$_____.

Inductive Step: Using the recurrence relation,

$$S(k) = \text{_____} \text{, by the recurrence relation}$$

$$= \text{_____} \text{, by inductive hypothesis}$$

$$= \text{_____} \text{, using algebra.}$$

$$= k^2$$

So, by induction, _____ for all $n \geq 1$.

2. Consider the following recurrence relation:

$$Q(n) = \begin{cases} 4 & \text{if } n = 0 \\ 2 \cdot Q(n - 1) - 3 & \text{if } n > 0 \end{cases}$$

Let $q(n) = 2^n + 3$. Write a proof by induction that $Q(n) = q(n)$, for all $n \geq 0$. Follow the template in question 1.

Mathematical induction is a difficult topic. In this section we have taken a very narrow view of the subject: verifying a closed-form solution. There are many other uses of mathematical induction, and these proofs can be quite challenging to write. The methods in this section will provide a foundation for more complicated inductive proofs.

We end this section with an example that shows why proofs are important.

Example 3.12 Let $P(n)$ be defined by the following recurrence relation:

$$P(n) = \begin{cases} 1 & \text{if } n = 0 \\ 3 \cdot P(n - 1) - (n - 1)^2 & \text{if } n > 0. \end{cases}$$

Does $P(n) = (n + 2) \cdot 2^{n-1}$ for all $n \geq 0$?

Solution: In order to show that $(\forall n \geq 0)(P(n) = (n + 2) \cdot 2^{n-1})$ is false, we need to show that its negation, $(\exists n \geq 0)(P(n) \neq (n+2) \cdot 2^{n-1})$, is true. That is, we need to find a value of n for which the closed-form formula does not match the recurrence relation. Using the recurrence relation,

$$a_0 = 1$$
$$a_1 = 3 \cdot 1 - (1 - 1)^2 = 3$$
$$a_2 = 3 \cdot 3 - (2 - 1)^2 = 8$$
$$a_3 = 3 \cdot 8 - (3 - 1)^2 = 20$$

and using the closed-form formula,

$$(0 + 2) \cdot 2^{0-1} = 1$$
$$(1 + 2) \cdot 2^{1-1} = 3$$
$$(2 + 2) \cdot 2^{2-1} = 8$$
$$(3 + 2) \cdot 2^{3-1} = 20,$$

the recurrence relation matches the closed-form solution for the first four values of n. Remember that we have always said that, while this may be good evidence that these two ways of calculating $P(n)$ will always agree, it is not a proof. Indeed, if we persist in our calculations, we find that

$$a_4 = 3 \cdot 20 - (4 - 1)^2 = 51$$

while

$$(4+2) \cdot 2^{4-1} = 48,$$

so the results do not match for $n = 4$. Therefore, it is not the case that $P(n) = (n+2) \cdot 2^{n-1}$ for all $n \geq 0$.   ◇

Once you have found a counterexample to a statement, you know that the statement is false in general. But failure to find a counterexample to a statement does not mean that the statement is true. In the previous example, we had to calculate five values of each formula to find a mismatch, but it could have taken 50, or 500, or any number of values to find our counterexample. This is why you will never know for sure that a closed-form formula matches a recurrence relation unless you prove it.

Exercises 3.2

1. Prove that the closed-form solution in Equation 3.2.2 matches the recurrence relation in Equation 3.2.1. (See Example 3.8.)

2. Prove that the closed-form solution in Equation 3.1.2 matches the recurrence relation in Equation 3.1.3. (See page 108.)

3. Consider the following recurrence relation:

$$B(n) = \begin{cases} 2 & \text{if } n = 1 \\ 3 \cdot B(n-1) + 2 & \text{if } n > 1. \end{cases}$$

Use induction to prove that $B(n) = 3^n - 1$ for all $n \geq 1$.

4. Consider the following recurrence relation:

$$P(n) = \begin{cases} 0 & \text{if } n = 0 \\ 5 \cdot P(n-1) + 1 & \text{if } n > 0. \end{cases}$$

Prove by induction that $P(n) = \dfrac{5^n - 1}{4}$ for all $n \geq 0$.

5. Consider the following recurrence relation:

$$C(n) = \begin{cases} 0 & \text{if } n = 0 \\ n + 3 \cdot C(n-1) & \text{if } n > 0. \end{cases}$$

Prove by induction that $C(n) = \dfrac{3^{n+1} - 2n - 3}{4}$ for all $n \geq 0$.

6. Consider the following recurrence relation:

$$Q(n) = \begin{cases} 4 & \text{if } n = 0 \\ 2 \cdot Q(n-1) - 3 & \text{if } n > 0. \end{cases}$$

Prove by induction that $Q(n) = 2^n + 3$, for all $n \geq 0$.

7. Consider the following recurrence relation:

$$R(n) = \begin{cases} 1 & \text{if } n = 0 \\ R(n-1) + 2n & \text{if } n > 0. \end{cases}$$

Prove by induction that $R(n) = n^2 + n + 1$ for all $n \geq 0$.

8. Guess a closed-form solution for the following recurrence relation:

$$K(n) = \begin{cases} 1 & \text{if } n = 0 \\ 2 \cdot K(n-1) - n + 1 & \text{if } n > 0. \end{cases}$$

Prove that your guess is correct.

9. Guess a closed-form solution for the following recurrence relation:

$$P(n) = \begin{cases} 5 & \text{if } n = 0 \\ P(n-1) + 3 & \text{if } n > 0. \end{cases}$$

Prove that your guess is correct.

10. Consider the following recurrence relation:

$$P(n) = \begin{cases} 1 & \text{if } n = 0 \\ P(n-1) + n^2 & \text{if } n > 0. \end{cases}$$

(a) Compute the first eight values of $P(n)$.

(b) Analyze the sequences of differences. What does this suggest about the closed-form solution?

(c) Find a good candidate for a closed-form solution.

(d) Prove that your candidate solution is the correct closed-form solution.

11. Consider the following recurrence relation:

$$G(n) = \begin{cases} 1 & \text{if } n = 0 \\ G(n-1) + 2n - 1 & \text{if } n > 0. \end{cases}$$

(a) Calculate $G(0)$, $G(1)$, $G(2)$, $G(3)$, $G(4)$, and $G(5)$.

(b) Use sequences of differences to guess at a closed-form solution for $G(n)$.

(c) Prove that your guess is correct.

12. Find a polynomial function $f(n)$ such that $f(1), f(2), \ldots, f(8)$ is the following sequence:

$$2, 7, 12, 17, 22, 27, 32, 37.$$

13. Find a polynomial function $f(n)$ such that $f(1), f(2), \ldots, f(8)$ is the following sequence:

$$1, 1, 2, 4, 7, 11, 16, 22.$$

14. Analyze the sequence

$$1, 6, 15, 100, 501, 1746, 4771, 11040, 22665, 42526, 74391$$

using sequences of differences. From what degree polynomial does this sequence appear to be drawn? (Don't bother finding the coefficients of the polynomial.)

15. Refer to Example 3.6. Guess at a closed-form solution to the recurrence relation for the number of nodes in a perfect binary tree of height n. Prove that your guess is correct.

16. Refer to Example 3.7. Guess at a closed-form solution to the recurrence relation for the number of edges in K_n, the complete graph on n vertices. Prove that your guess is correct.

17. Guess a closed-form solution for the following recurrence relation:

$$P(n) = \begin{cases} 1 & \text{if } n = 0 \\ P(n-1) + 2^n & \text{if } n > 0. \end{cases}$$

(Hint: Consider powers of 2.) Prove that your guess is correct.

18. Recall that $n! = 1 \cdot 2 \cdot 3 \cdots (n-1) \cdot n$ for $n > 0$, and by definition, $0! = 1$. Prove that $F(n) = n!$ for all $n \geq 0$, where

$$F(n) = \begin{cases} 1 & \text{if } n = 0 \\ n \cdot F(n-1) & \text{if } n > 0. \end{cases}$$

19. Consider the following recurrence relation:

$$H(n) = \begin{cases} 0 & \text{if } n = 0 \\ n \cdot H(n-1) + 1 & \text{if } n > 0. \end{cases}$$

Prove that $H(n) = n!(1/1! + 1/2! + 1/3! + \cdots + 1/n!)$ for all $n \geq 1$.

20. Is $1 + \frac{17}{6}n - 2n^2 + \frac{7}{6}n^3$ a closed-form solution for the following recurrence relation?

$$P(n) = \begin{cases} 1 & \text{if } n = 0 \\ 4 \cdot P(n-1) - n^2 & \text{if } n > 0. \end{cases}$$

Prove or disprove.

21. Recall the Fibonacci numbers defined in Definition 3.1 on page 110. Recall also that $\lceil x \rceil$ is the least integer k such that $k \geq x$, called the *ceiling* of x. Is it true that

$$F(n) = \left\lceil e^{\left(\frac{n-2}{2}\right)} \right\rceil$$

for all $n \geq 1$? Prove or disprove.

22. Let $f(n) = An^2 + Bn + C$. Show that the expression

$$f(n+1) - f(n)$$

is a linear function of n. (This calculation shows that a quadratic sequence has a linear sequence of differences.)

*23. Recall the definition of Fibonacci numbers in Definition 3.1.

   (a) Compute the sequence of differences of the first nine Fibonacci numbers. What seems to be true about this sequence?

   (b) Prove your assertion in part (a).

   (c) Explain why a closed-form formula for the Fibonacci numbers cannot be a polynomial function.

*24. Suppose you are given a sequence of numbers $a_1, a_2, a_3, \ldots, a_k$. Explain how to construct a polynomial $p(x)$ such that $p(n) = a_n$ for all $n = 1, 2, 3, \ldots, k$. (Note that this fact, along with Exercise 23, shows that it is possible for a closed-form formula to match a recurrence relation for arbitrarily many terms, without being a valid closed-form solution.)

3.3   Recursive Definitions

The definition of a recurrence relation is *self-referential*—we state a rule for calculating the values of a function in terms of itself. Recurrence relations have two parts: a base case that describes the simplest case of the function and a recursive step that describes the function in terms of a simpler version of itself. This is the essence of recursive thinking. In this section, we will apply this idea to an assortment of different objects.

Preview 3.3

1. Suppose that A is a set of numbers that contains 3 and 4, with the property that if $x \in A$ and $y \in A$, then $x + y$ is also in A. What other numbers must A contain?

2. Consider the pattern of numbers below. How is each row related to the row above it? What should the next row be?

```
               1
              1 1
             1 0 1
            1 1 1 1
           1 0 0 0 1
          1 1 0 0 1 1
         1 0 1 0 1 0 1
        1 1 1 1 1 1 1 1
       1 0 0 0 0 0 0 0 1
      1 1 0 0 0 0 0 0 1 1
     1 0 1 0 0 0 0 0 1 0 1
    1 1 1 1 0 0 0 0 1 1 1 1
   1 0 0 0 1 0 0 0 1 0 0 0 1
```

3.3.1   Definition and Examples

We will use the term *object* somewhat loosely; an object could be a number, a mathematical structure, a function, or almost anything else we want to describe. A *recursive definition* of a given object has the following parts:

B. A base case, which usually defines the simplest possible such object, and

R. A recursive case, which defines a more complicated object in terms of a simpler one.

The best way to understand recursive definitions is to see some examples.

Example 3.13 Any recurrence relation is a recursive definition of a function. For example, the recurrence relation

$$H(n) = \begin{cases} 1 & \text{if } n = 1 \\ H(n-1) + 6n - 6 & \text{if } n > 1 \end{cases}$$

for the hexagonal numbers (Example 3.4) can be written as a recursive definition with a base case and a recursive case:

B. $H(1) = 1$.

R. For any $n > 1$, $H(n) = H(n-1) + 6n - 6$.

Example 3.14 Let X be a set of actors and actresses, defined as follows.

B. Kevin Bacon $\in X$.

R. Let x be an actor or actress. If, for some $y \in X$, there has been a movie in which both x and y appear, then $x \in X$.

In other words, Kevin Bacon is in X, and anyone who has been in some movie with someone in X is also in X. For example, in order to show that Arnold Schwarzenegger $\in X$, we note that Arnold Schwarzenegger appeared in *Conan the Barbarian* with James Earl Jones, who appeared in *Clear and Present Danger* with Harrison Ford, who appeared in *The Fugitive* with Tommy Lee Jones, who appeared in *JFK* with Kevin Bacon.

Although this example might seem silly, it illustrates an important way to think about how things are connected. It is not hard to see how the same definition could describe the set of all computers exposed to a certain virus, or the collection of people who have heard about a tornado warning, etc. For more on the Kevin Bacon example and its relation to graph theory, see Hopkins [15].

A sequence of symbols written together in some order is called a *string*. The next example gives a useful recursive definition. Note that there are two base cases in this example.

Example 3.15 Given a list of symbols $a_1, a_2, \ldots, a_m$, a *string* of these symbols is:

   $\mathbf{B_1}$. the empty string, denoted by λ, or

   $\mathbf{B_2}$. any symbol a_i, or

   $\mathbf{R}$. xy, the *concatenation* of x and y, where x and y are strings.

Since λ represents the empty string, we do not write λ after it has been concatenated with another string. For example, `cubs`λ = `cubs`. It shouldn't be hard to convince yourself that this definition describes any possible "word" in the given symbols.

Example 3.16 A special kind of string called a *palindrome* can be defined as follows.

   $\mathbf{B_1}$. λ is a palindrome.

   $\mathbf{B_2}$. Any symbol a is a palindrome.

   $\mathbf{R}$. If x and y are palindromes, then yxy is a palindrome.

Note that any word that is the same forward as backward is a palindrome, such as `racecar` or `HANNAH`. We can build up the palindrome `racecar` from the definition as follows.

1. Since it is a symbol, `e` is a palindrome, by $\mathbf{B_2}$, the second part of the definition.
2. Similarly, `c` is a palindrome.
3. Using $\mathbf{R}$, `cec` is a palindrome.
4. By $\mathbf{B_2}$, `a` is a palindrome.
5. By $\mathbf{R}$, `aceca` is a palindrome.
6. By $\mathbf{B_2}$, `r` is a palindrome.
7. By $\mathbf{R}$, `racecar` is a palindrome.

As an exercise, think about why we have to define λ as a palindrome.

Example 3.17 The set X of all binary strings (strings with only 0s and 1s) having the same number of 0s and 1s is defined as follows.

   $\mathbf{B}$. λ is in X.

   $\mathbf{R_1}$. If x is in X, so are $1x0$ and $0x1$.

   $\mathbf{R_2}$. If x and y are in X, so is xy.

Notice that this definition has two recursive cases, both of which preserve the property of having the same number of 1s as 0s. These recursive cases form new strings from old by adding 0s and 1s, and they always add the same amount of each.

Strings can be useful in a number of contexts: text in word processing, genetic sequences in bioinformatics, etc. Thinking recursively can help us define operations that manipulate the symbols in a string. For example, the next recursive definition shows how to reverse the order of a string.

Example 3.18 If s is a string, define its *reverse* s^R as follows.

   $\mathbf{B}$. $\lambda^R = \lambda$.

   $\mathbf{R}$. If s has one or more symbols, write $s = ra$ where a is a symbol and r is a string (possibly empty). Then $s^R = ar^R$.

In other words, you reverse a string by moving the last symbol to the front and reversing the rest of the string. To see how this definition works, consider the string pit. Its reverse, $(\text{pit})^R$, is calculated as follows:

$$
\begin{aligned}
(\text{pit})^R &= \text{t}(\text{pi})^R \quad \text{by part } \mathbf{R} \\
&= \text{ti}(\text{p})^R \quad \text{by part } \mathbf{R} \\
&= \text{ti}(\lambda\text{p})^R \quad \text{(insertion of empty string)} \\
&= \text{tip}\lambda^R \quad \text{by part } \mathbf{R} \\
&= \text{tip}\lambda \quad \text{by part } \mathbf{B} \\
&= \text{tip} \quad \text{(removal of empty string)}.
\end{aligned}
$$

Most of the work in reversing pit was devoted to showing that $(\text{p})^R = \text{p}$. The definition doesn't say that the reversal of a one-symbol string is the same one-symbol string, but this fact follows from the definition by the above argument. It is a good idea to state such facts as theorems.

Theorem 3.1 *If a is a symbol, then $a^R = a$.*

Proof As above, $a^R = (\lambda a)^R = a\lambda^R = a\lambda = a.$ □

Example 3.19 Define a *line map* as follows.

   B. A blank rectangle is a line map.

   R. A line map with a straight line drawn all the way across it is a new line map.

The rectangle below shows an example of a line map with five lines. The recursive definitions of strings and line maps are similar: the base case is a blank object, and the recursive case defines how to add a new piece to an object to make it more complex. This is a useful way to think about objects that are built from identifiable pieces.

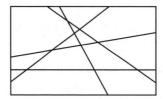

3.3.2   Writing Recursive Definitions

Just as some functions are easy to define using recurrence relations, some objects have natural recursive definitions. The trick to writing a recursive definition is to see the desired object as being built out of levels. The recursive case of the definition must describe a level in terms of the next simplest level. The base case should describe the simplest possible such object. Some examples will make this idea less abstract.

Example 3.20 Suppose you start browsing the Internet at some specified page p. Let X be the set of all pages you can reach by following links, starting at p. Give a recursive definition for the set X.

Solution: Observe that if you can reach some page x, then you can reach any page to which x has a link. This gives the recursive part of the definition:

   R. If $x \in X$ and y is some page such that x links to y, then $y \in X$.

The base case is the page where you start:

   B. $p \in X$.

Notice the similarity to Example 3.14.   ◇

The reasoning in this last example was "top-down." We thought about the recursive part first: what pages can you get to from any given page? The next example uses "bottom-up" thinking: start with the simplest case, and think about how to build up a slightly more complicated case.

Example 3.21 Give a recursive definition for the set of all odd natural numbers.

Solution: To find the base case, think about the simplest possible case of an odd natural number. A reasonable choice for the simplest odd number is 1. For the recursive case, think about how to get a new odd number from an old odd number. Observe that, if x is odd, then $x + 2$ is odd also. So we can define the set X of odd numbers as follows.

   B. 1 is in X.

   R. If x is in X, so is $x + 2$. $\diamond$

At this point you should object: we already have a definition for odd numbers (Definition 1.6). According to this definition, the set of odd natural numbers should be

$$\{n \in \mathbf{N} \mid n = 2k + 1 \text{ for some integer } k\}.$$

Fair enough. Definition 1.6 does stipulate what odd numbers are, once and for all. We should therefore view the recursive definition in Example 3.21 as an equivalent way to describe the set of odd natural numbers. Of course, we need to prove that these two definitions are equivalent; we'll do this in the next section.

Example 2.5 illustrated how to organize data into a binary search tree. More generally, any graph with this type of structure is called a *binary tree*. These graphs have a natural recursive definition.

Example 3.22 Give a recursive definition for the set of all binary trees.

Solution: For convenience, let's allow the "empty tree" consisting of no vertices and no edges to be a simple case of a binary tree. A single vertex could also be considered to be a binary tree. Using these two building blocks, a new tree can be formed from two existing trees by joining the two trees under a common root node. So we can write the following definition for a binary tree. Note that this definition also defines the root of the binary tree.

   B$_1$. The empty tree is a binary tree.

   B$_2$. A single vertex is a binary tree. In this case, the vertex is the root of the tree.

   R. If T_1 and T_2 are binary trees with roots r_1 and r_2, respectively, then the tree

   is a binary tree with root r. Here the circles represent the binary trees T_1 and T_2. If either of these trees T_i ($i = 1, 2$) is the empty tree, then there is no edge from r to T_i. $\diamond$

As we saw in Section 3.1, seeing the recursive structure of an object can be the key to defining a recurrence relation. In Example 3.6, we observed that a perfect binary tree is made of two smaller perfect binary trees. The definition in Example 3.22 generalizes this observation.

Activity 3.3.1: Binary Trees, Part I

Definition. A *binary tree* is:

   B$_1$. The empty tree, or

   B$_2$. A single root vertex, or

   R. A root vertex connected to two subtrees, either of which can be empty.

1. A vertex is called a *leaf* if both of its subtrees are empty. For the binary tree T pictured below, identify the leaves, the root v, the left and right subtrees T_1 and T_2, the roots v_1 and v_2 of the left and right subtrees, and the left and right subtrees of T_1 and T_2.

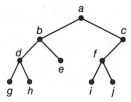

2. A *full* binary tree is a binary tree in which every non-leaf vertex has two non-empty subtrees.

   (a) Explain why the binary tree in Question 1 is not full.

   (b) Draw two different examples of full binary trees, each with 7 vertices.

3. The *level* of a vertex in a binary tree is the number of edges between the vertex and the root of the tree. A binary tree is *perfect* if it is full and all of its leaves are at the same level.

   (a) Draw three different perfect binary trees: one with leaves at level 1, one with leaves at level 2, and one with leaves at level 3.

   (b) If n is the level of the leaves in a perfect binary tree, how many vertices does the tree have (in terms of n)? Make a conjecture.

4. Notice that subtrees of a full binary tree are full, and the subtrees of a perfect binary tree are perfect.

   (a) Write a recursive definition for a full binary tree.

   (b) Write a recursive definition for a perfect binary tree.

3.3.3   Recursive Geometry

We can think of a recurrence relation $R(n)$ as a rule for constructing a sequence of numbers $R(1), R(2), R(3), \ldots$. For example, the recurrence relation

$$R(n) = \begin{cases} 2 & \text{if } n = 1 \\ \sqrt{R(n-1)} & \text{if } n > 1 \end{cases}$$

produces the sequence

$$2, 1.414, 1.189, 1.091, 1.044, 1.022, 1.011, 1.005, \ldots$$

to three decimal places. We say that the *limit* of this sequence is 1 because the numbers in this sequence get closer and closer to 1 as n gets larger.

Similarly, we can consider the limit of a recursive definition of geometric patterns. This is one way to construct *fractals*, a special type of shape with infinite layers of self-similarity. The following examples illustrate this process.

Example 3.23 Define a sequence of shapes as follows.

   B. $K(1)$ is an equilateral triangle.

   R. For $n > 1$, $K(n)$ is formed by replacing each line segment

   of $K(n-1)$ with the shape

   such that the central vertex points outward.

The first three terms of this sequence are as follows.

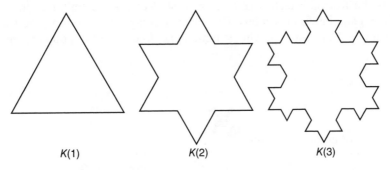

$K(1)$ $\qquad\qquad$ $K(2)$ $\qquad\qquad$ $K(3)$

The limit of this sequence of shapes is a fractal known as the *Koch snowflake:*

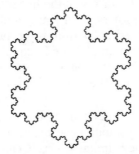

Example 3.24 Given a fractal, we can often examine it and describe its recursive structure. The following is a fractal model for the Badda-Bing axiomatic system of Example 1.17.

Notice that the pattern starts with a central square in the middle, with smaller squares on each vertex of this square, and smaller squares on all those vertices, and so on. Each time the squares get smaller, they do so by a factor of $1/2$. These observations lead to a definition for a sequence of shapes $B(1), B(2), B(3), \ldots$ whose limit is the Badda-Bing fractal.

B. $B(1)$ is a square.

R. For $n > 1$, $B(n)$ is formed from $B(n - 1)$ by adding squares to every vertex v that lies on only one square S. Such a new square must have v as a vertex, be oriented the same way as S, touch S at v only, and have side length $1/2$ the side length of S.

The first three terms of this sequence are as follows.

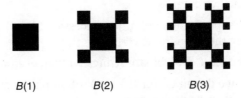

$B(1)$ $\qquad\quad$ $B(2)$ $\qquad\quad$ $B(3)$

The above definition defines a sequence of shapes $B(1), B(2), B(3), \ldots$ that approximate the Badda-Bing fractal. None of these shapes *is* the fractal, exactly. The actual fractal consists of infinitely many squares, while each approximating shape $B(n)$ contains finitely many. However, it is possible to define the fractal as a recursive set, following the idea in Example 3.21. The following statements define a set B of points in the plane.

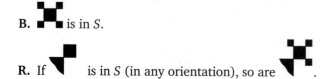

B. ▦ is in S.

R. If ◥ is in S (in any orientation), so are ▦ .

This definition is somewhat informal, but it helps us think about the recursive nature of the fractal. If you were to draw the fractal using this definition, you would start with the five squares in the base case, then you would apply the recursive case to the four squares on the corners, then you would apply the recursive case to the twelve little squares on the corners, and so on. This hypothetical "bottom-up" construction continues forever, with the squares becoming arbitrarily small and numerous, accounting for the fractal nature of the set B.

Of course, we haven't proved that the limit of the sequence $B(1), B(2), B(3), \ldots$ is the set B; we aren't going to study limits in enough detail to make such claims. The purpose of this example is to get us thinking recursively.

The mathematical study of fractals is relatively new; most of the important discoveries in this field weren't made until the second half of the 20th century, when computers became widely available to mathematicians. While these objects can be fascinating in themselves, their self-similar structure can help us visualize the concept of recursion. In a fractal, you can see copies of the fractal one layer down; each arm of the Koch snowflake has smaller, identically shaped arms coming off of it. This is the sort of observation you must make when you write recursive definitions. How does a string contain a smaller string on the inside? How can we build up a greater odd number from a lesser one? Fractals are pretty, but they are important because they show us a picture of recursive thinking.

3.3.4 Recursive Jokes

One measure of how well you understand a certain concept is whether you understand humor based on the concept. Here are some recursive jokes. Maybe these aren't very funny, but hopefully you don't need them explained to you.

> In order to understand recursion, you must understand recursion.

> It isn't unusual for the following to be in the index of a book:

>> Recursion, *see Recursion.*

Some acronyms are recursive jokes: VISA (VISA International Service Association), GNU (GNU's Not Unix), and PHP (PHP Hypertext Preprocessor). An early spin-off of the text editor EMACS was named EINE (EINE Is Not EMACS), and one of its successors was called ZWEI (ZWEI Was EINE Initially).

Certain well-known camp songs have recursive definitions, for example, "99 bottles of beer on the wall ...." This song is a good example of top-down thinking.

Exercises 3.3

1. Write the recurrence relation for the Fibonacci numbers (Definition 3.1) in the form of a recursive definition, with two base cases and one recursive case.

2. See Example 3.16. Why is the first part of the definition necessary? In other words, why must λ be defined as a palindrome? (Hint: Try forming the palindrome `otto`.)

3. Give a recursive definition for the set X of all binary strings with an even number of 0's.

4. See Example 3.17. Give a recursive definition for the set Y of all binary strings with *more* 0's than 1's. (Hint: Use the set X of Example 3.17 in your definition of Y.)

5. Define a set X of strings in the symbols 0 and 1 as follows.

   B. 0 and 1 are in X.

   R$_1$. If x and y are in X, so is $xxyy$.

   R$_2$. If x and y are in X, so is xyx.

   Using the definition, explain why the string $01001011 \in X$. Build up the string step by step, and justify each step by referring to the appropriate part of the definition.

6. Use the definition of the reverse of a string in Example 3.18 to compute $(\texttt{cubs})^R$. Justify each step using the definition.

7. Refer to Example 3.15. Suppose that the symbols can be compared, so for any i and j with $i \neq j$, either $a_i < a_j$ or $a_j < a_i$. Modify the definition so that it defines the set of all strings whose symbols are in increasing order.

8. Let K be the set of all cities that you can get to from Toronto by taking flights (or sequences of flights) on commercial airlines. Give a recursive definition of K.

9. Create your own example of an object or situation whose recursive definition is the same as the Kevin Bacon movie club in Example 3.14.

10. Define a set X of numbers as follows.

    B. $2 \in X$.

    R$_1$. If $x \in X$, so is $10x$.

    R$_2$. If $x \in X$, so is $x + 4$.

    (a) List all the elements of X that are less than 30.

    (b) Explain why there are no odd numbers in X.

11. Define a set X of integers recursively as follows.

    B. 10 is in X.

    R$_1$. If x is in X and $x > 0$, then $x - 3$ is in X.

    R$_2$. If x is in X and $x < 0$, then $x + 4$ is in X.

    List all elements of X.

12. Give a recursive definition for the set Y of all positive multiples of 5. That is,

    $$Y = \{5, 10, 15, 20, 25, 30, 35, 40, 45, 50, 55, \ldots\}.$$

    Your definition should have a base case and a recursive part.

13. The following recursive definition defines a set Z of ordered pairs.

    B. $(2, 4)$ is in Z.

    R$_1$. If (x, y) is in Z with $x < 10$ and $y < 10$, then $(x + 1, y + 1)$ is in Z.

    R$_2$. If (x, y) is in Z with $x > 1$ and $y < 10$, then $(x - 1, y + 1)$ is in Z.

    Plot these ordered pairs in the xy-plane.

14. Give a recursive definition for the set of even integers (including both positive and negative even integers).

15. Give a recursive definition for the set of all powers of 2.

16. Define a set X recursively as follows.

    B. 3 and 7 are in X.

    R. If x and y are in X, so is $x + y$. (Here it is possible that $x = y$.)

    Decide which of the following numbers are in X. Explain each decision.

    (a) 24

    (b) 1,000,000

    (c) 11

17. Define a set X recursively as follows.

    B. $12 \in X$.

    $\mathbf{R_1}$. If $x \in X$ and x is even, then $x/2 \in X$.

    $\mathbf{R_2}$. If $x \in X$ and x is odd, then $x + 1 \in X$.

    List all the elements of X.

18. Give a recursive definition for the set X of all natural numbers that are one or two more than a multiple of 10. In other words, give a recursive definition for the set $\{1, 2, 11, 12, 21, 22, 31, 32, \ldots\}$.

19. Let S be a set of sets with the following recursive definition.

    B. $\emptyset \in S$.

    R. If $X \subseteq S$, then $X \in S$.

    (a) List three different elements of S.

    (b) Explain why S has infinitely many elements.

20. In Example 3.22, we gave a recursive definition of a binary tree. Suppose we modify this definition by deleting part $\mathbf{B_1}$, so that an empty tree is not a binary tree. A tree satisfying this revised definition is called a *full binary tree*.

    (a) Give an example of a full binary tree with five nodes.

    (b) Give an example of a binary tree with five nodes that is not a full binary tree.

21. A *ternary* tree is a tree where every parent node has (at most) three child nodes. For example, the following are ternary trees.

    Give a recursive definition for a ternary tree.

22. Let G be an undirected graph, possibly not connected. The different pieces that make up G are called the *connected components* of G. More precisely, for any vertex v in G, the connected component G_v containing v is the graph whose vertices and edges are those that lie on some path starting at v. Give a recursive definition for G_v. (Hint: Mimic Example 3.14.)

23. Refer to Example 3.23. Suppose that the perimeter of $K(1)$ is 3. Give a recurrence relation for the perimeter $P(n)$ of the nth shape $K(n)$ in the sequence. Guess at a closed-form solution to $P(n)$. What does this say about the perimeter of the Koch snowflake fractal?

24. The following fractal is known as the *Sierpinski gasket*.

    In the first part of Example 3.24, we saw how to define a sequence of shapes to approximate a given fractal. Using this example as a guide, give a recursive definition for $S(n)$, where the limit of the sequence $S(1), S(2), S(3), \ldots$ is the Sierpinski gasket.

25. In the second part of Example 3.24, we saw an informal way to define a fractal as a recursively defined set. Using this example as a guide, give an informal definition of the Sierpinski gasket as a recursively defined set.

26. The following fractal resembles a tree. The "buds" at the top are actually tiny branches whose shape is similar to the larger branches lower in the tree. These branches become smaller and smaller (and more numerous) as you move up the tree.

This fractal tree is the limit of the sequence $T(1), T(2), T(3), \ldots$, where the first three terms are shown below. Give a recursive definition for $T(n)$.

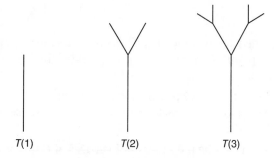

$T(1)$ $\qquad\qquad$ $T(2)$ $\qquad\qquad$ $T(3)$

27. Give an informal definition of the fractal tree in Exercise 26 as a recursively defined set.

28. The following fractal pattern is composed entirely of circles. The radius of each circle is twice as large as the radius of the next smallest circle in the pattern.

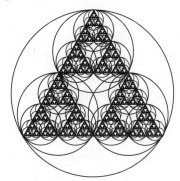

This pattern is the limit of the sequence $C(1), C(2), C(3), \ldots$, where the first and third terms of this sequence are shown below. Give a recursive definition for $C(n)$.

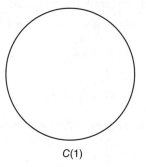
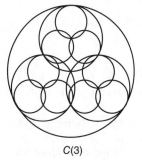

$C(1)$ $\qquad\qquad\qquad\qquad$ $C(3)$

29. Give an informal definition of the fractal in Exercise 28 as a recursively defined set.

3.4   Proof by Induction

In Section 3.2, we used induction to verify a closed-form solution to a recurrence relation. There are lots of other statements in mathematics that lend themselves to proofs by induction. Here are some examples.

- The sum of the first n natural numbers is $\dfrac{n(n+1)}{2}$.

- A binary tree of height n has less than 2^{n+1} nodes.

- A convex n-gon has $\dfrac{n(n-3)}{2}$ diagonals.

What do these examples have in common? They are all statements containing the variable n, and in each case, n stands for some natural number—each statement takes the form "Statement(n)" for all n. Furthermore, these statements all involve objects that have some sort of recursive structure. In this section we extend the technique of induction to prove facts about recursively defined objects.

Preview 3.4

1. A function $f : \mathbf{Z} \longrightarrow \mathbf{Z}$ is called *parity preserving* if $f(n)$ is even when n is even and if $f(n)$ is odd when n is odd. Give an example of a parity-preserving function (besides the identity). Explain how you know that the function preserves parity.

2. Consider the pattern of 0's and 1's given in preview question 3.3.2. Notice that all the rows are *palindromic*: they are the same forwards as backwards. Will all the subsequent rows also be palindromic? Explain why or why not.

3. For an undirected graph G, let $c(G)$ be the number of vertices of G minus the number of edges of G. Given a graph G, suppose you form a new graph G' by adding a vertex to G in the middle of one of its edges, as follows.

   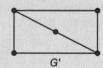

G G'

Notice that $c(G) = c(G')$. Explain why adding a vertex in this manner will always preserve the number of vertices minus the number of edges.

3.4.1   The Principle of Induction

To prove that a closed-form solution $f(n)$ matches a recurrence relation $R(n)$, we had to prove the following:

For all $n \geq 1$, $R(n) = f(n)$.

We did this by first checking the base case $R(1) = f(1)$, and then proving that $R(k) = f(k)$ follows from the inductive hypothesis $R(k-1) = f(k-1)$, for any $k > 1$. The principle of mathematical induction generalizes this approach.

The Principle of Mathematical Induction. To prove the statement "Statement(n), for all $n \geq 1$," it suffices to prove

1. Statement(1), and

2. Statement($k-1$) $\Rightarrow$ Statement(k), for $k > 1$.

This principle is plausible by the same reasoning used in Section 3.2: Step 2 establishes a chain of implications:

$$\text{Statement}(1) \Rightarrow \text{Statement}(2) \Rightarrow \text{Statement}(3) \Rightarrow \cdots ,$$

while step 1 gets the chain of implications started. It follows that these two steps, taken together, establish Statement(n) for all $n \geq 1$.

We label this a "principle" because, strictly speaking, we can't prove it as a theorem. In advanced treatments of the foundations of mathematics, this statement is usually assumed as an axiom.[2] Recall that part 1 of the principle is called the *base case* and part 2 is called the *inductive step*. In proving the inductive step, the assumption that Statement($k - 1$) is true is called the *inductive hypothesis*.

3.4.2 Examples

Mathematical induction is often the technique to use when you can think about a problem recursively. The discussion of the next result illustrates how to take a recursive viewpoint.

Theorem 3.2 *For any* $n \geq 1$, $1 + 2 + 3 + \cdots + n = \dfrac{n(n + 1)}{2}$.

Let $S_n = 1 + 2 + 3 + \cdots + n$ be the sum of the first n natural numbers. Then S_n has a recursive definition:

B. $S_1 = 1$.

R. $S_n = S_{n-1} + n$ for $n > 1$.

Understanding this definition is the key to following the inductive argument. Before digesting the proof, notice how we use the notation of the Principle of Mathematical Induction.

$$\text{Statement}(n): \quad 1 + 2 + 3 + \cdots + n = \frac{n(n + 1)}{2}.$$

$$\text{Statement}(1): \quad 1 = \frac{1(1 + 1)}{2}.$$

$$\text{Statement}(k - 1): \quad 1 + 2 + 3 + \cdots + (k - 1) = \frac{(k - 1)(k - 1 + 1)}{2}.$$

$$\text{Statement}(k): \quad 1 + 2 + 3 + \cdots + k = \frac{k(k + 1)}{2}.$$

Proof (Induction on n.)

Base Case: If $n = 1$, then the sum of the first n natural numbers is 1, and $n(n + 1)/2 = 1 \cdot 2/2 = 1$, so Statement(1) is true.

Inductive Hypothesis: Suppose as inductive hypothesis that

$$1 + 2 + \cdots + (k - 1) = \frac{(k - 1)(k - 1 + 1)}{2}$$

for some $k > 1$.

Inductive Step: Adding k to both sides of this equation gives

$$
\begin{aligned}
1 + 2 + \cdots + (k - 1) + k &= \frac{(k - 1)(k - 1 + 1)}{2} + k \\
&= \frac{(k - 1)(k) + 2k}{2} \\
&= \frac{k^2 + k}{2} \\
&= \frac{k(k + 1)}{2}
\end{aligned}
$$

as required. $\qquad\qquad\square$

---

2. Often, an equivalent condition called the *well-ordering principle* is assumed as an axiom: every nonempty set of positive integers contains a least element.

The recursive definition of S_n guides this proof: to move up one level from S_{k-1} to S_k, the definition says you just add k. This is exactly what we did to move from Statement($k-1$) to Statement(k) in the inductive step of the proof.

Theorem 3.2 is basically the statement that a certain recurrence relation has a certain closed-form solution, so the proof should remind you of those in Section 3.2. The next result looks different, but the underlying logic is the same, and we follow the same basic template.

Theorem 3.3 *Let $K(1), K(2), K(3), \ldots$ be the sequence of shapes whose limit is the Koch Snowflake of Example 3.23. Then $K(n)$, the nth term in this sequence, is composed of $4^{n-1} \cdot 3$ line segments.*

The recursive definition of this sequence is important:

B. $K(1)$ is an equilateral triangle.

R. For $n > 1$, $K(n)$ is formed by replacing each line segment

of $K(n-1)$ with the shape

such that the central vertex points outward.

The base case and the inductive steps of the following proof correspond to the base case and the recursive part of the definition, respectively.

Proof (Induction on n.)

Base Case: The base case of the definition states that $K(1)$ consists of three line segments, and $3 = 4^{1-1} \cdot 3$, so the theorem is true when $n = 1$.

Inductive Hypothesis: Suppose as inductive hypothesis that $K(k-1)$ is composed of $4^{k-1-1} \cdot 3 = 4^{k-2} \cdot 3$ line segments, for some $k > 1$.

Inductive Step: By the recursive part of the definition, $K(k)$ is formed by replacing each line segment with four others, so the number of line segments is multiplied by four. Therefore, $K(k)$ is composed of $4 \cdot 4^{k-2} \cdot 3 = 4^{k-1} \cdot 3$ line segments, as required.   □

The preceding proof closely resembles the proofs in Section 3.2 because Statement(n) was written in terms of a numerical formula, much like a closed-form solution. The next example is a little different because the claim is stated completely in the language of strings.

Theorem 3.4 *The string reversal function of Example 3.18 works. In other words, for any $n \geq 1$, $(a_1 a_2 \cdots a_{n-1} a_n)^R = a_n a_{n-1} \cdots a_2 a_1$.*

Proof (Induction on n.)

Base Case: If $n = 1$, then $a^R = a$ by Theorem 3.1, so the reversal function correctly reverses a one-element string.

Inductive Hypothesis: Suppose as inductive hypothesis that the reversal function works for any string of length $k - 1$, for some $k > 1$.

Inductive Step: Given a string $a_1 a_2 a_3 \cdots a_k$ of length k,

$$
\begin{aligned}
(a_1 a_2 a_3 \cdots a_{k-1} a_k)^R &= a_k (a_1 a_2 a_3 \cdots a_{k-1})^R && \text{by definition of } {}^R, \text{ part } \mathbf{R} \\
&= a_k (a_{k-1} \cdots a_3 a_2 a_1) && \text{by inductive hypothesis} \\
&= a_k a_{k-1} \cdots a_3 a_2 a_1
\end{aligned}
$$

as required.   □

Take another look at this last proof. It follows the template of the verification of a closed-form solution to a recurrence relation, but the recurrence relation is replaced by the recursive definition of the string reversal function. Otherwise, all the components are the same: check the base case, state the inductive hypothesis, use the recursive definition, apply the inductive hypothesis, and simplify to show the desired result.

Proofs involving recursive definitions often require induction. The next example is quite different; it indicates the diversity of results that can be proved using this technique.

Mathematicians say that a map can be N-colored if there is a way to color all of the regions of the map using only N colors so that no two regions with a common border share the same color. Recall the definition of a line map given in Example 3.19, and notice that the following example can be two-colored. The next theorem says that this is no accident.

Theorem 3.5 *Any line map can be two-colored.*

Proof (Induction on the number of lines.)

> **Base Case:** If a line map contains 0 lines, then it is just a blank rectangle, so it can be two-colored trivially using a single color.
>
> **Inductive Hypothesis:** Suppose as inductive hypothesis that any line map with $k - 1$ lines can be two-colored, for some $k > 0$.
>
> **Inductive Step:** Let M be a line map with k lines. Remove one line from M; call it l. By inductive hypothesis, the resulting map can be two-colored, so two-color it. Now put back l, and reverse the colors of all the regions on one side of the line l. Each side will still be correctly two-colored, and any regions having l as a border will be opposite colors. Hence the map M is correctly two-colored. □

In this proof, we started our induction at 0 instead of 1. We could have started at 1, and then the base case would read as follows.

> If a line map contains just 1 line, then one side of the line can be colored white and the other black, so the map can be two-colored.

The rest of the proof would be exactly the same. Sometimes there is a choice of where to start the base case of an inductive argument.

The following flow chart illustrates the reasoning in the inductive step of the proof of Theorem 3.5. To color a line map, remove a line l, apply the inductive hypothesis, put l back, and reverse the colors.

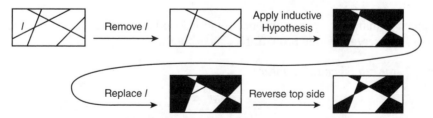

We have been following the same basic template for proofs by induction since Example 3.10, where we first verified the closed-form solution of a recurrence relation. Since then we have seen several examples. Although these examples differ in a variety of ways, they all match a basic pattern, which we can now state with more generality. In the following template, [object] stands for some sort of recursively defined object with "levels" for each natural number, and [property P] stands for the property of the [object] we are trying to justify.

Template for Inductive Proofs. An inductive proof of the statement "All [object]s have [property P]" should have the following components.

> **Base Case:** Prove that [property P] holds for the simplest [object].

Inductive Hypothesis: Suppose as inductive hypothesis that [property P] holds for an [object] of level $k - 1$, for some k.

Inductive Step: Suppose as given an [object] of level k. Use the inductive hypothesis and the recursive definition of [object] to conclude that the given level k [object] has [property P].

For example, this is how the template fits the proof of Theorem 3.5.

Base Case: Prove that a line map with 0 lines can be two-colored.

Inductive Hypothesis: Suppose as inductive hypothesis that a line map with $k - 1$ lines can be two-colored, for some $k > 0$.

Inductive Step: Suppose as given a line map with k lines. Follow the reasoning in the above flow chart.

If you are having trouble getting started with an inductive proof, try following this template.

Activity 3.4.1: Binary Trees, Part II

For this Activity, you will need to refer to the recursive definition of a perfect binary tree that you created in Activity 3.3.1.

1. Prove (by induction) that a perfect binary tree has $2^{n+1} - 1$ vertices, where n is the level of the leaves.

   Proof (by induction on n, the level of the leaves). If $n =$___, a perfect binary tree consists of a single root vertex, and $1 =$ _____. Let $k > 0$, and suppose as inductive hypothesis that a perfect binary tree with leaves of level $k - 1$ has _____ vertices. Let T be a perfect binary tree with leaves of level k. By the recursive definition, T consists of a root vertex connected to two subtrees with leaves of level _____. By inductive hypothesis, each of these subtrees has _____ vertices. Therefore, the total number of vertices in T is _____, which simplifies to _____, as required.

2. Prove (by induction) that a perfect binary tree has 2^n leaves, where n is the level of the leaves.

3.4.3   Strong Induction

So far, in all of the inductive proofs we have considered, the inductive step involved showing something about a level k object using a hypothesis about a level $k - 1$ object. However, there are times when we will need to use several previous levels ($k - 1, k - 2, \ldots$, etc.) to justify the inductive step. The verification of a closed-form solution for the Fibonacci sequence is a simple example.

Recall that the recurrence relation for these numbers,

$$F(n) = \begin{cases} 1 & \text{if } n = 1 \text{ or } n = 2 \\ F(n-1) + F(n-2) & \text{if } n > 2, \end{cases}$$

is a little more complicated than the other recurrence relations we have studied, since the recursive part refers to *two* previous values of F. Observe how the proof differs accordingly.

Theorem 3.6 *For $n \geq 1$, the nth Fibonacci number is*

$$F(n) = \frac{\alpha^n - \beta^n}{\alpha - \beta} \tag{3.4.1}$$

where

$$\alpha = \frac{1 + \sqrt{5}}{2} \text{ and } \beta = \frac{1 - \sqrt{5}}{2}.$$

Proof It is easy to check that α and β are the solutions to the following equation:

$$x^2 = x + 1. \tag{3.4.2}$$

Thus, we can use this equation as an identity for both α and β. We proceed by induction on n.

Base Case: If $n = 1$ or $n = 2$, the recurrence relation says that $F(1) = 1 = F(2)$. Formula 3.4.1 gives

$$F(1) = \frac{\alpha^1 - \beta^1}{\alpha - \beta} = \frac{\alpha - \beta}{\alpha - \beta} = 1$$

and

$$
\begin{aligned}
F(2) &= \frac{\alpha^2 - \beta^2}{\alpha - \beta} \\
&= \frac{(\alpha + 1) - (\beta + 1)}{\alpha - \beta}, \text{ using Equation 3.4.2} \\
&= \frac{\alpha - \beta}{\alpha - \beta} \\
&= 1,
\end{aligned}
$$

so the closed-form solution is correct for $n = 1$ and $n = 2$.

Inductive Hypothesis: Let $k > 2$. Suppose as inductive hypothesis that

$$F(i) = \frac{\alpha^i - \beta^i}{\alpha - \beta}$$

for all i such that $1 \leq i < k$.

Inductive Step: Using the recurrence relation,

$$
\begin{aligned}
F(k) &= F(k - 1) + F(k - 2) \\
&= \frac{\alpha^{k-1} - \beta^{k-1}}{\alpha - \beta} + \frac{\alpha^{k-2} - \beta^{k-2}}{\alpha - \beta}, \text{ by inductive hypothesis} \\
&= \frac{\alpha^{k-2}(\alpha + 1) - \beta^{k-2}(\beta + 1)}{\alpha - \beta} \\
&= \frac{\alpha^{k-2}(\alpha^2) - \beta^{k-2}(\beta^2)}{\alpha - \beta}, \text{ using Equation 3.4.2} \\
&= \frac{\alpha^k - \beta^k}{\alpha - \beta}
\end{aligned}
$$

as required. □

Look back at this proof. The inductive step requires us to use two previous values of $F(n)$. That's why the inductive hypothesis needs to be stronger. Instead of assuming "Statement($k - 1$), for some k," the inductive hypothesis has the form "Statement(i), for all $i < k$, for some k." This is known as *strong induction*; we state this as another principle.

The Second Principle of Mathematical Induction. To prove the statement "Statement(n), for all $n \geq 1$," it suffices to prove

1. Statement(1), and

2. Statement(1) $\wedge$ Statement(2) $\wedge \cdots \wedge$ Statement($k - 1$) $\Rightarrow$ Statement(k), for $k > 1$.

In other words, strong induction takes as its inductive hypothesis *all* previous cases, not just the immediate predecessor. As with simple induction, we are establishing a chain of implications that demonstrate Statement(n) for any value of n.

$$\text{Statement}(1) \Rightarrow \text{Statement}(2)$$

$$\text{Statement}(1) \wedge \text{Statement}(2) \Rightarrow \text{Statement}(3)$$

$$\text{Statement}(1) \wedge \text{Statement}(2) \wedge \text{Statement}(3) \Rightarrow \text{Statement}(4)$$

$$\cdots \Rightarrow \cdots$$

As before, each implication is of the form $P \Rightarrow Q$, but this time P is the conjunction of *all* previously established cases. In other words, P is a stronger assumption. This can make proving the inductive step easier, because you have more to work with.

The form of an inductive proof is the same with strong induction as it was with simple induction: prove the base case, state the inductive hypothesis, and use the recursive definition to prove the next case. Only the inductive hypothesis is different.

Example 3.25 Theorem 2.9 states that a connected graph with no simple circuits is a tree. We can use strong induction to show that binary trees (as defined in Example 3.22) are connected and have no simple circuits.

Proof (Strong induction on the height of the tree.)

> **Base Case:** A binary tree of height 0 consists of only a single vertex, so this graph is connected and has no simple circuits.
> **Inductive Hypothesis:** Suppose as inductive hypothesis that any binary tree with height less than k is connected and has no simple circuits, for some $k > 0$.
> **Inductive Step:** Suppose as given a binary tree T with height k. By the definition in Example 3.22, T consists of a root node r with edges going to two subtrees T_1 and T_2, each having height less than k. By inductive hypothesis, T_1 and T_2 are each connected and have no simple circuits. Since T_1 and T_2 are connected, there is a path from r to any vertex in T_1 and T_2, and therefore there is a path from any vertex in T to any other vertex. So T is connected, as required. Since T_1 and T_2 have no simple circuits, any simple circuit in T must pass through r. But in order for a circuit to begin and end in T_1 (or T_2), the circuit must pass through r twice—once to get out of T_1, and once to get back in. Such a circuit is not simple. So T has no simple circuits, as required. $\qquad\square$

We used strong induction in the preceding proof because it was necessary to apply the inductive hypothesis to the left and right subtrees, and it was possible that one of these subtrees could have had height less than $k - 1$. The strong induction hypothesis allowed us to conclude that each subtree was connected and had no simple circuits, for subtrees of any height up to $k - 1$.

In the following example, notice that we must suppose that *all* previous primes are products of primes in the inductive step. If we made only the weaker hypothesis that the preceding prime was a product of primes—as with simple induction—the argument wouldn't work.

Theorem 3.7 *Every integer $n \geq 2$ is either prime or the product of primes.*

Proof (Strong induction on n.)

> **Base Case:** The only factors of 2 are 1 and 2, so 2 is prime.
> **Inductive Hypothesis:** Let $k > 2$ be given. Suppose as inductive hypothesis that every i is such that $2 \leq i < k$ is either prime or the product of primes.
> **Inductive Step:** If k is prime, we are done. If k is not prime, then $k = pq$ for some $p \geq 2$ and $q \geq 2$. And since $k = pq$, p and q are both less than k. By inductive hypothesis, p and q are both either prime or products of primes, so $k = pq$ is the product of primes. $\qquad\square$

3.4.4 Structural Induction

In all of the previous examples, induction has been "on" some discrete quantity: proofs involving formulas of n tend to use induction on n; proofs about line maps use induction on the number of lines, etc. In some cases, however, it can be awkward to specify this quantity.

Example 3.26 Define a set $X \subseteq \mathbf{Z}$ recursively as

> **B.** $4 \in X$.
> **R_1.** If $x \in X$, then $x - 12 \in X$.
> **R_2.** If $x \in X$, then $x^2 \in X$.

Prove that every element of X is divisible by 4.

Before looking at the proof, notice that the two recursive cases move in opposite directions: changing x to $x - 12$ returns a smaller number, while changing x to x^2 returns a larger number. So it isn't natural to write the statement we are trying to prove in terms of n, for $n \geq 1$. The point of a structural induction proof is that the recursive case of the definition maintains the property of divisibility by 4.

Proof of Example 3.26. (Induction on the recursive definition of X.)

> **Base Case:** Since $4 = 1 \cdot 4$, $4 \mid 4$, so the claim holds for the base case of the definition.
> **Inductive Hypothesis:** Suppose as inductive hypothesis that some $x \in X$ is divisible by 4. Then $x = 4a$ for some integer a.
> **Inductive Step:** Now $x - 12 = 4a - 12 = 4(a - 3)$, and $x^2 = (4a)^2 = 4(4a^2)$, so both $x - 12$ and x^2 are divisible by 4. Therefore, cases R_1 and R_2 always produce integers that are divisible by 4 (given that $4 \mid x$), and the base case B gives an integer that is divisible by 4. So, by induction, all elements of X are divisible by 4. □

Pay particular attention to the inductive hypothesis in this proof: it is supposing that some element $x \in X$ has the desired property. In earlier proofs, we thought of x as an "object of level $k - 1$," and we proved something about all "objects of level k." Here we avoid the issue of how many levels an object has, focusing on the base and recursive cases of the definition. We call this "induction on the recursive definition" because we are really doing induction on the number of times the recursive part of the definition is used to obtain an element of X. We show that zero uses of the recursive part of the definition produces an element with the desired property, and then we suppose as inductive hypothesis that $k - 1$ uses of the recursive definition yields an element x with the desired property. Finally, we show that one more use of the recursive definition produces an element with the desired property. All this while, the variable k operates in the background, so it isn't really necessary to mention it in the proof.

This type of induction is also called "structural induction," because it uses the recursive structure of an object to guide the inductive argument.

Example 3.27 Theorem 3.5 states that any line map can be two-colored. Here is an alternate version of the proof of this theorem using structural induction.

Proof (Induction on the definition of a line map [Example 3.19].)

> **Base Case:** The base case of a line map is a blank rectangle, which can be two-colored because it can be one-colored.
> **Inductive Hypothesis:** Suppose as inductive hypothesis that some line map M' can be two-colored. Make a two-coloring of M'.
> **Inductive Step:** The recursive part of the definition says that a new line map M can be formed from M' by drawing some line l all the way across M'. Now reverse the colors of all the regions on one side of the line l. Each side will still be correctly two-colored, and any regions having l as a border will be opposite colors. Hence the map M is correctly two-colored. So by induction, the recursive definition of a line map always gives a two-colorable map. □

Remember that mathematical induction is a recursive technique; self-reference occurs in the inductive step of the proof. This is why many of the examples in this section make use of the recursive definitions from Section 3.3. Often, the presence of a recursive definition indicates the need for an inductive proof, and the key to constructing an inductive argument lies in thinking recursively about the problem.

Activity 3.4.2: Binary Trees, Part III

For this Activity, you will need to refer to the recursive definition of a full binary tree that you created in Activity 3.3.1.

1. Prove (by induction on the recursive definition) that a full binary tree has an odd number of vertices.

> Proof (by induction on the recursive definition). The base case of a nonempty full binary tree consists of _____, and 1 is odd. The recursive case of a full binary tree T consists of a root vertex r and two nonempty full binary subtrees T_1 and T_2. Suppose as inductive hypothesis

that T_1 and T_2 have _____ and _____ vertices, respectively, for some $k_1, k_2 \in \mathbf{N}$. By the recursive definition, the total number of vertices in T is _____, which is _____, as required.

2. Prove (by induction on the recursive definition) that a full binary tree has an even number of edges.

Exercises 3.4

1. Prove that the sum of the first n odd natural numbers is n^2.

2. You may already have a notion of what a *convex* region is, but here's a mathematical definition.

   Definition 3.2 A region R is *convex* if the line segment connecting any two points in R lies in R. A polygon is convex if it and its interior form a convex region.

   A consequence of this definition is that all the diagonals of a convex polygon lie inside the polygon. Use induction to prove that a convex n-gon has $n(n-3)/2$ diagonals. (Hint: Think of an n-gon as having an $(n-1)$-gon inside of it.)

3. Use induction to prove that the sum of the angles of a convex n-gon is $180(n-2)$ degrees.

4. Prove that any string of the form
   $$a_n a_{n-1} \cdots a_2 a_1 a_1 a_2 \cdots a_{n-1} a_n$$
   can be constructed using the definition in Example 3.16, for all $n \geq 1$.

5. Prove that any string of the form
   $$a_n a_{n-1} \cdots a_2 a_1 a_2 \cdots a_{n-1} a_n$$
   can be constructed using the definition in Example 3.16, for all $n \geq 1$.

6. Prove by induction that all of the hexagonal numbers are odd. (See Example 3.4.)

7. Recall the definition of a line map (Example 3.19).

   (a) Prove by induction that a line map with n distinct lines has at least $n + 1$ regions.

   (b) Prove by induction that a line map with n distinct lines has at most 2^n regions.

   (c) Part (a) gives a lower bound on the number of regions in a line map. For example, a line map with five lines must have at least six regions. Give an example of a line map that achieves this lower bound; that is, draw a line map with five lines and six regions.

   (d) Part (b) says that a line map with three lines can have at most eight regions. Can you draw a line map with three lines that achieves this upper bound? Do so, or explain why you can't.

8. Let the following definitions be given, where s is a string.

   Definition 1. Define the number $l(s)$ as follows.

   $\mathbf{B_1}$. $l(s) = 0$ if s is the empty string.

   $\mathbf{B_2}$. $l(s) = 1$ if s is a single symbol.

   $\mathbf{R}$. $l(s) = l(x) + l(y)$ if $s = xy$.

   Definition 2. Let n be a natural number. Define the string ns as follows:

   $\mathbf{B}$. $1s = s$.

   $\mathbf{R}$. $ns = (n-1)s\, s$ if $n > 1$.

   Use these definitions to prove that $l(ns) = nl(s)$ for all $n \geq 1$.

9. Use the recursive definition in Example 3.22 to prove that a binary tree with height n has less than 2^{n+1} nodes.

10. Refer to Exercise 20 of Section 3.3 for the definition of a full binary tree.

    (a) Use structural induction to prove that a full binary tree has an odd number of nodes.

    (b) Prove that a full binary tree has an even number of edges.

11. Let $C(n)$ be the constant term in the expansion of $(x + 5)^n$. Prove by induction that $C(n) = 5^n$ for all $n \in \mathbf{N}$.

12. Let $f : \mathbf{N} \longrightarrow \mathbf{N}$ be a function with the property that $f(1) = 2$ and $f(a + b) = f(a) \cdot f(b)$ for all $a, b \in \mathbf{N}$. Prove by induction that $f(n) = 2^n$ for all $n \in \mathbf{N}$.

13. In Exercise 3 of Section 3.1, we defined the following recurrence relation:

$$H(n) = \begin{cases} 0 & \text{if } n \leq 0 \\ 1 & \text{if } n = 1 \text{ or } n = 2 \\ H(n - 1) + H(n - 2) - H(n - 3) & \text{if } n > 2. \end{cases}$$

Prove that $H(2n) = H(2n - 1) = n$ for all $n \geq 1$.

14. The Lucas numbers $L(n)$ are defined in Exercise 4 of Section 3.1, and the Fibonacci numbers $F(n)$ are given by Definition 3.1. Prove that $L(n) = F(n - 1) + F(n + 1)$ for all $n \geq 2$.

15. Let $L(n)$ be defined as in Exercise 4 of Section 3.1, and let α and β be defined as in Theorem 3.6. Prove that $L(n) = \alpha^n + \beta^n$ for all $n \in \mathbf{N}$. Use strong induction.

16. Prove that $B(n)$, the nth term in the sequence of shapes whose limit is the Badda-Bing fractal of Example 1.17, has $4 \cdot 3^{n-1}$ free vertices (i.e., vertices that lie on only one square) for all $n \geq 1$.

17. Prove that $B(n)$, the nth term in the sequence of shapes whose limit is the Badda-Bing fractal of Example 1.17, consists of $2 \cdot 3^{n-1} - 1$ squares, for $n \geq 1$.

18. Prove that $K(n)$, the nth term in the sequence of shapes whose limit is the Koch snowflake fractal of Example 3.23, has perimeter $3 \cdot (4/3)^{n-1}$, where the equilateral triangle in $K(1)$ has side length of 1 unit.

19. Find a formula for the area of (the black part of) $S(n)$, the nth term in the sequence of shapes whose limit is the Sierpinski gasket fractal in Exercise 3.3.24 on page 134. Assume that $S(1)$ is a black equilateral triangle with area 1. Prove that your formula is correct.

20. Let X be the set defined in Example 3.21.

    (a) Prove, by induction on n, that $2n + 1 \in X$ for all $n \geq 0$. (This shows that X contains all the odd natural numbers.)

    (b) Prove by induction that every element in X is odd. (This shows that the set of all odd natural numbers contains X.)

    (c) Together, what do (a) and (b) show?

21. Define a set X recursively as follows.

    B. $2 \in X$.

    R. If $x \in X$, so is $x + 10$.

    Use induction to prove that every element of X is even.

22. Define a set X recursively as follows.

    B. 3 and 7 are in X.

    R. If x and y are in X, so is $x + y$. (Here it is possible that $x = y$.)

    Prove that, for every natural number $n \geq 12$, $n \in X$. (Hint: For the base case, show that 12, 13, and 14 are in X.)

23. Define a *Q-sequence* recursively as follows.

    B. $x, 4 - x$ is a Q-sequence for any real number x.

    R. If $x_1, x_2, \dots, x_j$ and $y_1, y_2, \dots, y_k$ are Q-sequences, so is

    $$x_1 - 1, x_2, \dots, x_j, y_1, y_2, \dots, y_k - 3.$$

    Use structural induction (i.e., induction on the recursive definition) to prove that the sum of the numbers in any Q-sequence is 4.

24. In the game of chess, a knight moves by jumping to a square that is two units away in one direction and one unit away in another. For example, on the following chessboard, the knight at K can move to any of the squares marked with an asterisk $*$.

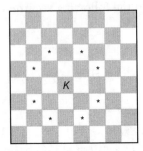

Prove by induction that a knight can move from any square to any other square on an $n \times n$ chessboard via a sequence of moves, for all $n \geq 4$.

3.5   Recursive Data Structures

In this section we will see how thinking recursively about how to organize data can lead to elegant solutions. We will give recursive definitions for lists and trees, and we will use these definitions to define useful functions on these structures. Moreover, we will prove that these functions do what they are supposed to do. Since the definitions and functions are recursive, most of these proofs will use induction.

Preview 3.5

1. Example 2.5 on page 52 introduced the rules for constructing a binary search tree to organize data according to an alphabetical order. How many different four-node binary search trees can you construct containing the words `fee`, `fi`, `fo`, and `fum`?

2. Do the following two lists contain all the same words? Describe an efficient method to decide.

   abo ahu axa bai bee bia chg cog cor cui deb din din div doa dog don dpn dry ecg eda ede eft eph esd etc fao fat fec fey fla fox fry ful guy ich its jag jat jin jug kat ken kin koa kop ler lia lou lyc mab max mgr mhd mis mob mom mun ned nub oik oke olm ora ore osa oyo pau phr pip plr pru pss qkt qmc rad rms rom sam ser sfz shf shr spp sta sym tam ter tip tob tob too ute utu wan war wit yan yea

   mhd wan mun koa fao utu fla ora mom max oke din guy kin lou eda jin div plr tob ecg min pau eph war qkt its dog rad lyc kat mgr doa etc tob jag din esd rom bai lia ned ken ser fox sta jug mob ful spp kop yan tam nub cor eft oyo fat cui chg sam oik bia shr jat fey osa olm mab fec ore bee wit rms pip tip shf pru deb dpn yea ler don abo ich axa ahu qmc too ter cog phr pss sym dry ute fry ede sfz

---

3.5.1   Lists

Almost every computer application uses some kind of list object. A *list* is a set of data elements in some sequential order

$$x_1, x_2, x_3, \ldots, x_n$$

where all of the x_i's are of the same type (e.g., integers, strings). You can make a list of n elements by adding an element to the end of a list of $n - 1$ elements; this observation inspires the following recursive definition.

Definition 3.3 Let X be a set. A *list* of elements of X is:

B. x where $x \in X$.

R. L, x where $x \in X$ and L is a list of elements of X.

Notice that, unlike a set, a list may repeat the same element several times, and the order of the elements matters. Every symbol in this definition is important; the commas between the list elements are part of the structure of a list. For example, we can build up the list of strings

cubs, bears, bulls, cubs

in a bottom-up fashion using this definition.

$$
\begin{array}{lll}
L_1 = \text{cubs} & & \text{by part } \mathbf{B} \\
L_2 = L_1, \text{bears} = \text{cubs}, \text{bears} & & \text{by part } \mathbf{R} \\
L_3 = L_2, \text{bulls} = \text{cubs}, \text{bears}, \text{bulls} & & \text{by part } \mathbf{R} \\
L_4 = L_3, \text{cubs} = \text{cubs}, \text{bears}, \text{bulls}, \text{cubs} & & \text{by part } \mathbf{R}
\end{array}
$$

One advantage to defining lists recursively is that it makes it possible to define recursive functions that tell us something about the data in the list. For example, we can use recursion to add up all the elements in a list of integers.

Definition 3.4 Let L be a list as defined by Definition 3.3, where $X = \mathbf{R}$, the real numbers. Define a function $\text{Sum}(L)$ recursively as follows.

B. If $L = x$, a single number, then $\text{Sum}(L) = x$.

R. If $L = L', x$ for some list L', then $\text{Sum}(L) = \text{Sum}(L') + x$.

Notice how the base and recursive cases of this definition match the base and recursive cases of Definition 3.3. The recursive structure of a list determines the way we write recursive functions.

Example 3.28 To evaluate the Sum function on the list $3, 1, 4, 2$, it is natural to take a top-down approach.

$$
\begin{array}{ll}
\text{Sum}(3, 1, 4, 2) = \text{Sum}(3, 1, 4) + 2 & \text{by part } \mathbf{R} \\
= \text{Sum}(3, 1) + 4 + 2 & \text{by part } \mathbf{R} \\
= \text{Sum}(3) + 1 + 4 + 2 & \text{by part } \mathbf{R} \\
= 3 + 1 + 4 + 2 & \text{by part } \mathbf{B} \\
= 10.
\end{array}
$$

The Sum function returns the correct answer for the list $3, 1, 4, 2$, but will it always work? We can prove that it does, using induction.

Theorem 3.8 *Let L be the list $x_1, x_2, x_3, \ldots, x_n$, where the x_i's are numbers. Then*

$$
\text{Sum}(L) = x_1 + x_2 + x_3 + \cdots + x_n
$$

for all $n \geq 1$.

Proof (Induction on the size of the list.)

Base Case: If L contains only a single number x, then the base case of the definition stipulates that $\text{Sum}(L) = x$, as required.

Inductive Hypothesis: Let $k > 1$. Suppose as inductive hypothesis that

$$
\text{Sum}(L') = x_1 + x_2 + x_3 + \cdots + x_{k-1}
$$

for any list L' containing $k - 1$ elements.

Inductive Step: Suppose as given a list $L = x_1, x_2, x_3, \ldots, x_k$ with k elements. Then, by Definition 3.3, $L = L', x_k$, where L' is a list of $k - 1$ elements. Therefore,

$$
\begin{array}{ll}
\text{Sum}(L) = \text{Sum}(L') + x_k & \text{by part } \mathbf{R} \\
= (x_1 + x_2 + x_3 + \cdots + x_{k-1}) + x_k & \text{by inductive hypothesis} \\
= x_1 + x_2 + x_3 + \cdots + x_k &
\end{array}
$$

as required. $\square$

The next recursive definition is for educational purposes only; the object it defines is simple and somewhat limited. The point is to help us study ways to search for an element in a list.

Definition 3.5 An *SList* is

   B. x where $x \in \mathbf{R}$, the real numbers.

   R. (X, Y) where X and Y are SLists having the same number of elements, and the last number in X is less than the first number in Y.

For example, $(((1, 3), (8, 9)), ((12, 16), (25, 30)))$ is an SList. Notice that SLists always have 2^p elements, for some $p \geq 0$. (The proof of this fact is left as an exercise.) The number p counts the *depth* of parentheses of the SList, or more simply, the depth of the SList; every number in the list will be inside p pairs of parentheses. So the example SList above has depth 3 and contains 2^3 elements. Also notice that if $L = (X, Y)$ is an SList of depth p, then X and Y must have depth $p - 1$.

What's the "S" for? The elements of an SList must be *sorted* in order from left to right. That's another exercise.

Suppose we want to define a function that will tell us whether or not a given number is in the list. Since the list is defined recursively, it is natural to define the function recursively as well. Note that the base and recursive cases of the following function correspond to the base and recursive cases of Definition 3.5.

Definition 3.6 Define a true or false function Search(t, L), where t is a number (the "target") and L is an SList, as follows.

   B.   Suppose $L = x$, a list of depth 0. Then

$$\text{Search}(t, L) = \begin{cases} \text{true} & \text{if } t = x \\ \text{false} & \text{if } t \neq x. \end{cases}$$

   R.   Suppose the depth of L is greater than 0, so $L = (X, Y)$. Then

$$\text{Search}(t, L) = \text{Search}(t, X) \vee \text{Search}(t, Y).$$

The Search function is supposed to tell whether the given target element t is in the list. For example, let $L = (((1, 3), (8, 9)), ((12, 16), (25, 30)))$. The following calculation shows how to calculate the Search function on this list, with a target value of 8:

Search$[8, L]$ = Search$[8, ((1, 3), (8, 9))] \vee$ Search$[8, ((12, 16), (25, 30))]$

= Search$[8, (1, 3)] \vee$ Search$[8, (8, 9)] \vee$ Search$[8, (12, 16)] \vee$ Search$[8, (25, 30)]$

= Search$[8, 1] \vee$ Search$[8, 3] \vee$ Search$[8, 8] \vee$ Search$[8, 9] \vee$ Search$[8, 12] \vee$ Search$[8, 16] \vee$ Search$[8, 25] \vee$ Search$[8, 30]$

= false $\vee$ false $\vee$ true $\vee$ false $\vee$ false $\vee$ false $\vee$ false $\vee$ false

= true.

Notice how to evaluate a recursive function: rewrite the function in terms of itself using the recursive step, until (hopefully) you are able to evaluate the function using the base case. Once the recursion "bottoms out," you can evaluate the function because there are no more recursive references to the function.

Search$[8, L]$ worked because it returned "true" and 8 was indeed in the list. Here is a proof that the Search function works in general.

Theorem 3.9 Search$(t, L) \iff t$ *is in L.*

Proof (Induction on p, the depth of the SList L.)

   Base Case: If $p = 0$, the list L contains only a single number, say $L = x$. The base case of the Search function will set Search$(t, L) = $ true if and only if $t = x$. Therefore,

$$\text{Search}(t, L) \iff t = x \iff t \text{ is in } L$$

when the depth of the list is 0.

Inductive Hypothesis: Suppose as inductive hypothesis that the Search function works for any list L' of depth $k - 1$, for some $k > 0$. That is, if L' has depth $k - 1$, then we suppose that

$$\text{Search}(t, L') \iff t \text{ is in } L'.$$

Inductive Step: Given a list L of depth k, we know that $L = (X, Y)$ for some X and Y of depth $k - 1$. So

$$\text{Search}(t, L) = \text{Search}(t, X) \vee \text{Search}(t, Y)$$

by the recursive part of the function definition. Now

$$
\begin{array}{llll}
t \text{ is in } L & \iff & (t \text{ is in } X) \vee (t \text{ is in } Y) & \text{by the definition of SList} \\
& \iff & \text{Search}(t, X) \vee \text{Search}(t, Y) & \text{by inductive hypothesis} \\
& \iff & \text{Search}(t, L) & \text{by the definition of Search.}
\end{array}
$$

So for any SList of any depth, the Search function will be true if and only if the target is in the list.   □

This Search function isn't very clever: it does not use the fact that an SList has to be in order. Let's look at another function designed to test whether a given number is in an SList.

Definition 3.7 Define a true or false function $\text{BSearch}(t, L)$, where t is a number and L is an SList, as follows.

B. Suppose $L = x$, a list of depth 0. Then

$$
\text{BSearch}(t, L) = \begin{cases} \text{true} & \text{if } t = x \\ \text{false} & \text{if } t \neq x. \end{cases}
$$

R. Suppose L has depth $p > 0$, so $L = (X, Y)$. Let r be the last element of X. Then

$$
\text{BSearch}(t, L) = \begin{cases} \text{BSearch}(t, Y) & \text{if } t > r \\ \text{BSearch}(t, X) & \text{if } t \not> r. \end{cases}
$$

For example, let $L = (((1, 3), (8, 9)), ((12, 16), (25, 30)))$, and try finding the number 8 using BSearch. Compare this calculation to the same search using the old (not smart) Search function:

$$
\begin{array}{lll}
\text{BSearch}[8, L] & = \text{BSearch}[8, ((1, 3), (8, 9))] & \text{since } 8 \not> 9 \\
& = \text{BSearch}[8, (8, 9)] & \text{since } 8 > 3 \\
& = \text{BSearch}[8, 8] & \text{since } 8 \not> 8 \\
& = \text{true} & \text{since } 8 = 8.
\end{array}
$$

BSearch appears to be a more clever function. Apparently, the BSearch function takes less work (and time) to evaluate than the Search function.

3.5.2 Efficiency

If these two search functions were implemented on a computer, we would probably expect BSearch to run more efficiently. How much better is it? To answer this question, we can try to count the number of operations each function does. In practice, instead of counting every single operation, computer scientists try to count the number of occurrences of the most time-consuming operation. For our functions, assume that these are the comparisons $t \overset{?}{=} x$ and $t \overset{?}{>} r$.

First consider the Search function. Let $C(p)$ be the number of times the comparison $t \overset{?}{=} x$ is done when searching a list of depth p. If $p = 0$, then the list contains only a single item, so the base case **B** of the definition gets used and one comparison is made. Therefore, $C(0) = 1$.

Now suppose the Search function is evaluated on a list of depth p, for some $p > 0$. Then the recursive case **R** of the definition gets used, and the Search function is executed twice on lists of depth $p - 1$. Each of these two recursive calls uses $C(p - 1)$ comparisons. Therefore, $C(p)$ must satisfy the following recurrence relation:

$$C(p) = \begin{cases} 1 & \text{if } p = 0 \\ 2C(p-1) & \text{if } p > 0. \end{cases} \tag{3.5.1}$$

This recurrence relation is easy to solve: $C(p) = 2^p$. Since an SList of depth p contains 2^p elements, the number of comparisons made by the Search function equals the number of elements in the list.

Similarly, we can derive a recurrence relation for the BSearch function. For a list containing a single item, the base case of the function requires one comparison. On a list of depth p, $p > 0$, the recursive part of the definition first makes one comparison, and then calls the BSearch function on a list of depth $p - 1$. If we use $D(p)$ to represent the number of comparisons needed, we get the following recurrence relation:

$$D(p) = \begin{cases} 1 & \text{if } p = 0 \\ 1 + D(p-1) & \text{if } p > 0. \end{cases} \tag{3.5.2}$$

This recurrence relation is even easier to solve: $D(p) = p + 1$. So you need only $p + 1$ comparisons to find an element in a list of size 2^p. In other words, to find a number in a list of N elements using BSearch, you need to make $\log_2 N + 1$ comparisons.

As the size of the list gets large, BSearch becomes a much better alternative to Search. For example, a list containing 1,048,576 elements requires 1,048,576 comparisons using Search, but only 21 comparisons using BSearch. Such considerations are important when writing computer programs that use these functions. We will study these issues in more depth in Chapter 5.

Here's one more recursive function that will be used in the exercises.

Example 3.29 Define a numerical function Sum(L), where L is an SList, as follows.

B. If $L = n$, then Sum(L) $= n$.

R. If $L = (X, Y)$, then Sum(L) $=$ Sum(X) $+$ Sum(Y).

This version of the Sum function differs from Definition 3.4 in exactly the ways that SLists differ from lists; the recursive definition of the object guides the recursive definition of the function.

3.5.3 Binary Search Trees Revisited

We have already considered recursive definitions for binary trees in general (Example 3.22). Now that we are used to thinking recursively about data structures, it is natural to write down the following recursive definition for a binary search tree. (Compare this definition with the discussion in Example 2.5 on page 52.)

Definition 3.8 Let S be a set that is totally ordered by $\leq$. A *binary search tree* on S is

B$_1$. The empty tree, or

B$_2$. a single vertex $r \in S$. In this case, r is the root of the tree.

R. If T_1 and T_2 are binary search trees with roots r_1 and r_2, respectively, and if $a \leq r$ for all nodes $a \in T_1$ and $r \leq b$ for all nodes $b \in T_2$, then the tree

is a binary search tree with root r.

You should convince yourself that the procedure outlined in Example 2.5 on page 52 always produces a binary search tree. The key observation is that part **R** of the recursive definition is satisfied.

Activity 3.5.1: Binary Search Trees, Part I

A *binary search tree* is a binary tree with the property that the root vertex is greater than or equal to all of the vertices in its left subtree and less than or equal to all of the vertices in its right subtree. Furthermore, these subtrees must also be binary search trees.

The vertices of a binary search tree need to have some sort of $\leq$ relation defined on them that gives a total ordering. For example, the vertices could be numbers (which are ordered in the usual way), or they could be words (which can be ordered alphabetically).

1. Put the words `zork`, `snork`, `gork`, `fork`, `pork`, `cork`, `bork` into a binary search tree that has the shape of a perfect binary tree with seven vertices.

2. Suppose that a binary search tree has the following shape.

   Place the integers 1 through 10 on the nodes in a manner consistent with the definition of a binary search tree.

3. Based on the two examples of binary search trees in this activity, where is the smallest element in a binary search tree? Where is the largest element?

4. Suppose that the number 37 is in the following binary search tree, on one of the unlabeled nodes. Which nodes could it possibly be on? Give a reason for your answer.

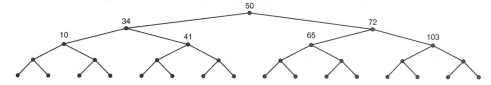

Given a binary search tree, we would like to be able to produce a listing of its nodes in order. We can define such a listing, separated by commas, as a recursive function.

Definition 3.9 Define a function InOrder(T), where T is a binary search tree,[3] as follows.

B₁. If T is the empty tree, then InOrder(T) = "" (the empty listing).

B₂. If T is a single node r, then InOrder(T) = "r".

 R. If T has root r and subtrees T_1 and T_2, then

$$\text{InOrder}(T) = \text{"InOrder}(T_1), r, \text{InOrder}(T_2)\text{"}$$

where the commas are part of the listing unless T_1 or T_2 is empty.

Let's step through this definition for the binary search tree in Figure 2.6 on page 53. Let T represent the whole tree; let L represent the subtree on the left containing complexify, clueless, and jazzed; and let R be the subtree on the right containing poset, phat, and sheafify. Then

InOrder(T) = InOrder(L), macchiato, InOrder(R)

= InOrder(clueless), complexify, InOrder(jazzed), macchiato, InOrder(phat), poset, InOrder(sheafify)

= clueless, complexify, jazzed, macchiato, phat, poset, sheafify.

So InOrder produces a listing of the words in alphabetical order. To see that InOrder always does this, observe that part **R** of Definition 3.9 always produces words that are in order, provided part **R** of Definition 3.8 holds.

---

3. Observe that this definition applies to a generic binary tree. We will discuss this and similar definitions further in Chapter 5.

Activity 3.5.2: Binary Search Trees, Part II

For the following questions, the symbol $\mathcal{P}$ denotes the set of all perfect binary trees, $\mathcal{S}$ denotes the set of all full binary search trees, and $\mathcal{L}$ denotes the set of all lists.

1. Let $S : \mathcal{S} \longrightarrow \{\text{true, false}\}$ be a function that inputs a full binary search tree and outputs either true or false, defined as follows.

    B. If X is a binary search tree consisting only of a single vertex, then $S(X) = \text{true}$ if this vertex equals pork and $S(X) = \text{false}$ otherwise.

    R. If X is a binary tree with root v, left subtree X_l and right subtree X_r, then $S(X) = \text{true}$ if v equals pork. Otherwise, if $v < \text{pork}$, then $S(X) = S(X_r)$. If $v > \text{pork}$, then $S(X) = S(X_l)$.

    If the input to S is the binary search tree from question 1 of Activity 3.5.1, what is the output? Illustrate with a top-down evaluation.

2. Let $T : \mathcal{P} \longrightarrow \mathcal{L}$ be a function that inputs a perfect binary tree and outputs a list of vertices, defined as follows.

    B. If X is a binary tree consisting only of a single vertex v, then $T(X) = v$, a list with only one entry.

    R. If X is a binary tree with root v, left subtree X_l and right subtree X_r, then $T(X)$ equals the list $T(X_l), T(X_r), v$.

    If the input to T is the binary search tree from Question 1 of Activity 3.5.1, what is the output? Illustrate with a top-down evaluation.

3. Modify the function in Question 2, so that, given the same input, the output is

    gork, cork, bork, fork, snork, pork, zork

    Check your answer by illustrating a top-down evaluation.

Exercises 3.5

1. Let L be a list, as in Definition 3.3. Define a numerical function f as follows.

    B. If $L = x$, a single element, then $f(L) = 1$.

    R. If $L = L', x$ for some list L', then $f(L) = f(L') + 1$.

    (a) Show the steps of a "top-down" computation, as in Example 3.28, to find the value of $f(\text{veni}, \text{vidi}, \text{vici})$.

    (b) What does the value of $f(L)$ tell you about the list L, in general?

    (c) Prove your assertion in part (b), using induction.

2. Consider the following function p, where L is a list.

    B. If $L = x$, a single element, then $p(L) = \text{"x"}$.

    R. If $L = L', x$ for some list L', then $p(L) = \text{"x}, p(L')\text{"}$.

    (a) If $L = \text{john}, \text{paul}, \text{george}, \text{ringo}$, what is $p(L)$?

    (b) What does the function p do, in general?

    (c) Prove your assertion in part (b), using induction.

3. Define a function max: $\mathbf{R} \times \mathbf{R} \longrightarrow \mathbf{R}$ by

$$\max(a, b) = \begin{cases} a & \text{if } a > b \\ b & \text{if } b \geq a. \end{cases}$$

(a) Use this function to write a recursive function LMax(L) that returns the greatest value in L, where L is a list of numbers.

(b) Prove that your LMax function works. In other words, prove that LMax(L) returns the greatest value in the list L.

4. Prove that the number of elements in any SList of depth p is 2^p. (Use induction on p.)

5. Prove that the elements of an SList are in strictly increasing order from left to right. That is, if $x_1, x_2, x_3, \ldots, x_{2^p}$ are the elements of the list, show that $x_1 < x_2 < x_3 < \cdots < x_{2^p}$. (Use induction on p.)

6. Prove that the BSearch function (Definition 3.7) works. In other words, prove that BSearch(t, L) $\Leftrightarrow$ t is in L.

7. Prove that the Sum function of Example 3.29 works. In other words, prove, for any $p \geq 0$, that if $a_1, a_2, \ldots, a_{2^p}$ are the elements of L, then Sum(L) $= a_1 + a_2 + \cdots + a_{2^p}$.

8. Suppose L is an SList of depth p. Find a recurrence relation for $A(p)$, the number of times two numbers are added when evaluating Sum(L).

9. Let L be an SList. Define a recursive function Flip as follows.

   B. Suppose $L = x$. Then Flip(L) $= x$.

   R. Suppose $L = (X, Y)$. Then Flip(L) $= $ (Flip(Y), Flip(X)).

   Compute Flip$[((2, 3), (7, 9))]$, showing all steps.

10. Let L be an SList. Define a recursive function Wham as follows.

   B. Suppose $L = x$. Then Wham(L) $= x \cdot x$.

   R. Suppose $L = (X, Y)$. Then Wham(L) $= $ Wham(X) $+$ Wham(Y).

   (a) Evaluate Wham$(((1, 2), (4, 5)))$, showing all work.

   (b) Give a recurrence relation for $S(p)$, the number of $+$ operations performed by Wham on an SList of depth p, for $p \geq 0$.

   (c) Give a recurrence relation for $M(p)$, the number of $\cdot$ operations performed by Wham on an SList of depth p, for $p \geq 0$.

11. Write a recursive function $d(L)$ that returns the depth of an SList L.

12. Write a recursive function $a(L)$ that computes the average of an SList L. Use the fact that the average of a list is the average of the averages of each half.

13. Let $L = ((10, 20), (30, 40))$ be an SList.

   (a) Compute Search$(15, L)$, showing all steps.

   (b) Compute BSearch$(15, L)$, showing all steps.

14. Let $L = (((15, 25), (35, 45)), ((50, 60), (70, 80)))$ be an SList.

   (a) Compute Search$(15, L)$, showing all steps.

   (b) Compute BSearch$(15, L)$, showing all steps.

15. Modify the InOrder function (Definition 3.9) so that it lists the items in a binary search tree in reverse order.

*16. Write a recursive search function for finding an element in a binary search tree. You should use the notion of a left or right subtree of a node in your definition. (In Definition 3.8, the left and right subtrees are T_1 and T_2, respectively.) Make sure you account for empty nodes.

17. Define a *UList* as follows. A *UList* is

   B. a number x, or

   R. a pair (X, Y), where X and Y are ULists.

   (a) Use induction to prove that, for any $n \geq 1$, a UList containing n numbers can be constructed.

   (b) Write a definition of a recursive function Product(L) that inputs a UList and returns the product of all the numbers in the UList.

   (c) Define a USearch function that tells whether a given number is in the list.

   (d) Prove that your USearch function works.

18. Define a *NumberSquare* as

    B. A single number x.

    R. A diagram

    $$\begin{bmatrix} S_1 & S_2 \\ S_3 & S_4 \end{bmatrix}$$

    where S_1, S_2, S_3, S_4 are NumberSquares each containing the same amount of numbers.

    Here are three examples of NumberSquares:

    $$4, \quad \begin{bmatrix} 4 & 17 \\ 13 & 1 \end{bmatrix}, \quad \begin{bmatrix} \begin{bmatrix} 3 & 12 \\ 11 & 7 \end{bmatrix} & \begin{bmatrix} 5 & 1 \\ 2 & 4 \end{bmatrix} \\ \begin{bmatrix} 6 & 10 \\ 7 & 3 \end{bmatrix} & \begin{bmatrix} 4 & 17 \\ 13 & 1 \end{bmatrix} \end{bmatrix}.$$

    Define a recursive function Trace(S) that returns the sum of the upper-left/lower-right diagonal of the NumberSquare S. (For the examples above, the Trace function should return 4, 5, and 15, respectively.)

19. Refer to the definition of NumberSquare in Exercise 18. The *depth* of a NumberSquare is the number of pairs of brackets needed to write the square. (So the given examples have depth 0, 1, and 2, respectively.) Prove, using induction on p, that a NumberSquare of depth p has 4^p numbers in it.

20. Define a *TGraph* as follows.

    B. This is a TGraph:

    R. If G is a TGraph and v is a vertex of G, then this is also a TGraph:

    Draw an example of a TGraph with seven vertices.

21. Refer to Exercise 20. Prove, by induction, that every vertex in a TGraph has even degree.

22. Refer to Exercise 20. Prove, by induction, that any TGraph can be three-colored.

23. Define a *Kgraph* as follows.

    B. 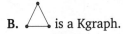 is a Kgraph.

    R₁. If ⊂ is a Kgraph, so is ⊂. (Any edge can be bisected.)

    R₂. If ⊂ is a Kgraph, so is ⊂. (Any two vertices can be joined.)

    Give reasons (**B**, **R₁**, or **R₂**) for each of the following five steps in the bottom-up construction of a Kgraph.

24. Refer to the definition of a Kgraph in the previous problem. Prove that in any Kgraph, the number of edges is greater than or equal to the number of vertices. Use induction on the recursive definition.

Chapter 4
Quantitative Thinking

Counting is important. Many problems in mathematics, computer science, and other technical fields involve counting the elements of some set of objects. But counting isn't always easy. In this chapter, we will investigate tools for counting certain types of sets, and we will learn how to think about problems from a quantitative point of view.

The goal of this chapter is to see how quantitative thinking is useful for analyzing discrete problems, especially in computer science. A course in combinatorics will teach you more about specific counting techniques; our aim here is not only to learn a few of these techniques but also to see why these techniques are important in the study of discrete processes.

Figure 4.1 A typical position in chess presents the players with several different possible moves. In order to look two or three moves ahead, players must consider hundreds of combinations, and the number of distinct 40-move games seems almost limitless. Enumerating these possibilities, even approximately, reveals the complex nature of the game.

4.1   Basic Counting Techniques

Preview 4.1

---

1. The small squares in the figure below represent the pixels needed to draw the figure on a raster display. Count the number of pixels. Explain your method of counting: did you just count, or did you also use arithmetic?

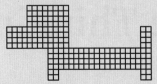

2. Recall that a *binary string* is a string using only the symbols 0 and 1. How many binary strings of length 4 are there? Write them down in some organized way that shows that you have included all of them.

3. A *ternary string* is a string made up of 0s, 1s, and 2s. How many ternary strings of length 4 are there? Without writing them all down, explain how your organizational method from preview question 4.1.2 could be used to confirm this result.

Most counting problems can be reduced to adding and multiplying. This sounds easy, but the hard part is knowing when to add and when to multiply. We'll start with some very simple examples.

4.1.1   Addition

In Section 2.2, we introduced the inclusion–exclusion principle. It states that if A and B are finite sets, then the size of their union is given by

$$|A \cup B| = |A| + |B| - |A \cap B|.$$

We say that A and B are *disjoint* if $A \cap B = \emptyset$. In this case, the inclusion–exclusion principle reduces to the equation $|A \cup B| = |A| + |B|$. In other words, if two sets have no elements in common, then you count the total number of elements in both sets by counting the elements in each and adding. This simple observation gives us our first counting principle.

> **Addition Principle.** Suppose A and B are finite sets with $A \cap B = \emptyset$. Then there are $|A| + |B|$ ways to choose an element from $A \cup B$.

In counting problems, disjoint sets usually take the form of mutually exclusive options or cases. If a person has an "either/or" choice, or a problem reduces to separate cases, the addition principle is probably called for.

Example 4.1 Ray owns five bicycles and three cars. He can get to work using any one of these vehicles. How many different ways can he get to work?

Solution: Since it is impossible to take *both* a car and a bicycle to work, these are disjoint sets. Thus, Ray has $5 + 3 = 8$ choices.   ◇

Example 4.2 On a certain day, a restaurant served 25 people breakfast and later served 37 people lunch. How many different customers did they have in total?

Solution: There isn't enough information to answer this question as stated. Before we can accurately count the total number of customers, we need to know whether any of the breakfast customers returned for lunch. If none did, then the breakfast customers are disjoint from the lunch customers, so the total is $25 + 37 = 62$. But suppose there were four breakfast customers who returned for lunch. Then by the inclusion–exclusion principle, there were only $25 + 37 - 4 = 58$ customers total. Another way to look at this situation is by thinking of the customers as belonging to three disjoint sets: those who ate only breakfast, those who ate only lunch, and those who ate both. The sizes of these three sets are 21, 33, and 4, respectively, so by the addition principle the total is $21 + 33 + 4 = 58$.   ◇

Strictly speaking, this last bit of reasoning used a slightly stronger version of the addition principle, which we will state as a theorem.

Theorem 4.1 *Suppose that $A_1, A_2, A_3, \ldots, A_n$ are pairwise disjoint finite sets, that is, $A_i \cap A_j = \emptyset$ for all i and j with $i \neq j$. Then*

$$|A_1 \cup A_2 \cup A_3 \cup \cdots \cup A_n| = |A_1| + |A_2| + |A_3| + \cdots + |A_n|.$$

Proof Exercise. Use induction on n.   □

In other words, no matter how many disjoint cases you have, you can account for them all by adding up the counts of each.

4.1.2 Multiplication

Counting the elements in a rectangular grid is easy: you multiply the number of rows by the number of columns.

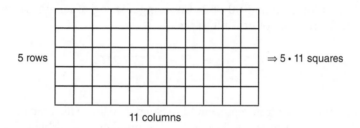

We can always think of a Cartesian product $A \times B$ of two finite sets A and B as a grid, where the columns are indexed by A and the rows are indexed by B. We state this observation as another principle.

> **Multiplication Principle.** Let A and B be finite sets. The number of elements (i.e., ordered pairs) in $A \times B$ is $|A| \cdot |B|$. So there are $|A| \cdot |B|$ ways to choose two items in sequence, with the first item coming from A and the second item from B.

Example 4.3 Ray owns five bicycles and three cars. He plans to ride a bicycle to and from work, and then take one of his cars to go to a restaurant for dinner. How many different ways can he do this?

Solution: Ray is making two choices in sequence, so he is forming an ordered pair of the form (bicycle, car). Thus, there are $5 \cdot 3 = 15$ ways possible.   ◇

The decision process in this last example has a nice graphical model in the form of the following tree.

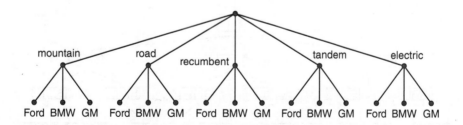

Let the root of the tree represent Ray's situation before he has made any decisions. The nodes of depth 1 correspond to the five different bicycles Ray can choose for his commute to work (mountain, road, recumbent, tandem, and electric), and the nodes of depth 2 represent the choice of car for dinner transportation (Ford, BMW, GM). Each path from the root to a leaf represents a choice of an ordered sequence of the form (bicycle, car), so the number of paths through this tree (i.e., the number of leaves) equals the number of different sequences Ray can choose. Such a model is called a *decision tree*.

Like the addition principle, the multiplication principle generalizes to collections of more than two sets.

Theorem 4.2 *Suppose that $A_1, A_2, A_3, \ldots, A_n$ are finite sets. Then*

$$|A_1 \times A_2 \times A_3 \times \cdots \times A_n| = |A_1| \cdot |A_2| \cdot |A_3| \cdots |A_n|.$$

Proof Exercise. Use induction on n.   □

Notice that unlike the addition principle, the sets in the multiplication principle need not be disjoint. The next example uses the fact that $|A \times A \times A| = |A| \cdot |A| \cdot |A|$.

Example 4.4 How many strings of length 3 can be formed from a 26-symbol alphabet?

Solution: There are three choices to be made in sequence: the first letter, the second letter, and the third letter. We have 26 options for each choice. Therefore, the total number of length 3 strings is $26 \cdot 26 \cdot 26 = 26^3 = 17,576$. ◇

Example 4.5 How many different binary strings of length 24 are there?

Solution: There are two choices for each digit: 0 or 1. Choosing a string of length 24 involves making this choice 24 times, in sequence. Thus, the number of possibilities is

$$\underbrace{2 \cdot 2 \cdots 2}_{24 \text{ two's}} = 2^{24} = 16,777,216.$$

In computer graphics, color values are often represented by such a string. This type of color is known variously as "true color," "24-bit color," or "millions of colors," reflecting the number of possible color choices.   ◇

The last two examples don't lend themselves well to decision trees; the trees would be much too large to draw. But we don't really need decision trees for such simple problems; it is easy to see how to apply Theorem 4.2 directly. However, for problems involving separate choices, in which later choices are restricted by earlier ones, decision trees are quite useful.

Example 4.6 How many designs of the form

are possible, if each square must be either red, green, or blue, and no two adjacent squares may be the same color?

Solution: If there were no restrictions on adjacent squares, then this problem would be just like forming a three-letter string from a three-letter alphabet (R, G, B), so the number of designs would be 3^3, reasoning as in Example 4.4. But this solution counts designs like RRG, which has two adjacent squares colored red, so it overcounts the correct number of designs. One way to avoid this error is to use a decision tree:

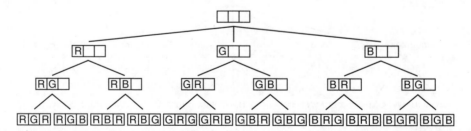

This tree shows that there are only $3 \cdot 2 \cdot 2 = 12$ designs that conform to the given restrictions.   ◇

The decision tree for Example 4.6 helps us see how to apply the multiplication principle. Think of the process of making a design as a sequence of three decisions. You can make the first square any color you wish: R, G, or B. But after this decision is made, the second square must be one of the other two colors. Similarly, the third square must be different than the second square, so there are only two choices for it as well. By applying Theorem 4.2, the total number of ways to make this sequence of three choices is $3 \cdot 2 \cdot 2 = 12$. We can therefore solve these types of problems without actually drawing the decision tree.

Example 4.7 How many different strings of length 7 can be formed from a 26-symbol alphabet, if no two adjacent symbols can be the same?

Solution: The decision tree for this problem is like the tree in Example 4.6, but with many more branches. There are 26 choices for the first symbol in the string, and then there are only 25 choices for each symbol thereafter. Hence, the total number of such strings is $26 \cdot 25^6 = 6{,}347{,}656{,}250$.   ◇

Example 4.8 Suppose that the streets of a shopping district form a grid, and that a customer enters the shopping district at point A in the diagram and begins walking in the direction of the arrow.

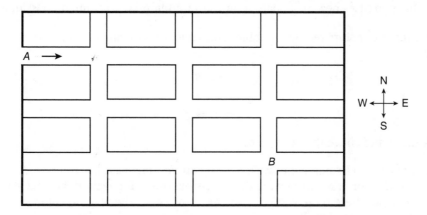

At each intersection, the customer chooses to go east or south, while taking as direct a path as possible to the bookstore at point B. How many different paths could the customer take?

Solution: The following decision tree enumerates all possible paths from A to B.

The root node represents the first intersection that the customer comes to. Each branch to the right represents a decision to go east, while a branch to the left represents a decision to go south. The nodes represent the intersections, with the leaves representing B. Whenever a move east or south would deviate from a direct path to B, there is no corresponding branch in the tree. Observe that there are six possible direct paths from A to B.   ◇

4.1.3   Mixing Addition and Multiplication

At face value, the addition and multiplication principles are pretty simple. Things get a little more tricky when a counting problem calls for a mixture of the two principles. The next few examples follow the same basic recipe: when a problem breaks up into disjoint cases, use multiplication to count each individual case, and then use addition to tally up the separate cases.

Example 4.9 How many (nonempty) strings of at most length 3 can be formed from a 26-symbol alphabet?

Solution: Reasoning as in Example 4.4, we see that there are 26 strings of length 1, 26^2 of length 2, and 26^3 of length 3. Since these cases are mutually exclusive, the total number of strings is $26 + 26^2 + 26^3 = 18{,}278$.   ◇

Example 4.10 Illinois license plates used to consist of either three letters followed by three digits or two letters followed by four digits. How many such plates are possible?

Solution: The two types of license plates can be thought of as two disjoint sets; the cases are mutually exclusive. The first case involves a choice of three letters (26^3) followed by a choice of three digits (10^3). For the second case, we first choose two letters (26^2) and then choose four digits (10^4). Putting these together, we have a total of

$$26^3 \cdot 10^3 + 26^2 \cdot 10^4 = 24{,}336{,}000$$

different possible license plates.   ◇

Example 4.10 is somewhat prototypical: it often helps to recognize certain counting problems as "license plate" problems. A license plate problem involves successive independent choices (multiplication), possibly divided up into disjoint cases (addition). All of the above examples could be thought of as license plate problems (although a system of 24-bit binary license plates, for example, would be a little strange).

Sometimes, it is easy to see how to break a counting problem into separate cases, but often it is not so obvious. In the next example, the two cases become apparent only after attempting to count all possibilities as a single case.

Example 4.11 Using the four colors red, green, blue, and violet, how many different ways are there to color the vertices of the graph

so that no two adjacent vertices have the same color?

Solution: Notice the similarity to Example 4.6; we'll start by attempting a similar solution. Color one vertex, say a, one of the four colors, R, G, B, or V. Now there are three possible colors for each of the adjacent vertices b and d, so we have $4 \cdot 3 \cdot 3$ ways to color these three vertices. We must now count the ways to color vertex c. But here we get stuck, for if b and d are the same color, then we have three choices for c, but if the colors of b and d are different, we are left with only two choices for c. Therefore, we should consider two disjoint cases:

Case 1. Suppose b and d are different colors. Then, as above, we have four choices for a, three choices for b, and then two choices for d, since it must differ from both b and a. We are left with only two choices for c, for a total of $4 \cdot 3 \cdot 2 \cdot 2 = 48$ different colorings.

Case 2. Suppose b and d are colored the same color. Then we have four choices for a, and then three choices for the color that b and d share. There are then three choices for c, for a total of $4 \cdot 3 \cdot 3 = 36$ ways to color this case.

By the addition principle, the total number of colorings is $48 + 36 = 84$.   ◇

Activity 4.1.1: Counting with Addition and Multiplication

1. The graph below (called a "word-chain automaton") defines a collection of sentences.

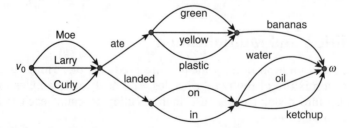

   To form a sentence using this graph, start at vertex v_0 and follow a directed path to vertex ω. The sentence is then formed by the words on the edges of this path. For example, the sentence "Moe ate green bananas" results from following the edges along the top of the graph. How many different sentences can be formed in this way? Express your answer as an unsimplified numeric expression that shows how addition and multiplication are used in this counting problem.

2. Create a simple word-chain automaton that produces exactly 19 sentences.

Exercises 4.1

1. Professor N. Timmy Date has 30 students in his Calculus class and 24 students in his Discrete Mathematics class.

   (a) Assuming that there are no students who take both classes, how many students does Professor Date have?

   (b) Assuming that there are eight students who take both classes, how many students does Professor Date have?

2. A restaurant offers two different kinds of soup and five different kinds of salad.

   (a) If you are having either soup or salad, how many choices do you have?

   (b) If you are having both soup and salad, how many choices do you have?

3. There are 18 major sea islands in the Queen Elizabeth Islands of Canada. There are 15 major lakes in Saskatchewan, Canada.

   (a) If you are planning a trip to visit one of these islands, followed by one of these lakes, how many different trips could you make?

   (b) If you plan to visit either one of these lakes or one of these islands, how many different visits could you make?

4. Bill has three one-piece jumpsuits, five pairs of work pants, and eight work shirts. He wears either a jumpsuit or pants and a shirt to work. How many different possible outfits does he have?

5. A new car is offered with 10 different optional packages. The dealer claims that there are "more than 1,000 different combinations" available. Is this claim justified? Explain.

6. Suppose that license plates in a certain municipality come in two forms: two letters (A ... Z) followed by three digits (0 ... 9) or three letters followed by two digits. How many different license plates are possible?

7. License plates in India begin with a code that identifies the state and district where the vehicle is registered, and this code is followed by a four-digit identification number. These identification numbers are given sequentially, starting with 0000, 0001, 0002, etc. Once this sequence reaches 9999, a letter from the set {A, ..., Z} is added (in order), and once these run out, additional letters are added, and so on. So the sequence of identification numbers proceeds as follows: 0000, 0001, ..., 9999, A0000, A0001, ..., A9999, B0000, B0001, ..., B9999, ..., Z0000, Z0001, ..., Z9999, AA0000, AA0001, ...

   (a) How many identification numbers are there that use two or fewer letters?

   (b) If a district registers 10 million cars, how many identification numbers must have three letters?

   (c) Suppose a district registers 500,000 cars. What percentage of identification numbers have exactly one letter?

   (d) Suppose a district registers 500,000 cars. What percentage of identification numbers have no letters?

   (e) Suppose you see a plate in Bangalore, India, with the identification number CR7812. How many vehicles were registered in this district before the vehicle with this plate?

8. License plates in China begin with a Chinese character designating the province, followed by a letter from the set {A, ..., Z}, followed by a five-character alphanumeric string (using symbols from the set {A, ..., Z, 0, 1, ... 9}). What is the maximum number of plates of this type for a given Chinese province?

9. The protein-coding strand of the average human gene consists of 1,350 nucleotides. Assuming that each nucleotide can take any of four values (A, T, C, or G), how many different genes with exactly 1,350 nucleotides are possible?

10. Refer to the previous problem. Assuming that gene strands can have between 1,200 and 1,500 nucleotides, write an expression for the number of possible genes. (Don't bother trying to evaluate this expression!)

11. How many numbers between 1 and 999 (inclusive) are divisible by either 2 or 5?

12. The following problems refer to strings in A, B, ..., Z.

    (a) How many different four-letter strings are there?

    (b) How many four-letter strings are there that begin with X?

   (c) How many four-letter strings are there that contain exactly two X's? (Hint: Consider the disjoint cases determined by where the X's are in the string.)

13. There is often more than one way to do a counting problem, and finding an alternate solution is a good way to check answers. Redo Example 4.11 by considering three disjoint cases: using two different colors, using three different colors, and using four different colors.

14. There are 16 soccer teams in Thailand's Premier League, and there are 22 teams in England's Premier League.

   (a) How many different ways are there to pair up a team from Thailand with a team from England?

   (b) How many different ways are there to pair up two teams from Thailand? (Careful: Pairing Bangkok Bank FC with Chonburi FC is the same as pairing Chonburi FC with Bangkok Bank FC.)

15. Use a decision tree to count the number of strings of length 3 using the symbols a, t, and e with the restriction that et, at, and ta do not appear anywhere in the string.

16. Using the nouns $N = \{\text{dog}, \text{man}, \text{mouse}, \text{bird}\}$ and the verbs $V = \{\text{bites}, \text{eats}, \text{kicks}\}$, how many "sentences" of the form

$$\langle \text{noun} \rangle \quad \langle \text{verb} \rangle \quad \langle \text{noun} \rangle$$

are there, with the restriction that every word in the sentence has a different length? (For example, "dog eats mouse" is such a sentence, but "man bites dog" is not, because it contains two words of length three.) Use a decision tree to arrive at your answer.

17. A five-digit number is formed according to the following rules:

   • The number contains only the digits 1, 2, 3, and 4, and these digits may be repeated or unused.

   • The first digit is 1.

   • If $D_1 D_2$ are consecutive digits and $D_1 \neq 4$, then $D_1 < D_2$.

   • If $D_1 D_2$ are consecutive digits and $D_1 = 4$, then $D_2 = 1$.

(In other words, digits must be in increasing order, except that any 4 must followed by 1. For example, 12413 is one such number.) How many numbers of this type are there? Use a decision tree to compute your answer.

18. How many different four-letter strings can be formed from the letters A,B,C,D,E (repeats allowed) if:

   (a) ... the first letter must be a vowel and the last letter must be a consonant?

   (b) ... the string must contain either all vowels or all consonants?

19. How many four-digit binary strings are there that do not contain 000 or 111? (Use a decision tree.)

20. Find an alternate solution to Exercise 19. (Count the number of strings that contain 000 or 111 and subtract from the total number of four-digit binary strings.)

21. Let X be a set containing 20 elements. Use the multiplication principle to compute $|\mathcal{P}(X)|$, the size of the power set of X. (Hint: To choose a subset of X, you must choose whether or not to include each element of X.)

22. In the directed graph below, how many directed paths are there beginning at a and ending at f? Use a decision tree to justify your answer.

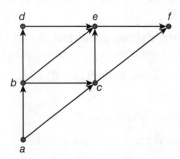

23. The *Museo de la Matemática* in Querétaro, Mexico, used to contain an exhibit with the following figure.

How many ways are there to choose a sequence of triangles starting at the top triangle and proceeding down to the bottom row, such that the sequence always proceeds down to an adjacent triangle?

24. Suppose that Omedi wants to get from point A on the following map to some point on the subway (represented by the thick dotted line).

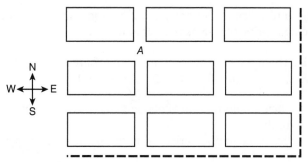

At each intersection, he can decide to go either south or east. How many different paths can he take? Draw a decision tree representing the different possible paths.

25. Two teams (A and B) play a best-of-five match. The match ends when one team wins three games. How many different win or loss scenarios are possible? (Use a decision tree.)

26. Prove Theorem 4.1.

27. Prove Theorem 4.2.

4.2 Selections and Arrangements

So far, we have seen how to enumerate sets using addition and multiplication. These basic principles apply to almost any counting problem in discrete mathematics, but there are many more counting techniques that we could study. While one could easily spend a semester learning these techniques, the next two sections focus on a few of the most important ideas for solving quantitative problems.

In this section, we will concentrate on two tasks: selecting and arranging. A selection problem involves choosing a subset of elements from a given set. An arrangement problem involves choosing a subset, and then putting its elements into some particular order. When you are able to think of a counting problem in terms of selections or arrangements, the solution is often easy to see.

Preview 4.2

1. In the graph below, every pair of vertices shares an edge. Count the number of edges. Did you employ a shortcut of some kind? If so, explain.

2. How many three-letter strings can you form using the letters O, A, T, and S, if you aren't allowed to use the same letter more than once in each string? Organize these strings in a way that shows you have included all the possibilities.

3. How many three-element subsets of $\{0, 1, 2, 3, 4\}$ are there? Write down these sets in some organized way to show that you have included them all.

4.2.1   Permutations: The Arrangement Principle

Here is an example of an arrangement problem:

Example 4.12 Yifan has 26 refrigerator magnets in the shapes of the letters from A to Z. How many different three-letter strings can he form with these?

Solution: This is a "license plate" problem (see Example 4.10), but with a restriction. Since Yifan has only one magnet per letter, he is not allowed to repeat letters. There are three slots to fill. He has 26 choices for the first slot. Since he can't reuse that letter, he has 25 choices for the second slot, and similarly, 24 for the third. So the total number of possible strings is $26 \cdot 25 \cdot 24$.   ◇

This solution applies the multiplication principle, but at each successive decision the number of letters is reduced by one. The arrangement principle states the general rule.

> **Arrangement Principle.** The number of ways to form an ordered list of r distinct elements drawn from a set of n elements is $P(n, r) = n \cdot (n - 1) \cdot (n - 2) \cdots (n - r + 1)$.

Such a list is called an *arrangement*. Note that arrangements have two key properties: the order of the elements matters, and all the elements are distinct.

The notation $P(n, r)$ comes from the mathematical term for arrangements: *permutations*. Notice that

$$P(n, r) = \frac{n!}{(n - r)!}$$

is a convenient way of expressing the number of permutations in terms of the factorial function. Recall that the factorial function is defined as $n! = n \cdot (n - 1) \cdots 3 \cdot 2 \cdot 1$, and, by convention, $0! = 1$. Note that $P(n, n) = n!$.

Example 4.13 A baseball team has a 24-man roster. How many different ways are there to choose a 9-man batting order?

Solution: A batting order is simply a list of nine players in order, so there are $P(24, 9) = 24!/15! = 474,467,051,520 \approx 4.74 \times 10^{11}$ ways to make such a list.   ◇

Example 4.14 How many different ways are there to rearrange the letters in the word GOURMAND?

Solution: The important thing to notice about the word GOURMAND is that all the letters are different. Hence they form a set of eight letters, and rearranging the letters amounts to choosing an ordered list of eight distinct elements from this set. The number of ways to do this is $P(8, 8) = 8! = 40,320$.   ◇

Rearranging the letters in the word GOURMAND is the same as finding a one-to-one correspondence:

$$f \colon \{G, O, U, R, M, A, N, D\} \longrightarrow \{G, O, U, R, M, A, N, D\}.$$

For any letter l in GOURMAND, $f(l)$ is the letter that replaces it in the rearrangement. In general, if X is a finite set with n elements, then the number of one-to-one correspondences $f \colon X \longrightarrow X$ is $n!$. Such a function is called a *permutation* of the set X.

Example 4.15 A kitchen drawer contains 10 different plastic food containers and 10 different lids, but any lid will fit on any container. How many different ways are there to pair up containers with lids?

Solution: The key to solving this problem is thinking about it the right way. In order to pair up each container with a lid, start by lining all the containers up in a row. (It doesn't matter how you line them up.) Now choose an arrangement of the 10 lids, and place the lids in this arrangement next to the containers. This determines a pairing, and all pairings are determined this way. The only choice was in the arrangement of the lids, so there are $P(10, 10) = 10! = 3,628,800$ ways to match up lids with containers.   ◇

The next example highlights the difference between the multiplication principle and the arrangement principle.

Example 4.16 An urn contains 10 ping-pong balls, numbered 1 through 10. Four balls are drawn from the urn in sequence, and the numbers on the balls are recorded. How many ways are there to do this, if (a) the balls are replaced before the next one is drawn, or (b) the balls are drawn and not replaced.

Solution: In case (a), there are always 10 balls in the urn, so there are always 10 choices. By the multiplication principle, the number of ways to draw four balls is $10^4 = 10,000$. In case (b), the balls are not replaced, so the number of choices goes down by one each time a ball is drawn. Hence there are $P(10, 4) = 10 \cdot 9 \cdot 8 \cdot 7 = 5,040$ ways to draw four balls. $\diamond$

Example 4.16 belongs to the arcane genre of "urn problems." Although we don't often encounter urns in real life, this type of problem is somewhat prototypical. Like license plate problems, urn problems provide a simple way to classify a certain type of enumeration tasks. And one often hears the terms "with replacement" and "without replacement" associated to arrangements or selections; this terminology makes sense in the context of urns.

4.2.2 Combinations: The Selection Principle

Here is a slight variation on Example 4.13.

Example 4.17 A baseball team has a 24-man roster. How many different ways are there to choose a group of nine players to start the game?

Solution: The only difference between this problem and Example 4.13 is that no order is imposed on the group of starters. Observe that any choice of nine starters accounts for exactly $P(9, 9) = 9!$ batting orders. Thus, the number of batting orders is 9! times as big as the number of choices for a group of starters. Hence, the number of ways to choose this group is

$$\frac{P(24, 9)}{9!} = \frac{24!}{15! \, 9!} = 1,307,504.$$

$\diamond$

The distinction between Examples 4.13 and 4.17 is important: in the latter, the group was an unordered set. This type of choice is called a *selection*.

Selection Principle. The number of ways to choose a subset of r elements from a set of n elements is

$$C(n, r) = \frac{n!}{r!(n - r)!}.$$

Since selections involve choosing a subset, we read the expression "$C(n, r)$" as "n choose r." Sometimes we use the notation

$$C(n, r) = \binom{n}{r}.$$

Note that $C(n, n) = 1$, because there is only one subset containing all the elements: the whole set. Similarly, $C(n, 0) = 1$, because the empty set is the only subset with zero elements.

Compare the formula for $C(n, r)$ to the formula for $P(n, r)$. In the selection principle, the $r!$ factor in the denominator accounts for the fact that no order is imposed on the elements of the subset. Arrangements and selections both involve choosing a subset of some set. The key distinction bears repeating: *In arrangements, the order of the elements in the subset matters; in selections, it doesn't.*

Example 4.18 As in Example 4.16, suppose an urn contains 10 ping-pong balls numbered 1 through 10. Instead of drawing four balls in sequence, reach in and grab a handful of four balls. How many different handfuls can you grab?

Solution: A "handful" of four ping-pong balls is an unordered set, so there are $C(10, 4) = 210$ different handfuls. $\diamond$

Take a moment to compare parts (a) and (b) of Example 4.16 with Example 4.18. The sizes of an ordered sequence with replacement, an ordered sequence without replacement, and an unordered set (without replacement) are 10,000, 5040, and 210, respectively.

Example 4.19 How many different ways are there to rearrange the letters in the word PFFPPPFFFF?

Solution: Although this example resembles Example 4.14, the solution is quite different because the letters of PFF-PPPFFFF are not all distinct. In fact, there are only two letters, P and F, and we must form a 10-letter word using four P's and six F's. In order to view this as a selection problem, notice that we have to fill 10 blanks

$$\underline{\quad} \; \underline{\quad} \; \underline{\quad} \; \underline{\quad} \; \underline{\quad} \; \underline{\quad} \; \underline{\quad} \; \underline{\quad} \; \underline{\quad} \; \underline{\quad}$$

using four P's and six F's. Once we choose where the P's go, there are no more choices to make, since the remaining blanks get filled up with the F's. The order of the blanks we choose doesn't matter, because we are putting P's in all of them. So the number of ways to fill in the blanks is $C(10, 4) = 210$. ◇

You may have noticed that we could also have solved this problem by choosing where the F's go, and then our answer would be $C(10, 6)$. Fortunately, $C(10, 6) = 210$ as well. In fact,

$$C(n, k) = C(n, n - k)$$

for all n and k with $n \geq k \geq 0$. The proof of this identity is left as an exercise.

Rearranging letters in a word may seem like a pointless diversion, but there are a variety of counting problems that are equivalent to Example 4.19. Two examples follow.

Example 4.20 In Example 4.8, we used a decision tree to count all the direct paths along a street grid traveling two blocks east and two blocks south. We could restate this problem as follows: how many different four-symbol strings are there using two E's and two S's? By the method of Example 4.19, there are $C(4, 2) = 6$ strings of this form.

Example 4.21 How many solutions are there to the equation $x_1 + x_2 + x_3 + x_4 + x_5 = 13$, if $x_1, \ldots, x_5$ must be nonnegative integers?

Solution: Such a solution corresponds to a distribution of 13 units among the five variables $x_1, \ldots, x_5$. For example, the solution

$$x_1 = 4, \quad x_2 = 0, \quad x_3 = 5, \quad x_4 = 1, \quad x_5 = 3$$

amounts to dividing up thirteen 1s into groups as follows:

$$1\,1\,1\,1\,|\,|\,1\,1\,1\,1\,1\,|\,1\,|\,1\,1\,1.$$

We can view this division into groups as a string containing four |s and thirteen 1s; every such string defines a different solution to the equation, and all solutions can be represented this way. So we just need to count the strings of this type. By the method of Example 4.19, the number of possible strings (and also the number of possible solutions) is $C(17, 4) = 2380$. ◇

Activity 4.2.1: Permutations and Combinations

The following notation is often useful for expressing the answers to counting problems.

$$k^n = \underbrace{k \cdot k \cdot k \cdots k}_{n} \qquad\qquad \text{power}$$

$$n! = \underbrace{n \cdot (n - 1) \cdot (n - 2) \cdots 3 \cdot 2 \cdot 1}_{n} \qquad\qquad \text{factorial}$$

$$P(n, r) = \underbrace{n \cdot (n - 1) \cdot (n - 2) \cdots (n - r + 1)}_{r} \qquad\qquad \text{permutation}$$

$$C(n, r) = \frac{P(n, r)}{r!} \qquad\qquad \text{combination}$$

1. A *quinary string* is a string made up of 0s, 1s, 2s, 3s, and 4s.

   (a) How many quinary strings of length 4 are there?

   (b) Suppose you are only allowed to use each digit once. Given this restriction, how many quinary strings of length 4 can you form?

   (c) Suppose you wish to select a set $\{d_1, d_2, d_3\}$ of quinary digits. How many such sets are there?

   If possible, express your answers using the notation given above.

2. A taco stand offers three types of taco: asada, pastor, and veggie. Don has enough money for 7 tacos. To make an order, you have to place checkmarks on an order form with three regions. For example, to order 3 asada, 2 pastor, and 2 veggie, you would fill out the form like this:

Asada	Pastor	Veggie
✓✓✓	✓✓	✓✓

   Notice that a taco order corresponds to an arrangement of the symbols in the string ✓✓✓ | ✓✓ | ✓✓. Use this observation to count how many different 7-taco orders Don can make.

The addition, multiplication, arrangement, and selection principles are powerful enough to solve most counting problems that arise in discrete mathematics. But this is easier said than done: it often takes quite a bit of skill to put these four principles together.

Example 4.22 Two teams, A and B, play a best-of-seven match. The match ends when one team wins four games. How many different win or loss scenarios are possible?

Solution: (Version #1.) The match could go four, five, six, or seven games, and these cases are all disjoint. There are only two ways the winners of a four-game match could go: $AAAA$ or $BBBB$. In a five-game match, the winning team must lose one of the first four games, so there are $2 \cdot C(4, 1) = 8$ ways this can happen; the $C(4, 1)$ factor accounts for choosing which game to lose, and the factor of 2 accounts for either A or B winning the match. Similarly, there are $2 \cdot C(5, 2) = 20$ scenarios for a six-game match, and $2 \cdot C(6, 3) = 40$ scenarios for a seven-game match. By the addition principle, there are $2 + 8 + 20 + 40 = 70$ different possible win or loss scenarios. ◇

This last solution is a nice illustration of using the addition principle in tandem with the selection principle. However, there is an alternate solution that is possibly simpler to understand.

Solution: (Version #2.) Regard every match as lasting seven games: once one team has won four games, that team forfeits the remaining games. This is the same as ending the match after four wins by one team, so the total number of win or loss scenarios should be the same. We must then count the number of seven-symbol strings using four A's and three B's (when A wins the match) and the number of seven-symbol strings using four B's and three A's (when B wins). This is just like Example 4.19; in each case there are $C(7, 4) = 35$ such strings, for a total of 70 win or loss scenarios. ◇

A third way of solving Example 4.22 would be to use a decision tree (though such a tree would be quite large). It is always a good idea to look for alternate solutions to a counting problem; it's a way of checking your answer.

4.2.3 The Binomial Theorem ‡

In high school algebra, you learned how to expand expressions like $(3x - 5)^4$ by multiplying polynomials:

$$(3x - 5)^4 = (3x - 5)(3x - 5)(3x - 5)(3x - 5)$$

$$= (9x^2 - 15x - 15x + 25)(3x - 5)(3x - 5)$$

$$= (27x^3 - 45x^2 - 45x^2 + 75x - 45x^2 + 75x + 75x - 125)(3x - 5)$$

$$= (27x^3 - 135x^2 + 225x - 125)(3x - 5)$$

$$= 81x^4 - 405x^3 + 675x^2 - 375x - 135x^3 + 675x^2 - 1125x + 625$$

$$= 81x^4 - 540x^3 + 1350x^2 - 1500x + 625.$$

After working through several problems like this one, patterns become apparent. You probably remember that $(a+b)^2 = a^2 + 2ab + b^2$, and you might even recall the formula $(a+b)^3 = a^3 + 3a^2b + 3ab^2 + b^3$. There is a general pattern for the expansion of $(a+b)^n$ that is worth knowing.

Theorem 4.3 *Let j and k be nonnegative integers such that $j+k = n$. The coefficient of the $a^j b^k$ term in the expansion of $(a+b)^n$ is $C(n,j)$.*

Proof We use induction on n. If $n = 1$, we have $(a+b)^1 = a+b$, so the coefficient of the $a^0 b^1$ term is $C(1,0) = 1$ and the coefficient of the $a^1 b^0$ term is $C(1,1) = 1$.

Suppose as inductive hypothesis that the coefficient of the $a^{j'} b^{k'}$ term in the expansion of $(a+b)^{n-1}$ is $C(n-1,j')$, for any j' and k' such that $j' + k' = n - 1$. Now let $j + k = n$. Now apply the inductive hypothesis to evaluate the expansion of $(a+b)^n$. In the calculation below, we need to keep track of only those terms that are capable of contributing to the $a^j b^k$ term:

$$(a+b)^n = (a+b)^{n-1}(a+b)$$

$$= \left(\cdots + \binom{n-1}{j-1} a^{j-1} b^k + \binom{n-1}{j} a^j b^{k-1} + \cdots \right)(a+b)$$

$$= \left(\cdots + \binom{n-1}{j-1} a^j b^k + \binom{n-1}{j} a^j b^k + \cdots \right).$$

Therefore, the coefficient of $a^j b^k$ is $C(n-1,j-1) + C(n-1,j)$. But this simplifies:

$$\binom{n-1}{j-1} + \binom{n-1}{j} = \frac{(n-1)!}{(j-1)!(n-1-(j-1))!} + \frac{(n-1)!}{j!(n-1-j)!}$$

$$= \frac{(n-1)!}{(j-1)!(n-j)!} \cdot \frac{j}{j} + \frac{(n-1)!}{j!(n-1-j)!} \cdot \frac{n-j}{n-j}$$

$$= \frac{(n-1)!(j)}{j!(n-j)!} + \frac{(n-1)!(n-j)}{j!(n-j)!}$$

$$= \frac{(n-1)!(j) + (n-1)!(n) - (n-1)!(j)}{j!(n-j)!}$$

$$= \frac{n!}{j!(n-j)!}$$

$$= \binom{n}{j}$$

as required.   □

This proof was a little messy, but the only tools we used were induction, algebra, and the definition of $C(n,j)$. However, there is another way to look at the result from the point of view of counting. If you were going to expand the product

$$\underbrace{(a+b)(a+b)\cdots(a+b)}_{n}$$

you would have to use the distributive property repeatedly to get a sum of a bunch of monomial terms, and then you would have to combine like terms. Each monomial is the product of a selection of a's and b's; to get a monomial, you must choose either an a or a b from each $(a+b)$ factor and multiply these together. The coefficient of the $a^j b^k$ term is therefore the number of ways you can get the monomial $a^j b^k$. But this is the number of ways you can choose j different $(a+b)$ factors—the factors that contribute an a to the monomial—out of n total: $C(n,j)$.

Often this result is stated as an equation.

Corollary 4.1 The Binomial Theorem.

$$(a+b)^n = \binom{n}{0}a^n + \binom{n}{1}a^{n-1}b + \binom{n}{2}a^{n-2}b^2 + \cdots + \binom{n}{j}a^j b^{n-j} + \cdots + \binom{n}{n}b^n.$$

Example 4.23 Use the binomial theorem to expand $(3x - 5)^4$.

Solution: Apply the corollary with $a = 3x$ and $b = -5$.

$$(3x - 5)^4$$

$$= (3x)^4 + \binom{4}{1}(3x)^3(-5) + \binom{4}{2}(3x)^2(-5)^2 + \binom{4}{3}(3x)(-5)^3 + (-5)^4$$

$$= 81x^4 + (4)(27x^3)(-5) + (6)(9x^2)(25) + (4)(3x)(-125) + (625)$$

$$= 81x^4 - 540x^3 + 1350x^2 - 1500x + 625$$

Notice that expanding $(3x - 5)^4$ by multiplying polynomials takes a lot more work. ◇

Activity 4.2.2: Poker Hands

A standard deck contains 52 cards, divided into four suits: spades, clubs, hearts, and diamonds. The thirteen cards in each suit are: 2, 3, 4, 5, 6, 7, 8, 9, 10, jack, queen, king, ace. These values are ordered as listed, but the ace can also function as a "1" for purposes of ordering.

1. A five-card *hand* (in stud or draw poker) is a set of five cards chosen from the 52-card deck. How many five-card hands are there? In this and in the questions that follow, use the notation introduced in Activity 4.2.1, and also give numerical answers.

2. A *flush* is a hand consisting of five cards of the same suit. How many flushes are there?

3. A *straight* is a hand consisting of five consecutive cards in order (aces, if used, can be either high or low). How many straights are there?

4. In poker, the rarest hand wins. Does a straight beat a flush, or does a flush beat a straight?

5. A *straight flush* is a straight that is also a flush. How many straight flushes are there?

6. A *full house* is a hand consisting of three cards of the same value and two cards of another value. How many full houses are there? Which wins: a full house or a straight flush?

7. *Two pair* is a hand consisting of two of one value and two of another, and a fifth card of a third value. How many two pairs are there?

8. *Four of a kind*, *three of a kind*, and *pair*, are hands consisting of 4, 3, or 2 cards, respectively, of the same value, and additional cards such that a full house or a two pair is not formed. How many of each of these hands are there?

9. Rank the eight poker hands mentioned above, in order from rarest to most common.

Exercises 4.2

---

1. Arturo can have pizza for dinner on any three of the next seven days. How many different ways can he select the days on which to have pizza?

2. There are 13 different pizza toppings, and Arturo must rank his top 5 in order. How many different possible rankings are there?

3. A committee of three is chosen from a group of 20 people. How many different committees are possible, if

   (a) the committee consists of a president, vice president, and treasurer?

   (b) there is no distinction among the three members of the committee?

4. Hugo and Viviana work in an office with eight other coworkers. Out of these 10 workers, their boss needs to choose a group of four to work together on a project.

(a) How many different working groups of four can the boss choose?

(b) Suppose Hugo and Viviana absolutely refuse, under any circumstances, to work together. Under this restriction, how many different working groups of four can be formed?

5. Ruth has the following set of refrigerator magnets: {A, B, C, D, E, F, G}.

(a) How many different three-letter strings can she form with these magnets?

(b) How many different three-letter strings can she form if the middle letter must be a vowel?

6. Refer to Example 4.22. Use the selection principle to count the number of different possible win or loss scenarios when two teams play a best-of-five match …

(a) using the method of Solution #1.

(b) using the method of Solution #2.

7. Form a seven-letter word by mixing up the letters in the word COMBINE.

(a) How many ways can you do this?

(b) How many ways can you do this if all the vowels have to be at the beginning?

(c) How many ways can you do this if no vowel is isolated between two consonants?

8. How many different strings can be formed by rearranging the letters in the word ABABA?

9. Lipid Fried Chicken offers a jumbo special with a choice of three side dishes from eight different side dishes on the menu. Assuming you must choose three different side dishes, how many different possibilities are there for your side dish selection?

10. Possible grades for a class are A, B, C, D, and F. (No +/−'s.)

(a) How many ways are there to assign grades to a class of seven students?

(b) How many ways are there to assign grades to a class of seven students if nobody receives an F and exactly one person receives an A?

11. The school board consists of three men and four women.

(a) When they hold a meeting, they sit in a row. How many different seating arrangements are there?

(b) How many different ways can the row be arranged if no two women sit next to each other?

(c) How many ways are there to select a subcommittee of four board members?

(d) How many ways are there to select a subcommittee of four board members if the subcommittee must contain at least two women?

12. The legislature of Puerto Rico consists of a 27-member Senate and a 51-member House of Representatives.

(a) How many ways are there to choose a group of six members from the Puerto Rican legislature?

(b) How many ways are there to choose a group of six members if three members must come from the Senate and three must come from the House of Representatives?

13. A men's field lacrosse team consists of 10 players: 3 attackmen, 3 midfielders, 3 defenders, and 1 goaltender. Given a set of 10 players, how many different ways are there to assign the roles of attackmen, midfielders, defenders, and goaltender?

14. There are 10 first-tier national rugby union teams: Argentina, Australia, England, France, Ireland, Italy, New Zealand, Scotland, South Africa, and Wales.

(a) How many different two-team pairings are possible among these 10 teams?

(b) How many different ways are there to select a first-, second-, and third-ranked team from these 10 teams?

(c) Suppose four teams will gather in Auckland, and the other six teams will gather in Melbourne. How many ways can this be done?

(d) Suppose five teams will gather in Sydney, and the other five teams will gather in Wellington. How many ways can this be done?

15. There are nine empty seats in a theater, and five customers need to find places to sit. How many different ways can these five seat themselves?

16. How many solutions (using only nonnegative integers) are there to the following equation?

$$x_1 + x_2 + x_3 + x_4 + x_5 = 32$$

17. How many solutions (using only nonnegative integers) are there to the following equation?

$$x_1 + x_2 + x_3 + x_4 + x_5 + x_6 + x_7 = 20$$

18. A certain brand of jellybean comes in four colors: red, green, purple, and yellow. These jellybeans are packaged in bags of 50, but there is no guarantee as to how the colors will be distributed; you might get a mixture of all four colors, or just some red and some green, or even (if you are very lucky) a whole bag of purple.

    (a) Explain how to view the color distribution of a bag of jellybeans as a solution to an equation like the one in Example 4.21.

    (b) Compute the total number of different possible color distributions.

19. Snow White has 50 one-dollar bills, which she wishes to divide up among seven different dwarves. Each dwarf may receive any (integral) number of bills, from 0 to 50. How many different ways can she distribute this money?

20. How many different ways are there to distribute 12 identical bones among three different dogs?

21. The North South Line of the Singapore Mass Rapid Transit system has 25 stations. How many different ways are there to divide this line into three segments, where each segment contains at least one station? (One possible such division is shown below.)

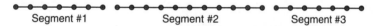

    Segment #1   Segment #2   Segment #3

22. The streets of many cities (e.g., Vancouver, British Columbia) are based primarily on a rectangular grid. In such a city, if you start at a given street corner, how many different ways are there to walk directly to the street corner that is 5 blocks north and 10 blocks east? For example, in the map below, how many ways can you walk from the corner of MacDonald and Broadway to the corner of 4th and Burrard?

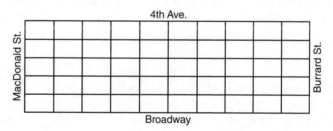

23. The following binary tree has as many nodes as possible for a tree of height 5.

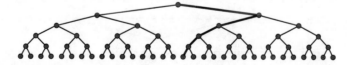

    Definition: A *climb* is a path that starts at the root and ends at a leaf.

    (a) How many different climbs are there in this tree?

    (b) Suppose you have a list of 100 names, and you need to assign a name from this list to each climb. You may not repeat names. How many different ways are there to do this?

    (c) Notice that as a climb goes from the root to a leaf, it must go either right or left at each node. We say that a climb has a *change of direction* if it goes right after having gone left, or left after having gone right. How many climbs are there with exactly two changes of direction?

    (d) Suppose you were given a binary tree like the one above, with as many nodes as possible, but with height 10. In this new tree, how many climbs are there with exactly two changes of direction?

24. Let $n \geq 0$ and let j and k be nonnegative integers such that $j + k = n$. Use algebra to prove that $C(n, j) = C(n, k)$.

25. Use the Binomial Theorem to expand $(2x + 7)^5$.

26. Use the Binomial Theorem to expand $(x + 1)^{10}$.

27. Compute the coefficient of x^8 in the expansion of $(3x - 2)^{13}$.

28. Compute the coefficient of z^4 in the expansion of $(2z + 5)^7$.

*29. Let $R(n, j)$ be a function of two variables that is defined recursively as follows.

   B. $R(n, 0) = R(n, n) = 1$ for all $n \geq 0$.

   R. $R(n, j) = R(n - 1, j) + R(n - 1, j - 1)$.

   Prove (using induction and one of the identities in the proof of Theorem 4.3) that $R(n, j) = C(n, j)$ for all $n \geq j \geq 0$.

*30. The following diagram is called *Pascal's Triangle*, named after the philosopher/theologian/mathematician Blaise Pascal (1623–1662). Explain what this diagram has to do with $C(n, j)$. (Use the result of the previous problem in your explanation.)

4.3   Counting with Functions

When faced with a new kind of mathematical problem, it often helps to relate it to something familiar. In Examples 4.17 and 4.21, our counting arguments were based on seeing relationships between mathematical objects. We observed that 9! batting orders correspond to each choice of nine starters, and we saw that every solution to a particular equation could be represented uniquely as a certain kind of string. These relationships can be thought of as functions. In this section, we explore how to count using this type of relational thinking.

Preview 4.3

1. A *quaternary string* is a string made up of 0s, 1s, 2s, and 3s. Devise a method for converting a quaternary string of length 2 to a binary string of length 4, and vice versa. If possible, ensure that your conversion methods return the original string when composed (both quaternary → binary → quaternary and binary → quaternary → binary).

2. How many triangular subgraphs are there in the following graph?

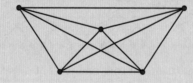

3. How many different paths are there through the following maze, starting at the opening at the bottom and ending in the shaded region, without backtracking?

4.3.1   One-to-One Correspondences

The next two observations are fairly easy to prove. The proofs are left as exercises.

Theorem 4.4 *Let* $|X| = m$ *and* $|Y| = n$. *If there is some* $f: X \longrightarrow Y$ *that is one-to-one, then* $m \leq n$.

Theorem 4.5 *Let* $|X| = m$ *and* $|Y| = n$. *If there is some* $f: X \longrightarrow Y$ *that is onto, then* $m \geq n$.

Together, they imply this corollary.

Corollary 4.2 *Let* $|X| = m$ *and* $|Y| = n$. *If there is a one-to-one correspondence* $f: X \longrightarrow Y$, *then* $m = n$.

The term "one-to-one correspondence" suggests exactly what this corollary states: if two finite sets are in one-to-one correspondence with each other, then the sets have the same number of elements. These formal theorems can help guide our thinking when solving counting problems.

Example 4.24 In a single-elimination tournament, players are paired up in each round, and the winner of each match advances to the next round. If the number of players in a round is odd, one player gets a bye to the next round. The tournament continues until only two players are left; these two players play the championship game to determine the winner of the tournament. In a tournament with 270 players, how many games must be played?

Solution: This problem is easy if you realize that there is a one-to-one correspondence $f: G \longrightarrow L$, where G is the set of all games played, and L is the set of players who lose a game. The function is defined for any game x as $f(x) = l$, where l is the loser of game x. Since every game has a single loser, the function is well defined. Since this is a single-elimination tournament, no player can lose two different games, so f is one-to-one. And since every loser lost some game, f is onto. So, by Corollary 4.2, the number of games equals the number of losers. The winner of the tournament is the only nonloser, so there are 269 losers, hence 269 games.   ◇

Example 4.25 Draw a diagram with six lines subject to the following conditions:

- Every line intersects every other line.
- No three lines intersect in a single point.

For example, the following diagram satisfies these two conditions.

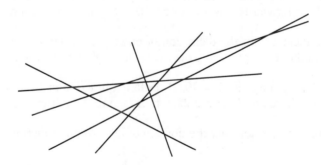

Your diagram will form lots of overlapping triangles. How many triangles are there?

Solution: Observe that every triangle is formed from three lines, and any set of three lines forms a triangle. Thus, there is a one-to-one correspondence

$$\{\text{triangles in figure}\} \longleftrightarrow \{\text{sets } \{l_1, l_2, l_3\} \mid l_i \text{ is a line}\}.$$

So instead of counting the number of triangles, we can just count the number of sets of three lines. There are $C(6, 3) = 20$ of these.   ◇

Activity 4.3.1: Counting with One-to-one Correspondences

1. Recall that a graph is called *complete* if every vertex shares an edge with every other vertex.

   (a) Explain why, in a complete graph, every three-element subset of vertices corresponds to a unique triangular subgraph.

   (b) Use this correspondence to count the number of triangular subgraphs in each of the following graphs.

   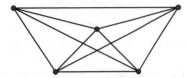   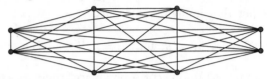

2. Consider the problem of counting all of the points of intersection that lie inside the circle in the figure.

   (a) Explain why a selection of four points on the circle determines a point of intersection inside the circle.

   (b) Explain why a point of intersection inside the circle determines a set of four points on the circle.

   (c) Use this one-to-one correspondence to count the number of intersection points inside the circle.

3. The grids on the right represent streets in a city with square-shaped blocks.

   (a) How many different 5-block routes are there from point A to point B?

   (b) Describe a one-to-one correspondence between the routes in part (a) and a certain set of strings.

   (c) How many different 11-block routes are there from point X to point Y?

   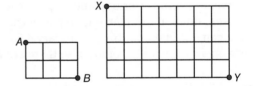

The idea in the above examples is clear: to count the elements in a set Y, find some one-to-one correspondence $f\colon X \longrightarrow Y$, and count X instead. We can extend this technique by considering functions with the following property.

Definition 4.1 A function $f\colon X \longrightarrow Y$ is called *n-to-one* if every y in the image of the function has exactly n different elements of X that map to it. In other words, f is n-to-one if $\big|\{x \in X \mid f(x) = y\}\big| = n$ for all $y \in f(X)$.

Note that this definition coincides with the definition of one-to-one when $n = 1$: if there is exactly one $x \in X$ such that $f(x) = y$ for every y in the image, then the only way $f(a) = f(b)$ can happen is if $a = b$.

Example 4.26 Let $X = \{1, 2, 3, 4, 5, 6\}$ and let $Y = \{0, 1\}$. Define a function $m\colon X \longrightarrow Y$ by $m(x) = x \mod 2$. This function is three-to-one, because there are three numbers that map to 0 and three numbers that map to 1.

The next theorem is just the observation that the domain of an n-to-one function must be n times as big as the image.

Theorem 4.6 Let $|X| = p$ and $|Y| = q$. If there is an n-to-one function $f\colon X \longrightarrow Y$ that maps X onto Y, then $p = qn$.

We have already used this idea to relate permutations and combinations. Let's revisit that discussion.

Example 4.27 Let S be a set with n elements, let X be the set of all arrangements of r elements of S, and let Y be the set of all selections (i.e., subsets) of r elements of S. Define a function $f\colon X \longrightarrow Y$ by

$$f(x_1 x_2 x_3 \cdots x_r) = \{x_1, x_2, x_3, \ldots, x_r\}.$$

This function is onto. Since there are exactly $r!$ ways to arrange any r elements, this function is also $r!$-to-one. Therefore, $|X| = r! \cdot |Y|$, or equivalently, $P(n, r) = r! \cdot C(n, r)$.

Example 4.28 How many different strings can you form by rearranging the letters in the word ENUMERATE?

Solution: This would be a simple arrangement problem, except that ENUMERATE contains repeated letters—three E's, to be precise. Let's pretend those E's are different for a moment: call them E_1, E_2, and E_3. Let X be the set of all strings you can form by rearranging the letters in the word E_1NUME$_2$RATE$_3$. Since the elements of X are just permutations of nine distinct symbols, $|X| = 9!$. Now let Y be the set of all rearrangements of ENUMERATE, and define a function $f : X \longrightarrow Y$ by $f(\lambda) = \lambda'$, where λ' is the string λ with the subscripts on the E's removed. This function is onto, because you can always take a string in Y and put the subscripts 1, 2, and 3 on the E's. Moreover, there are exactly $3! = 6$ ways to do this, so f is six-to-one. Therefore, by Theorem 4.6, $|X| = 6 \cdot |Y|$, so there are $|Y| = 9!/6 = 60{,}480$ arrangements.   ◇

Example 4.29 A group of 10 people sits in a circle around a campfire. How many different seating arrangements are there? In this situation, a seating arrangement is determined by who sits next to whom, not by where on the ground they sit. Let's also agree not to distinguish between clockwise and counterclockwise; all that matters is who your two neighbors are, not who is on your left and who is on your right.

Solution: First, consider the related problem of seating 10 people in a row. The set X of all such arrangements has 10! elements. Now define a function $f : X \longrightarrow Y$ from X to the set Y of all circular seating arrangements as follows. If λ is a row seating arrangement, then $f(\lambda)$ is the circular seating arrangement you get by curving the row into a circle and joining the endpoints:

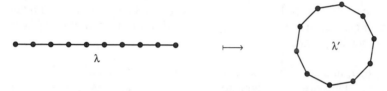

Notice that this map is onto, because given any $\lambda' \in Y$, you can find a $\lambda \in X$ that maps to it by breaking the circle between two people (say a and b) and straightening out the circle to form a row, with a on one end and b on the other. Also notice that this can be done in exactly 20 ways, because there are 10 different places to break the circle, and then there are two choices for where to put a: on the left end of the row or on the right end. Therefore, f is a twenty-to-one function. By Theorem 4.6, $|Y| = 10!/20 = 181{,}440$.   ◇

Activity 4.3.2: Counting with n-to-One Functions

A function $f : X \longrightarrow Y$ is called "n-to-one" if every $y \in Y$ is mapped to by n different elements of X. If X and Y are finite sets and $f : X \longrightarrow Y$ is both n-to-one and onto, then $|X| = n|Y|$.

1. Let X be the set of all arrangements of the letters LAKER, and let Y be the set of all arrangements of the letters RAKER.

   (a) Describe a 2-to-one and onto function $X \longrightarrow Y$. Given an arrangement of LAKER, your function should return an arrangement of RAKER. Explain why your function is 2-to-one and onto.

   (b) Determine the sizes of X and Y.

2. Count the number of arrangements of the letters RARER.

3. Count the number of arrangements of the letters HOPELESSNESS.

4. Each of the four regions in the design on the right needs to be colored a different color, chosen from red, orange, green, and blue.

   (a) Let X be the set of different colorings of these regions. Compute $|X|$.

   (b) Suppose this design is made into a token, manufactured of colored plastic. Two such tokens are indistinguishable if one can be rotated or flipped to coincide with the other. Let Y be the set of such tokens, and let $f : X \longrightarrow Y$ be the function that inputs a colored design (as in part (a)) and outputs a colored token. The function f is n-to-one and onto. What is n? What is $|Y|$, the number of distinct tokens?

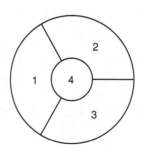

4.3.2   The Pigeonhole Principle

The Pigeonhole Principle is the simple observation that if you put n pigeons into r holes, and $n > r$, then some hole must contain multiple pigeons. We can state this a little more mathematically using functions.

Theorem 4.7 *Let $|X| = n$ and $|C| = r$, and let $f : X \longrightarrow C$. If $n > r$, then there are distinct elements $x, y \in X$ with $f(x) = f(y)$.*

Proof We proceed by contraposition. Suppose that for all pairs of distinct elements $x, y \in X, f(x) \neq f(y)$. This is the same as saying that f is one-to-one. By Theorem 4.4, this implies that $n \leq r$. □

Instead of pigeons and holes, it sometimes helps to think of X as a set of objects and C as a set of colors. The function f assigns a color to each object, and if $|X| > |C|$, there is some pair of objects with the same color. The following examples are direct applications of Theorem 4.7.

Example 4.30 In a club with 400 members, must there be some pair of members who share the same birthday?

Solution: Yes. Let X be the set of all people, and let C be the set of all possible birthdays. Let $f : X \longrightarrow C$ be the defined so that $f(x)$ is the birthday of person x. Since $|X| > |C|$, there must be two people x and y with the same birthday, that is, with $f(x) = f(y)$. ◇

Example 4.31 Chandra has a drawer full of 12 red and 14 green socks. In order to avoid waking his roommate, he must grab a selection of clothes in the dark and get dressed out in the hallway. How many socks must he grab to be assured of having a matching pair?

Solution: Let $C = \{\text{red}, \text{green}\}$ and let X be the set of socks Chandra selects. Let $f : X \longrightarrow C$ be the function that assigns a color to each sock. There are two colors, so he needs $|X| > 2$ socks. Three is enough. ◇

Example 4.32 In a round-robin tournament, every player plays every other player exactly once. Prove that, if no player goes undefeated, at the end of the tournament there must be two players with the same number of wins.

Solution: Apply Theorem 4.7 where X is the set of players, and let $|X| = n$. Each player plays $n - 1$ games, and no player wins every game, so the set of all possible numbers of wins is $C = \{0, 1, 2, \ldots, n - 2\}$. Define $f : X \longrightarrow C$ so that $f(x)$ is the number of times player x wins. Since $|C| < |X|$, there exists a pair of players with the same number of wins. ◇

4.3.3   The Generalized Pigeonhole Principle

We can extend the Pigeonhole Principle a little. If you have way more pigeons than holes, you would expect to find some hole with lots of pigeons in it.

Theorem 4.8 *Let $|X| = n$ and $|C| = r$, and let $f : X \longrightarrow C$. If $n > r(l - 1)$, then there is some subset $U \subseteq X$ such that $|U| = l$ and $f(x) = f(y)$ for any $x, y \in U$.*

Note that if $l = 2$, this is Theorem 4.7. We can restate the theorem in terms of colors: "Suppose each object in a set X of n objects is assigned a color from a set C of r colors. If $n > r(l - 1)$, then there is a subset $U \subseteq X$ with l objects, all of the same color."

Proof (By contraposition.) Suppose that when you group the elements of X according to color, the size of any of these groups is at most $l - 1$. Then the total number of elements of X is at most $r(l - 1)$. □

When you know n and r, it is handy to have a formula for l.

Corollary 4.3 *Let $|X| = n$ and $|C| = r$, and let $f : X \longrightarrow C$. Then there is some subset $U \subseteq X$ such that*

$$|U| = \left\lceil \frac{n}{r} \right\rceil$$

and $f(x) = f(y)$ for any $x, y \in U$.

Proof Let $l = \lceil n/r \rceil$. Then

$$r(l - 1) = (\lceil n/r \rceil - 1)r < (n/r)r = n,$$

so the result follows from Theorem 4.8.   □

Example 4.33 A website displays an image each day from a bank of 30 images. In any given 100-day period, show that some image must be displayed four times.

Solution: Apply Theorem 4.8, with X being the set of days and C being the set of images. Let $f: X \longrightarrow C$ be the function that returns the image $f(x)$ that gets displayed on day x. Since $100 > 30(4 - 1)$, there is some image that will be displayed four times.   ◇

Alternatively, we could have used Corollary 4.3: $\lceil 100/30 \rceil = \lceil 3.\overline{3} \rceil = 4$.

Example 4.34 Let G be the following complete graph on six vertices.

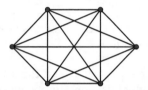

This graph has 15 edges. Suppose that some edges are colored red and the rest green. Show that there must be some triangular circuit whose edges are the same color.

Solution: Pick a vertex v. There are five edges on v, so by Theorem 4.8 three of these edges e_1, e_2, e_3 must be the same color (say green, without loss of generality). Let the other vertices of edges e_1, e_2, e_3 be x, y, z, respectively. If the triangular circuit formed by x, y, z has all red edges, we are done. But if one of the edges is green, then it forms a green triangular circuit with v.   ◇

4.3.4   Ramsey Theory ‡

Example 4.34 shows that no matter how mixed up the edge colors of G are, there will always be a monochromatic triangle. This example illustrates a general phenomenon: no matter how disordered something might be, there will always be some small part of it that has some kind of order. The following theorem (which we will not prove) states this mathematically.

Theorem 4.9 *(Ramsey) For any positive integers r, k, and l, there is a positive integer n such that if the k-element subsets of a set X with n elements are colored with r colors, then there is a subset $U \subseteq X$ with $|U| = l$ whose k-element subsets are all the same color.*

Given r, k, and l, the *Ramsey number* $R(r, k, l)$ is the smallest n satisfying the conclusion of the theorem. In Example 4.34, the edges in the graph represent all the two-element subsets of the set X of six vertices. Thus, we have $k = 2$ and $n = 6$. Since there are two colors, $r = 2$. The monochromatic triangle corresponds to a subset U with three elements, so $l = 3$. The example shows that for a set X with six elements there is always a three-element subset of X whose two-element subsets are all the same color. In other words, the example establishes that $R(2, 2, 3) \leq 6$. In the exercises, you will show that equality must hold by showing that $n = 5$ is not enough vertices to satisfy the conclusion of the theorem.

Exercises 4.3

1. Prove Theorem 4.4.
2. Prove Theorem 4.5.

3. Let G be the complete graph on n vertices. In other words, G is a simple graph with n vertices in which every vertex shares an edge with every other vertex.

   (a) Explain why there is a one-to-one correspondence between the set of all (unordered) pairs of vertices in G and the set of all edges of G.

   (b) Use part (a) to count the number of edges of G (in terms of n).

4. The following 8×24 grid is divided into squares that are 1 unit by 1 unit.

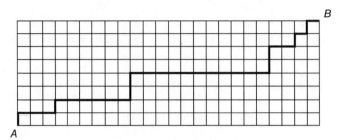

   The shortest possible path on this grid from A to B is 32 units long. One such path is shown in the figure. Let X be the set of all 32-unit-long paths from A to B.

   (a) There is a one-to-one correspondence between X and the set Y of all binary strings with 8 1s and 24 0s. Describe the function, and explain why it is a one-to-one correspondence.

   (b) Compute $|X|$, the number of 32-unit-long paths from A to B.

5. Why is there no such thing as a "one-to-n function" for $n > 1$?

6. The following figure consists of 7 horizontal lines and 13 vertical lines. The goal of this problem is to count the number of rectangles (squares are a kind of rectangle, but line segments are not).

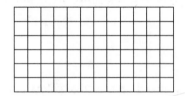

   Let V be the set of all sets of two vertical lines, and let H be the set of all sets of two horizontal lines. Let R be the set of all rectangles in the figure. Define a function $f : R \longrightarrow V \times H$ by

   $$A \quad C$$
   $$\begin{array}{c} \hline \\ \hline \end{array} \quad \overset{f}{\longmapsto} \quad (\{AB, CD\}, \{AC, BD\}).$$
   $$B \qquad D$$

   (a) Explain why f is well defined.

   (b) Explain why f is one-to-one.

   (c) Explain why f is onto.

   (d) Compute $|R|$, the number of rectangles in the figure.

   (e) The previous figure contains $7 \cdot 13 = 91$ intersection points. Let P be the set of all sets $\{X, Y\}$ of two intersection points. Suppose we tried counting R by defining a function $g : R \longrightarrow P$, which maps a rectangle to the set containing its lower left and upper right vertices:

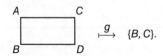

   Explain why g is not a one-to-one correspondence.

7. In the following graph, let S be the set of all squares formed by edges in the graph, and let V be the set of all sets of four vertices in the graph.

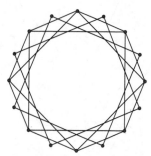

Define a function $f : S \longrightarrow V$ as follows: For any square $x \in S$, let $f(x)$ be the set containing the four vertices of the square x.

   (a) Is f one-to-one? Explain.

   (b) Is f onto? Explain.

8. Let S be a set of n numbers, and let k be a natural number less than or equal to n. Let X be the set of all subsets of S of size k, and let Y be the set of all ordered k-tuples $(s_1, s_2, \ldots, s_k)$ such that $s_1 < s_2 < \cdots < s_k$. That is,

$$X = \{ \{s_1, s_2, \ldots, s_k\} \mid s_i \in S \text{ and all } s_i\text{'s are distinct}\}, \text{ and}$$
$$Y = \{ (s_1, s_2, \ldots, s_k) \mid s_i \in S \text{ and } s_1 < s_2 < \cdots < s_k\}.$$

   (a) Define a one-to-one correspondence $f : X \longrightarrow Y$. Explain why f is one-to-one and onto.

   (b) Determine $|X|$ and $|Y|$.

9. Let X be a set with n elements, and let $\mathcal{P}(X)$ be its power set.

   (a) Describe a one-to-one correspondence

$$f : \mathcal{P}(X) \longrightarrow S$$

   where S is the set of all n-digit binary strings.

   (b) Use this one-to-one correspondence to compute $|\mathcal{P}(X)|$.

   *((iii)) Let $P_k \subseteq \mathcal{P}(X)$ be the set of all k-element subsets of X, for $0 \leq k \leq n$. The restriction

$$f|_{P_k} : P_k \longrightarrow S$$

   is one-to-one. What is the image of $f|_{P_k}$?

   *((iv)) How many elements are in the image of $f|_{P_k}$?

10. How many ways are there to rearrange the letters in FUNCTION?

11. How many ways are there to rearrange the letters in BANANA?

12. How many ways are there to rearrange the letters in INANENESS?

13. How many different strings can be formed by rearranging the letters in the word OZONOSPHERE? Explain your reasoning.

14. Use the one-to-one correspondence defined in Example 2.30 on page 71 to count the number of points of intersection in Figure 4.2, not counting the points that lie on the circle.

15. Refer to Figure 4.2. We say that a triangle is *inscribed* in the circle if its vertices all lie on the circle. How many inscribed triangles are there? Explain your reasoning.

16. In the following graph, every vertex in the left column shares an edge with every vertex in the right column. How many simple paths of two edges are there in this graph? (A simple path cannot repeat edges.)

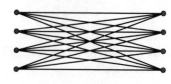

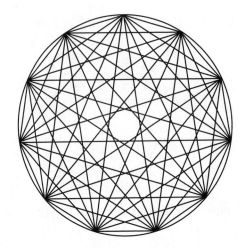

Figure 4.2 How many points of intersection are there? See Exercise 14.

17. Consider a diagram with n lines, all of which intersect, but no three of which pass through a single point. Here is an example with $n = 5$.

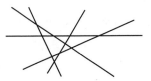

Let Y be the set of all points of intersection, and let X be the set of all sets of two lines. That is,

$$X = \{\{l_1, l_2\} \mid l_1 \text{ and } l_2 \text{ are distinct lines in the diagram}\}.$$

Define a function $f : X \longrightarrow Y$ by setting $f(\{l_1, l_2\})$ equal to the point where l_1 and l_2 intersect.

(a) Explain why f is one-to-one.

(b) Explain why f is onto.

(c) How many points of intersection are there? Give your answer in terms of n.

18. Suppose you have eight squares of stained glass, all of different colors, and you would like to make a rectangular stained glass window in the shape of a 2×4 grid.

How many different ways can you do this, taking symmetry into account? (Note that any pattern may be rotated 180°, flipped vertically, or flipped horizontally. You should count all the possible resulting patterns as the same window.)

19. Suppose you have four squares of stained glass, all of different colors, and you wish to make a 2×2 square stained glass window. How many different windows are possible? (Beware: a square has more symmetries than a rectangle.)

20. A certain board game uses tokens made of transparent colored plastic. Each token looks like

where each of the four different regions is a different color: either red, green, yellow, blue, orange, or purple. How many different tokens of this type are possible?

21. A different board game also uses tokens made of transparent colored plastic. In this game, each token looks like

    where each of the five different regions is a different color: either red, green, yellow, blue, orange, or purple. How many different tokens of this type are possible?

22. On the eve of an election, a radio station is forced to play 20 campaign ads in a row. Of these 20 ads, 15 are for the Tory candidate, and 5 are for the Labour candidate. Prove that the station must play at least three Tory ads in a row at some point. Use the generalized pigeonhole principle to justify your answer.

23. Explain why, in a class of 36, there will always be a group of at least 6 who were born on the same day of the week.

24. Let G be a simple graph with two or more vertices. Prove that there is a pair of vertices in G having the same degree.

25. Is it possible for a graph with 10 vertices and 50 edges to be simple? Explain.

26. Explain why any set of three natural numbers must contain a pair of numbers whose sum is even.

27. Let $\triangle ABC$ be an equilateral triangle whose sides are two inches long. Prove that it is impossible to place five points inside the triangle without two of them being within one inch of each other.

28. A small college offers 250 different classes. No two classes can meet at the same time in the same room, of course. There are 12 different time slots at which classes can occur. What is the minimum number of classrooms needed to accommodate all the classes?

*29. Use the pigeonhole principle to explain why every rational number has a decimal expansion that either terminates or repeats. In the case where a rational number m/n has a repeating decimal expansion, find an upper bound (in terms of the integer n) on the number of digits in the part that repeats. (Hint: In the long division problem

$$n \overline{)\, m}$$

    consider the possible remainders at each step of the algorithm for long division.)

30. Suppose that 100 lottery tickets are given out in sequence to the first 100 guests to arrive at a party. Of these 100 tickets, only 12 are winning tickets. The generalized pigeonhole principle guarantees that there must be a streak of at least l losing tickets in a row. Find l.

31. Show that $R(2, 2, 3) > 5$ by coloring the edges of the complete graph on five vertices red and green in such a way that no triangular circuit has edges of a single color.

*32. Show that if the edges of the complete graph on eight vertices are colored red and green, then there is either a three-circuit or a four-circuit whose edges are all the same color.

4.4 Discrete Probability

The previous three sections have introduced a range of tools for counting the elements in a finite set. While counting arguments are interesting and somewhat diverting, they also have important applications. One way to see connections between enumeration techniques and real-world problems is from the perspective of probability.

Intuitively, probability tells us how likely something is to occur. The probability of an event is a number between 0 and 1, with 0 representing impossibility and 1 representing certainty. We deal informally with probabilities often; statements like "there is a 40% chance of rain this weekend," or "the odds of winning are 1 in 200,000,000," are making quantitative predictions of some future event.

Preview 4.4

1. Danny, Lanny, and Manny are trying to decide who should get the last doughnut. Danny suggests that they flip two coins: if both are heads, Manny gets it. If both are tails, Lanny gets it. If one is heads and the other tails, Danny gets it. Is this fair? Explain.

2. Devise a fair scheme for choosing one winner from three candidates by flipping coins. Explain why your scheme is fair.

3. In a class that is half male and half female, the teacher chooses three students at random to present problems at the board. It turns out that all three of the students chosen are male. Do you think this is unusually unlikely? Does the size of the class make a difference?

4.4.1   Definitions and Examples

The mathematical definition of probability is based on enumeration. Most of the counting problems in the previous sections are of the form

How many ⟨blanks⟩ have ⟨some property⟩?

More formally, this question is asking

How many elements of set U are in some subset A?

which is basically the same as

What percentage of elements of U are in the subset A?

The answer to this last question is just a ratio based on a counting problem. This ratio can be thought of in terms of chance:

What is the probability that a randomly chosen element of U is in the subset A?

The following definition summarizes this discussion.

Definition 4.2 Suppose A is a subset of a nonempty finite set U. The *probability* that a randomly chosen element of U lies in A is the ratio

$$P(A) = \frac{|A|}{|U|}.$$

The set U is called the *sample space*, and the set A is called an *event*.

Example 4.35 Suppose you get a random license plate from all the possible plates described in Example 4.10. What is the probability that your plate contains the word CUB or the word SOX?

Solution: The sample space U is the set of all possible plates, which we found to have 24,336,000 elements. We are interested in the event A that a plate contains the word CUB or SOX, and these two cases are disjoint. If a plate contains one of these words, it must be the type that has three letters followed by three digits. There are 10^3 choices for the digits on such a plate, so there are 10^3 plates in each case. Thus, the desired probability is

$$\frac{|A|}{|U|} = \frac{10^3 + 10^3}{24,336,000} = \frac{1}{12168} \approx 0.000082,$$

which is not very likely.   ◇

Example 4.36 If you roll two standard six-sided dice, what is the probability that you roll an 8 (i.e., that the sum of the values on the two dice will be 8)?

Solution: It is important to be clear about our sample space. If D_1 represents the six possible values of the first die and D_2 represents the six values of the second, then our sample space is the Cartesian product $D_1 \times D_2$. (Note that although the dice may be identical, the outcome that the first is 3 and the second is 5 is different from the first being 5 and the second 3.) Thus, the size of the sample space is $|D_1 \times D_2| = |D_1| \cdot |D_2| = 36$. The following ordered pairs

$$\{(2,6),(3,5),(4,4),(5,3),(6,2)\}$$

represent the event of rolling an 8. Hence the probability of such a roll is $5/36 \approx 0.139$.   ◇

The next theorem presents an important fact that makes some probability calculations easier.

Theorem 4.10 *Let A be a subset of a nonempty finite set U. Let A' be the complement of A in U. If $P(A) = p$, then $P(A') = 1 - p$.*

Proof Exercise. (Use the Addition Principle.)   □

In other words, if p is the probability that some event A happens, then $1 - p$ is the probability that A does *not* happen. The following example shows how to use this trick.

Example 4.37 If you roll two standard six-sided dice, what is the probability of rolling 10 or less?

Solution: We could count up the ways of rolling 2, 3, 4, up to 10, and then add (since these cases are mutually exclusive) to get the size of this event. But it is easier to compute the probability of rolling more than 10. There are two ways to roll 11 and one way to roll 12, so the probability of rolling more than 10 is $(2+1)/36 = 1/12$. Thus, the probability of rolling 10 or less is $1 - 1/12 = 11/12$, by Theorem 4.10.   ◇

4.4.2   Applications

Many applications of enumeration techniques involve probability. In business, probability is important because it helps measure risk. For example, choosing the right location for a restaurant can play a major role in determining how many customers show up. A restaurant owner needs to plan accordingly. The next example shows how this situation can present a discrete problem.

Example 4.38 Suppose that the streets of a shopping district form a grid, and that a customer enters the shopping district at point A in the diagram and begins walking in the direction of the arrow.

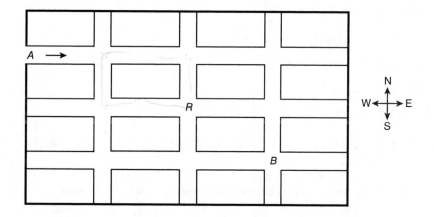

There is a restaurant at point B and a bookstore at point B. At each intersection, the customer chooses to go east or south, while taking as direct a path as possible to the bookstore at point B. Assuming that all such paths are equally likely, what is the probability that the customer passes by the restaurant at point R on the way to point B?

Solution: Since all the direct paths from A to B are equally likely, the set of these paths is our sample space. The event is the set of all such paths that contain point R. In Example 4.8, we used a decision tree to count all the possible paths from A to B. We can use the same tree to determine how many of these paths pass by the restaurant at R.

Recall from Example 4.8 that the nodes represent the intersections, with the leaves representing B and the labeled nodes representing R. Of the six possible direct paths, four pass through R, so the desired probability is $4/6 = 2/3$. ◇

Example 4.39 Suppose that there are 10 defective machines in a group of 200. A quality control inspector takes a sample of three machines and tests them for defects. How likely is it that the inspector discovers a defective machine?

Solution: We need to compute the probability that a defective machine shows up in the random sample. The sample space is the total number of selections of three machines: $C(200, 3)$. The event that at least one of the machines is defective is the opposite of the event that none are. There are 190 nondefective machines, so $C(190, 3)$ samples contain no defects. Therefore, the desired probability is

$$1 - \frac{C(190, 3)}{C(200, 3)} = 1 - \frac{1{,}125{,}180}{1{,}313{,}400} \approx 0.1433.$$

Thus, it isn't very likely that this method of testing reveals a defect. ◇

The previous two examples illustrate how discrete probability can apply to real-world situations. Compared to these applications, the following "urn problem" may seem more contrived, but it serves as an important template for future calculations.

Example 4.40 An urn contains seven red balls, seven white balls, and seven blue balls. A sample of five balls is drawn at random without replacement. What is the probability that the sample contains three balls of one color and two of another?

Solution: Nothing in this problem refers to the order of the sample, so we can consider the sample to be an unordered set—that is, a selection—of five balls from a total of 21. So there are $C(21, 5) = 20{,}349$ possible samples in the sample space. In order to count the number of samples with three balls of one color and two of another, we must make several choices in sequence.

1. Choose the color of the three balls.
2. Choose three balls of that color.
3. Choose the color of the two balls.
4. Choose two balls of that color.

There are three colors, so there are three options for the first choice. Then, no matter which color was chosen, there are $C(7, 3) = 35$ ways to choose three balls of this color. Similarly, choice number 3 has two options, since two colors remain. Then there are $C(7, 2) = 21$ ways to choose a pair of balls of the second color. Since these four choices are made in sequence, we use the multiplication principle to compute the size of the sample: $3 \cdot 35 \cdot 2 \cdot 21$. Therefore,

$$\frac{3 \cdot 35 \cdot 2 \cdot 21}{20{,}349} \approx 0.2167$$

is the desired probability. ◇

Real-world situations that involve *sampling*—choosing some elements of a population at random—can often be thought of as urn problems. While the study of random sampling lies beyond the scope of this book, the next example indicates the types of questions that courses in probability and statistics can address.

Example 4.41 Rodelio wants to know if a majority of the voters in his town will support his candidacy for mayor. Suppose, for the sake of this discussion, that out of the 300 voters in this town, 151 support Rodelio (but Rodelio doesn't know this information). Rodelio selects 20 voters at random from the population of 300. What is the probability that, out of this random sample, fewer than five support Rodelio?

Solution: Think of the 300 voters as 300 balls in an urn, 151 of which are colored red (for Rodelio) and 149 of which are colored blue. The random sample is then a selection of 20 balls at random from the urn. The sample space U is the set of all possible random samples, so $|U| = C(300, 20)$. The event A that fewer than 5 of the voters in this sample support Rodelio is the number of ways to draw 20 balls such that the number of red balls is 0, 1, 2, 3, or 4. Therefore,

$$|A| = C(149, 20) + C(151, 1) \cdot C(149, 19) + C(151, 2) \cdot C(149, 18) + C(151, 3) \cdot C(149, 17) + C(151, 4) \cdot C(149, 16).$$

The desired probability is $P(A) = |A|/|U| \approx 0.0042$.   ◇

   What can we infer from the above calculation? Assuming that a majority—even the slightest possible majority—supports Rodelio, it is very unlikely that a poll of 20 will reveal as few as four supporters. If Rodelio were to obtain such an outcome from his poll, he should be very discouraged: either the result was extremely unlucky, or the supposition that a majority supports Rodelio is false. A result of 4 out of 20 in this poll is strong evidence that Rodelio is going to lose the election.

Activity 4.4.1: Discrete Probability

Suppose A is a subset of a nonempty finite set U. The *probability* that a randomly chosen element of U lies in A is the ratio

$$P(A) = \frac{|A|}{|U|}.$$

The set U is called the *sample space*, and the set A is called an *event*.

1. Four-sided dice are tetrahedra that randomly determine a number from 1 to 4 when rolled. Suppose that you roll two four-sided dice.

   (a) The sample space for a roll of two dice is the set of all ordered pairs (r_1, r_2), where r_1 is the number indicated by the first die, and r_2 is the number indicated by the second. Write out all the elements in the sample space. Be organized.

   (b) Compute the probability of the event that the total $r_1 + r_2$ on the two dice is 5.

2. Suppose you flip a fair coin 10 times and observe whether each flip is heads or tails.

   (a) The sample space for 10 coin flips is the set of all strings of length 10 using the characters H and T. How many elements are in the sample space?

   (b) What is the probability of the event that three of the coin flips are heads and seven are tails?

   (c) What is the probability of the event that the number of heads does not equal three?

3. The grid below represents a street map in a city. There is a train station at point T and an office building at point B. There are several ways to walk directly from T to B by going four blocks east and three blocks south. Assuming that morning commuters walking from T to B choose their routes randomly from all possible direct routes, which intermediate intersection(s) will get the most foot traffic? What is the probability that a randomly chosen commuter passes this intersection?

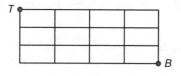

4.4.3   Expected Value

So far we have seen examples where probability quantifies how likely an event is to occur. Probability can also be used to make predictions about the value of a *random variable*.

Informally,[1] a random variable is a numerical result of a random experiment or process. We can extend our notation of probability to describe the probability that a random variable falls within a certain range. For example, $P(X = x)$ is the probability that the random variable X takes the particular value x.

Example 4.42 Rolling two standard six-sided dice is a random experiment. The sum of the values on the two dice is a random variable X. In Example 4.36, we showed that $P(X = 8) = 5/36$. In Example 4.37, we showed that $P(X \leq 10) = 11/12$.

Example 4.43 Select a random passenger on the London Underground and measure the passenger's nose. Let X be the length of the nose in centimeters. Then X is a random variable, and $P(0 \leq X \leq 50) = 1$ (assuming nobody has a nose larger than 50 cm).

Suppose that we repeat a random experiment several times and record the value of a random variable each time. If we averaged these results, we would get an estimate of the probabilistic "average" of the random variable. For example, if we measured the noses of 15 randomly selected passengers on the London Underground and averaged these measurements, we would probably get a number that was somewhat representative of the population of all Underground passengers. If we were somehow able to measure the noses of everyone on the Underground, we would get the average, or *expected*, nose size of the population.

Definition 4.3 Let $x_1, x_2, \ldots, x_n$ be all of the possible values of a random variable X. Then X's *expected value* $E(X)$ is the sum

$$\sum_{i=1}^{n} x_i \cdot P(X = x_i).$$

That is, $E(X) = x_1 \cdot P(X = x_1) + x_2 \cdot P(X = x_2) + \cdots + x_n \cdot P(X = x_n)$.

Example 4.44 In the "Both Ways" version of Australia's "Cash 3" lottery, you pick a three-digit number from 000 to 999, and a randomly chosen winning three-digit number is announced every evening at 5:55 p.m. If you pick a number with three distinct digits, you win \$580 if your number matches the winning number exactly, and you win \$80 if the digits of your number match the digits of the winning number, but in a different order. What is the expected value of the amount of money you win?

Solution: Let X be the amount of money you win. The possible values of X are 0, 580, and 80. Out of 1,000 possible winning numbers, only one matches your number exactly, and five ($3! - 1$) have the same digits, but in a different order. Therefore, your expected winnings are

$$E(X) = 0 \cdot P(X = 0) + 580 \cdot P(X = 580) + 80 \cdot P(X = 80)$$

$$= 0 \cdot \frac{994}{1000} + 580 \cdot \frac{1}{1000} + 80 \cdot \frac{5}{1000}$$

$$= 0.98.$$

Intuitively, this result means that if you play the lottery many times and average your winnings, in the long run you can expect the average to be around \$0.98. Given that it costs \$2 to play this game, playing the lottery is a losing venture (for you, but not for the Western Australia community, which receives the profits from Cash 3).   ◇

---

1. We omit the formal definition of a random variable.

Activity 4.4.2: Expected Value

A *random variable* is a numerical outcome of a random event. If X is a random variable, the probability that X takes the value a is denoted $P(X = a)$. Let $x_1, x_2, \ldots, x_n$ be all of the possible values of a random variable X. Then X's *expected value* $E(X)$ is the sum

$$\sum_{i=1}^{n} x_i \cdot P(X = x_i).$$

That is, $E(X) = x_1 \cdot P(X = x_1) + x_2 \cdot P(X = x_2) + \cdots + x_n \cdot P(X = x_n)$.

1. In the random experiment of rolling a single six-sided die, the random variable X takes the values 1, 2, 3, 4, 5, 6, and each of these values has probability 1/6.

   (a) Compute the expected value $E(X)$.

   (b) When all of the values of a random variable are equally likely, what is another name for the expected value?

2. Recall the random experiment of rolling two four-sided dice in Activity 4.4.1, Question 1. Let X be the random variable representing the sum of the numbers indicated by the two dice.

   (a) Compute the probability of each value of X.

   (b) Compute $E(X)$, the expected value of X.

   (c) Write one sentence interpreting the meaning of this value in the context of rolling two four-sided dice.

3. Recall Question 3 of Activity 4.4.1. In the street map below, compute the expected number of turns made by a commuter choosing a random direct route from point T to point B.

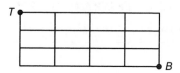

4.4.4 Conditional Probability

Often, the probability of an event changes if we have more information. For example, the probability that a good sports team will win on any given day might be around 0.6, but if we know that the team is facing a particularly strong opponent, the win probability would be closer to 0.5. In terms of enumeration, we can model the condition of additional information by restricting the sample space to a subset.

Example 4.45 Suppose that a number is drawn at random from the set $U = \{1, 2, \ldots, 50\}$, and we want to calculate the probability of the event E that the number is even. Since there are 25 even numbers in this sample space, we have $P(E) = 25/50 = 0.5$. Now suppose that a number is drawn at random from U, and we know that the number drawn has a two as one of its digits. That is, we know that the number is a member of the set $T = \{2, 12, 20, 21, \ldots 29, 32, 42\}$. There are 14 such numbers, and 9 of them are even, so the probability that the number drawn is even, given that it contains a 2, is $9/14 \approx 0.64$.

In symbols, we write $P(E \mid T)$ for the *conditional probability* of E, given T. Notice that we calculate such a conditional probability by counting an event as a subset of a restricted sample space. This observation motivates the following definition.

Definition 4.4 Let A and B be subsets of a sample space U, and suppose that $B \neq \emptyset$. The *conditional probability* of A given B is denoted $P(A \mid B)$, and is defined by the following equation.

$$P(A \mid B) = \frac{P(A \cap B)}{P(B)} \tag{4.4.1}$$

Often it is helpful to rewrite Equation 4.4.1 as $P(A \cap B) = P(B)P(A \mid B)$, or equivalently, as $P(A \cap B) = P(A)P(B \mid A)$. In this form, we have a *multiplication rule* for computing the probability of the intersection of two events if we are given information on conditional probabilities. Likewise, we can apply the Addition Principle for sets to obtain an *addition rule* for probability: if A and B are events with $A \cap B = \emptyset$, then $P(A \cup B) = P(A) + P(B)$. The following activity illustrates these rules.

Activity 4.4.3: Addition and Multiplication with Probabilities

---

Multiplication Rule: $P(A \cap B) = P(A)P(B \mid A) = P(B)P(A \mid B)$.
Addition Rule: If $A \cap B = \emptyset$, then $P(A \cup B) = P(A) + P(B)$.

1. A certain discount hardware store sells inexpensive LED bulbs. Five percent of these bulbs fail in the first week, but if a bulb lasts beyond the first week, it has a probability of 0.97 of lasting for more than two years.

   (a) Let W be the event that a randomly selected bulb does not fail in the first week. What is $P(W)$?

   (b) Let M be the event that a randomly selected bulb lasts more than two years. What is $P(M \mid W)$?

   (c) Use the multiplication rule to compute $P(M \cap W)$, and interpret your answer in the context of this problem.

2. Suppose that Urn #1 contains 5 red balls, 3 green balls, and 6 orange balls, and that Urn #2 contains 2 red balls, 2 green balls, and 3 orange balls. A coin is flipped. If the coin is heads, then a ball is chosen at random from Urn #1. If the coin is tails, then a ball is chosen at random from Urn #2. Let R, G, and O be the events that the chosen ball is red, green, and orange, respectively, and let H be the event that the coin is heads.

   (a) Compute $P(R \mid H)$ and $P(R \mid H')$.

   (b) Use the multiplication rule to compute $P(R \cap H)$ and $P(R \cap H')$.

   (c) Notice that $(R \cap H) \cup (R \cap H') = R$, and $(R \cap H) \cap (R \cap H') = \emptyset$. Use this information, and the addition rule, to compute $P(R)$.

   (d) Similarly, compute $P(G)$ and $P(O)$.

   (e) The following decision tree illustrates this situation. Label each of the leaves with its corresponding probability.

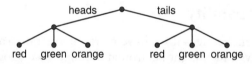

   (f) Events A and B are called *mutually exclusive* if $P(A \cap B) = 0$, and called *independent* if $P(A) = P(A \mid B)$. Consider the events R, G, and O, along with the event H that the coin flip is heads. Name a pair of mutually exclusive events and a pair of independent events.

In some situations, it is useful to reverse the order of a conditional probability. That is, given information about $P(B \mid A)$, we would like to deduce information about $P(A \mid B)$. The multiplication rule says that

$$P(A \cap B) = P(A)P(B \mid A) = P(B)P(A \mid B)$$

Let's solve for $P(A \mid B)$ and apply the addition rule.

$$P(A \mid B) = \frac{P(A)P(B \mid A)}{P(B)}$$

$$= \frac{P(A)P(B \mid A)}{P(A \cap B) + P(A' \cap B)}$$

$$= \frac{P(A)P(B \mid A)}{P(A)P(B \mid A) + P(A')P(B \mid A')}$$

The resulting formula is known as *Bayes's Rule*, which allows us to reverse a conditional probability. The next activity presents some applications.

Activity 4.4.4: Bayes's Rule

Bayes's Rule: $P(A \mid B) = \dfrac{P(A)P(B \mid A)}{P(A)P(B \mid A) + P(A')P(B \mid A')}$

1. Consider the urn-coin experiment from Question 2 in Activity 4.4.3. Compute the probability that the coin flip is heads, given that the chosen ball is red. That is, compute $P(H \mid R)$. (Use Bayes's Rule.)

2. Email data suggests that 80% of all email is spam. Furthermore, 10% of all spam emails contain the word "alert." By contrast, only 2% of non-spam emails contain the word "alert." What is the probability that a randomly chosen email message is spam, given that it contains the word "alert"?

3. A randomly chosen person has a probability of 0.005 of having a certain rare disease. A test for the disease will correctly detect the disease in an infected person 98% of the time. However, on healthy patients, the test will render a "false positive" 3% of the time. What is the probability that a randomly chosen person has the disease, given that the person tested positive for the disease?

Exercises 4.4

1. A computer generates a random four-digit string in the symbols A, B, C, ..., Z.

   (a) How many such strings are possible?

   (b) What is the probability that the random string contains no vowels (A, E, I, O, U)?

2. A multiple choice test consists of five questions, each of which has four choices. Each question has exactly one correct answer.

   (a) How many different ways are there to fill out the answer sheet?

   (b) How many ways are there to fill out the answer sheet so that four answers are correct and one is incorrect?

   (c) William guesses randomly at each answer. What is the probability that he gets three or fewer questions correct?

3. A random number generator produces a sequence of 20 digits (0, 1, ..., 9). What is the probability that the sequence contains at least one 3? (Hint: Consider the probability that it contains no 3's.)

4. Refer to Example 4.38. For each of the seven unlabeled intersections, find the probability that the customer passes through the intersection on the way to the bookstore.

5. If you roll two six-sided dice, what is the probability of rolling a 7?

6. If you roll two four-sided dice (numbered 1, 2, 3, and 4), what is the probability of rolling a 5?

7. If you roll a four-sided die and a six-sided die, which roll totals (2, 3, ..., 10) have the highest probability?

8. Refer to Example 4.10. Assume that all the different possible license plates are equally likely.

   (a) What is the probability that a randomly chosen plate contains the number 9999?

   (b) What is the probability that a randomly chosen plate contains the substring HI? (For example, HI4321 or PHI786 are two ways HI might appear.)

9. The tinyurl.com service lets you alias a long URL to a shorter one. For example, you can ask the service to send people to https://www.expensive.edu/departments/math/hard/discrete/ when they enter the URL https://tinyurl.com/sd8k4 in a web browser.

   (a) How many different URLs of the form https://tinyurl.com/***** are possible if ***** can be any string of the characters a, b, ..., z, and 0, 1, ..., 9? (Repeated characters are allowed.)

(b) How many different URLs of the form `https://tinyurl.com/*****` are possible if `*****` must be a string consisting of three letters (a, b, ..., z) followed by two digits (0, 1, ..., 9)? (Repeats allowed.) For example, `ace44`, `cub98`.

(c) Suppose that an arbitrary string `*****` of letters and digits (as in question 9(i)) is chosen at random. What is the probability that this string contains no digits?

10. In a suitable font, the letters A, H, I, M, O, T, U, V, W, X, and Y are all mirror images of themselves. A string made from these letters will be a mirror image of itself if it reads the same backward as forward: for example, MOM, YUMMUY, MOTHTOM. If a four-letter string in these letters is chosen at random, what is the probability that this string is a mirror image of itself?

11. In a class of 11 boys and 9 girls, the teacher selects three students at random to write problems on the board. What is the probability that all the students selected are boys?

12. Refer to Example 4.40. An urn contains seven red balls, seven white balls, and seven blue balls, and a sample of five balls is drawn at random without replacement.

(a) Compute the probability that the sample contains four balls of one color and one of another color.

(b) Compute the probability that all of the balls in the sample are the same color.

(c) Compute the probability that the sample contains at least one ball of each color.

13. An urn contains five red balls and seven blue balls. Four balls are drawn at random, without replacement.

(a) What is the probability that all four balls are red?

(b) What is the probability that two of the balls are red and two are blue?

14. In a class of 17 students, 3 are math majors. A group of four students is chosen at random.

(a) What is the probability that the group has no math majors?

(b) What is the probability that the group has at least one math major?

(c) What is the probability that the group has exactly two math majors?

15. Odalys sells eggs to restaurants. Before she sends a package of eggs to a customer, she selects five of the eggs in the package at random and checks to see if they are spoiled. She won't send the package if any of the eggs she tests are spoiled.

(a) Suppose the package contains 18 eggs, and half of them are spoiled. How likely is it that Odalys detects a spoiled egg?

(b) Suppose that a package contains 144 eggs, and half of them are spoiled. How likely is it that Odalys detects a spoiled egg?

(c) Suppose that a package contains 144 eggs, and 10 of them are spoiled. How likely is it that Odalys detects a spoiled egg?

(d) What seems to have a bigger effect on the probability of finding a spoiled egg: the size of the package or the percentage of spoiled eggs? Justify your answer.

*16. A game warden catches 10 fish from a lake, marks them, and returns them to the lake. Three weeks later, the warden catches five fish and discovers that two of them are marked.

(a) Let k be the number of fish in the lake. Find the probability (in terms of k) that two of five randomly selected fish are marked.

(b) What value of k will maximize this probability? (This sampling method is a way of estimating the number of fish in the lake.)

*17. Recall that K_n, the complete graph on n vertices, is the simple undirected graph in which every vertex shares an edge with every other vertex.

(a) Draw K_5. Suppose that three edges are chosen at random. What is the probability that these three edges form a circuit?

(b) Suppose that three edges of K_n are chosen at random. What is the probability that these edges form a circuit?

*18. Ten cards are numbered 1 through 10. The cards are shuffled thoroughly and placed in a stack. What is the probability that the numbers on the top three cards are in ascending order?

19. Refer to Example 4.44. If you pick a three-digit number with two repeated digits (e.g., 797), the payouts are more: you win $660 for an exact match and $160 if the digits match the winning digits, but in a different order. Show that this does not change the expected value of the amount of money you win.

20. An urn contains two red balls and five blue balls.

    (a) Draw three balls at random from the urn, without replacement. Compute the expected number of red balls in your sample.

    (b) Draw three balls at random from the urn, with replacement. Compute the expected number of red balls in your sample.

21. An urn contains 4 red balls and 6 green balls. Three balls are chosen randomly from the urn, without replacement.

    (a) What is the probability that all three balls are red?

    (b) Suppose that you win $10 for each red ball drawn and you lose $5 for each green ball drawn. Compute the expected value of your winnings.

22. An urn contains three red balls, four white balls, and two black balls. Three balls are drawn from the urn at random without replacement. For each red ball drawn, you win $10, and for each black ball drawn, you lose $15. Let X represent your net winnings.

    (a) Compute $P(X = 0)$.

    (b) Compute $P(X < 0)$.

    (c) Compute $E(X)$, your expected net winnings.

23. Refer to Exercise 7. Find the expected value of the roll total when rolling a four-sided die and a six-sided die.

24. To save time, Nivaldo's chemistry professor grades only two randomly chosen problems of a 10-problem assignment. Suppose that Nivaldo has 7 of 10 problems correct on the assignment.

    (a) Compute the probability that both randomly chosen problems are correct.

    (b) Compute the probability that both randomly chosen problems are incorrect.

    (c) Compute the expected value of the number of correct problems chosen by the professor.

25. A natural number n is chosen at random from the set $\{1, 2, 3, \ldots, 99, 100\}$. Let D be the number of digits that n has. What is the expected value of D?

26. Conduct the random experiment of flipping a coin five times. Let X be the number of heads.

    (a) Compute $P(X > 3)$.

    (b) Compute $E(X)$.

*27. Conduct the random experiment of flipping a coin until you get heads, or until you have flipped the coin five times. Let X be the number of flips.

    (a) Compute $P(X > 3)$.

    (b) Compute $E(X)$.

28. Prove Theorem 4.10.

4.5 Counting Operations in Algorithms

Counting techniques are used in lots of ways: DNA arrangements, risk assessment, and manufacturing optimization, to name a few. In this section we will see how enumeration strategies apply to the study of algorithms. We will learn how to describe some very simple algorithms, and then we will count the operations done by an algorithm. This study will give us a new perspective on the counting problems in the previous sections: any time we can enumerate a set, we can write an algorithm to describe the set. Counting the elements of the set and analyzing the algorithm are fundamentally related.

Preview 4.5

1. The following figure shows a "basketweave" brick pattern, often used for paths and floors. Count the bricks, and reflect on any shortcuts that you use.

2. Four penguins of different heights are standing in a row. Their owner would like to put them in order so that their height increases from left to right. The owner makes the following rearrangements in sequence:

   (a) If the first two on the left are out of order, switch them.

   (b) If the middle two are out of order, switch them.

   (c) If the last two on the right are out of order, switch them.

   Will the penguins be in order after these steps are applied? If not, is there a way to modify this method to guarantee that it always arranges the penguins in order?

4.5.1   Algorithms

An *algorithm* is a list of instructions for doing something. We use algorithms all the time; any time we follow an instruction manual or a recipe we are executing a well-defined sequence of operations in order to complete a certain task. Like a good instruction manual, a well-stated algorithm describes precisely what to do.

In mathematics and computer science, algorithms manipulate variables. A *variable* is an object of some type (e.g., integer, string, set) whose value can change. In mathematics, we usually think of variables as unknowns, like the symbol x in the equation $2x + 3 = 11$. In computer science, it is natural to think of variables as storage locations; a program changes the contents of various locations in the memory of a computer.

Algorithms are important for the modern study of almost any technical field. As computers have become commonplace, our understanding of the world has become more discrete. Our music is no longer pressed into the grooves of a vinyl record—it is encoded digitally as MP3s. Biologists can now understand living things by studying discrete genetic patterns. The hundreds of variables that influence the price of a commodity now fit neatly into a spreadsheet. Understanding how these things work requires some familiarity with algorithms.

4.5.2   Pseudocode

In order to discuss algorithms, we need some way of describing them. To avoid having to learn the syntax of a specific programming language (e.g., C++, Java, Python), we will give informal descriptions of program operations as *pseudocode*.

The nice thing about pseudocode is that there aren't very many rules. The variables can represent anything: numbers, strings, lists, or whatever is appropriate, considering the context. We change the values of the program variables using different commands, or *statements*. Note that we are using the word "statement" differently than we did in Chapter 1; in pseudocode, a statement is an instruction that does something, while in logic, a statement is a declarative sentence that is either true or false.

We'll use the $\leftarrow$ symbol to indicate the *assignment* of one variable to another. For example, the pseudocode statement $x \leftarrow y$ means "set the variable x equal to the value of the variable y." The arrow suggests the direction that the data is moving; in the context of computers, the value in storage location y is being copied into storage location x. Any preexisting data in x is lost (or "written over") when this assignment statement is executed, but the value of y doesn't change.

We can also use assignment statements to update the value of a single variable. For example, the statement

$$x \leftarrow x + 1$$

means "set x equal to the old value of x plus 1" or, more simply, "increment the value of x."

In the simple examples that follow, we are going to want our algorithms to report information back to the user. This type of information is called *output*. For our purposes, the print statement will suffice; imagine that whatever follows the word print gets written to the computer screen. If we print a variable, then the output is the value of the variable. If we print something enclosed in quotes, then the output consists of the quoted text.

We also want our algorithms to be able to execute certain statements depending on whether some condition holds. For example, the instructions for parking a car might include the following statement.

If the car is facing uphill, then turn the wheels away from the curb.

The if...then statement is the pseudocode version of this construction. When the statement

if ⟨condition⟩ then ⟨statement⟩

executes, the program first checks to see if the ⟨condition⟩ is true, and, if it is, the program executes the ⟨statement⟩.

The following example illustrates these simple commands.

Example 4.46 Suppose x is some integer. Consider the following pseudocode statement.

```
print "Old value of x:" x
if x > 5 then x ← x + 3
print "New value of x:" x
```

If initially $x = 10$, then the program will print the following.

```
Old value of x: 10
New value of x: 13
```

However, if instead the initial value of x is 4, the output will be as follows.

```
Old value of x: 4
New value of x: 4
```

In the second case, the condition that the if...then statement checked ($4 > 5$) was false, so the value of the variable x was not changed.

4.5.3 Sequences of Operations

Example 4.47 Consider the following pseudocode segment. The notation // stands for a *comment*—descriptive information that doesn't do anything.

```
y ← x + x + x + x + x      // line a
z ← y + y + y             // line b
```

First, five copies of x are added together and assigned to y, then three copies of y are added together and assigned to z. Line a requires four addition operations and line b requires two, so the total number of additions for this segment is 6.

This example is fairly simple, but it will be helpful to generalize it as our first counting principle for algorithms.

Addition Principle for Algorithms. If statement$_1$ requires m of a certain type of operation and statement$_2$ requires n operations, then the segment

```
statement₁
statement₂
```

requires $m + n$ operations.

Example 4.48 We can now revisit Example 4.2 from the perspective of algorithms. Let B be the set of breakfast customers and let L be the set of lunch customers. Let $|B| = 25$ and $|L| = 37$. Consider the following algorithm.

```
Serve everyone in B breakfast.
Serve everyone in L lunch.
```

By the addition principle, 62 meals were served.

4.5.4 Loops

Sometimes an algorithm needs to repeat the same process several times. For example, instructions for preparing to host a party might include the following statement.

For each guest that is invited to the party, prepare a name tag with the guest's name written on it.

The process of "preparing a name tag" must be repeated several times, once for each guest. In pseudocode, a for-*loop* is a convenient way to repeat a statement (or segment of statements) once for each element of some index set I.

Definition 4.5 Let I be a totally ordered set with n elements. Then the for-*loop*

```
for i ∈ I do
    statementₓ
```

will execute statement_x n times, once for each $i \in I$. Each time statement_x is executed, the value of i moves to the next element in I, according to the total ordering.

For example, the segment

```
for i ∈ {1,2,...n} do
    print i+i+i
```

will print out the first n multiples of three. Observe that the print statement is executed n times, and each time it does two additions, so the total number of additions performed by this segment is $2n$. Thus, we see that a loop requires us to multiply when counting operations in algorithms.

Multiplication Principle for Algorithms. If statement_x requires m of a certain type of operation, then a loop that repeats statement_x n times requires mn operations.

Example 4.49 The following pseudocode segment adds up the first n natural numbers.

```
s ← 0
for i ∈ {1,2,...,n} do
    s ← s+i
```

Each time through the loop, i gets added to the value of s. The loop runs through the first n natural numbers, so when the loop finishes, s contains the sum of these numbers. This algorithm performs one $+$ operation each time through the loop, so the total number of "$+$" operations is n, by the multiplication principle.

In the multiplication principle for algorithms, statement_x can be any kind of statement—in particular, it could be a loop. The next example illustrates this situation; the loops in this example are called *nested loops* because one is "nested" inside the other.

Example 4.50 Let $X = A \times B$, where A has m elements and B has n elements. The following pseudocode segment checks to see if $(a,b) \in X$. The $\ulcorner$ and $\llcorner$ symbols indicate that the bracketed lines together represent the statement that is inside the for-i-loop.

```
for i ∈ A do
  ⌐ for j ∈ B do
  ∟     if (i,j) = (a,b) then print "Found it."
```

How many comparisons does this segment perform?

Solution: The if...then statement performs a single comparison using the $=$ sign. This is inside the j-loop, which executes n times, and the j-loop is inside the i-loop, which executes m times. Therefore, this code segment performs mn comparisons.   ◇

Note that the `for`-loops in this example always run the same number of times, whether or not the pair (a, b) is found in X. This inefficiency points to a limitation of `for`-loops: there is no way to stop them from running for the predetermined number of iterations. A more clever algorithm would stop running once (a, b) is found. In Chapter 5, we'll see a different looping structure—a `while`-loop—with this capability.

There were several counting examples in Section 4.1 that used the addition and multiplication principles for counting sets. We can now revisit these examples from the point of view of algorithms.

Example 4.51 In Example 4.9 we counted the number of strings of at most length 3 that can be formed from a 26-symbol alphabet. Let the set A be this alphabet. The following algorithm prints out all 18,278 of these strings. Recall that if x and y are strings, their concatenation is written as xy.

```
for c ∈ A do
     print c
for c ∈ A do
     ⌐ for d ∈ A do
     L      print cd
for c ∈ A do
     ⌐ for d ∈ A do
            ⌐ for e ∈ A do
     L      L      print cde
```

Applying the addition and multiplication principles for algorithms is analogous to the solution of Example 4.9. The first `for`-c-loop prints one single-symbol string for every symbol in A, so it prints 26 strings. The second `for`-c-loop has another loop inside of it, which runs 26 times, so these nested loops print 26^2 strings. Finally, the third `for`-c-loop has a `for`-d-loop inside, which in turn has a `for`-e-loop inside of it. This nested trio therefore prints 26^3 strings. These three looping statements run in sequence, so by the addition principle, the total number of strings printed is $26 + 26^2 + 26^3 = 18{,}278$.

Example 4.52 In Example 4.6, we used a decision tree to determine that there are 12 designs of the form

where each square is colored either red, green, or blue, and no two adjacent squares are the same color. The following algorithm prints out strings in the symbols $A = \{\texttt{R}, \texttt{G}, \texttt{B}\}$ corresponding to these 12 designs. Recall that the set difference $U \setminus X$ is another way of writing $U \cap X'$.

```
for c ∈ A do
     ⌐ for d ∈ A \ {c} do
            ⌐ for e ∈ A \ {d} do
     L      L      print cde
```

These loops are very similar to the nested loops in Example 4.51. The only difference is that the index sets are modified so that d is drawn from a set that does not contain c, and likewise e comes from a set without d. This ensures that no two adjacent squares will be the same color. It also makes it easy to count the number of strings printed using the multiplication principle: $3 \cdot 2 \cdot 2$.

The following example first appeared in Section 4.2 as a counting problem. Let's revisit this example from an algorithmic point of view.

Example 4.53 Yifan has 26 refrigerator magnets in the shapes of the letters from A to Z. Write an algorithm to print all the different three-letter strings he can form with these letters.

Solution: The following algorithm will print out all the strings Yifan can form using his refrigerator magnets. The algorithm is very similar to the one used in Example 4.52. Let $A = \{\texttt{A}, \texttt{B}, \ldots, \texttt{Z}\}$.

```
for c ∈ A do
     ⌐ for d ∈ A \ {c} do
            ⌐ for e ∈ A \ {c, d} do
     L      L      print cde
```

In each successive loop, the index sets get smaller by one element; this ensures that no character is repeated. The sizes of the index sets are 26, 25, and 24, so by the multiplication principle for algorithms, $26 \cdot 25 \cdot 24$ strings are printed.   ◇

Activity 4.5.1: Counting in Algorithms

Consider the following algorithm, where n can be any natural number.

```
r ← 1
s ← 0
for i ∈ {1, 2, 3, ..., n} do
   ⌐ r ← r + 2
     for j ∈ {1, 2, 3, ... i} do
   └      s ← s + j * r
```

1. When $n = 3$, the values of i and j change as shown in the following table. Complete the rows for r and s.

i		1	2		3		
j		1	1	2	1	2	3
r	1						
s	0						

2. In terms of n, how many times is the line $r \leftarrow r + 2$ executed?

3. In terms of n, how many times is the line $s \leftarrow s + j * r$ executed?

4. How many "+" operations are done by this algorithm, in terms of n?

4.5.5   Arrays

A `for`-loop is a good tool for running through every item in a list of data. The following definition gives a way of representing a list in pseudocode.

Definition 4.6 An *array* is a sequence of variables $x_1, x_2, x_3, \ldots, x_n$.

An array is simply a notational convenience for a list of variables of the same type. Sometimes it is helpful to think of an array as a contiguous block of storage locations in a computer. For example, an array of 10 real numbers might look like this:

x_1	x_2	x_3	x_4	x_5	x_6	x_7	x_8	x_9	x_{10}
2.4	7.3	3.1	2.7	1.1	2.4	8.2	0.3	4.9	7.3

Notice that the order of the elements in an array matters, and an array can have duplicate entries.

Example 4.54 The following algorithm counts the number of duplicates in the array $x_1, x_2, x_3, \ldots, x_n$, where $n > 1$.

```
t ← 0
for i ∈ {1, 2, 3, ..., n − 1} do
   ⌐ for j ∈ {i + 1, ..., n} do
   └      if xᵢ = xⱼ then t ← t + 1
```

The variable t serves as a *counter*; its value gets incremented each time a duplicate is found. The loop indices are set up so that x_i always comes before x_j in the array. This avoids comparing the same pair of array elements more than once, while ensuring that every pair of elements gets compared.

The size of $\{i + 1, \ldots, n\}$, the index set for j, depends on i. Therefore, we can't use the multiplication principle to count the number of "=" comparisons, because the number of comparisons is different each time through the for-i-loop. The following table shows how the variables change in the case where $n = 4$ and the array has values $x_1 = 20$, $x_2 = 50$, $x_3 = 50$, and $x_4 = 18$.

x_1	x_2	x_3	x_4	t	i	j	Comparison
20	50	50	18	0	1	2	$20 \overset{?}{=} 50$
20	50	50	18	0	1	3	$20 \overset{?}{=} 50$
20	50	50	18	0	1	4	$20 \overset{?}{=} 18$
20	50	50	18	0	2	3	$50 \overset{?}{=} 50$
20	50	50	18	1	2	4	$50 \overset{?}{=} 18$
20	50	50	18	1	3	4	$50 \overset{?}{=} 18$

Such a table is called a *trace* of an algorithm. Notice that the only time that the counter t was incremented was after the two duplicates, x_2 and x_3, were compared. Also notice that each pair of array elements was compared exactly once. The number of comparisons is evidently $6 = 3 + 2 + 1$ in this case. In general, this algorithm will make

$$(n - 1) + (n - 2) + \cdots + 2 + 1$$

comparisons, by the addition principle.

Another way to count the number of comparisons is to notice that one comparison is done for each pair (x_i, x_j), where $i < j$. By the reasoning in Exercise 8 of Section 4.3, the number of such pairs is the same as the number of ways to choose a set of two elements from the set $\{1, 2, \ldots, n\}$, namely $C(n, 2)$. Recall that

$$C(n, 2) = \frac{n(n - 1)}{2},$$

which indeed equals $(n - 1) + (n - 2) + \cdots + 2 + 1$, by Exercise 2 of Section 3.2.

Example 4.54 works no matter what type of data is stored in the array $x_1, x_2, \ldots, x_n$—these variables could represent images, or sets, or people. But often the elements of an array are elements of a set on which some total ordering is defined, like the integers ($\leq$) or English words (alphabetical order). In this situation it is possible to find the maximum item in the list with respect to the total ordering.

Example 4.55 Let $x_1, x_2, \ldots, x_n$ be an array whose elements can be compared by the total ordering $\leq$. Write an algorithm for computing the maximum element in the array. How many "$<$" comparisons does your algorithm require?

Solution: The natural way to find the maximum element is to go through the list and keep track of the largest element as we go.

```
m ← x₁
for i ∈ {2, 3, ..., n} do
        if m < xᵢ then m ← xᵢ
```

The index set has $n - 1$ elements, so the algorithm makes $n - 1$ "$<$" comparisons, by the multiplication rule.   ◇

4.5.6 Sorting

Data is almost always easier to use if it is organized. For example, if we were working with an array containing a list of names, we would usually prefer to have the names listed alphabetically. In general, if the elements of an array can be compared by $\leq$, it is important to be able to rearrange the elements so that they are in order. A *sort* is an algorithm that guarantees that

$$x_1 \leq x_2 \leq x_3 \leq \cdots \leq x_n$$

after the algorithm finishes. The next example gives a very simple algorithm for sorting an array.

Example 4.56 Let $x_1, x_2, x_3, \ldots, x_n$ be an array whose elements can be compared by $\leq$. The following algorithm is called a *bubble sort*.

```
for i ∈ {1, 2, ..., n − 1} do
┌ for j ∈ {1, 2, ..., n − i} do
└     if xⱼ > xⱼ₊₁ then swap xⱼ and xⱼ₊₁
```

Step through this algorithm for the following list of four elements: $x_1 = 9$, $x_2 = 4$, $x_3 = 7$, and $x_4 = 1$.

Solution: The following table shows how the program variables change during execution. Each row of the table gives the value of the program variables before the if statement is executed. The last two columns show the result of each ">" comparison.

x_1	x_2	x_3	x_4	i	j	Comparison	Result
9	4	7	1	1	1	$x_1 \overset{?}{>} x_2$	yes
4	9	7	1	1	2	$x_2 \overset{?}{>} x_3$	yes
4	7	9	1	1	3	$x_3 \overset{?}{>} x_4$	yes
4	7	1	9	2	1	$x_1 \overset{?}{>} x_2$	no
4	7	1	9	2	2	$x_2 \overset{?}{>} x_3$	yes
4	1	7	9	3	1	$x_1 \overset{?}{>} x_2$	yes
1	4	7	9				

After the last comparison and swap, the loops are finished, and the list is in order.　　◇

The bubble sort is so named because the largest elements tend to "bubble" up to the end of the list, like the bubbles in a soft drink. Look back at the above trace and notice that the 9 bubbled to the end of the list when i was 1, then the 7 bubbled up next to it when i was 2, and so on.

Example 4.57 How many times does the bubble sort make the ">" comparison when sorting a list of n elements?

Solution: The if statement requires one comparison. The outside loop makes the inside loop execute $n − 1$ times, but each time the size of the index set for j gets smaller. Thus, the total number of comparisons is

$$(n − 1) + (n − 2) + \cdots + [n − (n − 2)] + [n − (n − 1)] = (n − 1) + (n − 2) + \cdots + 2 + 1$$
$$= \frac{(n − 1)n}{2}$$

as in Example 4.54.　　◇

Activity 4.5.2: Selection Sort

Consider the following algorithm on an array of numbers $x_1, x_2, x_3, \ldots, x_n$.

The element in the first position is compared to the $n − 1$ remaining elements; whenever one is found that is less, the first element is swapped with it. Then the element in the second position is compared with the remaining $n − 2$ elements. Whenever one is found that is less, the elements are swapped. This continues until the $(n − 1)$st element: if it is out of order with the nth element, the elements are swapped.

In pseudocode, the algorithm is as follows.

```
for i ∈ {1, 2, ..., n − 1} do
┌ for j ∈ {i + 1, i + 2, ..., n} do
└     if xᵢ > xⱼ then swap xᵢ and xⱼ
```

1. Step through this algorithm when applied to the array $x_1 = 9$, $x_2 = 4$, $x_3 = 7$, $x_4 = 1$.
2. In terms of n, how many "<" comparisons does this algorithm make on an array of length n?

Exercises 4.5

1. Look at pseudocode segment in Example 4.47. If $x = 3$ before this segment is executed, what is the value of z after execution?

2. Modify Example 4.49 so that it adds up the first n natural numbers using only $n - 1$ "+" operations. You may assume that $n \geq 1$.

3. Trace through the algorithm in Example 4.55 in the case when $n = 5$ and the array elements are $x_1 = 77$, $x_2 = 54$, $x_3 = 95$, $x_4 = 101$, and $x_5 = 62$.

4. Let x and n be integers greater than 1. Consider the following algorithm.

```
t ← 0,  s ← 0
for i ∈ {1, 2, ..., x} do
   ⌐ for j ∈ {1, 2, ..., n} do
         t ← t + x
   ∟ s ← s + t          // line A
```

   The ⌐ and ∟ symbols and the indentation are important: they tell you which lines are inside which loop. So, for example, line A is inside the i-loop, but outside the j-loop.

   (a) If $x = 3$ and $n = 5$ initially, what is the value of s after this segment executes?

   (b) Count the number of additions this segment performs. Your answer should be in terms of x and n.

5. How many words does each algorithm print? Explain your answers. Again, the indenting is important.

   (a)
```
for i ∈ {1, 2, ..., 9} do
   ⌐ for j ∈ {1, 2, ..., 6} do
         ⌐ for k ∈ {1, 2, 3} do
   ∟     ∟     print "Cubs Win"
```

   (b)
```
for i ∈ {1, 2, ..., 9} do
   ⌐ for j ∈ {1, 2, ..., 6} do
         print "Sox Win"
      for k ∈ {1, 2, 3} do
   ∟       print "Sox Win"
```

6. Consider the following algorithm.

```
for i ∈ {1, 2, 3, 4, 5, 6} do
   ⌐ beep
      for j ∈ {1, 2, 3, 4} do
         beep
      for k ∈ {1, 2, 3} do
         ⌐ for l ∈ {1, 2, 3, 4, 5} do
               beep
            for m ∈ {1, 2, 3, 4} do
   ∟     ∟       beep
```

   How many times does a beep statement get executed?

7. Let $n > 1$. Consider the following pseudocode segment.

```
for i ∈ {1, 2, ..., 10} do
   ⌐ statement_A
      for j ∈ {1, 2, ..., n} do
         statement_B
      for k ∈ {1, 2, 3, 4} do
         ⌐ for l ∈ {1, 2, ..., n} do
   ∟     ∟       statement_C
```

(a) Which statement (A, B, or C) gets executed the most number of times?

(b) Suppose that statement A requires $3n$ comparison operations, B requires n^2 comparisons, and C requires 30 comparisons. How many total comparisons does the entire pseudocode segment require?

8. For each algorithm below, compute the number of multiplications performed, as well as the final value of s.

(a)
```
p ← 1
s ← 0
for i ∈ {1, 2, 3, 4} do
    p ← p · 3
    s ← s + p
```

(b)
```
s ← 0
for i ∈ {1, 2, 3, 4} do
    p ← 1
    for j ∈ {1, ..., i} do
        p ← p · 3
    s ← s + p
```

9. Consider the following pseudocode segment.

```
x ← 3
for i ∈ {1, 2, ..., n} do
    for j ∈ {1, 2, ..., n} do
        x ← x + 5
        for k ∈ {1, 2, 3, 4, 5} do
            x ← x + k + 1
```

(a) How many times is the "+" operation executed?

(b) What is the value of x after this segment runs?

10. Consider the following algorithm.

```
x ← 1
for i ∈ {1, 2, 3} do
    for j ∈ {1, 2, 3, 4} do
        x ← x + x
        for k ∈ {1, 2, 3, 4, 5} do
            x ← x + 1
            x ← x + 5
```

(a) Count the number of + operations done by this algorithm.

(b) What is the value of x after the algorithm finishes?

11. Let $n > 3$. Consider the following pseudocode segment.

```
for i ∈ {1, 2, ..., n − 3} do
    w ← w + z + 10
    for j ∈ {1, 2, ..., n} do
        z ← y + y + y + 30
        for k ∈ {1, 2, ..., n²} do
            for l ∈ {1, 2, ..., n} do
                y ← x + l
            for m ∈ {1, 2, ..., n} do
                x ← w + y + z
```

How many "+" operations does this algorithm perform?

12. Interpret the following algorithm in the context of rolling two six-sided dice. What do the counters e and s count?

    ```
    s ← 0
    e ← 0
    for i ∈ {1, 2, 3, 4, 5, 6} do
        ⌐ for j ∈ {1, 2, 3, 4, 5, 6} do
              ⌐ if i + j = 7 then e ← e + 1
        ∟     ∟ s ← s + 1
    ```

13. Suppose $I = \emptyset$. According to Definition 4.5, how many times does $\texttt{statement}_x$ get executed in the following pseudocode segment?

    ```
    for i ∈ I do
        statementₓ
    ```

14. An urn containing n balls can be represented by the set $U = \{b_1, b_2, \ldots, b_n\}$. Interpret the following algorithm in the context of urn problems. Does it represent drawing with or without replacement? How many lines does it print?

    ```
    for i ∈ {1, 2, ..., n} do
        ⌐ for j ∈ {1, 2, ..., n} do
              ⌐ for k ∈ {1, 2, ..., n} do
        ∟     ∟     print bᵢ, bⱼ, bₖ
    ```

15. Let $U = \{b_1, b_2, \ldots, b_n\}$ with $n \geq 3$. Interpret the following algorithm in the context of urn problems. How many lines does it print?

    ```
    for i ∈ {1, 2, ..., n} do
        ⌐ for j ∈ {1, 2, ..., n} \ {i} do
              ⌐ for k ∈ {1, 2, ..., n} \ {i, j} do
        ∟     ∟     print bᵢ, bⱼ, bₖ
    ```

16. Let $U = \{b_1, b_2, \ldots, b_n\}$ with $n \geq 3$. Interpret the following algorithm in the context of urn problems. How many lines does it print?

    ```
    for i ∈ {1, 2, ..., n} do
        ⌐ for j ∈ {i + 1, i + 2, ..., n} do
              ⌐ for k ∈ {j + 1, j + 2, ..., n} do
        ∟     ∟     print bᵢ, bⱼ, bₖ
    ```

17. Write a pseudocode algorithm that runs through all possible outcomes when a four-sided die and a six-sided die are cast and prints all the ways of having a roll total of 8.

18. Write a pseudocode algorithm to compute the product of the first n positive integers. How many multiplications does your algorithm perform?

19. Write an algorithm in pseudocode that will print out all possible Illinois license plates, according to the description in Example 4.10.

20. Write an algorithm in pseudocode that will print out the first 500,000 license plates in a given district in India, according to the description in Exercise 7 of Section 4.1.

21. Trace through the bubble sort algorithm for the following data set: $x_1 = 5$, $x_2 = 4$, $x_3 = 2$, $x_4 = 1$, $x_5 = 3$.

22. The number of $\texttt{swap}$ statements executed by a bubble sort varies depending on the initial state of the array. Under what circumstances will the bubble sort make zero $\texttt{swaps}$?

23. Write a pseudocode algorithm to compute the following sum.

$$1 + 1 \cdot 2 + 1 \cdot 2 \cdot 3 + \cdots + 1 \cdot 2 \cdots n$$

How many multiplications does your algorithm perform?

24. Let $x_1, x_2, \ldots, x_n$ be an array. Consider the following algorithm.

$$
\begin{aligned}
&\texttt{for } i \in \{1, 2, \ldots, \lfloor n/2 \rfloor\} \texttt{ do} \\
&\quad \ulcorner \; t \leftarrow x_i \\
&\qquad x_i \leftarrow x_{n-i+1} \\
&\quad \llcorner \; x_{n-i+1} \leftarrow t
\end{aligned}
$$

   (a) How many "$\leftarrow$" operations does this algorithm perform?

   (b) What does this algorithm do to the array?

25. Let $x_1, x_2, \ldots, x_n$ be an array. Consider the following algorithm.

$$
\begin{aligned}
&t \leftarrow x_1 \\
&\texttt{for } i \in \{1, 2, \ldots, n-1\} \texttt{ do} \\
&\quad x_i \leftarrow x_{i+1} \\
&x_n \leftarrow t
\end{aligned}
$$

   (a) How many "$\leftarrow$" operations does this algorithm perform? (Give an answer in terms of n.)

   (b) Suppose that initially $n = 4$ and $x_1 = 12$, $x_2 = 19$, $x_3 = 23$, and $x_4 = 29$. What are the values of x_1, x_2, x_3, x_4 after the algorithm executes?

26. Let $x_1, x_2, \ldots, x_n$ be an array of integers. Write a pseudocode algorithm that will compute the probability that a randomly chosen element of this array is odd. (You may use a statement like "if k is odd then $\ldots$" in your algorithm.)

27. Write a pseudocode algorithm that will print out all three-letter palindromes with symbols from the set $A = \{A, B, \ldots, Z\}$. How many such palindromes are there?

28. Write a pseudocode algorithm that will print out all strings of four symbols from the set $A = \{A, B, \ldots, Z\}$ such that no symbol is repeated. How many such strings are there?

29. Recall Example 4.11. Write a pseudocode algorithm that prints out all allowable colorings of the vertices $a, b, c,$ and d as a four-symbol string using the symbols in $C = \{R, G, B, V\}$. Use the two disjoint cases given in the solution to Example 4.11: when b and d are the same color, and when b and d are different colors.

30. Repeat the previous problem using the three disjoint cases suggested in Exercise 13 of Section 4.1: using two different colors, using three different colors, and using four different colors.

4.6   Estimation

So far, we have usually been able to come up with an exact answer for counting problems. Some of our examples, such as rearranging the letters in a word or drawing balls from an urn, might seem somewhat distant from real-world situations. However, in many applications—and especially in algorithms—enumeration problems are too complicated to consider all the cases and get an exact count. Often, all we need is an estimate. In this section, we will practice estimating answers to counting problems, concentrating on the kind of answers that help solve discrete problems in computer science.

Preview 4.6

1. Which is bigger, $n!$ or 10^n? Explain.

2. In preview question 4.2.1, you counted the number of edges in K_8, the complete graph on eight vertices. In preview question 4.3.2, you counted the number of triangular subgraphs in K_5, the complete graph on five vertices. In general, are there more edges or triangular subgraphs in K_n? Does the answer depend on n?

3. Bert makes square coffee tables out of cubes, stacked two layers tall. For example, below is a 3×3 version.

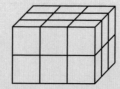

Bert paints the tops of the tables one color, and the sides another color. Which has more surface area, the tops or the sides? Is this true for the $n \times n$ version, for all n?

4.6.1 Growth of Functions

The concept of *scalability* is an important consideration in many applications in business and industry. Given a solution to a task or problem, how well will the solution work as the size of the task grows? For example, a system of inventory management might function well for a small retailer with a regional customer base, but will the same system continue to be effective as the company grows and its sales volume increases? The study of the growth of functions provides a mathematical foundation for approaching such questions.

In most discrete counting problems, the answer depends on some natural number n. We have seen several examples: the number of binary strings with n digits, the number of ways to choose three things from a set of n things, the number of socks needed to guarantee getting n of the same kind. The answer to these problems is a function

$$f : \mathbf{N} \longrightarrow \mathbf{R}.$$

This function usually maps into the integers, but for the purposes of estimation we use the codomain $\mathbf{R}$ to allow for the possibility of noninteger values. Sometimes we will also think of f as being defined on the domain $\mathbf{R}$ instead of $\mathbf{N}$, but for most discrete applications, we evaluate f only at integer values.

Example 4.58 Suppose that a certain networking algorithm must run through all the different possible groups of three computers (i.e., subsets of size 3) in a network of n computers. Give the number of groups as a function of n.

Solution: Let $f(n)$ be the number of subsets of three computers in a network of n computers. Using the Selection Principle, there are

$$f(n) = \binom{n}{3} = \frac{n!}{3!\,(n-3)!} = \frac{n(n-1)(n-2)}{3!}$$

different subsets of size 3.   ◇

Example 4.59 Suppose that a different networking algorithm must run through all the different possible (unordered) pairs of computers in a network of n computers. Give the number of pairs as a function of n.

Solution: Let $g(n)$ be the number of subsets of two computers in a network of n computers. Using the Selection Principle, there are

$$g(n) = \binom{n}{2} = \frac{n!}{2!\,(n-2)!} = \frac{n(n-1)}{2}$$

different subsets of size 2.   ◇

How do these two algorithms compare? More specifically, which one will run faster? Assuming that the running time depends mainly on the number of groups each algorithm must run through, the functions $f(n)$ and $g(n)$ should indicate the relative speed of the two algorithms. Figure 4.3 shows a plot of $f(n)$ and $g(n)$ versus n, for $0 \le n \le 6$. The two curves are fairly similar, suggesting that the running times of these two algorithms should be comparable for small networks.

However, the story is quite different for larger networks. Figure 4.4 shows a plot of the same two functions over the interval $0 \le n \le 50$. Notice that the $f(n)$ curve grows much more steeply than $g(n)$ over this range. Therefore, on larger networks, we would expect the algorithm on triples to run noticeably slower than the algorithm on pairs.

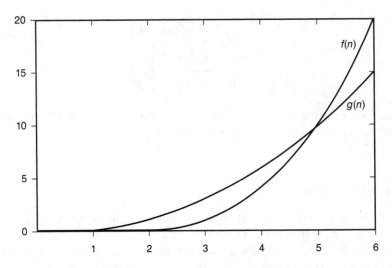

Figure 4.3 Plots of $f(n)$ and $g(n)$ for $0 \leq n \leq 6$.

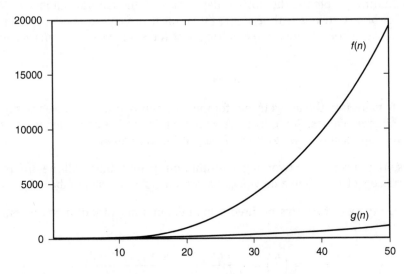

Figure 4.4 Plots of $f(n)$ and $g(n)$ for $0 \leq n \leq 50$.

Activity 4.6.1: Growth of Functions

1. Suppose that two different algorithms are written to perform the same processing task on data in the form of an image. The functions $f_1 : \mathbb{N} \longrightarrow \mathbb{N}$ and $f_2 : \mathbb{N} \longrightarrow \mathbb{N}$ output the time (in nanoseconds) that it takes for the algorithms to finish: the input to these functions is the size of the image data (in bytes). Suppose that $f_1(n) = 5000n^2$ and $f_2(n) = 10n^3$.

   (a) For what data sizes is the first algorithm faster? For what data sizes is the second algorithm faster?

   (b) What is the difference in running time on a small 8,000-byte thumbnail image?

   (c) What is the difference in running time on a large 2,600,000-byte high-definition image?

2. Suppose that the running times of five different algorithms are given by the following functions.

$$f(n) = n^2$$
$$g(n) = n^2 \ln(n)$$
$$h(n) = 10n$$
$$k(n) = n^2 + 2000$$
$$l(n) = 3n$$

Use a graphing calculator or app to plot these five functions on the same pair of axes. Set the graphing window to $1 \leq n \leq 500$ and $0 \leq y \leq 200000$. Sketch your graph and label each function. Rank the algorithms in order of speed, from fastest to slowest. Are any of the algorithms basically the same, in terms of running time?

The algorithms in Examples 4.58 and 4.59 illustrate a phenomenon that should seem plausible: differences in algorithm performance will be more noticeable when the algorithms are applied to big problems. For this reason, it is important to have a way of classifying and ranking functions of n based on their behavior for large values of n. This is the idea behind big-O ("big-oh"), big-Ω ("big-omega"), and big-Θ ("big-theta") notation.

For the remainder of this section, let's assume for simplicity that all the functions we consider map from domain $\mathbf{N}$ to codomain $\mathbf{R}^+$, the positive real numbers, unless noted otherwise.

Definition 4.7 Let $f: \mathbf{N} \longrightarrow \mathbf{R}^+$ be a function. Then $O(f)$ is the set of all functions g such that

$$g(n) \leq Kf(n)$$

for some constant $K > 0$, and for all $n \geq N$ for some $N > 0$. If $g \in O(f)$, we also say that "g is big-oh of f."

In other words, $O(f)$ is the set of all functions that are bounded above by some constant multiple of $f(n)$ for large values of n. Figure 4.4 illustrates this situation graphically; the following example shows how to apply the definition algebraically.

Example 4.60 Show that $g \in O(f)$, where

$$f(n) = \frac{n(n-1)(n-2)}{6} \quad \text{and} \quad g(n) = \frac{n(n-1)}{2}.$$

Solution: By Definition 4.7, we must show that there are constants K and N such that $g(n) \leq Kf(n)$ for all $n \geq N$. In order to establish this inequality, we construct a sequence of (in)equalities as follows:

$$\begin{aligned} g(n) &= \frac{n(n-1)}{2} \\ &\leq \frac{n(n-1)(n-2)}{2} \quad \text{for } n \geq 3 \\ &= 3 \cdot \frac{n(n-1)(n-2)}{6}. \end{aligned}$$

So $g(n) \leq 3f(n)$ for all $n \geq 3$, as required. $\diamond$

Notice that the second line of the above sequence holds because $n - 2 \geq 1$ for $n \geq 3$. In general, to establish a "$\leq$" inequality, start with an equation you know to be true, and think of ways to make the right-hand side bigger.

Activity 4.6.2: Big-O Notation

Let $f : \mathbf{N} \longrightarrow \mathbf{R}^+$ be a function. Then $O(f)$ is the set of all functions g such that

$$g(n) \leq Kf(n)$$

for some constant $K > 0$, and for all $n \geq N$, for some $N > 0$. If $g \in O(f)$, we also say that "g is big-oh of f."

1. Let $g(n) = 7n + 90$ and $f(n) = 2n$ be functions defined on the domain $\mathbf{N}$.

   (a) Suppose $K = 3$. Is there a value of $N > 0$ such that $g(n) \leq Kf(n)$ for all $n \geq N$? If so, what value works? If no such value exists, explain why.

(b) Suppose $K = 5$. Is there a value of $N > 0$ such that $g(n) \leq Kf(n)$ for all $n \geq N$? If so, what value works? If no such value exists, explain why.

(c) Is $g \in O(f)$? Justify your answer using the above definition.

2. Let $g(n) = 3n^2 + 100$. Use the above definition to show that $g \in O(n^2)$. Specifically, find values of K and N that satisfy the definition, where $f(n) = n^2$.

3. Let $g(n) = n^3$. Prove, by contradiction, that $g \notin O(n^2)$, by completing the following steps.

(a) Suppose to the contrary that $g \in O(n^2)$. Then the definition of big-O says that there are numbers K and N and an inequality involving K and n that must hold for all $n \geq N$. Write this inequality.

(b) Explain why the inequality from (a) leads to a contradiction.

In addition to big-O, there is a similar definition for functions that are bounded below by a multiple of f.

Definition 4.8 Let $f : \mathbf{N} \longrightarrow \mathbf{R}^+$ be a function. Then $\Omega(f)$ is the set of all functions g such that

$$g(n) \geq Kf(n)$$

for some constant $K > 0$, and for all $n \geq N$ for some $N > 0$. If $g \in \Omega(f)$, we also say that "g is big-omega of f."

Think of big-O and big-Ω as ways of comparing the long-term behavior of functions. They both stipulate that one function is at least as big as the other, up to a constant multiple K, for sufficiently large values of n. The two definitions are symmetric, as the following theorem shows.

Theorem 4.11 Let $f, g : \mathbf{N} \longrightarrow \mathbf{R}^+$. Then $f \in O(g) \Leftrightarrow g \in \Omega(f)$.

Proof Suppose $f \in O(g)$. Then there exist positive numbers K and N such that $f(n) \leq Kg(n)$ for all $n \geq N$. Let $K' = 1/K$. Then for all $n \geq N$, $g(n) \geq K'f(n)$, so $g \in \Omega(f)$. The proof of the converse is almost the same and is left as an exercise. □

Big-Θ notation combines big-O and big-Ω to form an equivalence relation on the set of all functions $\mathbf{N} \longrightarrow \mathbf{R}^+$.

Definition 4.9 Let $f : \mathbf{N} \longrightarrow \mathbf{R}^+$ be a function. The *big-theta class* $\Theta(f)$ is the set of all functions g such that

$$K_1 f(n) \leq g(n) \leq K_2 f(n)$$

for some positive constants K_1, K_2, and for all $n \geq N$ for some $N > 0$. In other words, $\Theta(f) = O(f) \cap \Omega(f)$. If $g \in \Theta(f)$, we also say that "g is big-theta of f" or "g is order f."

Observe that $f \in \Theta(g)$ if and only if $g \in \Theta(f)$. In this case we say that f and g are of the same order, and we often choose to write $\Theta(f) = \Theta(g)$. Functions of the same order grow in roughly the same way as n increases. For the purposes of estimation, big-Θ encapsulates just enough information to make useful comparisons between functions.

Example 4.61 See Example 4.56. Show that the number of comparisons required to do a bubble sort on a list of n items is in $\Theta(n^2)$.

Solution: In Example 4.57, we calculated that the number of comparisons performed by a bubble sort is $n(n-1)/2$. Since

$$\frac{n(n-1)}{2} = \frac{1}{2} \cdot (n^2 - n)$$

$$\leq \frac{1}{2} \cdot n^2 \quad \text{for } n \geq 1,$$

we conclude that $n(n-1)/2 \in O(n^2)$. Furthermore, the calculation

$$\frac{n(n-1)}{2} = \frac{1}{2} \cdot (n^2 - n)$$

$$\geq \frac{1}{2} \cdot \left(n^2 - \frac{n^2}{2}\right) \quad \text{for } n \geq 2$$

$$= \frac{1}{4} \cdot n^2$$

shows that $n(n-1)/2 \in \Omega(n^2)$. Therefore, $n(n-1)/2 \in \Theta(n^2)$.   ◇

In other words, using estimation, we say that "the number of comparisons done by the bubble sort is order n^2."

4.6.2 Estimation Targets

It is an exercise for you to show that big-Θ defines an equivalence relation on the set of all functions $\mathbf{N} \longrightarrow \mathbf{R}^+$. The Θ-classes are the equivalence classes determined by this relation. The next theorem lists some commonly used equivalence class representatives.

Theorem 4.12 *The following functions of n represent different Θ-classes. Furthermore, the functions are listed according to how fast they grow: if f comes before g on the list, then $f \in O(g)$.*

1. 1, *the constant function* $f(n) = 1$.
2. $\log_2 n$
3. n^p *for* $0 < p < 1$.
4. n
5. $n \log_2 n$
6. n^p *for* $1 < p < \infty$.
7. 2^n
8. $n!$

Cases (3) and (6) represent continuums of Θ-classes: if $0 < p < q$, then $n^p \in O(n^q)$ and $\Theta(n^p) \neq \Theta(n^q)$.

We'll skip proving this theorem, but you will find some parts of the proof left as exercises. The functions 1, $\log_2 n$, n, n^p, $n \log_2 n$, 2^n, $n!$ are called *estimation targets*. When we want to estimate the growth of a function, we will try to compare it to one of these target functions.

Example 4.62 Give a big-Θ estimate of $\log_2 n^{7n+1}$.

Solution: Using the identity $\log_b(a^k) = k \log_b a$, we obtain

$$\log_2 n^{7n+1} = (7n + 1) \log_2 n$$
$$\leq 8n \log_2 n, \text{ for } n \geq 1$$

and similarly,

$$\log_2 n^{7n+1} = (7n + 1) \log_2 n$$
$$\geq 7n \log_2 n, \text{ for } n \geq 1,$$

so $\log_2 n^{7n+1} \in \Theta(n \log_2 n)$.   ◇

Two functions in the same Θ-class grow at approximately the same rate, for large values of n. If these two functions describe the size of two tasks (in terms of input size n), then these tasks will "scale" up approximately equally well. We will explore this idea more carefully when we study the complexity of discrete processes in Chapter 5.

4.6.3 Properties of Big-Θ

There are several properties of Θ-classes that help make finding big-Θ estimates easier. The first property is the observation that constant multiples don't change the Θ-class.

Theorem 4.13 *Let $f : \mathbf{N} \longrightarrow \mathbf{R}^+$ be a function, and let $k > 0$ be a constant. Then $kf(n) \in \Theta(f(n))$.*

Proof Exercise.   □

The next theorem says that the big-Θ estimate of a sum is determined by the biggest summand.

Theorem 4.14 *Let $f, g : \mathbf{N} \longrightarrow \mathbf{R}^+$ be functions, and suppose that $g(n) \in O(f(n))$. Then $f(n) + g(n) \in \Theta(f(n))$.*

Proof Since g takes only positive values, $f(n) + g(n) \geq f(n)$, so $f(n) + g(n) \in \Omega(f(n))$. Since $g(n) \in O(f(n))$, there are positive constants K and N such that $g(n) \leq Kf(n)$ for all $n \geq N$. We can assume $K \geq 1$, for if it weren't, we could increase it, and the inequality $g(n) \leq Kf(n)$ would still hold. Therefore, $f(n) \leq Kf(n)$, and

$$f(n) + g(n) \leq Kf(n) + Kf(n) = 2Kf(n),$$

so $f(n) + g(n) \in O(f(n))$. Therefore, $f(n) + g(n) \in \Theta(f(n))$.   □

This theorem is a mathematical version of a rule from chemistry. In a chemical reaction involving several different stages, the rate-determining step is the step that takes the longest. A consequence of Theorem 4.14 is that the Θ-class of a polynomial is determined by its highest-degree term.

Corollary 4.4 *Let $f(n) = a_0 + a_1 n + a_2 n^2 + \cdots + a_p n^p$ and suppose all of the coefficients $a_i \geq 0$ and $a_p > 0$. Then $f \in \Theta(n^p)$.*

Actually, a stronger statement holds: the coefficients $a_0, a_1, \ldots, a_{p-1}$ need not be positive. It is left as an exercise to verify this fact.

Example 4.63 Give a big-Θ estimate of the number of strings with 10 or fewer letters that can be formed using n symbols if no symbol can be repeated.

Solution: Not counting the empty string, there are 10 cases to consider, and they are all arrangement problems. So we need an estimate for

$$f(n) = P(n, 1) + P(n, 2) + \cdots + P(n, 10).$$

Each term is a polynomial in n; as a product:

$$P(n, r) = n(n - 1)(n - 2) \cdots (n - r + 1).$$

There are r factors in this product, so the highest-degree term in $P(n, r)$ is n^r. Therefore, the highest-degree term in the polynomial $f(n)$ is n^{10}, so $f(n) \in \Theta(n^{10})$.   ◇

Activity 4.6.3: Big-Theta Estimation

The following simple functions are commonly used for big-theta estimates:

$$1, \ \log_2 n, \ n, \ n\log_2 n, \ n^2, \ n^3, \ \ldots, \ n^k, \ 2^n, \ n!$$

We refer to the above functions as *estimation targets*. These functions are listed in order of size: if f comes before g on the list, then $f \in O(g)$ and $g \notin O(f)$. The following rules can assist in choosing the correct estimation target.

Symmetry Rule:	If $f \in \Theta(g)$, then $g \in \Theta(f)$.
Reflexivity Rule:	$f \in \Theta(f)$.
Transitivity Rule:	If $f \in \Theta(g)$ and $g \in \Theta(h)$, then $f \in \Theta(h)$.
Sum Rule:	If $f \in O(g)$, then $f + g \in \Theta(g)$.
Constant Multiple Rule:	If $c > 0$ is a constant, then $cf \in \Theta(f)$.
Product Rule:	If $f_1 \in \Theta(g_1)$ and $f_2 \in \Theta(g_2)$, then $f_1 \cdot f_2 \in \Theta(g_1 \cdot g_2)$.

1. Use the above targets and rules to find simple big-theta estimates for each of the following functions. State which rules you apply.

   (a) $34n^4 + 9n^3 + 11n^2 + 20n + 70$

   (b) $(n^7 + n^4 + n^2)(n^{100} + 2^n)$

   (c) $n^{100} + 2^n + 10^n + n!$

   (d) $\log_2(n^{100}) + \log_2(n^n)$

   (e) $\log_2((n^3)(10^n))$

   (f) $(2n^2 + 3n + 1)^5 + n\log_2 n + \frac{1}{1000}n!$

2. A website requires users to choose a login name, which must consist of characters from a set of n symbols. Login names must be between 5 and 8 characters long. Give a big-theta estimate for the number of possible login names. Justify your answer.

3. At a college with n students, an honor council of 5 students must be chosen, and an activity committee of 12 students must also be chosen. How many different ways are there to form these two committees? Give an exact answer in terms of n, and also give a simple big-theta estimate.

4. Give a big-theta estimate for the number of nodes in a perfect binary tree with n levels. Explain your reasoning.

5. Give a big-theta estimate for the number of levels in a perfect binary tree with n nodes. Explain your reasoning.

6. Give a big-theta estimate for the number of ways to place 8 pawns on an $n \times n$ chessboard. Explain your reasoning.

Exercises 4.6

1. Give a big-Θ estimate of $\log_2(n^3)$ in terms of an estimation target. Use Definition 4.9 to justify your answer. (Hint: $\log_b(a^k) = k\log_b a$.)

2. Let $b > 1$. Show that $\log_b n \in \Theta(\log_2 n)$. (Hint: $\log_b n = \dfrac{\log_2 n}{\log_2 b}$.)

3. Find a big-Θ estimate for each function using an estimation target.

   (a) $3n^5 + 4n^2 + 17$.

   (b) $(12n + 17)^{23}$.

    (c) $n \log_2 n + n!$.

    (d) $n \log_2 n + n$.

    (e) $\log_2(n^{10})$.

4. Let $f_1, g_1, f_2, g_2 : \mathbf{N} \longrightarrow \mathbf{R}^+$ be functions such that $g_1 \in \Theta(f_1)$ and $g_2 \in \Theta(f_2)$. Use Definition 4.9 to verify the following identities.

    (a) $g_1 + g_2 \in \Theta(f_1 + f_2)$.

    (b) $g_1 \cdot g_2 \in \Theta(f_1 \cdot f_2)$.

    This exercise shows that big-Θ notation respects addition and multiplication: you can multiply (or add) first, and then estimate, or you can estimate first, and then multiply (or add).

5. Use the fact that big-Θ notation respects multiplication to give big-Θ estimates of the following. First estimate each factor, then multiply. Use estimation targets when possible.

    (a) $(10n + 100) \log_{10} n$.

    (b) $(4\sqrt{n} + 1)(\sqrt{n} + 10)$.

    (c) $(7n^3 + 3n^2 + 2n + 9)(9n^7 + 3n^5 + 2n + 4)$.

    (d) $(3n^5 + 7n^8) \log_2 n^3$.

6. Give a big-Θ estimate of each function. Use the estimation targets when possible.

    (a) $\log_2 n^3 + 3n \log_2 n$

    (b) $(3n^4 + 2n^3 + 7n + 10)(n^5 + 2n^4 + 7n^3 + 11n^2 + 8n + 9)$

7. Give a big-Θ estimate of each function. Use the estimation targets when possible.

    (a) $8n \log_2 n + (n - 1)^2 + 2^n$

    (b) $(1 + n + n^2 + n^3 + n^4 + n^5)(10 + n^2)$

8. Let $p, q \in \mathbf{N}$ with $0 < p < q$. Show that $n^p \in O(n^q)$ using Definition 4.6.

9. Let $m, b > 0$. Use Definition 4.8 to show that the linear function $l(n) = mn + b$ is in $\Theta(n)$.

10. Use the definition of big-Θ to show that $10n^3 + n^2 \in \Theta(n^3)$. Justify all of your assertions.

11. Each of the following statements can be used to justify a statement of the form $f \in \Omega(g)$, $f \in O(g)$, or $f \in \Theta(g)$ using the definition. For each statement below, give the appropriate statement in big-Ω, big-O, or big-Θ notation.

    (a) For every $n \geq 10$, $n^2 + 2n + 1 \leq 5n^3$.

    (b) For every $n \geq 1$, $\frac{1}{2}n \log_2 n \leq \log_2(n!) \leq n \log_2 n$.

12. Prove that $2^{n-1} \in \Theta(2^n)$.

13. Show that $2^n \in O(10^n)$.

14. In this exercise, we show that $2^n \notin \Omega(10^n)$. Suppose, to the contrary, that $2^n \in \Omega(10^n)$. By Definition 4.8, there are positive constants K and N such that $2^n \geq K \cdot 10^n$ for $n \geq N$. Therefore, $\frac{1}{K} \geq 5^n$ for all $n \geq N$. Explain why this is a contradiction.

15. Show that $2^n \in O(n!)$.

16. Prove by contradiction that $2^n \notin \Omega(n!)$.

17. Finish the proof of the assertion at the end of Theorem 4.12 by showing that $\Theta(n^p) \neq \Theta(n^q)$ for $0 < p < q$. (Hint: Use a proof by contradiction: suppose, to the contrary, that $n^p \in \Omega(n^q)$.)

18. Let $k > 0$ be a constant. Think of k as a constant function $f(n) = k$. Show that $k \in \Theta(1)$.

19. Prove Theorem 4.13.

20. Prove Corollary 4.4.

*21. Consider Corollary 4.4. Show that the result is still true even if negative coefficients are allowed, that is, if we remove the restriction that $a_i \geq 0$ for $i = 1, 2, \ldots, p - 1$.

22. Let X be a set with n elements, $n > 3$. Determine the sizes of each of the following sets in terms of n, and give a big-Θ estimate for each answer.

    (a) $\mathcal{P}(X)$, the power set of X.

    (b) The set of all one-to-one correspondences $X \longrightarrow X$.

    (c) The set of all subsets of X of size 3.

    (d) The set of all strings $x_1 x_2$, with $x_i \in X$.

23. Find a big-Θ estimate for the number of ways to choose a set of five or fewer elements from a set of size n.

24. An urn contains n distinct balls.

    (a) Give a big-Θ estimate for the number of ways to draw a sequence of three balls with replacement.

    (b) Give a big-Θ estimate for the number of ways to draw a sequence of three balls without replacement.

    (c) Give a big-Θ estimate for the number of ways to draw a sequence of n balls without replacement.

25. Recall that K_n, the complete graph on n vertices, is the simple undirected graph in which every vertex shares an edge with every other vertex. Give a big-Θ estimate for the number of edges in K_n.

26. Let $n \geq 3$. Give a big-Θ estimate for the number of circuits of length 3 in K_n.

27. Let $n > 1$. Consider the following pseudocode segment.

    ```
    w ← 1
    for i ∈ {1, 2, ..., n} do
        ┌ w ← w · 10
        │ for j ∈ {1, 2, ..., 2n} do
        │     w ← w · w
        │ for k ∈ {1, 2, ..., n⁵} do
        │     ┌ for l ∈ {1, 2, ..., n} do
        └     └     w ← l · w
    ```

    (a) How many multiplications does this algorithm perform? Show how you arrive at your answer.

    (b) Give a big-Θ estimate for your answer to part (a). Use one of the estimation targets.

28. A certain algorithm processes a list of n elements. Suppose that $\texttt{Subroutine}_a$ requires $n^2 + 2n$ operations and $\texttt{Subroutine}_b$ requires $3n^3 + 7$ operations. Give a big-Θ estimate for the number of operations performed by the following pseudocode segment.

    ```
    for i ∈ {1, 2, ..., n} do
        Subroutineₐ
        Subroutine_b
    ```

29. Consider a list of n names. Suppose that an algorithm on this list consists of the following tasks, and the big-Θ estimate of the number of operations in each step is as shown in the table.

	Task	Big-Θ
1.	Rearrange each name, putting last name first.	n
2.	Sort the list of names.	$n \log_2 n$
3.	Search the list for "Knuth, Donald."	$\log_2 n$

    Give a big-Θ estimate for the number of operations performed by the entire algorithm. Justify your answer with a theorem from this section.

30. Finish the proof of Theorem 4.11 by proving that $g \in \Omega(f) \Rightarrow f \in O(g)$.

31. Explain why the relation on functions $\mathbf{N} \longrightarrow \mathbf{R}^+$ defined by

$$f R g \iff f \in O(g)$$

is not a partial ordering.

32. Explain why the relation on functions $\mathbf{N} \longrightarrow \mathbf{R}^+$ defined by

$$f R g \;\Leftrightarrow\; f \in O(g)$$

is not an equivalence relation.

33. Show that the relation on functions $\mathbf{N} \longrightarrow \mathbf{R}^+$ defined by

$$f R g \;\Leftrightarrow\; f \in \Theta(g)$$

is an equivalence relation.

Chapter 5
Analytical Thinking

The ways of thinking we have studied so far—logical, relational, recursive, and quantitative—have highlighted different aspects of discrete problems in mathematics. In this chapter, we draw on many of the topics from earlier in the book to help us analyze algorithms. In addition to understanding what an algorithm does, we will study mathematical ways to determine the accuracy and efficiency of algorithms. This type of analysis is fundamentally important to computer scientists. And, as computing becomes increasingly important in other fields, scholars from many disciplines will need to be able to think this way.

5.1 Algorithms

We have already been dealing with simple algorithms. The recursive functions of Chapter 3 and the pseudocode segments of Chapter 4 defined short algorithms. In this section we will review and expand on these topics.

Figure 5.1 A raytraced image of three objects with mirrored surfaces. Raytracers use recursive algorithms to calculate reflections, and reflections of reflections, etc. How many reflections can you find?

Preview 5.1

1. Anthony and Berenice are playing a guessing game. Anthony thinks of a natural number between 1 and 10, inclusive. Berenice tries to guess the number. After each guess, Anthony tells Berenice if her guess was correct, too high, or too low. Devise an efficient strategy for Berenice to determine Anthony's number with the fewest possible guesses.

2. Eighteen spectators are sitting in a row at a football game. Nine white hats and nine black hats are distributed randomly to these 18 spectators. For the halftime show, the hats are supposed to alternate colors—black, white, black, white, etc.—across the entire row. Describe an efficient method for rearranging these hats to achieve this desired effect.

5.1.1   More Pseudocode

An algorithm is basically a list of instructions (statements) that need to be executed in sequence. Sometimes we need to be able to skip statements, or we might wish to repeat a statement several times. The following definitions will give us ways of doing this.

Definition 5.1 Let p be a logical statement that is either true or false. Then the if...then...else statement

```
if p then
    statement₁
else
    statement₂
```

will execute either statement₁ or statement₂, depending on whether p is true or false, respectively.

We used if...then statements in Chapter 4, but Definition 5.1 adds an else clause to this command. An if...then...else statement is the pseudocode equivalent of a binary branch in a decision tree.

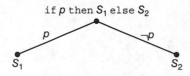

In Chapter 4 we used for-loops to repeat a statement a specified number of times. The following definition gives a more versatile looping structure.

Definition 5.2 Let $P(x)$ be a predicate statement. Then the while-loop

```
while P(x) do
    statement(x)
```

will continue to execute statement(x) as long as $P(x)$ remains true.

A while-loop will run forever unless statement(x) changes the value of x so that $P(x)$ can be false. If $P(x)$ is false to begin with, then statement(x) is never executed. The number of times a while-loop repeats depends on the pseudocode that changes the value of x. This behavior is different from a for-loop, which always executes a predetermined number of times.

The following algorithm illustrates if...then...else statements and while-loops. The purpose of this algorithm is to determine if a given *target* element t is present in an array. (For convenience, we omit the quotes from the print statements.)

Algorithm 5.1 Sequential Search. Let $x_1, x_2, \ldots, x_n$ be an array of elements from some set U, and let $t \in U$. The following algorithm performs a *sequential search* of this array.

```
i ← 1
x_{n+1} ← t
while t ≠ x_i do
        i ← i + 1
if i = n + 1 then
    print Element t was not found.
else
    print Element t was found in location i.
```

In the sequential search algorithm, the `while`-loop will continue to increment i while the statement $(t \neq x_i)$ is true. In other words, it will stop executing when $t = x_i$. Note that this must happen, since we put a copy of t at the end of the list as a "sentinel" value. If $i = n + 1$ after the loop finishes executing, then the loop will have run through all the values in the original array without finding one equal to t. In this case, t was not found in the array. Otherwise t was found, and $x_i = t$.

For example, suppose the array contains five integers ($n = 5$) whose values are as follows.

x_1	x_2	x_3	x_4	x_5
3	6	9	12	15

A *trace* of an algorithm is a step-by-step description of what happens when the algorithm executes. The following table describes a trace of the `while`-loop in the sequential search. Suppose that $t = 12$ is the target value we are searching for.

i	test
1	$12 \overset{?}{=} 3$
2	$12 \overset{?}{=} 6$
3	$12 \overset{?}{=} 9$
4	$12 \overset{?}{=} 12$

At this point, the `while`-loop terminates and the `if...then...else` statement executes. Since $4 \neq 5 + 1$, the `else` clause prints the message, "Element 12 was found in location 4."

5.1.2 Preconditions and Postconditions

Usually, an algorithm has a purpose. We can describe what an algorithm is supposed to do using *preconditions* and *postconditions*.

Definition 5.3 Let A be an algorithm. A *precondition* of A is a statement about algorithm variables before A executes. A *postcondition* of A is a statement about the algorithm variables after execution.

Writing good preconditions and postconditions is like writing clear mathematical statements. A precondition should specify exactly what needs to be true before an algorithm runs in order for it to do its job properly. Similarly, a postcondition should say precisely what will be true after the algorithm runs, assuming the preconditions are satisfied.

Example 5.1 Consider the bubble sort algorithm of Example 4.56. We'll reprint it here for convenience.

Algorithm 5.2 Bubble Sort.

```
for i ∈ {1, 2, ..., n − 1} do
   ⌐ for j ∈ {1, 2, ..., n − i} do
   ∟      if x_j > x_{j+1} then swap x_j and x_{j+1}
```

This (and any other sorting algorithm) is supposed to put the elements of an array in order. Mathematically speaking, we have the following preconditions.

Preconditions: The elements of the array $x_1, x_2, x_3, \ldots, x_n$ can be compared by $\leq$. In addition, $n \geq 2$.

In order for the algorithm to work, the comparison $x_j > x_{j+1}$ needs to make sense for any j. This explains the need for the first precondition. The second precondition ensures that the index sets $\{1, 2, \ldots, n-1\}$ and $\{1, 2, \ldots, n-i\}$ are well defined.

The only postcondition is that the array is in order after the algorithm executes.

Postcondition: $x_1 \leq x_2 \leq x_3 \leq \cdots \leq x_n$.

Think of preconditions and postconditions from the point of view of the user, or consumer, of an algorithm. The preconditions are the operating instructions in the owner's manual; they specify the proper way to use the algorithm. The postconditions are a performance guarantee; as long as the consumer upholds the preconditions, the algorithm promises to deliver the postconditions.

We can describe the roles of preconditions and postconditions more mathematically, in terms of logic. Consider an algorithm with preconditions $p_1, p_2, \ldots, p_k$ and postconditions $q_1, q_2, \ldots, q_l$. We say that the algorithm is *correct* if

$$p_1 \wedge p_2 \wedge \cdots \wedge p_k \Rightarrow q_1 \wedge q_2 \wedge \cdots \wedge q_l$$

where the preconditions p_i are evaluated before algorithm execution, and the postconditions q_i are evaluated after execution. This mathematical statement can be proved as a theorem; such a proof is called a *proof of correctness*. We will do these kinds of proofs in Sections 5.5 and 5.6.

Example 5.2 Any `while`-loop of the form

```
while P(x) do
        statement(x)
```

has

Postcondition: $\neg P(x)$

because the loop will continue to execute as long as $P(x)$ is true.

Example 5.3 Consider the sequential search (Algorithm 5.1). Before the algorithm executes, we are given a set $\{x_1, x_2, \ldots, x_n\}$ and a target value t. The algorithm is supposed to tell us if the target t is a member of the set. If it is, the value of i should be set so that $x_i = t$. In mathematical language, we have the following:

Preconditions: $\{x_1, x_2, \ldots, x_n\} \subseteq U$
$t \in U$
Postconditions: $t = x_i$
$i \in \{1, 2, \ldots, n+1\}$
$(i = n + 1) \Rightarrow (t \notin \{x_1, x_2, \ldots, x_n\})$.

We will prove that these conditions hold (i.e., that the algorithm is correct) in Section 5.6.

5.1.3   Iterative Algorithms

An algorithm that repeats a segment of code several times in a loop is called an *iterative* algorithm. The bubble sort and sequential search are iterative. Here is another searching algorithm.

Algorithm 5.3 Binary Search (iterative).

Preconditions: The set U is totally ordered by $<$, and $X = \{x_1, x_2, \ldots, x_n\} \subseteq U$,
   with $n \geq 1$,

$$x_1 < x_2 < \cdots < x_n,$$

   and $t \in U$.

Postconditions: $(t \notin \{x_1, x_2, \ldots, x_n\}) \vee (x_l = t)$

```
l ← 1,  r ← n
while l < r do
   ⌐ i ← ⌊(l + r)/2⌋
      if t > xᵢ then
         l ← i + 1
      else
   ∟    r ← i
if t = xₗ then
   print Element t was found in location l.
else
   print Element t was not found.
```

Let's trace the binary search algorithm when the program variables are initially as follows.

n	t	x_1	x_2	x_3	x_4	x_5
5	12	3	6	9	12	15

There are two tests, or comparisons, in this algorithm: $l < r$ and $t > x_i$. As we step through the pseudocode, each time we encounter a test we go on to a new line in the table.

l	r	i	test
1	5		$1 \overset{?}{<} 5$
		$\left\lfloor \frac{1+5}{2} \right\rfloor = 3$	$12 \overset{?}{>} 9$
$3 + 1 = 4$			$4 \overset{?}{<} 5$
		$\left\lfloor \frac{4+5}{2} \right\rfloor = 4$	$12 \overset{?}{>} 12$
	4		$4 \overset{?}{<} 4$

At this point, the `while`-loop finishes, and the program reports that 12 was found in location 4.

The binary search works by eliminating approximately half of the remaining items in the array from consideration each time through the `while`-loop. This is possible because the array items are in order; if the target t is greater than the middle array element, the algorithm eliminates the bottom half of the array, and *vice versa*. In Section 5.6, we will prove that the binary search always finds the target, if it is present in the array.

Activity 5.1.1: Iterative Binary Search

```
l ← 1,  r ← n
while l < r do
   ⌐ i ← ⌊(l + r)/2⌋
      if t > xᵢ then
         l ← i + 1
      else
   ∟    r ← i
```

Before the above algorithm executes, suppose that $t = 9$ and X is the following array.

x_1	x_2	x_3	x_4	x_5	x_6	x_7	x_8	x_9	x_{10}	x_{11}	x_{12}	x_{13}	x_{14}	x_{15}	x_{16}	x_{17}	x_{18}	x_{19}	x_{20}
2	3	5	7	11	13	17	19	23	29	31	37	41	43	47	53	59	61	67	71

1. Trace through the algorithm, and fill in the missing entries in the following table. Each row of the table corresponds to one pass through the while-loop.

t	l	r	i	x_i	$t > x_i$
9	1	20	10	29	false
9		10			
9					
9					
9					

2. What causes the while-loop to finish?

3. What is the value of x_l when the algorithm finishes?

4. The postcondition of this algorithm is $(t \notin \{x_1, x_2, \ldots, x_n\}) \lor (x_l = t)$. Given that the postcondition is true when the algorithm finishes, what does this postcondition imply about t?

5. Notice that the numbers l and r get closer together after each pass through the loop. Approximately how much does the distance $l - r$ decrease after each pass?

5.1.4 Functions and Recursive Algorithms

To write a function in pseudocode, we use a `return` statement.

Example 5.4 The following pseudocode defines the function $f(x) = x^2$.

```
function SquareIt (x ∈ R)
    t ← x²
    return t
```

This function inputs a real number x and outputs, or *returns*, x^2. The variable x is called a *parameter*; it stores a value of the domain that gets "plugged into" the function. The notation for functions in pseudocode is the same as the notation in mathematics: to evaluate $f(7)$, we use the *function call* `SquareIt(7)`.

When a call to function appears in a pseudocode statement, the effect is the same as if the returned value takes the place of the function call. So if

$$\text{SquareIt(7)}$$

appeared anywhere in a pseudocode statement, we could effectively replace it with 49. The statement

```
print SquareIt(4) + SquareIt(5)
```

would print the number 41.

In Chapter 3, we studied recursive functions. Recall that the definition of a recursive function includes a nonrecursive base case and a recursive part that defines the function in terms of itself. In this chapter we can think of recursive functions algorithmically; a recursive algorithm contains a call to itself.

Example 5.5 Recall that a recurrence relation is a simple type of recursive function. Let $S(n)$ be defined by the following recurrence relation:

$$S(n) = \begin{cases} 1 & \text{if } n = 1 \\ S(n-1) + 2n - 1 & \text{if } n > 1. \end{cases}$$

The pseudocode version of this recursive function is as follows.

```
function S (n ∈ N)
    if n = 1 then
        return 1
    else
        return S (n − 1) + 2n − 1
```

Notice how the base and recursive cases translate directly into pseudocode: The `if...then...else` statement tests the appropriate condition and chooses which case to apply.

Suppose the function call `S (5)` appears in some pseudocode segment. Since $5 \neq 1$, the `else` clause is executed, so this function call is effectively the same as `S (4)` +9, the return value. But now $S(4)$ needs to be evaluated, and its return value is `S (3)` +7. Similarly, `S (3)` returns `S (2)` +5 and `S (2)` returns `S (1)` +3. But now the call to `S (1)` invokes the nonrecursive `if` clause, and simply returns 1. Therefore, the return value of `S (2)` is effectively the same as $1 + 3 = 4$, since the `S (1)` can be replaced by 1. And now we can use 4 in place of `S (2)` to see that the return value of `S (3)` is equivalent to $4 + 5 = 9$. Continuing in this fashion, the return value of `S (4)` is $9 + 7 = 16$ and, finally, the return value of `S (5)` is $16 + 9 = 25$.

We can outline this calculation a little more concisely as follows:

$$
\begin{aligned}
S(5) &= S(4) + 9 \\
&= S(3) + 7 + 9 \\
&= S(2) + 5 + 7 + 9 \\
&= S(1) + 3 + 5 + 7 + 9 \\
&= 1 + 3 + 5 + 7 + 9 \\
&= 25 .
\end{aligned}
$$

This way of tracing through the execution of a recursive function is called a *top-down evaluation*. We start at the "top" with the original value of the parameter n, and we continue "down" until there are no more recursive calls. At this point we say that the recursive algorithm *bottoms out*, and we are able to compute the final return value.

You may have noticed that you have seen the recurrence relation in Example 5.5 before; in Exercise 1 in Section 3.4 you were asked to prove that the sum of the first n odd natural numbers is n^2. The recurrence relation for $S(n)$ computes this sum, so the pseudocode version can be thought of as a recursive algorithm for squaring a natural number. Many of the recursive definitions from Chapter 3 translate naturally into recursive algorithms in pseudocode.

Example 5.6 Recall the string reversal function of Example 3.18 on page 127. The pseudocode version is as follows.

```
function Reverse (s ∈ {strings})
    if s = λ then
        return λ
    else                        // assert: s = ra
        return a Reverse (r)
```

The `assert` comment tells us something that should be true at that point in the program. In this case, we know that if a string is not empty, it must be the concatenation of a (possibly empty) string r and a symbol a.

The structure of the `Reverse` function is typical of recursive algorithms. The `if...then...else` statement divides the body of the function into two parts: a base case and a recursive case.

Let's perform a top-down evaluation of this function. Compare the following calculation with Example 3.18 on page 127.

$$
\begin{aligned}
\text{Reverse(pit)} &= t\,\text{Reverse(pi)} && \text{using else clause} \\
&= ti\,\text{Reverse(p)} && \text{using else clause} \\
&= ti\,\text{Reverse}(\lambda p) && \text{inserting empty string} \\
&= tip\,\text{Reverse}(\lambda) && \text{using else clause} \\
&= tip\lambda && \text{using then clause} \\
&= tip && \text{removing empty string}
\end{aligned}
$$

The first three evaluations of the `Reverse` function send us to the `else` clause, since the parameter s is not the empty string. The evaluation of `Reverse (λ)`, however, uses the nonrecursive `then` clause, so the calculation bottoms out.

We can now revisit the binary search algorithm using recursion. In Algorithm 5.4, each recursive call eliminates the half of the remaining array in which t cannot lie.

Algorithm 5.4 Binary Search (recursive).

Preconditions: The set U is totally ordered by $<$, and $X = \{x_1, x_2, \ldots, x_n\} \subseteq U$, with $n \geq 1$,

$$x_1 < x_2 < \cdots < x_n,$$

and $t \in U$. Also, $1 \leq l \leq r \leq n$.
Postconditions: $\texttt{BinSearch}(t, X, l, r) = (t \in \{x_l, x_{l+1}, \ldots, x_r\})$

```
function BinSearch(t ∈ U,
                   X = {x₁,x₂,...,xₙ} ⊆ U,
                   l,r ∈ {1,2,...,n})
  i ← ⌊(l+r)/2⌋
  if t = xᵢ then
      return true
  else
    ⌐ if (t < xᵢ) ∧ (l < i) then
          return BinSearch(t,X,l,i−1)
      else
        ⌐ if (t > xᵢ) ∧ (i < r) then
              return BinSearch(t,X,i+1,r)
          else
  L     L     return false
```

The preconditions of this function are almost exactly the same as the preconditions for Algorithm 5.3. The only difference is the specification of the allowable range for l and r. The postconditions say that the function returns the true/false value of the statement "$t \in \{x_l, x_{l+1}, \ldots, x_r\}$." It is a common practice for a testing function like this one to return a true/false value. A typical call to this function would look like this:

```
if BinSearch(t,{3,6,9,12,15},1,n) then
    print Element t was found.
else
    print Element t was not found.
```

The choice of 1 and n for the last two parameters tell the function to search the whole array.

The following top-down evaluation of the recursive binary search looks for the target value 21 in the array $X = \{3, 6, 9, 12, 15, 18, 21, 24, 27, 30\}$.

$$
\begin{aligned}
\texttt{BinSearch}(21, X, 1, 10) &= \texttt{BinSearch}(21, X, 6, 10) \\
&= \texttt{BinSearch}(21, X, 6, 7) \\
&= \texttt{BinSearch}(21, X, 7, 7) \\
&= \texttt{true}
\end{aligned}
$$

Pay attention to how the values of the parameters l and r change in each recursive function call. First i is chosen to lie in the middle of l and r, then the new values of l and r span either the left or right side of i, depending on where the target must lie. As an exercise, trace through the pseudocode for this algorithm and determine what comparisons are made for each function call in the above calculation.

Activity 5.1.2: Recursive Binary Search

```
function BinSearch(t ∈ U,  X = {x₁,x₂,...,xₙ} ⊆ U,  l,r ∈ {1,2,...,n})
    i ← ⌊(l+r)/2⌋
    if t = xᵢ then
        return true
    else
      ┌ if (t < xᵢ) ∧ (l < i) then
      │     return BinSearch(t,X,l,i−1)
      │ else
      │   ┌ if (t > xᵢ) ∧ (i < r) then
      │   │     return BinSearch(t,X,i+1,r)
      │   │ else
      └   └     return false
```

x_1	x_2	x_3	x_4	x_5	x_6	x_7	x_8	x_9	x_{10}	x_{11}	x_{12}	x_{13}	x_{14}	x_{15}	x_{16}	x_{17}	x_{18}	x_{19}	x_{20}
2	3	5	7	11	13	17	19	23	29	31	37	41	43	47	53	59	61	67	71

1. For the given array X, trace through the algorithm and fill in the missing entries in the following table. Each row of the table corresponds to a recursive function call in a top-down evaluation.

function call	t	l	r	i	x_i	$(t < x_i) \wedge (l < i)$	$(t > x_i) \wedge (i < r)$
BinSearch$(32,X,1,20)$	32	1	20	10	29	false	true
BinSearch$(32,X,11,20)$							

2. What value is returned by the final function call?

3. The postcondition of this algorithm is BinSearch$(t,X,l,r) = (t \in \{x_l, x_{l+1}, \ldots, x_r\})$. Explain why this postcondition is true for the above example.

4. Notice that the numbers l and r get closer together after each function call, much as they did in the iterative version. Use this observation to give a big-Θ estimate of the number of function calls required on an array of size n.

Exercises 5.1

1. In the sequential search of Algorithm 5.1, suppose that $t = x_1$ before execution. How many times will the statement

$$i \leftarrow i + 1$$

be executed? Explain.

2. Give good preconditions and postconditions for the following pseudocode segment.

```
p ← 1
for i ∈ {1,2,3,...,n} do
    p ← p/b
```

3. Give a postcondition for the following algorithm that completely describes how the final value of i is related to x.

   Precondition: x is a positive real number.

   ```
   i ← 0
   while i < x do
           i ← i + 1
   ```

4. Give a postcondition for the following algorithm that completely describes how the final value of i is related to x.

   Precondition: x is a positive odd integer.

   ```
   i ← 0
   while i < x do
           i ← i + 2
   ```

5. Give preconditions on the variable t in the following algorithm so that the postcondition holds. Assume $x \in \mathbf{R}$.

   Postcondition: $p = xt$.

   ```
   p ← 0
   i ← 0
   while i < t do
           ⌐ i ← i + 1
           ∟ p ← p + x
   ```

6. Consider Example 5.3. If $t \in \{x_1, x_2, \ldots, x_n\}$, what do the postconditions say must be true about the value of i after execution? What derivation rules from propositional logic can you use to justify your answer?

7. Consider Algorithm 5.3. Rewrite the postconditions as an implication ($p \Rightarrow q$) using an equivalence rule from propositional logic.

8. Consider the following pseudocode function.

   ```
   function W(n ∈ Z)
       if n > 0 then
           ⌐ if n is odd then
                 return 2n
             else
           ∟      return n + 1
       else
           return n − 1
   ```

   Compute the values returned by the following function calls.

   (a) W(10)

   (b) W(−21)

   (c) W(7)

9. Let T be a binary search tree whose data can be compared using $<$. Consider the following algorithm.

   Precondition: Some node in T contains value t.

   ```
   l ← 0
   x ← the root of T
   while x ≠ t do
           ⌐ if x < t then
                 x ← x's right child
             else
                 x ← x's left child
           ∟ l ← l + 1
   ```

   Give a postcondition that accurately describes the value of l.

10. Consider the following algorithm

    Preconditions: $X = \{x_1, x_2, \ldots, x_n\} \subseteq \mathbf{N}$.

    $i \leftarrow 1$
    $t \leftarrow 0$
    while $i \leq n$ do
    ⌐ $s \leftarrow 1$
    $ j \leftarrow 1$
     while $j \leq i$ do
     ⌐ $s \leftarrow s \cdot x_i$
     ∟ $j \leftarrow j + 1$
     $t \leftarrow t + s$
    ∟ $i \leftarrow i + 1$

    (a) Give a postcondition that accurately describes the value of t.

    (b) Compute the number of times the algorithm performs a multiplication operation (in terms of n).

    (c) Give a big-Θ estimate of your answer to part (b).

11. Trace through Algorithm 5.3, given $X = \{3, 6, 10, 14, 20, 23\}$ and $t = 20$. Give a table showing the values of i, l, and r every time they change, along with any $\overset{?}{<}$ and $\overset{?}{>}$ comparisons.

12. Consider the following pseudocode function.

    ```
    function Crunch (x ∈ R)
        if x ≥ 100 then
            return x/100
        else
            return x + Crunch (10 · x)
    ```

    (a) Compute Crunch (137).

    (b) Compute Crunch (53).

    (c) Compute Crunch (4).

    (d) What happens if you try to compute Crunch (−26)? What does this suggest about an appropriate precondition for this function?

13. Look at the top-down evaluation of BinSearch $(21, X, 1, 10)$ that follows Algorithm 5.4. For each function call in this evaluation, give the value of i and say what $\overset{?}{<}, \overset{?}{>}$, and $\overset{?}{=}$ comparisons of list elements are made.

14. Consider Algorithm 5.4. Evaluate

    $$\text{BinSearch} (7, \{2, 4, 6, 8\}, 1, 4)$$

    using a top-down evaluation.

15. Consider Algorithm 5.4. Let $X = \{3, 6, 9, 12, 15, 18, 21, 24, 27, 30\}$. Evaluate

    $$\text{BinSearch} (3, X, 1, 10)$$

    using a top-down evaluation.

16. Consider the string reversal algorithm in Example 5.6. Evaluate

    $$\text{Reverse} (\text{prewt})$$

    using a top-down evaluation.

17. Trace through the following algorithm, if it is invoked as GCD $(42, 24)$. Use a top-down evaluation. (Recall that "$n \bmod m$" is the remainder when n is divided by m.)

```
function GCD (m, n ∈ {0, 1, 2, 3, ...})
    if n = 0 then
        return m
    else
        return GCD (n, m mod n)
```

18. The following is known as the Ackermann function.

```
function Ack (m, n ∈ {0, 1, 2, 3, ...})
    if m = 0 then
        return n + 1
    else
      ⌐ if n = 0 then
            return Ack (m − 1, 1)
        else
      ∟    return Ack (m − 1, Ack (m, n − 1))
```

Compute the values returned by the following function calls.

(a) Ack (0, 7)

(b) Ack (1, 0)

(c) Ack (1, 1)

(d) Ack (2, 1)

19. Write a pseudocode segment that is equivalent to

```
for i ∈ {1, 2, 3, ..., n} do
    print "YADA"
```

using a while-loop instead of a for-loop.

20. Rewrite the bubble sort (Algorithm 5.2) using nested while-loops instead of nested for-loops.

21. Write an iterative algorithm in pseudocode that satisfies the following preconditions and postconditions.

Preconditions: $X = \{x_1, x_2, \ldots, x_n\}$, $Y = \{y_1, y_2, \ldots, y_n\}$ are subsets of $\mathbf{N}$.

Postconditions: $k = |X \cap Y|$.

22. Write a recursive function in pseudocode that computes the value of the following recurrence relation:

$$H(n) = \begin{cases} 1 & \text{if } n = 1 \\ H(n - 1) + 6n - 6 & \text{if } n > 1. \end{cases}$$

Give descriptive preconditions and postconditions. (Hint: See Example 3.10.)

23. See Definition 3.1 on page 110. Translate the recurrence relation for the Fibonacci numbers $F(n)$ directly into pseudocode. Perform a top-down evaluation of $F(6)$. (Note: If you do the top-down evaluation correctly, you will find yourself writing down some redundant calculations.)

24. Write an iterative algorithm to compute $F(n)$, the nth Fibonacci number.

25. Write a pseudocode version of the factorial function ...

(a) iteratively.

(b) recursively.

5.2   Three Common Types of Algorithms

To the uninitiated, bird-watching might seem somewhat pointless. What is so fun about learning the difference between a junco and a chickadee, or distinguishing among the various species of hawks? But once you start trying to identify birds, you start noticing new things about them. The simple task of classification forces you to consider subtle differences in structure and behavior, and this leads to greater understanding and appreciation of these creatures.

In any scholarly pursuit, classifying objects supports the learning process. In this section we investigate three specific types of algorithms: traversal algorithms, greedy algorithms, and divide-and-conquer algorithms. While this list is by no means exhaustive, these three families of algorithms will provide some context for thinking about problems analytically.

Preview 5.2

1. A circular garden has the following design. Describe a method for walking through the garden, starting and ending in the center, in such a way that you travel along all its paths. Try to backtrack as little as possible. Does your method generalize to a larger garden with more rings in the same pattern?

2. Claude and Maude are playing a game with poker chips. The object of the game is to draw the last chip. The players take turns drawing chips. At each turn, a player must take at least 1 chip and at most 10 chips. Claude goes first. What is an optimal strategy? Does the strategy depend on the number of chips left?

3. An elementary school teacher needs to line up his class of 16 students in order of height. From experience, he knows his students are incapable of doing this on their own. However, when divided into groups of four, they can reliably sort themselves in order of height. What can this teacher do?

5.2.1 Traversal Algorithms

Data is usually arranged in some sort of structure. In order to do anything with the data—search it, print it out, manipulate it—you must be able to go through the data structure in some systematic way. An algorithm that does this is called a *traversal algorithm*. Think of the job of a traversal algorithm as executing the generic statement "visit x" for every element x in the data structure.

For example, a for-loop is all you need to traverse the elements of an array $x_1, x_2, \ldots, x_n$.

```
for i ∈ {1, 2, ..., n} do
    visit x_i
```

Similarly, the nested for-loops of Example 4.50 execute a traversal through a Cartesian product of sets. In fact, we can regard any of the enumeration algorithms in Section 4.5 as traversal algorithms; in order to get an accurate count of the elements in a set, an algorithm must visit each element exactly once.

More complicated data structures require more interesting traversal algorithms. Recall that a *binary tree* is a tree with a designated root in which each node has at most two children: a left child and a right child. Since binary trees are recursive structures, we can think of the left and right children as roots of binary subtrees. Thinking recursively suggests that a traversal of a binary tree should traverse each subtree and also visit the root. Choosing different orders for these tasks leads to the three standard ways to traverse a binary tree: the preorder, postorder, and inorder traversals (Algorithms 5.5, 5.6, and 5.7, respectively).

Algorithm 5.5 Preorder Traversal.

Preconditions: T is a binary tree.

Postconditions: Every node of T was visited exactly once.

```
function PreOrder(T ∈ {binary trees})
    if T ≠ ∅ then
        visit the root of T
        PreOrder(T's left subtree)
        PreOrder(T's right subtree)
    return
```

Algorithm 5.6 Postorder Traversal.

Preconditions: T is a binary tree.

Postconditions: Every node of T was visited exactly once.

```
function PostOrder(T ∈ {binary trees})
    if T ≠ ∅ then
        PostOrder(T's left subtree)
        PostOrder(T's right subtree)
        visit the root of T
    return
```

Algorithm 5.7 Inorder Traversal.

Preconditions: T is a binary tree.

Postconditions: Every node of T was visited exactly once.

```
function InOrder(T ∈ {binary trees})
    if T ≠ ∅ then
        InOrder(T's left subtree)
        visit the root of T
        InOrder(T's right subtree)
    return
```

We use a `return` statement without a value to indicate the end of the function. A function that doesn't return a value is sometimes called a *procedure* or *subroutine*. We are also "abusing" notation by representing the empty tree with the ∅ symbol. We studied the inorder traversal in Section 3.5, where we viewed it as a mathematical function.

Example 5.7 Do a preorder, postorder, and inorder traversal on the following binary tree.

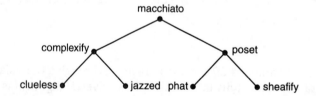

Solution: Tracing through these algorithms is a little tricky, but the resulting patterns are easy to recognize. Let $\mathcal{L}$ represent the subtree with root "complexify," and leaves "clueless" and "jazzed," and let $\mathcal{R}$ be the subtree with root "poset," and leaves "phat" and "sheafify." Then we can trace through the recursive function as follows, using indentation to show successive recursive calls.

```
PreOrder(T)
        visit macchiato
        PreOrder(L)
                visit complexify
                PreOrder(clueless)
                        visit clueless
                        PreOrder(∅)
                        PreOrder(∅)
                PreOrder(jazzed)
                        visit jazzed
                        PreOrder(∅)
                        PreOrder(∅)
```

```
PreOrder(R)
        visit poset
        PreOrder(phat)
                visit phat
                PreOrder(Ø)
                PreOrder(Ø)
        PreOrder(sheafify)
                visit sheafify
                PreOrder(Ø)
                PreOrder(Ø)
```

Notice that every nontrivial call to PreOrder spawns a visit followed by two more calls to PreOrder. The recursion bottoms out when PreOrder(Ø) is called, since the function skips the then clause for this value of the parameter. Therefore, the preorder traversal visits the nodes in the following order.

   macchiato, complexify, clueless, jazzed, poset, phat, sheafify.

A postorder traversal runs through

   clueless, jazzed, complexify, phat, sheafify, poset, macchiato

and an inorder traversal yields

   clueless, complexify, jazzed, macchiato, phat, poset, sheafify.

We'll leave it as an exercise to write a detailed trace of the postorder and inorder traversals.   ◇

To compare these three ways of traversing a tree, imagine making a path around the outside of the tree, as shown below.

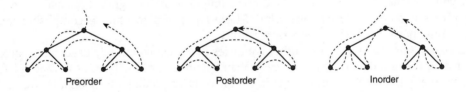

Preorder   Postorder   Inorder

All three traversal algorithms make their visits along roughly similar paths; the differences lie in the order of the visits. In a preorder traversal, the parent is always visited before the children, while in a postorder, the children are always visited before the parent. An inorder traversal visits the parent after visiting all of the left descendants and before visiting any of the right descendants.

In Section 3.5, we made the observation that, for binary search trees, an inorder traversal visits all the nodes in order. In the exercises we'll discuss some applications of the preorder and postorder traversals.

Activity 5.2.1: Tree Sort

The following algorithm will add a new node x to a binary search tree in the correct location. For simplicity, assume as a precondition that x is not already in the tree.

```
function AddToBST(T ∈ {binary search trees}, x ∈ U)
    if T = Ø then
        replace T with a single root node x and return
    else if x < the root of T
        AddToBST(T's left subtree, x)
    else
        AddToBST(T's right subtree, x)
```

1. Trace through the following algorithm and draw the tree that it produces.

   $$\mathcal{T} \leftarrow \emptyset$$
   ```
   for  x ∈ {17, 9, 25, 30, 12, 1, 20}  do
         AddToBST(T, x)
   ```

2. When adding a leaf at level k, how many $<$ comparisons does AddToBST make?

3. If a binary search tree contains n nodes, and the tree is approximately perfect, give a rough estimate for the level of the leaves, in terms on n.

4. Combine the previous two observations: When AddToBST adds a leaf to an approximately perfect binary tree with n nodes, give a rough estimate for the number of $<$ comparisons it makes.

5. The following algorithm describes a *Tree Sort*. Explain why the words "tree" and "sort" are appropriate descriptors of this algorithm.

   $$\mathcal{T} \leftarrow \emptyset$$
   ```
   for  x ∈ {x₁, x₂, …, xₙ}  do
         AddToBST(T, x)
   InOrder(T)
   ```

6. Give a rough estimate for the number of $<$ comparisons the Tree Sort requires on an array of size n, assuming the trees produced are approximately perfect.

7. Can you find a simple big-Θ estimate of your answer to Question 6?

5.2.2   Greedy Algorithms

Some things require planning. Even novice chess players know that capturing pieces whenever possible is not the way to win a game; a winning strategy requires thinking about the long term. On the other hand, maximizing the amount of candy you get when a piñata breaks is a much simpler task: just grab the most you can whenever you can. The latter strategy is a type of *greedy algorithm*. These types of algorithms accomplish a long-term goal by doing the most obvious short-term task at every opportunity.

In the United States, Canada, and several other countries, the most commonly used coins come in values of 1, 5, 10, and 25. Consider the problem of forming N cents using pennies (1¢), nickels (5¢), dimes (10¢), and quarters (25¢). We would normally like to have our change in as few coins as possible; for example, we prefer to have 30¢ as a nickel and a quarter $(5 + 25)$ rather than as three dimes $(10 + 10 + 10)$. Algorithm 5.8 greedily makes change by choosing the largest denomination of coin at each step.

Algorithm 5.8 Making Change.

Preconditions: $N \in \mathbf{N}$, $1 \le N \le 100$.

Postconditions: $p + 5n + 10d + 25q = N$, and $p + n + d + q$ is as small as possible.

```
p, n, d, q ← 0
T ← p + 5n + 10d + 25q
while T < N do
    ┌ if N − T ≥ 25 then
    │      q ← q + 1
    │  else
    │      if N − T ≥ 10 then
    │          d ← d + 1
    │      else
    │          if N − T ≥ 5 then
    │              n ← n + 1
    │          else
    │              p ← p + 1
    └ T ← p + 5n + 10d + 25q
```

The variable N represents the desired monetary value of change, while the indices p, n, d, q store running counts of the number of pennies, nickels, dimes, and quarters. At the end of each time through the loop, T is updated to give the monetary value of a collection of p pennies, n nickels, d dimes, and q quarters. Therefore, $N - T$ represents the discrepancy between the desired value of change and the current value of this collection. The nested if...then...else statements simply decide on the largest possible coin that is less than or equal to the difference $N - T$, and update the appropriate index.

It isn't obvious that this algorithm always gives an optimal amount of change. For example, suppose that dimes were worth 20¢ instead of 10¢. The optimal way to make 40¢ would be to use two of these "dimes" (20 + 20) but a greedy algorithm would take four coins: a quarter and three nickels (25 + 5 + 5 + 5). For standard U.S. currency, Algorithm 5.8 does minimize the number of coins, but the proof of this fact is a little messy. Our "20¢ dime" scenario suggests that the argument must rely on the relationship between 1, 5, 10, and 25.

Another classic application of greedy algorithms involves finding a minimal spanning tree in a network. Recall that a network is a graph with numerical weights on each edge. Given a network $\mathcal{N}$, it is often helpful to construct a connected subgraph T of $\mathcal{N}$ such that T spans all the vertices of $\mathcal{N}$ while the edges of T have the least possible total weight. Such a subgraph is called a *minimal spanning tree*. Note that any such T would have to be a tree, since any circuit would contain an unnecessary edge. The question is, which edges should we include? It turns out that a greedy algorithm will always give us the best tree. See Algorithm 5.9.

Algorithm 5.9 Prim's Algorithm for constructing a minimal spanning tree.

Preconditions: $\mathcal{N}$ is a connected network.

Postconditions: T is a minimal spanning tree of $\mathcal{N}$.

```
T ← •—e₁—•, where e₁ is the shortest edge of N.
while T does not contain all of N's vertices
      ⌈ e ← the shortest edge between a vertex in T and a vertex not in T.
      ⌊ Add edge e and the new vertex to T.
```

This algorithm makes the "greedy" choice of the shortest possible edge at every opportunity. (If there is a tie for the length of the shortest edge, any one of the shortest edges can be chosen.) The postconditions make three claims about the resulting tree T: it spans all the vertices, it is a tree, and it has minimal total weight. The first two claims are easy to verify; each new edge will never add a circuit, and the while-loop will not finish until all the vertices of $\mathcal{N}$ are in T. For the sake of brevity, we omit the proof that T is minimal, but it always is.

Example 5.8 In Example 2.4, we constructed the following network showing the driving distances between several California cities.

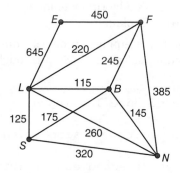

Suppose we are given the task of laying fiber-optic cable along these roads in such a way that all of these cities are connected. How can this be done with as little cable as possible?

Solution: To minimize the amount of cable and still connect all the cities, we need a minimal spanning tree. Using Algorithm 5.9, we begin with $\mathcal{T} = \overset{L}{\bullet}\!\!\!\!\underset{}{\text{—}}\!\!\!\!\overset{B}{\bullet}$, because *LB* is the edge with least weight. Looking at all the edges on *L* and all the edges on *B* reveals that *LS* is the edge with least weight, so we add it and its vertex to $\mathcal{T}$. Then after adding *BN*, *LF*, and *EF*, we have included all the vertices, so the minimal spanning tree $\mathcal{T}$ uses the edges *LB*, *LS*, *BN*, *LF*, and *EF*. The final tree (and hence the optimal layout of the cable network) is shown below.

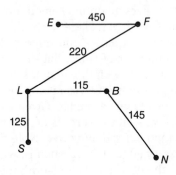

Its total weight is 1055; this is the least number of miles of cable needed to connect all the cities.   ◇

Activity 5.2.2: Greedy Algorithms

1. Use Prim's Algorithm to find a minimal spanning tree in the network below.

    > $\mathcal{T} \leftarrow \bullet\!\overset{e_1}{\text{———}}\!\bullet$, where e_1 is the shortest edge of $\mathcal{N}$.
    > while $\mathcal{T}$ does not contain all of $\mathcal{N}$'s vertices
    > ⌐ $e \leftarrow$ the shortest edge between a vertex in $\mathcal{T}$ and a vertex not in $\mathcal{T}$.
    > ∟ Add edge e and the new vertex to $\mathcal{T}$.

    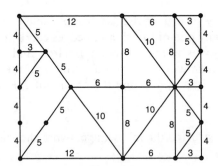

2. Is the spanning tree produced by Prim's Algorithm uniquely determined, or is there more than one possibility for a minimal spanning tree? Explain.

3. The following is a greedy algorithm that attempts to produce a directed path through a weighted directed graph, starting at vertex *A* and ending at vertex *B*. Step through the algorithm on the given directed graph.

    > $e \leftarrow$ the shortest directed edge leaving *A*.
    > $v \leftarrow$ the vertex e points at.
    > $\mathcal{P} \leftarrow$ the path consisting of edge e along with vertices *A* and v.
    > while $v \neq B$ do
    > ⌐ $e \leftarrow$ the shortest directed edge leaving v.
    > $\;\;\; v \leftarrow$ the vertex e points at.
    > ∟ Add edge e and the new vertex to $\mathcal{P}$.

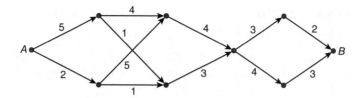

4. Give an example of a weighted directed graph for which the algorithm in Question 3 fails to produce the shortest path from A to B.

5.2.3 Divide-and-Conquer Algorithms

The recursive version of the binary search (Algorithm 5.4) works by dividing the list in half and calling itself recursively on each part. After enough divisions the list is small enough (one element) for the base case to apply. The recursive binary search is an example of a *divide-and-conquer* algorithm. This type of recursive algorithm divides the given problem (usually in half) and attempts to solve each part. Since the successive divisions rapidly become small, divide-and-conquer algorithms tend to work quickly.

The following is a recursive alternative to Example 4.55 of Section 4.5. If you keep the divide-and-conquer paradigm in mind, it is easy to see how to define the function.

Algorithm 5.10 Finding the largest element in a list.

Preconditions: $X = \{x_1, x_2, \ldots, x_n\}$ is a set of elements on which $\preceq$ defines a total ordering.

Postconditions: $\texttt{FindMax}(X) = \max\{x_1, x_2, \ldots, x_n\}$.

```
function FindMax (X)
    if X = {x} then
        return x
    else
        a ← FindMax ({x₁,x₂,...,x⌊n/2⌋})
        b ← FindMax ({x⌊n/2⌋+1,...,xₙ})
        if a ≺ b then
            return b
        else
            return a
```

A binary tree is a natural model for tracing the execution of a divide-and-conquer algorithm. Each node represents a function call, and the children of a node X represent the recursive calls made by X. The labels on each edge represent the return value of the lower node. When you draw such a tree, you start with the original call at the root and work down, and once you have drawn all the nodes you can start filling in the labels/return values from the bottom up.

Figure 5.2 shows such a tree. The first call to $\texttt{FindMax}(\{5,3,2,4\})$ spawns two recursive calls: $\texttt{FindMax}(\{5,3\})$ and $\texttt{FindMax}(\{2,4\})$. These in turn each make two calls to $\texttt{FindMax}\{n\}$ for some n, and since

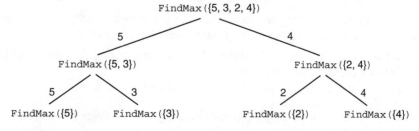

Figure 5.2 A binary tree models the trace of $\texttt{FindMax}(\{5,3,2,4\})$.

each of these parameter values is a set of the form $\{n\}$, each call returns n. When 5 and 3 are returned to the FindMax$(\{5,3\})$ call, it makes the comparison $5 \overset{?}{\prec} 3$ and returns 5. Similarly, FindMax$(\{2,4\})$ makes the comparison $2 \overset{?}{\prec} 4$ and returns 4. Finally, the original FindMax$(\{5,3,2,4\})$ call compares $5 \overset{?}{\prec} 4$ and returns 5, the maximum value in the set. Notice that the divide-and-conquer approach to finding the maximum element makes different comparisons than the iterative version in Example 4.55.

The divide-and-conquer paradigm leads to a nice algorithm for sorting the elements $x_1, x_2, \ldots, x_n$ in an array. In Section 4.5, we studied the bubble sort. This simple algorithm works well for small arrays, but it can be rather slow for large sets of data. The *merge sort* works more efficiently by dividing and conquering. The next activity introduces the merge sort algorithm in the special case when the size of the array is a power of 2.

Activity 5.2.3: Merge Sort

A Merge of two sorted arrays is a function that combines all the elements of both arrays into a single sorted array. The following recursive function M inputs an array L of size 2^p and outputs an array M(L) containing the same elements, but in order.

```
function M(x₁,x₂,…,x₂ₚ ∈ U)
    if p = 0 then
        return x₁
    else
        return Merge(M(x₁,x₂,…,x₂ₚ₋₁), M(x₂ₚ₋₁₊₁,x₂ₚ₋₁₊₂,…,x₂ₚ))
```

1. Compute M(dog, cat) using a top-down evaluation, showing all steps.

2. The function M is a version of the *merge sort*. Let L be the array $3, 1, 4, 1, 5, 9, 2, 6$. Compute M(L) with a top-down evaluation, showing all steps.

3. Model the steps of the execution in Question 2 with a binary tree. Each node represents a call of the function M. The children of each node represent the recursive calls made by the node call. The return values go on the edges. Work down from the root, and then add return values from the leaves going back up.

4. In your top-down evaluation in Question 2, you should have found that the evaluation of M(L) requires seven Merge calls. Since a Merge of k elements requires $\Theta(k)$ comparisons, the number of comparisons required by each Merge call can be approximated by the size of the resulting merged array. Complete the following table, and use it to estimate the total number of comparisons required by your evaluation in Question 2.

size of merged array $\approx$ # of comparisons	number of Merge calls	approximate total # of comparisons
8	1	8
4		
2		

5. Suppose you evaluated M(L) on a list L of size 16. Without writing out a top-down evaluation, construct a table like the one in Question 4 and use it to estimate the total number of comparisons required.

6. Generalize: Suppose L is an array with 2^p elements. How many comparisons would evaluating M(L) require?

7. Write your estimate from Question 6 in terms of n, where $n = 2^p$.

8. Since this estimate is an upper-bound, we should use big-O notation to express it. So give a big-O upper-bound estimate for the number of comparisons made by the Merge Sort when sorting an array of size n.

9. We have seen four sorting algorithms so far: Bubble Sort, Selection Sort, Tree Sort, and Merge Sort. Which of these do you think is/are the most efficient?

The main idea behind the merge sort is simple: divide the array into two smaller arrays, sort the smaller arrays (recursively), and merge the smaller arrays back together. When the size of the array is not a power of 2, the merging process can be slightly tricky; Algorithm 5.11 gives a general method.

Algorithm 5.11 Merge Subroutine.

Preconditions: $y_1, y_2, \ldots, y_l, z_1, z_2, \ldots, z_m \in U$, U is totally ordered by $<$, $y_1 \leq y_2 \leq \cdots \leq y_l$, and $z_1 \leq z_2 \leq \cdots \leq z_m$.

Postconditions: Returns $x_1, x_2, \ldots, x_n$, where $n = l + m$, $x_1 \leq x_2 \leq \cdots \leq x_n$, and $\{x_1, x_2, \ldots, x_n\} = \{y_1, y_2, \ldots, y_l, z_1, z_2, \ldots, z_m\}$.

```
function Merge (y₁,y₂,...,yₗ,z₁,z₂,...,zₘ ∈ U)
    i ← 1,  j ← 1,  k ← 1
    while k ≤ l+m do
        ┌ if i > l then
        │     ┌ xₖ ← zⱼ
        │     └ j ← j+1
        │   else if j > m then
        │         ┌ xₖ ← yᵢ
        │         └ i ← i+1
        │       else if yᵢ ≤ zⱼ then
        │             ┌ xₖ ← yᵢ
        │             └ i ← i+1
        │           else
        │             ┌ xₖ ← zⱼ
        │             └ j ← j+1
        └ k ← k+1
    return x₁,x₂,...,xₗ₊ₘ
```

We'll take a closer look at this algorithm in the next section; it really isn't as complicated as it might look at first glance. For now, just accept that it takes two ordered arrays and puts them together to make one big ordered array. Once you have this procedure for merging two ordered arrays, the merge sort is simple to write down using the divide-and-conquer paradigm. See Algorithm 5.12.

Algorithm 5.12 Merge Sort.

Preconditions: $x_1, x_2, \ldots, x_n \in U$, a set that is totally ordered by $<$.

Postconditions: Returns $\hat{x}_1, \hat{x}_2, \ldots, \hat{x}_n$, where $\{\hat{x}_1, \hat{x}_2, \ldots, \hat{x}_n\} = \{x_1, x_2, \ldots, x_n\}$ and $\hat{x}_1 \leq \hat{x}_2 \leq \cdots \leq \hat{x}_n$.

```
function MergeSort (x₁,x₂,...,xₙ ∈ U)
    if n = 1 then
        return x₁
    else
        l ← ⌊n/2⌋
        return Merge (MergeSort (x₁,x₂,...,xₗ), MergeSort (xₗ₊₁,xₗ₊₂,...,xₙ))
```

We can trace the merge sort with a top-down evaluation. To make things interesting, let's see what it does with a seven-element array with values 12, 3, 5, 17, 2, 8, 9.

```
  MergeSort (12,3,5,17,2,8,9)
= Merge (MergeSort (12,3,5), MergeSort (17,2,8,9))
= Merge (Merge (MergeSort (12), MergeSort (3,5)), Merge (MergeSort (17,2),
        MergeSort (8,9)))
= Merge (Merge (12, Merge (MergeSort (3), MergeSort (5))),
        Merge (Merge (MergeSort (17), MergeSort (2)), Merge (MergeSort (8),
        MergeSort (9))))
= Merge (Merge (12, Merge (3, 5)), Merge (Merge (17, 2), Merge (8, 9)))
= Merge (Merge (12, (3,5)), Merge ((2,17), (8,9)))
= Merge ((3,5,12), (2,8,9,17))
= 2,3,5,8,9,12,17
```

In the next section we will show that the merge sort is more efficient than the bubble sort. In fact, in a certain sense, you will never find a faster sorting algorithm. We'll see a mathematical reason why in Section 5.4.

Exercises 5.2

1. List the order in which the nodes are visited for (a) a preorder traversal, (b) a postorder traversal, and (c) an inorder traversal of the following binary tree.

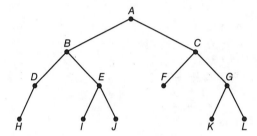

2. Make three copies of the tree in Figure 5.3 and draw paths that indicate the order in which the nodes are visited for (a) a preorder traversal, (b) a postorder traversal, and (c) an inorder traversal.

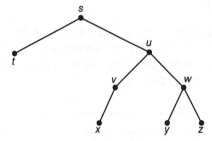

Figure 5.3 The binary tree for Exercises 2, 3, and 4.

3. Refer to the tree in Figure 5.3. Suppose each node of the tree represents a task, and each child node represents a task that must be done before the parent node's task. (Such a tree is sometimes called a *dependency tree*.) Which traversal method gives a suitable order in which to do these tasks?

4. Suppose that the tree in Figure 5.3 models the evolutionary relationships among a set of species of animals, where each node represents a species, and the descendants of a node represent its biological descendants. Which tree traversal method (preorder, postorder, or inorder) gives a possible chronological ordering for when these species could have appeared? Is this ordering unique? Explain.

5. Draw and label a single binary tree with six nodes ($A, \ldots, F$) such that an inorder traversal gives A, B, C, D, E, F and a preorder traversal gives C, B, A, E, D, F.

6. Draw and label a binary tree with six nodes ($A, \ldots, F$) such that an inorder traversal and a postorder traversal both give A, B, C, D, E, F.

7. (a) Place labels $A, \ldots, G$ in the following tree so that a preorder traversal will visit the nodes in the order A, B, C, D, E, F, G.

   (b) Do a postorder traversal of the tree in part (a) and list the nodes in the order that they are visited.

8. The three tree traversal algorithms (Algorithms 5.5, 5.6, and 5.7) can also be regarded as divide-and-conquer algorithms. Explain how the divide-and-conquer paradigm applies to these algorithms.

9. The solution to Example 5.7 includes a detailed trace of the preorder traversal algorithm using indentation to show all the recursive calls. Write out a similar trace for (a) the postorder traversal and (b) the inorder traversal of the binary tree in Example 5.7.

10. Let $X = \{x_1, x_2, \ldots, x_l\}$, $Y = \{y_1, y_2, \ldots, y_m\}$, and $Z = \{z_1, z_2, \ldots, z_n\}$ be finite sets. Write an algorithm that traverses the set $X \times Y \times Z$ using nested `for`-loops.

11. Refer to Definition 3.5 on page 148. Write a traversal algorithm for an SList.

12. Let G be a connected graph in which every vertex has degree 4. Write a recursive traversal algorithm in pseudocode that will visit all the vertices of G, starting at some specified vertex v. Include preconditions and postconditions.

13. Use Prim's algorithm (Algorithm 5.9) to construct a minimal spanning tree for the network in Figure 5.4. What is the total weight of the minimal spanning tree?

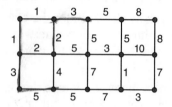

Figure 5.4 Network for Exercises 13 and 16b.

14. Use Prim's algorithm to construct a minimal spanning tree for the following network. Draw the minimal tree and compute its total weight.

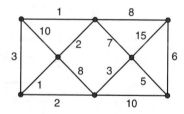

15. Use Prim's algorithm to construct a minimal spanning tree for the network in Figure 5.5. What is the total weight of the minimal spanning tree? Is there a unique minimal spanning tree? Explain.

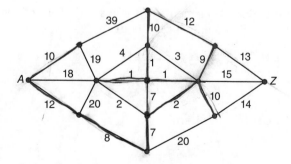

Figure 5.5 Network for Exercises 15, 16c, and 17.

16. *Kruskal's algorithm* gives another way to find a minimal spanning tree in a network.

Algorithm 5.13 Kruskal's Algorithm for constructing a minimal spanning tree.

Preconditions: $\mathcal{N}$ is a connected network with $n > 2$ vertices.

Postconditions: $\mathcal{T}$ is a minimal spanning tree of $\mathcal{N}$.

```
T ←  •——e₁——•  , where e₁ is the shortest edge of N.
for i ∈ {2,...,n − 1} do
    ⌐ eᵢ ← the shortest edge whose addition to T will not form a circuit.
    ⌊ Add edge eᵢ (and its vertices) to T.
```

(a) Is Kruskal's algorithm greedy? Explain.

(b) Use Kruskal's algorithm to construct a minimal spanning tree of the network in Figure 5.4.

(c) Use Kruskal's algorithm to construct a minimal spanning tree of the network in Figure 5.5.

17. Sometimes, greedy algorithms don't work at all. Consider the task of finding the shortest path between two nodes in a network. Write a greedy algorithm that inputs a network, a starting point A, and an ending point Z, and attempts to find a shortest path from A to Z. Try your algorithm on the graph in Figure 5.5. Show that it fails to find the shortest path.

18. Recall that a coloring of a graph is an assignment of colors to the vertices such that no two vertices of the same color are connected by an edge. The following algorithm attempts to produce a coloring for the vertices of a graph G using the fewest number of colors possible.

```
C ← ∅
while (G has vertices left to color) do
        Pick a new color x ∉ C.
        C ← C ∪ {x}
        Assign color x to as many vertices of G as possible, such that
            no edge connects vertices of the same color.
```

(a) Which type of algorithm is this?

(b) Find a graph for which this algorithm fails to produce a coloring with the fewest possible number of colors.

19. Consider the problem of tiling an $m \times n$ grid with tiles of the following shapes.

(a) Show that it is possible to tile a 3×4 grid using these tiles.

(b) Show that it is possible to tile a 2×4 grid using these tiles.

(c) Explain how a divide-and-conquer algorithm could construct a tiling of a 101×100 grid using these tiles.

20. Let $\mathcal{T}$ be a binary tree whose nodes are elements of some set U. The following algorithm searches $\mathcal{T}$ for a target value $t \in U$ and returns true if and only if t is a node in $\mathcal{T}$.

```
function Search(t ∈ U, T ∈ {binary trees})
    if T is empty then
        return false
    else
        if t = the root of T then
            return true
        else
            return (Search(t, left subtree of T) ∨ Search(t, right subtree of T))
```

(a) Write a top-down evaluation of Search$(17, \mathcal{T})$, where $\mathcal{T}$ is the following tree. (Note that this tree is not a binary search tree.)

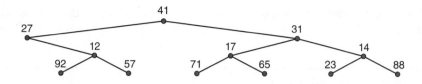

(b) Which type of algorithm is this? Explain.

21. Compare the comparisons made by the divide-and-conquer version of FindMax (Algorithm 5.10) with the comparisons made by the simple for-loop version in Example 4.55. Use $x_1, x_2, x_3, x_4 = 5, 3, 2, 4$.

22. There is a top-down evaluation of MergeSort $(12, 3, 5, 17, 2, 8, 9)$ on page 233. Write this trace in the form of a binary tree, as in Figure 5.2.

23. Do a trace of MergeSort $(23, 5, 7, 13, 43, 21, 17, 2)$ using a top-down evaluation.

24. Write a divide-and-conquer algorithm that computes the sum of all elements of a finite set $K = \{k_1, k_2, \ldots, k_n\}$ of integers.

*25. Write a greedy algorithm that constructs the base two expansion of a given natural number. (Hint: This is like change-making, using coins of denominations $1, 2, 4, 8, 16, \ldots$.)

5.3 Algorithm Complexity

In Sections 3.5 and 4.5, we counted the number of operations in some simple algorithms. In Section 4.6, we practiced the art of estimating quantities. In this section, we will put these two skills together to develop a mathematical way of predicting how fast a given algorithm will work.

There are many factors that influence how fast a given algorithm will run on a given computer. Technical considerations such as computer architecture, processor speed, and memory access require knowing the current state of affairs in the hardware industry, and this is a moving target. Given all of these variables, the most we should expect to get from mathematical analysis of algorithms is a means for making broad comparisons between algorithms. Counting the exact number of operations isn't so important, but being able to make good estimates is crucial.

Preview 5.3

1. Matheus drives one mile to work along a single road. He never exceeds 30 miles per hour, and there are three stoplights along the way. Matheus can never predict how many lights he will have to stop for, but he knows that each light stays red for 45 seconds before turning green again. What can you say about the time it takes him to complete the trip?

2. In three-dimensional computer graphics, the faces of an object are often divided into a triangular mesh, like the boxes below. When an object is rendered to the screen, the program needs to draw only the triangles that would be visible to the viewer. How does the orientation of these boxes determine how many triangles need to be drawn? In general, if a triangular mesh object is composed of n triangular faces, how many triangles would you expect the program to have to draw?

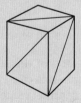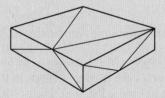

3. Define a function $\sigma : \mathbf{N} \longrightarrow \mathbf{N}$ such that $\sigma(n)$ counts the natural numbers that divide n. For example, $\sigma(6) = 4$, because 1, 2, 3, and 6 are the divisors of 6. What can you say about the range of possible values for $\sigma(n)$? Consider several different values of n.

The following activity reviews the practice of counting operations, using the sequential search (Algorithm 5.1). It also introduces the idea of three cases to consider when analyzing algorithms: best case, worst case, and average case.

Activity 5.3.1: Best, Worst, and Average

Suppose that $x_1, x_2, \ldots, x_n$ is a list of data (e.g, numbers, words), and t is an item of the same type of data. Consider the following algorithm.

$$i \leftarrow 1$$
$$x_{n+1} \leftarrow t$$
$$\texttt{while } t \neq x_i \texttt{ do}$$
$$\quad i \leftarrow i + 1$$

1. If $n = 7$, $t = \texttt{dog}$, and $\{x_1, x_2, \ldots, x_n\} = \{\texttt{ape}, \texttt{ewe}, \texttt{pig}, \texttt{bat}, \texttt{dog}, \texttt{cat}, \texttt{fox}\}$, then how many "$\neq$" comparisons does this algorithm make?

2. If $n = 7$, $t = \texttt{emu}$, and $\{x_1, x_2, \ldots, x_n\} = \{\texttt{ape}, \texttt{ewe}, \texttt{pig}, \texttt{bat}, \texttt{dog}, \texttt{cat}, \texttt{fox}\}$, then how many "$\neq$" comparisons does this algorithm make?

3. If $i = n + 1$ after this algorithm finishes, what can you conclude about t?

4. If $i \neq n + 1$ after this algorithm finishes, what can you conclude about t?

5. What is the fewest number of "$\neq$" comparisons this algorithm could make? (This is the *best case* number of comparisons.)

6. What is the greatest number of "$\neq$" comparisons this algorithm could make, in terms of n? (This is the *worst case* number of comparisons.)

7. Suppose that the probability that the item t is in the list is 0.2. In addition, for $1 \leq i \leq n$, suppose that the conditional probability that the item is in location i, given that the item is in the list, is $1/n$. What is the expected value of the number of "$\neq$" comparisons made by this algorithm, in terms of n? (This is the *average case* number of comparisons.)

5.3.1 The Good, the Bad, and the Average

Often, we want to know the answer to the question, "Will Algorithm A finish in time to do X?" Here X could be "finish my report by 5 pm" or "render the next animation frame" or some other constraint on the time of execution. In this situation, a *worst-case* analysis of the algorithm is useful.

Definition 5.4 Let D be the set of all possible inputs of size n for a given algorithm. For $d \in D$, let $c(d)$ be the number of operations performed by the algorithm on data set d. (Note that $c(d)$ depends on n also.) The *worst-case* number of operations performed by the algorithm is the maximum value of $c(d)$ as d ranges through all elements of D.

The *time complexity* of an algorithm is a measure of how the running time of an algorithm increases as a function of n, the size of the input data. We calculate the worst-case time complexity by calculating the worst-case number of some representative operation in the algorithm. We usually estimate this number using big-O or big-Θ notation.

Example 5.9 Calculate the worst-case time complexity of the sequential search (Algorithm 5.1).

Solution: Let's count the number of $\neq$ comparisons. The `while`-loop in this algorithm continues to run until the target item t is found, so the worst-case is when t is not in the list. In this case, the algorithm will have to make the $\neq$ comparison with every element on the list, and finally with the sentinel value. That's a total of $n+1$ comparisons for a list of size n, so the worst-case complexity is $\Theta(n)$.   ◇

How do we know which operation to count? Here we have some latitude. We would like to count the operation that will make the most demands on a computer implementation of the algorithm, but we won't always be sure what this is. If there is a block of operations that gets repeated more than any other part of the algorithm, it is usually a good idea to count one of the operations in this block. The good news is that most reasonable choices will produce the correct result, especially after passing to big-Θ or big-O notation.

We will generally strive to report the complexity of an algorithm in big-Θ notation, but there are times when we will have to use big-O instead. It follows immediately from Definitions 4.7 and 4.9 that $f \in O(g)$ if $f \in \Theta(g)$. It is also easy to show that if $f(n) \leq g(n)$ for all n, then $f \in O(g)$. (Just take $K = 1$ in Definition 4.7.) Therefore, if we are forced to overestimate an operation count in a worst-case analysis, we should report our estimate using big-O notation. Just remember that big-O is reporting an upper bound on complexity, not the complexity itself.

Calculating the complexity of the Euclidean algorithm illustrates this way of using big-O notation. In Exercise 17 of Section 5.1, we saw a recursive function for finding the greatest common divisor of two natural numbers. Here is an iterative version.

Algorithm 5.14 The Euclidean Algorithm.

Preconditions: $m, n \in \{0, 1, 2, 3, \ldots\}$
Postconditions: d is the greatest integer such that $d \mid m$ and $d \mid n$.

$d \leftarrow m$
$e \leftarrow n$
while $e \neq 0$ do
    ┌ $r \leftarrow d \bmod e$
       $d \leftarrow e$
    └ $e \leftarrow r$

Example 5.10 Show that the worst-case complexity of the Euclidean algorithm is $O(n)$.

Solution: Like the recursive version, this algorithm makes repeated divisions until the remainder is zero. Let's try to count the worst-case number of "$d \bmod e$" operations in terms of n. The algorithm starts with e equal to n, and each time through the loop, e gets replaced by the remainder r when d is divided by e. To distinguish the old and new values of e, let $\hat{e}$ represent the value of e after this replacement, where e is its value before the loop iteration. In this notation,

$$\hat{e} = d \bmod e.$$

In particular, this implies that $\hat{e} < e$, since it is the remainder of division by e. So e gets smaller (by at least 1) each time through the loop, and the loop will terminate when $e = 0$. This shows that the worst-case number of "$d \bmod e$" operations is at most n, so the worst-case complexity is $O(n)$. $\diamond$

It is important to note that reporting complexity in terms of big-O notation only makes the claim of an upper bound on complexity. The next example shows that the Euclidean algorithm is actually more efficient than $O(n)$.

Example 5.11 Show that the worst-case complexity of the Euclidean algorithm is $O(\log_2 n)$.

Solution: We'll improve on the solution to the previous example by showing that e must decrease by at least a factor of $1/2$ every two times through the loop; that is, we will show that

$$\hat{\hat{e}} \leq e/2.$$

We can apply the $\hat{\ }$ notation to other variables as well: $\hat{d} = e$ expresses the fact that the new value of d is the old value of e. Now consider going through the loop a second time. We then have

$$\hat{\hat{e}} = \hat{d} \bmod \hat{e}$$
$$= e \bmod \hat{e}$$
$$= e \bmod (d \bmod e).$$

If $\hat{e} \geq e/2$, then $\hat{e}$ goes into e once with remainder at most $e/2$, so

$$\hat{\hat{e}} = e \bmod \hat{e} \leq e/2.$$

On the other hand, if $\hat{e} < e/2$, then $\hat{\hat{e}} < e/2$ also, since $\hat{\hat{e}}$ is the remainder of division by $\hat{e}$.

Therefore, the value of e is (at least) halved after two iterations of the loop. Since

$$n \left(\frac{1}{2}\right)^{\log_2 n} = 1,$$

it will take at most $1 + 2 \log_2 n$ iterations for the value of e to reach zero. So the worst-case complexity is $O(\log_2 n)$.   ◇

In both of the above solutions, we were only able to establish that the number of operations was *at most* some value; we bounded the number of operations above by a function of n. Since we were unable to get an exact count, and we never established a lower bound, we were forced to report the complexity in big-O notation.

Worst-case complexity analyses will tell you if your algorithm is good enough, but they won't always tell you how good it is. We can also calculate *best-case* complexity, making the obvious modifications to Definition 5.4.

Definition 5.5 Let D be the set of all possible inputs of size n for a given algorithm. For $d \in D$, let $c(d)$ be the number of operations performed by the algorithm on data set d. (Note that $c(d)$ depends on n also.) The *best-case* number of operations performed by the algorithm is the minimum value of $c(d)$ as d ranges through all elements of D.

Example 5.12 For the sequential search (Algorithm 5.1), the best-case number of $\neq$ operations happens when the target t is x_1, the first item in the array. In this case, only one $\neq$ comparison is made, since the while-loop is never entered. So the best-case complexity is $\Theta(1)$.

Worst-case and best-case complexity analyses together don't always tell the whole story, because most data sets in the real world will be somewhere between these two extremes. Actual data tends to fluctuate randomly, and algorithm speed can vary accordingly. The *average-case* complexity of an algorithm accounts for the range of different possible data sets.

Definition 5.6 Suppose that there are k different possible data sets of size n for a given algorithm, and that these different data sets occur randomly. For each $i \in \{1, 2, \ldots, k\}$, let p_i be the probability that data set i occurs, and let c_i be the number of operations performed by the algorithm on data set i. (Typically, c_i is a function of n.) Then the *average-case* number of operations performed by the algorithm is

$$p_1 c_1 + p_2 c_2 + \cdots + p_k c_k.$$

In particular, if all the data sets are equally likely, the average-case number of operations is

$$\frac{c_1 + c_2 + \cdots + c_k}{k}.$$

In general, computing the average-case complexity is much trickier than computing the best-case or worst-case complexity. For starters, we have to know more about the set of all possible input data sets, and we have to incorporate this information into our analysis.

Example 5.13 Calculate the average-case time complexity of the sequential search (Algorithm 5.1). Assume that the probability that the target value is in the list is 0.90, and that all list positions are equally likely.

Solution: Notice that if the item is in position i, the algorithm makes i comparisons. Since 90% of the sample space consists of the equally likely list positions $1, 2, \ldots, n$, each of these has probability $0.9/n$. The remaining 10% of the sample space requires $n + 1$ comparisons, by the worst-case analysis. Using Definition 5.6, the average-case number of comparisons is

$$\left(\frac{0.9}{n}\right)(1 + 2 + \cdots + n) + 0.1(n + 1) = \left(\frac{0.9}{n}\right)\left(\frac{n(n+1)}{2}\right) + 0.1(n + 1),$$

which simplifies to a linear function of n. So the average-case complexity of the sequential search is $\Theta(n)$.   ◇

In this example, it doesn't really matter what we assume about the probability of the target being in the list: this number goes away when we pass to big-Θ notation. The next example illustrates another situation in which probabilities can be ignored: some algorithms always do the same amount of work, regardless of the data set.

Example 5.14 Recall the bubble sort of Example 4.56. This algorithm always makes $n(n-1)/2$ comparisons on a list of n items, no matter what. Therefore, the best-case, worst-case, and average-case complexity of the bubble sort is $\Theta(n^2)$.

Activity 5.3.2: Binary Search Complexity

The following recursive function performs a binary search for a target value t in a sorted list of data $x_1, x_2, \ldots, x_n$.

```
function BinSearch(t ∈ U,  l, r ∈ {1, 2, ..., n})
    i ← ⌊(l + r)/2⌋
    if t = x_i then
        return true
    else
        ⌈ if (t < x_i) ∧ (l < i) then
              return BinSearch(t, l, i − 1)
          else
              ⌈ if (t > x_i) ∧ (i < r) then
                    return BinSearch(t, i + 1, r)
                else
        ⌊     ⌊     return false
```

1. Suppose that, initially, $x_1 = 3$, $x_2 = 13$, $x_3 = 23$, and $x_4 = 33$. Evaluate `BinSearch(23, 1, 4)` using a top-down evaluation.

2. What is the best-case number of list comparisons ($=$, $<$, or $>$) made by this algorithm, regardless of list and target value?

3. Suppose that $n = 16$, and that the target value t is less than every item in the list $x_1, x_2, \ldots, x_n$. How many list comparisons does the algorithm make when invoked as `BinSearch(t, 1, 16)`?

4. Suppose that $n = 16$, and that the target value t is greater than every item in the list $x_1, x_2, \ldots, x_n$. How many list comparisons does the algorithm make when invoked as `BinSearch(t, 1, 16)`?

5. Suppose that $n = 2^p$ for some $p \in \mathbf{N}$. What is the worst-case number of list comparisons made by this algorithm, when invoked as `BinSearch(t, 1, n)`? Give an exact answer in terms of p and also in terms of n, and give a big-Θ estimate of the latter.

5.3.2 Approximate Complexity Calculations

For many important algorithms, counting the number of operations exactly can be tedious, difficult, or impossible. However, judicious use of approximation can help us explore the basic ideas of algorithm complexity without getting too bogged down in the details. The trade-off is that approximation techniques are not mathematically rigorous, so it is important to treat their results with caution. But understanding rough calculations of complexity will help develop the capacity to think analytically about algorithms.

Example 5.15 Approximate the complexity of the iterative binary search (Algorithm 5.3).

Solution: We have a choice of which operation to count. Since the `while`-loop is the only part of this algorithm that repeats, it makes sense to count an operation that gets repeated inside this loop. Let's agree to count the $>$ comparisons on the elements of U. This comparison happens once every time the loop is entered.

The algorithm works by eliminating *approximately* half of the items in the list from consideration each time through the loop. The problem is that $(l+r)/2$ may not be an integer, so $\lfloor (l+r)/2 \rfloor$ is not exactly in the middle of the list. Sometimes we eliminate a little more than half of the items, sometimes we eliminate a little less. So to say that the list is "halved" at each stage is an approximation.

At any point in the execution of this algorithm, the number of items under consideration is $r - l + 1$, and the loop terminates when $l = r$. In other words, the loop terminates when there is only one item left under consideration.

So we can approximate the number of times through the loop by computing the number of times n needs to be halved to obtain 1. Call this number c. Then

$$\left(\frac{1}{2}\right)^c n \approx 1,$$

so $c \approx \log_2 n$. We conclude that the complexity of the binary search is approximately $\Theta(\log_2 n)$. Note that this approximation holds for best-case, worst-case, and average-case, since the number of times through the loop depends only on the size of the list and not on the arrangement of the data set.   ◇

Our approximation works exactly when n is a power of 2. It is a little tedious to compute this complexity when n is not a power of 2, but you shouldn't be surprised that the exact calculation shows the complexity of the binary search to be $\Theta(\log_2 n)$.

Example 5.16 Compute (or approximate) the best- and worst-case complexity of the recursive binary search function (Algorithm 5.4).

Solution: Again, let's agree to count the number of comparisons of elements of U. The best case occurs when the target item is found right away by the very first if-statement. Thus, the best-case complexity is $\Theta(1)$. For the worst case, approximate the number of comparisons $C(n)$ done on a list of size n by a recurrence relation. If $n = 1$, the worst our algorithm does is make three comparisons: $t \overset{?}{=} x_i$, $t \overset{?}{<} x_i$, and $t \overset{?}{>} x_i$.[1] For a list of size n, the algorithm will also make at most three comparisons, followed by a call to BinSearch on a list of approximately half the size. Hence the recurrence relation

$$C(n) = \begin{cases} 3 & \text{if } n = 1 \\ 3 + C(n/2) & \text{if } n > 1 \end{cases}$$

gives an approximate measure of the number of comparisons. As long as we are approximating, we might as well make it easy on ourselves by assuming that $n = 2^p$ for some p. Let $D(p) = C(2^p)$. This related recurrence relation has the following formula:

$$D(p) = \begin{cases} 3 & \text{if } p = 0 \\ 3 + D(p - 1) & \text{if } p > 0. \end{cases}$$

It is easy to verify the closed-form solution $D(p) = 3p + 3$. This means that a list of size 2^p requires approximately $3p + 3$ comparisons, in the worst case. Substituting $p = \log_2 n$, we get that $C(n) \approx 3\log_2 n + 3$, so we can approximate the worst-case complexity of this algorithm as $\Theta(\log_2 n)$.   ◇

The above calculations show that the binary search is more efficient than the sequential search, as far as time complexity is concerned. It is often the case that divide-and-conquer algorithms outperform simpler sequential algorithms. For another example, recall the merge sort.

Example 5.17 Approximate the worst-case complexity of the merge sort algorithm.

Solution: First, take another look at the Merge subroutine of Algorithm 5.11. Its job is to take two ordered arrays $y_1, y_2, \ldots, y_l$ and $z_1, z_2, \ldots, z_m$ and merge them into one big array $x_1, x_2, \ldots, x_n$, where $n = l + m$. Think of the data as standing in two lines, arranged by "height," as in Figure 5.6. Each time through the loop, the algorithm compares the data elements at the front of each line and chooses the shortest one to become the next element in the list of x_k's.

If we count array item assignments, there are always n, one for each of the x_k's. However, it is customary to count array-item comparisons instead, and this is a bit more tricky. Once $i > l$, there are no more items left in the y_i list, so no more array-item comparisons need to be made; in this event the rest of the x_k's must be taken from the z_j list. Similarly, we run out of z_j's when $j > m$, in which case we fill up the rest of the x_k's using the remaining y_i's without making any more array-item comparisons. Since one of the lists must run out before the other, there will always be fewer than n comparisons. Things get even more confusing when you take into account that the two lists might not be exactly the same size (when $l \neq m$), so determining an exact count of the operations in the Merge

---

1. The third of these comparisons is redundant, but we'll ignore this inefficiency.

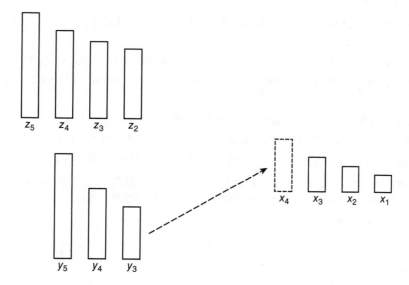

Figure 5.6 The `Merge` subroutine combines two ordered arrays. Here $y_3 < z_2$, so y_3 is taken to be the next element x_4 of the combined array.

algorithm is hard. Let's just say that this subroutine requires n operations, and remember that we are making a conservative overestimate.

Now consider the recursive `MergeSort` function (Algorithm 5.12). To make the calculation easier, assume the size of our array is $n = 2^p$. A merge sort on a list of 2^p elements performs a `Merge` on a 2^p-element list after performing two merge sorts on lists of size 2^{p-1}. Therefore, by the addition principle for algorithms, we have the following recurrence relation for $C(p)$, the approximate number of comparison operations done on a list of size 2^p:

$$C(p) = \begin{cases} 0 & \text{if } p = 0 \\ 2^p + 2C(p-1) & \text{if } p > 0. \end{cases}$$

It is left as an exercise to show that $C(p) = p \cdot 2^p$ is the closed-form solution. Therefore, a list of 2^p items requires at most $p \cdot 2^p$ comparisons in the worst case. Substituting $p = \log_2 n$, this says that a `MergeSort` on list of n items requires approximately

$$(\log_2 n)2^{(\log_2 n)} = (\log_2 n)(n)$$

$$\in O(n \log_2 n)$$

comparisons.[2] We are using big-O here instead of big-Θ because we overestimated the number of comparisons done by the `Merge` subroutine. In the next section, we will see that *every* sorting algorithm must have complexity at least $\Theta(n \log_2 n)$. This fact, combined with the above result, implies that the merge sort has complexity $\Theta(n \log_2 n)$.   ◇

Exercises 5.3

1. Look back at Example 5.12 and Algorithm 5.1. Count the best- and worst-case number of assignment statements involving items of the array. In other words, count the number of times the statement

$$x_{n+1} \leftarrow t$$

is executed. Why is this statement a bad choice for calculating the complexity of this algorithm?

---

2. Again, we omit the proof that this formula holds for all n, not just powers of 2.

2. Step through Algorithm 5.14 using $m = 42$ and $n = 24$. Compare this trace with the result of Exercise 17 of Section 5.1.

3. Explain why the results of Example 5.10 and Example 5.11 do not contradict each other.

4. Which statement is stronger: "this algorithm has complexity $\Theta(n^3)$" or "this algorithm has complexity $O(n^3)$"? Explain.

5. Consider Algorithm 5.8 for making change. Let $1 \leq N \leq 100$.

   (a) What is the best-case number of $\geq$ comparisons? For what N does this occur? Justify your answer.

   (b) What is the worst-case number of $\geq$ comparisons? For what N does this occur? Justify your answer.

6. Consider Algorithm 5.8 for making change. Suppose $N \in \{10, 15, 20, 25\}$, and all these values are equally likely. Compute the average-case number of $\geq$ comparisons. (Use Definition 5.6.)

7. Consider the following algorithm.

   ```
   i ← 2
   while (N mod i) ≠ 0 do
       i ← i + 1
   ```

   (a) Suppose that $N \in \{2, 3, 4, 5, \ldots, 100\}$. Find the best- and worst-case number of "N mod i" operations made by this algorithm.

   (b) Suppose instead that $N \in \{2, 3, 4, 5, 6, 7, 8\}$, and all these values are equally likely. Find the average-case number of "N mod i" operations made by this algorithm.

8. Find the (a) best-case, (b) worst-case, and (c) average-case number of $<$ comparisons performed by the following pseudocode segment. For parts (a) and (b), tell which values of n produce the best and worst cases. For part (c), assume that all possible values of n are equally likely.

   Preconditions: $n \in \{5, 10, 15, 20, 25\}$.

   ```
   while n < 17 do
       n ← n + 5
   ```

9. Count the (a) best-case, (b) worst-case, and (c) average-case number of $+$ operations performed by the following pseudocode segment. Assume that all possible data sets are equally likely.

   Preconditions: $X = \{x_1, x_2, x_3, x_4, x_5\} \subseteq \{10, 20, 30, 40, 50, 60\}$, where $x_1 < x_2 < x_3 < x_4 < x_5$.

   ```
   t ← 0
   i ← 1
   while t < 101 do
       ⌐ t ← t + x_i
       ∟ i ← i + 1
   ```

10. Find the (a) best-case, (b) worst-case, and (c) average-case number of $<$ comparisons performed by the following pseudocode segment. For parts (a) and (b), tell which data sets produce the best and worst cases. For part (c), assume that all possible data sets are equally likely.

    Preconditions: $X = \{x_1, x_2, x_3\} \subseteq \{5, 10, 15, 20, 25\}$ and $x_1 < x_2 < x_3$.

    ```
    i ← 1
    while x_i < 12 do
        i ← i + 1
    ```

11. In Example 4.55 we observed that the following algorithm performs $n - 1$ "$\prec$" comparisons.

    ```
    m ← x_1
    for i ∈ {2, 3, ..., n} do
        if m ≺ x_i then m ← x_i
    ```

    (a) Find the best-case number of "$\leftarrow$" operations.

    (b) Find the worst-case number of "$\leftarrow$" operations.

12. The bubble sort that we introduced in Example 4.56 is sometimes called the "dumb" bubble sort because it will continue to run even after the array has been put in order. The following algorithm checks a true/false variable s each time through the loop to see if any more sorting is necessary.

Algorithm 5.15 The Smart Bubble Sort.

Preconditions: $x_1, x_2, \ldots, x_n \in U$, a set that is totally ordered by $<$, and $n \geq 2$.

Postconditions: $x_1 \leq x_2 \leq \cdots \leq x_n$.

```
s ← false    // s = "array is sorted"
i ← 1
while ¬s do
    ⌐ j ← 1
      s ← true    // array is sorted UNLESS ...
      while j ≤ n − i do
          ⌐ if xⱼ > xⱼ₊₁ then
              ⌐ swap xⱼ and xⱼ₊₁
              L s ← false    // ... a swap is made
          L j ← j + 1
    L i ← i + 1
```

This algorithm takes advantage of the observation that if no swaps are made, then the array must be in order.

   (a) Trace through this algorithm for the array $x_1 = 1, x_2 = 7, x_3 = 4, x_4 = 9$.

   (b) What is the best-case number of array item comparisons in this algorithm, in terms of n? For what kind of data sets does it occur?

   (c) What is the worst-case number of array item comparisons in this algorithm, in terms of n? For what kind of data sets does it occur?

13. Suppose that two arrays $x_1, x_2, \ldots, x_n$ and $y_1, y_2, \ldots, y_n$ have at least one element in common. The following algorithm finds i, j such that $x_i = y_j$. Compute its best-case and worst-case complexity. (Count the number of $\neq$ comparisons.)

```
i ← 0
j ← n + 1
while j = n + 1 do
    ⌐ i ← i + 1
      yₙ₊₁ ← xᵢ
      j ← 1
      while xᵢ ≠ yⱼ do
    L        j ← j + 1
```

14. Consider the following way of sorting an array X with n elements.

```
Put the elements of X into a binary search tree.
Do an inorder traversal of your tree.
```

   (a) Approximate the average-case complexity of this algorithm. (For the average case, assume that you get a balanced binary search tree. Don't bother with Definition 5.6.)

   (b) Compute the worst-case complexity of this algorithm. (Hint: The worst case occurs when the array is in order to begin with!)

15. The following algorithm can be applied to a weighted, directed graph with starting nodes $\{A_1, A_2, A_3, A_4\}$ and ending nodes $\{B_1, B_2, B_3, B_4\}$. It finds a directed path starting at some starting node A and ending at some B_i, and it computes w, the total weight of the path.

```
w ← 0
while A ∉ {B₁,B₂,B₃,B₄} do
   ┌ e ← the shortest edge starting at A
   │ w ← w + the weight of e
   └ A ← the vertex e points to
```

For example, when applied to the following graph, if $A = A_2$ initially, the algorithm follows the edges labeled 3, 1, and 1, and computes $w = 3 + 1 + 1 = 5$.

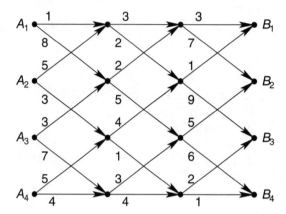

(a) Which kind of algorithm is this (traversal, greedy, or divide-and-conquer)? Explain.

(b) Compute the average-case value of w over the possible inputs A_1, A_2, A_3, A_4. Assume that each of these inputs is equally likely.

(c) Does the algorithm always succeed in finding the shortest directed path from A to some B_i? Why or why not?

16. In this problem we will approximate the complexity of Prim's algorithm for finding a minimal spanning tree of a network $\mathcal{N}$ (Algorithm 5.9). Let the input size n be the number of vertices in $\mathcal{N}$.

(a) Suppose that no vertex has degree greater than 5. Use Theorem 2.6 to explain why the number of edges is at most a linear function of n.

(b) Use Example 4.55 to approximate the worst-case number of comparisons needed for the following part of the algorithm.

```
e ← the shortest edge between a vertex in T
    and a vertex not in T.
```

(c) Give an approximate big-O estimate for the worst-case complexity of Prim's algorithm.

17. Use a recurrence relation to approximate the number of comparisons done by the recursive FindMax function (Algorithm 5.10).

18. Consider the following algorithm for finding a target element t in an array $x_1, x_2, \ldots, x_n$. Assume as a precondition that exactly one of the x_i's is equal to t.

```
Choose i at random from {1, 2, ..., n}.
while xᵢ ≠ t do
        Choose i at random from {1, 2, ..., n}.
print Element t was found in location i.
```

This algorithm continues to guess randomly until it finds where t is. Note that it does not keep track of its previous guesses, so it may check the same location more than once.

(a) Find the best-case number of $\neq$ comparisons made by this algorithm.

(b) *Warning: Tricky.* Find the worst-case number of $\neq$ comparisons made by this algorithm.

(c) *Calculus required.* Use the sum of an infinite series to find the average-case number of $\neq$ comparisons made by this algorithm.

19. Use induction to prove that the recurrence relation

$$C(i) = \begin{cases} 0 & \text{if } i = 0 \\ 2^i + 2C(i-1) & \text{if } i > 0 \end{cases}$$

has the closed-form solution $C(i) = i \cdot 2^i$.

20. The concept of best-, worst-, and average-case analyses extends beyond algorithms to other counting problems in mathematics. Recall that the height of a binary tree is the number of edges in the longest path from the root to a leaf.

    (a) Find the best-case height of a binary tree with five nodes.

    (b) Find the worst-case height of a binary tree with five nodes.

    (c) Find the average-case height of a binary tree with five nodes. For this problem, you will have to list all possible binary trees with five nodes. Assume that each of these is equally likely to occur.

    (d) Find the worst-case height of a binary tree with n nodes.

    (e) Approximate the best-case height of a binary tree with n nodes.

21. Suppose you have 100 square tiles, each measuring 1 foot by 1 foot. These tiles can be arranged in the shape of a solid rectangle in five different (i.e., noncongruent) ways.

    (a) Find the best-case (i.e., smallest) perimeter of such a rectangle.

    (b) Find the worst-case perimeter of such a rectangle.

    (c) Find the average-case perimeter of such a rectangle, assuming that the five cases are equally likely to occur.

22. Find the best-, worst-, and average-case values for rolling two standard six-sided dice. (Hint: Refer to Example 4.36.)

23. An urn contains three red marbles and two green marbles. Four marbles are drawn at random from the urn. Find the best-, worst-, and average-case number of red marbles in this random drawing. (In probability, the average-case number of red marbles is called the *expected value*.)

5.4   Bounds on Complexity

So far, our study of complexity has centered on counting or estimating the number of operations a given algorithm performs. In this section we take a different point of view: given a task (e.g., sorting a list), what is the best we can expect *any* algorithm to do? More specifically, given sets of preconditions and postconditions, what is a lower bound on the worst-case complexity of an algorithm that satisfies those preconditions and postconditions?

This question is much harder, in general, than the question of how a specific algorithm will perform. To answer it, we must focus on the intrinsic difficulty of the given algorithmic task, not on the algorithm. This kind of question belongs to the study of *computational complexity*. While most of the techniques in computational complexity theory are beyond the scope of this book, this section presents some relatively simple examples that are now within our grasp.

Preview 5.4

1. There are many ways to design a tournament. A fair tournament gives every participant an equal chance to win the tournament and guarantees that there will be a clear winner. What is the minimum number of games that need to be played in a fair tournament with 16 players? Why can't you have a fair tournament with fewer games?

2. Design a fair tournament for four players that establishes a clear first-place winner and also a clear second-place winner. What is the fewest number of games that need to be played?

3. There are many different Euler circuits in the following graph. Find one. Notice that at each degree-four vertex, you have the option of continuing your path straight through the vertex or turning one way or the

other. Can you minimize the number of "turns" your circuit makes? How can you tell if you have found the circuit with the fewest number of turns?

5.4.1 Algorithms as Decisions

Sometimes, we can think of an algorithm as a sequence of decisions. A program accepts some input values and then, through a sequence of mathematical operations, decides on some output values. If we understand the types of decisions necessary to solve a problem, we can determine—in some cases—whether an algorithm is working as efficiently as possible.

To illustrate this idea, consider the problem of identifying a particular species of bird. Suppose we are given an unknown bird B to identify, and for simplicity assume that we know that B must belong to one of four species: Steller's Jay, Western Scrub Jay, California Thrasher, and California Towhee. We are given the following facts about these species.

Species	Facts
Steller's Jay	Mostly blue, with a black crest.
Western Scrub Jay	Mostly blue, without a crest.
California Thrasher	Mostly brown, with a curved bill.
California Towhee	Mostly brown, with a conical bill.

The following two algorithms present two ways to identify the bird B.

Algorithm 5.16 Identifying a bird B.

```
if B has a crest then
    print B is a Steller's Jay.
else
    if B is mostly blue then
        print B is a Western Scrub Jay.
    else
        if B has a curved bill then
            print B is a California Thrasher.
        else
            print B is a California Towhee.
```

Algorithm 5.17 Identifying a bird B.

```
if B is mostly blue then
  ┌ if B has a crest then
         print B is a Steller's Jay.
    else
  └      print B is a Western Scrub Jay.
  else
  ┌ if B has a curved bill then
        print B is a California Thrasher.
    else
  └     print B is a California Towhee.
```

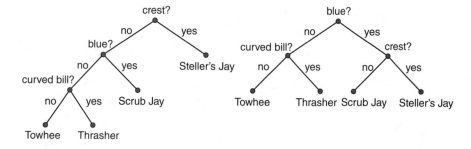

Figure 5.7 Decision-tree models for Algorithms 5.16 (left) and 5.17 (right).

Both of these algorithms identify the bird through a sequence of "yes or no" questions; these are decisions with two possible outcomes. However, they do so in slightly different ways. To compare these algorithms, consider the decision trees in Figure 5.7.

Both decision trees have four leaves; these correspond to the four different possible outcomes of the algorithm: bird B belongs to one of the four species. However, the height of the tree for Algorithm 5.16 is greater than the height of the tree for Algorithm 5.17, so Algorithm 5.16 may have to answer more questions to correctly identify the bird. The worst-case number of questions answered by Algorithm 5.16 is three, while Algorithm 5.17 needs to answer at most two.

If we measure efficiency by the worst-case number of questions answered, then Algorithm 5.17 is more efficient. But we can say more. The decision-tree analysis shows that Algorithm 5.17 is the *most* efficient possible algorithm for solving this problem, because its decision tree has the smallest possible height. Any algorithm that answers "yes or no" questions can be modeled with a binary tree, as in Figure 5.7. Since identifying B requires distinguishing among four possible outcomes, such a tree must have (at least) four leaves. The tree for Algorithm 5.17 is the shortest possible binary tree with four leaves; you can't do any better.

Definition 5.7 An algorithm that, in the worst case, solves a given problem using the fewest possible operations of a given type is called *optimal*.

Algorithm 5.17 is an optimal solution to our (contrived) bird identification problem with respect to the number of "yes or no" question operations. In general, proving the optimality of an algorithm is very difficult, but the following examples explore some cases for which we have the necessary tools.

Example 5.18 Consider the problem of identifying a counterfeit coin from among a set of 10 coins using only a balance scale. Suppose that all the genuine coins weigh the same, but the counterfeit coin weighs slightly less than the real coins. How many weighings are needed to identify the fake?

Solution: The balance scale is an operation with three possible outcomes: it could tilt left, tilt right, or balance evenly. We could attempt a divide-and-conquer algorithm for finding the counterfeit coin: divide the coins in half and weigh them. The lighter group contains the fake coin. Repeat until you find the coin. If you ever have to weigh an odd number of coins, keep one coin apart and weigh the rest; if the balance stays level, the separate coin is the fake.

Figure 5.8 illustrates this process. The left branch represents the event that the left side is lighter, the right branch represents the right being lighter, and the middle branch represents the two sides balancing. Note that this method requires three weighings, worst case.

This divide-and-conquer approach isn't the only way to do the problem. For example, we could have begun by setting two or more coins apart, in hope of finding the coin faster. Since there are lots of other ways to do this task, we should wonder whether it is possible to identify the coin in fewer than three weighings. But any scheme we devise must produce a decision tree with 10 leaves, because there are 10 choices for the counterfeit coin.

Since weighing on a balance scale is a 3-ary (or *ternary*) operation, a sequence of two weighings can produce a tree with at most nine leaves. Therefore, no matter how clever we are, there is no way to distinguish between 10 different outcomes using only two weighings. Thus, the solution outlined in Figure 5.8 using three weighings is optimal. ◇

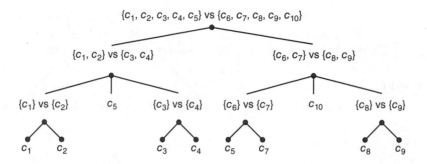

Figure 5.8 Decision tree for finding a counterfeit coin.

Activity 5.4.1: Counterfeit Coins

A balance scale allows the user to compare the weights of two objects. The scale will read one of three ways: it will tilt to the left if the object on the left is heavier, it will tilt to the right if the object on the right is heavier, or it will remain balanced if the two objects weigh the same amount.

1. Suppose that one coin in a collection of 3 coins is fake, and weighs less than the others. Explain how you can identify the fake coin with a balance scale using only one weighing.

2. Illustrate the strategy in Question 1 with a decision tree consisting of a root vertex with three children.

3. Suppose that one coin in a collection of 6 coins $c_1, c_2, c_3, c_4, c_5, c_6$ is fake, and weighs less than the others. Ned devises the following strategy. Weigh c_1 versus c_2. If one of these coins is lighter, it is fake. Otherwise, weigh c_1 versus c_3. If c_3 is lighter, it is fake. Otherwise, continue in this manner, weighing c_1 versus c_4, c_5, etc., until the fake coin is found.

   (a) Illustrate Ned's strategy with a decision tree.

   (b) What is the best-case number of weighings required by Ned's strategy?

   (c) What is the worst-case number of weighings required by Ned's strategy?

   (d) Devise a strategy for identifying the fake coin with a balance scale using at most two weighings. Illustrate your strategy with a decision tree.

4. What is the largest value of n such that, in a collection of n coins, a fake (lighter) coin can be identified with at most three weighings? Illustrate a strategy that works with this value of n.

5. An algorithm that, in the worst case, solves a problem in the fewest possible operations of a given type is called *optimal*. Are any of the above strategies optimal? Explain.

6. What properties should an optimal decision tree have?

5.4.2   A Lower Bound

In both the bird identification and counterfeit coin examples, we needed to know the maximum number of leaves possible in a decision tree. The number of children of each node equals the number of possible options for each decision; a decision tree where each decision has m options produces an m-ary tree. A standard induction argument will establish the following observation.

Lemma 5.1 Let $m \geq 2$ and $p \geq 0$ be integers. An m-ary tree with height p has at most m^p leaves.[3]

Proof Exercise. (Use induction on p.)   □

In other words, a sequence of p decisions, each of which has m choices, can produce at most m^p different outcomes. We used this lemma implicitly in the above solutions. The following theorem describes our technique more generally.

---

3. Recall that the height of a binary tree is the number of edges in the longest path from the root to a leaf. So a tree of height p represents a sequence of at most p decisions.

Theorem 5.1 *Let n measure the size of the input for a certain task, and suppose that any algorithm that solves this task must distinguish between $f(n)$ different possibilities. If an algorithm is based on an operation X that has m different outcomes, then the worst-case number of X operations this algorithm performs must be at least $\log_m(f(n))$.*

Proof The work of the algorithm can be modeled in terms of an m-ary decision tree: every time the algorithm performs operation X, it makes a decision among m choices. Since there are $f(n)$ possible outcomes, the algorithm must perform enough X operations so that this tree has at least $f(n)$ leaves. Let p be the worst-case number of times operation X is performed, so the decision tree has height p. By Lemma 5.1, the decision tree has at most m^p leaves. Therefore, $f(n) \leq m^p$, so $\log_m(f(n)) \leq p$.   □

This theorem tends to give a very conservative lower bound; in most cases an algorithm will perform many more operations than the theorem guarantees. However, for two important examples—searching and sorting—we have already seen algorithms that are as efficient as possible, in the sense that their worst-case complexity is in the same Θ-class as the lower bound given by Theorem 5.1.

Definition 5.8 Suppose that the worst-case number of operations of a given type needed to solve a given problem is at least $w(n)$. An algorithm is called *asymptotically optimal* if the number of operations it uses to solve the problem is in $\Theta(w(n))$.

In other words, an asymptotically optimal algorithm is optimal up to a big-Θ estimate.

Activity 5.4.2: Asymptotic Optimality

The Lower Bound Theorem. Let n measure the size of the input for a certain task, and suppose that any algorithm that solves this task must distinguish between $f(n)$ different possibilities. If an algorithm is based on an operation X that has m different outcomes, then the worst-case number of X operations this algorithm performs must be at least $\log_m(f(n))$.

Asymptotic Optimality. Suppose that the worst-case number of operations of a given type needed to solve a given problem is at least $w(n)$. An algorithm is called *asymptotically optimal* if the number of operations it uses to solve the problem is in $\Theta(w(n))$.

1. Consider the task of searching a list of n words to determine whether a particular target word is present. An algorithm must distinguish between the following possibilities: the target word could be in one of n different locations, or the target word may not be in the list. Suppose that such an algorithm is based on "if $a = b$ then" operations; such operations have two outcomes: yes or no. Apply the above theorem. What is $f(n)$? What is m? Give a lower bound on the number of "if $a = b$ then" operations the algorithm must perform.

2. Suppose that one coin in a collection of n coins is fake, and weighs less than the others. You have a balance scale that reads three ways: left, right, or balanced. Find a lower bound on the worst-case number of weighings needed to identify the counterfeit coin.

3. A sorting algorithm can be thought of as a function s that inputs a list L given in some order and returns a list $s(L)$ with the same elements, but in order. In terms of decisions, a sorting algorithm is deciding which rearrangement of the list will result in an ordered list.

   (a) How many different possibilities must a sorting algorithm distinguish between? That is, how many ways are there to arrange the elements of an n-element list?

   (b) Use the Lower Bound Theorem to find a lower bound of the number of comparisons ($<$, $>$, or $=$) required by a sorting algorithm.

   (c) Is the Bubble Sort asymptotically optimal? Explain.

   (d) Is the Merge Sort asymptotically optimal? Explain.

5.4.3 Searching an Array

Recall the two algorithms for searching an array: the sequential search (Algorithm 5.1) and the binary search (Algorithm 5.3). Both of these algorithms were based on *binary* comparisons, that is, operations having two different outcomes. In Example 5.9, we counted the $\neq$ operations to show that the worst-case complexity of the sequential search is $\Theta(n)$. Example 5.16 analyzed the $<$ operation to estimate the complexity of the binary search at $\Theta(\log_2 n)$. The next theorem says that you can't do better than a binary search.

Proposition 5.1 Any algorithm that uses binary comparisons to search an array of size n for a target element must require at least $w(n) \in \Theta(\log_2 n)$ comparisons, in the worst case.

Proof A searching algorithm must be able to distinguish between $n + 1$ possibilities: the target element could be in any of the positions $1, 2, \ldots, n$, or it could fail to be in the list. Theorem 5.1 tells us that the worst-case number of comparisons must be at least $\log_2(n + 1)$, which is in $\Theta(\log_2 n)$. □

Since the binary search has worst-case complexity $\Theta(\log_2 n)$, it achieves the lower bound set by Proposition 5.1. In other words, the binary search is an asymptotically optimal solution to the searching problem, with respect to the number of comparisons.

5.4.4 Sorting

The key to viewing sorting an array as a decision problem is to see it as choosing a correct arrangement from among all the possible arrangements of data. A sorting algorithm must rearrange the data, and there is only one way to put the list in order. Since there are $n!$ different ways to arrange an array of n elements, we have the following result.

Proposition 5.2 Any sorting algorithm based on binary comparisons must perform at least $w(n) \in \Theta(n \log_2 n)$ comparisons in the worst case to sort an array of n elements.

Proof By the above discussion, Theorem 5.1 shows that a sorting algorithm must perform at least $\log_2(n!)$ comparisons to sort a list of n elements, worst case. Since

$$
\begin{aligned}
\log_2(n!) &= \log_2 1 + \log_2 2 + \cdots + \log_2 n \\
&\leq \underbrace{\log_2 n + \log_2 n + \cdots + \log_2 n}_{n} \\
&\leq n \log_2 n,
\end{aligned}
$$

we have $\log_2(n!) \in O(n \log_2 n)$. Since

$$
\begin{aligned}
(n!)^2 &= \begin{matrix} 1 \\ n \end{matrix} \cdot \begin{matrix} 2 \\ (n-1) \end{matrix} \cdot \begin{matrix} 3 \\ (n-2) \end{matrix} \cdots \begin{matrix} (n-1) \\ 2 \end{matrix} \cdot \begin{matrix} n \\ 1 \end{matrix} \cdot \\
&\geq \underbrace{n \cdot n \cdots n}_{n} \\
&= n^n
\end{aligned}
$$

and, since $\log_2(n!)^2 = 2 \log_2(n!)$, it follows that

$$
\log_2(n!) \geq \frac{1}{2} \log_2(n^n) = \frac{1}{2} n \log_2 n,
$$

so $\log_2(n!) = \Omega(n \log_2 n)$. By Definition 4.9, we have shown that $\log_2(n!) \in \Theta(n \log_2 n)$, as required. □

We have already seen an asymptotically optimal sorting algorithm: the merge sort has worst-case complexity $\Theta(n \log_2 n)$.

5.4.5 *P vs. NP*

Don't let the foregoing discussion give you the impression that finding optimal algorithms is always easy. It isn't. In fact, there are many important questions in computational complexity theory that nobody knows how to answer.

One famous example is the question, "Does P equal NP?" We'll try to explore this question meaningfully without wading too deeply into the technical details.

The class P is the collection of all problems that can be solved with an algorithm whose complexity is at most polynomial: $\Theta(n^r)$ for some r. Many of the problems we have seen, including searching and sorting, belong to the class P, because we have solved them using polynomial-time algorithms.

The class NP is the collection of all problems whose solution can be *checked* (but not necessarily *found*) in polynomial time.[4] One example of a problem in NP is the task of finding a Hamilton circuit in a graph. It is easy to check that a given circuit is Hamiltonian, but it isn't always easy to find such a circuit. Another example is determining whether a given integer n is composite; you can easily check to see if d divides n, but it may take a long time to find d.

A problem x in NP is called *NP-complete* if a polynomial-time solution to x would yield a polynomial-time solution to *any* problem in NP. So NP-complete problems are in a sense the hardest problems in NP; solving just one of them would solve all the others. The following are some well-known NP-complete problems.

- Does a given graph have a Hamilton circuit?

- Can the vertices of a given graph be colored with a given number of colors?

- Can the variables in a given formula in propositional logic be given true/false values that will make the value of the formula true?

- Given a set U of integers, is there some subset of U whose elements add up to 0?

- Given two graphs G_1 and G_2, is G_1 isomorphic to a subgraph of G_2?

Hundreds of other problems are known to be NP-complete. If someone could find a polynomial-time algorithm to solve any one of them, there would be a polynomial-time solution to all problems in NP. In other words, P would equal NP. But, to date, nobody has found such an algorithm. Mathematicians today generally suspect that $P \neq NP$, but a valid proof of this assertion has never been found. This is arguably the greatest open question in modern mathematics.[5]

Exercises 5.4

1. Use a decision tree to describe an optimal procedure for identifying a bird B from among the six species below, using "yes or no" questions only. Explain how you know that your procedure is optimal.

Species	Facts
Yellow Warbler	Mostly yellow, no cap.
Wilson's Warbler	Mostly yellow, black cap, olive back.
American Goldfinch	Mostly yellow, black cap, yellow back.
Oak Titmouse	Mostly gray, with a crest.
Hutton's Vireo	Mostly gray, olive back, no crest.
Blue-gray Gnatcatcher	Mostly gray, dark gray back, no crest.

2. Algorithm 5.18 gives a (rather inelegant) method for printing three numbers in increasing order.

   (a) Draw a decision tree to model the choices made by this algorithm.

   (b) Is this algorithm optimal with respect to the number of $<$ comparisons? Explain.

3. In a collection of 10 coins, 4 coins are counterfeit and weigh less than the genuine coins. Find a good lower bound on the number of balance scale weighings needed to identify all the fake coins. (Assume the balance scale has three states: tilted left, tilted right, or balanced.)

---

4. The "N" in NP stands for "nondeterministic." If you guess randomly (not in some determined order) and you happen to guess correctly, you can prove that your solution is right in polynomial time.

5. The Riemann Hypothesis is probably the closest rival. Two famous results, Fermat's Last Theorem and the Poincaré Conjecture, have only recently been proved.

Algorithm 5.18 Printing three numbers in order by brute force.

Preconditions: $a, b, c \in \mathbf{R}$.

Postconditions: The elements of $\{a, b, c\}$ are printed in increasing order.

```
if a < b then
  ┌ if b < c then
        print a,b,c
    else
      ┌ if a < c then
            print a,c,b
        else
  └   └     print c,a,b
else
  ┌ if a < c then
        print b,a,c
    else
      ┌ if b < c then
            print b,c,a
        else
  └   └     print c,b,a
```

4. Consider the problem of identifying a counterfeit coin with a balance scale. Suppose, as we did in Example 5.18, that 1 coin out of a set of 10 is fake, but this time suppose that the fake coin could be *either* too heavy or too light, and it must be determined which is the case. What does Theorem 5.1 say about the minimum number of weighings in this case?

5. In a collection of 200 coins, one is counterfeit and weighs either more or less than the genuine coins. Find a good lower bound on the number of balance scale weighings needed to identify the fake coin and determine whether it is too heavy or too light. Assume the balance scale has three states: tilted left, tilted right, or balanced.

6. Suppose that one coin in a set of eight coins is fake, and that the fake coin is lighter than the other coins.

   (a) Use Theorem 5.1 to find a lower bound on the number of balance-scale weighings needed to identify the fake.

   (b) Find a strategy that identifies the fake coin in the optimal number of weighings. Draw a decision tree to show how your strategy works.

7. Suppose that 1 coin out of a set of 16 is fake and has a different weight than the others. Instead of a balance scale with three positions, you have a device that tells only whether or not two quantities weigh the same. In other words, your device has only two positions: "same" or "different."

   (a) Use Theorem 5.1 to find a lower bound on the number of times you need to use this device to identify the fake.

   (b) Find a strategy that identifies the fake coin in the optimal number of weighings. Draw a decision tree to show how your strategy works.

8. Let X be a set of n natural numbers. Consider the task of finding a pair of numbers in X whose difference is 100. Use Theorem 5.1 to find a lower bound on the worst-case number of binary comparisons needed to accomplish this task. Give an exact answer, and also a big-Θ estimate.

9. A string of 24 Christmas lights has one defective bulb and one special bulb. The string of lights can be tested by removing any subset of the 24 bulbs and leaving the rest connected. If the defective bulb is connected, none of the lights will work. If the special bulb is connected (and the defective one is not), then all of the bulbs will blink. If neither the defective nor the special bulb is connected, all of the bulbs will light up normally. Use Theorem 5.1 to find a good lower bound for the number of tests needed to identify the defective bulb and the special bulb. Explain your reasoning. (Don't draw the whole tree!)

10. Consider the task of selecting a person at random from a group of n people by repeatedly rolling a single six-sided die.

    (a) Use Theorem 5.1 to find a lower bound on the worst-case number of rolls needed to select a person from a group of $n = 72$ people.

    (b) Describe an optimal algorithm for selecting a person from a group of $n = 72$ people.

    (c) What is the greatest value of n for which a person can be selected at random using five rolls?

11. Compute the best-case number of questions answered by Algorithms 5.16 and 5.17.

12. Compute the average-case number of questions answered by Algorithms 5.16 and 5.17. Assume that each of the four species is equally likely to occur.

13. Consider the problem of searching for a target element in an ordered list. Is the sequential search (Algorithm 5.1) asymptotically optimal? Why or why not?

14. Is the Bubble Sort asymptotically optimal? Why or why not?

15. The Quick Sort is a recursive sorting algorithm that has average-case complexity $\Theta(n \log_2 n)$ and worst-case complexity $\Theta(n^2)$. Is the Quick Sort asymptotically optimal? Why or why not?

16. Refer to Exercise 15 of Section 5.3. Consider the general problem of finding the shortest directed path from some $A \in \{A_1, A_2, A_3, A_4\}$ and ending at some B_i in a weighted directed graph of the following form, where the graph is n edges wide (instead of 3 edges wide, as in Exercise 15). (The weights of this graph are not shown below.)

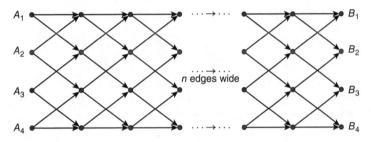

    (a) In terms of n, how many different directed paths are there that start at a given $A \in \{A_1, A_2, A_3, A_4\}$ and end at the rightmost column (at any B_i)?

    (b) Give a good lower bound on the number of two-way comparisons required by any algorithm that finds the overall shortest directed path from the A column to the B column. Give an exact answer in terms of n, and also give a big-Θ estimate for your answer.

17. Prove Lemma 5.1 using induction on p.

18. Suppose s and t are two strings of length 5 in the alphabet a $\ldots$ z. An algorithm checks to see if $s = t$ by comparing corresponding symbols in each string, from left to right. Draw the decision tree that models this algorithm.

19. Does the set

$$U = \{-15, -12, -9, -4, 2, 5, 6, 14, 23\}$$

have a subset whose elements add up to 0? If so, find such a subset. If not, explain why not.

20. Suppose U is a set of n integers. Approximate the worst-case complexity of an algorithm that runs through all possible subsets of U and adds up the elements in each subset to see if there is a subset whose elements add up to 0.

21. Is there an assignment of true/false values for the variables p, q, r, s, and t such that the formula

$$[(p \lor q) \land (\neg p \lor \neg r)] \to [(s \lor t) \land (\neg s \lor \neg t)]$$

takes the value true? If so, find such an assignment. If not, explain why not.

22. Suppose P is a formula in propositional logic containing n variables. Approximate the worst-case complexity of an algorithm that runs through all possible true/false values of the n variables to see if there is an assignment that makes P true.

23. Let G_1 and G_2 be graphs with vertex sets V_1 and V_2, respectively, with $|V_1| = |V_2| = n$. Approximate the worst-case complexity of an algorithm that runs through all possible one-to-one correspondences $V_1 \longrightarrow V_2$ to see if there is an isomorphism $G_1 \longrightarrow G_2$.

5.5   Program Verification

Up to this point, we have been using preconditions and postconditions to describe what a given algorithm is supposed to do. This is good practice, because it gives a mathematically precise way of summarizing the work of a segment of pseudocode. However, aside from appealing to intuition and "common sense," we have not yet proved that any of our preconditions and postconditions accurately describe their algorithms. In this section and the next, we will learn how to write mathematical proofs of correctness to verify that a given algorithm works according to its specifications.

Preview 5.5

1. Suppose you have a stack of two boxes, a small one on top of a larger one. There are three platforms capable of bearing the weight of the boxes, and you want to move the stack to the third platform. However, you can move only one box at a time, and you can't put the big box on top of the smaller one. Find a sequence of moves to accomplish this task. Invent your own notation to represent your sequence.

2. Now suppose you have a stack of three boxes, and you want to move the stack to the third platform under the same constraints as in preview question 5.5.1: move one box at a time, and never put a box on one that is smaller. Find an appropriate sequence of moves.

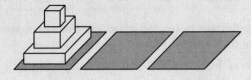

5.5.1   Verification vs. Testing

Generally speaking, there are two ways to check that an algorithm will behave properly. The first, and most common, is *program testing*. We enter our algorithm into a computer, enter some data that satisfies the preconditions, and check to see if the output satisfies the postconditions. Programmers always test their programs; they try to concoct as many different kinds of sets of input data as needed to convince themselves that their program works. The problem with program testing is that it can never, with 100% certainty, tell you that a program will always work (unless you are able to test every possible data set—an unlikely circumstance).

The second method, *program verification*, tells us more than testing can tell us: it gives a mathematical proof that, no matter what data is input into the program, the output will always satisfy the postconditions.

It is always better to verify than to test. Unfortunately, program verification is hard, except for small, self-contained routines. The primary value of learning program verification lies in applying logical thinking to algorithms. A programmer who understands program verification is more likely to write correct code.

Recall from Section 5.1 that an algorithm is *correct* if

$$\text{Preconditions} \Rightarrow \text{Postconditions},$$

where the preconditions are evaluated before program execution, and the postconditions are evaluated after. Therefore, to prove that an algorithm is correct, you assume the preconditions as given, and you try to deduce the postconditions by analyzing the code.

5.5.2   Verifying Recursive Algorithms

Recursive algorithms can be easy to verify if you understand induction. The examples in this section should remind you of the proofs in Chapter 3. In fact, the following example first appeared in Section 3.4, only with different notation.

Example 5.19 Prove that the string reversal algorithm of Example 5.6 is correct.

Solution: In order to write a proof of correctness, we need to state the preconditions and postconditions.

Preconditions: $s = c_1c_2c_3 \cdots c_n$ is a string, possibly empty.
Postconditions: $\texttt{Reverse}(s) = c_nc_{n-1}c_{n-2} \cdots c_2c_1$.

Before looking at the proof, let's remind ourselves about mathematical induction. The preconditions and postconditions are statements about a string of length n, so it seems natural to do induction on n. We are trying to conclude the postconditions, so the base case needs to check the postconditions for the string with $n = 0$ symbols—the empty string λ.

> **Base Case:** $\texttt{Reverse}(\lambda) = \lambda$.

The inductive hypothesis looks like the statement we are trying to prove, but with n replaced by $k - 1$.

> **Inductive Hypothesis:** If $c_1c_2c_3 \cdots c_{k-1}$ is a string of length $k - 1$ for some $k > 0$, then $\texttt{Reverse}$
> $(c_1c_2c_3 \cdots c_{k-1}) = c_{k-1} \cdots c_2c_1$.

Once we have proved the base case and stated the inductive hypothesis, all that is left to do is to prove the postconditions for $n = k$.

> **Need to Show:** $\texttt{Reverse}(c_1c_2c_3 \cdots c_k) = c_k \cdots c_3c_2c_1$.

Now that we have identified these key parts, writing down the inductive proof is fairly straightforward.

Proof We use induction on n, the length of the string. If $n = 0$, $s = \lambda$, the empty string. In this case, the first return statement is executed, and the function returns λ, the correct reversal of itself. In other words,

$$\texttt{Reverse}(\lambda) = \lambda.$$

Suppose as inductive hypothesis that, for any string of length $k - 1$,

$$\texttt{Reverse}(c_1c_2c_3 \cdots c_{k-1}) = c_{k-1}c_{k-2} \cdots c_2c_1$$

for some $k > 0$. Now suppose $\texttt{Reverse}$ is sent a string of length k.

$$\texttt{Reverse}(c_1c_2c_3 \cdots c_{k-1}c_k) = c_k \texttt{Reverse}(c_1c_2c_3 \cdots c_{k-1}) \qquad \text{using the algorithm}$$
$$= c_kc_{k-1}c_{k-2} \cdots c_2c_1 \qquad \text{by inductive hypothesis}$$

as required. □

Compare this proof with the proof of Theorem 3.4. ◇

Our first look at inductive proofs was back in Section 3.2, where we used induction to verify a closed-form solution to a recurrence relation. The following example recasts such a proof in the language of algorithms.

Example 5.20 Prove the correctness of the following algorithm for computing the Triangular Numbers.

Preconditions: $n \geq 1$.
Postconditions: $\texttt{Trinum}(n) = \dfrac{n(n + 1)}{2}$.

```
function Trinum (n ∈ N)
    if n = 1 then
        return 1
    else
        return n + Trinum (n − 1)
```

Proof (Induction on n.) Since $\texttt{Trinum}(1) = 1 = (1+1)/2$, the postconditions hold when $n = 1$. Suppose as inductive hypothesis that

$$\texttt{Trinum}(k-1) = \frac{(k-1)(k)}{2}$$

for some $k > 1$. Then

$$
\begin{aligned}
\texttt{Trinum}(k) &= k + \texttt{Trinum}(k-1) && \text{using algorithm} \\
&= k + (k-1)(k)/2 && \text{by inductive hypothesis} \\
&= (2k + k^2 - k)/2 \\
&= k(k+1)/2
\end{aligned}
$$

as required. □

To get started with an inductive proof, you need to identify the variable on which to perform the induction. Notice that in both of the preceding examples, this variable measures the size of the input. This is typically the case; remember that inductive arguments are appropriate for proving assertions of the form

$$\text{Statement}(n) \text{ for all } n.$$

When the input to an algorithm depends on n, the statement

$$\text{Preconditions} \Rightarrow \text{Postconditions}$$

will usually be of this form.

5.5.3 Searching and Sorting

We now have enough tools at our disposal to look at two important divide-and-conquer algorithms—the binary search and the merge sort—from the point of view of program correctness.

The next example is a little tricky. Although the size n of the set X is specified in the preconditions, the postconditions make a claim about a subset $\{x_l, x_{l+1}, \ldots, x_r\} \subseteq X$. The size of this subset, $r - l + 1$, is the quantity on which we perform the induction.

Example 5.21 Prove the correctness of Algorithm 5.4, the recursive binary search. (The algorithm is copied below for convenience.)

Preconditions: The set U is totally ordered by $<$, and $X = \{x_1, x_2, \ldots, x_n\} \subseteq U$, with $x_1 < x_2 < \cdots < x_n$ and $t \in U$. Also, $1 \le l \le r \le n$.
Postconditions: $\texttt{BinSearch}(t, X, l, r) = (t \in \{x_l, x_{l+1}, \ldots, x_r\})$

```
function BinSearch (t ∈ U,
                    X = {x₁, x₂, ..., xₙ} ⊆ U,
                    l, r ∈ {1, 2, ..., n})
    i ← ⌊(l + r)/2⌋
    if t = xᵢ then
        return true
    else
        ⌐ if (t < xᵢ) ∧ (l < i) then
              return BinSearch (t, X, l, i − 1)
```

```
        else
          ┌ if (t > xᵢ) ∧ (i < r) then
                return BinSearch(t,X,i+1,r)
             else
    └   └       return false
```

Proof We use induction on $r - l + 1$, the size of the list. If the list contains one element, then $l = r$, so i is set to $\lfloor (l+l)/2 \rfloor = l$. If $t = x_l$, the function returns true. If not, the comparisons $l < i$ and $i < r$ will fail, so the function will return false. In other words,

$$\text{BinSearch}(t,X,l,l) = (t \in \{x_l\}),$$

so the algorithm is correct for lists of size 1. Suppose, as inductive hypothesis, that the function returns true exactly when t is in the list, for lists of size $n - 1$ or less. In other words, suppose that

$$\text{BinSearch}(t,X,l,r) = (t \in \{x_l, x_{l+1}, \ldots, x_r\})$$

for any l, r satisfying $r - l + 1 < n$. Given a list $x_l, x_{l+1}, \ldots, x_r$ with $r - l + 1 = n$, the function will return true if $x_i = t$, where $i = \lfloor (l+r)/2 \rfloor$. If $t < x_i$, we know that t is in the list if and only if it is in $\{x_l, x_{l+1}, \ldots, x_{i-1}\}$. In this case,

$$\begin{aligned} \text{BinSearch}(t,X,l,r) &= \text{BinSearch}(t,X,l,i-1) && \text{by 2nd return statement} \\ &= (t \in \{x_l, x_{l+1}, \ldots, x_{i-1}\}) && \text{by inductive hypothesis} \\ &= (t \in \{x_l, x_{l+1}, \ldots, x_r\}) \end{aligned}$$

as required. A similar statement holds if $t > x_i$. □

This proof wasn't easy. Writing down rigorous proofs of correctness usually takes quite a bit of work. However, we can employ the same inductive technique slightly less formally to check just one part of the specified behavior of an algorithm.

Example 5.22 Assuming that the Merge subroutine (Algorithm 5.11) is correct, prove that the MergeSort function (Algorithm 5.12) returns an ordered list.

Proof We use strong induction on n, the size of the array to be sorted. If $n = 1$, MergeSort returns x_1, which is trivially in order. Suppose, as inductive hypothesis, that MergeSort$(x_1, x_2, \ldots, x_i)$ always returns an ordered list of size i, for any array of size $i < k$, for some $k > 1$. Given a list A of size k, MergeSort(A) returns Merge(MergeSort(L), MergeSort(R)), where L and R are lists of size less than k. By inductive hypothesis, MergeSort(L) and MergeSort(R) are also of size less than k and are ordered. Thus, the preconditions of the Merge subroutine are satisfied, so the postconditions imply that Merge(MergeSort(L), MergeSort(R)), is in order, as required. □

Although we haven't yet proved that the Merge subroutine works, we have shown that, if it does, the MergeSort will work also.

Learning to prove the correctness of recursive algorithms has an important side benefit: it develops the ability to write accurate recursive programs. For starters, the base case of a correct recursive function must satisfy the postconditions. Furthermore, any recursive call can make use of the assumption that the postconditions hold for simpler cases. For example, the call

$$\text{Merge}(\text{MergeSort}(x_1, x_2, \ldots, x_l), \ \text{MergeSort}(x_{l+1}, x_{l+2}, \ldots, x_n))$$

inside the MergeSort function returns a sorted list, assuming that MergeSort works on the smaller lists. This is the crux of the above inductive argument, but it is also a key principle that guides the recursive paradigm of algorithm design.

Activity 5.5.1: Quick Sort

Consider the following recursive algorithm, which accepts a list of sortable elements $x_1, x_2, x_3, \ldots, x_n$ (possibly empty) and returns a list of the same elements, but in order from least to greatest.

```
function QuickSort(L = (x₁,x₂,...,xₙ))
    if L is empty or L is a single element then
        return L
    else
        Make new empty lists L₁ and L₂
        for i ∈ {2,3,...,n} do
          ⌐ if xᵢ < x₁ then
                Add xᵢ to the end of L₁
             else
          └     Add xᵢ to the end of L₂
        return(QuickSort(L₁), x₁, QuickSort(L₂))
```

1. Compute `QuickSort(7)`.

2. Compute `QuickSort(∅)`.

3. What is the base case of `QuickSort`? Explain why the algorithm correctly sorts a list in the base case.

4. Write a top-down evaluation of `QuickSort(3,4,2)`. Construct a binary tree illustrating this evaluation. The nodes represent calls to `QuickSort`, and the return values go on the edges (e.g., as in Figure 5.2).

5. Construct a binary tree to illustrate the evaluation of `QuickSort(5,9,3,10,6,4,2,7)`.

6. Consider `QuickSort(L)`, where L is a list with more than one element. Suppose as inductive hypothesis that `QuickSort` correctly sorts any list shorter than L. Explain why `QuickSort(L)` returns a correctly sorted list.

5.5.4   Towers of Hanoi

We wrap up this section on recursion, induction, and program verification with a look at a classic mathematical puzzle: the Towers of Hanoi. This puzzle is worth pondering because it illustrates the power and elegance of recursive thinking, and because it gives us an example of an algorithm that is easy to verify, but hard to test.

The puzzle consists of three pegs and a stack of disks of descending sizes. (See Figure 5.9.) To begin, the disks are all stacked on the leftmost peg in order of size, with the largest on the bottom. The object is to move the entire pile of disks to the rightmost peg, subject to the following rules:

1. The top disk on any of the pegs may be moved to either of the other two pegs, where it then becomes the top disk.

2. Only one disk may be moved at a time.

3. A disk must never be placed on top of a smaller disk.

Figure 5.9 A version of the Towers of Hanoi puzzle with $n = 5$ disks.

In order to discuss how to solve this puzzle, we need to develop a little notation. Number the three pegs 1, 2, and 3 from left to right. A single move of a disk from one peg to another can then be represented by an ordered pair (p, q), with $\{p, q\} \subseteq \{1, 2, 3\}$. For example, in the case $n = 4$, the move sequence $(1, 2), (1, 3), (2, 1)$ proceeds as follows.

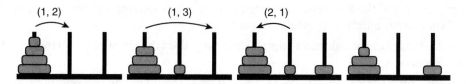

Our goal here is to write and prove the correctness of an algorithm to solve this puzzle for any value of n. As we think about how to write the algorithm, we can think ahead to how the inductive proof of correctness will go. The base case is easy to solve: when there is only $n = 1$ disk, we can just move it to the rightmost peg. The inductive hypothesis will be, roughly, that we can solve the puzzle for $n = k - 1$ disks. The trick to solving the $n = k$ disk case is to use the $n = k - 1$ case to do most of the work. Suppose k disks are initially stacked up on peg #1.

- Move the top $k - 1$ disks from peg #1 to peg #2, using the solution for $n = k - 1$.

- Move the remaining disk from peg #1 to peg #3.

- Use the $n = k - 1$ case again to move the stack from peg #2 to peg #3.

The formal pseudocode version of this algorithm, using the above ordered-pair notation, is shown in Algorithm 5.19.

Algorithm 5.19 Solving the Towers of Hanoi puzzle.

Preconditions: $n \in \mathbf{N}$, $p_{\text{from}}, p_{\text{to}} \in \{1, 2, 3\}$, $p_{\text{from}} \neq p_{\text{to}}$.

Postconditions: Returns a sequence of ordered pairs that represent legal moves that solve the Towers of Hanoi puzzle for n disks, where the disks are initially stacked on peg p_{from} and moved to peg p_{to}.

```
function Hanoi (n ∈ N, p_from, p_to ∈ {1, 2, 3})
    if n = 1 then
        return (p_from, p_to)
    else
        p_other ← other peg (not p_from or p_to)
        return Hanoi (n − 1, p_from, p_other),
               (p_from, p_to),
               Hanoi (n − 1, p_other, p_to)
```

The following top-down evaluation tests this algorithm for the case $n = 2$. Initially, the two disks are stacked on peg #1.

$$\begin{aligned} \text{Hanoi}\,(2, 1, 3) &= \text{Hanoi}\,(1, 1, 2), (1, 3), \text{Hanoi}\,(1, 2, 3) \\ &= (1, 2), (1, 3), (2, 3) \end{aligned}$$

This sequence of moves does, in fact, solve the puzzle for the $n = 2$ case. Testing the $n = 3$ case is left as an exercise, as well as proving the correctness of this algorithm for all n.

Another exercise will ask you to verify that this function always returns a sequence of $2^n - 1$ moves. So, for example, our algorithm will require

$$1,267,650,600,228,229,401,496,703,205,375$$

moves to solve the puzzle in the case of $n = 100$ disks. Suppose (generously) that a computer is able to produce and check this sequence at a speed of one nanosecond per move. Such a test would take about 40 trillion years! This calculation illustrates the power of program verification. Testing this program—even for relatively small values of n—is practically impossible, but proving its correctness for *all* values of n is easy to do.

Exercises 5.5

1. Can program testing ever prove that an algorithm is *not* correct? Explain.

2. The proof of correctness of the Reverse algorithm in Example 5.19 uses different notation than the proof of Theorem 3.4. What else is different about these two proofs?

3. See Example 5.21. What kind of induction (simple or strong) does the proof of correctness of the binary search algorithm use? Explain.

4. Suppose a recursive function Median $(x_1, x_2, \ldots, x_n \in \mathbf{R})$ has the following preconditions and postconditions.

   Preconditions: $x_1, x_2, \ldots, x_n \in \mathbf{R}$.

   Postconditions: Returns the median of $x_1, x_2, \ldots, x_n$.

   Answer the following questions regarding a possible proof of correctness by induction.

   (a) What is the base case?

   (b) What is the inductive hypothesis, assuming the proof uses simple induction?

   (c) What is the inductive hypothesis for strong induction?

   (d) What would you then have to show to finish the proof?

5. Let U be a set whose elements can be put into a binary search tree. A recursive function MakeTree $(u_1, u_2, \ldots, u_n \in U)$ for making a binary search tree has the following preconditions and postconditions.

   Preconditions: $u_1, u_2, \ldots, u_n \in U$.

   Postconditions: Returns a binary search tree whose nodes are $u_1, u_2, \ldots, u_n$.

   Answer the following questions regarding a possible proof of correctness by induction.

   (a) What is the base case?

   (b) What is the inductive hypothesis for simple induction?

   (c) What is the inductive hypothesis for strong induction?

   (d) What would you then have to show to finish the proof?

6. Prove that the following algorithm is correct.

   Preconditions: n is an odd natural number.

   Postconditions: Square $(n) = \left(\dfrac{n+1}{2}\right)^2$.

   ```
   function Square (n ∈ N)
       if n = 1 then
           return 1
       else
           return n + Square (n − 2)
   ```

7. Prove the correctness of the following algorithm.

   Preconditions: $n \geq 1$.

   Postconditions: P $(n) = (n^2 + n)/2$.

   ```
   function P (n ∈ N)
       if n = 1 then
           return 1
       else
           return n + P(n − 1)
   ```

8. Prove the correctness of the following algorithm.

   Preconditions: $n \geq 1$.

   Postconditions: MyNum $(n) = 2^n - 1$.

```
function MyNum (n ∈ N)
    if n = 1 then
        return 1
    else
        return 2 · MyNum (n − 1) + 1
```

9. Prove that the following algorithm is correct.

   Preconditions: $n \geq 0$.

   Postconditions: $P(n) = 2 - \left(\dfrac{1}{2}\right)^n$.

   ```
   function P (n ∈ Z)
       if n = 0 then
           return 1
       else
           return 1 + 1/2 · P (n − 1)
   ```

10. In Exercise 22 of Section 5.1, you wrote a pseudocode version of the recurrence relation for the hexagonal numbers, and you gave descriptive preconditions and postconditions. Prove that your algorithm is correct.

11. Prove that the following algorithm is correct.

    Preconditions: $n = 2^p$ for some integer $p \geq 0$.

    Postconditions: $\text{PLog}(n) = \log_2 n$.

    ```
    function PLog (n ∈ N)
        if n = 1 then
            return 0
        else
            return 1 + PLog (n/2)
    ```

*12. Prove that the following algorithm is correct.

    Preconditions: $n \geq 1$.

    Postconditions: $\text{ILog}(n) = \lfloor \log_2 n \rfloor$.

    ```
    function ILog (n ∈ N)
        if n = 1 then
            return 0
        else
            return 1 + ILog (⌊n/2⌋)
    ```

13. Prove that the following algorithm for computing powers is correct.

    Preconditions: $n \geq 0$, $x \in \mathbf{R}$, and n, x are not both zero.

    Postconditions: $\text{Power}(x, n) = x^n$.

    ```
    function Power (x ∈ R,  n ∈ Z)
        if n = 0 then
            return 1
        else
            return x · Power (x,  n − 1)
    ```

14. The following algorithm is a "quicker" version of the algorithm in Problem 13. Notice that the preconditions and postconditions are the same. Prove that this faster algorithm is correct.

    Preconditions: $n \geq 0$, $x \in \mathbf{R}$, and n, x are not both zero.

    Postconditions: $\text{QPower}(x, n) = x^n$.

```
function QPower (x ∈ R,  n ∈ Z)
    if n = 0 then
        return 1
    else
      ┌ if n is even then
            return (QPower(x, n/2))²
          else
      └     return x · (QPower(x, (n − 1)/2))²
```

15. Refer to the algorithms in Problems 13 and 14. Use top-down evaluations to compute the following.

   (a) Power(2, 10)

   (b) QPower(2, 10)

16. Prove that the preorder traversal of Algorithm 5.5 visits every node in the tree exactly once.

17. Prove that the FindMax function of Algorithm 5.10 is correct.

18. Prove that the following recursive sequential search algorithm is correct.

Algorithm 5.20 Recursive Sequential Search.

Preconditions: The set U is totally ordered by $<$, and $X = \{x_1, x_2, \ldots, x_n\}$ is a (possibly empty) subset of U.

Postconditions: RSearch$(t, X) = (t \in X)$.

```
function RSearch (t ∈ U, X ⊆ U)
    if X = ∅ then
        return false
    else
        return (t = xₙ) ∨ RSearch(X \ {xₙ})
```

---

19. In Exercise 24 of Section 5.2, you wrote a divide-and-conquer algorithm that computes the sum of all elements of a finite set $K = \{k_1, k_2, \ldots, k_n\}$ of integers. Prove that your algorithm is correct.

20. Prove: If $x \mid m$ and $x \mid (n \bmod m)$, then $x \mid n$.

21. Prove that the GCD function in Exercise 17 of Section 5.1 returns a number that divides both m and n. (Use strong induction on m.)

22. Test Algorithm 5.19 for solving the Towers of Hanoi puzzle in the case of $n = 3$ disks using a top-down evaluation.

23. Prove the correctness of Algorithm 5.19. You will need to check that the algorithm always makes legal moves, and that the returned sequence of moves represents a valid solution for all $n \geq 1$.

24. Use a recurrence relation to show that Algorithm 5.19 will always return a sequence of $2^n - 1$ ordered pairs.

5.6   Loop Invariants

Recursive algorithms are relatively easy to verify because it is easy to think of a recursive algorithm as a recursive definition, so it is natural to apply induction. In practice, however, iterative algorithms tend to be more common. In this section we will see how loop invariants can be used to prove the correctness of iterative algorithms. This study has an important side effect. As you begin to think more mathematically about looping structures, your ability to write accurate algorithms will improve.

Preview 5.6

---

1. Tim and Kim work in an ice cream shop. At the beginning of the year, Tim makes $5 per hour and Kim makes $10 per hour. Each month, Tim gets a $0.20 raise and Kim gets a $0.40 raise. Use algebra to explain why Kim always makes twice as much as Tim.

2. The *Euler characteristic* χ of a polygonal mesh is the number of faces minus the number of edges plus the number of vertices. For example, the triangular mesh of the octagon below has $\chi = 6 - 13 + 8 = 1$. Refine this mesh by adding an edge to split one of the faces into two faces. How does the value of χ change? Make a conjecture.

3. Construct two different triangular meshes of a cube and compute the Euler characteristic χ of each. Make a conjecture.

5.6.1 Verifying Iterative Algorithms

The basic idea behind loop invariants is simple: if we can isolate what each iteration of the loop does, then we have a good chance of knowing the cumulative effect of the loop. Stating this idea precisely takes a little bit of patience.

Definition 5.9 Let S represent a segment of pseudocode inside a loop. A *loop invariant* is a predicate statement P in the program variables with the property that, if P is true before S executes, P will be true after S executes. More formally, let $x_1, x_2, \ldots, x_n$ be the program variables. For all i, let $\underline{x_i}$ denote the value of the program variable x_i before S executes, and let $\bar{x_i}$ denote the value of x_i after S executes. Then the predicate $P(x_1, x_2, \ldots, x_n)$ is an invariant if

$$P(\underline{x}_1, \underline{x}_2, \ldots, \underline{x}_m) \Rightarrow P(\bar{x}_1, \bar{x}_2, \ldots, \bar{x}_m).$$

The notation in this definition is a necessary evil. For variables that change inside the loop, we keep track of before and after values using underlines and overlines. The notation is meant to be suggestive:

```
// assert: x = x
pseudocode inside loop that changes the value of x
// assert: x = x
```

Think of the line (over or under) as representing the pseudocode inside the loop. Then $\underline{x}$ is the value of x before executing this "line" of pseudocode, and $\bar{x}$ is the value after.

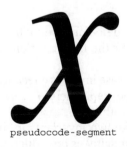

pseudocode-segment

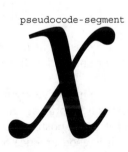

The $\underline{x}$ on the left denotes the value of x before the `pseudocode-segment` is executed, and the $\bar{x}$ on the right denotes the value after the segment is executed. The bar in the notation represents the segment of pseudocode: x takes its value before (above) or after (below) the segment.

We use the word "invariant" because the predicate P stays true, no matter how many times the loop is executed. As long as P is true to begin with, its truth doesn't vary, even though the values of the program variables are changing. If you can show that an invariant is true before a loop starts, then it will be true after any number of iterations of the loop. In particular, the invariant will be true after the loop terminates. In other words, the invariant will give you a postcondition on the loop.

The hardest thing about loop invariants is finding a useful (and valid) one that yields a good postcondition. We'll start with a simple example.

Example 5.23 Consider the following algorithm.

```
i ← 0
j ← 0
while i < n do
       ⌐ i ← i + 1
       ⌐ j ← j + 2
```

Show that the statement $j = 2i$ is an invariant for this `while`-loop.

Proof Let $i = \underline{i}$ and $j = \underline{j}$ before the segment

```
⌐ i ← i + 1
⌐ j ← j + 2
```

executes, and let $\bar{i}$ and $\bar{j}$ denote the values of i and j after execution. To prove that $j = 2i$ is an invariant, we need to show that

$$\underline{j} = 2\underline{i} \implies \bar{j} = 2\bar{i}.$$

The first assignment statement is the only statement that changes the value of i. Therefore,

$$\bar{i} = \underline{i} + 1,$$

or equivalently, $\underline{i} = \bar{i} - 1$. Similarly, $\bar{j} = \underline{j} + 2$. Suppose $\underline{j} = 2\underline{i}$. Then

$$\bar{j} = \underline{j} + 2$$
$$= 2\underline{i} + 2$$
$$= 2(\bar{i} - 1) + 2$$
$$= 2\bar{i}$$

as required.   □

We have proved—rather formally—a fact that we could have easily checked informally. Notice that if you trace through this algorithm, the values of i and j are as follows.

i	0	1	2	3	...
j	0	2	4	6	...

It seems clear that j is always twice as big as i. Certainly this is true before the loop executes: $0 = 2 \cdot 0$. We have proved that $j = 2i$ is a loop invariant, so $j = 2i$ remains true after the first iteration, and the second, and so on, until the loop terminates.

Notice that this is essentially an inductive argument. The base case involves checking that $j = 2i$ before entering the loop. The proof that $j = 2i$ is a loop invariant is the inductive step. Therefore, by induction, $j = 2i$ after any number of loop iterations, so $j = 2i$ is a postcondition on this algorithm.

When writing algorithms, it is good practice to include any known invariants in the code as comments, as in the next example. Note also that the following proof is written explicitly as an inductive argument.

Example 5.24 Prove the correctness of the following routine using the given loop invariant.

Preconditions: $m, n \in \mathbf{Z}$, $m \geq 0$, $n > 0$.

Postconditions: $q = \lfloor m/n \rfloor$, $r = m \bmod n$.

```
q ← 0, r ← m
// invariant: m = qn + r, r ≥ 0
while r ≥ n do
    q ← q + 1
    r ← r - n
```

Proof We use induction on the number of times through the loop. Before the loop executes, $q = 0$ and $r = m$, so we check that $m = 0 \cdot n + m$, which is true. Let $\underline{q}$ and $\underline{r}$ be the values of q and r before going through the loop, and suppose as inductive hypothesis that $m = \underline{q}n + \underline{r}$ with $\underline{r} \geq 0$. After one more iteration,

$$\overline{q} = \underline{q} + 1 \tag{5.6.1}$$

$$\overline{r} = \underline{r} - n \tag{5.6.2}$$

and $\overline{r} \geq 0$, since $r \geq n$ was a condition of entering the loop. Therefore,

$$
\begin{aligned}
m &= \underline{q}n + \underline{r} && \text{by inductive hypothesis} \\
&= (\overline{q} - 1)n + \overline{r} + n && \text{using Equations 5.6.1 and 5.6.2} \\
&= \overline{q}n + \overline{r}
\end{aligned}
$$

By induction, the invariant will be true after every iteration of the loop, and therefore, also at loop termination, when $r < n$. So when the routine finishes, $m = qn + r$ with $0 \leq r < n$, which means that $q = \lfloor m/n \rfloor$ and $r = m \bmod n$. □

You might be wondering why, in the last proof, the variables q and r sometimes have lines above or below them, but the variables m and n do not. The answer points to a good rule of thumb: the loop changes the value of q and r, but the values of m and n remain constant during loop execution. Therefore, we need to keep track of the before/after values of q and r with the underlines/overlines, but this notation is unnecessary for the fixed variables m and n.

Activity 5.6.1: Loop Invariants

The precondition for the following algorithm is that n is a natural number. The goal of this activity is to determine, with proof, a formula for the output value x in terms of the input value n.

```
x ← 0
k ← n
while k > 1 do
  ⌈ x ← x + 1
  ⌊ k ← ⌊k/2⌋
```

1. Let $\underline{x}$ be the value of x before the two lines inside the while-loop are executed, and let $\overline{x}$ be the value of x after these lines execute. Write an equation relating $\underline{x}$ and $\overline{x}$.

2. Similarly, write an equation relating $\underline{k}$ and $\overline{k}$.

3. When k is even, $\lfloor k/2 \rfloor = k/2$. Use this fact to write a version of your equation from Question 2 that applies when $\underline{k}$ is even.

4. When k is odd, $\lfloor k/2 \rfloor = (k-1)/2$. Use this fact to write a version of your equation from Question 2 that applies when $\underline{k}$ is odd.

5. Suppose that $\underline{k}$ is even, and that $2^{\underline{x}} \cdot \underline{k} \leq n$. Use your equations from Questions 1 and 3 to prove that $2^{\overline{x}} \cdot \overline{k} \leq n$.

6. Suppose that $\underline{k}$ is odd, and that $2^{\underline{x}} \cdot \underline{k} \leq n$. Use your equations from Questions 1 and 4 to prove that $2^{\overline{x}} \cdot \overline{k} \leq n$.

7. Questions 5 and 6 establish that the statement $2^x \cdot k \leq n$ is an invariant for the while-loop. Show that this statement is true before the while-loop executes.

8. Determine the value of k when the loop exits, and use this value to derive an inequality that must hold when the above algorithm finishes.

9. Similarly, prove that the statement $2^x(k+1) > n$ is also an invariant for the while-loop.

10. Check that the statement $2^x(k+1) > n$ is true before the while-loop begins, and use the exit value of k to derive another inequality that must hold when the algorithm finishes.

11. Apply $\log_2$ to both sides of the two inequalities you derived in Questions 8 and 10. What do you conclude about the final value of x?

5.6.2   Searching and Sorting

In the last section, we verified some recursive algorithms for searching and sorting. We now verify iterative versions using loop invariants.

Example 5.25 Consider the iterative binary search (Algorithm 5.3). The pseudocode routine inside the `while`-loop is as follows.

$$i \leftarrow \lfloor (l + r)/2 \rfloor$$

```
if  t > x_i  then
    l ← i + 1
else
    r ← i
```

Prove the following loop invariant for the `while`-loop.

$$(t \in \{x_1, x_2, \ldots, x_n\}) \Rightarrow (t \in \{x_l, x_{l+1}, \ldots, x_r\}), \text{ with } 1 \le l \le r \le n.$$

Proof Let $\underline{l}$ and $\underline{r}$ represent the values of l and r before the above pseudocode segment executes. Suppose that the invariant holds for these values of l and r; that is, suppose that

$$(t \in \{x_1, x_2, \ldots, x_n\}) \Rightarrow (t \in \{x_{\underline{l}}, x_{\underline{l}+1}, \ldots, x_{\underline{r}}\})$$

with $1 \le \underline{l} \le \underline{r} \le n$. Set $i = \lfloor (\underline{l} + \underline{r})/2 \rfloor$, and note that this implies that $\underline{l} \le i \le \underline{r}$. Suppose that $t \in \{x_1, x_2, \ldots, x_n\}$, so by assumption, $t \in \{x_{\underline{l}}, x_{\underline{l}+1}, \ldots, x_{\underline{r}}\}$. If $t > x_i$, then t must be in the subset $\{x_{i+1}, x_{i+2}, \ldots, x_{\underline{r}}\}$, since the list is in order. In this case, the pseudocode segment sets $\bar{l} = i + 1$ (which is still less than $\underline{r}$) and sets $\bar{r} = \underline{r}$. If $t \le x_i$, then t must be in the subset $\{x_{\underline{l}}, x_{\underline{l}+1}, \ldots, x_i\}$, so the segment sets $\bar{l} = \underline{l}$ and $\bar{r} = i$. In either case,

$$t \in \{x_{\bar{l}}, x_{\bar{l}+1}, \ldots, x_{\bar{r}}\}$$

with $1 \le \bar{l} \le \bar{r} \le n$ as required. □

This invariant expresses the fact that t remains in the set $\{x_l, x_{l+1}, \ldots, x_r\}$ even as the values of l and r change. Once the invariant has been established, it is easy to prove the correctness of the algorithm.

Example 5.26 Use the above loop invariant to prove the correctness of the iterative binary search (Algorithm 5.3).

Proof Before the loop executes, $l = 1$ and $r = n$, so the loop invariant becomes

$$(t \in \{x_1, x_2, \ldots, x_n\}) \Rightarrow (t \in \{x_1, x_2, \ldots, x_n\}), \text{ with } 1 \le 1 \le n \le n,$$

which is true. Therefore, by induction, the invariant is true when the loop finishes. At loop termination, $l = r$, so the invariant implies that

$$(t \in \{x_1, x_2, \ldots, x_n\}) \Rightarrow (t \in \{x_l\}),$$

which is equivalent to the postconditions. □

The loop invariant in this last proof was a sort of "postcondition in progress." The binary search algorithm works by moving l and r closer together, all the while keeping the target in the set $\{x_l, x_{l+1}, \ldots, x_r\}$. Once $l = r$, the postcondition in progress becomes the desired postcondition.

When a loop manipulates an array, a good loop invariant often makes a statement about the desired result for part of the array. For example, consider the following sorting algorithm.

Algorithm 5.21 Selection Sort.

Preconditions: The elements of the array $x_1, x_2, x_3, \ldots, x_n$ can be compared by $\leq$. In addition, $n \geq 1$.

Postconditions: $x_1 \leq x_2 \leq x_3 \leq \cdots \leq x_n$.

```
i ← 1
while i < n do
    ⌐ m ← i
      j ← i + 1
      while j ≤ n do
          ⌐ if xj < xm then
                m ← j
          ∟ j ← j + 1
      swap xi and xm
    ∟ i ← i + 1
```

The selection sort works by searching the list for the smallest element, putting it in front, then searching for the next smallest element, putting it in the next position, and so on. Since this process builds up the ordered list from left to right, a good invariant for the while-i loop is the statement that the first i elements are in order. But before we can prove anything about the while-i loop, we must first show that the while-j loop correctly locates the smallest element in the set $\{x_i, x_{i+1}, \ldots, x_n\}$. This is also done with a loop invariant.

Lemma 5.2 Suppose $1 \leq i < n$. The statement

$$x_m = \text{minimum}\{x_i, x_{i+1}, \ldots, x_{j-1}\}$$

is an invariant for the loop in the following pseudocode segment.

```
m ← i
j ← i + 1
while j ≤ n do
    ⌐ if xj < xm then
          m ← j
    ∟ j ← j + 1
```

Furthermore, when the loop terminates, $x_m = \text{minimum}\{x_i, x_{i+1}, \ldots, x_n\}$.

Proof Exercise.   □

We can now use this lemma to verify the selection sort algorithm.

Example 5.27 Prove the correctness of the selection sort (Algorithm 5.21).

Proof We begin by showing that the following statement is an invariant for the while-i loop in Algorithm 5.21.

The smallest $i - 1$ elements of $x_1, x_2, \ldots, x_n$ are in order at the front of the list.[6]

Let $i = \underline{i}$, and, for $1 \leq k \leq n$, let $x_k = \underline{x_k}$ before the following segment executes.

```
⌐ m ← i
  j ← i + 1
  while j ≤ n do
        ⌐ if xj < xm then
              m ← j
        ∟ j ← j + 1
  swap xi and xm
∟ i ← i + 1
```

---

6. More formally, this invariant says that $x_1 \leq x_2 \leq \cdots \leq x_{i-1}$, and $x_{i-1} \leq x_k$ for $i \leq k \leq n$, where the case $i = 1$ is vacuous; the invariant makes no claims about the list when $i = 1$.

Suppose that the smallest $i - 1$ elements of $\underline{x}_1, \underline{x}_2, \ldots, \underline{x}_n$ are in order at the front of the list. By Lemma 5.2, the segment finds m such that

$$\underline{x}_m = \mathrm{minimum}\{\underline{x}_i, \underline{x}_{i+1}, \ldots, \underline{x}_n\}.$$

Then the values of x_i and x_m are swapped, so $\overline{x}_i = \underline{x}_m$. Finally, i is incremented, so $\overline{i} = \underline{i} + 1$, which means that $\overline{x}_{\overline{i}-1} = \underline{x}_m$.

Now the values of $x_1, x_2, \ldots, x_{i-1}$ have not changed, so the smallest $\overline{i} - 2$ elements of $\overline{x}_1, \overline{x}_2, \ldots, \overline{x}_n$ are in order at the front of the list. Furthermore, $\overline{x}_{\overline{i}-1}$ is the next smallest element, since $\underline{x}_m$ was chosen to be the minimum of the remaining elements. Therefore, the invariant holds: the smallest $\overline{i} - 1$ elements of $\overline{x}_1, \overline{x}_2, \ldots, \overline{x}_n$ are in order at the front of the list.

To finish the proof of correctness, we need to show that the invariant holds before the loop begins, and then evaluate the invariant at loop termination. Before the loop begins, $i = 1$, so the invariant makes a claim about "the smallest 0 elements" of the list. Since this claim is true vacuously, there is nothing to prove. At loop termination $i = n$, so the loop invariant implies that

$$x_1 \leq x_2 \leq \cdots \leq x_{n-1}$$

and $x_{n-1} \leq x_n$, the only remaining element. This statement is equivalent to the postconditions, as required.   □

Activity 5.6.2: Polynomial Evaluation

Suppose that $f(x) = a_n x^n + a_{n-1} x^{n-1} + \cdots + a_2 x^2 + a_1 x + a_0$ is a polynomial function, where the coefficients a_i are real numbers. Consider the following algorithm, where t is some real number.

```
y ← aₙ
i ← n
while i > 0 do
  ┌ i ← i − 1
  └ y ← aᵢ + yt
```

1. Write an equation giving $\underline{i}$ in terms of $\overline{i}$.

2. Write an equation relating y and $\overline{y}$. Make sure that you correctly choose between $a_{\underline{i}}$ and $a_{\overline{i}}$ when writing this equation. (Note that the value of t does not change, so it doesn't need before/after versions.)

3. Prove that the equation $y = a_n t^{n-i} + a_{n-1} t^{n-i-1} + \cdots + a_i$ is an invariant for the while-loop.

4. Check that this equation holds before the loop begins.

5. What is the value of i when the loop finishes? Write the invariant using this value of i.

6. Suppose that, before the algorithm executes, $f(x) = x^3 - 3x^2 + 10x - 4$, and $t = 2$. What is the value of y when the algorithm finishes?

5.6.3   Using Invariants to Design Algorithms

Understanding loop invariants can help you think about how to write algorithms. As an illustration, consider the problem of finding a zero of a continuous function $f(x)$, i.e., a point x where $f(x) = 0$.

Suppose that we start with two points a and b, $a < b$, such that $f(x)$ changes sign as x goes from a to b; that is, $f(a)f(b) \leq 0$. Since f is continuous, this implies that $f(x)$ has a zero in the interval $[a, b]$. We would like to close in on the zero of the function until we get within a certain desired accuracy. One approach would be to try to shrink the interval down in some systematic way, all the while making sure that the zero stays inside the interval. The condition that the zero remains in the interval will be our loop invariant; in symbols: $f(a)f(b) \leq 0$.

Now we need to decide on a way to shrink the interval down. Dividing it in half is probably the most straightforward thing to do. Thus, our algorithm will look something like this:

```
while (not done) do
    cut the interval in half
```

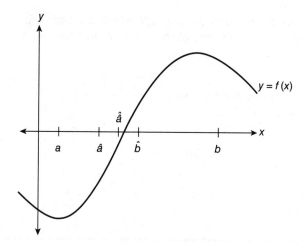

Figure 5.10 Finding a zero of a function by iteration.

When we cut the interval in half, we need to maintain the loop invariant. If we halve the interval by taking the midpoint, we can make sure the new interval contains the zero of f by replacing the appropriate endpoint (a or b) with the midpoint. We choose which endpoint to replace by making sure $f(x)$ changes signs over the new interval. If ε is some small error tolerance, we can repeat our loop until the interval has width ε. The result is shown in Algorithm 5.22.

Algorithm 5.22 Finding a zero of a continuous function.

Preconditions: $f : \mathbf{R} \longrightarrow \mathbf{R}$ is a continuous function, with $f(a)f(b) \leq 0$, and $\varepsilon > 0$.
Postconditions: $f(x) = 0$ for some x with $|x - a| < \varepsilon$ and $|x - b| < \varepsilon$.

```
while b − a ≥ ε do
  ⌐ m ← (a + b)/2
    if f(m)f(b) ≤ 0 then
        a ← m
    else
  ∟      b ← m
```

At loop termination, $f(a)f(b) \leq 0$, because we have designed our loop so that the above invariant holds. Furthermore, the exit conditions for the loop ensure that $b - a < \varepsilon$. Thus, both a and b are within ε of the desired zero of $f(x)$. Figure 5.10 illustrates this procedure.

Activity 5.6.3: Greatest Common Divisor

Recall that a natural number x *divides* a natural number y if $y = kx$ for some $k \in \mathbf{N}$. In this case, we write $x \mid y$.

The *greatest common divisor* of two natural numbers a and b is the number g such that $g \mid a$ and $g \mid b$ and, for any other common divisor d such that $d \mid a$ and $d \mid b$, we have $d \mid g$. We write $g = \gcd(a, b)$.

1. Find $\gcd(36, 20)$.

2. Prove that if $a > b$ and $g \mid a$ and $g \mid b$, then $g \mid (a - b)$.

3. Prove that if $a > b$ and $d \mid b$ and $d \mid (a - b)$, then $d \mid a$.

4. It follows from Questions 2 and 3 that $\gcd(a, b) = \gcd(a - b, b)$ whenever $a > b$. Similarly, if $a < b$, then $\gcd(a, b) = \gcd(a, b - a)$. Check that these identities are true for $\gcd(36, 20)$.

5. Consider the pseudocode skeleton below. Determine a *condition* for the while-loop and a *loop body* so that the statement

$$\gcd(a, b) = \gcd(x, y)$$

is an invariant for the `while`-loop, and so that, upon loop termination, $a = \gcd(x, y)$. (Hint: The *loop body* should modify a and/or b, making use of the identities in Question 4.)

$$
\begin{aligned}
&a \leftarrow x \\
&b \leftarrow y \\
&\texttt{// invariant: } \gcd(a, b) = \gcd(x, y) \\
&\texttt{while } [\textit{condition on a and b}] \texttt{ do} \\
&\qquad [\textit{loop body}]
\end{aligned}
$$

6. Test your algorithm when $x = 36$ and $y = 20$.

Exercises 5.6

1. For the following line of pseudocode, let $\underline{z}$ denote the value of the variable z before execution, and let $\bar{z}$ denote the value of z after execution.

   $$z \leftarrow 2z - 7$$

   (a) Suppose that $\underline{z} = 11$. What is $\bar{z}$?

   (b) Suppose that $\bar{z} = 3$. What is $\underline{z}$?

   (c) Write an equation giving $\bar{z}$ in terms of $\underline{z}$.

   (d) Write an equation giving $\underline{z}$ in terms of $\bar{z}$.

2. Consider the following loop.

   $$
   \begin{aligned}
   &\texttt{while } i < n \texttt{ do} \\
   &\qquad \ulcorner i \leftarrow i + 1 \\
   &\qquad\ \ j \leftarrow j + 1 \\
   &\qquad \llcorner k \leftarrow 10 \cdot k
   \end{aligned}
   $$

   Prove that each of the following statements is a loop invariant.

   (a) $i = j$

   (b) $i < j + 10$

   (c) $k = 10^i$

3. Let $n \in \mathbf{N}$. Consider the following algorithm.

   $$
   \begin{aligned}
   &i \leftarrow 0 \\
   &j \leftarrow 0 \\
   &k \leftarrow 1 \\
   &\texttt{while } i < n \texttt{ do} \\
   &\qquad \ulcorner i \leftarrow i + 1 \\
   &\qquad\ \ j \leftarrow j + 1 \\
   &\qquad \llcorner k \leftarrow 10 \cdot k
   \end{aligned}
   $$

   Use appropriate loop invariants from Exercise 2 to prove that each of the following statements is true after the algorithm executes.

   (a) $i = j = n$

   (b) $k = 10^n$

4. Show that the statement

   $$m \geq x \text{ for all } x \in \{x_1, x_2, \ldots, x_i\}$$

   is a loop invariant for the loop in the following pseudocode segment.

   Preconditions: $\{x_1, x_2, \ldots, x_n\} \subseteq \mathbf{Z}$

```
i ← 1
m ← x₁
while i < n do
   ⌐ i ← i + 1
      if xᵢ > m then
   ∟     m ← xᵢ
```

5. Use the invariant in Exercise 4 to give a postcondition on the algorithm.

6. In Section 5.2, we made the claim that the algorithm

```
for i ∈ {1, 2, ..., n} do
    visit xᵢ
```

   visits each element in the array $x_1, x_2, \ldots, x_n$ exactly once. Prove this claim formally using a loop invariant. (Hint: First, rewrite the algorithm using a while-loop instead of a for-loop.)

7. Use a loop invariant to prove that the following algorithm is correct.

   Preconditions: n is an odd natural number.

   Postconditions: $s = \left(\dfrac{n+1}{2}\right)^2$.

```
s ← 1
i ← 1
while i < n do
   ⌐ i ← i + 2
   ∟ s ← s + i
```

8. Use a loop invariant to prove that the following algorithm is correct.

   Preconditions: $n \in \mathbf{N}$

   Postconditions: $x = n!$

```
x ← 1
i ← 1
while i < n do
   ⌐ i ← i + 1
   ∟ x ← x · i
```

9. Consider the following algorithm.

   Preconditions: N is an even natural number.

```
i ← N
x ← N
y ← 0
while i > 0 do
   ⌐ i ← i - 2
     x ← x - 1
   ∟ y ← y + 1
```

   (a) Prove that the conjunction of statements

$$x + y = N \quad \wedge \quad x - y = i$$

   is an invariant for the while-loop.

   (b) Use the invariant to prove the correctness of a good postcondition on this algorithm.

   (c) Suppose that $N = 300$ before the algorithm begins. What is the value of x when the algorithm terminates?

10. Consider the following algorithm.

Preconditions: $n \in \mathbb{Z}$.

```
i ← 0
j ← 0
while i < n² do
   ⌐ i ← i + 1
   ∟ j ← j + 2i
```

(a) Prove that the statement $j = i^2 + i$ is an invariant for the `while`-loop.

(b) Use the invariant to find a postcondition on this algorithm that gives the value of j in terms of n.

11. Consider the iterative sequential search of Algorithm 5.1.

(a) Prove that the statement $t \notin \{x_1, x_2, \ldots, x_{i-1}\}$ is an invariant for the `while`-loop in this algorithm. (Interpret this statement as "$t \notin \emptyset$" when $i = 1$.)

(b) Suppose that $i = n + 1$ at loop termination. What can you conclude from this loop invariant?

12. Recall (Definition 3.1) that the Fibonacci numbers are defined by the following recurrence relation.

$$F(n) = \begin{cases} 1 & \text{if } n = 1 \text{ or } n = 2 \\ F(n-1) + F(n-2) & \text{if } n > 2 \end{cases}.$$

The following algorithm computes $F(n)$, the nth Fibonacci number.

Algorithm 5.23 Computing $F(n)$ iteratively.

Preconditions: $n \in \mathbb{N}$ and $n \geq 2$.

Postconditions: $x = F(n)$

```
x ← 1
y ← 1
i ← 2
while i < n do
   ⌐ t ← x
     x ← x + y
     y ← t
   ∟ i ← i + 1
```

(a) Prove that the statement

$$x = F(i) \text{ and } y = F(i-1)$$

is an invariant for the `while`-loop.

(b) Prove that the algorithm is correct.

13. Consider the following recursive algorithm for computing the nth Fibonacci number.

Algorithm 5.24 Computing $F(n)$ recursively.

Preconditions: $n \in \mathbb{N}$ and $n \geq 1$.

Postconditions: $x = F(n)$

```
function FibNum (n ∈ N)
    if (n = 1) ∨ (n = 2) then
        return 1
    else
        return FibNum (n − 1)  +  FibNum (n − 2)
```

(a) Use a recurrence relation to compute (in terms of n) the number of "+" operations performed by Algorithm 5.24.

(b) Compute (in terms of n) the number of "+" operations performed by the iterative Algorithm 5.23.

(c) Which algorithm is more efficient?

*14. Consider the merge subroutine of Algorithm 5.11. The goal of this exercise is to prove that this algorithm is correct.

(a) State an appropriate loop invariant. (Hint: It will be similar to [but not the same as] the invariant used to verify the selection sort in Example 5.27.)

(b) Prove that your proposed statement is a loop invariant. (Hint: Your proof can [and should] make use of the preconditions of the algorithm.)

(c) Prove that the Merge algorithm is correct.

*15. Use a loop invariant to prove the correctness of the bubble sort (Algorithm 5.2).

16. Use an invariant to show that Prim's algorithm (5.9) always produces a tree.

17. Use a loop invariant to prove that the following algorithm is correct.

Preconditions: $f(x) = a_0 + a_1 x + a_2 x^2 + \cdots + a_n x^n$, $t \in \mathbf{R}$.

Postconditions: $y = f(t)$.

$y \leftarrow a_n$
$i \leftarrow n$
while $i > 0$ do
⌐ $i \leftarrow i - 1$
∟ $y \leftarrow a_i + yt$

18. Trace through the selection sort (Algorithm 5.21) for $n = 4$ given initial values $x_1 = 5$, $x_2 = 2$, $x_3 = 7$, and $x_4 = 1$.

19. Approximate the complexity of the selection sort (Algorithm 5.21).

20. Prove Lemma 5.2.

21. Trace Algorithm 5.22 given initial values $a = 1$, $b = 5$, $\varepsilon = 0.7$, and $f(x) = \sin x$. (Make sure your calculator is in radians.)

22. Suppose Algorithm 5.22 is used with $f(x) = x^2 - 2$ for initial values $a = 1$, $b = 2$, and $\varepsilon = 0.00001$.

(a) What is the value of a, approximately, at loop termination?

(b) How many iterations does the loop perform?

23. Prove, formally, that the statement $f(a)f(b) \leq 0$ is an invariant for the loop in Algorithm 5.22.

Chapter 6
Thinking Through Applications

In the 1970s, music came on vinyl. The best way to get high-fidelity recordings of your favorite tunes was to invest in a good turntable and buy the LP—the "long playing" ($33\frac{1}{3}$-rpm) record. The grooves in an LP are a copy of the vibrations of the recorded sound; the turntable needle vibrates as it runs over these rising and falling grooves, and these vibrations are amplified and transmitted to the speakers, whose diaphragms vibrate to produce the desired sound waves. This method of recording is called *analog* because the form of the recording medium (the LP) is analogous to the form of the data (the sound waves). The grooves in an LP are continuous and relatively smooth; their shape matches the changes in frequency and amplitude of the sound.

In 1982, the introduction of the compact disc (CD) marked the beginning of a transition in consumer audio from analog to digital. The CD is a *digital* format because it encodes the sound wave data as a string of binary digits—0's and 1's. A CD player is basically a computer that is able to read this code and create the appropriate electronic signals to send to the speakers. Consequently, the mechanics of storage and playback became discrete processes, eventually leading to the streaming music industry that dominates the market today.

The transformation of sound recording technology illustrates the modern shift from the continuous to the discrete. The realm of continuous mathematics—most notably calculus—deals with things you measure: speed, distance, volume, and temperature. Discrete mathematics, in contrast, applies to things you can count: binary strings, sequences of operations, lists of data, and connections between objects. As computers have become better and more common, the discrete point of view has become more applicable to problems in science and industry.

This final chapter has a different character from the rest. In Chapters 1–5, we have studied the essential principles of discrete mathematics. Our perspective has been primarily mathematical; the chapters are organized around different types of mathematical thinking. In this chapter we consider a selection of applications of discrete

Figure 6.1 Digital recording formats use discrete mathematics.

mathematics to a range of different fields of study. This selection is by no means exhaustive, but hopefully it will convince you of the power and utility of discrete mathematical thinking.

A note to instructors and students: you will probably want to use the material in this chapter differently than the material in the other chapters. The case studies here are appropriate for individual or group projects, and the exercises are more involved and open-ended. The sections are not self-contained; they are designed to introduce applications and encourage further study. If you get frustrated, take a look at the references, and go from there.

6.1   Patterns in DNA

One of the most dramatic shifts from continuous to discrete techniques has taken place over the past 50 years in the discipline of biology. Ever since biologists began to discover and decipher the genetic code in DNA (deoxyribonucleic acid), they have had to grapple with the information hidden in gigantic strings of nucleotides—discrete data. The fields of molecular biology, and more specifically, bioinformatics, are now extremely active; increasingly, biology's microscope is being replaced by mathematics. [8]

6.1.1   Mutations and Phylogenetic Distance

A guiding principle in molecular biology is that two organisms are closely related if their DNA is similar. This principle is routinely applied to show, for example, that a child has a certain biological parent, or that two types of virus have a common ancestor. So it is important to be able to compare two genetic sequences and quantify how closely they match.

At a simple level, genetic information comes as a string in the symbols A, T, C, and G, which represent the four nucleotide bases: adenine, thymine, cytosine, and guanine. These strings naturally undergo changes, or *mutations*, during the process of cell division, or through external factors such as chemicals or radiation. Since some of these mutations are passed on to offspring, the descendant DNA will be slightly different from the parent, though similarities should be evident.

For example, the strings $a = $ TCTGGCGAGT and $b = $ TCTGGCTAGT differ in only one position, but the string $c = $ AAGACCGTGA looks completely unrelated to the others. So we would expect that it takes fewer mutations to get from a to b than from a to c. To quantify these differences, we could simply count the number of positions where the symbols don't match. This gives a discrete measure of the "distance" $d(x, y)$ between two strings x and y. For example, the diagram

```
    T  C  T  G  G  C  G  A  G  T
    A  A  G  A  C  C  G  T  G  A
    ↑  ↑  ↑  ↑  ↑        ↑     ↑
```

shows that $d($TCTGGCGAGT, AAGACCGTGA$) = 7$. Such a function is called a *phylogenetic distance* measure, because it quantifies how far apart two organisms are in the *phylogeny*, or evolutionary history, of a group of species.

In practice, phylogenetic distance measures are much more complicated than this basic example. For one thing, geneticists routinely work with much longer sequences, often consisting of hundreds or thousands of nucleotide bases. More significant, however, is the fact that mutations are more mysterious than the above portrayal suggests. A mutation may consist of a simple replacement of one base by another, but strings can also mutate by adding, deleting, or reversing substrings. For instance, the strings TCTGGCGAGT and TTGGCGAGT differ only by a single deletion, so counting differences in corresponding positions

```
    T  C  T  G  G  C  G  A  G  T
    T  T  G  G  C  G  A  G  T
       ↑  ↑     ↑  ↑  ↑  ↑  ↑  ↑
```

gives a misleading measure of distance. If we account for the possibility of deleted bases, these two strings should be regarded as closely related.

```
    T  C  T  G  G  C  G  A  G  T
    T     T  G  G  C  G  A  G  T
       ↑
```

Given a string of length 10 and a string of length 9, there are 10 ways to insert a blank into the shorter string to look for matches. In general, these problems require thinking about discrete quantities, using the techniques of Chapter 4.

Example 6.1 Let x be a string of length n, and let y be a string of length $n - k$, for $1 \leq k < n$. We wish to line up the symbols in x with the symbols in y by adding k blanks to y. How many ways are there to do this? Devise an algorithm.

Solution: The exercises have you explore some of the issues involved.   ◇

For more information about phylogenetic distance measures from a biological point of view, see Hillis et al. [14]. For a more mathematical perspective, take a look at the epilogue of Maurer et al. [20], which contains a nice study of some algorithms for pattern matching in DNA.

6.1.2   Phylogenetic Trees

The information hidden in the DNA of present-day species can give valuable clues about how these species may have evolved. The basic technique is simple: use the genetic data to estimate the phylogenetic distance between each pair of species, then find a weighted tree that best fits this data. Of course, the details of this technique are quite complicated. To get an idea of the issues involved, let's consider a simple example.

	A	B	C
A	0		
B	5.4	0	
C	3.2	5.0	0

Table 6.1 Pairwise phylogenetic distances of three related species.

Suppose A, B, and C are three related species, and suppose that we have estimates of the pairwise phylogenetic distances, shown in Table 6.1. In other words, $d(A, B) = 5.4$, $d(A, C) = 3.2$, and $d(B, C) = 5.0$. Since $d(x, y) = d(y, x)$ for all x and y, we don't bother filling in symmetric entries of the table.

For this example and the others in this section, let's operate under the assumption that the species we are studying have evolved from earlier, possibly unknown species. Thus, we need to find a tree whose leaves are A, B, and C, and whose internal nodes are hypothetical ancestral species. It seems reasonable, then, to consider trees with as few internal nodes as possible, so as to introduce as few hypothetical species as possible. If we further restrict our attention to binary trees (a common convention), there is really only one possible shape to consider: a full binary tree with three leaves:[1]

Without making further assumptions, we can assign A, B, and C to the leaves of this tree—in any order—and weight the edges appropriately to fit the data in Table 6.1. Figure 6.2 shows three possible configurations.

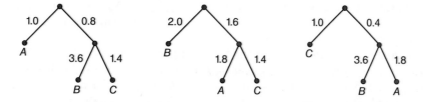

Figure 6.2 Three ways to assign leaves and weights to fit the data in Table 6.1.

---
1. See Exercise 20 of Section 3.3 for the definition of a full binary tree.

Which one of the three trees in Figure 6.2 is the most plausible phylogeny for species *A*, *B*, and *C*? In order to answer such a question, we need to make some more biological assumptions. For example, we might decide that the tree in the middle is the most reasonable, because its edges are roughly the same length. The biological assumption guiding this decision is that two different descendants of a common ancestor should be approximately equidistant from the ancestor; each descendant's DNA should have undergone roughly the same number of mutations.

There are many different methods for inferring a phylogenetic tree from distance data. Choosing the correct method involves knowing the assumptions that guide the method, and knowing which assumptions are reasonable for the given biological situation. The remainder of this section discusses one such method: the Unweighted Pair Group Method with Arithmetic Mean (UPGMA).

6.1.3   UPGMA

In order to discuss the UPGMA algorithm accurately, we need to have a precise definition of an evolutionary tree. The following definition should remind you of the recursive definitions we studied in Chapter 3.

Definition 6.1 An *evolutionary tree* for a set $\mathcal{T} = \{X_1, X_2, \ldots, X_n\}$ of organisms is

B. X_1, if $n = 1$.

R. $\{T_1, T_2\}$, where T_1 and T_2 are evolutionary trees for nonempty sets $\mathcal{T}_1$ and $\mathcal{T}_2$ such that $\mathcal{T}_1 \cap \mathcal{T}_2 = \emptyset$ and $\mathcal{T}_1 \cup \mathcal{T}_2 = \mathcal{T}$, if $n > 1$.

Graphically, an evolutionary tree can be represented by a binary tree whose leaves are $X_1, X_2, \ldots, X_n$. To draw a diagram of an evolutionary tree, interpret the recursive step **R** in the definition as introducing some unspecified internal node *r*, with subtrees T_1 and T_2. Biologically, *r* is a common ancestor of the organisms in $\mathcal{T}_1$ and $\mathcal{T}_2$.

Definition 6.1 is very similar to the recursive definition of binary trees (Example 3.22). The main difference is that we make no distinction between the left and right subtrees in an evolutionary tree, so we use the (unordered) set $\{T_1, T_2\}$ to represent the evolutionary tree with subtrees T_1 and T_2. Two trees are the same if they are the same as sets. For example, the following tree diagrams are equivalent; both represent the tree $\{\{A, \{B, C\}\}, D\}$.

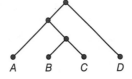 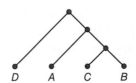

Since part **R** of Definition 6.1 always puts two smaller trees together by adding a common root, evolutionary trees (as we have defined them) are always binary trees. Since we don't allow empty subtrees, these binary trees are full. Notice that we usually draw them a bit differently from other binary trees; all the leaves, regardless of depth, appear on the same horizontal line. This drawing convention suggests that the leaves are known present-day organisms, while the internal nodes are (possibly unknown or extinct) ancestors.

Now that we have a mathematical definition of evolutionary trees, we can return to the problem of inferring a phylogenetic tree from pairwise distance data. The Unweighted Pair Group Method with Arithmetic Mean (UPGMA) [27, pp. 230–234] will produce a binary tree whose leaves are $X_1, X_2, \ldots, X_n$ and whose edges are weighted so that each internal node is the same distance from all its descendant leaves. This distance is called the *height* of the node.[2] The height of any leaf X_i is 0.

The formal description of this algorithm is intimidating at first. Informally, the algorithm works by gradually building up a tree from a set $\mathcal{P}$ of smaller trees. Initially, $\mathcal{P}$ contains only the one-node trees X_i. At each stage, the two closest trees are joined under a common root to form a new tree, and a distance from this new tree to all the other trees in $\mathcal{P}$ is calculated. This process repeats until $\mathcal{P}$ contains only a single tree.

---

2. Unfortunately, this standard biological terminology conflicts slightly with the standard mathematical use of "height" of a tree and "depth" of a node. When working across disciplines, you will often encounter differences in the way words are used.

Algorithm 6.1 UPGMA (adapted from [14]).

Preconditions: $X_1, X_2, \ldots, X_n$ represent n organisms, and the pairwise phylogenetic distance $d(X_i, X_j)$ is defined for all i, j.

Postconditions: The set $\mathcal{P}$ contains a single evolutionary tree, and each node in this tree is assigned a height that equals the distance to all its descendant leaves.

```
𝒫 ← {X₁, X₂, ..., Xₙ}
while |𝒫| > 1 do
    ⌐ Choose T,U in 𝒫 so that d(T,U) is minimized.
      Add the tree {T,U} to 𝒫 at height d(T,U)/2.
      // Let n_T, n_U denote the number of leaves in T,U.
      for W ∈ 𝒫 \ {{T,U}} do
```
$$d(\{T,U\}, W) \leftarrow \frac{n_T d(T,W) + n_U d(U,W)}{n_T + n_U}$$
```
      d({T,U}, {T,U}) ← 0
    ∟ Remove T and U from 𝒫.
```

The following statement is an invariant for the `while`-loop in Algorithm 6.1.

> $\mathcal{P}$ is a set of evolutionary trees, and the distance $d(T, U)$ is defined for any pair $T, U \in \mathcal{P}$.

Note that this statement is true before the loop begins, since each X_i can be regarded as a base-case evolutionary tree, and the pairwise distance data is given. The following example should help clarify how this algorithm works.

Example 6.2 The following table gives pairwise phylogenetic distances of seven fish-parasite species [32]. Calculate the UPGMA tree for this data.

	K	G	M	J	A	L	P
kobayashii	0						
gracilihamatus	20.0	0					
macronychus	31.0	31.1	0				
jussii	29.8	26.1	12.1	0			
aphyae	22.4	25.5	32.4	31.9	0		
leucisci	24.4	25.1	29.5	30.5	9.4	0	
pannonicus	23.8	25.2	31.2	30.1	8.3	7.3	0

Reproduced from Zietara, M. S., and Lumme, J. Speciation by host switch and adaptive radiation in a fish parasite genus *Gyrodactylus* (Monogenea, Gyrodactylidae). *Evolution* 56 (2002), 2445–2458.

Solution: In Algorithm 6.1, let $X_1, \ldots, X_7$ be K, G, M, J, A, L, P, respectively, representing the seven species. For each iteration of the `while`-loop, the following table lists the new tree that is added to $\mathcal{P}$.

$\lvert\mathcal{P}\rvert$	Minimum d	Tree added
7	7.30	$\{L, P\}$
6	8.85	$\{\{L, P\}, A\}$
5	12.10	$\{M, J\}$
4	20.00	$\{K, G\}$
3	24.40	$\{\{K, G\}, \{\{L, P\}, A\}\}$
2	30.25	$\{\{\{K, G\}, \{\{L, P\}, A\}\}, \{M, J\}\}$
1	—	—

As an exercise, you should complete this trace by computing the result of the `for`-loop at each step. Figure 6.3 shows the structure of the UPGMA tree. The height of each internal node forces the distance labels on the edges. ◇

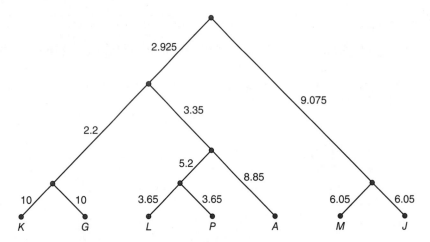

Figure 6.3 UPGMA tree for the data in Example 6.2.

In Figure 6.3, notice that the distances between leaves defined by the labels only approximate the given distance data; they don't fit the data exactly. For example, *K* and *A* were given as 22.4 units apart, but on the tree they appear 24.4 units apart.

By construction, any UPGMA tree has the property that every leaf is equidistant from the root. In biological terms, this means that all present-day organisms have undergone the same amount of evolutionary change from some common ancestor. So it only makes sense to use this algorithm if we are reasonably confident that evolutionary change occurs at a constant rate, as measured by our chosen phylogenetic distance measure.

Example 6.3 Construct a weighted tree that the UPGMA algorithm fails to reconstruct. That is, construct a weighted tree, and write down the distance data that your tree defines. Compute the UPGMA tree for this data. Find an example where these two trees are different as unweighted trees.

Solution: It is possible to construct a solution with as few as three leaves. The key is to construct a weighted tree in which the leaves are decidedly *not* equidistant from the root. ◇

In cases where the rate of evolutionary change is not constant, there are other tree reconstruction algorithms that are more appropriate. One common technique is the *neighbor-joining* method of Saitou and Nei [26]. Interested students can investigate the following.

Example 6.4 Read about the neighbor-joining algorithm in Saitou and Nei [26], Allman and Rhodes [2], or Hillis et al. [14]. Step through this algorithm using the distance data from the tree you created for Example 6.3. Explain why this algorithm handles nonconstant rates of evolutionary change better than UPGMA.

There are many more problems in bioinformatics that inspire interesting applications of mathematics. But the material in this brief case study alone should convince you that modern biology requires discrete mathematical thinking. In this section we have used logic, mathematical definitions, sets, functions, graphs, recursive definitions, counting techniques, algorithms, and loop invariants—a representative sample of the material in the first five chapters of this book. As technology continues to advance the study of biology, discrete ideas are likely to become even more essential to life scientists.

Exercises 6.1

1. Consider Example 6.1.

    (a) Suppose that we decide to add the *k* blanks in one continuous block. How many ways are there to do this?

    (b) Suppose that we add two separate blocks of blanks, one of size *i* and one of size $k - i$, for $1 \leq i < k$. How many ways are there to do this?

    (c) Design a recursive algorithm for traversing all the ways to add blanks to the smaller string. Investigate the complexity of your algorithm.

2. Compare the definition of an evolutionary tree (Definition 6.1) to the definition of an SList (Definition 3.5).

3. Draw two different full binary trees that both represent the evolutionary tree $\{\{\{A, B\}, C\}, \{D, \{E, F\}\}\}$.

4. Modify the weights on the middle tree in Figure 6.2 so that three of the edges have the same weight. Make sure the tree still fits the data of Table 6.1.

5. Consider the evolutionary tree $\{\{A, B\}, \{C, D\}\}$ for organisms A, B, C, D.

   (a) Draw a graph that represents this tree.

   (b) Label the edges of your tree to fit the following distance data exactly. Is your answer unique? Explain.

	A	B	C	D
A	0			
B	2.2	0		
C	4.3	4.5	0	
D	4.9	5.1	2.6	0

6. Is it possible to fit the data of Table 6.1 with a weighted tree of the following shape such that the two edges labeled "x" have the same weight? Exhibit such an assignment, or show that it is impossible.

7. Calculate the UPGMA tree for the data in Table 6.1. Does the tree fit the data exactly?

8. Complete the trace in Example 6.2 by computing the results of the for-loop for each iteration of the while-loop. The line

$$d(\{T, U\}, W) \leftarrow \frac{n_T d(T, W) + n_U d(U, W)}{n_T + n_U}$$

computes the new distance from the added tree $\{T, U\}$ to the tree W. For each $W \in \mathcal{P}$, compute these distances.

9. Can the loop invariant given after Algorithm 6.1 be strengthened? Explain.

10. Complete Example 6.3.

11. **Project:** Investigate pattern matching in DNA. Find (or write) an algorithm that searches for the largest substring that two strings (possibly of different lengths) have in common. Modify your algorithm to allow for the possibility that substrings may be reversed.

12. **Project:** Do what Example 6.4 says to do.

13. **Project:** Investigate the number of different possible evolutionary trees for a set of n organisms. You may wish to start with small values of n (like $1, 2, 3, \ldots$) and look for a pattern. See if you can find and solve a recurrence relation using a proof by induction.

14. **Project:** Make up your own algorithm for constructing a phylogenetic tree from distance data. What biological assumptions does your method make? Compare your method to UPGMA.

6.2   Social Networks

Sociology—the study of human society—addresses questions about the nature of interactions between people and the roles of individuals in social groups. While sociologists employ many different methods of research, mathematical ideas and techniques are becoming increasingly important to modern sociological theory. Many of these ideas are discrete: human interactions can be represented by mathematical relationships between the elements of a discrete set of individuals.

A *social network* is a graph model for the interactions among the members of a group. Ideas from graph theory apply directly to such models, and sociological concerns raise interesting mathematical questions about graphs. In this section we will consider a sample of topics in social network analysis, highlighting applications of the various ways of thinking we have studied in the first five chapters of this book.

6.2.1 Definitions and Terminology

Ideally, an application of mathematics involves three steps.

1. Construct a faithful model of a problem from another discipline.

2. Use a mathematical theorem to conclude something about the model.

3. Interpret the results to answer an important question in the other discipline.

While many interdisciplinary uses of mathematics fall short of this ideal, there is value in simply trying to express concepts from another field of study in mathematical language.

In this brief look at social network analysis, we will make lots of definitions while considering only a few theorems. But the definitions are quite useful in themselves; couching sociological ideas in mathematical language helps motivate new ways of describing social phenomena. Although we might not always be applying mathematical theory, we are applying the mathematical way of thinking.

Definition 6.2 A *social network* is a graph whose vertices are called *actors* and whose edges are called *ties*.

A social network can be almost any type of graph: directed or undirected, with weighted or unweighted edges. The actors are meant to represent individual units in society; actors can be people, teams, organizations, or any entity that interacts socially. The ties model social relationships: marriage, authority, collaboration, friendship, dependence, etc. Some relationships are symmetric (e.g., a is married to b if and only if b is married to a), so the ties are undirected. Other relationships may not be symmetric (e.g., a is the father of b), in which case the ties are directed. Sometimes a relationship carries with it some measure of strength (e.g., a argues with b on p percent of occasions), calling for ties that are labeled with numerical weights.

There are certain features of a social network that have socially significant interpretations. A *clique* can be defined as a complete subgraph of a social network that is not part of some larger complete subgraph.[3] For example, suppose that actors in the network shown in Figure 6.4 represent children in an elementary school. Two actors have a tie between them if they were observed eating lunch at the same cafeteria table during some observation period. The sets of actors $\{u, v, w, x\}$, $\{s, t, u\}$, and $\{y, z\}$ are cliques in this network; we might expect to see these groups of children playing together at recess.

A *liaison* is an actor whose removal would disconnect the graph. In Figure 6.4, u is a liaison between $\{s, t\}$ and the rest of the actors. For example, if the ties represent lines of communication, then a message from one of the actors in $\{v, w, x, y, z\}$ must pass through u in order to reach s or t.

Definitions can help identify the actors that play the most important roles in a social network. In an undirected network, an actor is *central* if it has many ties; one obvious measure of centrality is the degree of a vertex. By this measure, u is the most central actor in the network in Figure 6.4, followed by w and x. More sophisticated centrality measures also take into account other indicators of actor importance, such as the degrees of the neighboring actors. See Wasserman et al. [29], Chapter 5, for examples.

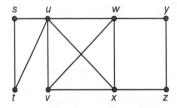

Figure 6.4 A social network with three cliques: $\{s, t, u\}$, $\{u, v, w, x\}$, and $\{y, z\}$.

---

3. Other definitions of "clique" exist.

In a directed network, an actor with many ties coming in is often called *prestigious*, while an actor with many ties going out may be called *influential*. Therefore, prestige and influence are most easily approximated by indegree and outdegree, respectively. Again, more complicated definitions can refine these measures.

In the following social network, suppose that the actors represent universities, and that a tie goes from university a to university b if a's best undergraduates go to b for graduate school. The most prestigious university in this social network is apparently v, while the most influential is w.

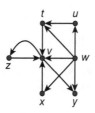

Depending on the context, the labels "prestigious" and "influential" may or may not be apt. For example, if the actors in a directed social network are teenagers, where a has a tie to b if a wants to be friends with b, then "popularity" may be a better descriptor than "prestige," and "gregariousness" might replace "influence." Notice that the task of finding appropriate names for indegree and outdegree helps us think about some facets of social interaction. Teenagers can be both popular and gregarious; these two qualities are somehow related, but they affect interpersonal relationships in distinct ways.

Social network theory also uses statistical techniques in interesting ways. Any time you deal with a sample of data, it is important to take into account the randomness of the sampling process. An observed social network may exhibit certain qualities, but in order to argue that these qualities are likely to occur in other networks, you need to use inferential statistics. This type of analysis goes far beyond the scope of this section, but the underlying structures are fundamentally discrete.

6.2.2   Notions of Equivalence

An important idea in sociology is the role that an individual plays in a group. We can explore this idea in social networks by defining ways in which actors are equivalently tied to other actors. One of the earliest definitions appears in Lorrain and White [19]. (Recall that a graph is *simple* if it has no loops or multiple edges.)

Definition 6.3 Two actors, a and b, in a simple social network are *structurally equivalent* if, for all actors v in the network, a has a tie to (resp. from) v if and only if b has a tie to (resp. from) v.

In other words, two actors are structurally equivalent if they are tied to the same set of actors, or in the case of a directed network, if they have ties out to the same set and ties in to the same set. Another definition helps formalize this statement.

Definition 6.4 In an undirected network, the *neighborhood* $N(a)$ of an actor a is the set of all actors that a is tied to. In a directed network, the *in-neighborhood* $N_{\text{in}}(a)$ is the set of all actors with ties coming in to a, and the *out-neighborhood* $N_{\text{out}}(a)$ is the set of all actors to which a has ties going out.

In this notation, actors a and b in a simple undirected network are structurally equivalent if $N(a) = N(b)$. Similarly, in a simple directed network, actors a and b are structurally equivalent if $N_{\text{in}}(a) = N_{\text{in}}(b)$ and $N_{\text{out}}(a) = N_{\text{out}}(b)$.

Structural equivalence is a very strong notion. Structurally equivalent actors in a network relate in exactly the same way to all other actors. In Figure 6.5, actors v and y are structurally equivalent: $N(v) = \{u, x, w, z\} = N(y)$.

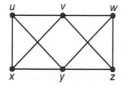

Figure 6.5 This social network illustrates different notions of equivalence.

However, even though actors u and x play very similar roles in this network, they are not structurally equivalent, because $N(u) = \{v, x, y\}$ while $N(x) = \{u, v, y\}$. This fact points out a strange quirk in the definition of structural equivalence.

Lemma 6.1 Suppose a and b are actors in a simple network, directed or undirected. If a has a tie to b, then a and b are not structurally equivalent.

Proof Exercise.   □

The following definition gives a weaker equivalence condition that fixes this quirk.

Definition 6.5 [31] Let N be a simple social network with actor set A. Two actors $a, b \in A$ are *automorphically equivalent* (written $a \equiv b$) if there is a one-to-one correspondence

$$f : A \longrightarrow A$$

such that $f(a) = b$ and having the following property: for any $x, y \in A$, x has a tie to y if and only if $f(x)$ has a tie to $f(y)$.

Compare this definition with the condition for graph isomorphism given in Theorem 2.5. Informally, an automorphism of a graph is a way of permuting the labels on the vertices without changing the structure of the graph. For example, we can define a one-to-one correspondence

$$f : \{u, v, w, x, y, z\} \longrightarrow \{u, v, w, x, y, z\}$$

by $f(u) = x$, $f(x) = u$, $f(v) = y$, $f(y) = v$, $f(w) = z$, and $f(z) = w$, and this defines an automorphism of the graph in Figure 6.5. This map also shows that $u \equiv x$, and that $v \equiv y$ and $w \equiv z$.

It is left as an exercise to check that Definitions 6.3 and 6.5 define equivalence relations on the set of actors in a social network. These equivalence relations partition the actors of a network into subsets.

Example 6.5 Consider the social network in Figure 6.5. The automorphism defined above shows that $v \equiv y$, $u \equiv x$, and $w \equiv z$. There is no automorphism mapping u to v, since u and v have different degrees, so $u \not\equiv v$. We can define another automorphism

$$g : \{u, v, w, x, y, z\} \longrightarrow \{u, v, w, x, y, z\}$$

by setting $g(u) = w$, $g(w) = u$, $g(x) = z$, $g(z) = x$, $g(v) = v$, and $g(y) = y$. This shows, in particular, that $u \equiv w$, so by transitivity, $x \equiv u \equiv w \equiv z$. Therefore, the automorphic equivalence classes are $\{v, y\}$ and $\{u, w, x, z\}$.

The goal of these definitions of equivalence is to capture the idea of the role of an actor in mathematical terms. The equivalence classes represent groups of actors that play the same role.

Example 6.6 Suppose that the ties in the social network in Figure 6.5 represent friendships between actors. The actors in the automorphic equivalence class $\{v, y\}$ both have more friends than the others, but v and y are not friends with each other. They play the role of rivals. The actors in the other equivalence class $\{u, x, w, z\}$ also have similar roles: they are the friends for whom v and y compete.

Actors that are automorphically equivalent play identical roles in a network, because any graph-theoretical property of a vertex (e.g., degree, membership in a clique) is preserved under graph isomorphism. But in many applications, the conditions for automorphic equivalence are too strong. For example, consider the graph in Figure 6.6. Suppose that the actors represent individuals who communicate with each other, and the ties represent two-way lines of communication.

The actors on the edges—the v_i's and z_i's—play similar roles. They can only communicate with one other actor, and nobody needs to communicate with them in order to get a message through to somebody else. In the language of graph theory, they are all leaves in this unrooted tree. However, they are not all automorphically equivalent to each other. Some are: for example, $v_5 \equiv v_6$; but many are not. Note, for instance, that $z_1 \not\equiv z_2$, because z_1 has a tie to an actor of degree 2, but z_2 does not.

We would like to define a type of equivalence that captures the essential idea of role without constraining the equivalence classes as tightly as automorphic equivalence does. Instead of trying to define a new equivalence relation on the set of actors, sociologists define a desirable property that some equivalence relations have.

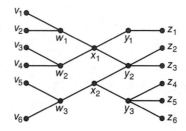

Figure 6.6 A social network representing lines of communication.

Definition 6.6 Let N be a social network with actor set A, and suppose R is an equivalence relation on A. Then R is called *regular* if, for all $a, b \in A$, $a R b$ implies that, for any $c \in A$ that has a tie to (resp. from) a, there is some $d \in A$ that has a tie to (resp. from) b such that $c R d$ [30].

In a regular equivalence relation, if one member of an equivalence class X has a tie to or from another equivalence class, then all members of X do. This property motivates the following definition.

Definition 6.7 Let R be a regular equivalence relation on a set of actors A in a social network N, and let $X_1, X_2, \ldots, X_n$ be the equivalence classes of A. The *quotient network* of N by R is the social network whose vertices correspond to the equivalence classes $X_1, X_2, \ldots, X_n$, where X_i has a tie to X_j if and only if some element of X_i has a tie to some element of X_j.

Definition 6.6 ensures that the ties in the quotient network are consistent with the ties in the original network. Although Definition 6.7 requires a weaker condition, it is in fact the case that *every* element of X_i has a tie to some element of X_j whenever X_i has a tie to X_j in the quotient graph. These definitions give us a way to see how the different roles in a social network interact.

Example 6.7 Define an equivalence relation R on the actors A in the social network in Figure 6.6 as follows: For actors $a, b \in A$, $a R b$ if and only if a and b are denoted with the same letter (though possibly with a different subscript). In other words, the equivalence classes of R are the sets $V = \{v_1, \ldots, v_6\}$, $W = \{w_1, w_2, w_3\}$, $X = \{x_1, x_2\}$, $Y = \{y_1, y_2, y_3\}$, and $Z = \{z_1, \ldots, z_6\}$. Clearly, R is an equivalence relation, because we have defined it by giving its partition. Checking formally that R is regular is a bit more tedious, but one can easily verify that it is by looking at Figure 6.6: the equivalence classes are drawn in columns, and it is easy to see that every member of every column has a tie to some member of every adjacent column, and every tie is accounted for in this way.[4]

The following graph is the quotient network of N by R.

Notice that the quotient network isolates the structure of how the different roles (i.e., equivalence classes) are related. Actors in the equivalence classes V and Z are peripheral communicators who must depend on actors in W and Y to get messages through the network. Actors in X are the most central; messages can't get from one side of the network to the other without passing through X.

It is left as an exercise to show that there are other regular equivalence relations on this network. In general, a network can have many regular equivalence relations, so part of the job of the sociologist is to find the regular equivalence relation that best describes the structure of the roles in the network. For large graphs, finding interesting regular equivalence relations isn't easy. See Borgatti and Everett [5] for descriptions of two possible algorithms.

6.2.3 Hierarchical Clustering

Social network data can come in many forms. So far, we have seen social networks modeling *dichotomous* relationships: either two actors are related, or they aren't. However, in many applications, sociological data may come with a natural measure of the strength of the relationship.

---

4. This is called verification "by inspection."

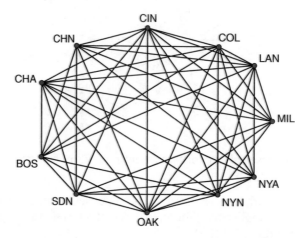

	BOS	CHA	CHN	CIN	COL	LAN	MIL	NYA	NYN	OAK	SDN
BOS											
CHA	7										
CHN	6	0									
CIN	15	4	5								
COL	14	6	4	16							
LAN	2	13	8	4	6						
MIL	0	8	14	3	7	7					
NYA	0	5	5	19	8	11	0				
NYN	4	6	0	7	20	12	10	8			
OAK	2	10	11	4	10	3	3	6	5		
SDN	25	5	9	5	0	0	6	15	9	5	

Figure 6.7 A social network representing trades between baseball franchises. The table lists the weights on each edge. (Data on Major League Baseball transactions can be found in the transaction file archive of Retrosheet [25].)

Example 6.8 Figure 6.7 shows a social network in which the actors are Major League Baseball franchises. Two franchises are connected by an edge if the two franchises have traded players during the years 2000–2006. The weights on each edge represent the total number of players involved in all trades between the two franchises. To keep the diagram uncluttered, the weights are given in the accompanying table.

The graph in Figure 6.7 is nearly complete; all of these franchises have made trades with most of the other franchises. There are only seven pairs of teams that never made any trades with each other. These pairs correspond to 0's in the table, which indicate the absence of a tie. The strongest relationship in this network is BOS–SDN; 25 players have been involved in trades between these two franchises over this seven-year period.

Algorithm 6.2 Hierarchical Clustering.

Preconditions: N is a weighted, undirected social network with actor set A.

Postconditions: A sequence of clusterings has been printed.

```
G ← the graph with vertex set A and no edges
Mark all edges of N as unused.
while G is not connected do
┌   e ← an unused edge in N of largest weight
│   u,v ← the vertices of e
│   Add an edge between u and v in graph G.
│   Mark e as used.
└   Print the connected components of G.
```

When a social network has weighted edges that indicate the strength of the ties, Algorithm 6.2 gives a simple way to identify *clusters* of closely related actors. Each time through the loop, the algorithm prints a clustering into progressively larger groups, culminating with a single cluster.

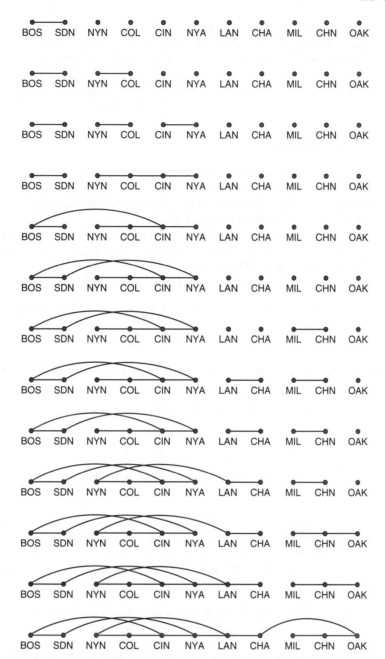

Figure 6.8 Algorithm 6.2 prints out the connected components of G at each stage.

Example 6.9 Applying Algorithm 6.2 to the social network in Figure 6.7 amounts to searching through the table for the largest entry and connecting the corresponding vertices in the graph G. Figure 6.8 shows the result of this process: the algorithm prints the connected components of G each time through the loop.

The hierarchical clustering algorithm doesn't define a particular clustering; it gives a sequence of clusters, and it is up to the researcher to interpret this sequence. In this example, notice that the cluster containing BOS, SDN, NYN, COL, CIN, and NYA forms fairly early, so we would expect that players tend to move somewhat freely among these six franchises. This is surprising when you notice that two pairs of these franchises, NYA–BOS and SDN–COL, never trade with each other. Both of these pairs consist of teams in the same division of Major League Baseball, and as such they are rivals who play each other often during the regular season. Apparently these franchises want to avoid trading players with each other for some reason; perhaps they fear giving a key opponent some competitive advantage. However, the above cluster analysis suggests that the structure of the trading network obviates this strategy; it seems quite likely that some players will move to a rival within the division, despite efforts to the contrary.

The technique of hierarchical clustering applies to problems in many other disciplines. In marketing, producers can use cluster analysis to identify groups of consumers that are likely to be interested in a particular product. Databases that contain many related data points use clustering to make searching and retrieval more efficient. And biologists use clustering in a variety of ways; in the exercises, you have the opportunity to explore the relationship between the hierarchical clustering algorithm and the UPGMA algorithm (Algorithm 6.1) for finding a phylogenetic tree.

6.2.4   Signed Graphs and Balance

Sometimes problems from another discipline can motivate new questions that are interesting for their own sake, as mathematical questions. For example, consider a social network that models how a group of people feel about each other. Two actors in this network might like each other, or they might dislike each other, or they may have no opinion whatsoever about each other. So it makes sense to label the ties with + for "like" and − for "dislike," where "no opinion" is represented by the absence of a tie. This kind of network is called a *signed graph*. Signed graphs are mathematically interesting; they are useful in other areas of mathematics, such as knot theory and group theory [1].

Suppose a signed network N models likes and dislikes among a set of actors. It is natural to wonder whether it is possible to divide the actors of N into conflict-free groups. One possible notion of such a division is called *balance*.

Definition 6.8 A simple, undirected, signed graph is *balanced* if the vertices can be divided into two sets U and V such that all ties between elements of the same set are positive, while all ties between a member of U and a member of V are negative.

For example, following the signed graph is balanced: take $U = \{r, s, t, u, w\}$ and $V = \{q, v, x, y, z\}$.

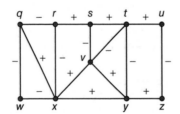

If we put all the actors from U in one room and all the actors from V in another, we would expect everybody to get along. It is even possible that the actors would split themselves up into these two groups in the course of normal interaction; people tend to avoid people they dislike and associate with people they like.

Given a signed graph, it can be hard to determine whether it is balanced. The following theorem gives a necessary condition.

Theorem 6.1 *Let G be a simple, undirected, signed graph. If G is balanced, then every circuit in G has an even number of − edges.*

Proof Suppose G is balanced. Then the actors of G are partitioned into two sets U and V such that every + edge connects two elements of U or two elements of V, and every − edge connects an element of U with an element of V. Any circuit must begin and end in one of these sets, and every − edge in the circuit switches sets, so the number of − edges must be even.   □

The contrapositive of this theorem gives us an easy condition to check: if there is a circuit with an odd number of − edges, then the graph is not balanced. The converse is also true; a proof appears in Harary [11].

Theorem 6.1 suggests that balance is a very strong condition; most signed graphs that model real-life social networks probably won't be balanced. All it takes is one bad circuit. However, there is a slightly weaker notion that is easier to satisfy.

Definition 6.9 A simple, undirected, signed graph is *k-balanced* if the vertices can be partitioned into k sets $U_1, U_2, \ldots, U_k$ such that all ties between elements of the same set are positive, while all ties between a member of U_i and a member of U_j are negative whenever $i \neq j$.

This definition gives us more options than Definition 6.8. Notice that a balanced graph is a 2-balanced graph.

Example 6.10 The following social network is not balanced, because the sequence of vertices v, y, z, w form a circuit with an odd number of − edges.

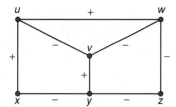

However, this graph is 3-balanced: $U_1 = \{u, w, x\}$, $U_2 = \{v, y\}$, and $U_3 = \{z\}$. If the ties represent likes/dislikes between actors, then the sets U_1, U_2, and U_3 might represent alliances. Actor z doesn't like anybody, and all the actors that are neutral toward z become allied with someone who z dislikes. Therefore, z is isolated.

There is a corresponding theorem about k-balanced graphs and circuits.

Theorem 6.2 *Let G be a simple, undirected, signed graph. If G is k-balanced for some $k > 0$, then G contains no circuits having exactly one $-$ edge.*

Proof Exercise.   □

The converse of this theorem is also true, and is proved in Davis [9]. The smallest example of a signed graph that is not k-balanced is the following triangle.

Think about this triangle from the perspective of likes/dislikes. Actor a likes two people who dislike each other—an awkward social situation.

Exercises 6.2

1. Give an example of an undirected social network containing a vertex x that is a liaison between two cliques of four actors.

2. Consider the social network in Figure 6.9. Using degree as a measure of centrality, which vertices are the most central?

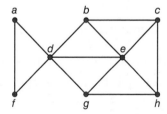

Figure 6.9 Social network for Exercises 2 and 3.

3. For an actor x in a social network, let $C(x)$ be the sum of the degrees of all the actors that x is tied to. Using $C(x)$ as a measure of centrality, which vertices are the most central in the social network in Figure 6.9?

4. Consider a directed social network in which the actors are nations. Nation x has a tie to nation y if x sells more to y than y sells to x. (In other words, the ties point in the direction of net trade.) Find appropriate adjectives to describe the nation with the largest indegree and the nation with the largest outdegree.

5. Prove Lemma 6.1. Make sure you account for both the directed and undirected cases.

6. Let a and b be actors in a simple social network. Prove the following:

   If a and b are structurally equivalent, then a and b are automorphically equivalent.

7. Prove the following statements.

   (a) Structural equivalence (Definition 6.3) is an equivalence relation on the set of actors in a social network.

   (b) Automorphic equivalence (Definition 6.5) is an equivalence relation on the set of actors in a social network.

8. Consider the social network N in Figure 6.6.

   (a) In addition to the regular equivalence of Example 6.7, find three other regular equivalence relations on the actors of N.

   (b) For each regular equivalence relation R in part (a), draw the graph of the quotient network of N by R.

9. Let N be a simple, undirected social network with actor set A.

   (a) Define a trivial equivalence relation R_1 on A as follows: for all $a, b \in A$, $a\,R_1\,b$. Prove that R_1 is a regular equivalence relation. What is its quotient network?

   (b) Define a trivial equivalence relation R_2 on A as follows: for all $a, b \in A$, $a\,R_2\,b$ if and only if $a = b$. Prove that R_2 is a regular equivalence relation. What is its quotient network?

10. Let N be the following directed social network. Find a regular equivalence relation on the actors of N having exactly three equivalence classes, and give the quotient network.

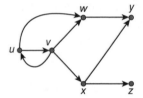

11. Apply hierarchical clustering (Algorithm 6.2) to the network in Figure 5.5 on page 235.

12. For some applications, it makes sense to change the line

    ```
    e ← the unused edge in N of largest weight
    ```

    in Algorithm 6.2 to

    ```
    e ← the unused edge in N of smallest weight
    ```

    Apply this modified version of hierarchical clustering to the network in Figure 2.5 on page 52.

13. Represent the steps of the hierarchical clustering trace in Example 6.9 as a tree whose leaves are the actors in a network. The joining of two subtrees in your tree should correspond to the connection of two components of G in the trace of the algorithm. Sociologists call such a tree a *dendrogram*.

14. Prove Theorem 6.2.

15. **Project:** Experiment with the CATREGE algorithm described in Borgatti and Everett [5]. Implement this algorithm on a computer, or download the software from the authors' website. See what equivalence relations it finds for the examples in this section. How does the choice of initial partition affect the output of the algorithm?

16. **Project:** Compare UPGMA (Algorithm 6.1) and hierarchical clustering (Algorithm 6.2). Explain how to produce a phylogenetic tree by making appropriate modifications to Algorithm 6.2. Does this always produce a tree with the same structure as the UPGMA tree?

17. **Project:** Compare the neighbor-joining algorithm of Saitou and Nei [26] with the hierarchical clustering algorithm.

18. **Project:** There is a simple way to transform a projection of a knot into a signed graph: consult Adams [1]. Which knots have balanced signed graphs? Investigate by computing some examples.

19. **Project:** Use some of the data from the transaction file archive of Retrosheet [25] to construct a social network, and analyze your network using some of the ideas in this section.

6.3   Structure of Languages

Human language is a discrete phenomenon. Written words are strings of symbols from a finite alphabet, and sentences are well-defined strings of words. Even spoken language can be broken down into discrete segments of sounds, combined in very specific ways to convey information. Therefore, linguistics—the study of human language—uses many ideas from discrete mathematics.

Linguistics is a very broad and diverse field. Language can be analyzed from many different perspectives: historical, anthropological, biological, psychological, to name just a few. In this section, we will take a very brief tour of some topics in structural linguistics that highlight how a mathematical point of view can help explain how language works.

One of the goals of studying language structure is to create an abstract framework that models how humans form strings of words into sentences. Ideally, this framework should have two properties.

1. It should be mathematically precise.

2. It should be detailed enough to describe the structure of any human language. In particular, it should be able to describe English grammar.

This goal is extremely ambitious, because these two properties pull in different directions. While every human language is governed by some system of well-defined rules, finding a universal model is a daunting task. In addition, humans form sentences intuitively in a way that is hard to pin down mathematically. But any progress we can make toward this goal will give us some insight into the mysterious and uniquely human activity of language.

6.3.1   Terminology

As we saw in Chapter 1, definitions are an essential part of mathematical writing. The following definition helps narrow the scope of the problem of modeling language with mathematics.

Definition 6.10 A *language* is a set L whose elements are finite-length strings of some finite set W of symbols.

The elements of the set L are called the *grammatical sentences* of the language. The symbols in W can be thought of as the words in the language, and we say that "L is a language over W." The assumption that W is a finite set is reasonable—dictionaries exist, for example.

Example 6.11 Let $W = \{a, b\}$. The set

$$L_1 = \{ab, abab, ababab, \ldots\} = \{(ab)^n \mid n \in \mathbf{N}\}$$

and the set

$$L_2 = \{ab, aabb, aaabbb, \ldots\} = \{a^n b^n \mid n \in \mathbf{N}\}$$

are both languages over W. Note that $L_1 \neq L_2$, because, for example, $abab \in L_1$ but $abab \notin L_2$. These two languages illustrate a fairly obvious but important point: a language with a finite number of words can have an infinite number of grammatical sentences.

The languages L_1 and L_2 in Example 6.11 seem more like mathematical sets than human languages. We use the term *formal language* to describe a language with an explicit mathematical definition that stipulates the grammatical sentences L given W.

Example 6.12 English, or more specifically, *Standard American English* (SAE), fits the definition of a language if we are willing to make a few assumptions. We need to decide on a vocabulary W; we could take W to be the set of all words defined in the *Oxford English Dictionary*. It is a much more difficult task to determine which strings of words are grammatical sentences, but it is reasonable to assume that, given a string of words, there is a standard way of determining whether the string is in L. For example, we could appoint our third-grade teacher, Mrs. Crabapple, arbiter of what constitutes a grammatical sentence: a string of words belongs to L if and only if Mrs. Crabapple says it does.

Note that a grammatical sentence doesn't have to make sense. For example, the sentence

Colorless green ideas sleep furiously.

is a famous instance of a grammatical sentence in SAE whose meaning is nonsensical [6]. This sentence is an element of L. However, the string

> This sentence make sense but not good grammar.

conveys its meaning clearly enough, but isn't a grammatical sentence. So the set of meaningful strings in W is quite a different thing from the set L.

Examples 6.11 and 6.12 represent two extremes, from very simple to very complicated. These two examples illustrate how broad our definition of language is. But this definition is at least a first step toward describing human language structure with an abstract model.

6.3.2   Finite-State Machines

The crux of describing a language L over a set W is determining which strings belong to L and which do not. One way of doing this is by specifying a method for constructing all the grammatical sentences. We will give a graph-theoretic definition.

Definition 6.11 A *word-chain automaton* is a directed graph with a finite number of vertices V, satisfying the following properties.

1. There is a specified *initial node* $v_0 \in V$.

2. There is a subset $F \subseteq V$ of *terminal nodes*.

3. Each edge is labeled with a symbol from a finite set W.

A string $w_1 w_2 \cdots w_k$ of symbols in W is *recognized* by the automaton if there is a directed path starting at the initial node v_0 and ending at a terminal node $\omega \in F$ such that the sequence of edges in this directed path is $w_1, w_2, \ldots, w_k$. The set L of all strings recognized by the automaton is called the *language recognized* by the automaton.[5]

A word-chain automaton is a special type of *finite-state automaton*, which, in turn, is a type of *finite-state machine*. These mathematical structures have a variety of applications in economics, biology, sociology, and other sciences.

Example 6.13 Let $W = \{a, b\}$. The following word-chain automaton has two nodes, so $V = \{v_0, \omega\}$. The only terminal node is ω, so $F = \{\omega\}$.

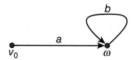

Any string produced by this automaton must begin with a, since any directed path from v_0 to ω must include the edge labeled a. Such a path may also include any number of loops from ω to ω before terminating. Therefore, the language recognized by this automaton is the set $L = \{ab^n \mid n \geq 0\}$.

In addition to formal languages, word-chain automata are able to synthesize a variety of grammatical sentences in human languages.

Example 6.14 The graph in Figure 6.10 is a word-chain automaton using the words in the set $W = \{$fear, know, I, they, that, Eileen's, her, his, dog, hamster, friend, and, is, but, very, happy, unruly, dead$\}$. There is only one terminal node ω, so $F = \{\omega\}$. The following strings are recognized by this automaton.[6]

---

5. The plural of "automaton" is "automata."
6. To avoid making this discussion overly complicated, we will usually ignore issues involving punctuation and capitalization.

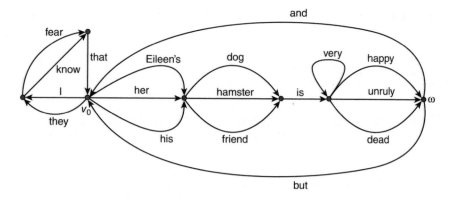

Figure 6.10 A word-chain automaton defines a set of sentences.

Eileen's hamster is unruly.

Her dog is very very happy but her hamster is dead.

I fear that they know that Eileen's hamster is dead and her dog is very unruly but they fear that I know that his friend is happy.

These strings are all grammatical sentences in the language L recognized by this automaton. Since the graph contains circuits, this language has infinitely many grammatical sentences.

A language that is recognized by a word-chain automaton is called *regular*. Example 6.14 illustrates that relatively simple word-chain automata are capable of representing quite convoluted sentence structures, so you might wonder whether it is possible (in principle, if not in practice) to recognize the English language with a huge word-chain automaton. Are all languages regular? The following theorem shows that the answer is "no."

Theorem 6.3 *Let $L = \{a^n b^n \mid n \in \mathbf{N}\}$ be a language over $W = \{a, b\}$. Then L is not recognized by any word-chain automaton.*

Proof Suppose we are given a word-chain automaton that recognizes $a^n b^n$ for all $n \in \mathbf{N}$. We will prove the theorem by showing that this automaton must recognize some sentence that is not in L. Since the number of states in this automaton is finite, choose N to be larger than the number of states. The path P that recognizes the sentence $a^N b^N$ consists of a sequence of N edges labeled a followed by a sequence of N edges labeled b. Since there are more edges labeled b than there are states, one of the states visited by the sequence of b edges must be visited twice, by the pigeonhole principle. There is, therefore, a circuit C beginning and ending at this state, all of whose edges are labeled b. The length k of this circuit is nonzero. Therefore, we can recognize the sentence $a^M b^{N+k}$ by modifying the path P to follow the circuit C one additional time. But $a^N b^{N+k} \notin L$, so L is not recognized by the given automaton. $\square$

Noam Chomsky [6] observes that nonrecognizable languages like the one in Theorem 6.3 show that the English language can't be recognized by a word-chain automaton. Chomsky's argument is that English (and other human languages) contain structures like

If S_1 then S_2.

that are grammatical sentences, provided that S_1 and S_2 are grammatical sentences. For example, if S_1 = "roses are red" and S_2 = "violets are blue" are grammatical sentences, so is the sentence

S_3 = "If S_1 then S_2."
  = "If roses are red then violets are blue."

Now granting that the "if ... then" structure is grammatical, we must also grant that the sentence

S_4 = "If S_3 then S_2."

is grammatical, and likewise,

$$S_5 = \text{"If } S_4 \text{ then } S_2\text{."}$$
$$= \text{"If if } S_3 \text{ then } S_2 \text{ then } S_2\text{."}$$
$$= \text{"If if if } S_1 \text{ then } S_2 \text{ then } S_2 \text{ then } S_2\text{."}$$

must also be considered grammatical, even though we would probably never choose to say such a sentence. Continuing in this fashion, our set L of grammatical sentences in English must include sentences of the form

$$\underbrace{\text{If if} \ldots \text{if}}_{n} \; S_1 \; \underbrace{\text{then } S_2 \text{ then } S_2 \ldots \text{then } S_2}_{n}$$

which has basically the same form as $a^n b^n$. It isn't exactly the same, but a similar argument to the proof of Theorem 6.3 will show that this sentence can't be recognized by an automaton.

Chomsky notes that human languages normally feature such "long-distance dependencies," meaning that something much later in a sentence may depend on something much earlier. There is no way an automaton can keep track of a dependency like this: as an automaton builds a sentence, the only constraints on the next word are determined by the current word, not any words earlier in the sentence.

Less arcane examples of long-distance dependencies occur often in everyday language. For example, in the sentence

> The fact that Bill thinks that if someone needs glasses to read a magazine then that person shouldn't be allowed to drive makes me want to scream.

contains a dependency between "The fact that" at the beginning and "makes me want to scream" at the end. Putting any statement, no matter how complicated, between these two phrases will result in a grammatical sentence.

While it is conceivable that we could create a library of automata large enough to handle every reasonable construction involving dependencies, such a model for language is unnaturally cumbersome. The previous examples illustrate the limitations of an automata-based model; there is something fundamental to the structure of human language that demands more than word-chains.

6.3.3 Recursion

The problems raised by this discussion have to do with constructions where a sentence is placed inside another sentence. These problems indicate that natural language is somehow recursive. Following Chomsky [6], we describe a model that allows for recursive sentence structure.

Definition 6.12 A *grammar* is a pair $[\Sigma, F]$ consisting of a finite set Σ of *initial strings* and a set F of *instruction formulas*. An instruction formula must look like

$$X \rightarrow Y$$

meaning that X may be rewritten as Y. A *derivation* is a sequence of strings beginning with an initial string and formed by repeatedly applying instruction formulas.

This definition is quite abstract. A simple example may help illustrate how it works.

Example 6.15 Define a grammar by setting $\Sigma = \{\sigma\}$ and let F consist of the following three formulas.

1. $\sigma \rightarrow N V N$.

2. $N \rightarrow n$, for some $n \in \{\text{Moe, Larry, Curly}\}$.

3. $V \rightarrow v$, for some $v \in \{\text{hit, poked, spanked, kicked, punched}\}$.

An example of a derivation in this grammar is the following.

	σ	initial string
$\rightarrow$	$N\ V\ N$	formula 1
$\rightarrow$	Moe $V\ N$	formula 2
$\rightarrow$	Moe punched N	formula 3
$\rightarrow$	Moe punched Curly	formula 2

A derivation is *terminated* if its last line cannot be rewritten further by any instruction formula in the grammar. The string "Moe punched Curly" is called a *terminal* string in the grammar of Example 6.15 because it is the last line of a terminated derivation. Given these terms, we can now state the connection between grammar and languages.

Definition 6.13 A set L of strings is a *terminal language* if it consists of all the terminal strings for some grammar $[\Sigma, F]$.

The terminal language defined by the grammar of Example 6.15 contains sentences that describe various ways that Moe, Larry, and Curly can attack each other. The next example shows that grammars can define languages that automata cannot.

Example 6.16 Let $L = \{a^n b^n \mid n \in \mathbf{N}\}$ be a language over $W = \{a, b\}$. Show that L is a terminal language.

Solution: Let $\Sigma = \{\sigma\}$, and let F consist of the following instruction formulas.

1. $\sigma \rightarrow ab$

2. $\sigma \rightarrow a\sigma b$

We claim that L is the terminal language defined by the grammar $[\Sigma, F]$: if you start with σ and apply the second formula k times and then apply the first formula, you end up with the terminal string $a^{k+1}b^{k+1}$. A rigorous proof of this claim (using induction) is left as an exercise. $\diamond$

The grammar given in the solution to Example 6.16 is actually a recursive definition in disguise. In the notation of Chapter 3, the terminal language L is described by the following base and recursive cases.

B. $ab \in L$

R. If $X \in L$, so is aXb.

Notice the analogy between the parts of this recursive definition and the instruction formulas for the above grammar. In the notation of instruction formulas, the symbol σ acts as a placeholder for a general grammatical sentence, while in set notation the general element X plays the same role. Grammars contain the power of recursive definitions. In particular, a terminal language defined by a grammar is capable of expressing the kind of recursion found in human languages.

Example 6.17 Let $\Sigma = \{\sigma\}$, and let F consist of the following instruction formulas.

1. $\sigma \rightarrow N\ V$

2. $N \rightarrow n$, for some $n \in \{$he, she, José, Sal, Anna$\}$.

3. $V \rightarrow v$, for some $v \in \{$runs, jumps, skips, falls, swims$\}$.

4. $\sigma \rightarrow \sigma\ P\ \sigma$

5. $P \rightarrow p$, for some $p \in \{$and, while, until$\}$.

6. $\sigma \rightarrow$ either σ or σ.

Construct a terminated derivation for the following sentence.

Either José runs until he falls or Sal swims while Anna jumps and José skips.

Solution:

σ	initial string
$\rightarrow$ Either σ or σ	formula 6
$\rightarrow$ Either $\sigma\,P\,\sigma$ or σ	formula 4
$\rightarrow$ Either $\sigma\,P\,\sigma$ or $\sigma\,P\,\sigma$	formula 4
$\rightarrow$ Either $\sigma\,P\,\sigma$ or $\sigma\,P\,\sigma\,P\,\sigma$	formula 4 (on rightmost σ)
$\rightarrow$ Either $N\,V\,P\,N\,V$ or $N\,V\,P\,N\,V\,P\,N\,V$	formula 1 (5 times)
$\rightarrow$ Either José $V\,P$ he V or Sal V	
$\quad P$ Anna $V\,P$ José V	formula 2 (5 times)
$\rightarrow$ Either José runs P he falls or Sal swims	
$\quad P$ Anna jumps P José skips	formula 3 (5 times)
$\rightarrow$ Either José runs until he falls or Sal swims	
$\quad$ while Anna jumps and José skips	formula 5 (3 times)

$\diamond$

A derivation in grammar has a natural tree representation. Every time we apply an instruction formula, we replace part of an expression with a new, generally more complicated, expression. To model a derivation in a grammar with a tree, let the root be the initial string, and let the children of any node be the strings making up their replacement. In other words, each instruction formula is interpreted as

$$\text{parent} \;\rightarrow\; \text{child}\;\;\text{child}\;\ldots\;\text{child},$$

starting with the root and proceeding down the tree. The following tree corresponds to the derivation in Example 6.17. You can read the terminal sentence off such a tree by reading the leaves in order from left to right.

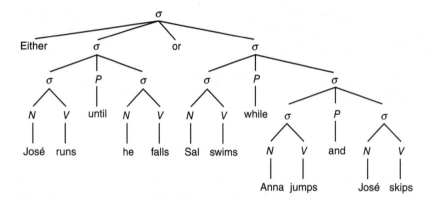

Example 6.17 illustrates the recursive nature of grammar; any sentence σ can appear inside another sentence, and even the final sentence in the above derivation could appear as one part of a much larger sentence. This grammar even contains a construction for a long-distance dependency: "either σ or σ." Once the phrase "either σ" appears in a sentence, the sentence must eventually include an "or σ" phrase to complete the sentence. We could even construct a sentence with an $a^n b^n$ pattern using this grammar.

$$\underbrace{\text{Either either} \ldots \text{either}}_{n} \; \sigma \; \underbrace{\text{or } \sigma \text{ or } \sigma \ldots \text{or } \sigma}_{n}.$$

This construction presents the same problem as the if ... then construction we saw before: no automaton can recognize this terminal language.

6.3.4   Further Issues in Linguistics

So far, we have taken only a few baby steps into the field of linguistics; actual definitions of grammar have many more components and are much more complex. However, we have made some progress. We have identified a feature of human language—recursion—that appears to explain how our minds naturally keep track of complex sentence structures. And this progress illustrates the power of the search for an abstract model of language: as we develop mathematical models for language, we get a clearer picture of how everything related to language works.

How is it that young children are able to develop linguistic competence so quickly? Are humans the only animals that communicate with languages that contain recursive structures? Do all human languages exhibit recursion? How did the capacity for human language evolve? Is it possible to program a computer to carry on an authentic conversation with a human? These questions are motivated and informed by discrete mathematical models.

Attempts to describe language with mathematics highlight how incredibly complicated language is. For example, computer-generated translations based only on the syntactic structure of a sentence are often substandard. Consider the following sentence.

> Whenever my back is giving me problems, I find that lying down makes it feel better.

A early version of a syntax-based translation engine renders the following version in Italian.

> Ogni volta che la mia parte posteriore sta dandomi i problemi, trovo che trovandosi giù le marche esso tatto più meglio.

If we ask for an English translation of this Italian sentence, we get a mixture of parts of our original sentence along with some complete nonsense.

> Every time that my posterior part is giving the problems to me, I find that finding the Marches down it tact more better.

In recent years, the accuracy of translation engines has been greatly improved by combining syntax-based approaches with searches of human-translated data. One of these services renders our original sentence as follows.

> Ogni volta che la schiena mi dà problemi, trovo che sdraiarsi lo fa sentire meglio.

Translating back to English yields a more comprehensible sentence, but with a slightly different meaning.

> Whenever my back gives me trouble, I find that lying down makes him feel better.

Despite recent advances, reliable translation still requires human intelligence.

Exercises 6.3

1. Use the word-chain automaton given in Figure 6.10 to construct several sentences of varying complexity. Are these sentences grammatically correct according to your understanding of standard English?

2. Let $L = \{(ab)^n \mid n \in \mathbf{N}\}$ be a language over $W = \{a, b\}$. Construct a word-chain automaton that recognizes L.

3. Construct a grammar that shows that $L = \{(ab)^n \mid n \in \mathbf{N}\}$ is a terminal language.

4. Construct a word-chain automaton that is able to recognize the string $a^n b^n$ for all $n \in \mathbf{N}$. Find a string that your automaton recognizes that is not of the form $a^n b^n$. (Such a string must exist, by Theorem 6.3.)

5. Describe a "machine" with an infinite number of states that is able to recognize the string $a^n b^n$ for all $n \in \mathbf{N}$.

6. Consider the following word-chain automaton using symbols from the set $W = \{a, b, c\}$.

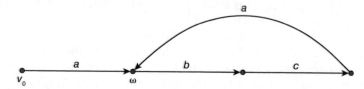

   (a) Write the language recognized by this automaton in set-builder notation.

   (b) Using only three vertices, construct another automaton that recognizes the same language.

7. Let $\mathcal{A}$ be a word-chain automaton with initial node v_0 and terminal node ω. Suppose that there is a directed path in $\mathcal{A}$ from v_0 to ω that contains a circuit. Prove that the language L recognized by $\mathcal{A}$ contains an infinite number of strings.

8. How many different grammatical sentences are there in the terminal language defined by the grammar of Example 6.15?

9. Describe an automaton that recognizes the terminal language defined by Example 6.15.

10. Let $[\Sigma, F]$ be the grammar defined in Example 6.16. Use induction to prove the following.

    (a) The string $a^n b^n$ is a terminal string for $[\Sigma, F]$.

    (b) Every terminal string for $[\Sigma, F]$ has the form $a^n b^n$.

    Note that parts (a) and (b) together prove that $L = \{a^n b^n \mid n \in \mathbf{N}\}$ is a terminal language.

11. Give derivations for the following strings in the grammar of Example 6.17.

    (a) Sal runs while Anna jumps.

    (b) Either José runs or he swims.

    (c) José runs and either Anna swims or Sal skips.

    (d) Either Anna jumps while she runs or either Sal skips or José falls.

12. For each derivation in Exercise 11, draw the corresponding tree.

13. Define a grammar that contains both the if ... then construction and the either ... or construction. Give a derivation in your grammar for a sentence that uses both of these constructions.

14. Explain why every language that is recognized by an automaton must be a terminal language. (Chomsky [7] proves this fact.) Explain why the converse is false.

15. **Project:** Construct a word-chain automaton that parodies a certain genre of sentence (e.g., rock lyrics, warning labels, telemarketers). Implement this automaton as a computer program that generates random sentences in your chosen genre.

16. **Project:** In Hauser et al. [12], the authors argue that the use of recursion in language is a distinctly human trait. Read this article. Design an experiment to test the hypothesis that animals don't understand recursion. Perform your experiment, if possible.

17. **Project:** Experiment with online translation software, either by translating text into a language that you know, or by translating to and from some intermediate language. What grammatical structures does the software tend to translate correctly? What structures does it fail to translate accurately? Make a guess at how the software works.

6.4   Discrete-Time Population Models

In this section we will explore how ideas from earlier in the book can explain how populations change over time. The study of population growth applies to many disciplines: sociology and economics (human populations), biology and medicine (organism or disease populations), chemistry and physics (populations of particles or substances), and so on.

If you have taken calculus, you have probably seen some models for population growth using differential equations. These types of models are called *continuous-time* models, because they regard time t as occurring on a continuum; the model attempts to predict the size of the population at any time t over an interval of real numbers. This approach has the advantage of admitting *analytical* solutions. You can use integrals to find a formula for a function $P(t)$ that describes the population in terms of t.

But calculating integrals analytically can be quite difficult, and even impossible at times. So here we will sidestep the use of calculus by using *discrete-time models*. Instead of viewing time as a continuum, we will view it as a sequence $t_0, t_1, t_2, \ldots$ of regular "snapshots," where $t_i - t_{i-1} = \Delta t$, some fixed increment of time. The smaller we set Δt, the closer our model will approximate a continuous-time model. Graphically, a discrete-time model will produce a sequence of points, while a continuous-time model results in a function $\mathbf{R} \longrightarrow \mathbf{R}$. See Figure 6.11.

You might be worried that discrete-time models can't possibly be realistic. But in practice, many continuous-time models can't be solved without resorting to some kind of numerical technique (such as Euler's method), and

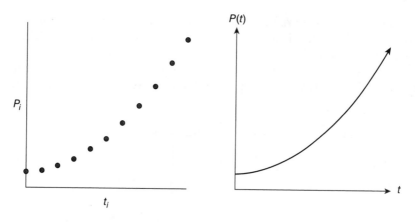

Figure 6.11 A discrete-time model produces a sequence (t_0, P_0), (t_1, P_1), (t_2, P_2), ... of points (left), while a continuous-time model yields a function $P(t)$ over a real interval (right).

these techniques generally produce approximations by breaking time into discrete intervals. In effect, a numerical solution for a continuous-time model is really a discrete-time approximation.

The discrete-time approach has the advantage of allowing us to use relational and recursive thinking to understand population dynamics. Furthermore, discrete-time models are natural to implement on a computer, so graphs and simulations are easy to produce.

6.4.1 Recursive Models for Population Growth

Population growth is a recursive phenomenon. The key observation is that tomorrow's population depends (at least in part) on today's population. In other words, the population P_n depends on the populations P_{n-1}, P_{n-2}, etc. This observation leads to a general recursive definition.

$$P_n = \begin{cases} \text{The initial population} & \text{if } n = 0 \\ \text{Some function of } P_i\text{'s, } i < n & \text{if } n > 0 \end{cases}$$

In fact, this recursive definition is really just a recurrence relation, in slightly different notation. We use P_n to denote the population at time $t_n = n\Delta t$, for $n \geq 0$. We use subscripts because the alternative, $P(n)$, might give the (false) impression that we are talking about the population at time n.

Example 6.18 We have already discussed a discrete-time model for population growth: Fibonacci's rabbits (page 110). In the above notation, let t be measured in months, with $\Delta t = 1$ month. Let P_n be the number of rabbits present at time $t_n = n\Delta t = n$. Then we can rewrite Definition 3.1 as follows:

$$P_n = \begin{cases} 1 & \text{if } n = 0 \text{ or } n = 1 \\ P_{n-1} + P_{n-2} & \text{if } n > 1 \end{cases}$$

If you have been paying close attention, you may have noticed that in this definition, we have started indexing the Fibonacci numbers at 0, while in Definition 3.1, the indexing starts at 1. In general, it makes sense to have a population model start at time $t = 0$, so t can represent the elapsed time.

Example 6.19 A very useful model for population growth results from assuming that, at each time step, the population increases by a fixed multiple $r > 0$. In other words,

$$P_n = \begin{cases} A & \text{if } n = 0 \\ rP_{n-1} & \text{if } n > 0 \end{cases}$$

where A is the population at time $t = 0$. We have seen similar recurrence relations in Chapter 3. It is easy to prove by induction that the population at time $n\Delta t$ is $P_n = Ar^n$. This *exponential* population model applies to a wide range of situations; we saw it applied to compound interest in Example 3.3.

The constant r is called a *parameter*. You can change the behavior of the model by choosing different values of the parameter r. For $r > 1$, $P_n = Ar^n$ increases without bound as time increases (i.e., $P_n \to \infty$ as $n \to \infty$). This choice of parameter models *exponential growth*. However, setting the parameter $r < 1$ results in entirely different behavior: $P_n \to 0$ as $n \to \infty$, modeling *exponential decay*. For example, the following graphs illustrate the difference between growth ($r = 1.03$ in the left graph) and decay ($r = 0.97$ in the right graph) for an initial population $A = 25$.

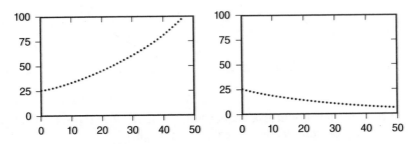

The exponential growth model is a good fit for populations that have nothing to stop them from growing. The next model can account for a population whose size is limited by competition for limited resources.

Example 6.20 Let P_n be given by the following formula:

$$P_n = \begin{cases} A & \text{if } n = 0 \\ rP_{n-1}(1 - P_{n-1}) & \text{if } n > 0. \end{cases}$$

Here $0 \le A \le 1$ and $0 \le r \le 4$. It is left as an exercise to show that these constraints ensure that $0 \le P_n \le 1$ for all $n \ge 0$. Since P_n can never exceed 1, we can think of P_n as giving the population at time $n\Delta t$ as a percentage of some fixed maximum population. This model is often called the *logistic* population model.

The recursive definition in Example 6.20 is very similar to the definition in Example 6.19; the only difference is the presence of the $(1 - P_{n-1})$ term. This factor becomes small as P_n approaches 1, so it can model a phenomenon that restrains growth for large populations, such as competition for food or habitat.

The following graphs give a comparison of these two models for $A = 0.001$ and $r = 1.08$. Notice that, for smaller values of n (up to approximately $n = 40$), the two models produce very similar results. However, once n gets larger, the exponential model (left) continues to increase faster and faster, while the growth of the logistic model (right) starts to level out. Apparently, the $(1 - P_{n-1})$ term begins to have a noticeable effect on the graph once the population rises above 0.02 or so.

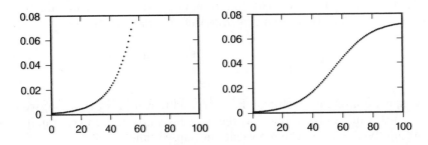

6.4.2   Fixed Points, Equilibrium, and Chaos

The graph of the logistic model suggests that the population might stabilize as $n \to \infty$. Indeed, for $A = 0.001$ and $r = 1.08$, the following table indicates that the values of P_n tend toward 0.0741, approximately.

n	0	1	2	3	$\cdots$	99	100	$\cdots$	199	200
P_n	0.001	0.0011	0.0012	0.0013	$\cdots$	0.0721	0.0723	$\cdots$	0.0741	0.0741

The following definition will help explain this phenomenon.

Definition 6.14 Let $f: X \longrightarrow X$ be a function. An element $a \in X$ is called a *fixed point* if $f(a) = a$.

Given a function $f(x)$, you can find the fixed points by solving the equation $f(a) = a$.

Example 6.21 Find the fixed points of $f(x) = x^2$, a function $\mathbf{R} \longrightarrow \mathbf{R}$.

Solution: The only solutions of $a^2 = a$ over the real numbers are $a = 0$ and $a = 1$, so these are the fixed points. ◇

Now consider the logistic model with $A = 0.001$ and $r = 1.08$. The recursive part of the definition of P_n states that

$$P_n = 1.08P_{n-1}(1 - P_{n-1}) \quad \text{if } n > 0.$$

In other words, given P_{n-1} for $n > 0$, you compute P_n by evaluating the function

$$f(x) = 1.08x(1 - x)$$

with $x = P_{n-1}$. The logistic model is a type of *iterated function system*, because the sequence it generates can be found by repeatedly applying the function f. The fixed points of this function are easy to calculate.

$$x = 1.08x(1 - x)$$
$$x = 1.08x - 1.08x^2$$
$$0 = 0.08x - 1.08x^2$$
$$0 = x(0.08 - 1.08x)$$

So $x = 0$ and $x = 0.08/1.08 \approx 0.0741$ are the fixed points. It makes sense that the long-term behavior of this model stabilizes to the fixed point 0.0741, because once P_{n-1} reaches this value, P_n will be the same as P_{n-1}. When a system reaches a state where the population no longer changes, it is said to be at *equilibrium*.

Finding fixed points of an iterated function system can sometimes give a hint of the long-term behavior. However, in general, fixed points don't tell the whole story. Figure 6.12 shows two graphs of the logistic model where the population fails to converge to a single fixed point. The graph on the top shows what happens when $r = 3.2$ and $A = 0.1$. Close inspection of the graph reveals that once n is greater than 20, the value of P_n alternates between two values: roughly 0.8 and 0.5. The long-term behavior of this system is *periodic*.

The graph on the bottom shows quite different behavior for $r = 3.8$ and $A = 0.1$. Since there is no obvious pattern to this sequence, it can be called *chaotic*. The study of chaos is deep and fascinating; chaotic systems may explain many seemingly random phenomena in nature.

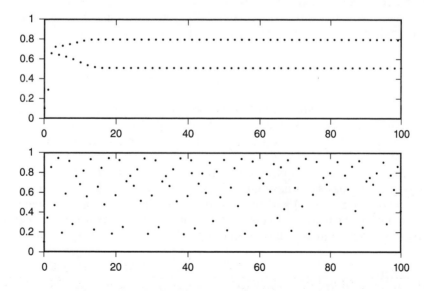

Figure 6.12 Two graphs of P_n versus n for the logistic model with $A = 0.1$. The top graph shows a periodic sequence in the $r = 3.2$ case, while the bottom shows a chaotic sequence for $r = 3.8$.

6.4.3 Predator–Prey Systems

The recursive paradigm for modeling population change extends naturally to systems of several interrelated populations. The relationship between predators and their prey is a classic example. The predator (traditionally represented by foxes) depends on its prey (traditionally rabbits) for food, while the prey's survival is limited by the predator's success. This competition is naturally self-referential, that is, recursive.

Example 6.22 Let F_n be the population of a predator (foxes), and let R_n be the population of its prey (rabbits). Let initial values R_0 and F_0 be given. For $n > 0$, R_n and F_n are given by the following system of equations:

$$\begin{cases} R_n = rR_{n-1}(1 - R_{n-1}) - aR_{n-1}F_{n-1} \\ F_n = F_{n-1} + bR_{n-1}F_{n-1} - cF_{n-1}. \end{cases}$$

The parameter r is the growth rate of the rabbit population. Notice that if there were no foxes ($F_n = 0$ for all n), we are assuming that the rabbit population would follow the logistic model. So the restrictions on R_0 and r are the same as in Example 6.20: $0 \leq R_0 \leq 1$ and $0 \leq r \leq 4$.

On the other hand, we are assuming that the foxes depend on rabbits for their food. In the absence of rabbits ($R_n = 0$ for all n) the foxes will die off. Therefore, the parameter c is the associated death rate. Taking $0 < c \leq 1$ ensures that the fox population would decay exponentially without rabbits.

To understand the parameters a and b, recall that the number of ways to form a rabbit/fox pair from R rabbits and F foxes is RF, by the multiplication principle. Therefore, the number of predation events (foxes eating rabbits) should be proportional to $R_{n-1}F_{n-1}$. The parameter a reflects how effective the foxes are at eating rabbits; this is why the term $aR_{n-1}F_{n-1}$ gets subtracted from the rabbit population at each stage. Similarly, the term $bR_{n-1}F_{n-1}$ gets added to the fox population at each stage, so the parameter b measures the extent to which eating rabbits keeps the foxes from starving.

We haven't been very careful about the units associated with these four parameters; in practice, one would have to modify the parameters or scale the population sizes to fit some empirical observations.

Figure 6.13 shows the behavior of this system when $R_0 = 0.02$, $F_0 = 1$, $r = 1.5$, $a = 0.3$, $b = 2$, $c = 0.2$, and $0 \leq n \leq 100$. The top two graphs show how the fox and rabbit populations change over time. Notice that both populations rise and fall, with the peaks of the fox population occurring slightly after the peaks of the rabbit population. This should seem intuitively correct: the foxes do well when there are lots of rabbits, but then the rabbits get eaten, so the foxes don't do as well until the rabbits start doing better, and so on.

For this choice of parameters, it appears that both populations are converging to some equilibrium values. The graph of F_n versus R_n in Figure 6.13 shows how the ordered pairs (R_n, F_n) spiral inward toward this equilibrium value as $n \to \infty$.

We can compute fixed points for the predator–prey model in much the same way that we did for the logistic model. The main difference is that any fixed point must be an ordered pair (x, y), where x is the number of rabbits and y is the number of foxes. We can regard the recursive definition of Example 6.22 as an iterated function system in x and y, so the fixed points must satisfy the following system of equations:

$$\begin{cases} x = 1.5x(1 - x) - 0.3xy \\ y = y + 2xy - 0.2y. \end{cases}$$

It is an easy exercise to solve this system: the only fixed points are $(0, 0)$, $(1/3, 0)$, and $(1/10, 7/6)$. The first is trivial, the second corresponds to the logistic model (no foxes), and the third matches the apparent equilibria in Figure 6.13. Remember that, as with the logistic model, fixed points are not always equilibria. Different parameters can produce oscillating or even chaotic behavior.

The predator–prey model can apply to other competitive relationships. For example, an economic model of established and emerging technologies can have the same dynamics as the rabbit and fox populations above [23]. A new, emerging technology (the predator) benefits by cutting into the market share of the established technology (the prey). The above model predicts that the market shares of these two technologies will oscillate in a pattern similar to Figure 6.13 before eventually reaching equilibrium.

6.4.4 The SIR Model

Often, the members of a single, homogeneous population can move between two or more subpopulations. For example, the students at a college are divided into several different majors, and students can change from one

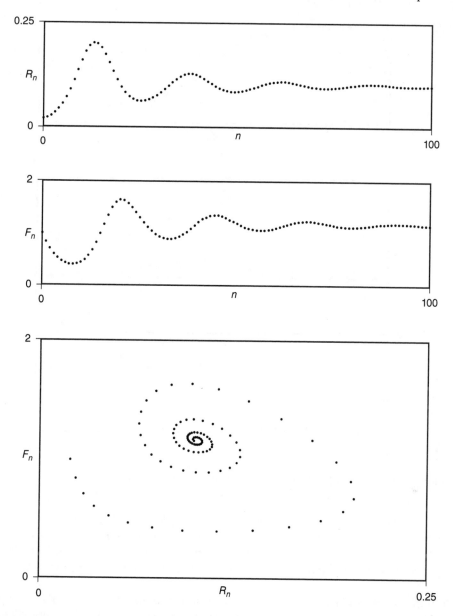

Figure 6.13 Graphs of R_n versus n, F_n versus n, and F_n versus R_n for the predator–prey model.

major to another. Exercise 23 of Section 2.1 gives another example: rental cars move among three different rental locations.

In their seminal 1927 paper, Anderson Gray McKendrick and William Kermack [18] proposed a model for the spread of disease through a population in terms of three subpopulations: susceptible, infected, and recovered. The Kermack–McKendrick SIR model uses differential equations; the following is a discrete-time version.

Example 6.23 Suppose that a disease is spreading through a population of P individuals. At time $n\Delta t$, let S_n be the number of individuals who are susceptible to the disease, let I_n be the number who are infected, and let R_n be the number who have recovered from the disease (and are therefore immune). Let's assume that initially some individuals have been infected and none have yet recovered, so $0 < I_0 \leq P$, $R_0 = 0$, and $S_0 = P - I_0$. For $n > 0$, S_n, I_n, and R_n are given by the following system of equations:

$$\begin{cases} S_n = S_{n-1} - aS_{n-1}I_{n-1} \\ I_n = I_{n-1} + aS_{n-1}I_{n-1} - bI_{n-1} \\ R_n = R_{n-1} + bI_{n-1}. \end{cases}$$

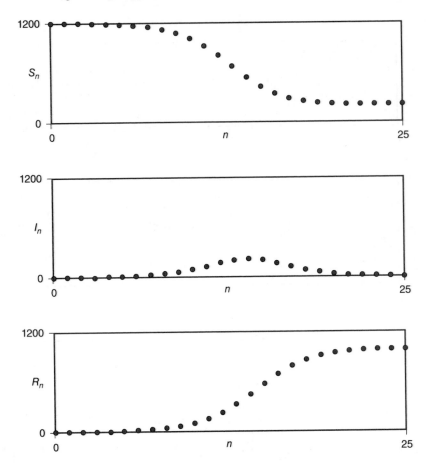

Figure 6.14 Plots of the three populations in the SIR model for $a = 0.001$, $b = 0.6$, $I_0 = 1$, and $P = 1200$.

The parameter a is the coefficient of transmission; its value models how likely the disease is to spread when an infected individual meets a susceptible one. By the multiplication rule, the number of possible susceptible/infected meetings is $S_{n-1}I_{n-1}$, so the term $aS_{n-1}I_{n-1}$ represents the number of newly infected individuals at time-step n. The parameter b is the fraction of infected individuals who recover at each time step; at time step n, bI_{n-1} individuals recover.

It is left as an exercise to show that $S_n + I_n + R_n = P$ for all $n \geq 0$. In other words, the total population doesn't change; individuals simply move among the three different roles. We can represent this model as a simple, directed graph.

We don't really need subscripts to understand the meaning of this graph. At each time step, aSI individuals move from susceptible to infected, while bI individuals move from infected to recovered.

Suppose that, at a college of 1200 students, one student returns from vacation with a strange new disease. Assuming a transmission coefficient of $a = 0.001$ and a recovery rate of $b = 0.6$, Figure 6.14 shows the plots of the three subpopulations over a 25-day period. Notice that it takes about 14 days for the number of infected students to peak, and after 25 days the disease appears to have run its course. However, a look at the number of recovered students at day 25 reveals that a large majority of the college's students (about 1000) ended up getting the disease.

In their article, Kermack and McKendrick [18] observe that their model is very sensitive to changes in the parameter a, the transmission coefficient. For the above example, if we change the value of a from 0.001 to 0.0005, the total number of students who get the disease drops from 1000 to about 50. Reducing the transmission coefficient by 50% reduces the total number of cases by 95%. This mathematical observation has an important public health implication: controlling the factors that cause a disease to spread—even a little—can have a large effect on whether the disease becomes an epidemic.

Exercises 6.4

1. Write a formula relating the sequences given by Definition 3.1 and Example 6.18.

2. Radioactive substances decay exponentially. For example, a sample of Carbon-14 (^{14}C) will lose half of its mass every 5730 years. (In other words, the *half-life* of ^{14}C is 5730 years.) Let A be the initial mass of the sample. Model the decay of ^{14}C using a discrete-time model ...

   (a) using $\Delta t = 5730$ years.

   (b) using $\Delta t = 1$ year.

3. Let P_n be defined as in Example 6.20. Prove that $0 \leq P_n \leq 1$ for all $n \geq 0$. (Hint: Use induction on n, and make use of the fact that the maximum value of $f(x) = x - x^2$ is $1/4$ on the interval $[0, 1]$.)

4. Implement the logistic model (Example 6.20) using a spreadsheet. Test your implementation by recreating the graphs in Figure 6.12. Using $A = 0.1$, find a value of r such that P_n appears to cycle among four different values as $n \to \infty$.

5. Let r be a constant with $0 < r < 1$. Find all fixed points (in terms of r) of the function $f(x) = r(1 - x)$.

6. Consider the following discrete-time population model:

$$P_n = \begin{cases} A & \text{if } n = 0 \\ r(1 - P_{n-1}) & \text{if } n > 0. \end{cases}$$

   Both the initial population A and the parameter r are between 0 and 1, noninclusive.

   (a) Implement this model on a spreadsheet, and experiment with different values of r and A. Describe the long-term behavior.

   (b) Let x_∞ be the fixed point that you found in Exercise 5. Prove that

   $$P_{n-1} \geq x_\infty \implies P_n \leq x_\infty \quad \text{and} \quad P_{n-1} \leq x_\infty \implies P_n \geq x_\infty.$$

   (c) Suppose that $P_{n-1} \neq x_\infty$. Prove that

   $$|x_\infty - P_n| < |x_\infty - P_{n-1}|.$$

   (d) Do parts (b) and (c) confirm your observations from part (a)? Explain.

7. Find all solutions to the following system of equations:

$$\begin{cases} x = 1.5x(1 - x) - 0.3xy \\ y = y + 2xy - 0.2y. \end{cases}$$

8. Implement the SIR model (Example 6.23) on a spreadsheet.

   (a) Check your implementation by recreating the plots in Figure 6.14.

   (b) Experiment with different values of I_0, the initial number of infected students. How does the value of I_0 affect the spread of the disease?

   (c) Experiment with different values of the parameter b, the recovery rate. Remember that $0 < b < 1$. How does this parameter affect the spread of the disease?

   (d) For the scenario in Example 6.23, which is more effective: reducing the transmission coefficient by 10% (to $a = 0.0009$) or increasing the recovery rate by 10% (to $b = 0.66$)? Explain.

   (e) What are the public health implications of part (d)?

9. In the SIR model (Example 6.23), prove by induction that $S_n + I_n + R_n = P$ for all $n \geq 0$.

10. Explain why, in any fixed point in the SIR model, the number of infected individuals must equal zero.

11. In Exercise 23 of Section 2.1, you were asked to model the following scenario with a directed network.

> A car rental company has three locations in Mexico City: the International Airport, Oficina Vallejo, and Downtown. Customers can drop off their vehicles at any of these locations. Based on prior experience, the company expects that, at the end of each day, 40% of the cars that begin the day at the Airport will end up Downtown, 50% will return to the Airport, and 10% will be at Oficina Vallejo. Similarly, 60% of the Oficina Vallejo cars will end up Downtown, with 30% returning to Oficina Vallejo and 10% to the Airport. Finally, 30% of Downtown cars will end up at each of the other locations, with 40% staying at the Downtown location.

This scenario can also be investigated using a discrete-time population model.

(a) Let A_n, V_n, and D_n be the number of cars at the Airport, Oficina Vallejo, and Downtown, respectively, on day n. Write a system of three equations (as in Example 6.23) giving A_n, V_n, and D_n each as functions of A_{n-1}, V_{n-1}, and D_{n-1}.

(b) Suppose that, initially, $A_0 = 1000$, $V_0 = 0$, and $D_0 = 0$. Use your system to compute A_2, V_2, and D_2.

(c) Solve a system of three equations in three variables to find all fixed points of this system.

(d) Implement your system on a spreadsheet. Does the rental car population appear to stabilize at a fixed point?

This kind of population model—where each subpopulation is a linear function of the others and the total population remains constant—is called a *Markov chain*.

12. **Project:** (This project is an extension of Exercise 4. Start with that.) In the logistic population model (Example 6.20), different values of r result in different types of long-term behavior. As $n \to \infty$, the population may stabilize to a single point, it may cycle among two or more values, or it may behave chaotically. A *bifurcation diagram* is a plot with the range of values for the parameter r on the horizontal axis and population on the vertical axis. A point (r, P) in the bifurcation diagram indicates that P is a long-term population value for parameter value r. For example, Figure 6.12 suggests that for $r = 3.2$, the population cycles between 0.8 and 0.5, so the points $(3.2, 0.8)$ and $(3.2, 0.5)$ should appear in the bifurcation diagram. We would also expect many different points of the form $(3.8, P)$, since $r = 3.8$ appears chaotic.

Using a spreadsheet or other software, create a bifurcation diagram for Example 6.20. The range on the horizontal axis should be $0 \le r \le 4$. Experiment with bifurcation diagrams of other population models.

13. **Project:** (Calculus required.) Find a discussion of Euler's method in a calculus textbook. Show that you can replace a differential equation model with a discrete-time model using a recurrence relation. Find a specific example, and compare the solution you get by using Euler's method with the solution of the discrete-time equivalent.

14. **Project:** Create your own discrete-time population model for a set of subpopulations about which you have data. (For example, the subpopulations of different majors at your college, or the membership in various organizations.) Implement your model on a spreadsheet. Experiment with the parameters of your model to get it to fit your data reasonably closely. Use algebra to find any fixed points of your model. Can you make any predictions based on your model?

6.5   Twelve-Tone Music

Mathematics is sometimes described as the study of patterns. So far in this chapter, we have seen how discrete mathematical ideas can help identify patterns in DNA, natural language, social structures, and population change. This last section on applications presents a change of pace, as we take a mathematical look at what could be called the *art* of patterns: music.

Mathematics and music are intertwined in many ways. The recursive and symmetric patterns in the music of Johann Sebastian Bach, for example, are well-chronicled in Hofstadter [13]. In this section we will take a look at music by composers who are probably less familiar to you: the founders of the Viennese school of twelve-tone composition. This avant-garde, atonal music is somewhat less accessible than most music, and it can even be difficult to listen to at first, but it employs discrete mathematical ideas in interesting ways. In particular, we will make extensive use of functions and algorithms on discrete sets. And, while we aren't going to use any tools or jargon from more advanced mathematics courses, this section provides a gentle introduction to some ideas from abstract algebra.

6.5.1   Twelve-Tone Composition

In the early 20th century, the Austrian composer Arnold Schoenberg pioneered a new way of writing music. Schoenberg's method dictated rigid rules that force a composer to use all of the twelve *pitch classes*—C, C♯, D, D♯, E, F, F♯, G, G♯, A, A♯, B—in such way that each pitch class appears as often as the others. The resulting music is *atonal*; it isn't written in a key, and it lacks many familiar characteristics that we are accustomed to hearing in music.

A twelve-tone composition is based on a single permutation of the twelve pitch classes, called a *tone row*. Throughout the entire piece, the composer must use the tone row, or a transformation of the tone row, to form all of the melodies and harmonies. For example, Schoenberg's Serenade, opus 24, movement 5, uses the following tone row.

The entire movement uses this pattern of notes, transformed in certain ways: transposed (shifted up or down), inverted (flipped upside-down), and/or retrograded (played backward). We'll take a closer look at the definitions of these transformations later in this section.

A tone row can be represented mathematically as an ordered 12-tuple. Let the pitch classes C, C♯, D, ..., B correspond to the integers $0, 1, 2, \ldots, 11$, respectively. The above tone row from Schoenberg's Serenade can then be written as

$$(9, 10, 0, 3, 4, 6, 5, 7, 8, 11, 1, 2).$$

Since each pitch class must be used exactly once in any tone row, these 12-tuples must contain every integer in $\{0, 1, 2, \ldots, 11\}$; they are permutations of this set.

6.5.2   Listing All Permutations

The theory of twelve-tone music naturally centers on the study of permutations and the transformations that act on them. From Chapter 4, we know that there are $12! = 479{,}001{,}600$ different twelve-tone rows. As a first step, let's see how to create a list of all the permutations in a systematic way.

In order to design an algorithm that will list all possible permutations of the set $\{0, 1, 2, \ldots, n-1\}$, it helps to think recursively. Each permutation of this set looks like a permutation of the smaller set $\{0, 1, 2, \ldots, n-2\}$, with the symbol $n-1$ inserted somewhere in this shorter permutation. This observation motivates Algorithm 6.3.

Algorithm 6.3 Make a list of all permutations of $\{0, 1, 2, \ldots, n-1\}$.

Preconditions: $n \in \mathbf{N}$.

Postconditions: Returns the set S_n of all permutations of $\{0, 1, 2, \ldots, n-1\}$, listed as ordered n-tuples.

```
function ListPerms (n ∈ N)
    if n = 1 then
        return {(0)}
    else
      ⌐ Sₙ ← ∅
        X ← ListPerms (n − 1)
        for (p₀, p₁, ..., pₙ₋₂) ∈ X do
            Sₙ ← Sₙ ∪ InsertEverywhere (n − 1, (p₀, p₁, ..., pₙ₋₂))
      ∟ return Sₙ
```

The helper algorithm InsertEverywhere returns the set containing all the permutations that can be formed by inserting a new symbol t into a k-tuple $(p_0, p_1, \ldots, p_{k-1})$. See Algorithm 6.4.

Algorithm 6.4 Make a list of permutations by inserting a new symbol.

Preconditions: $t \in \mathbf{N}$ and $(p_0, p_1, \ldots, p_{k-1})$ is a k-tuple of natural numbers.

Postconditions: Returns the set

$$
\begin{aligned}
Y = \{ &(t, p_0, p_1, \ldots, p_{k-1}), \\
&(p_0, t, p_1, \ldots, p_{k-1}), \\
&(p_0, p_1, t, \ldots, p_{k-1}), \\
&\cdots \\
&(p_0, p_1, \ldots, p_{k-1}, t) \}
\end{aligned}
$$

```
function InsertEverywhere (t ∈ N, (p₀,p₁,...,p_{k-1}) ∈ N × ··· × N)
                                                        \_____ k _____/
    Y ← ∅
    for i ∈ {0,1,2,...,k} do
        Y ← Y ∪ {(p₀,p₁,...,p_{i-1},t,p_i,...,p_{k-1})}
    return Y
```

In the `for`-loop in this algorithm, let it be understood that t goes at the beginning of the k-tuple when $i = 0$ and at the end when $i = k$.

The `ListPerms` function lends itself nicely to bottom-up evaluation. The base case, `ListPerms(1)`, returns the set $\{(0)\}$. For $n = 2$, `ListPerms(2)` returns

$$\texttt{InsertEverywhere}(1, (0)),$$

which is the set $\{(1, 0), (0, 1)\}$. Similarly, `ListPerms(3)` returns

$$
\begin{aligned}
&\texttt{InsertEverywhere}(2, (1, 0)) \cup \texttt{InsertEverywhere}(2, (0, 1)) \\
&= \{(2, 1, 0), (1, 2, 0), (1, 0, 2)\} \cup \{(2, 0, 1), (0, 2, 1), (0, 1, 2)\} \\
&= \{(2, 1, 0), (1, 2, 0), (1, 0, 2), (2, 0, 1), (0, 2, 1), (0, 1, 2)\}.
\end{aligned}
$$

The $n = 4$ case is left as an exercise. It is also an exercise to show that this algorithm really does produce all $n!$ permutations, and it shouldn't be surprising that the time and space complexity are both $\Theta(n!)$.

Making a list of all twelve-tone rows is a large problem for a computer. If we decide to store the tone rows in a file, for example, we might require about 12 bytes for each row, producing a file with $12 \cdot 12!$ bytes, which is more than 5 gigabytes. Any further analysis of this data (e.g., sorting, clustering) presents significant computational challenges.

6.5.3   Transformations of Tone Rows

Once a composer decides on a tone row for a piece of music, the art of composition lies in applying various transformations to the tone row to form the melodies and harmonies of the piece. A transformation turns a tone row into another tone row. Therefore, the twelve pitch classes remain evenly distributed after transformations are applied, preserving the atonal quality of the music.

We will consider four types of tone row transformations that were used by early twelve-tone composers. *Transposition* T_k shifts the row up k semitones. Modular arithmetic is convenient for expressing the effect of T_k on a tone row.

$$T_k((p_0, p_1, p_2, \ldots, p_{11})) = (p_0 + k, p_1 + k, \ldots, p_{11} + k) \mod 12$$

Inversion I turns the pattern of notes on the staff upside-down. We'll adopt the convention that inversion fixes the first pitch class of a tone row.

$$I((p_0, p_1, p_2, \ldots, p_{11})) = (p_0, 2p_0 - p_1, 2p_0 - p_2, \ldots, 2p_0 - p_{11}) \mod 12$$

Retrograde R reverses the order of the notes.

$$R((p_0, p_1, p_2, \ldots, p_{11})) = (p_{11}, p_{10}, \ldots, p_1, p_0)$$

Schoenberg and his students Alban Berg and Anton Webern used transposition, inversion, and retrograde extensively in their compositions. Berg, and to a lesser extent Schoenberg, also employed a fourth transformation, *cyclic shift*. Cyclic shift C_k moves the last k notes from the end of a tone row to the beginning.

$$C_k((p_0, p_1, p_2, \ldots, p_{11})) = (p_{0+k}, p_{1+k}, \ldots, p_{11+k})$$

where the subscripts are taken modulo 12.

Notice that I and R can both "undo" themselves: for any tone row p, $I(I(p)) = p = R(R(p))$. In other words, $I \circ I$ and $R \circ R$ are both the identity, or *trivial*, transformation. Similarly, $C_i \circ C_j$ and $T_i \circ T_j$ are trivial whenever $i + j = 12$. In the language of functions, all the transformations are invertible. If there is a transformation sending p to q, then there is a transformation sending q to p.

6.5.4 Equivalence Classes and Symmetry

Let S_{12} denote the set of all twelve-tone rows. Define a relation $\cong$ on S_{12} as follows: For $p, q \in S_{12}$, $p \cong q$ if there is some composite A of transpositions, inversions, retrogrades, and cyclic shifts such that $A(p) = q$. It is left as an exercise to show that $\cong$ is an equivalence relation.

Suppose a composer has chosen a tone row p and begins to write down all possible transformations of p using transposition, inversion, retrograde, and cyclic shift. The set of all tone rows formed in this way is the $\cong$-equivalence class, or *row class*, of p. It doesn't really matter if the composition is based on p or an equivalent tone row; the set of available rows will be the same.

How many different tone rows can be formed in this way? How big is the row class of p? The answer to this question isn't easy. It depends on p.

First of all, notice that given any row p, the list

$$p, T_1(p), T_2(p), \ldots, T_{11}(p)$$

always contains 12 distinct tone rows, since, in particular, the first pitch class of these rows are all distinct. Therefore, every row class must have at least 12 elements. Now you might think that taking the retrograde of each element on this list would produce a list

$$R(p), R(T_1(p)), R(T_2(p)), \ldots, R(T_{11}(p))$$

of 12 new tone rows, but this isn't always the case.

Example 6.24 Webern's Chamber Symphony, opus 21, is based on the tone row $p = (5, 8, 7, 6, 10, 9, 3, 4, 0, 1, 2, 11)$. To form the retrograde $R(p)$, we just need to reverse the order of the pitch classes:

$$R(p) = (11, 2, 1, 0, 4, 3, 9, 10, 6, 7, 8, 5).$$

However, this row has a curious property: reversing its order is the same as transposing it.

$$\begin{aligned}
T_6(p) &= (5+6, 8+6, 7+6, 6+6, 10+6, 9+6, 3+6, 4+6, 0+6, 1+6, 2+6, 11+6) \quad \text{mod } 12 \\
&= (11, 14, 13, 12, 16, 15, 9, 10, 6, 7, 8, 17) \quad \text{mod } 12 \\
&= (11, 2, 1, 0, 4, 3, 9, 10, 6, 7, 8, 5),
\end{aligned}$$

which is the same as $R(p)$. (Tone rows that are transpositions of their retrogrades are called *palindromic*.)

This example reveals the difficulty of counting the elements of a row class. For this value of p, the list of retrograded transpositions contains exactly the same tone rows as the list of transpositions.

For most tone rows, however, the list of transpositions is distinct from the list of retrograded transpositions; together, these two transformations usually produce 24 distinct tone rows. Suppose now that p is such a row, and take the inversion of these 24 elements. Normally, this will produce 24 new elements, but—again—there are exceptions. It is left as an exercise to show that the tone row from Schoenberg's Serenade is the same as an inverted retrograde of a transposition.

However, for most tone rows p, the list

$$
\begin{array}{ccccc}
p, & T_1(p), & T_2(p), & \ldots, & T_{11}(p), \\
R(p), & R(T_1(p)), & R(T_2(p)), & \ldots, & R(T_{11}(p)), \\
I(p), & I(T_1(p)), & I(T_2(p)), & \ldots, & I(T_{11}(p)), \\
I(R(p)), & I(R(T_1(p))), & I(R(T_2(p))), & \ldots, & I(R(T_{11}(p)))
\end{array}
$$

contains 48 distinct tone rows [17]. Furthermore, additional applications of inversion, retrograde, and transposition to the items on this list will only produce duplicates. The following example begins to explain why.

Example 6.25 Let p be a tone row, and let $k, j \in \{1, 2, \ldots, 11\}$. Prove that $T_j(I(R(T_k(p)))) = I(R(T_l(p)))$ for some l.

Proof The key part of this proof is left for you to do in the exercises: for any tone row q and any i, you are asked to show that $T_i(R(q)) = R(T_i(q))$ and $T_i(I(q)) = I(T_i(q))$. In other words, transposition *commutes* with both inversion and retrograde.

Using this fact,

$$
\begin{aligned}
T_j(I(R(T_k(p)))) &= I(T_j(R(T_k(p)))) \\
&= I(R(T_j(T_k(p)))) \\
&= I(R(T_l(p)))
\end{aligned}
$$

for $l = j + k \mod 12$. This last step follows from the observation that a composite of transpositions is another transposition. □

The upshot of this example is that applying a transposition to something in the last row of the above list will not give you a new tone row. Similar facts hold about the other transformations. When the rows of the above list are transformed via cyclic shift, the total number of distinct rows has the potential to reach at most $12 \cdot 48 = 576$.

The main result is the following.

Theorem 6.4 *For any tone row p, the row class of p contains at most 576 tone rows. If the size of the row class is less than 576, then there is some nontrivial composite transformation A such that $A(p) = p$.*

Rows that transform back into themselves via a nontrivial composite transformation are called *symmetric*. The row from Webern's Chamber Symphony (Example 6.24) is one example; its row class contains only 288 tone rows. We saw above that this tone row is the same backward as forward, up to a transposition. Webern extends this idea to the entire piece, using palindromic rhythms and dynamics, to give the Chamber Symphony a palindromic theme [4].

Theorem 6.4 illustrates mathematically that the four transformations—transposition, inversion, retrograde, and cyclic shift—are closely related. It is actually quite remarkable that any composite of these four transformations will yield such a small fraction (576/12!) of the total number of tone rows. The choice of these four transformations was musically motivated; it is interesting that this musical relatedness appears to express itself in mathematics.

Exercises 6.5

1. Perform a bottom-up evaluation of `ListPerms(4)`.

2. Use induction to prove that Algorithm 6.3 returns a set of $n!$ distinct n-tuples.

3. Use Exercise 2 to compute (in terms of n) the number of union ($\cup$) operations that Algorithm 6.3 performs.

4. Show that the row $p = (9, 10, 0, 3, 4, 6, 5, 7, 8, 11, 1, 2)$ from Schoenberg's Serenade has the property that $p = I(R(T_7(p)))$.

5. Let p be the row from Schoenberg's Serenade. Use the result of Exercise 4 to show that $p = T_5(R(I(p)))$, without doing any additional tone row calculations. (Hint: Apply inverse functions to both sides of the equation $p = I(R(T_7(p)))$.)

6. The tone row from Berg's Violin Concerto is $p = (7, 10, 2, 6, 9, 0, 4, 8, 11, 1, 3, 5)$. Show that $p = T_4(C_3(R(I(p))))$.

7. Let $p = (4, 6, 11, 7, 0, 8, 1, 9, 2, 10, 3, 5)$ and let $q = (10, 0, 5, 1, 6, 2, 7, 3, 8, 4, 9, 11)$ be tone rows. Verify that $p = T_k(R(I(q)))$ for some k, and find this value of k.

8. Prove that the relation $\cong$ on S_{12} is an equivalence relation. (For $p, q \in S_{12}$, $p \cong q$ if there is some composite K of transpositions, inversions, retrogrades, and cyclic shifts such that $K(p) = q$.)

9. Compute all 24 tone rows in the row class of $(0, 1, 2, 3, 4, 5, 6, 7, 8, 9, 10, 11)$, the *chromatic scale*.

10. Show that the row class of the *circle of fifths* $(0, 7, 2, 9, 4, 11, 6, 1, 8, 3, 10, 5)$ contains 24 tone rows.

11. Prove, for any tone row p and any k, that $T_k(R(p)) = R(T_k(p))$. (We say that transposition *commutes* with retrograde.)

12. Prove, for any tone row p and any k, that $T_k(I(p)) = I(T_k(p))$.

13. Prove, for any tone row p, that $R(I(p))$ is a transposition of $I(R(p))$. (We say that retrograde and inversion commute *up to* a transposition.)

14. Let p be a tone row, and let $k, j \in \{1, 2, \dots, 11\}$. Prove that $R(I(R(T_k(p)))) = I(T_l(p))$ for some l.

15. **Project:** (Programming skill required.) Implement Algorithm 6.3 on a computer. Try different ways of traversing the set S_n: writing the permutations to a file, storing them in memory, and simply counting them. Record the running time of your program for different values of n in the range $1 \le n \le 25$. What is the largest n for which the program finishes in a reasonable amount of time?

16. **Project:** Twelve-tone composers use other transformations in addition to the ones described here. Research some of these, or try your hand at designing your own. Relate these other transformations to transposition, inversion, retrograde, and cyclic shift. Do the new transformations commute with each other, or with the old transformations? What mathematical and musical qualities of transformations are desirable?

17. **Project:** A tone row can be represented geometrically with a *clock diagram*: Place 12 vertices evenly around the circumference of a circle, and label them with the numbers $0, 1, 2, \dots, 11$, as they would appear on a clock (with 0 replacing 12). A tone row $(p_0, p_1, p_2, \dots, p_{11})$ can then be represented as a sequence of directed edges, starting at p_0 and passing through vertices $p_1, p_2, \dots, p_{11}$ in order. For example, the tone row $(9, 10, 0, 3, 4, 6, 5, 7, 8, 11, 1, 2)$ from Schoenberg's Serenade has the following clock diagram.

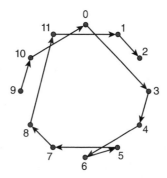

Other examples appear in Hunter and von Hippel [17], along with a discussion of how to recognize tone row symmetry by looking at the clock diagram. Experiment with clock diagrams. See if you can create symmetric rows by creating symmetric clock diagrams, and for each symmetric row p, identify the composite transformation A such that $A(p) = p$. Investigate other uses of clock diagrams in music theory, starting with McCartin [21].

Hints, Answers, and Solutions to Selected Exercises

1.1 Formal Logic

1. (a) $(q \wedge p) \to \neg r$

   (b) If the car will start, then there isn't a blown head gasket or water in the cylinders.

3. (a) $(q \vee r) \to \neg p$

   (b) $\neg\neg p \to \neg(q \vee r)$

   (c) If you can vote, then you aren't under 18 or from Mars.

5. (a) If the ground is wet, then it is raining.

   (b) If the ground is not wet, then it is not raining.

7. (a) Yes, the first components of equal ordered pairs must be equal.

   (b) If $a = c$, then $(a, b) = (c, d)$.

   (c) No. For example, $1 = 1$, but $(1, 2) \neq (1, 5)$.

9.

p	q	$p \leftrightarrow q$	$p \to q$	$q \to p$	$(p \to q) \wedge (q \to p)$
T	T	T	T	T	T
T	F	F	F	T	F
F	T	F	T	F	F
F	F	T	T	T	T

11. The statements $\neg(p \to q)$ and $\neg p \to \neg q$ are not logically equivalent:

p	q	$\neg p$	$\neg q$	$\neg p \to \neg q$	$\neg(p \to q)$
T	T	F	F	T	F
T	F	F	T	T	T
F	T	T	F	F	F
F	F	T	T	T	F

13.

p	q	$p \vee q$	$\neg p$	$(p \vee q) \wedge (\neg p)$	$[(p \vee q) \wedge (\neg p)] \to q$
T	T	T	F	F	T
T	F	T	F	F	T
F	T	T	T	T	T
F	F	F	T	F	T

15. (a)

p	q	r	$q \wedge \neg r$	$p \to (q \wedge \neg r)$	$q \leftrightarrow r$
T	T	T	F	F	T
T	T	F	T	T	F
T	F	T	F	F	F
T	F	F	F	F	T
F	T	T	F	T	T
F	T	F	T	T	F
F	F	T	F	T	F
F	F	F	F	T	T

(b) There are only two rows in which statements A and B are both true. In both rows, p is false.

17. (a)

p	q	r	$p \vee q$	$q \vee r$	$p \vee (q \vee r)$	$(p \vee q) \vee r$
T	T	T	T	T	T	T
T	T	F	T	T	T	T
T	F	T	T	T	T	T
T	F	F	T	F	T	T
F	T	T	T	T	T	T
F	T	F	T	T	T	T
F	F	T	F	T	T	T
F	F	F	F	F	F	F

(b) Hint: mimic part (a).

19. The first statement is stronger, since all squares are rectangles, but not all rectangles are squares.

21. The second statement is stronger, since any number that is divisible by 12 will also be divisible by 3, but not *vice versa*.

23. For $n + 2$ to be a prime number, it is necessary that n be odd. This is not sufficient because, for example, 7 is odd but $7 + 2$ is not prime.

25. $P \leftrightarrow Q$

27. (a)

p	q	$\neg(p \to q)$	$\neg(p \vee q)$	S
T	T	F	F	F
T	F	T	F	T
F	T	F	F	F
F	F	F	T	T

(b) The statement $\neg q$ is logically equivalent to S.

29. (a)

p	q	$p \uparrow q$	$(p \uparrow q) \uparrow (p \uparrow q)$	$p \wedge q$
T	T	F	T	T
T	F	T	F	F
F	T	T	F	F
F	F	T	F	F

31. (a) A's report is $\neg b \wedge c$; B's report is $a \leftrightarrow b$; C's report is $\neg a \vee \neg b$.

(b)

a	b	c	A's report	B's report	C's report
T	T	T	F	T	F
T	T	F	F	T	F
T	F	T	T	F	T
T	F	F	F	F	T
F	T	T	F	F	T
F	T	F	F	F	T
F	F	T	T	T	T
F	F	F	F	T	T

(c) Hint: Consider the seventh row of the truth table.

(d) Hint: In which row are all processors working?

(e) Hint: Construct a truth table for the statement

$$S = (A\text{'s report} \leftrightarrow a) \land (B\text{'s report} \leftrightarrow b) \land (C\text{'s report} \leftrightarrow c)$$

1.2   Propositional Logic

1.

p	q	$\neg q$	$p \to q$	$(\neg q) \land (p \to q)$	$\neg p$	$[(\neg q) \land (p \to q)] \to \neg p$
T	T	F	T	F	F	T
T	F	T	F	F	F	T
F	T	F	T	F	T	T
F	F	T	T	T	T	T

3.

Statements	Reasons
1. $(p \land q) \to r$	given
2. $\neg(p \land q) \lor r$	implication, 1
3. $(\neg p \lor \neg q) \lor r$	De Morgan, 2
4. $\neg p \lor (\neg q \lor r)$	associativity, 3
5. $p \to (\neg q \lor r)$	implication, 4

5. Yes, the proof is reversible because it uses only equivalence rules.

7. (a) *modus tollens*   (b) simplification   (c) *modus ponens*   (d) De Morgan's laws

9. If $x \le y$, then x is odd.

11. $x > 3$ or y is found.

13. This soup tastes funny, or I'm feeling sick. (Answers may vary.)

15.

Statements	Reasons
1. $p \to \neg q$	given
2. $r \to (p \land q)$	given
3. $\neg p \lor \neg q$	implication, 1
4. $\neg(p \land q)$	De Morgan's laws, 3
5. $\neg r$	*modus tollens*, 4, 2

17.

Statements	Reasons
1. $p \to q$	given
2. $p \land r$	given
3. p	simplification, 2
4. q	*modus ponens*, 3, 1
5. $r \land p$	commutativity, 2
6. r	simplification, 5
7. $q \land r$	conjunction, 4, 6

19.

Statements	Reasons
1. $p \land p$	given
2. p	simplification, 1

Statements	Reasons
1. p	given
2. $p \land p$	conjunction, 1, 1

21.

Statements	Reasons
1. $\neg(\neg p \to q) \lor (\neg p \land \neg q)$	given
2. $\neg(\neg(\neg p) \lor q) \lor (\neg p \land \neg q)$	implication, 1
3. $\neg(p \lor q) \lor (\neg p \land \neg q)$	double negation, 2
4. $(\neg p \land \neg q) \lor (\neg p \land \neg q)$	De Morgan, 3
5. $\neg p \land \neg q$	Exercise 20, 4

23. (a) $\neg\neg p \land \neg q$ follows from the given by De Morgan's laws.

(b) The goal will follow from p, by the addition rule.

25. (a)

Statements	Reasons
1. $p \to (q \to r)$	given
2. $\neg p \lor (q \to r)$	implication, 1
3. $\neg p \lor (\neg q \lor r)$	implication, 2
4. $(\neg p \lor \neg q) \lor r$	associativity, 3
5. $\neg(p \land q) \lor r$	De Morgan, 4
6. $(p \land q) \to r$	implication, 5

(c) $\left. \begin{array}{c} p \land (q \to r) \\ q \end{array} \right\} \Rightarrow p \land r$

27.

a	b	$a \to b$	$\neg b$	$a \land \neg b$	$(a \to b) \land (a \land \neg b)$
T	T	T	F	F	F
T	F	F	T	T	F
F	T	T	F	F	F
F	F	T	T	F	F

1.3   Predicate Logic

1. (a) True   (c) True   (e) False

3. (a) $(\exists x)V(x)$ (c) $\neg(\exists x)V(x)$

5. (a) All heavy books are confusing.

(c) All books are confusing or heavy.

7. (a) True: Given y, set $x = y$, and $x/y = 1$ is an integer.

(b) False. (Why?)

9. (a) $(\exists x)(\exists y)(\forall z)\neg P(x, y, z)$

(b) Yes. (Explain.)

(c) No. (Explain.)

11. (a) In the domain of all real numbers, let $N(x)$ be "x is a natural number" and let $I(x)$ be "x is an integer." Then the statement becomes $(\forall x)(N(x) \to I(x))$.

(c) In the domain of all streets, let $O(x)$ be "x is one-way" and let $C(x)$ be "x is in Cozumel." The the statement becomes $(\forall x)(C(x) \to O(x))$.

13. (a) $(\exists x)(C(x) \land R(x))$

(b) $\neg(\exists x)(C(x) \land R(x)) \Leftrightarrow (\forall x)(\neg C(x) \lor \neg R(x)) \Leftrightarrow (\forall x)(C(x) \to \neg R(x))$

(c) All children are pleasant.

15. (a) $(\forall y)(\exists x)P(x, y)$

(b) $(\exists y)(\forall x)\neg P(x, y)$

(c) There is a number that all numbers are less than or equal to.

17. (a) $(\forall x)(\neg P(x) \to (\exists y)(P(y) \land Q(y, x)))$

(b) $(\exists x)(\neg P(x) \land (\forall y)(P(y) \to \neg Q(y, x)))$

(c) There is a nonprime x such that no prime y divides it.

19. (a)

$\quad \neg[(\forall x)(P(x) \to (\exists y)(H(y) \land B(x, y)))]$
$\Leftrightarrow \quad (\exists x)[\neg(P(x) \to (\exists y)(H(y) \land B(x, y)))]$, univ. neg.
$\Leftrightarrow \quad (\exists x)[\neg(\neg P(x) \lor (\exists y)(H(y) \land B(x, y)))]$, implication
$\Leftrightarrow \quad (\exists x)[\neg\neg P(x) \land \neg(\exists y)(H(y) \land B(x, y))]$, De Morgan
$\Leftrightarrow \quad (\exists x)[\neg\neg P(x) \land (\forall y)\neg(H(y) \land B(x, y))]$, exist. neg.
$\Leftrightarrow \quad (\exists x)(P(x) \land (\forall y)\neg(H(y) \land B(x, y)))$, double neg.
$\Leftrightarrow \quad (\exists x)(P(x) \land (\forall y)(\neg H(y) \lor \neg B(x, y)))$, De Morgan
$\Leftrightarrow \quad (\exists x)(P(x) \land (\forall y)(H(y) \to \neg B(x, y)))$, implication

21. (a)   iii $(\forall x)[I(x) \rightarrow (\forall y)(\neg I(y) \rightarrow M(x,y))]$

    (c) $\neg(\exists x)[I(x) \wedge (\forall y)(H(x,y) \rightarrow M(y,x))]$
    $\Leftrightarrow (\forall x)\neg[I(x) \wedge (\forall y)(H(x,y) \rightarrow M(y,x))]$, exist. neg.
    $\Leftrightarrow (\forall x)[\neg I(x) \vee \neg(\forall y)(H(x,y) \rightarrow M(y,x))]$, De Morgan
    $\Leftrightarrow (\forall x)[\neg I(x) \vee (\exists y)\neg(H(x,y) \rightarrow M(y,x))]$, univ. neg.
    $\Leftrightarrow (\forall x)[I(x) \rightarrow (\exists y)(H(x,y) \wedge \neg M(y,x))]$, imp., D.M.

23. (a) $p \wedge q$ (b) $p \vee q$ (c) De Morgan

25. (a) (Answers may vary.) In the domain of real numbers, let $P(x)$ denote "$x \geq 0$" and let $Q(x)$ denote "$x < 0$." The statement that $(\forall x)(P(x) \vee Q(x))$ is true: every number is either nonnegative or negative. However, the statement that $(\forall x)P(x) \vee (\forall x)Q(x)$ is false: not every number is nonnegative, and not every number is negative.

1.4   Logic in Mathematics

1. Answers may vary.

3. $104 = 2 \cdot 52$.

5. (a) $n_1 = 2k_1$ and $n_2 = 2k_2$ for some k_1, k_2.

    (b) $n_1 n_2 = 4k_1 k_2$.

    (c) $n_1 + n_2 = 2(k_1 + k_2)$.

7. Answers may vary.

9. The lines have the point $(1,3)$ in common.

11. $(\forall n)(E(n) \leftrightarrow (\exists k)(n = 2k))$.

13. A theorem must be proved, while an axiom is assumed without proof.

15. Answers may vary. For example,

    (b) An equilateral triangle.   (d) $n = 9$.

17. None can be proved, since all have counterexamples.

19.

21. No. Given two different points x and y, there is a *unique* line (Axiom 1) passing through x and y.

23. Two lines intersect if there is a point that is on both lines.

25. There is at least one bing; call it x. By Axiom 2, x is hit by exactly two baddas, call them a and b. These two baddas hit exactly four bings each: call these bings x, y_1, y_2, y_3 and x, z_1, z_2, z_3. Now a and b are distinct baddas, each hitting bing x, so there are no other bings hit by both a and b, by Axiom 3. Therefore the distinct bings y_1, y_2, y_3 must be different from the distinct bings z_1, z_2, z_3, so the seven bings $x, y_1, y_2, y_3, z_1, z_2, z_3$ are all distinct.

27. $(\forall x)(\forall y)(\forall q)(D(x) \wedge D(y) \wedge G(q) \wedge N(x,y) \wedge H(x,q) \wedge H(y,q) \rightarrow \neg(\exists r)(G(r) \wedge N(r,q) \wedge H(x,r) \wedge H(y,r)))$.

29. The model satisfies Axioms 1, 3, and 4, but not Axiom 2. (Explain.)

1.5   Methods of Proof

1. (a) Let $D(a,b)$ denote "$a \mid b$," and let $E(a)$ denote "a is even." Then we are trying to prove that $(\forall x)(D(4,x) \rightarrow E(x))$.

    (b) Let x be an integer, and suppose that $4 \mid x$.

(c) Therefore $x = 4k$ for some integer k.

(d) Since $x = 2(2k)$, x is even.

3. **Proof** Suppose a, b, c are integers with $(a \cdot b) \mid c$. Then $c = k(a \cdot b)$ for some integer k, so $c = (k \cdot b)a$, so $a \mid c$. $\square$

5. **Proof** Let $ABCD$ be a parallelogram. By Theorem 1.2, the sums of the angle measures of triangles $\triangle ABC$ and $\triangle BCD$ are both $180°$. The sum of the angle measures of parallelogram $ABCD$ is the sum of these two sums: $180 + 180 = 360$. $\square$

7. **Proof** (By contraposition.) Let x be an integer. Suppose that x is even, so $x = 2k$ for some integer k. Then $x^2 + x + 1 = 4k^2 + 2k + 1 = 2(2k^2 + k) + 1$ is odd. $\square$

9. **Proof** Let n_1 be an even integer, and let n_2 be an odd integer. So $n_1 = 2k_1$ and $n_2 = 2k_2 + 1$ for some integers k_1 and k_2. Then $n_1 + n_2 = 2k_1 + 2k_2 + 1 = 2(k_1 + k_2) + 1$ is odd. $\square$

11. **Proof** (By contradiction.) Let x and y be integers that satisfy the equation $3x + 5y = 153$. Suppose, to the contrary, that both x and y are even. Then $x = 2k_1$ and $y = 2k_2$ for some integers k_1 and k_2. Then $153 = 3x + 5y = 6k_1 + 10k_2 = 2(3k_1 + 5k_2)$ is even. But $153 = 76 \cdot 2 + 1$ is also odd. This contradicts Axiom 1.2. $\square$

13. **Proof** (By contraposition.) Let a and b be integers. Suppose that $5 \mid a$ or $5 \mid b$. If $5 \mid a$, then $a = 5k$ for some k. Therefore $ab = 5kb$, so $5 \mid ab$. Similarly, if $5 \mid b$, then $5 \mid ab$. $\square$

15. **Proof** Suppose that $a \lhd b$ and $c \lhd d$. Then there exist integers k_1 and k_2 such that $3a + 5b = 7k_1$ and $3c + 5d = 7k_2$. Adding equations gives $3(a + c) + 5(b + d) = 7(k_1 + k_2)$. Therefore $a + c \lhd b + d$. $\square$

17. **Proof** Let a and b be rational numbers. Then $a = p/q$ and $b = r/s$ for some integers p, q, r, s. Therefore,

$$a \cdot b = \frac{p}{q} \cdot \frac{r}{s} = \frac{pr}{qs},$$

which is the ratio of two integers pr and qs, using Axiom 1.1. So $a \cdot b$ is rational. $\square$

19. **Proof** (By contradiction.) Suppose that $x \neq 0$ is rational and y is irrational, and suppose, to the contrary, that xy is rational. Therefore $x = p/q$ and $xy = r/s$ for some integers p, q, r, s. Then,

$$y = \frac{xy}{x}$$
$$= \frac{r}{s} \cdot \frac{q}{p}$$
$$= \frac{rq}{sp}$$

which contradicts that y is irrational. $\square$

21. **Proof** (By contraposition.) Suppose n is an even integer, so $n = 2k$ for some integer k. Then $n^2 + 2n = 4k^2 + 4k = 2(2k^2 + 2k)$ is even, so n is not frumpable. $\square$

23. **Proof** (By contradiction.) Let l, m, n be lines, and suppose $l \parallel m$ and $m \parallel n$. Suppose, to the contrary, that l is not parallel to n. By the definition of "parallel," this means there is some point x on both l and n. And since $l \parallel m$, x is not on m. So Axiom 2 says that there is a *unique* line such that x is on the line and the line is parallel to m. This contradicts that l and n are *both* lines that x is on and that are parallel to m. $\square$

25. (c) **Proof** By Axiom 3, there are four points w, x, y, z, no three of which are on the same line. By Axiom 1, there is a unique line through each one of the pairs (w, x), (x, y), (y, z), and (z, w) of points: denote these lines as wx, wy, wz, xy. Since no three of w, x, y, z are on the same line, these four lines are distinct. Suppose, to the contrary, that there is a point on three of them. Without loss of generality, suppose

point p is on wx, xy, and yz. By part (b), there is exactly one point on both wx and xy, so this point x must be the same as p. Therefore x is also on yz. But this contradicts that no three of w, x, y, z are on the same line. $\square$

2.1 Graphs

1. (a) 9

   (b) $a : 4, b : 4, c : 2, d : 4, e : 4$

   (c) Yes: $4 + 4 + 2 + 4 + 4 = 2 \cdot 9$

3. Any such graph must have six edges. Drawings may vary.

5. Drawings may vary. For example:

   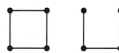

7. There are only two odd-degree vertices, so it is possible to travel an Euler path, for example: B, C, D, A, B, D.

   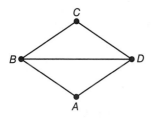

9. For example: (a) add an edge between e and c, and (b) add an edge between b and h.

11. The vertices for Math, Chem, Soc, and Psych are all joined to each other, so these four must use four different colors.

13. Three colors suffice. (Do it.) Three colors are needed. (Explain why.)

    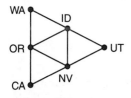

15. Hint: Construct a graph in which each vertex represents a word, and two vertices are joined if their words have a letter in common.

17. Hint: Starting at the top and proceeding around the perimeter, the colors must alternate.

19. The graph can be colored with three colors. (Do it.) Three colors are needed, because the graph contains triangles.

21. Hint: The minimal weight is 1925. (Find a circuit with this weight.)

23. After two days, 38% will be at the Airport, 42% will be Downtown, and 20% will be at Oficina Vallejo.

25. (a) 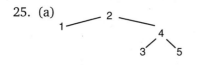   (b)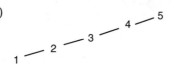

27.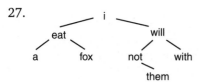

29. (a) A, B, H, I (or B, G, H, I)

(b) Answers may vary. For example: Because G has the most ties, and G's removal would disconnect the network, G is important.

(c) Actors G and A have three mutual friends, so they should become acquainted soon. Actors E and A are four ties apart, so they will likely take a while to become acquainted.

2.2   Sets

1.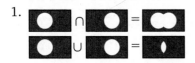

3. (a) $\{1, 7, 8, 9\}$

(b) $\{(3, 2), (3, 3), (3, 4), (4, 2), (4, 3), (4, 4)\}$

(c) $\{\emptyset, \{5\}, \{6\}, \{5, 6\}\}$

5. (a) $B \cap C = \emptyset$ (b) $D \subseteq A$ (c) $3 \in B \cap A'$ (d) $(A \cup B \cup C \cup D)' \neq \emptyset$

7. (a) $x \in A \cap B'$ (b) $(A \cup D)' \neq \emptyset$ (c) $(B \cup C) \subseteq A$

9. $E \cap P = \{2\}$

11. $34 + 9 - 40 = 3$

13. (a) By the inclusion–exclusion principle, $|X \cap C| = |A \cap C| + |B \cap C| - |A \cap B \cap C|$.

(b) By the inclusion–exclusion principle, $|A \cup B \cup C| = |X \cup C| = |X| + |C| - |X \cap C| = |A \cup B| + |C| - (|A \cap C| + |B \cap C| - |A \cap B \cap C|) = |A| + |B| - |A \cap B| + |C| - |A \cap C| - |B \cap C| + |A \cap B \cap C| = |A| + |B| + |C| - |A \cap B| - |A \cap C| - |B \cap C| + |A \cap B \cap C|$.

15. $2, 3, 6, 7$

17. (a) $S \times S = \{(a, a), (a, b), (a, c), (b, a), (b, b), (b, c), (c, a), (c, b), (c, c)\}$

(b) $\mathcal{P}(S) = \{\emptyset, \{a\}, \{b\}, \{c\}, \{a, b\}, \{b, c\}, \{a, c\}, \{a, b, c\}\}$

19. $\{n \in \mathbf{Z} \mid n = 2k + 1 \text{ for some } k \in \mathbf{Z}\}$

21. $\{1, 2, 3\}, \{1, 2, 4\}, \{1, 3, 4\}, \{2, 3, 4\}$

23. **Proof**   Let $x \in (A \cap B)'$. In other words, if $P(x)$ is the statement "$x \in A$" and $Q(x)$ is the statement "$x \in B$," we are starting with the assumption $\neg(P(x) \wedge Q(x))$. By De Morgan's laws for propositional logic, this is equivalent to $\neg P(x) \vee \neg Q(x)$, which, in the language of set theory, is the same as $x \in A' \cup B'$. We have shown that $x \in (A \cap B)' \Leftrightarrow x \in A' \cup B'$, hence the sets $(A \cap B)'$ and $A' \cup B'$ are equal. $\square$

25. (a) Even integers and odd integers are integers.

(b) Every integer is either even or odd. (Axiom 1.2.)

27. **Proof**   Let $x \in X \cap (Y \cup Z)$. In other words, if $P(x)$ is the statement "$x \in X$," $Q(x)$ is the statement "$x \in Y$," and $R(x)$ is the statement "$x \in Z$," we are starting with the assumption $P(x) \wedge (Q(x) \vee R(x))$. By the distributive property for propositional logic, this is equivalent to $(P(x) \wedge Q(x)) \vee (P(x) \wedge R(x))$, which, in the language of set theory, is the same as $x \in (X \cap Y) \cup (X \cap Z)$. $\square$

29. $|P_1| > |P_2|$. (Why?)

31.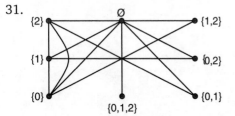

2.3 Functions

1. (a)    (b)

3. For example, $s(\{1,2\}) = s(\{3\})$, but $\{1,2\} \neq \{3\}$.

5. A resident may speak more than one language.

7. The function m is not one-to-one, because two people can have the same mother (i.e., siblings exist). The function m is not onto, because not all people are mothers.

9. The function is not onto because there are dots in Y that have no arrows to them.

11. The number $(y-1)/2$ may fail to be an integer.

13. Yes. $n = n^{-1}$.

15. For example, $g(4,2) = g(2,1)$, so g is not one-to-one.

17. (a) **Proof** Let $a, b \in \mathbf{Z}$, and suppose $f(a) = f(b)$. Then $(2a+3, a-4) = (2b+3, b-4)$, so $a-4 = b-4$, and $a = b$. □

    (b) The function f is not onto, because there is no x such that $f(x) = (2x+3, x-4) = (0,0)$. Suppose, to the contrary, that $2x+3 = 0$. Then $x = -3/2$ is not an integer.

19. (a) Yes. Suppose $d(a) = d(b)$. Then $(a,a) = (b,b)$, so $a = b$.

    (b) No (assuming X has more than one element). For any a, b with $a \neq b$, $(a,b) \neq d(x)$ for any x.

21. (a) The set $f(e)$ is always a set $\{v_1, v_2\}$, with $v_1 \neq v_2$, because simple graphs have no loops.

    (b) **Proof** Let a, b be edges such that $f(a) = f(b)$. Then a and b join the same two vertices. Since simple graphs have no multiple edges, a must equal b. □

    (c) The function f is not onto, in general. If G is not a complete graph, then there is some set of vertices $\{a, b\}$ that do not share an edge.

23. (a) Suppose $f(a) = f(b)$. Then $30030/a = 30030/b$, so $a = b$.

    (b) Let $y \in X$. Since $y \mid 30030$, there is some k such that $30030 = ky$. Therefore $k \mid 30030$ also, so $k \in X$. So we have $f(k) = 30030/k = ky/k = y$.

25. (a) **Proof** Suppose $f(a) = f(b)$. If a and b are both even, then $a/2 = b/2$, so $a = b$. If a and b are both odd, then $(1-a)/2 = (1-b)/2$, so $a = b$. Finally, suppose (without loss of generality) that a is even and b is odd. Then $a/2 = (1-b)/2$, so $a+b = 1$. But this can't happen, since a and b are both in $\mathbf{N}$. Therefore f is one-to-one.
    Let $y \in \mathbf{Z}$. If $y > 0$, then $f(2y) = 2y/2 = y$. If $y \leq 0$, then $1 - 2y = 2(-y) + 1$ is an odd natural number, and $f(1-2y) = (1-1+2y)/2 = y$. So f is onto. □

    (b) $f^{-1}(x) = \begin{cases} 2x & \text{if } x > 0 \\ 1 - 2x & \text{if } x \leq 0 \end{cases}$

27. $f^{-1}(x) = \sqrt[3]{x-1}$. (Check your answer.)

29. No. For example, $(f \circ g)(5) = 4$, but $(g \circ f)(5) = 5$.

31. For any $(x,y) \in D^*$, $p(x,y) = (x/\sqrt{x^2+y^2}, y/\sqrt{x^2+y^2})$ because p just converts the vector $\langle x,y \rangle$ to a unit vector. If $(x,y) \in H$, then $\sqrt{x^2+y^2} = 1/2$, so $p|_H(x,y) = (x/(1/2), y/(1/2)) = (2x, 2y)$.

33. **Proof** Let $z \in Z$. Since g is onto, there is some $y \in Y$ such that $g(y) = z$. Since f is onto, there is some $x \in X$ such that $f(x) = y$. Therefore $(g \circ f)(x) = g(y) = z$. □

35. Let $f \colon X \longrightarrow Y$ and $g \colon Y \longrightarrow Z$ be functions such that $h = g \circ f$ is a one-to-one correspondence.

(a) **Proof**   Suppose $f(a) = f(b)$. Then $g(f(a)) = g(f(b))$, that is, $h(a) = h(b)$. Since h is one-to-one, $a = b$.   □

(b) **Proof**   Let $z \in Z$. Since h is onto, there is some $x \in X$ such that $h(x) = z$. But then $f(x) \in Y$, and $g(f(x)) = h(x) = z$.   □

2.4   Relations and Equivalences

1. Since $<$ is not symmetric, the graph should be directed.

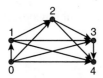

3. Since $\rightleftharpoons$ is symmetric, this graph is undirected.

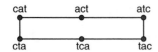

5. It does not have an Euler path, because every vertex has degree three.

7. The graph would be undirected, since equivalence relations are symmetric. The equivalence classes would be the connected components of the graph.

9. (a) **Proof**   Since $a^2 = a^2$, aRa for any $a \in \mathbf{Z}$, so R is reflexive. Suppose aRb. Then $a^2 = b^2$, so $b^2 = a^2$ and bRa. Thus R is symmetric. Finally, suppose aRb and bRc. Then $a^2 = b^2$ and $b^2 = c^2$, so $a^2 = c^2$, and aRc. Therefore R is transitive.   □

(b)   The equivalence classes are all the sets of the form $\{-n, n\}$, for $n \in \mathbf{Z}$.

11. (Answers may vary.) A web page need not link to itself, so the relation is not reflexive. (It isn't transitive or symmetric, either.)

13. $\{1\}, \{2, 3\}$

15. The relation is not transitive: $0R1$, $1R2$, but $0\not R2$.

17. (a) Hint: There are 16 subsets. (List them.)

(b) $\{(0, 0), (1, 1)\}$ and $\{(0, 0), (0, 1), (1, 0), (1, 1)\}$

19. Since a province can't border itself, the relation isn't reflexive. The relation is symmetric but not transitive. (Explain.)

21. The relation is reflexive and symmetric, but not transitive. (Explain.)

23. $\{\emptyset\}, \{\{1\}, \{2\}, \{3\}\}, \{\{1, 2\}, \{2, 3\}, \{1, 3\}\}$, and $\{\{1, 2, 3\}\}$

25. **Proof**   A vertex is related to itself, since there is always a path with zero edges going nowhere, so R is reflexive. Since G is undirected, a path from a to b with an even number of edges can be reversed to form a path from b to a with an even number of edges, so R is symmetric. Finally, if there is an even-edged path from a to b, and another even-edged path from b to c, then the two paths can be combined to form an even-edged path from a to c. So R is transitive.   □

27. (a) Since $x + x = 2x$ is even, xRx, so R is reflexive. Since $x + y = y + x$, $x + y$ will be even whenever $y + x$ is, so R is symmetric. Suppose that xRy and yRz. Then $x + y = 2k_1$ and $y + z = 2k_2$ for some $k_1, k_2 \in \mathbf{Z}$. Therefore $x + z = 2k_1 - y + 2k_2 - y = 2(k_1 + k_2 - y)$ is even, so xRz. Therefore R is transitive.

(b) They are the sets E and O of even and odd numbers.

29. (a) [2]   (b) [2]   (c) [5]

31. Onto: For any $[n]$, $p(n) = [n]$. It is not one-to-one (for $n \neq 0$) because $p(0) = [0] = p(n)$.

33.

·	0	1	2	3	4	5	6	7	8	9	10
0	0	0	0	0	0	0	0	0	0	0	0
1	0	1	2	3	4	5	6	7	8	9	10
2	0	2	4	6	8	10	1	3	5	7	9
3	0	3	6	9	1	4	7	10	2	5	8
4	0	4	8	1	5	9	2	6	10	3	7
5	0	5	10	4	9	3	8	2	7	1	6
6	0	6	1	7	2	8	3	9	4	10	5
7	0	7	3	10	6	2	9	5	1	8	4
8	0	8	5	2	10	7	4	1	9	6	3
9	0	9	7	5	3	1	10	8	6	4	2
10	0	10	9	8	7	6	5	4	3	2	1

35. Since $a_1 a_2 a_3 a_4 a_5 a_6 a_7 a_8 a_9 a_{10}$ is valid, we have (mod 11)

$$a_{10} \equiv 1a_1 + 2a_2 + 3a_3 + 4a_4 + 5a_5 + 6a_6 + 7a_7 + 8a_8 + 9a_9$$

$$0 \equiv 1a_1 + 2a_2 + 3a_3 + 4a_4 + 5a_5 + 6a_6 + 7a_7 + 8a_8 + 9a_9 - a_{10}$$

$$0 \equiv 1a_1 + 2a_2 + 3a_3 + 4a_4 + 5a_5 + 6a_6 + 7a_7 + 8a_8 + 9a_9 + 10a_{10}$$

37. The check digits will be different if $(1a_1 + \cdots + ka_k + (k+1)a_{k+1} + \cdots + 9a_9) - (1a_1 + \cdots + ka_{k+1} + (k+1)$ $a_k + \cdots + 9a_9)$ is nonzero, mod 11. This difference equals $a_{k-1} - a_k$, which will be an integer between -9 and 9, since $0 \le a_i \le 9$. This integer will be nonzero as long as $a_k \ne a_{k+1}$, so it will be nonzero mod 11.

39. As in Exercise 38, the check digit will change if $k(a_k - a'_k)$ is nonzero, mod 14. But in $\mathbf{Z}/14$, there are nonzero numbers whose product is zero, for example, $2 \cdot 7$. Therefore, changing 111111111111 to 181111111111 will not change the check digit. (The check digit is 8 in both cases.)

2.5 Partial Orderings

1. Reflexivity: For any n, $n = 1 \cdot n$, so $n \mid n$. Transitivity: Suppose $a \mid b$ and $b \mid c$. Then $b = k_1 a$ and $c = k_2 b$ for some natural numbers k_1 and k_2. Therefore $c = k_2(k_1 a) = (k_2 k_1)a$, so $a \mid c$. Antisymmetry: Suppose $a \mid b$ and $b \mid a$. Then $b = k_1 a$ and $a = k_2 b$ for some natural numbers k_1 and k_2. Therefore $b = k_1 k_2 b$, so $k_1 k_2 = 1$. Since $k_i \in \mathbf{N}$, this forces $k_1 = k_2 = 1$. Hence $a = b$.

3. The minimal element is 1. There are no maximal elements.

5. Antisymmetry fails. There are many examples of web pages where it is possible to navigate back and forth between two distinct pages.

7. Transitivity fails: $0 R 2$, $2 R 3$, but $0 \not{R} 3$.

9. $\{(0,0), (1,1), (2,2), (3,3), (0,1), (1,3), (0,2), (2,3), (0,3)\}$

11. The maximal elements are 6, 8, and 10.

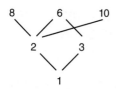

13. **Proof** Since a can be obtained from a by adding an empty collection of coins, $a \models a$, so $\models$ is reflexive. Suppose $a \models b$ and $b \models c$. Then, starting with a, adding a collection of dimes and quarters will yield b, then adding another collection of dimes and quarters will yield c. These two collections can be combined, showing that $a \models c$, so $\models$ is transitive. Finally, suppose that $a \models b$ and $b \models a$. Then $a \le b$, since it is possible to add coins to a to get b. Similarly, $b \le a$. Therefore $a = b$, so $\models$ is antisymmetric. $\square$

15. (a)

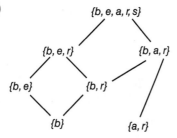

(b) $\{b\}$, $\{a, r\}$

(c) $\{a, r\}$ and $\{b, r\}$ (Answers may vary.)

17. (a)

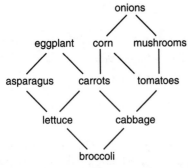

(b) Favorites: onions and eggplant. Least favorite: broccoli.

(c) Possible ranking: broccoli, lettuce, cabbage, asparagus, carrots, tomatoes, eggplant, corn, mushrooms, onions. The ranking is not unique, because incomparables (such as lettuce and cabbage) could be switched.

19.

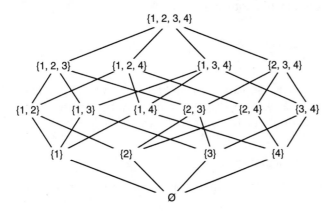

21. Let $n = p^2 q$, with p, q prime. For example, $n = 45 = 3^2 \cdot 5$.

A	1	2	3	4	6	12
B	1	p	q	p^2	pq	n

23. Hint: Define $f: \mathcal{P}(\{1, 2, 3, 4\}) \longrightarrow B$ by setting $f(X) = x_1 x_2 x_3 x_4$, where $x_i = 1$ if and only if $i \in X$.

25. Answers may vary. For example, 0000, 0001, 0010, 0100, 1000, 1100, 1010, 1001, 0110, 0101, 0011, 0111, 1011, 1101, 1110, 1111.

27. (a) f and h.   (b) c and e.   (c) f and i.

29.

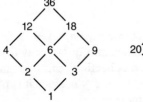 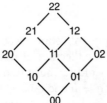

31. Hints: For reflexivity, use the identity function. For symmetry, use the inverse function. For transitivity, use function composition and Exercises 2.3/33,34.

2.6 Graph Theory

1. Since e joins vertex v to vertex w if and only if $\beta(e)$ joins vertex $\alpha(v)$ to vertex $\alpha(w)$, the number of edges joined to (and from) x is the same as the number of edges joined to (and from) $\alpha(x)$.

3. $a, b, c, d, e \mapsto r, t, s, u, q$

5. Hint: Define $f: V_G \longrightarrow V_H$ by $f(S) = S'$, and use Theorem 2.5.

7. **Definition.** Let R_1 and R_2 be relations on a set X. Then $(X, R_1) \cong (X, R_2)$ if there is a one-to-one correspondence $f: X \longrightarrow X$ such that $a R_1 b \Leftrightarrow f(a) R_2 f(b)$ for all $a, b \in X$.

9. Hint: Let G be the graph whose vertices correspond to the 13 teams in a conference, and let two teams be joined by an edge if the two teams play a game. Find a contradiction using Theorem 2.6.

11. The number of edges is $(n-1)n/2$. (Why?)

13. There are m vertices of degree n, and n vertices of degree m, so the sum of the degrees is $2mn$. Therefore the number of edges is mn.

15. **Proof** Let $v_0, e_1, v_1, e_2, v_2, \ldots, v_{k-1}, e_k, v_0$ be a circuit in $K_{m,n}$. Notice that every edge of the graph joins a vertex in V_1 with a vertex in V_2. Without loss of generality, let $v_0 \in V_1$. Then $v_1, v_3, \ldots, v_{k-1} \in V_2$, and $v_0, v_2, \ldots, v_k \in V_1$. Thus k is even. $\square$

17. **Proof** Let G be a graph with exactly two vertices, v and w, of odd degree. Let G' be the graph formed from G by adding an edge from v to w. By Theorem 2.7, G' has an Euler circuit, which becomes an Euler path in G when the edge from v to w is removed. $\square$

19. No. All the vertices (more than two) have odd degree.

21. **Proof** Let $v_1, \ldots, v_n$ be the vertices in K_n. Then there is a circuit visiting these vertices in order, since every pair of vertices is connected by an edge. $\square$

23. Both m and n must be even.

25. Since vertices a, d, and g all have degree 2, any Hamilton circuit must use the edges that touch these vertices. But this would require visiting f more than once, since three of these edges touch f.

27.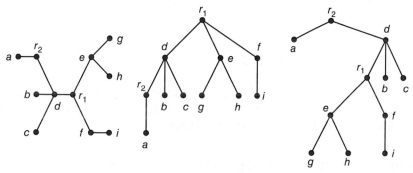

29. No. Counterexamples are possible where E contains edges whose vertices are not included in V.

3.1 Recurrence Relations

1. (a) 144   (b) $F(1000) = F(999) + F(998)$ (c) $F(1000) = 2 \cdot F(998) + F(997)$

3. (a) $1, 1, 2, 2, 3, 3, 4, 4, 5, 5$ (b) 50

5. (a) $1, 2, 4, 8, 16, 32, 64$ (b) $1, 3, 7, 15, 31, 63, 127$
   (c) $0, 1, 3, 6, 10, 15, 21$

7. 24

9. (a) $M(n) = \begin{cases} 500 & \text{if } n = 0 \\ 1.10 \cdot (M(n-1) - 100) & \text{if } n > 0 \end{cases}$

   (b) \$221.54

11. $C(n) = \begin{cases} 10000 & \text{if } n = 0 \\ 50 + 0.90 \cdot C(n-1) & \text{if } n > 0 \end{cases}$

13. $T(n) = \begin{cases} 1 & \text{if } n = 1 \\ T(n-1) + n & \text{if } n > 1 \end{cases}$

15. $W(n) = \begin{cases} 8 & \text{if } n = 0 \\ \frac{2}{3}[W(n-1) + 1] & \text{if } n > 0 \end{cases}$

17. $S(n) = \begin{cases} 1 & \text{if } n = 1 \\ S(n-1) + n^2 & \text{if } n > 1 \end{cases}$

19. (a) $P(n) = \begin{cases} 5 & \text{if } n = 1 \\ P(n-1) + 5 & \text{if } n > 1 \end{cases}$

   (b) $Q(n) = \begin{cases} 5 & \text{if } n = 1 \\ Q(n-1) + 4 + n & \text{if } n > 1 \end{cases}$

21. $P(n) = \begin{cases} 1 & \text{if } n = 1 \text{ or } n = 2 \\ P(n-2) + 2 & \text{if } n > 2 \end{cases}$

23. (a) $\displaystyle\prod_{k=1}^{n} k$ (b) $P(n) = \begin{cases} f(1) & \text{if } n = 1 \\ P(n-1) \cdot f(n) & \text{if } n > 1 \end{cases}$

25. (a) $V(n) = \begin{cases} 1 & \text{if } n = 1 \\ V(n-1) + 2 \cdot V(n-1) & \text{if } n > 1 \end{cases}$

   (b) There are several unrealistic aspects: For example, nobody ever gets better, and there is no limit on the number of people who get infected. More realistic models can be found in Chapter 6.

27. (a) $E(n) = \begin{cases} 3 & \text{if } n = 1 \\ 3 + E(n-1) & \text{if } n > 1 \end{cases}$

   (b) $F(n) = \begin{cases} 1 & \text{if } n = 1 \\ F(n-1) + 2n - 1 & \text{if } n > 1 \end{cases}$

3.2 Closed-Form Solutions and Induction

1. **Proof** We use induction on n. Let $f(n) = 500(1.10)^n$. If $n = 0$, the recurrence relation says that $M(0) = 500$, and the formula says that $f(0) = 500(1.10)^0 = 500$, so they match. Suppose as inductive hypothesis that $M(k-1) = 500(1.10)^{k-1}$ for some $k > 0$. Using the recurrence relation,

$$M(k) = 1.10 \cdot M(k-1), \text{ by the second part of the recurrence relation}$$

$$= 1.10 \cdot 500(1.10)^{k-1}, \text{ by inductive hypothesis}$$

$$= 500(1.10)^k$$

so, by induction, $M(n) = f(n)$ for all $n \geq 0$. $\qquad\qquad\square$

3. **Proof** (Induction on n.) Let $f(n) = 3^n - 1$. If $n = 1$, the recurrence relation says that $B(1) = 2$, and the formula says that $f(1) = 3^1 - 1 = 2$, so they match. Suppose as inductive hypothesis that $B(k-1) = 3^{k-1} - 1$ for some $k > 1$. Using the recurrence relation,

$$B(k) = 3 \cdot B(k-1) + 2, \text{ by the second part of the recurrence relation}$$

$$= 3(3^{k-1} - 1) + 2, \text{ by inductive hypothesis}$$

$$= (3^k - 3) + 2 = 3^k - 1$$

so, by induction, $B(n) = f(n)$ for all $n \geq 1$. $\qquad\square$

5. **Proof** (Induction on n.) Let $f(n) = (3^{n+1} - 2n - 3)/4$. If $n = 0$, the recurrence relation says that $C(0) = 0$, and the formula says that $f(0) = (3^1 - 2 \cdot 0 - 3)/4 = 0$, so they match. Suppose as inductive hypothesis that $C(k-1) = (3^k - 2(k-1) - 3)/4$ for some $k > 0$. Using the recurrence relation,

$$C(k) = k + 3 \cdot C(k-1), \text{ by the second part of the recurrence relation}$$

$$= k + 3 \left(\frac{3^k - 2(k-1) - 3}{4} \right), \text{ by inductive hypothesis}$$

$$= \frac{4k}{4} + \frac{3^{k+1} - 6k + 6 - 9}{4} = \frac{3^{k+1} - 2k - 3}{4}$$

so, by induction, $C(n) = f(n)$ for all $n \geq 0$. $\qquad\square$

7. **Proof** (Induction on n.) Let $f(n) = n^2 + n + 1$. If $n = 0$, the recurrence relation says that $R(0) = 1$, and the formula says that $f(0) = 0^2 + 0 + 1 = 1$, so they match. Suppose as inductive hypothesis that $R(k-1) = (k-1)^2 + (k-1) + 1$ for some $k > 0$. Using the recurrence relation,

$$R(k) = R(k-1) + 2k, \text{ by the second part of the recurrence relation}$$

$$= (k-1)^2 + (k-1) + 1 + 2k, \text{ by inductive hypothesis}$$

$$= k^2 + k + 1$$

so, by induction, $R(n) = f(n)$ for all $n \geq 0$. $\qquad\square$

9. **Proof** (Induction on n.) Let $f(n) = 3n + 5$. If $n = 0$, the recurrence relation says that $P(0) = 5$, and the formula says that $f(0) = 3 \cdot 0 + 5 = 5$, so they match. Suppose as inductive hypothesis that $P(k-1) = 3(k-1) + 5$ for some $k > 0$. Using the recurrence relation,

$$P(k) = P(k-1) + 3, \text{ by the second part of the recurrence relation}$$

$$= 3(k-1) + 5 + 3, \text{ by inductive hypothesis}$$

$$= 3k + 5$$

so, by induction, $P(n) = f(n)$ for all $n \geq 0$. $\qquad\square$

11. (a) $1, 2, 5, 10, 17, 26$

(b) First differences: $1, 3, 5, 7, 9$. Second differences: $2, 2, 2, 2$. So a quadratic formula is suggested. Guess: $f(n) = n^2 + 1$.

(c) **Proof** (Induction on n.) Let $f(n) = n^2 + 1$. If $n = 0$, the recurrence relation says that $G(0) = 1$, and the formula says that $f(0) = 0^2 + 1 = 1$, so they match. Suppose as inductive hypothesis that $G(k-1) = (k-1)^2 + 1$ for some $k > 0$. Using the recurrence relation,

$$G(k) = G(k-1) + 2k - 1, \text{ by the 2nd part of the recurrence relation}$$

$$= (k-1)^2 + 1 + 2k - 1, \text{ by inductive hypothesis}$$

$$= k^2 - 2k + 1 + 1 + 2k - 1 = k^2 + 1$$

so, by induction, $G(n) = f(n)$ for all $n \geq 0$. $\qquad\square$

13. $f(n) = n^2/2 - 3n/2 + 2$

15. **Proof**   (Induction on n.) Let $f(n) = 2^{n+1} - 1$. If $n = 0$, the recurrence relation says that $V(0) = 1$, and the formula says that $f(0) = 2^1 - 1 = 1$, so they match. Suppose as inductive hypothesis that $V(k - 1) = 2^k - 1$ for some $k > 0$. Using the recurrence relation,

$$V(k) = 2 \cdot V(k - 1) + 1, \text{ by the second part of the recurrence relation}$$

$$= 2(2^k - 1) + 1, \text{ by inductive hypothesis}$$

$$= 2^{k+1} + 1$$

so, by induction, $V(n) = f(n)$ for all $n \geq 0$.   □

17. **Proof**   (Induction on n.) Let $f(n) = 2^{n+1} - 1$. If $n = 0$, the recurrence relation says that $P(0) = 1$, and the formula says that $f(0) = 2^1 - 1 = 1$, so they match. Suppose as inductive hypothesis that $P(k - 1) = 2^k - 1$ for some $k > 0$. Using the recurrence relation,

$$P(k) = P(k - 1) + 2^k, \text{ by the second part of the recurrence relation}$$

$$= 2^k - 1 + 2^k, \text{ by inductive hypothesis}$$

$$= 2^{k+1} + 1$$

so, by induction, $P(n) = f(n)$ for all $n \geq 0$.   □

19. Hint: The inductive step uses the following algebra:

$$H(k) = k \cdot H(k - 1) + 1$$

$$= k \cdot (k - 1)!(1/1! + 1/2! + 1/3! + \cdots + 1/(k - 1)!) + 1$$

$$= k!(1/1! + 1/2! + 1/3! + \cdots + 1/(k - 1)!) + k!/k!$$

$$= k!(1/1! + 1/2! + 1/3! + \cdots + 1/(k - 1)! + 1/k!)$$

21. Hint: Try $n = 11$.

23. (a) $F(n + 1) - F(n) = F(n - 1)$.

   (b) This follows from the definition, as $F(n + 1) = F(n) + F(n - 1)$.

   (c) The sequence of differences is always the Fibonacci sequence, which is never constant.

3.3   Recursive Definitions

1. B_1. $F(1) = 1$. B_2. $F(2) = 1$.   R. $F(n) = F(n - 1) + F(n - 2)$.

3. B_1. λ is in X. B_2. 1 is in X. R_1. If x is in X, so is $0x0$.
   R_2. If x and y are in X, so is xy. (Answers may vary.)

5. 0 (B), 1 (B), 010 (R_2), 01001011 (R_1)

7.   R. xy, the *concatenation* of x and y, where x and y are strings, and the last symbol in x is less than or equal to the first symbol in y.

9. Answers may vary.

11. $10, 7, 4, 1, -2, 2, -1, 3, 0$

13.

15. **B.** $1 \in X$. **R.** If $p \in X$ so is $2p$.

17. $12, 6, 3, 4, 2, 1$

19. (a) $\emptyset, \{\emptyset\}, \{\{\emptyset\}, \emptyset\}$ (b) Hint: $\{\{\{\emptyset\}\}\} \in S$.

21. Hint: Mimic Example 3.22.

23. The closed form solution of

$$P(n) = \begin{cases} 3 & \text{if } n = 1 \\ (4/3) \cdot P(n-1) & \text{if } n > 1 \end{cases}$$

   is $P(n) = 3 \cdot (4/3)^{n-1}$. Thus the perimeter of the fractal is infinite.

25. The Sierpinski gasket is the complement of the set C defined as follows.

   B. ▼ $\in C$. **R.** If ▼ $\in C$, so is ▼▼▼.

27. **B.** | $\in T$. **R.** If — $\in T$, so is —$<$.

29. **B.** ◯ $\in C$. **R.** If ◯ $\in C$, so is ⊛.

3.4 Proof by Induction

1. **Proof** (Induction on n.) Let $S(n)$ denote the sum of the first n odd natural numbers. Note that the nth odd natural number is $2n - 1$, for $n \geq 1$. $S(1) = 1 = 1^2$. Suppose as inductive hypothesis that $S(k-1) = (k-1)^2$ for some $k > 1$. Then $S(k) = S(k-1) + 2k - 1 = (k-1)^2 + 2k - 1 = k^2 - 2k + 1 + 2k - 1 = k^2$ so by induction, $S(n) = n^2$ for all $n \geq 1$. □

3. Hint: For the inductive step, draw a diagonal in a k-gon to form a triangle and a $k-1$-gon.

5. **Proof** (Induction on n, where $2n - 1$ is the length of the string.) For any symbol a, a can by constructed by **B$_2$**. Suppose as inductive hypothesis that any string $a_{k-1} \cdots a_2 a_1 a_2 \cdots a_{k-1}$ of length $2(k-1) - 1$ can be constructed, for some $k > 1$. Suppose as given a string $P = a_k a_{k-1} \cdots a_2 a_1 a_2 \cdots a_{k-1} a_k$ of length $2k - 1$. By inductive hypothesis, $a_{k-1} \cdots a_2 a_1 a_2 \cdots a_{k-1}$ can be constructed. By **B$_2$**, the symbol a_k can be constructed. Then P can be constructed by **R**. □

7. (a) **Proof** (Induction on the number of lines.) If a line map contains 0 lines, then it has 1 region, and $1 \geq 0 + 1$. Suppose as inductive hypothesis that any line map with $k - 1$ lines has at least k regions, for some $k > 0$. Let M be a line map with k lines. Remove one line from M, call it l. By inductive hypothesis, the resulting map M' has k regions. Now put l back. Since l crosses the whole rectangle, it must pass through at least one region of M', dividing this region into two regions. Hence M has at least one more region than M', so M has at least $k + 1$ regions, as required. □

   (b) Hint: Mimic part (a).

   (c) ▱▱▱▱▱

   (d) You can't. (Explain why not.)

9. **Proof** (Induction on the number of levels.) A binary tree with one level has one node, and $1 < 2^1$. Suppose as inductive hypothesis that any binary tree with $k - 1$ levels has less than 2^{k-1} nodes, for some $k > 1$. Suppose as given a binary tree T with k levels. By the definition in Example 3.22, T consists of a root node and two subtrees T_1 and T_2, each with at most $k - 1$ levels. By inductive hypothesis, T_1 and T_2 each have less than 2^{k-1} nodes, so each has at most $2^{k-1} - 1$ nodes. Therefore the number of nodes in T is at most $2(2^{k-1} - 1) + 1 = 2^k - 1$, which is less than 2^k, as required. □

11. **Proof** (Induction on n.) The constant term of $(x + 5)^1$ is $5 = 5^1$. Suppose as inductive hypothesis that the constant term of $(x + 5)^{k-1}$ is 5^{k-1} for some $k > 1$. Then $(x + 5)^k = (x + 5)^{k-1}(x + 5)$, so its constant term is $5^{k-1} \cdot 5 = 5^k$, as required. □

13. **Proof** (Strong induction on n.) By definition, $H(2 \cdot 0) = 0 = H(2 \cdot 0 - 1)$ and $H(2 \cdot 1) = 1 = H(2 \cdot 1 - 1)$. Note that $H(3) = H(2) + H(1) - H(0) = 1 + 1 - 0 = 2$ and $H(4) = H(3) + H(2) - H(1) = 2 + 1 - 1 = 2$, so $H(2 \cdot 2) = 2 = H(2 \cdot 2 - 1)$. Suppose as inductive hypothesis that $H(2k) = H(2k - 1) = k$ for all k such that $1 \leq k < n$, for some $n > 2$.

$$H(2n) = H(2n - 1) + H(2n - 2) - H(2n - 3), \text{ by definition}$$
$$= H(2n - 1) + H(2(n - 1)) - H(2(n - 1) - 1)$$
$$= H(2n - 1) + (n - 1) - (n - 1), \text{ by inductive hypothesis}$$
$$= H(2n - 1)$$

Furthermore,

$$H(2n - 1) = H(2n - 2) + H(2n - 3) - H(2n - 4), \text{ by definition}$$
$$= H(2(n - 1)) + H(2(n - 1) - 1) - H(2(n - 2))$$
$$= (n - 1) + (n - 1) - (n - 2), \text{ by inductive hypothesis}$$
$$= n$$

so $H(2n) = H(2n - 1) = n$, as required. $\square$

15. **Proof** First, note that $L(1) = 1 = \alpha + \beta$, and $\alpha^2 + \beta^2 = (\alpha + 1) + (\beta + 1) = \alpha + \beta + 2 = 3 = L(2)$. Suppose as inductive hypothesis that $L(i) = \alpha^i + \beta^i$ for all $i < k$, for some $k > 2$. Then $L(k) = L(k - 1) + L(k - 2) = \alpha^{k-1} + \beta^{k-1} + \alpha^{k-2} + \beta^{k-2} = \alpha^{k-2}(\alpha + 1) + \beta^{k-2}(\beta + 1) = \alpha^{k-2}(\alpha^2) + \beta^{k-2}(\beta^2) = \alpha^k + \beta^k$, as required. $\square$

17. **Proof** (Induction on n.) The first term $B(1)$ is a single square, and $2 \cdot 3^{1-1} - 1 = 1$. Suppose as inductive hypothesis that $B(k - 1)$ consists of $2 \cdot 3^{k-2} - 1$ squares, for some $k > 1$. By the previous problem, $B(k - 1)$ has $4 \cdot 3^{k-2}$ free vertices, and $B(k)$ is formed by adding one square to each free vertex. Therefore $B(k)$ contains $2 \cdot 3^{k-2} - 1 + 4 \cdot 3^{k-2} = 6 \cdot 3^{k-2} - 1 = 2 \cdot 3^{k-1} - 1$ squares, as required. $\square$

19. The area of $S(n)$ is $(3/4)^{n-1}$. (Prove it.)

21. **Proof** (Induction on the recursive definition of X.) Since $2 = 2 \cdot 1$, 2 is even. Suppose as inductive hypothesis that some $x \in X$ is even. Then $x = 2k$ for some k, so $x + 10 = 2k + 10 = 2(k + 5)$ is also even. Therefore, by induction, all elements of X are even. $\square$

23. **Proof** Any base-case Q-sequence has sum $x + (4 - x) = 4$. Suppose as inductive hypothesis that $x_1, x_2, \ldots, x_j$ and $y_1, y_2, \ldots, y_k$ are Q-sequences, each of which sums to 4. Then the Q-sequence formed by the recursive part of the definition is $x_1 - 1, x_2, \ldots, x_j, y_1, y_2, \ldots, y_k - 3$, which has sum $x_1 + x_2 + \cdots + x_j - 1 + y_1 + y_2 + \cdots + y_k - 3 = 4 - 1 + 4 - 3 = 4$. $\square$

3.5   Recursive Data Structures

1. (a) $f(\text{veni}, \text{vidi}, \text{vici}) = 1 + f(\text{veni}, \text{vidi}) = 1 + 1 + f(\text{veni}) = 1 + 1 + 1 = 3$

   (b) It gives the length of the list.

   (c) **Proof** (Induction on the length of the list.) If list L contains a single element, then $f(L) = 1$, so it gives the length of the list. Suppose as inductive hypothesis that $F(L') = k - 1$ for any list L' with $k - 1$ elements, for some $k > 1$. Let $L = L', x$ be a list of length k. Then $f(L) = f(L') + 1 = (k - 1) + 1 = k$, as required. $\square$

3. (a) Define LMax(L) as follows.

   B. If $L = x$, a single number, then LMax(L) $= x$.

   R. If $L = L', x$ for some list L', then LMax(L) $= \max(\text{LMax}(L'), x)$.

   (b) **Proof** (Induction on the recursive definition.) If $L = x$, a single number, then LMax(L) $= x \geq x$. Suppose as inductive hypothesis that LMax(L') returns the greatest value in L', for some list L'. Then

LMax(L', x) = max(LMax(L'), x). Therefore LMax(L', x) $\geq x$, and LMax(L', x) $\geq$ LMax(L'), which is the greatest value in L', by inductive hypothesis. So LMax(L', x) returns the greatest value in the list L', x, as required. $\qquad\square$

5. An SList of depth $p = 0$ contains a single number, so it is in order. Suppose as inductive hypothesis that any SList of depth $k - 1$ is in order, for some $k > 0$. Any SList L of depth k has the form $L = (X, Y)$, where X and Y are SLists of depth $k - 1$. By inductive hypothesis, both X and Y are in order. By definition, the last element of X is less than the first element of Y, so the elements of $L = (X, Y)$ are all in order.

7. Hint: Use induction on p.

9. Flip$[((2, 3), (7, 9))]$ = (Flip$[(7, 9)]$, Flip$[(2, 3)]$) = ((Flip$[9]$, Flip$[7]$), (Flip$[3]$, Flip$[2]$)) = ((9, 7), (3, 2)).

11. **B.** If $L = x$, then $d(L) = 0$.

  R. If $L = (X, Y)$, then $d(L) = d(X) + 1$.

13. (a) Search$[15, L]$ = Search$[15, (10, 20)]$ $\vee$ Search$[15, (30, 40)]$
  = Search$[15, 10]$ $\vee$ Search$[15, 20]$ $\vee$ Search$[15, 30]$ $\vee$ Search$[15, 40]$
  = false $\vee$ false $\vee$ false $\vee$ false = false.

  (b) BSearch$[15, L]$ = BSearch$[15, (10, 20)]$ = BSearch$[15, 20]$ = false.

15. InOrder(T) = "InOrder(T_2), r, InOrder(T_1)"

17. (b) **B.** If $L = x$, then Product(L) = x.

  R. If $L = (X, Y)$, then Product(L) = Product(X) $\cdot$ Product(Y).

  (d) The proof is almost the same as the proof of Theorem 3.9.

19. **Proof**   A NumberSquare of depth 0 has $4^0 = 1$ element. Suppose as inductive hypothesis that a Number-Square of depth $k - 1$ has 4^{k-1} elements, for some $k > 0$. A NumberSquare of depth k is made of four NumberSquares of depth $k - 1$, and therefore has $4 \cdot 4^{k-1} = 4^k$ elements, as required. $\qquad\square$

21. **Proof**   (Induction on the recursive definition of a TGraph.) A base-case TGraph is a triangle, and each vertex has degree 2, which is even. Suppose as inductive hypothesis that all the vertices in some TGraph G' have even degree. Applying the recursive definition to G' produces a TGraph G by adding two vertices of even degree and increasing the degree of vertex v by two. Thus the degree of v remains even, so all the vertices of G have even degree. $\qquad\square$

23. **B, R$_1$, R$_2$, R$_1$, R$_2$**

4.1   Basic Counting Techniques

1. (a) $30 + 24 = 54$ (b) $30 + 24 - 8 = 46$

3. (a) $18 \cdot 15 = 270$ (b) $18 + 15 = 33$

5. Yes. There are $2^{10} = 1{,}024$ different package choices.

7. (a) 7,030,000   (b) 2,970,000   (c) 52%   (d) 2%   (e) 967,812

9. 4^{1350}

11. $499 + 199 - 99 = 599$

13. Two colors: 12. Three colors: 48. Four colors: 24.

15. The following tree shows that there are 12 such strings.

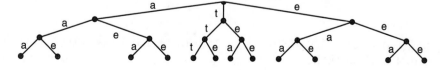

17. The following tree shows that there are 11 such numbers.

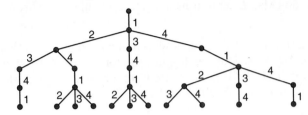

19. The following tree shows that there are 10 such strings.

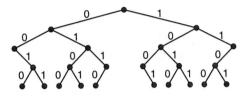

21. 1,048,576

23. 2,048

25. In the tree below, a path to the right represents a win by Team A, and a path to the left represents a win by Team B. There are 20 possible scenarios.

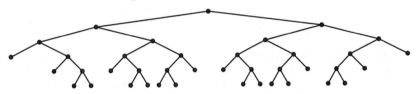

27. Hint: Use the multiplication principle for the base case when $n = 2$, and also for the inductive step.

4.2   Selections and Arrangements

1. $C(7, 3) = 35$

3. (a) $P(20, 3) = 6,840$ (b) $C(20, 3) = 1,140$

5. (a) $P(7, 3) = 210$ (b) $2 \cdot 6 \cdot 5 = 60$

7. (a) 5,040   (b) 144   (c) 1,872

9. $C(8, 3) = 56$

11. (a) 5,040   (b) 144   (c) 35   (d) 31

13. $C(10, 3) \cdot C(7, 3) \cdot C(4, 3) = 16,800$

15. $P(9, 5) = 15,120$

17. $C(26, 6) = 230,230$

19. $C(56, 6) = 32,468,436$

21. $C(24, 2) = 276$

23. (a) $2^5 = 32$ (b) $P(100, 32) \approx 3.76 \times 10^{61}$
    (c) $2 \cdot C(4, 2) = 12$ (d) $2 \cdot C(9, 2) = 72$

25. $32x^5 + 560x^4 + 3920x^3 + 13720x^2 + 24010x + 16807$

27. $-270,208,224$

29. Hint: For the inductive step, $R(k, j) = R(k - 1, j) + R(k - 1, j - 1) = C(k - 1, j) + C(k - 1, j - 1) = C(k, j)$, using the identity from the proof of Theorem 4.3.

4.3 Counting with Functions

1. **Proof**   Let $X = \{x_1, x_2, \ldots, x_m\}$. Since f is one-to-one, $f(x_1), f(x_2), \ldots, f(x_m)$ are distinct elements of Y. Therefore Y has at least m elements. $\square$

3. (a) Hint: Let P be the set of all unordered pairs of vertices, and let E be the set of all edges. Define $f : P \longrightarrow E$ by setting $f(\{v_1, v_2\})$ to be the edge between v_1 and v_2. Show that f is well defined, one-to-one, and onto.

   (b) $C(n, 2)$

5. Such a function would not be well defined.

7. (a) Yes. (Explain.)   (b) No. (Explain.)

9. (a) Let $X = \{x_1, x_2, \ldots, x_n\}$. For each subset $H = \{x_{i_1}, \ldots, x_{i_k}\}$, let $f(H)$ be the n-digit binary string with 1's in positions $i_1, \ldots, i_k$ and 0's elsewhere.

   (b) 2^n

   (c) The image is the set of n-digit binary strings with exactly k 1's.

   (d) $C(n, k)$

11. $6!/(3! \cdot 2!) = 60$

13. 3,326,400

15. 165

17. (a) The function is one-to-one because no three lines pass through a single point, so every point is at the intersection of exactly one pair of lines.

   (b) The function is onto because each point is a point of intersection.

   (c) $C(n, 2)$

19. $4!/8 = 3$

21. $P(6, 5)/8 = 90$

23. Let the "pigeons" be birthdays of the 36 students, and let the "holes" be the 7 days of the week. Then there must be $\lceil 36/7 \rceil = 6$ birthdays on the same day of the week.

25. Without multiple edges or loops, there can be at most $C(10, 2)$ edges.

27. Hint: Divide $\triangle ABC$ into four regions by drawing lines connecting the midpoints of the sides of the triangle, then use the pigeonhole principle.

29. When dividing m by n, the possible nonzero remainders are $1, 2, \ldots, n-1$. Thus the algorithm could not produce a string of more than $n-1$ digits in a row without repeating, by the pigeonhole principle.

31. Answers may vary.

4.4 Discrete Probability

1. (a) $26^4 = 456,976$ (b) $21^4/26^4 \approx 0.4256$

3. $1 - 9^{20}/10^{20} \approx 0.8784$

5. $6/36$

7.

Roll total	2	3	4	5	6	7	8	9	10
Probability	1/24	2/24	3/24	4/24	4/24	4/24	3/24	2/24	1/24

9. (a) 60,466,176   (b) 1,757,600   (c) ≈ 0.1965

11. $C(11, 3)/C(20, 3) \approx 0.1447$

13. (a) ≈ 0.0101 (b) ≈ 0.4242

15. (a) ≈ 0.9853 (b) ≈ 0.9709 (c) ≈ 0.3059
    (d) The percentage of spoiled eggs seems to have a greater effect.

17. (a) $C(5,3)/C(10,3) \approx 0.0833$ (b) $C(n,3)/(C(C(n,2),3))$

19. $E(X) = 0 \cdot P(X=0) + 660 \cdot P(X=660) + 160 \cdot P(X=160)$
    $= 0 \cdot \frac{997}{1000} + 660 \cdot \frac{1}{1000} + 160 \cdot \frac{2}{1000} = 0.98.$

21. (a) $C(4,3)/C(10,3) \approx 0.0333$ (b) 3

23. 6

25. $1 \cdot \frac{9}{100} + 2 \cdot \frac{90}{100} + 3 \cdot \frac{1}{100} = 1.92$

27. (a) 1/8   (b) 1.9375

4.5 Counting Operations in Algorithms

1. $z = 45$

3.

m	i	x_1	x_2	x_3	x_4	x_5	Comparison
		77	54	95	101	62	
77		77	54	95	101	62	
77	2	77	54	95	101	62	$77 < 54$?
77	3	77	54	95	101	62	$77 < 95$?
95	4	77	54	95	101	62	$95 < 101$?
101	5	77	54	95	101	62	$101 < 62$?
101	5	77	54	95	101	62	

5. (a) $2 \cdot 3 \cdot 6 \cdot 9 = 324$ (b) $(2 \cdot 3 + 2 \cdot 6) \cdot 9 = 162$

7. (a) C (b) $10n^3 + 1230n$

9. (a) $n^2 + 10n$ (b) $5n^2 + 20n + 3$

11. $(n-3)(2 + 3n + n^2(n+2n)) = 3n^4 - 9n^3 + 3n^2 - 7n - 6$

13. 0

15. The algorithm prints out all the possible ways to draw three balls in sequence, without replacement. It prints $P(n,3)$ lines.

17.
```
for a ∈ {1,2,3,4} do
      for b ∈ {1,2,3,4,5,6} do
            if a+b = 8 then print a,b
```

19. Let $A = \{A, B, \ldots, Z\}$ and let $N = \{0, 1, \ldots, 9\}$.
```
for a ∈ A do
      for b ∈ A do
            for c ∈ A do
                  for d ∈ A do
                        for x ∈ N do
                              for y ∈ N do
                                    print abcdxy
for a ∈ A do
      for b ∈ A do
            for c ∈ A do
                  for x ∈ N do
                        for y ∈ N do
                              for z ∈ N do
                                    print abcxyz
```

21.

x_1	x_2	x_3	x_4	x_5	i	j	Comparison	Result
5	4	2	1	3	1	1	$x_1 > x_2$?	yes
4	5	2	1	3	1	2	$x_2 > x_3$?	yes
4	2	5	1	3	1	3	$x_3 > x_4$?	yes
4	2	1	5	3	1	4	$x_4 > x_5$?	yes
4	2	1	3	5	2	1	$x_1 > x_2$?	yes
2	4	1	3	5	2	2	$x_2 > x_3$?	yes
2	1	4	3	5	2	3	$x_3 > x_4$?	yes
2	1	3	4	5	3	1	$x_1 > x_2$?	yes
1	2	3	4	5	3	2	$x_2 > x_3$?	no
1	2	3	4	5	4	1	$x_1 > x_2$?	no

23. $s \leftarrow 0$
$p \leftarrow 1$
for $i \in \{1, 2, \ldots, n\}$ do
  ┌ $p \leftarrow p \cdot i$
  └ $s \leftarrow s + p$
This algorithm performs n multiplications.

25. (a) $n + 1$ (b) 19, 23, 29, 12

27. for $x \in A$ do
      for $y \in A$ do
        print xyx
There are $26^2 = 676$ such palindromes.

29. for $a \in C$ do
      for $b \in C \setminus \{a\}$ do
        for $d \in C \setminus \{a, b\}$ do
          for $c \in C \setminus \{d, b\}$ do
            print $abcd$
    for $a \in C$ do
      for $b \in C \setminus \{a\}$ do
        for $c \in C \setminus \{b\}$ do
          print $abcb$

4.6 Estimation

1. Since $1 \cdot \log_2 n \le \log_2 n^3 \le 3 \cdot \log_2 n$, $\log_2 n^3 \in \Theta(\log_2 n)$.

3. (a) $\Theta(n^5)$ (b) $\Theta(n^{23})$ (c) $\Theta(n!)$ (d) $\Theta(n \log_2 n)$
   (e) $\Theta(\log_2 n)$

5. (a) $\Theta(n \log_2 n)$ (b) $\Theta(n)$ (c) $\Theta(n^{10})$ (d) $\Theta(n^8 \log_2 n)$

7. (a) $\Theta(2^n)$ (b) $\Theta(n^7)$

9. Let M be the larger of m and b. Then $l(n) = mn + b \le Mn + M \le Mn + Mn = (2M)n$. Furthermore, $mn \le mn + b$, so $l(n) \in \Theta(n)$.

11. (a) $n^2 + 2n + 1 \in O(n^3)$ (b) $\log_2(n!) \in \Theta(n \log_2 n)$

13. Since $2 < 10$, it follows that $2^n \le 1 \cdot 10^n$, so $2^n \in O(10^n)$.

15. Hint: $\underbrace{2 \cdot 2 \cdot 2 \cdot 2 \cdot 2 \cdots 2}_{n} \le 2 \cdot 2 \cdot 3 \cdot 4 \cdot 5 \cdots n$.

17. Let $0 < p < q$, and suppose, to the contrary, that $n^p \in \Omega(n^q)$. Then there are positive constants K and N such that $n^p \ge K \cdot n^q$ for $n \ge N$. Therefore $1/K \ge n^q/n^p = n^{q-p}$ for $n \ge N$. This is a contradiction: $1/K$ is fixed, while n^{q-p} increases without bound, since $q - p > 0$.

19. Hint: $k \cdot f(n) \le kf(n) \le k \cdot f(n)$.

21. Hint: $a_0 + a_1 n + \cdots + a_{p-1} n^{p-1} \le |a_0| + |a_1| n + \cdots + |a_{p-1}| n^{p-1}$.

23. $\Theta(n^5)$

25. $\Theta(n^2)$

27. (a) $(1 \cdot n \cdot n^5 + 2n + 1) \cdot n$ (b) $\Theta(n^7)$

29. $n + n \log_2 n + \log_2 n = \Theta(n \log_2 n)$ by Theorem 4.14.

31. Antisymmetry fails. (Give a counterexample.)

33. The relation is reflexive because $f \in \Theta(f)$ for any function f. It is symmetric by the observation following Definition 4.8. To see that it is transitive, suppose $f \in \Theta(g)$ and $g \in \Theta(h)$. Then there are constants K_1 and K_2 such that $K_1 g(n) \le f(n) \le K_2 g(n)$ and constants L_1 and L_2 such that $L_1 h(n) \le g(n) \le L_2 h(n)$, for sufficiently large n. Then $f(n) \le K_2 g(n) \le K_2 L_2 h(n)$, and $f(n) \ge K_1 g(n) \ge K_1 L_1 h(n)$, so $f \in \Theta(h)$, as required.

5.1   Algorithms

1. Zero. The `while`-loop is never entered.

3. $i = \lceil x \rceil$

5. Precondition: t is a nonnegative integer.

7. $(t \in \{x_1, x_2, \ldots, x_n\}) \Rightarrow (x_l = t)$

9. Postcondition: l is the depth of the node containing t.

11.

l	r	i	test
1	6		$1 < 6$?
		$\left\lfloor \frac{1+6}{2} \right\rfloor = 3$	$20 > 10$?
$3 + 1 = 4$			$4 < 6$?
		$\left\lfloor \frac{4+6}{2} \right\rfloor = 5$	$20 > 20$?
	5		$5 < 6$?
		$\left\lfloor \frac{4+5}{2} \right\rfloor = 4$	$20 > 14$?
$4 + 1 = 5$			$5 < 5$?

13.

function call	l	r	i	comparisons
BinSearch $(21, X, 1, 10)$	1	10	5	$21 = 15$? $21 < 15$? $21 > 15$?
BinSearch $(21, X, 6, 10)$	6	10	8	$21 = 24$? $21 < 24$?
BinSearch $(21, X, 6, 7)$	6	7	6	$21 = 18$? $21 < 18$? $21 > 18$?
BinSearch $(21, X, 7, 7)$	7	7	7	$21 = 21$?

15. BinSearch $(3, X, 1, 10)$ = BinSearch $(3, X, 1, 4)$ = BinSearch $(3, X, 1, 1)$ = true

17. GCD $(42, 24)$ = GCD $(24, 18)$ = GCD $(18, 6)$ = GCD $(6, 0)$ = 6.

19.
```
i ← 1
while i ≤ n do
      ⌐ print "YADA"
      ⌊ i ← i + 1
```

21.
```
k ← 0
for i ∈ {1, 2, 3, ..., n} do
      for j ∈ {1, 2, 3, ..., n} do
            if xᵢ = yⱼ then k ← k + 1
```

23.
```
function F (n ∈ N)
      if (n = 1) ∨ (n = 2) then
            return 1
      else
            return F (n − 1) + F (n − 2)
```

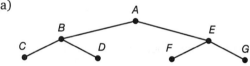

$F(6) = F(5) + F(4) = F(4) + F(3) = F(3) + F(2) + F(2) + F(1) + F(2) + F(1) + 1 = F(2) + F(1) + 1 + 1 + 1 + 1 + 1 + 1 = 1 + 1 + 6 = 8.$

25. Precondition: $n \geq 0$.

    (a) function FactI $(n \in \mathbf{Z})$
    $\quad p \leftarrow 1$
    $\quad i \leftarrow 1$
    $\quad$ while $i < n$ do
    $\quad\quad \ulcorner \; i \leftarrow i+1$
    $\quad\quad \llcorner \; p \leftarrow p \cdot i$
    $\quad$ return p

    (b) function FactR $(n \in \mathbf{Z})$
    $\quad$ if $n = 0$ then
    $\quad\quad$ return 1
    $\quad$ else
    $\quad\quad$ return $n \cdot$ FactR $(n-1)$

5.2 Three Common Types of Algorithms

1. (a) Preorder: $A, B, D, H, E, I, J, C, F, G, K, L$

   (b) Postorder: $H, D, I, J, E, B, F, K, L, G, C, A$

   (c) Inorder: $H, D, B, I, E, J, A, F, C, K, G, L$

3. A postorder traversal is appropriate, because the child tasks must be done before their parent tasks.

5.

7. (a)

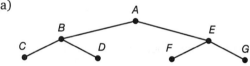

   (b) C, D, B, F, G, E, A

9. Hint: The traces for parts (a) and (b) both resemble the trace in Figure 5.4; the visit statements need to be moved.

11. function SLTraverse $(\mathcal{L} \in \{$SLists$\})$
    $\quad$ if $\mathcal{L} = x$ then
    $\quad\quad$ visit x
    $\quad$ else // $\mathcal{L} = (X, Y)$
    $\quad\quad$ SLTraverse (X)
    $\quad\quad$ SLTraverse (Y)
    $\quad$ return

13. The minimum weight is 51. Spanning trees may vary.

15. The minimum weight is 84. Spanning trees may vary.

17. $c \leftarrow A$
    while $c \neq Z$ do
    $\quad \ulcorner$ Find shortest edge from c to a new vertex n.
    $\quad \llcorner \; c \leftarrow n$
    On the network in Figure 5.12, this algorithm gets stuck (paths may vary).

19. (a)

    (b)

    (c) A 101×100 grid can be divided into a collection of 3×4 and 2×4 grids, each of which can be tiled using the above patterns.

21. The divide-and-conquer version makes the comparisons $5 < 3$, $2 < 4$, $5 < 4$. The for-loop version makes the comparisons $5 < 3$, $5 < 2$, $5 < 4$.

23. MergeSort $(23, 5, 7, 13, 43, 21, 17, 2)$
    $=$ Merge (MergeSort $(23, 5, 7, 13)$, MergeSort $(43, 21, 17, 2)$)
    $=$ Merge (Merge (MergeSort $(23, 5)$, MergeSort $(7, 13)$),
            Merge (MergeSort $(43, 21)$, MergeSort $(17, 2)$))
    $=$ Merge (Merge (Merge (MergeSort (23), MergeSort (5)),
                Merge (MergeSort (7), MergeSort (13))),
            Merge (Merge (MergeSort (43), MergeSort (21)),
                Merge (MergeSort (17), MergeSort (2))))
    $=$ Merge (Merge (Merge $(23, 5)$, Merge $(7, 13)$),
            Merge (Merge $(43, 21)$, Merge $(17, 2)$))
    $=$ Merge (Merge $((5, 23), (7, 13))$, Merge $((21, 43), (2, 17))$)
    $=$ Merge $((5, 7, 13, 23), (2, 17, 21, 43))$ $=$ $2, 5, 7, 13, 17, 21, 23, 43$

25. Preconditions: $n \in \mathbf{N}$. Postconditions: The string $d_p d_{p-1} \cdots d_2 d_1 d_0$ is the base-2 expansion of n.

    $p \leftarrow \lfloor \log_2 n \rfloor$
    while $p \geq 0$ do
        ⌐ if $n \geq 2^p$ then
            $n \leftarrow n - 2^p$
            $d_p = 1$
        else
            $d_p = 0$
        ∟ $p \leftarrow p - 1$

5.3 Algorithm Complexity

1. There is exactly 1 such assignment, in all cases. This is a bad choice because it is outside of the main loop of the algorithm.

3. The second result is stronger, but both are correct.

5. (a) There is 1 comparison in the best case, when $N = 25$. (Why?)

   (b) There are 20 comparisons in the worst case, when $N = 94$. (Why?)

7. (a) Best case: 1 operation when $N = 2$ (or any even number). Worst case: 96 operations when $N = 97$.

   (b) $(1 + 2 + 1 + 4 + 1 + 6 + 1)/7 = 16/7$.

9. (a) 8   (b) 10   (c) $52/6 \approx 8.67$.

11. (a) 1   (b) n

13. Best case: $\Theta(1)$. Worst case: $O(n^2)$.

15. (a) greedy   (b) 7.25   (c) No. (Why not?)

17. Let n be the number of elements in the list. For simplicity, assume that n is a power of 2.

$$C(n) = \begin{cases} 0 & \text{if } n = 1 \\ 2 \cdot C(n/2) + 1 & \text{if } n > 1 \end{cases}$$

Let $D(p) = C(2^p)$. Then

$$D(p) = \begin{cases} 0 & \text{if } p = 0 \\ 2 \cdot D(p-1) + 1 & \text{if } p > 0 \end{cases}$$

It is easy to check, using induction, that $D(p) = 2^p - 1$. Thus $C(n) = n - 1 \in \Theta(n)$.

19. **Proof** (Induction on i.) When $i = 0$, $C(0) = 0$ and $0 \cdot 2^0 = 0$, so the formulas match. Suppose as inductive hypothesis that $C(k-1) = (k-1) \cdot 2^{k-1}$. Using the recurrence relation, $C(k) = 2^k + 2C(k-1) = 2^k + 2(k-1) \cdot 2^{k-1} = 2^k + k \cdot 2^k - 2^k = k \cdot 2^k$, as required. □

21. (a) 40   (b) 202   (c) 90.8

23. Best: 3. Worst: 2. Average: 2.4.

5.4 Bounds on Complexity

1.

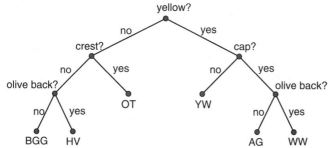

3. At least $\left\lceil \log_3 \binom{10}{4} \right\rceil = 5$ weighings are needed.

5. At least $\lceil \log_3(400) \rceil = 6$ weighings are needed.

7. (a) A lower bound is $\log_2 16 = 4$.

    (b) Hint: Begin by weighing $\{c_1, c_2, c_3, c_4\}$ versus $\{c_5, c_6, c_7, c_8\}$.

9. At least $\lceil \log_3(24 \cdot 23) \rceil = 6$ tests are required.

11. Algorithm 5.16: 1. Algorithm 5.17: 2.

13. No. The sequential search has worst-case complexity $\Theta(n)$, while an asymptotically optimal search has worst-case complexity $\Theta(\log_2 n)$.

15. No. The Quick Sort has worst-case complexity $\Theta(n^2)$. An asymptotically optimal sorting algorithm has worst-case complexity $\Theta(n \log_2 n)$.

17. **Proof** (Induction on p.) An m-ary tree with height 0 has $1 = m^0$ leaves. Suppose as inductive hypothesis that an m-ary tree with height i has at most m^i leaves, for $0 \le i < k$, for some $k > 0$. Any m-ary tree of height k consists of a root node with at most m subtrees, each having height at most $k - 1$. By inductive hypothesis, each of these subtrees has at most m^{k-1} leaves, so the total number of leaves is at most $m \cdot m^{k-1} = m^k$. $\square$

19. Answers may vary. For example, $\{-15, -4, 5, 14\}$.

21. Any assignment of values where p and q are both false will make the value of the formula true.

23. Since there are $n!$ one-to-one correspondences $V_1 \longrightarrow V_2$, the complexity of the algorithm must be at least $\Omega(n!)$, depending on assumptions about the number of edges.

5.5 Program Verification

1. Yes. A counterexample can show that the preconditions do not guarantee the postconditions.

3. The proof uses strong induction because the inductive hypothesis is supposed "for lists of size $n - 1$ or less."

5. (a) MakeTree(u) returns a binary search tree whose only node is u.

    (b) MakeTree$(u_1, u_2, \ldots, u_{k-1})$ returns a binary search tree whose nodes are $u_1, u_2, \ldots, u_{k-1}$, for some $k > 1$.

    (c) MakeTree$(u_1, u_2, \ldots, u_i)$ returns a binary search tree whose nodes are $u_1, u_2, \ldots, u_i$, for $1 \le i < k$, for some $k > 1$.

    (d) MakeTree$(u_1, u_2, \ldots, u_k)$ returns a binary search tree whose nodes are $u_1, u_2, \ldots, u_k$.

7. **Proof** (Induction on n.) For the base case, check that $P(1) = (1^2 + 1)/2 = 1$. Suppose as inductive hypothesis that $P(k - 1) = [(k - 1)^2 + (k - 1)]/2$ for some $k > 1$. Then $P(k) = k + P(k - 1) = k + [(k - 1)^2 + (k - 1)]/2 = (2k + k^2 - 2k + 1 + k - 1)/2 = (k^2 + k)/2$, as required. $\square$

9. **Proof** (Induction on n.) First, note that $P(0) = 1 = 2 - (1/2)^0$. Suppose as inductive hypothesis that $P(k-1) = 2 - (1/2)^{k-1}$ for some $k > 0$. Then $P(k) = 1 + \frac{1}{2} \cdot P(k-1) = 1 + \frac{1}{2} \cdot \left[2 - \left(\frac{1}{2}\right)^{k-1}\right] = 2 - \left(\frac{1}{2}\right)^k$, as required.   □

11. **Proof** (Induction on p.) If $p = 0$, we have $\text{PLog}(1) = 0 = \log_2 1$. Suppose as inductive hypothesis that $\text{PLog}(2^{k-1}) = \log_2(2^{k-1}) = k - 1$, for some $k > 0$. Then $\text{PLog}(2^k) = 1 + \text{PLog}(2^{k-1}) = 1 + k - 1 = k$, as required.   □

13. **Proof** (Induction on n.) If $n = 0$, we have $\text{Power}(x, 0) = 1 = x^0$. Suppose as inductive hypothesis that $\text{Power}(x, k-1) = x^{k-1}$, for some $k > 0$. Then $\text{Power}(x, k) = x \cdot \text{Power}(x, k-1) = x \cdot x^{k-1} = x^k$, as required.   □

15. (a) $\text{Power}(2, 10) = 2 \cdot \text{Power}(2, 9) = 4 \cdot \text{Power}(2, 8) = 8 \cdot \text{Power}(2, 7)$
    $= 16 \cdot \text{Power}(2, 6) = 32 \cdot \text{Power}(2, 5) = 64 \cdot \text{Power}(2, 4)$
    $= 128 \cdot \text{Power}(2, 3) = 256 \cdot \text{Power}(2, 2) = 512 \cdot \text{Power}(2, 1)$
    $= 1024 \cdot \text{Power}(2, 0) = 1024 \cdot 1 = 1024.$

    (b) $\text{QPower}(2, 10) = (\text{QPower}(2, 5))^2 = (2 \cdot (\text{QPower}(2, 2))^2)^2$
    $= (2 \cdot ((\text{QPower}(2, 1))^2)^2)^2 = (2 \cdot ((2 \cdot (\text{QPower}(2, 0))^2)^2)^2)^2$
    $= (2 \cdot ((2 \cdot (1)^2)^2)^2)^2 = (2 \cdot 16)^2 = 1024.$

17. **Proof** (Induction on n.) If $n = 1$, then $\text{FindMax}(\{x\}) = x$, which is the maximum of $\{x\}$. Suppose as inductive hypothesis that $\text{FindMax}(X') = \max(X')$ for any X' with $|X'| < k$, for some $k > 1$. Let X be a set with k elements. By inductive hypothesis, $a = \max\{x_1, x_2, \ldots, x_{\lfloor n/2 \rfloor}\}$ and $b = \max\{x_{\lfloor n/2 \rfloor + 1}, \ldots, x_n\}$. The function returns m such that m is the larger of a and b, so $m = \max(X)$, as required.   □

19. Answers may vary.

21. Hint: For the inductive step, use Exercise 20.

23. Hint: For your inductive hypothesis, suppose that $\text{Hanoi}(k-1, p_1, p_2)$ returns a legal sequence of moves taking the top $k-1$ disks from peg p_1 and placing them on p_2, for some $k > 1$.

5.6 Loop Invariants

1. (a) $\bar{z} = 15$ (b) $\underline{z} = 5$ (c) $\bar{z} = 2\underline{z} - 7$ (d) $\underline{z} = (\bar{z} + 7)/2$

3. (a) **Proof** Before the loop executes, $i = j$, so the invariant from (2a) holds. Therefore the invariant will be true after the loop finishes, when $i = n$. So $i = j = n$ is a postcondition on the algorithm.   □

    (b) **Proof** Before the loop executes, $k = 1$ and $i = 0$, and $1 = 10^0$, so the invariant from (2c) holds. Therefore the invariant will be true after the loop finishes, when $i = n$. So $k = 10^n$ is a postcondition on the algorithm.   □

5. Postcondition: $m = \max(\{x_1, x_2, \ldots, x_n\})$.

7. **Proof** First, we claim that $s = \left(\frac{i+1}{2}\right)^2$ is an invariant for the while-loop. To prove invariance, suppose that $\underline{s} = ((\underline{i} + 1)/2)^2$ before a pass through the loop. After one pass, $\bar{i} = \underline{i} + 2$ and $\bar{s} = \underline{s} + \bar{i}$. Therefore, $\bar{s} = \left(\frac{\underline{i}+1}{2}\right)^2 + \bar{i} = \left(\frac{\bar{i}-1}{2}\right)^2 + \bar{i} = \frac{\bar{i}^2 - 2\bar{i} + 1}{4} + \frac{4\bar{i}}{4} = \left(\frac{\bar{i}+1}{2}\right)^2$, proving invariance. Before the loop executes, $s = 1 = ((1+1)/2)^2$, so the invariant holds before loop execution. After the loop terminates, i must be an odd number that equals n or $n+1$. Since n is odd, $i = n$. Since the invariant will be true at loop termination, $s = ((n+1)/2)^2$, as required.   □

9. (a) Suppose that $\underline{x} + \underline{y} = N$ and $\underline{x} - \underline{y} = \underline{i}$ before a pass through the loop. After one pass, $\bar{i} = \underline{i} - 2$, $\bar{x} = \underline{x} - 1$, and $\bar{y} = \underline{y} + 1$. Therefore, $\bar{x} + \bar{y} = \underline{x} - 1 + \underline{y} + 1 = \underline{x} + \underline{y} = N$. Similarly, $\bar{x} - \bar{y} = \underline{x} - 1 - (\underline{y} + 1) = (\underline{x} - \underline{y}) - 2 = \underline{i} - 2 = \bar{i}$. This proves invariance.

(b) Before the loop executes, $x + y = N + 0 = N$ and $x - y = N - 0 = i$, so the invariant holds. At loop termination, $i = 0$, so a postcondition is that $x + y = N$ and $x - y = 0$, or equivalently, $x = y = N/2$.

(c) 150

11. (a) **Proof** Suppose that $t \notin \{x_1, x_2, \ldots, x_{i-1}\}$ before the segment of code inside the loop executes. The algorithm will step through the loop as long as $t \neq x_i$, in which case $\bar{i} = i + 1$. So $t \neq x_{\bar{i}-1}$, and since $t \notin \{x_1, x_2, \ldots, x_{\bar{i}-2}\}$, it follows that $t \notin \{x_1, x_2, \ldots, x_{\bar{i}-1}\}$, as required. $\qquad \square$

(b) You can conclude that t is not in the array.

13. (a) Let $P(n)$ be the number of $+$ operations performed by Algorithm 5.24. By inspection, $P(n)$ satisfies the following recurrence relation.

$$P(n) = \begin{cases} 0 & \text{if } n = 1 \text{ or } n = 2 \\ 1 + P(n-1) + P(n-2) & \text{if } n > 1 \end{cases}$$

A standard induction argument shows that $P(n) = F(n) - 1$.

(b) $2n - 4$

(c) Algorithm 5.23 is more efficient.

15. $i \leftarrow 1$
```
while i < n do
   ⌐ j ← 1
     while j < n − i + 1 do
        ⌐ if xⱼ > xⱼ₊₁ then swap xⱼ and xⱼ₊₁
        ∟ j ← j + 1
   ∟ i ← i + 1
```
Hints: To prove correctness, an invariant for the while-i-loop is that the greatest $i - 1$ elements of the array are in order at the end of the array. An invariant for the while-j loop is that x_j is larger than all the elements before it.

17. Hint: $y = a_n t^{n-i} + a_{n-1} t^{n-i-1} + \cdots + a_i$ is an invariant for the while-loop.

19. $\Theta(n^2)$

21.

a	b	m	$\sin(m)\sin(b)$
1	5	3	-0.1353
3		4	0.7257
	4	3.5	0.2655
	3.5		

23. **Proof** Suppose that $f(\underline{a})f(\underline{b}) \leq 0$ before passing through the loop. After one pass, $m = (\underline{b} - \underline{a})/2$. If $f(m)f(\underline{b}) \leq 0$, then $\bar{a} = m$ and $\bar{b} = \underline{b}$, so $f(\bar{a})f(\bar{b}) \leq 0$. If $f(m)f(\underline{b}) > 0$, then $\bar{b} = m$ and $\bar{a} = \underline{a}$. Furthermore, this inequality implies that $f(m)$ and $f(\underline{b})$ have the same sign. And since $f(\underline{a})f(\underline{b}) \leq 0$, $f(\underline{a})$ and $f(\underline{b})$ have different signs (or $f(\underline{a}) = 0$, in which case $f(\underline{a})f(\bar{b}) = f(\bar{a})f(\bar{b}) = 0 \leq 0$). If $f(\underline{a})$ and $f(\underline{b})$ have different signs, then $f(m)$ (a.k.a. $f(\bar{b})$) and $f(\underline{a})$ (a.k.a. $f(\bar{a})$) have different signs, so $f(\bar{a})f(\bar{b}) \leq 0$. This proves invariance. $\qquad \square$

Selected References

[1] Adams, Colin. *The Knot Book: An Elementary Introduction to the Mathematical Theory of Knots*, reprinted edition, (2004) American Mathematical Society.

[2] Allman, Elizabeth, and Rhodes, John. *Mathematical Models in Biology: An Introduction*, (2004) Cambridge University Press.

[3] Atela, Pau, and Golé, Cristophe. *Phyllotaxis*. Retrieved September 6, 2007 from the Smith College website: `http://maven.smith.edu/~phyllo/index.html`

[4] Bailey, Kathryn. *The Twelve-Note Music of Anton Webern: Old Forms in a New Language*, (1991) Cambridge University Press.

[5] Borgatti, Stephen, and Everett, Martin. Two algorithms for computing regular equivalence. *Social Networks* **15** (1993), 361–376.

[6] Chomsky, Noam. *Syntactic Structures*, 12th printing, (1976) Mouton.

[7] Chomsky, Noam. Three models for the description of language. *IRE Transactions on Information Theory* **2** (1956), 113–124.

[8] Cohen, Joel E. Mathematics is biology's next microscope, only better; biology is mathematics' next physics, only better. *PLoS Biology* **2(12):e439** (2004), 2017–2023.

[9] Davis, James A. Clustering and structural balance in graphs. *Human Relations* **20** (1967), 181–187.

[10] Fauvel, John, and Gray, Jeremy. *The History of Mathematics: A Reader*, (1997) Mathematical Association of America.

[11] Harary, Frank. On the notion of balance in a signed graph. *Michigan Mathematical Journal* **2** (1953), 143–146.

[12] Hauser, Marc D., Chomsky, Noam, and Fitch, W. Tecumseh. The faculty of language: What is it, who has it, and how did it evolve? *Science* **298:5598** (2002), 1569–1579.

[13] Hofstadter, Douglas. *Gödel, Escher, Bach: An Eternal Golden Braid*, (1979) Basic Books, Inc.

[14] Hillis, David M., Moritz, Craig and Mable, Barbara K., editors. *Molecular Systematics*, 2nd edition, (1996) Sinauer.

[15] Hopkins, Brian. Kevin Bacon and Graph Theory. *PRIMUS: Problems, Resources, and Issues in Mathematics Undergraduate Studies* **XIV:1** (2004), 5–11.

[16] Hopkins, Brian, and Wilson, Robin. The truth about Königsberg. *College Mathematics Journal* **35:3** (2004), 198–207.

[17] Hunter, David, and von Hippel, Paul. How rare is symmetry in musical 12-tone rows? *American Mathematical Monthly* **110:2** (2003), 124–132.

[18] Kermack, William O., and McKendrick, Anderson G. A contribution to the mathematical theory of epidemics. *Proceedings of the Royal Society of London. Series A, Containing Papers of a Mathematical and Physical Character* **115:772** (1927), 700–721.

[19] Lorrain, Francois, and White, Harrison C. Structural equivalence of individuals in social networks. *Journal of Mathematical Sociology* **1** (1971), 49–80.

[20] Maurer, Steven, and Ralston, Anthony. *Discrete Algorithmic Mathematics*, 3rd edition, (2004) A. K. Peters.

[21] McCartin, Brian. Prelude to musical geometry. *College Mathematics Journal* **29:5** (1998), 354–370.

[22] Nei, Masatoshi, and Kumar, Sudhir *Molecular Evolution and Phylogenetics*, (2000) Oxford University Press.

[23] Pistorius, Carl, and Utterback, James. A Lotka-Volterra model for multi-mode technological interaction: Modeling competition, symbiosis, and predator prey modes. *Working Papers #155–96, Massachusetts Institute of Technology, Sloan School of Management* (1996) 62–71.

[24] Reid, Constance. *Hilbert*, (1996) Springer.

[25] Retrosheet (2007). *Transaction file archive.* Retrieved July 7, 2007 from Retrosheet on the World Wide Web: `http://www.retrosheet.org/transactions/tranDB.zip`

[26] Saitou, Naruya, and Nei, Masatoshi. The neighbor-joining method: A new method for reconstructing phylogenetic trees. *Molecular Biology and Evolution* **4** (1987), 406–425.

[27] Sneath, Peter H. A., and Sokal, Robert R. *Numerical Taxonomy*, (1973) W. H. Freeman.

[28] Tucker, Alan. *Applied Combinatorics*, 3rd edition, (1995) Wiley.

[29] Wasserman, Stanley, and Faust, Katherine. *Social Network Analysis: Methods and Applications*, (1994) Cambridge University Press.

[30] White, Douglas R., and Reitz, Karl P. Graph and semigroup homomorphisms on networks of relations. *Social Networks* **5** (1983), 193–234.

[31] Winship, Christopher, and Mandell, Michael. Roles and positions: A critique and extension of the blockmodeling approach. *Sociological Methodology* **14** (1983–1984), 314–344.

[32] Zietara, Marek S., and Lumme, Jaakko. Speciation by host switch and adaptive radiation in a fish parasite genus *Gyrodactylus* (Monogenea, Gyrodactylidae). *Evolution* **56** (2002), 2445–2458.

Index

Addition principle, 156
  for algorithms, 193
Algorithms, 192–199, 213–237
  asymptotic optimality of, 251
  complexity of, 208, 238
  correctness, 216
  divide-and-conquer, 231
  division, 43
  efficiency of, 149, 249, 251
  Euclidean, 239
  greedy, 228
  Kruskal's, 236
  optimality of, 249
  postconditions, 215
  preconditions, 215
  Prim's, 229
  pseudocode, 192, 213
  searching, 148, 215, 217
  subroutines, 226
  traversal, 225
And, 4
Antisymmetry, 87
Arrangements, 163–164
Arrays, 196
Assignment, 192
Associative properties
  in logic, 9
Asymptotic optimality, 251
Australia, 170, 186
Automata, 294
Axiomatic systems, 34
  models for, 35
Axioms, 32

Bacon, Kevin, 126
Balance, 290
Bayes Rule, 189
Bifurcations, 308

Big-Ω notation, 206
Big-Θ notation, 206
Big-O notation, 205
Bijections, *see* One-to-one correspondences
Binary search, 217, 220
Binary search trees, 53, 150
Binary trees, 112, 129, 225
  full, 134, 279
Binomial Theorem, 168
Bioinformatics, 127, 278
Biology, 278, 282, 294, 300
  bioinformatics, 127, 278
  diseases, 300, 305
  DNA, 191, 278
  evolutionary trees, 234, 280
  morphogenesis, 110
  neighbor-joining method, 282
  phyllotaxis, 110
  phylogenetic trees, 279
  predator–prey system, 304
  SIR model, 305
  UPGMA method, 280
Bipartite graphs, 105, 116
Boolean algebras, 93, 94
Bottom-up evaluation, 108
Bubble sort, 197, 215

Canada, 18, 56, 85, 133, 161, 171
Cartesian products, 61, 157
Centrality, 284
Chaos, 303
Chemistry, 208, 300
China, 161
Chomsky, Noam, 295
Circuits, 49
  simple, 100
Cliques, 284
Closed-form formulas, 116

Clustering, 288
   hierarchical, 288
Codomain, 66
Coloring graphs, 51, 139
Combinations, 165
Complete graphs, 54, 112
Complexity, 208, 238
   average-case, 240
   best-case, 240
   worst-case, 238
Composition of functions, 72
Computational complexity, 247
Concatenation, 127
Concept image, 31
Conditional probability, 187
Conjectures, 33
Connected graphs, 49
Connectives, 3
   and, 4
   if and only if, 4
   implies, 4
   negation, 4
   or, 4
Constructive proofs, 100
Contingency, 13
Continuous-time models, 300
Contradiction, 13
   proof by, 43
Contraposition, 41
Contrapositive, 6, 16
Converse, 6
Convex, 144
Convex set, 144
Corollaries, 33
Correctness of algorithms, 216
Counterexamples, 33, 123
Counting, *see* Enumeration

De Morgan's laws, 8
   for logic, 8, 13
   for sets, 62
Decision trees, 157, 214
Deduction method, 20
Definitions, 31
Degrees, 49, 99
Dendrograms, 292
Dependency tree, 234
Depth
   of a vertex, 104, 112
Difference, of sets, 63
Direct proofs, 39
Directed graphs, 48, 77
Discrete-time models, 300
Diseases, 300, 305
Disjoint sets, 65, 156

Distributive properties
   in logic, 9, 20
   in set theory, 66
Divide-and-conquer algorithms, 231
Divides relation, 41
Divisibility of integers, 41
Division algorithm, 43
DNA, 191, 278
Domain
   of a function, 66
   of a predicate, 21

Edges, 48, 97
Efficiency, 149, 249, 251
Empty set, 59
Enumeration, 155
   addition principle, 156, 193
   arrangements, 163–164
   combinations, 165
   inclusion–exclusion principle, 63, 65
   inclusion-exclusion principle, 156
   multiplication principle, 157, 194
   permutations, 164
   pigeonhole principle, 176
   Ramsey theory, 177
   selections, 163, 165
Equilibrium, 303
Equivalence classes, 81
   representatives, 83
Equivalence relation, 79
Equivalence rules, 13
Estimation, 202
Estimation targets, 207
Euclidean algorithm, 239
Euler paths/circuits, 49, 100
Euler's method, 300, 308
Euler, Leonhard, 48
Even numbers, 32
Events, 182
Evolutionary trees, 234, 280
Exclusive or, 8
Existential quantifier, 21
Expected value, 186, 247
Exponential growth and decay, 302

Factorials, 115, 164
Fibonacci (Leonardo Pisano), 109
Fibonacci sequence, 109, 116, 140
   rabbits and, 110, 301
Fixed points, 303
Floor function, 70
For-loops, 194
Formal logic, *see* Logic, formal
Formalism, 2
Forward-backward method, 15
Four color theorem, 51

Fractal, 135
Fractals, 36, 131, 132, 134, 145
Free variables, 3
Full binary tree, 134, 279
Functions, 66
   codomain of, 66
   composition, 72
   domain of, 66
   fixed points, 303
   identity, 68
   image of, 70
   inverse, 73
   one-to-one, 69
   one-to-one correspondences, 71
   onto, 69
   restriction of, 73
   well-defined, 68

Geometry, 5, 31, 34, 35, 37, 130
   Euclidean, 37, 42
   four-point, 34
   projective, 46
   taxicab, 37
Grammars, 293
Graphs, 48, 97
   bipartite, 105, 116
   circuits in, 49
   coloring, 51, 139
   complete, 54, 112
   connected, 49
   degree in, 49, 99
   directed, 48, 77
   edges, 48, 97
   Euler paths/circuits in, 49, 100
   Hamilton paths/circuits in, 101, 253
   indegree in, 49, 99
   isomorphisms, 98
   networks, 52, 229
   outdegree in, 49, 99
   paths in, 49, 100
   planar, 51
   signed, 290
   simple, 54
   subgraphs, 106
   trees, 102
   undirected, 48, 78
   vertices, 48, 49, 97
   weighted, 52
Greatest integer function, 70
Greatest lower bound, 93
Greedy algorithms, 228

Hamilton paths/circuits, 101, 253
Hasse diagrams, 88
Height
   of a tree, 57, 104, 112

Hexagonal numbers, 111
Hierarchical clustering, 288
Hilbert, David, 35

Identity function, 68
If and only if, 4
If...then statement, 193
Iff, 4
Image, of a function, 70
Implication, 4
Inclusion-exclusion principle, 63, 65, 156
Incomparable elements, 87
Indegree, 49, 99
India, 64, 74, 161
Induction, 119, 136, 257, 266
   principle of, 136
   strong, 141
   structural, 142
Inductive hypothesis, 119
Inference rules, 13, 14
Injectivity, *see* One-to-one functions
Inorder traversal, 151
Integers, 41, 58
   closure properties, 41
   divisibility, 41
Intersection, 59
Invariants, 265
Inverse of a function, 73
Inversion, 310
ISBN numbers, 86
Isomorphisms, 91, 99, 104, 286
   of graphs, 98
   of posets, 91
Italy, 109
Iterated function systems, 303

Join, 93

Kermack, William, 305
Königsberg bridges, 48
Korea, 8
Kruskal's algorithm, 236

Languages, 292
Lattices, 93
Lemmas, 33
Liaisons, 284
Linguistics, 293
   automata, 294
   grammars, 293
   languages, 292
   recursion, 296
   word-chain automata, 294
Logic, 1
   connectives, *see* Connectives
   equivalences, 5, 13
   formal, 2

implication, 4
inference rules, 13, 14
modus ponens, 12
modus tollens, 12
necessary conditions, 9
predicates, 20, 21
proposition, 2
propositional, 11
statement, 2
sufficient conditions, 9
tautologies, 12
translation, 2, 3, 22
truth tables, 4
vacuous truth, 4, 269, 270
Logic gates, 10
Logical equivalences, 5, 13
Logistic growth, 302
Loops
    for-, 194
    invariants of, 265
    nested, 194
    sentinels, 215, 238
    while-, 214
Lucas numbers, 114

Map, 67
Markov chains, 308
Mathematical statements, 1, 31
    definitions, 31
    axioms, 32
    conjectures, 33
    corollaries, 33
    counterexamples, 33, 123
    lemmas, 33
    propositions, 33
    theorems, 33
Maximal elements, 89
McKendrick, Anderson Gray, 305
Meet, 93
Merge sort, 232, 242, 259
Mexico, 28, 57, 163
Minimal elements, 89
Models, 35
Modular arithmetic, 82, 83, 310
Modus ponens, 12, 14
Modus tollens, 12, 14
Morphogenesis, 110
Multiplication principle, 157, 194
Music, 110, 277, 308
    twelve-tone, 308

Natural numbers, 58
Necessary conditions, 9
Negation, 4
    of a quantified statement, 23, 24
Neighbor-joining method, 282

Nested loops, 194
Networks, 52, 229
    social, 57, 284
    spanning trees of, 106, 229
New Zealand, 170
Not, 4
NP-completeness, 102, 253

Odd numbers, 32
One-to-one, 69
One-to-one correspondences, 71
One-to-one functions, 69
Onto, 69
Onto functions, 69
Optimality, 249
Or, 4
Ordered pairs
    equality of, 8, 61
Outdegree, 49, 99
Output, 193

Palindromes, 127, 311, 312
Parallel lines, 31, 35
Partially ordered sets, *see* Posets
Partitions
    of a set, 80
    of an integer, 96
Pascal's Triangle, 172
Paths, 49, 100
Permutations, 164
    of a set, 164
Phyllotaxis, 110
Phylogenetic trees, 279
Physics, 300
Pigeonhole principle, 176
Planar graphs, 51
Population, 300
Population growth, 300
Posets, 87
    Boolean algebras, 93, 94
    Hasse diagrams, 88
    incomparable elements in, 87
    isomorphisms, 91
    join, 93
    lattices, 93
    maximal elements in, 89
    meet, 93
    minimal elements in, 89
    topological sorting, 89
    total ordering, 87
Postconditions, 215
Postorder traversal, 226
Power sets, 61, 112
Preconditions, 215
Predator–prey system, 304
Predicates, 20, 21
    free variables in, 3

Preorder traversal, 225
Prestige, 285
Preview questions, 2
Prim's algorithm, 229
Prime numbers, 142
Print statement, 193
Probability, 181, 182
  addition rule, 188
  Bayes's Rule, 189
  conditional, 187
  events, 182
  expected value, 186, 247
  multiplication rule, 188
  random variables, 186
  sample space, 182
  sampling, 184
Product notation, 115
Program verification, 256
Proof sequences, 15
Proofs, 11, 15, 33, 39
  by contradiction, 43
  by contraposition, 41
  by induction, 119, 136, 257, 266
  constructive, 100
  direct, 39
  forward-backward method, 15
Propositional calculus, 11
Propositional logic
  equivalence rules, 13
Propositions, 33
Pseudocode, 192, 213
  assignment statement, 192
  if...then statement, 193
  print statement, 193
Puerto Rico, 18, 170

Quantified statements, 21
Quantifiers, 21
  existential, 21
  scope of, 22
  universal, 21
Quick sort, 255

Ramsey theory, 177
Random variables, 186
Rational numbers, 44, 58
Recurrence relations, 108, 116, 301
  closed-form formulas, 116
  closed-form solutions, 117
  modeling with, 111
Recursion, *see also* Self-reference, 108
  bottom-up, 108
  defining sets with, 129, 132
  definitions involving, 108, 126
  Fibonacci sequence, 109
  fractals, 36, 131

  in linguistics, 296
  induction and, 119, 136, 257, 266
  recurrence relations, 108, 116, 301
  top-down, 109, 219
  towers of Hanoi, 260
Recursive definitions, 108, 126
Reflexivity, 79, 80
Relations, 76, 77
  antisymmetric, 87
  divides, 41
  equivalence, 79
  reflexive, 79, 80
  symmetric, 78, 80
  transitive, 79, 80
Representatives, 83
Restriction, 73
Retrograde, 311
Roots (of a tree), 53, 102

Sample space, 182
Sampling, 184
Scalability, 203
Scheduling, 50
Schoenberg, Arnold, 309
Schwarzenegger, Arnold, 126
Scope, 22
Searching algorithms, 148, 215, 217
  binary, 217, 220
  sequential, 215
Selection Principle, 165
Selection sort, 269
Selections, 163, 165
Self-reference, *see* Recursion
Sentinels, 215, 238
Sequences of differences, 118
Sequential search, 215
Sets, 58
  builder notation, 58
  Cartesian products, 61, 157
  complement, 60
  containment, 59
  difference of, 63
  disjoint, 65, 156
  empty, 59
  equality of, 60, 62
  finite, 63
  integers, 58
  intersection of, 59
  membership, 58
  natural numbers, 58
  power sets, 61, 112
  rational numbers, 58
  recursively defined, 129, 132
  subsets, 59
  union of, 59
Venn diagrams, 59

Shortest path, 236
Sigma notation, 115
Signed graphs, 290
Simple circuit, 100
Simple graph, 54
Singapore, 171
SIR model, 305
Social networks, 57, 284
    balance, 290
    centrality, 284
    cliques, 284
    clustering, 288
    dendrograms, 292
    liaisons, 284
    prestige, 285
Sociology, 284
Sorting, 197
    bubble sort, 197, 215
    merge sort, 232, 242, 259
    quick sort, 255
    selection sort, 269
    topological, 89
Spanning trees, 106, 229
Statements
    in logic, 2
    in mathematics, *see* Mathematical statements
    in pseudocode, 192
    mathematical, 31
    quantified, 21
    strength of, 9
Strings, 126
    concatenation of, 127
    reversal, 127
Strong induction, 141
Structural induction, 142
Subgraphs, 106
Subroutines, 226
Subsets, 59
Substitution, 19
    using equivalence rules, 14, 15
Subtrees, 151, 225
Sufficient conditions, 9
Surjectivity, *see* Onto functions
Symmetry, 78, 80

Tautologies, 12
Thailand, 162
Theorems, 33
Tone rows
    inversion, 310

Tone-rows, 309
    retrograde, 311
    transpositions, 310
Top-down evaluation, 109, 219
Topological sorting, 89
Total orderings, 87
Towers of Hanoi, 260
Transitive properties
    in logic, 15
    in set theory, 87
Transitivity, 79, 80
Translation, 2, 3, 22
Transpositions, 310
Traversal algorithms, 225
Tree traversals
    inorder, 151
    postorder, 226
    preorder, 225
Trees, 102
    binary, 112, 129, 225
    binary search, 53, 150
    decision, 157, 214
    depth in, 104, 112
    full binary, 134, 279
    height of, 57, 104, 112
    roots of, 53, 102
    subtrees, 151, 225
Triangular numbers, 257
Truth tables, 4
Twelve-tone music, 308

Undefined terms, 34
Undirected graphs, 48, 78
Union, 59
United Kingdom, 9, 28, 162, 170, 186
Universal quantifier, 21
Universal set, 60
UPGMA method, 280

Vacuous truth, 4, 269, 270
Venn diagrams, 59
Vertices, 48, 49, 97
    degrees of, 49, 99
    depth of, 104, 112

Weighted graphs, 52
Well-defined functions, 68
While-loops, 214
Word-chain automata, 294

Index of Symbols

Notation	Description	Page
$\neg p$	Not p	4
$p \wedge q$	p and q	4
$p \vee q$	p or q	4
$p \leftrightarrow q$	p if and only if q	4
$p \rightarrow q$	p implies q	4
$A \Rightarrow B$	Implies tautology	12
$A \Leftrightarrow B$	If and only if tautology	12
$\forall$	Universal quantifier	21
$\exists$	Existential quantifier	21
$a \mid b$	a divides b	41
$a \nmid b$	a does not divide b	45
$x \in S$	x is in S	58
$x \notin S$	x is not in S	58
$\{\ \}$	Set definition	58
$\{\ \mid\ \}$	Set builder notation	58
$\mathbf{Z}$	Set of integers	58
$\mathbf{N}$	Set of natural numbers	58
$\mathbf{R}$	Set of real numbers	58
$\mathbf{Q}$	Set of rational numbers	58
$A \subseteq B$	A is a subset of B	59
$\emptyset$	Empty set	59
$A \cup B$	A union B	59
$A \cap B$	A intersect B	59
A'	Complement of A	60
$A \times B$	Cartesian product of A and B	61
$\mathcal{P}(X)$	Power set of X	61
$|X|$	Number of elements in X	63
$A \setminus B$	Set difference of A and B	63
$f : X \longrightarrow Y$	Function from X to Y	66
1_X	Identity function	68
$\lfloor x \rfloor$	Greatest integer $\leq x$	70
$g \circ f$	Function composition	72

Notation	Description	Page
f^{-1}	Inverse of a function	73
$f\|_H$	Restriction of f to H	73
(X, R)	Relation R on set X	77
$a R b$	a is related to b	77
$a \not{R} b$	a is not related to b	77
$\equiv \mod n$	Equivalence modulo n	77
$\mathbf{Z}/n$	Integers modulo n	82
$(X, \preceq)$	Partial order $\preceq$ on set X	87
$a \preceq b$	a is related to b in a poset	87
$a \prec b$	$a \preceq b$ and $a \neq b$	87
$X \cong Y$	X is isomorphic to Y	91
V_G	Vertex set of G	97
E_G	Edge set of G	97
λ	Empty string	127
s^R	Reverse of string s	127
$P(n, r)$	Permutations	164
$n!$	n factorial	164
$C(n, r)$	Combinations	165
$\binom{n}{r}$	Combinations	165
$P(A)$	Probability of A	182
$E(X)$	Expected value	186
$x \leftarrow y$	Assign the value of y to x	192
$O(f)$	Big-oh of f	205
$\Omega(f)$	Big-omega of f	206
$\Theta(f)$	Big-theta of f	206
$\underline{x}, \bar{x}$	Before and after values of x	265